OXFORD SHAKESPEARE CONCORDANCES

OXFORD SHAKESPEARE CONCORDANCES

II HENRY VI

A CONCORDANCE TO THE TEXT
OF THE FIRST FOLIO

OXFORD
AT THE CLARENDON PRESS
1970

Oxford University Press, Ely House, London W. 1

GLASGOW NEW YORK TORONTO MELBOURNE WELLINGTON
CAPE TOWN SALISBURY IBADAN NAIROBI DAR ES SALAAM LUSAKA ADDIS ABABA
BOMBAY CALCUTTA MADRAS KARACHI LAHORE DACCA
KUALA LUMPUR SINGAPORE HONG KONG TOKYO

FILMSET BY COMPUTAPRINT LIMITED
AND PRINTED IN GREAT BRITAIN
AT THE UNIVERSITY PRESS, OXFORD
BY VIVIAN RIDLER
PRINTER TO THE UNIVERSITY

GENERAL INTRODUCTION

IN this series of Oxford Shakespeare Concordances, a separate volume is devoted to each of the plays. The text for each concordance is the one chosen as copy-text by Dr. Alice Walker for the Oxford Old Spelling Shakespeare now in preparation.

Each concordance takes account of every word in the text, and represents their occurrence by frequency counts, line numbers, and reference lines, or a selection of these according to the interest of the particular word. The number of words which have frequency counts only has been kept as low as possible. The introduction to each volume records the facsimile copy of the text from which the concordance was prepared, a table of Folio through line numbers and Globe edition act and scene numbers, a list of the misprints corrected in the text, and an account of the order of printing, and the proof-reading, abstracted from Professor Charlton Hinman's *The Printing and Proof-Reading of the First Folio of Shakespeare* (Oxford, 1963).

The following notes on the main features of the concordances may be helpful.[1]

A. *The Text*

The most obvious misprints have been corrected, on conservative principles, and have been listed for each play in the introduction to the corresponding concordance. Wrong-fount letters have been silently corrected.

Obvious irregularities on the part of the original compositor—for example the anomalous absence of full stops after speech prefixes—have been normalized and noted. Colons, semicolons, exclamation and interrogation marks after italicized words have been modernized to roman fount after current practice, since this aspect of

[1] An account of the principles and methods by which the concordances were edited appears in *Studies in Bibliography*, vol. 22, 1969.

compositorial practice would not normally be studied from a concordance. The spacing of words in the original printed texts, particu-
larly in 'justified' lines, is extremely variable; spacing has been
normalized on the basis of the compositor's practice as revealed in
the particular column or page.

For ease of reference, the contractions *S.*, *L.*, *M.*, and forms such
as *Mist.* and tildes, have been expanded when the compositor's own
preferred practice is clear, and the expansion has been noted in the
text. For M^r, the superior character has been lowered silently.
Superior characters like the circumflex in *baâ* and those in $\overset{t}{y}$, $\overset{e}{y}$, $\overset{u}{y}$, and
$\overset{c}{w}$, have been ignored. The reader should find little difficulty in dis-
tinguishing the original form of the pronominal contractions when
they are encountered in the text. They are listed under Y and W
respectively.

B. *Arrangement of entries*

The words in the text are arranged alphabetically, with numerals
and & and &c listed at the end. Words starting with I and J, and U
and V, will be found together under I and V respectively. The reader
should note that the use of U for the medial V (and I for J) leads in
some cases to an unfamiliar order of entry. For example, ADUISED is
listed before ADULTERY. The reader will usually find the word he
wants if he starts his inquiry at the modern spelling, for when the old
spelling differs considerably from the modern spelling, a reference
such as 'ENFORCE *see* inforce' will direct the reader to the entry in the
concordance.

In hyphenated compounds where the hyphen is the second or third
character of the heading-word (as in A-BOORD), the hyphenated form
may be listed some distance from other occurrences of the same word
in un-hyphenated form. In significant cases, references are given to
alert the user.

Under the heading-word, the line numbers or lines of context are
in the order of the text. The heading-word is followed by a frequency
count of the words in short and long (that is, marked with an
asterisk) lines, and the reference lines. When a word has been treated
as one to have a frequency count only, or a list of the line numbers

and count, any further count which follows will refer to the reference lines listed under the same heading. Where there are two counts but no reference lines (as with AN), the first count refers to the speech prefix.

C. *Special Forms*

(*a*) The following words have not been given context lines and line references but are dealt with only by the counting of their frequency:

A AM AND ARE AT BE BY HE I IN IS IT OF ON SHE THE THEY TO WAS WE WITH YOU

These forms occur so often in most texts that the reader can locate them more easily by examining the text of the play than he could by referring to an extensive listing in the concordance.

Homographs of these words (for example I = *ay*) have been listed in full and are given separate counts under the same heading-word.

(*b*) A larger number of words, consisting mainly of variant spellings, have been given line references as well as frequency counts.

These words are: ACTUS AN AR ART ATT AU BEE BEEING BEEN BEENE BEING BENE BIN BUT CAN CANST CE COULD COULDST DE DECIMA DES DID DIDD DIDDEST DIDDST DO DOE DOES DOEST DOETH DONE DOO DOOE DOOES DOOEST DOOING DOON DOONE DOOS DOOST DOOTH DOS DOST DOTH DU E EN EST ET ETC FINIS FOR FROM HA HAD HADST HAH HAS HAST HATH HAUE HEE HEEL HEELE HEL HELL HER HIM HIR HIS IE IF IL ILL ILLE INTO LA LE LES MA MAIE MAIEST MAIST MAY ME MEE MIGHT MIGHTEST MIGHTST MINE MOI MOY MY NE NO NOE NON NONA NOR NOT O OCTAUA OFF OH OR OU OUR OUT PRIMA PRIMUS QUARTA QUARTUS QUE QUINTA QUINTUS SCAENA SCENA SCOENA SECUNDA SECUNDUS SEPTIMA SEPTIMUS SEXTA SHAL SHALL SHALT SHEE SHOLD SHOLDE SHOLDST SHOULD SHOULDE SHOULDST SIR SO SOE TE TERTIA TERTIUS THAT THEE THEIR THEIRE THEM THEN THER THERE THESE THEYR THIS THOSE THOU THY TIS TU VN VNE VOS VOSTRE VOUS VS WAST WEE WER WERE WERT WHAT WHEN WHER WHERE WHICH WHO WHOM WHOME WHY WIL WILL WILT WILTE WOLD WOLDE WOLDST WOULD WOULDE WOULDEST WOULDST YE YEE YF YOUE YOUR YT & &C 1 2 3 4.

Homographs of words on this list (e.g. *bee* = n.) have been listed in full, and also have separate counts.

(*c*) All speech prefixes, other than *All.*, *Both.*, and those which represent the names of actors, have been treated as count-only words. In some cases, however, where a speech prefix corresponds to a form already on the count-only list (e.g. *Is.*), a full entry has been given. In some other cases, when two counts are given for the same heading-word for no apparent reason, the count which does not correspond to the following full references or to the list of line references is that of the speech prefix form (for example AN in *The Tempest*).

(*d*) Hyphenated compounds such as *all-building-law* have been listed under the full form, and also under each main constituent after the first. In this example there are entries under ALL-BUILDING-LAW, BUILDING, and LAW. When, however, one of the constituents of the compound is a word on the count- or location-only list ((*a*) or (*b*) above), it is dealt with in whichever of these two lists applies. References such as 'AT *see also* bemock't-at-stabs' are given to assist the reader in such cases.

Simple or non-hyphenated compounds such as *o'th'King* have been listed only under the constituent parts—in this example under OTH and KING.

(*e*) 'Justified' lines where the spellings *may* have been affected by the compositor's need to fit the text to his measure are distinguished by an asterisk at the beginning of the reference line. If only location is being given, the asterisk occurs before the line reference. If only frequency counts are being given, the number *after* the asterisk records the frequency of forms occurring in 'justified' lines. Lines which do not extend to the full width of the compositor's measure have not been distinguished as 'justified' lines, even though in many cases the shorter line may have affected the spelling.

D. *Line Numbers*

The lines in each text have been numbered from the first *Actus Primus* or stage direction and thereafter in normal reading order, including all stage directions and act and scene divisions. Each typographical line has been counted as a unit when it contains matter for inclusion in the concordance. Catchwords are not included in the count. The only general exception is that turn-overs are regarded as belonging to their base-lines; where a turn-over occurs on a line by itself, it has been reckoned as part of the base-line, and the line containing only the turn-over has not been counted as a separate line. Turn-overs may readily be distinguished by vertical stroke and single bracket after the last word of the base-line; for example *brought with* | (*child,*.

When two or more lines have been joined in order to provide a fuller context, the line-endings are indicated by a vertical stroke |, and the line reference applies to that part of the line before the vertical stroke. For the true line-numbers of words in the following part of the context line, the stated line-number should be increased by one each time a vertical stroke occurs, save when the next word is a turn-over.

The numbering of the quarto texts has been fitted to that of the corresponding Folio texts; lines in the Quarto which do not occur in the Folio are prefixed by +. The line references are similarly specified. The line references of these concordances therefore provide a consistent permanent numbering of each typographical line of text, based on the First Folio.

PROGRAM CHANGES

Preparation of concordances to the first few texts, and the especial complexity of *Wiv.*, have enabled some improvements to be made to the main concordance program. For texts other than *Tmp.*, *TGV*, *MM*, and *Err.*, the concordances have been prepared with the improved program.

Speech-prefixes now have separate entries under the appropriate heading-word and follow any other entry under the same heading-word. Entries under AN in *Wiv.*, AND and TO in *TN*, and AD in *AYL* offer examples. This alteration provides a clearer record of the total number of occurrences of words which occur both as speech-prefixes and also as forms on the 'count only' or 'locations only' lists.

Another modification supplies a more precise reference to the location of words such as BEENE for which line numbers but no full lines are given. When a 'location only' word is encountered to the right of the 'end-of-line' bar (which shows that lines of text have been joined together in order to provide a sufficient context), the line number is now adjusted to supply the exact reference. In the concordances to the texts listed above, users will find that in some instances the particular occurrence of a 'location only' word which they wish to consult in the text is to be found in the line after the one specified in the concordance; this depends on whether lines have been joined in the computer-readable version of the text from which the concordance was made. It is not expected that readers will be seriously inconvenienced by this. Should a concordance to the First Folio be published, it will, of course, incorporate all improvements.

HENRY VI PART II

Lee's facsimile of the First Folio (Oxford, 1902) provided the copy for the concordance to *2H6*. It shows the corrected states of m3 and m3^v of which Professor Charlton Hinman (*Printing and Proof-Reading*. Oxford, 1963. V. 1, p. 274) records variants, but the text is not materially affected. The order of printing which Professor Hinman gives for this section of F (v. 2, p. 515) reads as follows:

By Ax $m3^v$:4	By Ax $m3$:4^v	By Ax $m2^v$:5	By Ax $m2$:5^v	By Ax $m1^v$:6	By Ax $m1$:6^v	By Ax $n3^v$:4	Ax By $n3$:4^v
Ax By $n2^v$:5	Ax By $n2$:5^v	Ax By $n1^v$:6	Ax By $n1$:6^v	By Ax $o3^v$:4	By Ax $o3$:4^v	By Ax $o2^v$:5	By Ax $o2$:5^v
By Ax $o1$:6^v	By Ax $o1^v$:6						

[Here a jump back to quire d, but no delay is in evidence.]

TABLE OF LINE AND ACT/SCENE NUMBERS

Page	Col.	Comp.	F line nos.	Globe act/scene nos.
$m2^v$	a	B	1–45	1.1.1–1.1.38
	b	B	46–90	1.1.83
m3	a	B	91–156	1.1.149
	b	B	157–222	1.1.211
$m3^v$	a	B	223–88	1.2.15
	b	B	289–354	1.2.79
m4	a	A	355–416	1.3.35
	b	A	417–82	1.3.99
$m4^v$	a	A	483–545	1.3.154
	b	A	546–607	1.3.214
m5	a	A	608–68	1.4.43
	b	A	669–730	2.1.14
$m5^v$	a	A	731–94	2.1.67
	b	A	795–858	2.1.114
m6	a	A	859–920	2.1.168
	b	A	921–84	2.2.25
$m6^v$	a	A	985–1050	2.2.82
	b	A	1051–114	2.3.58
n1	a	A	1115–76	2.4.5
	b	A	1177–240	2.4.64
$n1^v$	a	A	1241–305	3.1.11
	b	A	1306–71	3.1.77

Page	Col.	Comp.	F line nos.	Globe act/scene nos.
n2	a	A	1372–435	3.1.135
	b	A	1436–501	3.1.200
n2ᵛ	a	A	1502–67	3.1.265
	b	A	1568–631	3.1.326
n3	a	A	1632–91	3.2.5
	b	A	1692–761	3.2.61
n3ᵛ	a	B	1762–825	3.2.123
	b	B	1826–91	3.2.187
n4	a	A	1892–954	3.2.242
	b	A	1955–2020	3.2.306
n4ᵛ	a	B	2021–84	3.2.367
	b	B	2085–148	3.3.14
n5	a	B	2149–212	4.1.43
	b	B	2213–78	4.1.110
n5ᵛ	a	B	2279–342	4.2.26
	b	B	2343–406	4.2.95
n6	a	B	2407–70	4.2.158
	b	B	2471–533	4.4.1
n6ᵛ	a	B	2534–96	4.4.59
	b	B	2597–656	4.7.25
o1	a	B	2657–720	4.7.92
	b	B	2721–80	4.8.5
o1ᵛ	a	B	2781–845	4.8.70
	b	B	2846–904	4.9.49
o2	a	B	2905–65	4.10.15
	b	B	2966–3027	5.1.35
o2ᵛ	a	B	3028–90	5.1.95
	b	B	3091–154	5.1.155
o3	a	B	3155–220	5.2.2
	b	B	3221–86	5.2.64
o3ᵛ	a	B	3287–318	5.2.90
	b	B	3319–56 (Finis)	5.3.33

The following misprints, etc. were corrected in the text:

m3	193	Cardinall.		2563	Southwatke:
m3ᵛ	268	in in		2637	*Rut.*
	281	Inehac'd	o1ᵛ	22802	Fteedome.
	294	worid.		22870	Aduertised,
m4ᵛ	503	*Buekingham*			(turned n)
n2	1402	' Tis	o2	2990	*with*
n4ᵛ	2065	Aduenrure	o2ᵛ	3067	rhou
	2121	Ir		3133	atrested,
n5	2179	theit	o3	3207	io
n5ᵛ	2304	*Brutsn*		3215	*Yo∧Clif.*
	2373	*Weauer·*		3238	theee
n6ᵛ	2551	huae			

December, 1969   T. H. H.

HENRY VI   PART II

A = 295*77, 6*3
*Peter. Here a comes me thinkes, and the Queene with | him: Ile be the
first sure.   392
King. A Gods Name see the Lysts and all things fit,   1110
Sirs, what's a Clock? | Seru. Tenne, my Lord.   1175
Weauer. A must needs, for beggery is valiant.   2373
is but a Knight, is a? | Mich. No.   2436
*his Tongue, he speakes not a Gods name. Goe, take   2741
*for a stray, for entering his Fee-simple without leaue. A   2930
But I must make faire weather yet a while,   3022
By what we can, which can no more but flye. | Alarum a farre off. 3303
ABASE = 1
And neuer more abase our sight so low,   288
ABHOMINABLE = *1
*Nowne and a Verbe, and such abhominable wordes, as   2673
ABIDES = 1
For none abides with me: my Ioy, is Death;   1268
ABIECT = 3
The abiect People, gazing on thy face,   1182
Vpon these paltry, seruile, abiect Drudges: 2273
I am so angry at these abiect tearmes.   3017
ABLE = 3*5
*O Lord haue mercy vpon me, I shall neuer be able to | fight a blow: O
Lord my heart.   612
Simpc. Alas Master, I am not able to stand alone: 892
*Simpc. Alas Master, what shall I doe? I am not able to | stand.   900
*God, for I am neuer able to deale with my Master, hee   1138
*Weauer. But now of late, not able to trauell with her   2366
Cade. I am able to endure much.   2374
*matters they were not able to answer. Moreouer,   2676
Is able with the change, to kill and cure.   3096
ABOORD = 1
Whitm. I lost mine eye in laying the prize aboord,   2194
ABORTIUE = 1
I, and alay this thy abortiue Pride: 2228
ABOUE = 4*1
Aboue the reach or compasse of thy thought?   320
And what a pytch she flew aboue the rest: 722
And beares his thoughts aboue his Faulcons Pitch.   728

1

ABOUE *cont.*
  *Card. I thought as much, hee would be aboue the | Clouds.   731
  Murther indeede, that bloodie sinne, I tortur'd | Aboue the Felon, or
  what Trespas else.   1431
ABOUND = 1
  So Cares and Ioyes abound, as Seasons fleet.   1174
ABOUT = 6*3
  With walking once about the Quadrangle,   548
  You goe about to torture me in vaine.   893
  That he should come about your Royall Person,   1320
  and Inke-horne about his necke. | *Exit one with the Clearke*   2427
  *that thou hast men about thee, that vsually talke of a   2672
  *Iustices of Peace, to call poore men before them, a-|bout   2675
  Least they consult about the giuing vp   2767
  *be hang'd with your Pardons about your neckes? Hath   2798
  Enter Multitudes with Halters about their | *Neckes.*   2860
ABROAD = 1
  His hands abroad display'd, as one that graspt   1876
ABROOKE = 1
  Sweet *Nell*, ill can thy Noble Minde abrooke   1181
ABSIRTIS = 1
  As wilde *Medea* yong *Absirtis* did.   3281
ABUSE = 3
  In thine owne person answere thy abuse.   760
  Knowing how hardly I can brooke abuse?   3087
  Or wherefore doest abuse it, if thou hast it?   3172
ACCEPT = 1*1
  Armorer. And I accept the Combat willingly.   609
  *Yor. Humfrey of Buckingham, I accept thy greeting.   3007
ACCOMPLICES *see* complices
ACCOMPT = 1
  *Weauer. The Clearke of Chartam: hee can write and | reade, and cast
  accompt.   2403
ACCORDETH = 1
  But that my heart accordeth with my tongue,   1571
ACCORDING = 3
  There to be vs'd according to your State.   1275
  According to that State you shall be vs'd.   1279
  According as I gaue directions? | 1. 'Tis, my good Lord.   1703
ACCUSATION = 1
  away an honest man for a Villaines accusation.   599
ACCUSD = 2
  falsely accus'd by the Villaine.   586
  Who being accus'd a craftie Murtherer,   1556
ACCUSE = 4
  Yorke. Doth any one accuse *Yorke* for a Traytor?   575
  That doth accuse his Master of High Treason;   579
  Who can accuse me? wherein am I guiltie?   1401
  By false accuse doth leuell at my Life.   1460
ACCUSED = 1
  Suff. Because here is a man accused of Treason,   573
ACCUSER = *1
  *words: my accuser is my Prentice, and when I did cor-|rect   595
ACHIEUE *see* atcheeue
ACHILLES = 1
  Whose Smile and Frowne, like to *Achilles* Speare   3095

ACQUIT = 1
Pray God he may acquit him of suspition.   1719
ACT = 1
Perswaded him from any further act: 3331
ACTE = 1
And with the same to acte controlling Lawes: 3098
ACTION = 2
I cannot giue due action to my words,   2999
Clif. My soule and bodie on the action both.   3247
ACTIUE = 1
The People Liberall, Valiant, Actiue, Wealthy,   2697
ACTS = 2
And Brother Yorke, thy Acts in Ireland,   202
His Fathers Acts, commenc'd in burning Troy.   1818
ACTUS *l*.1 = 1
AD = 1
Spirit. Ad sum. | *Witch. Asmath*, by the eternall God,   648
ADAM = 1
Cade. And *Adam* was a Gardiner. | *Bro.* And what of that?   2454
ADDE = 1
Thou wilt but adde encrease vnto my Wrath.   2006
ADDER = 1
What? Art thou like the Adder waxen deafe?   1776
ADDRESSE = 1
Yor. A dreadfull lay, addresse thee instantly.   3248
ADIUDGD = 1
Such as by Gods Booke are adiudg'd to death.   1057
ADMIRD = 1
That all the Court admir'd him for submission.   1306
ADMITTED = 1
Or be admitted to your Highnesse Councell.   1321
ADUANCE = 1
Aduance our halfe-fac'd Sunne, striuing to shine;   2266
ADUANTAGE = 2
And when I spy aduantage, claime the Crowne,   254
And his aduantage following your decease,   1319
ADUANTAGES *see* vantages
ADUENTURE = 1
Aduenture to be banished my selfe: 2065
ADUERTISED = 1
Mes. Please it your Grace to be aduertised,   2876
ADUICE = 2
Hume. But by the grace of God, and *Humes* aduice,   347
But with aduice and silent secrecie.   1034
ADUISD = 1
Glost. True Vnckle, are ye aduis'd?   769
ADUISED = 2
And bid me be aduised how I treade.   1212
To loose thy youth in peace, and to atcheeue | The Siluer Liuery of
aduised Age,   3268
AEACIDA = 1
Why this is iust, *Aio Aeacida Romanos vincere posso.*   691
AENEAS = 2
As did *Aeneas* old *Anchyses* beare,   3284
But then, *Aeneas* bare a liuing loade;   3286
AEOLUS = 1
Yet Aeolus would not be a murtherer,   1792

3

AFEARD = 1
Death, at whose Name I oft haue beene afear'd,   1269
AFFABLE = 1
We know the time since he was milde and affable,   1303
AFFAIRES = 2
Henry, my Lord, is cold in great Affaires,   1526
Whiles I take order for mine owne affaires.   1625
AFFAYRES = 1
I come to talke of Common-wealth Affayres.   549
AFFECT = 1
How they affect the House and Clayme of *Yorke*.   1681
AFFECTED = 1
Haue I affected wealth, or honor? Speake.   2731
AFFIANCE = *1
Qu. Ah what's more dangerous, then this fond affiance?   1368
AFFLICT = *1
Glost. Ambitious Church-man, leaue to afflict my heart: 934
AFFLICTION = 1
Hearts Discontent, and sowre Affliction,   2015
AFFOORDS = 1
With ruder termes, such as my wit affoords,   37
AFFRIGHT *see also* fright = 2
How now? why starts thou? What doth death affright?   2201
Euen to affright thee with the view thereof.   3207
AFFRIGHTS = 1*1
Their touch affrights me as a Serpents sting.   1747
Suf. Thy name affrights me, in whose sound is death: 2202
AFFYE = 1
For daring to affye a mighty Lord   2248
AFOOT *see* a-foot
AFRAID = 1*1
Or more afraid to fight, then is the Appellant,   1113
1.Prent. Here *Peter*, I drinke to thee, and be not a-|fraid.   1129
AFTER = 11
And listen after *Humfrey*, how he proceedes: 542
After the Beadle hath hit him once, he leapes ouer   902
Who after *Edward* the third's death, raign'd as King,   979
Shall, after three dayes open Penance done,   1064
And after Summer, euermore succeedes   1172
Looke after him, and cannot doe him good: 1520
And after all this fearefull Homage done,   1929
If after three dayes space thou here bee'st found,   2009
The Rascall people, thirsting after prey,   2588
What sayes Lord Warwicke, shall we after them?   3349
War. After them: nay before them if we can: 3350
AGAINE = 20*2
For were there hope to conquer them againe,   124
Deliuer'd vp againe with peacefull words? | *Mort Dieu.*   129
Hum. Nay be not angry, I am pleas'd againe.   329
And neuer mount to trouble you againe.   477
That could restore this Cripple to his Legges againe.   880
To morrow toward London, back againe,   953
You foure from hence to Prison, back againe;   1058
You vse her well: the World may laugh againe,   1260
And vndiscouer'd, come to me againe,   1675
Suff. He doth reuiue againe, Madame be patient.   1734
Droue backe againe vnto my Natiue Clime.   1784

4

AGAINE *cont.*

To blush and beautifie the Cheeke againe.	1871
Aliue againe? Then shew me where he is,	2146
Who in contempt shall hisse at thee againe.	2246
*the Lent shall bee as long againe as it is, and thou shalt	2518
But stay, Ile read it ouer once againe.	2546
And so farwell, for I must hence againe. *Exeunt*	2612
*Cade. Giue him a box o'th'eare, and that wil make'em | red againe.	2719
When they were aliue. Now part them againe,	2766
Alarum, and Retreat. Enter againe Cade, | *and all his rabblement.*	2773
We are thy Soueraigne *Clifford,* kneele againe;	3124
* *War.* You were best to go to bed, and dreame againe,	3196

AGAINST *see also* 'gainst = 12*6

Against my King and Nephew, vertuous *Henry,*	293
*1.*Pet.* Mine is, and't please your Grace, against *Iohn*	401
*What's yours? What's heere? Against the Duke of	405
* *Peter.* Against my Master *Thomas Horner,* for saying,	410
King. Sweet Aunt be quiet, 'twas against her will.	535
Duch. Against her will, good King? looke to't in time,	536
*pitty my case: the spight of man preuayleth against me.	611
Against this prowd Protector with my Sword,	756
Haue practis'd dangerously against your State,	923
Be brought against me at my Tryall day.	1414
And trie your hap against the Irishmen?	1619
Oppose himselfe against a Troupe of Kernes,	1667
Against the senselesse windes shall grin in vaine,	2245
*thousand diuelles come against me, and giue me but the	2966
Against thy Oath, and true Allegeance sworne,	3012
And fight against that monstrous Rebell *Cade,*	3055
Makes him oppose himselfe against his King.	3130
Yorke. So let it helpe me now against thy sword,	3245

AGE = 9*1.

He being of age to gouerne of himselfe.	173
Warwicke my sonne, the comfort of my age,	198
Ah *Humfrey,* this dishonor in thine age,	1072
Sorrow would sollace, and mine Age would ease.	1075
* *Beuis.* O miserable Age: Vertue is not regarded in | Handy-crafts men.	2329
Became a Bricklayer, when he came to age.	2465
And shame thine honourable Age with blood?	3170
That bowes vnto the graue with mickle age.	3174
To loose thy youth in peace, and to atcheeue | The Siluer Liuery of	
aduised Age,	3268
Shall be eterniz'd in all Age to come.	3353

AGED = 1

That Winter Lyon, who in rage forgets | Aged contusions, and all brush	
of Time:	3322

AGENT = 1

(The agent of thy foule inconstancie)	1815

AGREE = *1

*apparrell them all in one Liuery, that they may agree like	2392

AGREED = 1*2

Glo. Reads. Inprimis, *It is agreed betweene the French K.*(ing)	50
* *Win.* Item, *It is further agreed betweene them, That the*	63
The Peeres agreed, and *Henry* was well pleas'd,	230

AGREES = 1

Agrees not with the leannesse of his purse.	119

AH *see also* a = 15*4
Ah *Humfrey*, this dishonor in thine age,	1072
Ah *Gloster*, hide thee from their hatefull lookes,	1199
Elianor. Ah *Gloster*, teach me to forget my selfe:	1203
Ah *Humfrey*, can I beare this shamefull yoake?	1213
Glost. Ah *Nell*, forbeare: thou aymest all awry.	1234
Qu. Ah what's more dangerous, then this fond affiance?	1368
Glost. Ah gracious Lord, these dayes are dangerous:	1442
Glost. Ah, thus King *Henry* throwes away his Crutch,	1489
Ah that my feare were false, ah that it were;	1493
Ah Vnckle *Humfrey*, in thy face I see	1503
Suff. Ah *Yorke*, no man aliue, so faine as I.	1546
King. Ah woe is me for Gloster, wretched man.	1772
King. Ah, what a signe it is of euill life,	2139
Qu. Ah barbarous villaines: Hath this louely face,	2547
Qu. Ah were the Duke of Suffolke now aliue,	2577
*Ah thou Say, thou Surge, nay thou Buckram Lord, now	2659
Say. Ah Countrimen: If when you make your prair's,	2747
Ah *Sancta Maiestas!* who would not buy thee deere?	2996

AIAX = 1
And now like *Aiax Telamonius*,	3018

AID *see* ayd
AIDANCE *see* aydance
AIMEST *see* aymest
AIO = 1
Why this is iust, *Aio Aeacida Romanos vincere posso.*	691

AIRE *see also* ayre = 1
That makes him gaspe, and stare, and catch the aire,	2088

ALANSON = *1
*The Dukes of *Orleance, Calaber, Britaigne,* and *Alanson,*	14

ALARUM = 6
Sound Trumpets, Alarum to the Combattants.	1154
Alarum. Fight at Sea. Ordnance goes off.	2168
Alarum, and Retreat. Enter againe Cade,	*and all his rabblement.*	2773
Now when the angrie Trumpet sounds alarum,	3221
By what we can, which can no more but flye.	*Alarum a farre off.*	3303
Alarum. Retreat. Enter Yorke, Richard, Warwicke,	*and Soldiers, with Drum & Colours.*	3319

ALARUMS = 2
Alarums to the fight, wherein both the Staffords are slaine.	*Enter Cade and the rest.*	2511
Alarums. Mathew Goffe is slain, and all the rest.	*Then enter Iacke Cade, with his Company.*	2633

ALAS = 4*5
*2. *Pet.* Alas Sir, I am but a poore Petitioner of our	whole Towneship.	408
Armorer. Alas, my Lord, hang me if euer I spake the	594
Peter. Alas, my Lord, I cannot fight; for Gods sake	610
Simpc. Alas, good Master, my Wife desired some	842
Glost. Tell me Sirrha, what's my Name?	*Simpc.* Alas Master, I know not.	862
Simpc. Alas Master, I am not able to stand alone:	892
Simpc. Alas Master, what shall I doe? I am not able to	stand.	900
Wife. Alas Sir, we did it for pure need.	908
Alas, he hath no home, no place to flye too:	2815

ALAY = 1
I, and alay this thy abortiue Pride:	2228

ALBIONS = 2
    And this the Royaltie of *Albions* King?   431
    For loosing ken of *Albions* wished Coast.   1813
ALBON = 1
    In my sleepe, by good Saint *Albon*:   824
ALBONE = 1
    My Lords, Saint *Albone* here hath done a Miracle: 878
ALBONES = 6
    When from Saint *Albones* we doe make returne,   358
    The King is now in progresse towards Saint *Albones*,   702
    One. Forsooth, a blinde man at Saint *Albones* Shrine,   790
    Enter the Maior of Saint Albones, and his Brethren, | *bearing the man*
    betweene two in a Chayre.   795
    **Simpc.* Yes Master, cleare as day, I thanke God and | Saint *Albones.*   848
    Glost. My Masters of Saint *Albones*,   882
ALBONS = 3
    You do prepare to ride vnto S.(aint) *Albons*,   332
    The Castle in S.(aint) *Albons*, Somerset   3291
    Saint Albons battell wonne by famous Yorke,   3352
ALDER = 1
    With you mine *Alder liefest* Soueraigne,   35
ALEXANDER = 2
    That *Alexander Iden* an Esquire of Kent,   2947
    Iden. Alexander Iden, that's my name,   3068
ALE-HOUSE = 2
    And make my Image but an Ale-house signe.   1781
    For vnderneath an Ale-house paltry signe,   3290
ALIUE = 5*1
    Suff. Ah *Yorke*, no man aliue, so faine as I.   1546
    And all to haue the Noble Duke aliue.   1764
    Aliue againe? Then shew me where he is,   2146
    *the brickes are aliue at this day to testifie it: therefore | deny it not.   2469
    Qu. Ah were the Duke of Suffolke now aliue,   2577
    When they were aliue. Now part them againe,   2766
ALL = 129*21
    **All kneel.* Long liue Qu.(eene) *Margaret*, Englands happines.   44
    Queene. We thanke you all. *Florish*   45
    We thanke you all for this great fauour done,   76
    Come, let vs in, and with all speede prouide | To see her Coronation be
    perform'd.   78
    Your greefe, the common greefe of all the Land.   84
    With all the Learned Counsell of the Realme,   96
    Your Deeds of Warre, and all our Counsell dye?   104
    Defacing Monuments of Conquer'd France, | Vndoing all as all had
    neuer bin.   109
    Sal. Now by the death of him that dyed for all,   120
    Nay more, an enemy vnto you all,   156
    And all the wealthy Kingdomes of the West,   161
    I feare me Lords, for all this flattering glosse,   170
    Then all the Princes in the Land beside,   183
    As stout and proud as he were Lord of all,   195
    I cannot blame them all, what is't to them?   232
    Still reuelling like Lords till all be gone,   236
    While all is shar'd, and all is borne away,   240
    Inchac'd with all the Honors of the world?   281
    Sort how it will, I shall haue Gold for all. *Exit.*   383
    and Lands, and Wife and all, from me.   403

ALL *cont.*

All. Come, let's be gone. *Exit.*	427
But all his minde is bent to Holinesse,	441
Suff. And he of these, that can doe most of all,	458
Queene. Not all these Lords do vex me halfe so much,	461
Was better worth then all my Fathers Lands,	472
So one by one wee'le weed them all at last,	485
Buck. All in this presence are thy betters, *Warwicke.*	501
Warw. Warwicke may liue to be the best of all.	502
And all the Peeres and Nobles of the Realme	516
Let him haue all the rigor of the Law.	593
Elianor. Well said my Masters, and welcome all: To	633
Buck. True Madame, none at all: what call you this?	679
Wee'le see your Trinkets here all forth-comming. | All away. *Exit.*	683
To see how God in all his Creatures workes,	723
Or all my Fence shall fayle.	776
Simpc. But that in all my life, when I was a youth.	838
Wife. Neuer before this day, in all his life.	861
Thou might'st as well haue knowne all our Names,	873
But suddenly to nominate them all, | It is impossible.	876
The Ring-leader and Head of all this Rout,	922
Sorrow and griefe haue vanquisht all my powers;	935
And him to Pumfret; where, as all you know,	985
At *Buckingham,* and all the Crew of them,	1038
King. A Gods Name see the Lysts and all things fit,	1110
Armorer. Let it come yfaith, and Ile pledge you all, | and a figge for	
Peter.	1127
Peter. I thanke you all: drinke, and pray for me, I pray	1133
*take all the Money that I haue. O Lord blesse me, I pray	1137
For *Suffolke,* he that can doe all in all	1227
With her, that hateth thee and hates vs all,	1228
Haue all lym'd Bushes to betray thy Wings,	1230
Glost. Ah *Nell,* forbeare: thou aymest all awry.	1234
All these could not procure me any scathe,	1238
Elianor. Art thou gone to? all comfort goe with thee,	1267
That all the Court admir'd him for submission.	1306
'Tis to be fear'd they all will follow him.	1324
Take heed, my Lord, the welfare of vs all.	1374
Som. All health vnto my gracious Soueraigne.	1377
Som. That all your Interest in those Territories,	1380
Is vtterly bereft you: all is lost.	1381
Glost. All happinesse vnto my Lord the King:	1391
Pittie was all the fault that was in me:	1425
That you will cleare your selfe from all suspence,	1440
I would expend it with all willingnesse.	1450
I, all of you haue lay'd your heads together,	1465
And all to make away my guiltlesse Life.	1467
Buck. Hee'le wrest the sence, and hold vs here all day.	1486
Wer't not all one, an emptie Eagle were set,	1550
Som. If *Yorke,* with all his farre-fet pollicie,	1596
Yorke. No, not to lose it all, as thou hast done.	1599
By staying there so long, till all were lost.	1602
Yorke. What, worse then naught? nay, then a shame | take all.	1610
For there Ile shippe them all for Ireland.	1634
The King and all the Peeres are here at hand.	1701
Haue you layd faire the Bed? Is all things well,	1702
King. Lords take your places: and I pray you all	1713

ALL *cont.*
And all to haue the Noble Duke aliue.	1764
Is all thy comfort shut in Glosters Tombe?	1778
King. Ô thou that iudgest all things, stay my thoghts:	1838
But all in vaine are these meane Obsequies, | *Bed put forth.*	1848
For with his soule fled all my worldly solace:	1855
Being all descended to the labouring heart,	1867
The least of all these signes were probable.	1882
And after all this fearefull Homage done,	1929
Set all vpon me, mightie Soueraigne.	1951
But all the Honor *Salisbury* hath wonne,	1988
* *Within.* An answer from the King, or wee will all | breake in.	1991
King. Goe *Salisbury*, and tell them all from me,	1993
All the foule terrors in darke seated hell -- -	2043
King. Forbeare to iudge, for we are sinners all.	2165
And let vs all to Meditation. *Exeunt.*	2167
The Princely Warwicke, and the *Neuils* all,	2259
And all by thee: away, conuey him hence.	2271
*small Beere. All the Realme shall be in Common, and in	2386
All. God saue your Maiesty. | *Cade.* I thanke you good people. There	
shall bee no	2389
*mony, all shall eate and drinke on my score, and I will	2391
*apparrell them all in one Liuery, that they may agree like	2392
But. The first thing we do, let's kill all the Lawyers.	2394
* *All.* He hath confest: away with him: he's a Villaine | and a Traitor.	2424
All. I marry will we: therefore get ye gone.	2473
All. No, no, and therefore wee'l haue his head.	2493
But. They are all in order, and march toward vs.	2508
All Schollers, Lawyers, Courtiers, Gentlemen,	2572
Killing all those that withstand them:	2603
Alarums. Mathew Goffe is slain, and all the rest. | *Then enter Iacke*	
Cade, with his Company.	2633
Others to'th Innes of Court, downe with them all.	2636
*burne all the Records of the Realme, my mouth shall be | the	
Parliament of England.	2647
* *Cade.* And hence-forward all things shall be in Com-|mon. *Enter a*	
Messenger.	2651
Is term'd the ciuel'st place of all this Isle:	2695
All. It shall be done.	2746
Cade. Marry presently. | *All.* O braue.	2761
Alarum, and Retreat. Enter againe Cade, | *and all his rabblement.*	2773
And heere pronounce free pardon to them all,	2785
Henry the fift, that made all France to quake,	2793
All. God saue the King, God saue the King.	2795
*all Recreants and Dastards, and delight to liue in slauerie	2803
*make shift for one, and so Gods Cursse light vppon you | all.	2807
All. Wee'l follow *Cade*,	2809
Crying *Villiago* vnto all they meete.	2823
All. A Clifford, a Clifford,	2830
To reconcile you all vnto the King. *Exeunt omnes.*	2847
* *Clif.* He is fled my Lord, and all his powers do yeeld,	2862
And so with thankes, and pardon to you all,	2872
All. God saue the King, God saue the King.	2874
As all things shall redound vnto your good.	2901
*I hid me in these Woods, and durst not peepe out, for all	2908
*fiue men, and if I doe not leaue you all as dead as a doore	2944
My foote shall fight with all the strength thou hast,	2954

9

ALL *cont.*

*ten meales I haue lost, and I'de defie them all. Wither	2967
*Garden, and be henceforth a burying place to all that do	2968
*Kent from me, she hath lost her best man, and exhort all	2978
That I haue giuen no answer all this while:	3025
Souldiers, I thanke you all: disperse your selues:	3037
Command my eldest sonne, nay all my sonnes,	3041
Ile send them all as willing as I liue:	3043
Yorke. In all submission and humility,	3051
Clif. Health, and all happinesse to my Lord the King.	3121
Yorke. Call Buckingham, and all the friends thou hast,	3193
And tread it vnder foot with all contempt,	3209
War. How now my Noble Lord? What all a-foot.	3227
Clif. Shame and Confusion all is on the rout,	3253
Of all our Fortunes: but if we haply scape,	3306
Reignes in the hearts of all our present parts.	3315
That Winter Lyon, who in rage forgets | Aged contusions, and all brush	
of Time:	3322
By'th'Masse so did we all. I thanke you *Richard*.	3338
Shall be eterniz'd in all Age to come.	3353
Sound Drumme and Trumpets, and to London all,	3354

ALLEGATION = 1

My Lord of Suffolke, Buckingham, and Yorke, | Reproue my	
allegation, if you can,	1333

ALLEGATIONS = 1

False allegations, to o'rethrow his state.	1481

ALLEGEANCE = 2

Against thy Oath, and true Allegeance sworne,	3012
King. Hast thou not sworne Allegeance vnto me? | *Sal.* I haue.	3179

ALLS = 1

Or *Somerset*, or *Yorke*, all's one to me.	492

ALMIGHTIE = 1

Card. What, art thou lame? | *Simpc.* I, God Almightie helpe me.	830

ALMOST = 2

And so breake off, the day is almost spent,	1630
Were almost like a sharpe-quill'd Porpentine:	1669

ALOFT = 4*1

Then will I raise aloft the Milke-white-Rose,	266
Hume, that you be by her aloft, while wee be busie be-|low;	627
Enter Elianor aloft.	632
They know their Master loues to be aloft,	727
This day Ile weare aloft my Burgonet,	3204

ALONE = 3*1

We are alone, here's none but thee, & I. *Enter Hume.*	344
Simpc. Alas Master, I am not able to stand alone:	892
Cade. Let me alone: Dost thou vse to write thy name?	2419
And liue alone as secret as I may.	2584

ALONG = 3

Me thinkes I should not thus be led along,	1206
Qu. Mischance and Sorrow goe along with you,	2014
And still proclaimeth as he comes along,	2881

ALOOFE = 1

And shakes his head, and trembling stands aloofe,	239

ALOWD = 2

That euen now he cries alowd for him.	2095
Ring Belles alowd, burne Bonfires cleare and bright	2994

ALREADIE = 1
    Me thinkes alreadie in this ciuill broyle,   2821
ALREADY = 2
    hath learnt so much fence already.   1139
    Thy graue is digg'd already in the earth: 2956
ALTERD = 1
    The strangenesse of his alter'd Countenance?   1299
ALTHAEA = 1
    As did the fatall brand *Althaea* burnt,   246
ALTHOUGH = 5
    Although we fancie not the Cardinall,   480
    Although by his sight his sinne be multiplyed.   800
    Although thou hast beene Conduct of my shame.   1281
    Although the Duke was enemie to him,   1757
    Although the Kyte soare with vnbloudied Beake?   1897
ALTOGETHER = 1
    And altogether with the Duke of Suffolke,   175
ALWAYES = 1
    Iustice with fauour haue I alwayes done,   2701
AM = 50*13
AMAINE = 2
    Post. Great Lords, from Ireland am I come amaine,   1585
    Qu. Call hither *Clifford*, bid him come amaine,   3109
AMBASSADOR *see also* embassador = *1
    Charles, and William de la Pole Marquesse of Suffolke, Am-|bassador   51
AMBASSADORS = 1
    Know *Cade*, we come Ambassadors from the King   2783
AMBITION = 5
    Sal. Pride went before, Ambition followes him.   188
    The pride of Suffolke, and the Cardinall,| With Somersets and
    Buckinghams Ambition,   209
    Queene. And thy Ambition, *Gloster.*   751
    At *Beaufords* Pride, at *Somersets* Ambition,   1037
    Vertue is choakt with foule Ambition,   1443
AMBITIONS = *1
    Cade. Fye on Ambitions: fie on my selfe, that haue a   2906
AMBITIOUS = 4*1
    Banish the Canker of ambitious thoughts: 291
    Card. Ambitious *Warwicke*, let thy betters speake.   499
    Glost. Ambitious Church-man, leaue to afflict my heart: 934
    And like ambitious Sylla ouer-gorg'd,   2252
    King. I Clifford, a Bedlem and ambitious humor   3129
AMBITIOUSLY = 1
    As others would ambitiously receiue it.   1091
AMISSE = 2*1
    Gold cannot come amisse, were she a Deuill.   368
    *picke a Sallet another while, which is not amisse to coole   2913
    Buc. So please it you my Lord, 'twere not amisse   3070
AMONGST *see* 'mongst
AN *l.*156 160 306 416 464 582 599 *626 672 *992 *1149 1309 1426 1550
    1560 1648 1781 1827 1845 1889 1893 1910 *1982 1987 *1991 2046 2098
    2124 *2345 2360 2368 *2396 *2485 *2491 *2627 *2834 2850 *2933 2947
    3093 3123 *3181 3279 3290 = 31*13, 1
    Mine haire be fixt an end, as one distract: 2033
ANCHORS = 1
    For whilst our Pinnace Anchors in the Downes,   2178

ANCHYSES = 1
 As did *Aeneas* old *Anchyses* beare,   3284
ANCIENT = 3*1
 So in the Famous Ancient City, *Toures*,   12
 We shall begin our ancient bickerings: 151
 The ancient Prouerbe will be well effected,   1470
 *you had recouered your ancient Freedome. But you are   2802
AND *see also* &. = 765*143, 3*3
 Suff. No maruell, and it like your Maiestie,   725
 Glost. What's thine owne Name? | *Simpc. Saunder Simpcoxe*, and if it
 please you, Master.   868
 *World. Here *Robin*, and if I dye, I giue thee my Aporne;   1135
 *Ile bridle it: he shall dye, and it bee but for pleading so   2739
 *fiue men, and if I doe not leaue you all as dead as a doore   2944
 And if thou dost not hide thee from the Beare,   3220
ANDT = 2*4
 *1.*Pet.* Mine is, and't please your Grace, against *Iohn*   401
 Armorer. And't shall please your Maiestie, I neuer sayd   584
 Simpc. Borne blinde, and't please your Grace. | *Wife.* I indeede was he.   806
 Suff. What Woman is this? | *Wife.* His Wife, and't like your Worship.   808
 Simpc. At Barwick in the North, and't like your | Grace.   813
 Sh. And't please your Grace, here my Commission stayes: 1253
ANEW' = 1
 Begin your Suites anew, and sue to him. | *Teare the Supplication.*   424
ANGRIE = 1
 Now when the angrie Trumpet sounds alarum,   3221
ANGRY = 7
 Hum. Nay be not angry, I am pleas'd againe.   329
 He knits his Brow, and shewes an angry Eye,   1309
 The Commons like an angry Hiue of Bees   1827
 Bro. But angry, wrathfull, and inclin'd to blood,   2446
 I am so angry at these abiect tearmes.   3017
 Nay, do not fright vs with an angry looke: 3123
 Whom angry heauens do make their minister,   3256
ANIMIS = 1
 Tantaene animis Coelestibus irae, Church-men so hot?   742
ANIOU = 5*2
 *Item, *That the Dutchy of Aniou, and the County of Main,*   56
 Dutchesse of Aniou and Maine, shall be released and deliuered   64
 Hath giuen the Dutchy of *Aniou* and *Mayne*,   117
 Aniou and *Maine*? My selfe did win them both: 126
 Yorke. Aniou and *Maine* are giuen to the French,   226
 Aniou and *Maine* both giuen vnto the French?   248
 By thee *Aniou* and *Maine* were sold to France.   2254
ANNE = 2
 Roger had Issue, *Edmond, Anne*, and *Elianor*.   999
 Yorke. His eldest Sister, *Anne,* | My Mother, being Heire vnto the
 Crowne,   1005
ANNOY = 1
 To mowe downe Thornes that would annoy our Foot,   1361
ANON = 1
 Yor. Nay we shall heate you thorowly anon.   3158
ANOTHER = 4*1
 Yet haue I Gold flyes from another Coast: 369
 Enough to purchase such another Island,   2137
 Enter another Messenger.   2585
 Let them kisse one another: For they lou'd well   2765

ANOTHER *cont.*
*picke a Sallet another while, which is not amisse to coole 2913
ANSWER = 1*6
 Commons within. An answer from the King, my Lord | of Salisbury. 1982
 Within. An answer from the King, or wee will all | breake in. 1991
 Cade. Nay answer if you can: The Frenchmen are our 2489
 Buc. What answer makes your Grace to the Rebells | Supplication? 2539
 *What canst thou answer to my Maiesty, for giuing vp of 2661
 *matters they were not able to answer. Moreouer, 2676
 That I haue giuen no answer all this while: 3025
ANSWERD = *1
 Suff. My Lord, these faults are easie, quickly answer'd: 1433
ANSWERE = 3
 That shall make answere to such Questions, 355
 Answere that I shall aske: for till thou speake, 651
 In thine owne person answere thy abuse. 760
ANSWERES = 1
 And call these foule Offendors to their Answeres; 955
ANSWERS = 1
 As for words, whose greatnesse answer's words, 2957
ANT = 2
 An't like your Lordly Lords Protectorship. 749
 Iden. I was, an't like your Maiesty. 3066
ANY = 16*4
 Englands owne proper Cost and Charges, without hauing any | Dowry. 66
 Suff. How now fellow: would'st any thing with me? 396
 That *Yorke* is most vnmeet of any man. 559
 Yorke. Doth any one accuse *Yorke* for a Traytor? 575
 *nor thought any such matter: God is my witnesse, I am 585
 *take my death, I neuer meant him any ill, nor the King, 1150
 All these could not procure me any scathe, 1238
 Or any Groat I hoorded to my vse, 1413
 Queene. God forbid any Malice should preuayle, 1717
 On any ground that I am Ruler of, 2010
 Stoope to the blocke, then these knees bow to any, 2293
 And now henceforward it shall be Treason for any, 2620
 Dare any be so bold to sound Retreat or Parley 2779
 King. In any case, be not to rough in termes, 2898
 *the World to be Cowards: For I that neuer feared any, 2979
 Lands, Goods, Horse, Armor, any thing I haue 3044
 Who can be bound by any solemne Vow 3184
 Then any thou canst coniure vp to day: 3199
 That keepes his leaues inspight of any storme, 3206
 Perswaded him from any further act: 3331
ANYONE *see* one
ANYTHING *see* thing
APART = 1*1
 And *Henry* put apart: the next for me. *Exit.* 1689
 Salisb. Sirs stand apart, the King shall know your | minde. 1953
APORNE = *1
 World. Here *Robin*, and if I dye, I giue thee my Aporne; 1135
APOSTLES = 1
 His Champions, are the Prophets and Apostles, 443
APOTHECARIE = 1
 Giue me some drinke, and bid the Apothecarie 2151
APPARANT = 1
 And heyre apparant to the English Crowne: 159

APPARRELL = 1*1
    *apparrell them all in one Liuery, that they may agree like   2392
    Is my Apparrell sumptuous to behold?   2733
APPEALE = *1
    *Glost. Madame, for my selfe, to Heauen I doe appeale,   942
APPEASD = 1
    These Kentish Rebels would be soone appeas'd.   2578
APPELLANT = 2
    And ready are the Appellant and Defendant,   1105
    Or more afraid to fight, then is the Appellant,   1113
APPLYED = 1
    It is applyed to a deathfull wound.   2121
APPOINTED = 5*1
    Next, if I be appointed for the Place,   562
    And let these haue a day appointed them   604
    This is the day appointed for the Combat,   1104
    Glost. Tenne is the houre that was appointed me,   1177
    And Sir Iohn Stanly is appointed now,   1254
    *no Christian eare can endure to heare. Thou hast appoin-|ted   2674
APPREHENDED = 1
    Whom we haue apprehended in the Fact,   925
APPRENTICE see prentice
APPROACH = 1
    Where death's approach is seene so terrible.   2140
APPROUD = 1
    He be approu'd in practise culpable.   1716
APRON see aporne
APRONS = 1
    *Hol. The Nobilitie thinke scorne to goe in Leather | Aprons.   2331
ARE = 68*18
ARGO = 1
    Hol. And Smith the Weauer. | Beu. Argo, their thred of life is spun.   2347
ARGUES = 1
    War. So bad a death, argues a monstrous life.   2164
ARGUMENT = 2
    Eli. Tut, this was nothing but an argument,   306
    And yet we haue but triuiall argument,   1543
ARISE = 1
    King. Suffolke arise. Welcome Queene Margaret,   24
ARMD = 1
    Thrice is he arm'd, that hath his Quarrell iust;   1939
ARME = 5
    Whose ouer-weening Arme I haue pluckt back,   1459
    And if mine arme be heaued in the Ayre,   2955
    That thus he marcheth with thee arme in arme?   3050
    King. Call Buckingham, and bid him arme himselfe.   3192
ARMES = 14*1
    Those Prouinces, these Armes of mine did conquer,   127
    And in my Standard beare the Armes of Yorke,   268
    Th'vnciuill Kernes of Ireland are in Armes,   1615
    Will make him say, I mou'd him to those Armes.   1684
    Broke be my sword, my Armes torne and defac'd,   2211
    As hating thee, and rising vp in armes.   2261
    The Commons heere in Kent are vp in armes,   2268
    *I thought ye would neuer haue giuen out these Armes til   2801
    His Armes are onely to remoue from thee   2882
    And now is Yorke in Armes, to second him.   2889

ARMES *cont.*

And aske him what's the reason of these Armes:	2891
To know the reason of these Armes in peace.	3010
But if thy Armes be to no other end,	3031
Yo.Clif. And so to Armes victorious Father,	3211
Warwicke is hoarse with calling thee to armes.	3225

ARMIE = 1

The cause why I haue brought this Armie hither,	3027

ARMOR = 2

*them to me in the Garret one Night, as wee were scow-│ring my Lord of Yorkes Armor.	588
Lands, Goods, Horse, Armor, any thing I haue	3044

ARMORER = 3*1

Enter Armorer and his Man.	572
The Armorer and his Man, to enter the Lists,	1106
The seruant of this Armorer, my Lords.	1114
Enter at one Doore the Armorer and his Neighbors, drinking	1115

ARMORER = 1*5
ARMORERS = 1

Enter three or foure Petitioners, the Armorers │ Man being one.	384

ARMY = 4*1

Assaile them with the Army of the King.	2495
His Army is a ragged multitude	2568
Dicke. My Lord, there's an Army gathered together │ in Smithfield.	2627
Vntill his Army be dismist from him.	2894
Enter Yorke, and his Army of Irish, with │ Drum and Colours.	2990

AROUSE = 1

And now loud houling Wolues arouse the Iades	2172

ARRAY = 1

Is marching hitherward in proud array,	2880

ARREST = 4

I doe arrest thee of High Treason here.	1395
Nor change my Countenance for this Arrest:	1397
I doe arrest you in his Highnesse Name,	1436
Som. O monstrous Traitor! I arrest thee Yorke	3101

ARRESTED = 1

Qu. He is arrested, but will not obey:	3133

ARROGANT = 1

Nor cease to be an arrogant Controller,	1910

ART *l.*317 830 1267 1273 *1393 1394 1639 1776 1919 1935 2062 2077 2079 2104 2123 2182 2235 2251 2453 *2660 *2666 2951 3008 *3062 3065 3067 3088 3171 3242 *3250 = 25*5

ARTICLES = 2

Heere are the Articles of contracted peace,	47
Suffolke concluded on the Articles,	229

ARTUS = 1

Suf. Pine gelidus timor occupat artus, it is thee I feare.	2285

AS = 153*21

Suffolke. │ As by your high Imperiall Maiesty,	7
As Procurator to your Excellence, │ To marry Princes *Margaret* for your Grace;	10
With ruder termes, such as my wit affoords,	37
Defacing Monuments of Conquer'd France, │ Vndoing all as all had neuer bin.	109
As stout and proud as he were Lord of all,	195
And as we may, cherish Duke Humfries deeds,	211
War. So God helpe Warwicke, as he loues the Land,	213

AS *cont.*

And would haue kept, so long as breath did last:	222
While as the silly Owner of the goods	237
As did the fatall brand *Althaea* burnt,	246
Euen as I haue of fertile Englands soile.	250
As frowning at the Fauours of the world?	277
As to vouchsafe one glance vnto the ground.	289
But as I thinke, it was by'th Cardinall,	301
Where as the King and Queene do meane to Hawke.	333
Elia. What saist thou man? Hast thou as yet confer'd	349
As by your Grace shall be propounded him.	356
Queene. And as for you that loue to be protected	422
Suff. Madame be patient: as I was cause	451
As that prowd Dame, the Lord Protectors Wife:	462
Contemptuous base-borne Callot as she is,	469
As for the Duke of Yorke, this late Complaint	483
Since thou wert King; as who is King, but thou?	513
Haue beene as Bond-men to thy Soueraigntie.	517
If they were knowne, as the suspect is great,	526
As for your spightfull false Obiections,	550
As I in dutie loue my King and Countrey.	553
*them to me in the Garret one Night, as wee were scow-|ring my Lord	
of Yorkes Armor.	588
Elianor. Not halfe so bad as thine to Englands King,	677
Thither goes these Newes, | As fast as Horse can carry them:	704
Card. I thought as much, hee would be aboue the | Clouds.	731
Glost. As who, my Lord? | *Suff.* Why, as you, my Lord,	747
Simpc. Yes Master, cleare as day, I thanke God and | Saint *Albones.*	848
Simpc. Red Master, Red as Blood.	852
Simpc. Black forsooth, Coale-Black, as Iet.	855
Thou might'st as well haue knowne all our Names,	873
As thus to name the seuerall Colours we doe weare.	874
Buck. Such as my heart doth tremble to vnfold:	918
As more at large your Grace shall vnderstand.	929
And vanquisht as I am, I yeeld to thee, | Or to the meanest Groome.	936
As like to Pytch, defile Nobilitie;	948
And giue her as a Prey to Law and Shame,	950
Who after *Edward* the third's death, raign'd as King,	979
And him to Pumfret; where, as all you know,	985
As I haue read, layd clayme vnto the Crowne,	1001
Doe you as I doe in these dangerous dayes,	1035
Such as by Gods Booke are adiudg'd to death.	1057
As willingly doe I the same resigne,	1088
As ere thy Father *Henry* made it mine;	1089
And euen as willingly at thy feete I leaue it,	1090
As others would ambitiously receiue it.	1091
Armorer. Masters, I am come hither as it were vpon	1147
So Cares and Ioyes abound, as Seasons fleet.	1174
As he stood by, whilest I, his forlorne Duchesse,	1221
Hang ouer thee, as sure it shortly will.	1226
So long as I am loyall, true, and crimelesse.	1239
As next the King, he was successiue Heire,	1343
Our Kinsman *Gloster* is as innocent,	1363
As is the sucking Lambe, or harmelesse Doue:	1365
For hee's disposed as the hatefull Rauen.	1370
For hee's enclin'd as is the rauenous Wolues.	1372
As firmely as I hope for fertile England.	1385

AS *cont.*

As I am cleare from Treason to my Soueraigne.	1400
So helpe me God, as I haue watcht the Night,	1410
As if she had suborned some to sweare	1480
Doe, or vndoe, as if our selfe were here.	1496
And as the Butcher takes away the Calfe,	1511
And as the Damme runnes lowing vp and downe,	1515
Beguiles him, as the mournefull Crocodile	1528
Or as the Snake, roll'd in a flowring Banke,	1530
Suff. Ah *Yorke*, no man aliue, so faine as I.	1546
Say as you thinke, and speake it from your Soules:	1549
As place Duke *Humfrey* for the Kings Protector?	1552
As *Humfrey* prou'd by Reasons to my Liege.	1562
Yorke. That *Somerset* be sent as Regent thither:	1593
Yorke. No, not to lose it all, as thou hast done.	1599
To make Commotion, as full well he can,	1664
Shaking the bloody Darts, as he his Bells.	1672
Say that he thriue, as 'tis great like he will,	1685
For *Humfrey*; being dead, as he shall be,	1688
We haue dispatcht the Duke, as he commanded.	1693
According as I gaue directions? | 1. 'Tis, my good Lord.	1703
If he be guiltie, as 'tis published.	1711
Their touch affrights me as a Serpents sting.	1747
And for my selfe, Foe as he was to me,	1759
Looke pale as Prim-rose with blood-drinking sighes,	1763
With teares as salt as Sea, through thy vnkindnesse.	1796
As farre as I could ken thy Chalky Cliffes,	1801
To sit and watch me as *Ascanius* did,	1816
War. As surely as my soule intends to liue	1857
His hands abroad display'd, as one that graspt	1876
As guilty of Duke *Humfries* timelesse death.	1891
As being thought to contradict your liking,	1964
From such fell Serpents as false *Suffolke* is;	1978
Yet did I purpose as they doe entreat:	1996
Would curses kill, as doth the Mandrakes grone,	2025
I would inuent as bitter searching termes,	2026
As curst, as harsh, and horrible to heare,	2027
With full as many signes of deadly hate,	2029
As leane-fac'd enuy in her loathsome caue.	2030
Mine haire be fixt an end, as one distract:	2033
Their softest Touch, as smart as Lyzards stings:	2040
Their Musicke, frightfull as the Serpents hisse,	2041
As one that surfets, thinking on a want:	2063
Sometime he talkes, as if Duke *Humfries* Ghost	2090
And whispers to his pillow, as to him,	2092
As milde and gentle as the Cradle-babe,	2109
Euen as a splitted Barke, so sunder we:	2129
Lieu. But Ioue was neuer slaine as thou shalt be,	2217
Lieu. First let my words stab him, as he hath me.	2234
As hating thee, and rising vp in armes.	2261
By such a lowly Vassall as thy selfe.	2279
Farre be it, we should honor such as these	2291
Lieu. And as for these whose ransome we haue set,	2308
*which is as much to say, as let the Magistrates be la-|bouring	2336
*Cheapside shall my Palfrey go to grasse: and when I am | King, as	
King I will be.	2387
*shall be encountred with a man as good as himselfe. He	2435

17

AS *cont.*

Cade. As for these silken-coated slaues I passe not,	2448
Spare none, but such as go in clouted shooen,	2505
As would (but that they dare not) take our parts.	2507
*thou behaued'st thy selfe, as if thou hadst beene in thine	2516
*the Lent shall bee as long againe as it is, and thou shalt	2518
And liue alone as secret as I may.	2584
Scales. Such ayd as I can spare you shall command,	2606
*that must sweepe the Court cleane of such filth as thou	2665
*Nowne and a Verbe, and such abhominable wordes, as	2673
Dicke. And worke in their shirt to, as my selfe for ex-|ample, that am	
a butcher.	2685
Cade. Nay, he noddes at vs, as who should say, Ile be	2727
God should be so obdurate as your selues:	2748
Cade. Away with him, and do as I command ye: the	2751
*And we charge and command, that their wiues be as free	2756
as heart can wish, or tongue can tell. | *Dicke.* My Lord,	2757
*as this multitude? The name of Henry the fift, hales them	2833
As I do long and wish to be a Subiect.	2855
And still proclaimeth as he comes along,	2881
As all things shall redound vnto your good.	2901
And may enioy such quiet walkes as these?	2922
*fiue men, and if I doe not leaue you all as dead as a doore	2944
As for words, whose greatnesse answer's words,	2957
But thou shalt weare it as a Heralds coate,	2975
And as I thrust thy body in with my sword,	2983
Or why, thou being a Subiect, as I am,	3011
As pledges of my Fealtie and Loue,	3042
Ile send them all as willing as I liue:	3043
As crooked in thy manners, as thy shape.	3157
As on a Mountaine top, the Cedar shewes,	3205
As I intend Clifford to thriue to day,	3237
As I in iustice, and true right expresse it.	3246
Shall be to me, euen as the Dew to Fire,	3275
Into as many gobbits will I cut it	3280
As wilde *Medea* yong *Absirtis* did.	3281
As did *Aeneas* old *Anchyses* beare,	3284
Nothing so heauy as these woes of mine.	3287
(As well we may, if not through your neglect)	3307
But Noble as he is, looke where he comes.	3335
For (as I heare) the King is fled to London,	3346
And more such dayes as these, to vs befall. *Exeunt.*	3355

ASCANIUS = 1

To sit and watch me as *Ascanius* did,	1816

ASHES = 1

The Witch in Smithfield shall be burnt to ashes,	1060

ASHFORD = 2

I haue seduc'd a head-strong Kentishman, | *Iohn Cade* of Ashford,	1662
Cade. Where's Dicke, the Butcher of Ashford? | *But.* Heere sir.	2513

ASHY = 1

Of ashy semblance, meager, pale, and bloodlesse,	1866

ASK = *2

*enemies: go too then, I ask but this: Can he that speaks	2490
York. Wold'st haue me kneele? First let me ask of thee,	3104

ASKD = 2

Glost. And my consent ne're ask'd herein before?	1249
And neuer ask'd for restitution.	1418

ASKE = 2*1
Answere that I shall aske: for till thou speake,   651
*Spirit. Aske what thou wilt; that I had sayd, and | done.   653
And aske him what's the reason of these Armes: 2891
ASKETH = 1
The businesse asketh silent secrecie.   366
ASLEEPE = 1
Watch thou, and wake when others be asleepe,   261
ASMATH = 1
Spirit. Ad sum. | Witch. Asmath, by the eternall God,   648
ASPIRING = 1
They (knowing Dame Elianors aspiring humor)   373
ASSAILE = 1
Assaile them with the Army of the King.   2495
ASSAYD = 1
The Rebels haue assay'd to win the Tower.   2608
ASSURD = 2
I take it kindly: yet be well assur'd,   1652
I will repeale thee, or be well assur'd,   2064
ASSURE = 2
Yorke. And Neuill, this I doe assure my selfe,   1047
Assure your selues will neuer be vnkinde: 2871
ASSURES = *1
*Warw. My heart assures me, that the Earle of Warwick   1045
ASTONISH = 1
They may astonish these fell-lurking Curres,   3143
ASUNDER = 1
And kept asunder: you Madame shall with vs.   681
AT = 62*8
ATCHEEUE = 1
To loose thy youth in peace, and to atcheeue | The Siluer Liuery of
aduised Age,   3268
ATILT see a-tilt
ATTAIND = 1
These Oracles are hardly attain'd, | And hardly vnderstood.   700
ATTAINTED = 1
I must offend, before I be attainted: 1235
ATTAINTURE = 1
And her Attainture, will be Humphreyes fall: 382
ATTEND = 2
May honorable Peace attend thy Throne.   1093
And will, that thou henceforth attend on vs.   3074
ATTENDANCE = 1
Last time I danc't attendance on his will,   566
ATTENDANTS = 2
Sound Trumpets. Enter the King, the Queene, | Cardinall, Suffolke,
Somerset, with | Attendants.   1706
Enter King and Attendants.   3048
ATTRACTS = 1
Attracts the same for aydance 'gainst the enemy,   1869
ATTYRE = 2*1
*Som. Thy sumptuous Buildings, and thy Wiues Attyre   520
And goe we to attyre you for our Iourney.   1287
And shew it selfe, attyre me how I can.   1290
AUDACIOUS = 1
Obey audacious Traitor, kneele for Grace.   3103

AUENGD = 1
Shall I not liue to be aueng'd on her?   468
AUE-MARIES = 1
To number *Aue-Maries* on his Beades: 442
AUGHT *see* ought
AUGMENT = 1
Nor store of Treasons, to augment my guilt: 1469
AUKWARD = 1
And twice by aukward winde from Englands banke   1783
AUNT = 1
King. Sweet Aunt be quiet, 'twas against her will.   535
AUOIDE = 1
False Fiend auoide. | *Thunder and Lightning. Exit Spirit.*   667
AUTHORITIE = 1
Suff. Why, our Authoritie is his consent,   1621
AWAIT = 1
Bulling. What fates await the Duke of Suffolke?   659
AWAITS = 1
Well, to the rest: | Tell me what fate awaits the Duke of Suffolke?   692
AWAY = 44*14
And our King *Henry* giues away his owne,   137
Salisbury. Then lets make hast away,   217
'Tis thine they giue away, and not their owne.   233
While all is shar'd, and all is borne away,   240
Away from me, and let me heare no more.   324
Away, base Cullions: *Suffolke* let them goe.   426
And stol'st away the Ladies hearts of France;   438
away an honest man for a Villaines accusation.   599
King. Away with them to Prison: and the day of   615
Somerset, wee'le see thee sent away. | *Flourish. Exeunt.*   617
Away with them, let them be clapt vp close,   680
Wee'le see your Trinkets here all forth-comming. | All away. *Exit.*   683
To suppe with me to morrow Night. Away. | *Exeunt.*   713
*leape me ouer this Stoole, and runne away.   891
the Stoole, and runnes away: and they | *follow, and cry, A Miracle.*   903
Glost. Follow the Knaue, and take this Drab away.   907
Suff. True: made the Lame to leape and flye away.   913
Yorke. Take away his Weapon: Fellow thanke God,   1158
Why yet thy scandall were not wipt away,   1241
And Caterpillers eate my Leaues away: 1387
And all to make away my guiltlesse Life.   1467
Card. Sirs, take away the Duke, and guard him sure.   1488
Glost. Ah, thus King *Henry* throwes away his Crutch,   1489
And as the Butcher takes away the Calfe,   1511
Suff. Away, be gone. *Exeunt.*   1705
Can chase away the first-conceiued sound?   1744
Yet doe not goe away: come Basiliske,   1752
It may be iudg'd I made the Duke away,   1767
What, Dost thou turne away, and hide thy face?   1774
Warw. Away euen now, or I will drag thee hence: 1934
Well could I curse away a Winters night,   2050
To wash away my wofull Monuments.   2057
Queen. Away: Though parting be a fretfull corosiue,   2120
Oh beate away the busie medling Fiend,   2155
But with our sword we wip'd away the blot.   2209
And all by thee: away, conuey him hence.   2271
Lieu. Hale him away, and let him talke no more: 2299

AWAY *cont.*

*All. He hath confest: away with him: he's a Villaine | and a Traitor.	2424
*Cade. Away with him I say: Hang him with his Pen	2426
Was by a begger-woman stolne away,	2463
Staf. Herald away, and throughout euery Towne,	2496
Therefore away with vs to Killingworth.	2580
Buc. Then linger not my Lord, away, take horse.	2591
Come, let's away. *Exeunt omnes.*	2632
*Cade. I haue thought vpon it, it shall bee so. Away,	2646
*Cade. Away with him, away with him, he speaks La-|tine.	2690
a pole, or no: Take him away, and behead him.	2729
*well for his life. Away with him, he ha's a Familiar vn-|der	2740
*him away I say, and strike off his head presently, and then	2742
*Cade. Away with him, and do as I command ye: the	2751
Haue them kisse. Away. *Exit*	2772
And chop away that factious pate of his.	3132
*Qu. Away my Lord, you are slow, for shame away.	3297
Away for your releefe, and we will liue	3316
Away my Lord, away. *Exeunt*	3318

AWE = 1

How France and Frenchmen might be kept in awe,	99

AWEFULL = 1

And not to grace an awefull Princely Scepter.	3093

AWHILE *see* a-while

AWKWARD *see* aukward

AWRY = 1

Glost. Ah *Nell*, forbeare: thou aymest all awry.	1234

AXE = 2

Nor stirre at nothing, till the Axe of Death	1225
And sees fast-by, a Butcher with an Axe,	1893

AY *see* I

AYD = 1*1

*The L.(ord) Maior craues ayd of your Honor from the Tower	2604
Scales. Such ayd as I can spare you shall command,	2606

AYDANCE = 1

Attracts the same for aydance 'gainst the enemy,	1869

AYE = 3

This get I by his death: Aye me vnhappie,	1770
Aye me, I can no more: Dye *Elinor*,	1820
Aye me! What is this World? What newes are these?	2097

AYMEST = 1

Glost. Ah *Nell*, forbeare: thou aymest all awry.	1234

AYRE = 6

With whose sweet smell the Ayre shall be perfum'd,	267
He shall not breathe infection in this ayre,	2001
Heere could I breath my soule into the ayre,	2108
Breath foule contagious darknesse in the ayre:	2176
And if mine arme be heaued in the Ayre,	2955
And dead mens cries do fill the emptie ayre,	3222

A-FOOT = 1

War. How now my Noble Lord? What all a-foot.	3227

A-TILT = 1

Thou ran'st a-tilt in honor of my Loue,	437

A-WHILE = 1

Then Yorke be still a-while, till time do serue:	260

BABE = 1

As milde and gentle as the Cradle-babe,	2109

BABES = 1
No more will I their Babes, Teares Virginall,   3274
BABY = 1
Shee'le hamper thee, and dandle thee like a Baby: 537
BACK = 4
To morrow toward London, back againe,   953
You foure from hence to Prison, back againe;   1058
Mayl'd vp in shame, with Papers on my back,   1207
Whose ouer-weening Arme I haue pluckt back,   1459
BACKE = 5*1
*2. Pet. Come backe foole, this is the Duke of Suffolk, | and not my
Lord Protector.   394
She beares a Dukes Reuenewes on her backe,   466
Droue backe againe vnto my Natiue Clime.   1784
When from thy Shore, the Tempest beate vs backe,   1802
But now is Cade driuen backe, his men dispierc'd,   2888
Run backe and bite, because he was with-held,   3151
BACKES = *1
*to the Nobility. Let them breake your backes with bur-|thens,   2804
BAD = 5
Elianor. Not halfe so bad as thine to Englands King,   677
So good a Quarrell, and so bad a Peere.   746
Elianor. That's bad enough, for I am but reproach: 1276
Suf. You bad me ban, and will you bid me leaue?   2048
War. So bad a death, argues a monstrous life.   2164
BADE see bad
BADGE = 3*1
Hum. Me thought this staffe mine Office-badge in | Court   298
That slanders me with Murthers Crimson Badge.   1904
Might I but know thee by thy housed Badge.   3201
War. Now by my Fathers badge, old *Neuils* Crest,   3202
BAGGE = 1*1
Drumme before him, and his Staffe, with a Sand-bagge   1117
Drumme and Sand-bagge, and Prentices drinking to him.   1119
BAGS = *1
Card. The Commons hast thou rackt, the Clergies Bags   518
BAILE = 2
Shall be their Fathers baile, and bane to those   3115
Qu. And here comes *Clifford* to deny their baile.   3120
BALE = 1
Sirrah, call in my sonne to be my bale: 3106
BALEFULL = 1
Thou balefull Messenger, out of my sight: 1748
BALLANCE = 1
Except a Sword or Scepter ballance it.   3000
BALLES = 1
His eye-balles further out, than when he liued,   1873
BALLS = 1
Vpon thy eye-balls, murderous Tyrannie   1749
BAN = 2
I, euery ioynt should seeme to curse and ban,   2034
Suf. You bad me ban, and will you bid me leaue?   2048
BAND = 2
To Ireland will you leade a Band of men,   1617
Whiles I in Ireland nourish a mightie Band,   1654

22

BANDETTO = 1
A Romane Sworder, and Bandetto slaue | Murder'd sweet *Tully. Brutus*
Bastard hand   2303
BANDOGS = 1
The time when Screech-owles cry, and Bandogs howle,   638
BANE = 1
Shall be their Fathers baile, and bane to those   3115
BANISH = 3
Banish the Canker of ambitious thoughts: 291
I banish her my Bed, and Companie,   949
Sound Trumpets. Enter the King and State, | *with Guard, to banish the*
Duchesse.   1051
BANISHD = 1
Now by the ground that I am banish'd from,   2049
BANISHED = 4
Or banished faire Englands Territories,   1957
Aduenture to be banished my selfe: 2065
And banished I am, if but from thee.   2066
Suf. Thus is poore Suffolke ten times banished,   2072
BANISHMENT = 2*1
Liue in your Countrey here, in Banishment,   1065
Elianor. Welcome is Banishment, welcome were my | Death.   1067
Makes them thus forward in his Banishment.   1965
BANISHT = 2
His Lady banisht, and a Limbe lopt off.   1098
If it be banisht from the frostie head,   3167
BANKE = 2
Or as the Snake, roll'd in a flowring Banke,   1530
And twice by aukward winde from Englands banke   1783
BANNE = 1
And banne thine Enemies, both mine and thine.   1201
BARBAROUS = 2
1.Gent. O barbarous and bloudy spectacle,   2315
Qu. Ah barbarous villaines: Hath this louely face,   2547
BARE = 2*1
Hol. So he had need, for 'tis thred-bare. Well, I say,   2326
Die damned Wretch, the curse of her that bare thee: 2982
But then, *Aeneas* bare a liuing loade;   3286
BARE-HEADED = 1
Bare-headed plodded by my foot-cloth Mule,   2222
BARGAIND = 1
While his owne Lands are bargain'd for, and sold: 243
BARGULUS = 1
Then *Bargulus* the strong Illyrian Pyrate.   2276
BARKE = 1
Euen as a splitted Barke, so sunder we: 2129
BARKES = 1
The Fox barkes not, when he would steale the Lambe.   1349
BARONS = *1
*Seuen Earles, twelue Barons, & twenty reuerend Bishops   15
BARREN = 1
Barren Winter, with his wrathfull nipping Cold;   1173
BARWICK = 1*1
Simpc. At Barwick in the North, and't like your | Grace.   813
Till they come to Barwick, from whence they came. | *Exit.*   910
BASE = 6*4
While Gloster beares this base and humble minde.   337

BASE *cont.*

Away, base Cullions: *Suffolke* let them goe.	426
Yorke. Base Dunghill Villaine, and Mechanicall,	590
Glost. My Lord, 'tis but a base ignoble minde,	729
Neuer yet did base dishonour blurre our name,	2208
Suf. Base slaue, thy words are blunt, and so art thou.	2235
*Small things make base men proud. This Villaine heere,	2274
Staf. And will you credit this base Drudges Wordes,	2471
*And you base Pezants, do ye beleeue him, will you needs	2797
*base and ignominious treasons, makes me betake mee to | my heeles.	
Exit	2840

BASE-BORNE = 2

Contemptuous base-borne Callot as she is,	469
Better ten thousand base-borne *Cades* miscarry,	2824

BASILISKE = 1

Yet doe not goe away: come Basiliske,	1752

BASILISKES = 1

Their cheefest Prospect, murd'ring Basiliskes:	2039

BASIMECU = *1

*Normandie vnto Mounsieur *Basimecu*, the Dolphine of	2662

BASTARD = 2

A Romane Sworder, and Bandetto slaue | Murder'd sweet *Tully. Brutus*	
Bastard hand	2303
To say, if that the Bastard boyes of Yorke	3110

BASTARDIE = 1

That thou thy selfe wast borne in Bastardie;	1928

BATE = *1

Clif. Are these thy Beares? Wee'l bate thy Bears to death,	3147

BATTELL = 3

That those which flye before the battell ends,	2498
To die in Ruffian battell? Euen at this sight,	3271
Saint Albons battell wonne by famous Yorke,	3352

BAYTING = 1

If thou dar'st bring them to the bayting place.	3149

BE = 205*43

BEADES = 2

In Courtly company, or at my Beades,	34
To number *Aue-Maries* on his Beades:	442

BEADLE = 3*1

Maior. Sirrha, goe fetch the Beadle hither straight. | *Exit.*	887
Enter a Beadle with Whippes.	894
*Sirrha Beadle, whippe him till he leape ouer that same | Stoole.	896
After the Beadle hath hit him once, he leapes ouer	902

BEADLE = 1

BEADLES = 1

Haue you not Beadles in your Towne, | And Things call'd Whippes?	883

BEAKE = 1

Although the Kyte soare with vnbloudied Beake?	1897

BEAME = *1

*Whose Beame stands sure, whose rightful cause preuailes. | *Flourish.*	
Exeunt.	957

BEAMES = 2

Queene. Free Lords: | Cold Snow melts with the Sunnes hot Beames:	1524
Like to the glorious Sunnes transparant Beames,	1659

BEARARD = 1

Despight the Bearard, that protects the Beare.	3210

BEARD = 1*1
His well proportion'd Beard, made ruffe and rugged,	1879
*broach'd, and beard thee to. Looke on mee well, I haue	2942

BEARE = 16*3
Did beare him like a Noble Gentleman:	192
Beare that proportion to my flesh and blood,	245
And in my Standard beare the Armes of Yorke,	268
Ah *Humfrey*, can I beare this shamefull yoake?	1213
The reuerent care I beare vnto my Lord,	1328
Before his Legges be firme to beare his Body.	1490
And beare the name and port of Gentlemen?	2188
More can I beare, then you dare execute.	2298
His body will I beare vnto the King:	2316
*This Monument of the victory will I beare, and the bo-|dies	2522
*Say. Heare me but speake, and beare mee wher'e you | will:	2692
Which I will beare in triumph to the King,	2988
Old Clif. I am resolu'd to beare a greater storme,	3198
The rampant Beare chain'd to the ragged staffe,	3203
Old Clif. And from thy Burgonet Ile rend thy Beare,	3208
Despight the Bearard, that protects the Beare.	3210
And if thou dost not hide thee from the Beare,	3220
As did *Aeneas* old *Anchyses* beare,	3284
So beare I thee vpon my manly shoulders:	3285

BEARES = 8*1
While Gloster beares this base and humble minde.	337
She beares a Dukes Reuenewes on her backe,	466
And beares his thoughts aboue his Faulcons Pitch.	728
That beares so shrewd a mayme: two Pulls at once;	1097
With what a Maiestie he beares himselfe,	1300
Respecting what a rancorous minde he beares,	1318
Call hither to the stake my two braue Beares,	3141
Clif. Are these thy Beares? Wee'l bate thy Bears to death,	3147
Who being suffer'd with the Beares fell paw,	3152

BEAREST = 1
King. O God, seest thou this, and bearest so long?	905

BEARING = 3
Enter the Maior of Saint Albones, and his Brethren, | bearing the man	
betweene two in a Chayre.	795
Bearing it to the bloody Slaughter-house;	1513
Yorke. With thy braue bearing should I be in loue,	3241

BEARS = *1
Clif. Are these thy Beares? Wee'l bate thy Bears to death,	3147

BEAST = 1
Euen of the bonnie beast he loued so well.	3231

BEAT = 2
Beat on a Crowne, the Treasure of thy Heart,	737
A Staffe is quickly found to beat a Dogge.	1471

BEATE = 2
When from thy Shore, the Tempest beate vs backe,	1802
Oh beate away the busie medling Fiend,	2155

BEATEN = 2
Thus is the Shepheard beaten from thy side,	1491
Mine eyes should sparkle like the beaten Flint,	2032

BEATS = 1
And binds the Wretch, and beats it when it strayes,	1512

BEAU = 1

BEAUFORD see also *Beau.* = 6*3
* *Enter King, Duke Humfrey, Salisbury, Warwicke, and Beau-|ford on*
  the one side. 3
Or hath mine Vnckle *Beauford*, and my selfe, ... 95
* *Queene.* Beside the haughtie Protector, haue we *Beauford* 454
And *Yorke*, and impious *Beauford*, that false Priest, ... 1229
My selfe and *Beauford* had him in protection, ... 1884
Is *Beauford* tearm'd a Kyte? where are his Tallons? 1900
That Cardinall *Beauford* is at point of death: 2086
* *King.* How fare's my Lord? Speake *Beauford* to thy | Soueraigne. .. 2134
War. Beauford, it is thy Soueraigne speakes to thee. 2141
BEAUFORDS = 3
At *Beaufords* Pride, at *Somersets* Ambition, ... 1037
Beaufords red sparkling eyes blab his hearts mallice, ... 1454
By Suffolke, and the Cardinall *Beaufords* meanes: 1826
BEAUTEOUS = 1
For thou hast giuen me in this beauteous Face 28
BEAUTIE = 3
Could I come neere your Beautie with my Nayles, ... 533
That for the beautie thinkes it excellent. 1532
And Beautie, that the Tyrant oft reclaimes, ... 3276
BEAUTIFIE = 1
To blush and beautifie the Cheeke againe. 1871
BECAME = 1
Became a Bricklayer, when he came to age. 2465
BECAUSE = 10*2
Queene. Because the King forsooth will haue it so. 505
Suff. Because here is a man accused of Treason, ... 573
Because in *Yorke* this breedes suspition; 603
Because I wish'd this Worlds eternitie. 1270
Because I would not taxe the needie Commons, ... 1416
Because his purpose is not executed. 1558
Because thy flinty heart more hard then they, ... 1799
*thou hast put them in prison, and because they could not 2677
Sweet is the Country, because full of Riches, ... 2696
Because my Booke preferr'd me to the King. 2706
*dwell in this house, because the vnconquered soule of | *Cade* is fled. .. 2969
Run backe and bite, because he was with-held, ... 3151
BECOME = 2*1
* *Bulling.* First of the King: What shall of him be-|come? 655
How insolent of late he is become, ... 1301
That Head of thine doth not become a Crowne: 3091
BECOMES = 1
Suff. No mallice Sir, no more then well becomes 745
BED = 8*1
I banish her my Bed, and Companie, ... 949
Haue you layd faire the Bed? Is all things well, ... 1702
Suff. Dead in his Bed, my Lord: *Gloster* is dead. | *Queene.* Marry God
  forfend. 1725
But all in vaine are these meane Obsequies, | *Bed put forth.* 1848
Thy Mother tooke into her blamefull Bed 1917
Enter the King, Salisbury, and Warwicke, to the | Cardinal in bed. .. 2132
Dy'de he not in his bed? Where should he dye? 2143
What wilt thou on thy death-bed play the Ruffian? 3164
* *War.* You were best to go to bed, and dreame againe, ... 3196
BEDFORD = 1
And did my brother *Bedford* toyle his wits, ... 90

26

BEDFORDS = 1
Shall *Henries* Conquest, *Bedfords* vigilance,   103
BEDLAM = 1
Did instigate the Bedlam braine-sick Duchesse,   1345
BEDLEM = 2
To Bedlem with him, is the man growne mad.   3128
King. I Clifford, a Bedlem and ambitious humor   3129
BEE *l*.*2390 *2518 *2638 *2646 *2739 = *5, *1
*should vndoe a man. Some say the Bee stings, but I say,   2398
BEEFE = *1
*cut not out the burly bon'd Clowne in chines of Beefe,   2961
BEEN *l*.*810 = *1
BEENE *see also* bene, bin *l*.517 805 816 835 872 1002 1269 1281 1337
1597 1608 1995 *2516 2556 *2679 *2917 = 13*3
BEERE = *2
*3.*Neighbor*. And here's a Pot of good Double-Beere   1125
*small Beere. All the Realme shall be in Common, and in   2386
BEES = 1*1
The Commons like an angry Hiue of Bees   1827
*'tis the Bees waxe: for I did but seale once to a thing, and   2399
BEESOME = *1
*the presence of Lord *Mortimer*, that I am the Beesome   2664
BEEST = 1*1
If after three dayes space thou here bee'st found,   2009
*Ca. If thou beest death, Ile giue thee Englands Treasure,   2136
BEE-HIUES = 1
Drones sucke not Eagles blood, but rob Bee-hiues: 2277
BEFALL = 4
Bulling. What shall befall the Duke of Somerset?   661
Oh let me stay, befall what may befall.   2119
And more such dayes as these, to vs befall. *Exeunt.*   3355
BEFORE = 18*10
Before I would haue yeelded to this League.   134
Hum. A proper iest, and neuer heard before,   139
She should haue staid in France, and steru'd in France | Before --- 142
Sal. Pride went before, Ambition followes him.   188
Follow I must, I cannot go before,   336
*presently: wee'le heare more of your matter before | the King. *Exit.* 420
Suff. Before we make election, giue me leaue   557
A man that ne're saw in his life before.   792
Glost. But Cloakes and Gownes, before this day, a | many.   859
Wife. Neuer before this day, in all his life.   861
Edward the Black-Prince dyed before his Father,   977
Succeed before the younger, I am King.   1016
Drumme before him, and his Staffe, with a Sand-bagge   1117
I must offend, before I be attainted: 1235
Glost. And my consent ne're ask'd herein before?   1249
Before his Legges be firme to beare his Body.   1490
Before his Chaps be stayn'd with Crimson blood,   1561
Before the Wound doe grow vncurable;   1589
Wal. Thou shalt haue cause to feare before I leaue thee.   2286
Cade. For our enemies shall faile before vs, inspired   2355
That those which flye before the battell ends,   2498
Cade. They fell before thee like Sheepe and Oxen, &   2515
*London, where we will haue the Maiors sword born be-|fore vs.   2524
*before, our Fore-fathers had no other Bookes but the   2668
*Iustices of Peace, to call poore men before them, a-|bout   2675

BEFORE *cont.*

For with these borne before vs, in steed of Maces,	2770
*Wiues and Daughters before your faces. For me, I will	2806
War. After them: nay before them if we can:	3350

BEGAN = 2

Vpon my Life began her diuellish practises:	1340
And when the duskie sky, began to rob	1804

BEGGE = 2

I care not whither, for I begge no fauor;	1272
Make thee begge pardon for thy passed speech,	1926

BEGGERIE = 1

And to conclude, Reproach and Beggerie, | Is crept into the Pallace of our King,	2269

BEGGERY = 1

Weauer. A must needs, for beggery is valiant.	2373

BEGGER-WOMAN = 1

Was by a begger-woman stolne away,	2463

BEGIN = 2*1

We shall begin our ancient bickerings:	151
Begin your Suites anew, and sue to him. | *Teare the Supplication.*	424
Warw. Sweet *Yorke* begin: and if thy clayme be good,	966

BEGINS = 1*1

Yorke. Dispatch, this Knaues tongue begins to double.	1153
Whose floud begins to flowe within mine eyes;	1500

BEGUILES = 1

Beguiles him, as the mournefull Crocodile	1528

BEHALFE = 2

For euery word you speake in his behalfe,	1913
This hand of mine hath writ in thy behalfe,	2231

BEHAUEDST = *1

*thou behaued'st thy selfe, as if thou hadst beene in thine	2516

BEHEAD = 1

a pole, or no: Take him away, and behead him.	2729

BEHEADED = *1

Cade. Well, hee shall be beheaded for it ten times:	2658

BEHINDE = 1*1

And left behinde him *Richard*, his onely Sonne,	978
Geo. O monstrous Coward! What, to come behinde | Folkes?	2716

BEHOLD = 4

her Ladyship behold and heare our Exorcismes?	623
So please your Highnesse to behold the fight.	1107
That were vnworthy to behold the same.	2550
Is my Apparrell sumptuous to behold?	2733

BEHOOFE = 1

This Tongue hath parlied vnto Forraigne Kings | For your behoofe.	2711

BEHOOUES = 1

Behooues it vs to labor for the Realme.	190

BEING *l.*71 173 341 385 547 823 990 1006 1404 1556 1590 1670 1688 1867 1964 1974 2206 2275 *2381 *2397 2462 3011 3063 3152 3344 = 23*2

BELDAM = 1

Beldam I thinke we watcht you at an ynch.	672

BELEEUE = 4*1

Queene. Beleeue me Lords, for flying at the Brooke,	717
Card. Beleeue me, Cousin *Gloster*,	765
Beleeue me Lords, were none more wise then I,	1533
I do beleeue that violent hands were laid	1860
*And you base Pezants, do ye beleeue him, will you needs	2797

28

BELEEUING = 1
King. Now God be prays'd, that to beleeuing Soules   793
BELIKE = 1
Queen. Than you belike suspect these Noblemen,   1890
BELLES = 1
Ring Belles alowd, burne Bonfires cleare and bright   2994
BELLS = 1
Shaking the bloody Darts, as he his Bells.   1672
BELONG = 1
For iudgement onely doth belong to thee: 1842
BELONGING = 1
Here doe the Ceremonies belonging, and make the Circle,   643
BELONGS = 1
Disdaining dutie that to vs belongs.   1311
BELOUD = 2
And the Protectors wife belou'd of him?   318
And goe in peace, *Humfrey,* no lesse belou'd,   1081
BELOW = 1*1
Hume, that you be by her aloft, while wee be busie be-|low;   627
Enter Lord Scales vpon the Tower walking. Then enters | two or three
Citizens below.   2598
BEND = 1
For shame in dutie bend thy knee to me,   3173
BENDED = 1
And humbly now vpon my bended knee,   17
BENE *l.*2321 *2916 = 1*1
BENEFIT = 1
Will make but little for his benefit: 484
BENT = 2
But all his minde is bent to Holinesse,   441
A sort of naughtie persons, lewdly bent,   919
BERARD = 1
And manacle the Berard in their Chaines,   3148
BEREFT = 3
Is vtterly bereft you: all is lost.   1381
Whose dismall tune bereft my Vitall powres: 1741
They say is shamefully bereft of life.   1981
BESEECH = 2*2
I doe beseech your Royall Maiestie,   592
*of this; therefore I beseech your Maiestie, doe not cast   598
I beseech your Maiestie giue me leaue to goe;   1074
*ere thou sleepe in thy Sheath, I beseech Ioue on my knees   2962
BESHREW = 1
Beshrew the winners, for they play'd me false,   1484
BESIDE = 1*1
Then all the Princes in the Land beside,   183
* *Queene.* Beside the haughtie Protector, haue we *Beauford*   454
BESIEGD = 1
Till Paris was besieg'd, famisht, and lost.   567
BESPOTTED = 1
Yorke. O blood-bespotted Neopolitan,   3112
BEST = 5*4
Warw. Warwicke may liue to be the best of all.   502
That time best fits the worke we haue in hand.   640
And looke thy selfe be faultlesse, thou wert best.   941
Where it best fits to be, in *Henries* hand.   1100
And with your best endeuour haue stirr'd vp   1463

BEST   *cont.*
  King. My Lords, what to your wisdomes seemeth best,   1495
  Cade. Braue thee? I by the best blood that euer was   2941
  *Kent from me, she hath lost her best man, and exhort all   2978
  War. You were best to go to bed, and dreame againe,   3196
BESTEAD = 1
  Yorke. I neuer saw a fellow worse bestead,   1112
BESTOWD = 1
  Large gifts haue I bestow'd on learned Clearkes,   2705
BESTRID = 1
  Three times bestrid him: Thrice I led him off,   3330
BESTS = *1
  Hol. I see them, I see them: There's *Bests* Sonne, the | Tanner of
  Wingham.   2340
BETAKE = *1
  *base and ignominious treasons, makes me betake mee to | my heeles.
  Exit   2840
BETIDE = 1
  What shall betide the Duke of Somerset?   695
BETIME = 1
  Send Succours (Lords) and stop the Rage betime,   1588
BETIMES = 1
  I rather would haue lost my Life betimes,   1600
BETRAID = 1
  Buc. Trust no body for feare you betraid.   2595
BETRAY = 2*1
  Haue all lym'd Bushes to betray thy Wings,   1230
  *Villaine, thou wilt betray me, and get a 1000. Crownes   2931
  I know thee not, why then should I betray thee?   2936
BETTER = 9*2
  Was better worth then all my Fathers Lands,   472
  Warw. The Cardinall's not my better in the field.   500
  this geere, the sooner the better.   634
  I saw not better sport these seuen yeeres day: 718
  Glost. Hadst thou been his Mother, thou could'st haue | better told.   810
  Elianor. Sherife farewell, and better then I fare,   1280
  Which feare, if better Reasons can supplant,   1331
  Beuis. Thou hast hit it: for there's no better signe of a | braue minde,
  then a hard hand.   2338
  Better ten thousand base-borne *Cades* miscarry,   2824
  King. Come wife, let's in, and learne to gouern better,   2902
  I am farre better borne then is the king: 3020
BETTERS = 3
  Card. Ambitious *Warwicke*, let thy betters speake.   499
  Buck. All in this presence are thy betters, *Warwicke.*   501
  The sonnes of Yorke, thy betters in their birth,   3114
BETWEENE = 3*3
  *Betweene our Soueraigne, and the French King *Charles,*   48
  Glo. Reads. Inprimis, *It is agreed betweene the French K.(ing)*   50
  Win. Item, *It is further agreed betweene them, That the*   63
  Enter the Maior of Saint Albones, and his Brethren, | bearing the man
  betweene two in a Chayre.   795
  Dying with mothers dugge betweene it's lips.   2110
  Hath clapt his taile, betweene his legges and cride,   3153
BETWIXT   *see* 'twixt
BEU = 1

BEUIS see also Beu. = 1
  Enter Beuis, and Iohn Holland. 2319
BEUIS = *7
BEWAYLES = 1
  Euen so my selfe bewayles good *Glosters* case 1518
BEWITCH = 1
  Bewitch your hearts, be wise and circumspect. 164
BEWITCHT *see* witcht
BEYOND = 1
  The Dolphin hath preuayl'd beyond the Seas, 515
BEZONIONS = 1
  Great men oft dye by vilde Bezonions. 2302
BICKERINGS = 1
  We shall begin our ancient bickerings: 151
BID = 10*1
  And bid me be aduised how I treade. 1212
  *Elianor. What, gone my Lord, and bid me not fare-|well? 1263
  And bid them blow towards Englands blessed shore, 1790
  And bid mine eyes be packing with my Heart, 1811
  Suf. You bad me ban, and will you bid me leaue? 2048
  Giue me some drinke, and bid the Apothecarie 2151
  Go bid her hide him quickly from the Duke. 3079
  Qu. Call hither *Clifford*, bid him come amaine, 3109
  Bid Salsbury and Warwicke come to me. 3144
  King. Call Buckingham, and bid him arme himselfe. 3192
  I would speake blasphemy ere bid you flye: 3313
BILL = *1
  *a Sallet, my brain-pan had bene cleft with a brown Bill; 2916
BILLES = 1
  *When shall we go to Cheapside, and take vp commodi-|ties vpon our
  billes? 2759
BIN *l.*110 *2422 = 1*1
BINDS = 1
  And binds the Wretch, and beats it when it strayes, 1512
BIRD = 2
  That mounts no higher then a Bird can sore: 730
  But may imagine how the Bird was dead, 1896
BIRDS = 2
  And plac't a Quier of such enticing Birds, 475
  Yea Man and Birds are fayne of climbing high. 724
BIRTH = 4
  A cunning man did calculate my birth, 2203
  Cade. By her he had two children at one birth. | *Bro.* That's false. 2459
  And ignorant of his birth and parentage, 2464
  The sonnes of Yorke, thy betters in their birth, 3114
BIRTH-RIGHT = 1
  With honor of his Birth-right to the Crowne. 1026
BISHOP = 1
  King. Ile send some holy Bishop to intreat: 2541
BISHOPS = *1
  *Seuen Earles, twelue Barons, & twenty reuerend Bishops 15
BITE = 2
  So Yorke must sit, and fret, and bite his tongue, 242
  Run backe and bite, because he was with-held, 3151
BITING *see also* byting = 1
  Iohn. Then we are like to haue biting Statutes 2649

BITTER = 1
I would inuent as bitter searching termes,   2026
BLAB = 1
Beaufords red sparkling eyes blab his hearts mallice,   1454
BLABBING = 1
Lieu. The gaudy blabbing and remorsefull day,   2170
BLACK = 3
Simpc. Black forsooth, Coale-Black, as Iet.   855
I will stirre vp in England some black Storme,   1655
BLACKE = 2
But see, his face is blacke, and full of blood: 1872
And from his bosome purge this blacke dispaire.   2157
BLACK-PRINCE = 2
The first, *Edward* the Black-Prince, Prince of Wales;   970
Edward the Black-Prince dyed before his Father,   977
BLAME = 1
I cannot blame them all, what is't to them?   232
BLAMEFULL = 1
Thy Mother tooke into her blamefull Bed   1917
BLANKE = *1
*art thou within point-blanke of our Iurisdiction Regall.   2660
BLASPHEMING = 1
Blaspheming God, and cursing men on earth.   2089
BLASPHEMY = 1
I would speake blasphemy ere bid you flye: 3313
BLAST = 1
Now let the generall Trumpet blow his blast,   3265
BLASTED = 1
Thus are my Blossomes blasted in the Bud,   1386
BLEEDING = 1*1
**Warw.* Who finds the Heyfer dead, and bleeding fresh,   1892
With gobbets of thy Mother-bleeding heart.   2253
BLESSE = 1*1
*2.*Pet.* Marry the Lord protect him, for hee's a good | man, Iesu blesse
him.   389
*take all the Money that I haue. O Lord blesse me, I pray   1137
BLESSED = 3
For blessed are the Peace-makers on Earth.   754
Card. Let me be blessed for the Peace I make   755
And bid them blow towards Englands blessed shore,   1790
BLESSINGS = 1
A world of earthly blessings to my soule,   29
BLINDE = 7
One. Forsooth, a blinde man at Saint *Albones* Shrine,   790
What, hast thou beene long blinde, and now restor'd?   805
Simpc. Borne blinde, and't please your Grace. | *Wife.* I indeede was he. 806
Glost. How long hast thou beene blinde? | *Simpc.* O borne so, Master.   835
If thou hadst beene borne blinde,   872
I would be blinde with weeping, sicke with grones,   1762
And call'd them blinde and duskie Spectacles,   1812
BLINDED = 1
He hath no eyes, the dust hath blinded them.   2148
BLISSE = 1
Lord Card'nall, if thou think'st on heauens blisse,   2161
BLOCKE = 1
Stoope to the blocke, then these knees bow to any,   2293

BLOCKES = 1
I would remoue these tedious stumbling blockes,   339
BLOOD = 18*1
My sword should shed hot blood, mine eyes no teares.   125
Consider Lords, he is the next of blood,   158
Beare that proportion to my flesh and blood,   245
Were I a Man, a Duke, and next of blood,   338
Simpc. Red Master, Red as Blood.   852
With heart-blood of the House of *Lancaster*:   1032
Before his Chaps be stayn'd with Crimson blood,   1561
And temper Clay with blood of Englishmen.   1616
War. See how the blood is setled in his face.   1864
But see, his face is blacke, and full of blood: 1872
Suff. Thou shalt be waking, while I shed thy blood,   1932
Or with their blood staine this discoloured shore.   2180
Obscure and lowsie Swaine, King *Henries* blood.   2218
Suf. The honourable blood of Lancaster   2219
Drones sucke not Eagles blood, but rob Bee-hiues: 2277
Bro. But angry, wrathfull, and inclin'd to blood,   2446
*Cade. Braue thee? I by the best blood that euer was   2941
Ne're shall this blood be wiped from thy point,   2974
And shame thine honourable Age with blood?   3170
BLOODIE = 1
Murther indeede, that bloodie sinne, I tortur'd | Aboue the Felon, or
what Trespas else.   1431
BLOODLESSE = 1
Of ashy semblance, meager, pale, and bloodlesse,   1866
BLOODSHEDDING = 1
These hands are free from guiltlesse bloodshedding,   2735
BLOODY = 6
Vnlesse it were a bloody Murtherer,   1428
Bearing it to the bloody Slaughter-house;   1513
Shaking the bloody Darts, as he his Bells.   1672
And sooner dance vpon a bloody pole,   2295
Rather then bloody Warre shall cut them short,   2544
Out-cast of *Naples*, Englands bloody Scourge,   3113
BLOODY-MINDED = 1
Yet let not this make thee be bloody-minded,   2205
BLOOD-BESPOTTED = 1
Yorke. O blood-bespotted Neopolitan,   3112
BLOOD-CONSUMING = 1
Or blood-consuming sighes recall his Life;   1761
BLOOD-DRINKING = 1
Looke pale as Prim-rose with blood-drinking sighes,   1763
BLOOD-SUCKER = 1
Pernicious blood-sucker of sleeping men.   1931
BLOSSOMES = 1
Thus are my Blossomes blasted in the Bud,   1386
BLOT = 1
But with our sword we wip'd away the blot.   2209
BLOTTING = 1
Blotting your names from Bookes of memory,   107
BLOUDY = 1
1.*Gent.* O barbarous and bloudy spectacle,   2315
BLOW = 4*1
*O Lord haue mercy vpon me, I shall neuer be able to | fight a blow: O
Lord my heart.   612

BLOW *cont.*

*nor the Queene: and therefore *Peter* haue at thee with a | downe-right
blow.   1151
And bid them blow towards Englands blessed shore,   1790
**Cade.* Tut, when struck'st thou one blow in the field?   2713
Now let the generall Trumpet blow his blast,   3265
BLOWE = 1
Shall blowe ten thousand Soules to Heauen, or Hell: 1656
BLOWES = *1
**Salisb.* Come, leaue your drinking, and fall to blowes.   1140
BLOWNE = 1 *1
Humf. Now Lords, my Choller being ouer-blowne,   547
**Cade.* Was euer Feather so lightly blowne too & fro,   2832
BLUNT = 1
Suf. Base slaue, thy words are blunt, and so art thou.   2235
BLUNT-WITTED = 1
Suff. Blunt-witted Lord, ignoble in demeanor,   1915
BLURRE = 1
Neuer yet did base dishonour blurre our name,   2208
BLUSH = 3
But be thou milde, and blush not at my shame,   1224
Glost. Well *Suffolke*, thou shalt not see me blush,   1396
To blush and beautifie the Cheeke againe.   1871
BOADED = 1
What boaded this? but well fore-warning winde   1785
BOADING = 1
And boading Screech-Owles, make the Consort full.   2042
BOATS = 1
Lieu. Conuey him hence, and on our long boats side,   2236
BODE = 1
This was my dreame, what it doth bode God knowes.   305
BODIE = 2
Wal. There let his head, and liuelesse bodie lye,   2313
Clif. My soule and bodie on the action both.   3247
BODIES = *1
*This Monument of the victory will I beare, and the bo-|dies   2522
BODY = 12
Before his Legges be firme to beare his Body.   1490
My Body round engyrt with miserie: 1501
Som. Rere vp his Body, wring him by the Nose.   1732
And so I wish'd thy body might my Heart: 1809
**Warw.* Come hither gracious Soueraigne, view this | body.   1852
Or I should breathe it so into thy body,   2115
Manet the first Gent. Enter Walter with the body.   2312
His body will I beare vnto the King: 2316
But where's the body that I should imbrace?   2538
Buc. Trust no body for feare you betraid.   2595
And as I thrust thy body in with my sword,   2983
So was his Will, in his old feeble body,   3334
BOLD = 4
For I am bold to counsaile you in this;   479
Here in our presence? Dare you be so bold?   1948
And therefore am I bold and resolute. *Exeunt.*   2597
Dare any be so bold to sound Retreat or Parley   2779
BOLDER = 1
Makes me the bolder to salute my King,   36

34

BOLDLY = 1
But boldly stand, and front him to his face. 3081
BOLLINGBROOKE = 1
With *Roger Bollingbrooke* the Coniurer? 351
BONA = 1
Dic. What say you of Kent. | *Say.* Nothing but this: 'Tis *bona terra,*
mala gens. 2688
BOND = *1
*cut not out the burly bon'd Clowne in chines of Beefe, 2961
BOND-MEN = 1
Haue beene as Bond-men to thy Soueraigntie. 517
BONES = *1
* *Peter.* By these tenne bones, my Lords, hee did speake 587
BONFIRES = 1
Ring Belles alowd, burne Bonfires cleare and bright 2994
BONNIE = 1
Euen of the bonnie beast he loued so well. 3231
BOOKE = 2*1
Such as by Gods Booke are adiudg'd to death. 1057
* *Wea.* Ha's a Booke in his pocket with red Letters in't 2408
Because my Booke preferr'd me to the King. 2706
BOOKES = 1*1
Blotting your names from Bookes of memory, 107
*before, our Fore-fathers had no other Bookes but the 2668
BOOKISH = 1
Whose bookish Rule, hath pull'd faire England downe. | *Exit Yorke.* 271
BOORD = 1
Fed from my Trencher, kneel'd downe at the boord, 2225
BOORDED = 1
Is straight way calme, and boorded with a Pyrate. 2887
BOOTE = 1
And thou that art his Mate, make boote of this: 2182
BORN = *1
*London, where we will haue the Maiors sword born be-|fore vs. 2524
BORNE = 13*2
While all is shar'd, and all is borne away, 240
Contemptuous base-borne Callot as she is, 469
Simpc. Borne blinde, and't please your Grace. | *Wife.* I indeede was he. 806
King. Where wert thou borne? 812
Glost. How long hast thou beene blinde? | *Simpc.* O borne so, Master. 835
If thou hadst beene borne blinde, 872
You Madame, for you are more Nobly borne, 1062
Euen so remorselesse haue they borne him hence: 1514
Let pale-fac't feare keepe with the meane-borne man, 1641
That thou thy selfe wast borne in Bastardie; 1928
*was he borne, vnder a hedge: for his Father had neuer a | house but
the Cage. 2370
For with these borne before vs, in steed of Maces, 2770
Better ten thousand base-borne *Cades* miscarry, 2824
*Sallet was borne to do me good: for many a time but for 2915
I am farre better borne then is the king: 3020
BORROWD = 1
Seemes he a Doue? his feathers are but borrow'd, 1369
BOSOME = 2
And from his bosome purge this blacke dispaire. 2157
Is crept into the bosome of the Sea: 2171

35

BOSOMES = 1
Throw in the frozen bosomes of our part, 3257
BOTH = 10*3
Aniou and *Maine*? My selfe did win them both: 126
Aniou and *Maine* both giuen vnto the French? 248
And hauing both together heau'd it vp, 286
Wee'l both together lift our heads to heauen, 287
To call them both a payre of craftie Knaues. 379
Both. Long liue our Soueraigne *Richard,* Englands | King. 1027
And banne thine Enemies, both mine and thine. 1201
War. But both of you were vowed D.(uke) Humfries foes, 1886
Cut both the Villaines throats, for dy you shall: 2189
Alarums to the fight, wherein both the Staffords are slaine. | Enter Cade and the rest. 2511
*and strike off his head, and bring them both vppon two | poles hither. 2744
War. Of one or both of vs the time is come. 3233
Clif. My soule and bodie on the action both. 3247
BOTTOME = 1
If you be tane, we then should see the bottome 3305
BOUGHT = 2*1
*With his new Bride, & Englands deere bought Queen, 264
Wife. Too true, and bought his climbing very deare. 839
Bring the strong poyson that I bought of him. 2152
BOUND = 3
A Hart it was bound in with Diamonds, 1807
Who can be bound by any solemne Vow 3184
But that he was bound by a solemne Oath? 3190
BOUNTIE = 1
Iden. May *Iden* liue to merit such a bountie, 3075
BOW = 2*1
Stoope to the blocke, then these knees bow to any, 2293
If they can brooke I bow a knee to man: 3105
King. Why Warwicke, hath thy knee forgot to bow? 3161
BOWES = 1
That bowes vnto the graue with mickle age. 3174
BOX = 1*1
Giue me my Fanne: what, Mynion, can ye not? | *She giues the Duchesse a box on the eare.* 529
Cade. Giue him a box o'th'eare, and that wil make'em | red againe. 2719
BOYES = 3*1
Cade. O monstrous. | *Wea.* We tooke him setting of boyes Copies. 2405
*the fift, (in whose time, boyes went to Span-counter 2477
To say, if that the Bastard boyes of Yorke 3110
That for my Surety will refuse the Boyes. 3116
BRAINE-SICK = 1
Did instigate the Bedlam braine-sick Duchesse, 1345
BRAIN-PAN = *1
*a Sallet, my brain-pan had bene cleft with a brown Bill; 2916
BRAIN-SICKE = 1
Thou mad misleader of thy brain-sicke sonne, 3163
BRAND = 1
As did the fatall brand *Althaea* burnt, 246
BRAUE = 7*4
Glo. Braue Peeres of England, Pillars of the State, 82
Braue *Yorke, Salisbury,* and victorious *Warwicke,* 93
Beuis. Thou hast hit it: for there's no better signe of a | braue minde, then a hard hand. 2338

BRAUE *cont.*

Cade. Be braue then, for your Captaine is Braue, and	2382
Cade. Marry presently. | *All.* O braue.	2761
Cade. What Buckingham and Clifford are ye so braue?	2796
But thou wilt braue me with these sawcie termes?	2940
Cade. Braue thee? I by the best blood that euer was	2941
Call hither to the stake my two braue Beares,	3141
Yorke. With thy braue bearing should I be in loue,	3241

BRAUELY = *1

*and many a time when I haue beene dry, & brauely mar-|ching,	2917

BRAUER = 1

Cade. But is not this brauer:	2764

BRAYNE = 2

And buzze these Coniurations in her brayne.	375
My Brayne, more busie then the laboring Spider,	1645

BRAZEN = 2

Are brazen Images of Canonized Saints.	446
And he that loos'd them forth their Brazen Caues,	1789

BREACH = 2*1

But I in danger for the breach of Law.	1242
Card. A Breach that craues a quick expedient stoppe.	1591
And where this breach now in our Fortunes made | May readily be stopt.	3309

BREAKE = 6*4

And Spirits walke, and Ghosts breake vp their Graues;	639
Enter the Duke of Yorke and the Duke of Buckingham | with their Guard, and breake in.	669
Salisb. My Lord, breake we off; we know your minde | at full.	1043
And so breake off, the day is almost spent,	1630
Within. An answer from the King, or wee will all | breake in.	1991
And euen now my burthen'd heart would breake	2035
But. If we meane to thriue, and do good, breake open	2526
*breake into his Sonne in Lawes house, Sir *Iames Cromer*,	2743
*to the Nobility. Let them breake your backes with bur-|thens,	2804
Is't not enough to breake into my Garden,	2937

BREAKES = 1

That he that breakes a sticke of Glosters groue,	307

BREAKFAST = 1

A sorry Breakfast for my Lord Protector.	706

BREAST = 2

By crying comfort from a hollow breast,	1743
This breast from harbouring foule deceitfull thoughts.	2736

BREASTS = 1

Who cherisht in your breasts, will sting your hearts.	1650

BREATH = 3*1

And would haue kept, so long as breath did last:	222
Heere could I breath my soule into the ayre,	2108
Breath foule contagious darknesse in the ayre:	2176
Smith. Nay *Iohn*, it wil be stinking Law, for his breath | stinkes with eating toasted cheese.	2644

BREATHD = *1

*Through whom a thousand sighes are breath'd for thee.	2060

BREATHE = 2

He shall not breathe infection in this ayre,	2001
Or I should breathe it so into thy body,	2115

BREATHING = 1

Be my last breathing in this mortall world.	294

BREATHLESSE = 1
   Enter his Chamber, view his breathlesse Corpes,   1834
BRED = 1
   Doe calme the furie of this mad-bred Flawe.   1660
BREECHES = 1
   Though in this place most Master weare no Breeches,   538
BREEDES = 1
   Because in *Yorke* this breedes suspition;   603
BREST = 1
   Heere may his head lye on my throbbing brest: 2537
BREST-PLATE = *1
   King. What stronger Brest-plate then a heart vntainted?   1938
BRETHREN = 1
   Enter the Maior of Saint Albones, and his Brethren, | bearing the man
   betweene two in a Chayre.   795
BRIBE = 1
   Nor euer had one penny Bribe from France.   1409
BRIBES = 1
   Yorke. 'Tis thought, my Lord, | That you tooke Bribes of France,   1402
BRICKE = *1
   *could stay no longer. Wherefore on a Bricke wall haue   2911
BRICKES = *1
   *the brickes are aliue at this day to testifie it: therefore | deny it not.   2469
BRICKLAYER = 2
   But. He was an honest man, and a good Bricklayer.   2360
   Became a Bricklayer, when he came to age.   2465
BRIDE = *1
   *With his new Bride, & Englands deere bought Queen,   264
BRIDGE = 3
   Mess. Iacke Cade hath gotten London-bridge.   2586
   For they haue wonne the Bridge,   2602
   But first, go and set London Bridge on fire,   2630
BRIDLE = 1*1
   In what we can, to bridle and suppresse   208
   *Ile bridle it: he shall dye, and it bee but for pleading so   2739
BRIGHT = 1
   Ring Belles alowd, burne Bonfires cleare and bright   2994
BRIGHTEST = *1
   Glost. Thus sometimes hath the brightest day a Cloud: 1171
BRING = 8*4
   Dame *Elianor* giues Gold, to bring the Witch: 367
   Glost. Stand by, my Masters, bring him neere the King,   801
   Will bring thy head with sorrow to the ground.   1073
   *Which time will bring to light in smooth Duke *Humfrey*.   1359
   Then bring a burthen of dis-honour home,   1601
   Beau. Bring me vnto my Triall when you will.   2142
   Bring the strong poyson that I bought of him.   2152
   Therefore bring forth the Souldiers of our prize,   2177
   *and strike off his head, and bring them both vppon two | poles hither. 2744
   Or dare to bring thy Force so neere the Court?   3014
   K. Then what intends these Forces thou dost bring?   3053
   If thou dar'st bring them to the bayting place.   3149
BRINGING = 1
   In bringing them to ciuill Discipline: 203
BRINGS = 2
   To match with her that brings no vantages.   138
   And he that brings his head vnto the King,   2843

BRISTOW = 1
| At Bristow I expect my Souldiers, | 1633 |
BRITAIGNE = *1
| *The Dukes of *Orleance, Calaber, Britaigne,* and *Alanson,* | 14 |
BRITAINES = 1
| Is this the Gouernment of Britaines Ile? | 430 |
BRO = 4*1
BROACHD = *1
| *broach'd, and beard thee to. Looke on mee well, I haue | 2942 |
BROKE = 2*1
Was broke in twaine: by whom, I haue forgot,	300
Broke be my sword, my Armes torne and defac'd,	2211
*my sword therefore broke through London gates, that	2799
BROKEN = 2
And on the peeces of the broken Wand	302
False King, why hast thou broken faith with me,	3086
BROKER = 2
They say, A craftie Knaue do's need no Broker,	376
Yet am I *Suffolke* and the Cardinalls Broker.	377
BROOD = 1
Clif. Why what a brood of Traitors haue we heere?	3138
BROOKE = 6
Car. This weighty businesse will not brooke delay,	177
Queene. Beleeue me Lords, for flying at the Brooke,	717
Smooth runnes the Water, where the Brooke is deepe,	1347
For he is fierce, and cannot brooke hard Language.	2899
Knowing how hardly I can brooke abuse?	3087
If they can brooke I bow a knee to man:	3105
BROTHER *see also Bro.* = 4*1
What? did my brother *Henry* spend his youth,	85
And did my brother *Bedford* toyle his wits,	90
And Brother Yorke, thy Acts in Ireland,	202
Mich. Fly, fly, fly, Sir *Humfrey Stafford* and his brother	2432
Enter Sir *Humfrey Stafford, and his Brother,* | *with Drum and Soldiers.*	2440
BROTHERS = 2
Brothers, and worship me their Lord.	2393
Sir *Humfrey Stafford,* and his Brothers death,	2570
BROUGHT = 4*1
Till we haue brought Duke *Humphrey* in disgrace.	482
Be brought against me at my Tryall day.	1414
If Wind and Fuell be brought, to feed it with:	1606
Clearke. Sir I thanke God, I haue bin so well brought | vp, that I can write my name.	2422
The cause why I haue brought this Armie hither,	3027
BROW = 3
He knits his Brow, and shewes an angry Eye,	1309
And *Suffolks* cloudie Brow his stormie hate:	1455
And like a Gallant, in the brow of youth,	3324
BROWES = 2
Why doth the Great Duke *Humfrey* knit his browes,	276
That Gold, must round engirt these browes of mine,	3094
BROWN = *1
*a Sallet, my brain-pan had bene cleft with a brown Bill:	2916
BROYLE = 1
Me thinkes alreadie in this ciuill broyle,	2821

BUILDINGS = *1
  Som. Thy sumptuous Buildings, and thy Wiues Attyre   520
BUILT = *1
  *hast built a Paper-Mill. It will be prooued to thy Face,   2671
BULLIN = *1
BULLING = 2*4
BULLINGBROOKE *see also Bollingbrooke, Bullin., Bulling.* = 4
  Enter the Witch, the two Priests, and Bullingbrooke.   619
  Bullingbrooke or Southwell reades, Coniuro | te, &c. *It Thunders and*
  Lightens   644
  Till *Henry Bullingbrooke,* Duke of Lancaster,   980
  Salisb. This *Edmond,* in the Reigne of *Bullingbrooke,*   1000
BURGONET = 2*1
  And that Ile write vpon thy Burgonet,   3200
  This day Ile weare aloft my Burgonet,   3204
  Old Clif. And from thy Burgonet Ile rend thy Beare,   3208
BURLY = *1
  *cut not out the burly bon'd Clowne in chines of Beefe,   2961
BURNE = 3*1
  And if you can, burne downe the Tower too.   2631
  *burne all the Records of the Realme, my mouth shall be | the
  Parliament of England.   2647
  Ring Belles alowd, burne Bonfires cleare and bright   2994
  Clif. Take heede least by your heate you burne your | selues: 3159
BURNES = 1
  Burnes with reuenging fire, whose hopefull colours   2265
BURNING = 2*1
  Bulling. Discend to Darknesse, and the burning Lake: 666
  burning in her hand, with the Sherife | and Officers.   1189
  His Fathers Acts, commenc'd in burning Troy.   1818
BURNT = 3
  As did the fatall brand *Althaea* burnt,   246
  The Witch in Smithfield shall be burnt to ashes,   1060
  burnt i'th hand for stealing of Sheepe.   2381
BURTHEN = 1
  Then bring a burthen of dis-honour home,   1601
BURTHEND = 1
  And euen now my burthen'd heart would breake   2035
BURTHENS = *1
  *to the Nobility. Let them breake your backes with bur-|thens,   2804
BURY = 3
  Holden at Bury, the first of this next Moneth.   1248
  Suff. The trayt'rous *Warwick,* with the men of Bury,   1950
  Vntill the Queene his Mistris bury it. *Exit Walter.*   2314
BURYING = *1
  *Garden, and be henceforth a burying place to all that do   2968
BUSH = 1
  Suff. Madame, my selfe haue lym'd a Bush for her,   474
BUSHES = 1
  Haue all lym'd Bushes to betray thy Wings,   1230
BUSIE = 2*1
  Hume, that you be by her aloft, while wee be busie be-|low;   627
  My Brayne, more busie then the laboring Spider,   1645
  Oh beate away the busie medling Fiend,   2155
BUSINESSE = 3
  Car. This weighty businesse will not brooke delay,   177
  The businesse asketh silent secrecie.   366

BUSINESSE *cont.*

To looke into this Businesse thorowly,	954

BUT *l.*39 115 122 135 148 191 201 223 301 306 309 326 344 346 347 364
365 *408 441 457 484 513 552 554 *626 658 690 721 729 818 838 845
*859 876 914 946 *992 1002 1004 1021 1030 1034 1049 1186 1224 1232
1242 1276 1304 1307 1313 1362 1369 *1382 1388 1406 1434 1451 1482
1517 1538 1540 1543 1548 1557 1571 1574 *1575 1627 1644 1649 1755
1766 1781 1785 1788 1793 1833 1848 1851 1872 1881 *1886 1894 1896
1902 1921 1940 1973 1986 1988 2002 2006 2007 2008 2053 2062 2066
2081 2098 2104 2107 2117 2209 2216 2217 2277 *2366 2371 *2380 *2398
*2399 2436 2446 2461 *2478 *2483 *2490 2505 2507 *2509 2536 2538
2546 2553 *2558 2607 2609 2618 2630 *2668 2689 *2692 2710 *2738
*2739 *2754 2764 *2802 2816 *2839 2853 2859 2888 *2909 *2915 *2932
2940 2952 *2966 2975 2998 3022 3031 3076 3081 3127 3133 3183 3190
3201 3229 3242 3244 3261 3286 3294 3303 3306 3312 3314 3332
3335 = 146*27

BUT = 9*9

BUTCH = 1

BUTCHER see also *But.*, *Butch.* = 5*3

And as the Butcher takes away the Calfe,	1511
And sees fast-by, a Butcher with an Axe,	1893
* *Qu.* Are you the Butcher, *Suffolk?* where's your Knife?	1899
Hol. And Dicke the Butcher.	2344
* *Drumme. Enter Cade, Dicke Butcher, Smith the Weauer,* | *and a*	
Sawyer, with infinite numbers.	2350
* *Butcher.* And furthermore, wee'l haue the Lord *Sayes*	2480
Cade. Where's Dicke, the Butcher of Ashford? | *But.* Heere sir.	2513
* *Dicke.* And worke in their shirt to, as my selfe for ex-|ample, that am	
a butcher.	2685

BUY = 1

Ah *Sancta Maiestas*! who would not buy thee deere?	2996

BUZZE = 1

And buzze these Coniurations in her brayne.	375

BY *see also* fast-by = 102*13, 1*1

*will come this way by and by, and then wee may	387
Glost. Now fetch me a Stoole hither by and by.	889

BYTH = 2

But as I thinke, it was by'th Cardinall,	301
By'th'Masse so did we all. I thanke you *Richard.*	3338

BYTING = 1

Where byting cold would neuer let grasse grow,	2052

CA = *1

CADE = 24*8

I haue seduc'd a head-strong Kentishman, | *Iohn Cade* of Ashford,	1662
In Ireland haue I seene this stubborne *Cade*	1666
* *Beuis.* I tell thee, *Iacke Cade* the Cloathier, meanes to	2323
* *Drumme. Enter Cade, Dicke Butcher, Smith the Weauer,* | *and a*	
Sawyer, with infinite numbers.	2350
* *Cade.* Wee *Iohn Cade*, so tearm'd of our supposed Fa-|ther.	2352
But. Or rather of stealing a Cade of Herrings.	2354
* *Bro. Iacke Cade*, the D.(uke) of York hath taught you this.	2474
Proclaime them Traitors that are vp with *Cade*,	2497
Alarums to the fight, wherein both the Staffords are slaine. | *Enter Cade*	
and the rest.	2511
Will parley with *Iacke Cade* their Generall.	2545
King. Lord *Say*, *Iacke Cade* hath sworne to haue thy | head.	2551
Iacke Cade proclaimes himselfe Lord *Mortimer*,	2564

CADE *cont.*
    Mess. Iacke Cade hath gotten London-bridge.   2586
    Scales. How now? Is *Iacke Cade* slaine?   2600
    Enter Iacke Cade and the rest, and strikes his | staffe on London stone.   2613
    Soul. Iacke Cade, Iacke Cade. | Cade. Knocke him downe there. *They*
    kill him.   2623
    Cade more, I thinke he hath a very faire warning.   2626
    Alarums. Mathew Goffe is slain, and all the rest. | Then enter Iacke
    Cade, with his Company.   2633
    Alarum, and Retreat. Enter againe Cade, | and all his rabblement.   2773
    Know *Cade*, we come Ambassadors from the King   2783
    All. Wee'l follow *Cade*,   2809
    Wee'l follow *Cade*.   2810
    Clif. Is *Cade* the sonne of *Henry* the fift,   2811
    **Kin.* Why Buckingham, is the Traitor *Cade* surpris'd?   2858
    **King.* Thus stands my state, 'twixt Cade and Yorke | distrest,   2884
    But now is Cade driuen backe, his men dispierc'd,   2888
    Enter Cade.   2905
    **Iden.* Is't *Cade* that I haue slain, that monstrous traitor?   2971
    And fight against that monstrous Rebell *Cade*,   3055
    The head of *Cade*, whom I in combat slew.   3061
    **King.* The head of *Cade*? Great God, how iust art thou?   3062
CADE = 24*38
CADES = 2
    Better ten thousand base-borne *Cades* miscarry,   2824
    Enter Iden with Cades head.   3057
CAESAR = 2
    Stab'd *Iulius Caesar. Sauage* Islanders   2305
    Kent, in the Commentaries *Caesar* writ,   2694
CAGE = 1
    *was he borne, vnder a hedge: for his Father had neuer a | house but
    the Cage.   2370
CALABER = *1
    *The Dukes of *Orleance, Calaber, Britaigne,* and *Alanson*,   14
CALCULATE = 1
    A cunning man did calculate my birth,   2203
CALFE = 2
    And as the Butcher takes away the Calfe,   1511
    **Beuis.* Then is sin strucke downe like an Oxe, and ini-|quities throate
    cut like a Calfe.   2345
CALIDON = 1
    Vnto the Princes heart of *Calidon*:   247
CALL = 17*3
    To call them both a payre of craftie Knaues.   379
    Buck. True Madame, none at all: what call you this?   679
    And many time and oft my selfe haue heard a Voyce, | To call him so.   828
    And call these foule Offendors to their Answeres;   955
    If it be fond, call it a Womans feare: 1330
    King. Goe call our Vnckle to our presence straight: 1709
    Suff. Ile call him presently, my Noble Lord. *Exit.*   1712
    King. Vngentle Queene, to call him gentle *Suffolke.*   2004
    Disdaine to call vs Lord, and *Piccardie*   2256
    They call false Catterpillers, and intend their death.   2573
    **But.* If this Fellow be wise, hee'l neuer call yee *Iacke*   2625
    *Iustices of Peace, to call poore men before them, a-|bout   2675
    King did I call thee? No: thou art not King: 3088
    Sirrah, call in my sonne to be my bale: 3106

CALL *cont.*

Qu. Call hither *Clifford*, bid him come amaine,	3109
Yorke. Looke in a Glasse, and call thy Image so.	3139
Call hither to the stake my two braue Beares,	3141
King. Call Buckingham, and bid him arme himselfe.	3192
*Yorke. Call Buckingham, and all the friends thou hast,	3193
To call a present Court of Parliament:	3347

CALLD = 4

Being call'd a hundred times, and oftner,	823
Haue you not Beadles in your Towne, | And Things call'd Whippes?	883
And call'd them blinde and duskie Spectacles,	1812
King. How art thou call'd? And what is thy degree?	3067

CALLES = 3*1

Were by his side: Sometime, he calles the King,	2091
And calles your Grace Vsurper, openly,	2566
That calles me other then Lord *Mortimer.*	2621
* War. Clifford of Cumberland, 'tis Warwicke calles:	3219

CALLING = 2

Calling him, *Humfrey the good Duke of Gloster,*	166
Warwicke is hoarse with calling thee to armes.	3225

CALLOT = 1

Contemptuous base-borne Callot as she is,	469

CALMD = 1

My selfe haue calm'd their spleenfull mutinie,	1830

CALME = 3

Doe calme the furie of this mad-bred Flawe.	1660
Qu. He dares not calme his contumelious Spirit,	1909
Is straight way calme, and boorded with a Pyrate.	2887

CAMBRIDGE = 1

Marryed *Richard*, Earle of Cambridge,	1007

CAME = 5*1

Your Highnesse came to England, so will I	452
Till they come to Barwick, from whence they came. | *Exit.*	910
*Sent his poore Queene to France, from whence she came,	984
Came he right now to sing a Rauens Note,	1740
*it was neuer merrie world in England, since Gentlemen | came vp.	2327
Became a Bricklayer, when he came to age.	2465

CAMST = 2

Cam'st thou here by Chance, or of Deuotion, | To this holy Shrine?	820
Suff. How cam'st thou so? | *Simpc.* A fall off of a Tree.	832

CAN *l.*25 61 114 208 457 458 529 568 665 705 730 744 1042 1181 1213
1227 1290 1298 1331 1334 1401 1482 1517 1576 1664 1683 1744 1820
2080 2144 2298 2300 *2403 *2410 2423 2466 *2486 *2489 *2490 2536
2606 2631 *2674 2757 *2912 3015 3087 3105 3184 *3298 3303 3321
3350 = 47*8

CANCELLING = 1

Fatall this Marriage, cancelling your Fame,	106

CANDLE = *1

*Cade. Ye shall haue a hempen Candle then, & the help | of hatchet.	2723

CANKER = 1

Banish the Canker of ambitious thoughts:	291

CANNOT = 15*1

I cannot blame them all, what is't to them?	232
Follow I must, I cannot go before,	336
Gold cannot come amisse, were she a Deuill.	368
Cannot doe more in England then the *Neuils*:	459
First, for I cannot flatter thee in Pride:	561

CANNOT *cont.*

Peter. Alas, my Lord, I cannot fight; for Gods sake	610
I cannot iustifie whom the Law condemnes:	1070
Glost. Witnesse my teares, I cannot stay to speake. | *Exit Gloster.*	1265
Who cannot steale a shape, that meanes deceit?	1373
Whereof you cannot easily purge your selfe.	1435
Looke after him, and cannot doe him good:	1520
It cannot be but he was murdred heere,	1881
Suf. If I depart from thee, I cannot liue,	2105
You cannot but forbeare to murther me:	2710
For he is fierce, and cannot brooke hard Language.	2899
I cannot giue due action to my words,	2999

CANONIZED = 1

Are brazen Images of Canonized Saints.	446

CANST *l.*1231 *2661 2950 3090 *3181 3199 3216 = 5*2

CAP = 1

Fling vp his cap, and say, God saue his Maiesty.	2791

CAPITALL = 1

Of Capitall Treason 'gainst the King and Crowne:	3102

CAPITE = *1

*ere they haue it: Men shall hold of mee in Capite.	2755

CAPRE = 1

Him capre vpright, like a wilde Morisco,	1671

CAPTAINE = 1*2

Whit. Speak Captaine, shall I stab the forlorn Swain.	2233
Being Captaine of a Pinnace, threatens more	2275
Cade. Be braue then, for your Captaine is Braue, and	2382

CAPTIUITIE = 1

Who kept him in Captiuitie, till he dyed. | But, to the rest.	1003

CAR = 3*1

CARD = 16*7

CARDINAL = 1

Enter the King, Salisbury, and Warwicke, to the | Cardinal in bed.	2132

CARDINALL *see also Ca., Car., Card.* = 21

Ile to the Duke of Suffolke presently. *Exit Cardinall.*	178
Yet let vs watch the haughtie Cardinall,	181
Despite Duke *Humfrey,* or the Cardinall. | *Exit Buckingham, and Somerset.*	186
Oft haue I seene the haughty Cardinall,	193
The pride of Suffolke, and the Cardinall, | With Somersets and Buckinghams Ambition,	209
But as I thinke, it was by 'th Cardinall,	301
I dare not say, from the rich Cardinall,	370
Although we fancie not the Cardinall,	480
Enter the King, Duke Humfrey, Cardinall, Bucking-|ham,	488
Buck. Lord Cardinall, I will follow *Elianor,*	541
Enter the King, Queene, Protector, Cardinall, and | Suffolke, with Faulkners hallowing.	715
Glost. I my Lord Cardinall, how thinke you by that?	733
Glost. What, Cardinall? | Is your Priest-hood growne peremptorie?	740
The East side of the Groue: | Cardinall, I am with you.	770
Sound a Senet. Enter King, Queene, Cardinall, Suffolke,	1292
And here commit you to my Lord Cardinall	1437
Lord Cardinall, he is your Prisoner.	1487
But my Lord Cardinall, and you my Lord of Suffolke,	1548
Sound Trumpets. Enter the King, the Queene, | Cardinall, Suffolke, Somerset, with | Attendants.	1706

CARDINALL cont.

By Suffolke, and the Cardinall *Beaufords* meanes:	1826
That Cardinall *Beauford* is at point of death:	2086

CARDINALLS = 3

Yet am I *Suffolke* and the Cardinalls Broker.	377
I would the Colledge of the Cardinalls	447
Warw. The Cardinall's not my better in the field.	500

CARDINALS = *1

Goodman, my Lord Cardinals Man, for keeping my House,	402

CARDNALL = 1

Lord Card'nall, if thou think'st on heauens blisse,	2161

CARE = 11

King. For my part, Noble Lords, I care not which,	491
I care not whither, for I begge no fauor;	1272
The reuerent care I beare vnto my Lord,	1328
King. My Lords at once: the care you haue of vs,	1360
If those that care to keepe your Royall Person	1473
And care not who they sting in his reuenge.	1829
They say, in care of your most Royall Person,	1966
I thanke them for their tender louing care;	1994
'Tis not the Land I care for, wer't thou thence,	2074
Whit. Gualtier or *Walter*, which it is I care not,	2207
Or gather wealth I care not with what enuy:	2926

CARES = 1

So Cares and Ioyes abound, as Seasons fleet.	1174

CARRION = 1

And made a prey for Carrion Kytes and Crowes	3230

CARRY = 2

Would chuse him Pope, and carry him to Rome,	448
Thither goes these Newes, | As fast as Horse can carry them:	704

CARRYING = *1

*of the King by carrying my head to him, but Ile make	2932

CASE = 2*1

*pitty my case: the spight of man preuayleth against me.	611
Euen so my selfe bewayles good *Glosters* case	1518
King. In any case, be not to rough in termes,	2898

CASKE = 1

Suf. A Iewell lockt into the wofulst Caske,	2127

CAST = 2*1

*of this; therefore I beseech your Maiestie, doe not cast	598
* *Weauer.* The Clearke of Chartam: hee can write and | reade, and cast	
accompt.	2403
Out-cast of *Naples*, Englands bloody Scourge,	3113

CASTLE = 1

The Castle in S.(aint) *Albons*, Somerset	3291

CASTLES = 4

Spirit. Let him shun Castles,	662
Then where Castles mounted stand.	664
Let him shunne Castles,	696
Then where Castles mounted stand.	698

CATCH = 2

That makes him gaspe, and stare, and catch the aire,	2088
Like Lime-twigs set to catch my winged soule:	2150

CATERPILLERS = 1

And Caterpillers eate my Leaues away:	1387

CATHEDRALL = 1

In the Cathedrall Church of Westminster,	311

CATTERPILLERS = 1
They call false Catterpillers, and intend their death. 2573
CAUE = 1
As leane-fac'd enuy in her loathsome caue. 2030
CAUES = 1
And he that loos'd them forth their Brazen Caues, 1789
CAUSE = 7*3
Yor. And so sayes Yorke, | For he hath greatest cause. 215
With thy Confederates in this weightie cause. | *Exit Elianor.* 361
Suff. Madame be patient: as I was cause 451
Iniurious Duke, that threatest where's no cause. 678
And poyse the Cause in Iustice equall Scales, 956
*Whose Beame stands sure, whose rightful cause preuailes. | *Flourish.*
Exeunt. 957
What counsaile giue you in this weightie cause? 1592
* *Wal.* Thou shalt haue cause to feare before I leaue thee. 2286
*that cause they haue beene most worthy to liue. Thou 2679
The cause why I haue brought this Armie hither, 3027
CAUSED = *1
*Score and the Tally, thou hast caused printing to be vs'd, 2669
CAUSELESSE = 1
Causelesse haue lay'd disgraces on my head, 1462
CAUSES = 1
Say. Long sitting to determine poore mens causes, 2721
CEASE = 7
And this fell Tempest shall not cease to rage, 1657
Nor cease to be an arrogant Controller, 1910
Suff. Cease, gentle Queene, these Execrations, 2019
Qu. Oh, let me intreat thee cease, giue me thy hand, 2054
Thinke therefore on reuenge, and cease to weepe. 2535
But who can cease to weepe, and looke on this. 2536
Particularities, and pettie sounds | To cease. Was't thou ordain'd (deere
Father) 3266
CEDAR = 1
As on a Mountaine top, the Cedar shewes, 3205
CENSURE = 2
To giue his Censure: These are no Womens matters. 507
Say you consent, and censure well the deed, 1577
CEREMONIES = 1
Here doe the Ceremonies belonging, and make the Circle, 643
CERES = 1
Hanging the head at Ceres plenteous load? 275
CHACE = *1
* *Yor.* Hold Warwick: seek thee out some other chace 3234
CHAFE = 1
Faine would I go to chafe his palie lips, 1843
CHAIND = 1
The rampant Beare chain'd to the ragged staffe, 3203
CHAINES = 2
That with the very shaking of their Chaines, 3142
And manacle the Berard in their Chaines, 3148
CHAIRE = *1
*And in that Chaire where Kings & Queens wer crownd, 312
CHAIRE-DAYES = 1
And in thy Reuerence, and thy Chaire-dayes, thus 3270
CHALKY = 1
As farre as I could ken thy Chalky Cliffes, 1801

CHAMBER = 1
   Enter his Chamber, view his breathlesse Corpes,   1834
CHAMPION = *1
   *Cade. By my Valour: the most compleate Champi-|on   2959
CHAMPIONS = 1
   His Champions, are the Prophets and Apostles,   443
CHANCE = 2
   Main-chance father you meant, but I meant *Maine*,   223
   Cam'st thou here by Chance, or of Deuotion, | To this holy Shrine?   820
CHANGE = 3*1
   *To change two Dukedomes for a Dukes faire daughter.   231
   Nor change my Countenance for this Arrest: 1397
   And change misdoubt to resolution;   1638
   Is able with the change, to kill and cure.   3096
CHANNELL = 1
   I charge thee waft me safely crosse the Channell.   2282
CHAPS = 1
   Before his Chaps be stayn'd with Crimson blood,   1561
CHARACTERD = 1
   Shew me one skarre, character'd on thy Skinne,   1603
CHARGE = 6*2
   I had in charge at my depart for France,   9
   *Stanly. So am I giuen in charge, may't please your | Grace.   1257
   But mightier Crimes are lay'd vnto your charge,   1434
   Suff. A charge, Lord *Yorke*, that I will see perform'd.   1626
   And charge, that no man should disturbe your rest,   1968
   I charge thee waft me safely crosse the Channell.   2282
   I charge and command, that of the Cities cost   2617
   *And we charge and command, that their wiues be as free   2756
CHARGED = 2
   Or like an ouer-charged Gun, recoile,   2046
   The secrets of his ouer-charged soule,   2093
CHARGES = 1*1
   *Englands owne proper Cost and Charges, without hauing any | Dowry.   66
   For Costs and Charges in transporting her: 141
CHARIOT-WHEELES = 1
   That erst did follow thy prowd Chariot-Wheeles,   1184
CHARITIE = 2
   And Charitie chas'd hence by Rancours hand;   1444
   Rich. Fie, Charitie for shame, speake not in spight,   3213
CHARLES = *2
   *Betweene our Soueraigne, and the French King *Charles*,   48
   *Charles, and William de la Pole Marquesse of Suffolke, Am-|bassador   51
CHARME = 1
   And therefore shall it charme thy riotous tongue.   2232
CHARNECO = 1
   *2.Neighbor. And here Neighbour, here's a Cuppe of | Charneco.   1123
CHARRACTERS = 1
   Racing the Charracters of your Renowne,   108
CHARTAM = *1
   *Weauer. The Clearke of Chartam: hee can write and | reade, and cast
   accompt.   2403
CHASD = 1
   And Charitie chas'd hence by Rancours hand;   1444
CHASE = 1
   Can chase away the first-conceiued sound?   1744

CHASTITIE = 1
To force a spotlesse Virgins Chastitie,   3186
CHAYRE = 1
Enter the Maior of Saint Albones, and his Brethren, | bearing the man
betweene two in a Chayre.   795
CHEAPE = 1
Pirates may make cheape penyworths of their pillage,   234
CHEAPSIDE = *2
*Cheapside shall my Palfrey go to grasse: and when I am | King, as
King I will be.   2387
*When shall we go to Cheapside, and take vp commodi-|ties vpon our
billes?   2759
CHECKD = 1
Next time Ile keepe my dreames vnto my selfe, | And not be check'd.   327
CHECKERD = 1
With shining checker'd slough doth sting a Child,   1531
CHEEFEST = 1
Their cheefest Prospect, murd'ring Basiliskes: 2039
CHEEKE = 1
To blush and beautifie the Cheeke againe.   1871
CHEEKES = *1
*Say. These cheekes are pale for watching for your good   2718
CHEEREFULL = 1
Lords, with one cheerefull voice, Welcome my Loue.   43
CHEESE = 1
*Smith. Nay *Iohn*, it wil be stinking Law, for his breath | stinkes with
eating toasted cheese.   2644
CHERISH = 1
And as we may, cherish Duke Humfries deeds,   211
CHERISHT = 1
Who cherisht in your breasts, will sting your hearts.   1650
CHESTS = 1
Are my Chests fill'd vp with extorted Gold?   2732
CHICKEN = 1*1
To guard the Chicken from a hungry Kyte,   1551
*Queene. So the poore Chicken should be sure of death.   1553
CHID = 1
Be thus vpbrayded, chid, and rated at,   1475
CHIDE = 2
Hum. Nay *Elinor*, then must I chide outright: 315
Qu. But I can giue the loser leaue to chide.   1482
CHILD = 2
Should be to be protected like a Child,   1084
With shining checker'd slough doth sting a Child,   1531
CHILDISH = 1
Nor hold the Scepter in his childish Fist,   257
CHILDREN = 1
Cade. By her he had two children at one birth. | *Bro.* That's false.   2459
CHILDRENS = 1
May euen in their Wiues and Childrens sight,   2499
CHIMNEY = *1
* *Wea.* Sir, he made a Chimney in my Fathers house, &   2468
CHINES = *1
*cut not out the burly bon'd Clowne in chines of Beefe,   2961
CHIRPING = 1
And thinkes he, that the chirping of a Wren,   1742

CHOAKE = 1
And choake the Herbes for want of Husbandry.   1327
CHOAKT = 1
Vertue is choakt with foule Ambition,   1443
CHOLLER = 2
Humf. Now Lords, my Choller being ouer-blowne,   547
Yor. Scarse can I speake, my Choller is so great.   3015
CHOLLERICKE = 1
Elia. What, what, my Lord? Are you so chollericke   325
CHOP = 1
And chop away that factious pate of his.   3132
CHOSEN = 1
A pretty Plot, well chosen to build vpon.   686
CHOYCELY = 1
Collected choycely, from each Countie some,   1618
CHRIST = 1
For you shall sup with Iesu Christ to night.   3214
CHRISTENDOME = 1
The lying'st Knaue in Christendome.   871
CHRISTIAN = *1
*no Christian eare can endure to heare. Thou hast appoin-|ted   2674
CHRISTIAN-LIKE = 1
Yet he most Christian-like laments his death: 1758
CHURCH = 2
More like a Souldier then a man o'th'Church,   194
In the Cathedrall Church of Westminster,   311
CHURCHMAN = 1
The imperious Churchman; *Somerset, Buckingham,*   455
CHURCH-LIKE = 1
Whose Church-like humors fits not for a Crowne.   259
CHURCH-MAN = *1
Glost. Ambitious Church-man, leaue to afflict my heart: 934
CHURCH-MEN = 1
Tantaene animis Coelestibus irae, Church-men so hot?   742
CHURLE = 1
Some sterne vntutur'd Churle; and Noble Stock   1918
CHUSE = 1
Would chuse him Pope, and carry him to Rome,   448
CIRCLE = 1
Here doe the Ceremonies belonging, and make the Circle,   643
CIRCLED = 1
Vntill thy head be circled with the same.   283
CIRCUIT = 1
Vntill the Golden Circuit on my Head,   1658
CIRCUMSPECT = 1
Bewitch your hearts, be wise and circumspect.   164
CIRCUMSTANCE = 3
This preroration with such circumstance: 112
King. Good-fellow, tell vs here the circumstance,   803
Hath not essentially, but by circumstance   3261
CITED = 1
And had I not beene cited so by them,   1995
CITIE = 2
I tell thee *Poole,* when in the Citie *Tours*   436
Deferre the spoile of the Citie vntill night: 2769
CITIES = 1
I charge and command, that of the Cities cost   2617

50

CITIZEN see 1.*Cit.*
CITIZENS = 2
    The Citizens flye and forsake their houses: 2587
    Enter Lord Scales vpon the Tower walking. Then enters | two or three
    Citizens below.   2598
CITTIES = 1
    And are the Citties that I got with wounds,   128
CITTY = 1
    And therefore in this Citty will I stay,   2583
CITY = 4
    So in the Famous Ancient City, *Toures,*   12
    To spoyle the City, and your Royall Court.   2590
    To defend the City from the Rebels.   2605
    Cade. Now is *Mortimer* Lord of this City,   2615
CIUELST = 1
    Is term'd the ciuel'st place of all this Isle: 2695
CIUILL = 2
    In bringing them to ciuill Discipline: 203
    Me thinkes alreadie in this ciuill broyle,   2821
CLAD *see* yclad
CLAIM = *1
    * *Yor.* From Ireland thus comes York to claim his right,   2992
CLAIME = 2
    A day will come, when Yorke shall claime his owne,   251
    And when I spy aduantage, claime the Crowne,   254
CLAMOR = 1
    Why what tumultuous clamor haue we here?   1949
CLAPPING = 1
    Clapping their hands, and crying with loud voyce,   167
CLAPT = 2
    Away with them, let them be clapt vp close,   680
    Hath clapt his taile, betweene his legges and cride,   3153
CLARENCE = 5
    Lionel, Duke of Clarence; next to whom,   972
    Yorke. The third Sonne, Duke of Clarence,   994
    Who marryed *Phillip,* sole Daughter | Vnto *Lionel,* Duke of Clarence.   1013
    married the Duke of *Clarence* daughter, did he not? | *Staf.* I sir.   2457
    Descended from the Duke of *Clarence* house,   2565
CLARKELY = 1
    With ignominious words, though Clarkely coucht?   1479
CLARRET = 1
    The pissing Conduit run nothing but Clarret Wine   2618
CLAY = 1
    And temper Clay with blood of Englishmen.   1616
CLAYME = 5*1
    * *Warw.* Sweet *Yorke* begin: and if thy clayme be good,   966
    From whose Line I clayme the Crowne,   995
    As I haue read, layd clayme vnto the Crowne,   1001
    By her I clayme the Kingdome: 1010
    Henry doth clayme the Crowne from *Iohn* of Gaunt,   1018
    How they affect the House and Clayme of *Yorke.*   1681
CLAYMES = 1
    The fourth Sonne, *Yorke* claymes it from the third: 1019
CLEANE = *1
    *that must sweepe the Court cleane of such filth as thou   2665
CLEAPE = 1
    Cleape dead-mens graues, and from their misty Iawes,   2175

CLEARE = 3*1
*Simpc. Yes Master, cleare as day, I thanke God and | Saint *Albones*.   848
As I am cleare from Treason to my Soueraigne.   1400
That you will cleare your selfe from all suspence,   1440
Ring Belles alowd, burne Bonfires cleare and bright   2994
CLEARKE = 2*1
Enter a Clearke.   2402
Weauer. The Clearke of Chartam: hee can write and | reade, and cast
accompt.   2403
and Inke-horne about his necke. | *Exit one with the Clearke*   2427
CLEARKE = 1*1
CLEARKES = 1
Large gifts haue I bestow'd on learned Clearkes,   2705
CLEFT = *1
*a Sallet, my brain-pan had bene cleft with a brown Bill;   2916
CLERGIES = *1
Card. The Commons hast thou rackt, the Clergies Bags   518
CLIF = 13*6
CLIFFES = 1
As farre as I could ken thy Chalky Cliffes,   1801
CLIFFORD *see also Clif., Yo.Clif.* = 17*3
Enter Buckingham, and old Clifford.   2781
Cade. What Buckingham and Clifford are ye so braue?   2796
All. A Clifford, a Clifford,   2830
Wee'l follow the King, and Clifford.   2831
Enter Buckingham and Clifford.   2856
Qu. Call hither *Clifford*, bid him come amaine,   3109
Enter Clifford.   3119
Qu. And here comes *Clifford* to deny their baile.   3120
Yor. I thanke thee *Clifford*: Say, what newes with thee?   3122
We are thy Soueraigne *Clifford*, kneele againe;   3124
King. I Clifford, a Bedlem and ambitious humor   3129
War. Clifford of Cumberland, 'tis Warwicke calles: 3219
Clifford I say, come forth and fight with me,   3223
Proud Northerne Lord, Clifford of Cumberland,   3224
Yor. The deadly handed Clifford slew my Steed: 3228
Enter Clifford.   3232
As I intend Clifford to thriue to day,   3237
Enter yong Clifford.   3252
Enter Clifford.   3311
CLIFFORDS = 1
Come thou new ruine of olde Cliffords house: 3283
CLIMBD = *1
*I climb'd into this Garden, to see if I can eate Grasse, or   2912
CLIMBE = 1*1
Glost. What, and would'st climbe a Tree?   837
*Damsons, and made me climbe, with danger of my | Life.   843
CLIMBING = 3
Yea Man and Birds are fayne of climbing high.   724
Wife. Too true, and bought his climbing very deare.   839
Climbing my walles inspight of me the Owner,   2939
CLIME = 1
Droue backe againe vnto my Natiue Clime.   1784
CLOAKE = *2
Glost. Say'st thou me so: what Colour is this Cloake | of?   850
*a Cloake, when honester men then thou go in their Hose | and
Doublets.   2683

CLOAKES = 1*1
  Glost. But Cloakes and Gownes, before this day, a | many. 859
  Enter Duke Humfrey and his Men in | Mourning Cloakes. 1169
CLOATHIER = *1
  Beuis. I tell thee, *Iacke Cade* the Cloathier, meanes to 2323
CLOCK = 1
  Sirs, what's a Clock? | *Seru.* Tenne, my Lord. 1175
CLOSE = 6*1
  1.Pet. My Masters, let's stand close, my Lord Pro-|tector 386
  Away with them, let them be clapt vp close, 680
  In this close Walke, to satisfie my selfe, 962
  This is close dealing. Well, I will be there. 1250
  And cry out for thee to close vp mine eyes: 2112
  Close vp his eyes, and draw the Curtaine close, 2166
CLOSET = 1
  And in thy Closet pent vp, rue my shame, 1200
CLOTH = 2
  Bare-headed plodded by my foot-cloth Mule, 2222
  dost ride in a foot-cloth, dost thou not? | *Say.* What of that? 2680
CLOUD = *1
  Glost. Thus sometimes hath the brightest day a Cloud: 1171
CLOUDIE = 1
  And *Suffolks* cloudie Brow his stormie hate; 1455
CLOUDS = 2
  Card. I thought as much, hee would be aboue the | Clouds. 731
  And with the Southerne clouds, contend in teares? 2101
CLOUTED = 1
  Spare none, but such as go in clouted shooen, 2505
CLOWNE = *1
  *cut not out the burly bon'd Clowne in chines of Beefe, 2961
COALES = 1
  Hot Coales of Vengeance. Let no Souldier flye. 3258
COALE-BLACK = 1
  Simpc. Black forsooth, Coale-Black, as Iet. 855
COAST = 3
  Yet haue I Gold flyes from another Coast: 369
  For loosing ken of *Albions* wished Coast. 1813
  Spare England, for it is your Natiue Coast: 2827
COATE = 1*1
  Wea. He neede not feare the sword, for his Coate is of | proofe. 2378
  But thou shalt weare it as a Heralds coate, 2975
COATED = 1
  Cade. As for these silken-coated slaues I passe not, 2448
COBHAM = 1
  King. Stand forth Dame *Elianor Cobham,* | *Glosters* Wife: 1053
COELESTIBUS = 1
  Tantaene animis Coelestibus irae, Church-men so hot? 742
COINE = 1
  His valour, coine, and people in the warres? 86
COLD = 7*1
  In Winters cold, and Summers parching heate, 88
  Cold newes for me: for I had hope of France, 249
  Barren Winter, with his wrathfull nipping Cold; 1173
  King. Cold Newes, Lord *Somerset:* but Gods will be | done. 1382
  Yorke. Cold Newes for me: for I had hope of France, 1384
  Queene. Free Lords: | Cold Snow melts with the Sunnes hot Beames: 1524
  Henry, my Lord, is cold in great Affaires, 1526

COLD *cont.*
Where byting cold would neuer let grasse grow,   2052
COLLECT = 1
Made me collect these dangers in the Duke.   1329
COLLECTED = 1
Collected choycely, from each Countie some,   1618
COLLEDGE = 1
I would the Colledge of the Cardinalls   447
COLOUR = 1*3
Glost. Say'st thou me so: what Colour is this Cloake | of?   850
Glost. Why that's well said: What Colour is my | Gowne of?   853
King. Why then, thou know'st what Colour Iet is | of?   856
But yet we want a Colour for his death: 1538
COLOURS = 5
As thus to name the seuerall Colours we doe weare.   874
Sight may distinguish of Colours: 875
Burnes with reuenging fire, whose hopefull colours   2265
Enter Yorke, and his Army of Irish, with | Drum and Colours.   2990
Alarum. Retreat. Enter Yorke, Richard, Warwicke, | and Soldiers, with
Drum & Colours.   3319
COMBAT = 4*1
For single Combat, in conuenient place,   605
Armorer. And I accept the Combat willingly.   609
*Combat, shall be the last of the next moneth. Come   616
This is the day appointed for the Combat,   1104
The head of *Cade*, whom I in combat slew.   3061
COMBATE = 1
Tooke oddes to combate a poore famisht man.   2948
COMBATTANTS = 1
Sound Trumpets, Alarum to the Combattants.   1154
COMBE = *1
*Combe downe his haire; looke, looke, it stands vpright,   2149
COME = 44*24
Come, let vs in, and with all speede prouide | To see her Coronation be
perform'd.   78
A day will come, when Yorke shall claime his owne,   251
Hu. I go. Come *Nel* thou wilt ride with vs? *Ex. Hum*   334
Gold cannot come amisse, were she a Deuill.   368
*will come this way by and by, and then wee may   387
2.Pet. Come backe foole, this is the Duke of Suffolk, | and not my
Lord Protector.   394
All. Come, let's be gone. *Exit.*   427
Could I come neere your Beautie with my Nayles,   533
I come to talke of Common-wealth Affayres.   549
*Combat, shall be the last of the next moneth. Come   616
Hume. Come my Masters, the Duchesse I tell you ex-|pects
performance of your promises.   620
Come, come, my Lords,   699
Glost. Faith holy Vnckle, would't were come to that.   757
Come with thy two-hand Sword.   768
Suffolke. Come to the King, and tell him what Mi-|racle.   788
Who said; *Symon,* come; come offer at my Shrine,   825
Come on Sirrha, off with your Doublet, quickly.   899
Till they come to Barwick, from whence they came. | *Exit.*   910
Armorer. Let it come yfaith, and Ile pledge you all, | and a figge for
Peter.   1127
Salisb. Come, leaue your drinking, and fall to blowes.   1140

COME *cont.*

Armorer. Masters, I am come hither as it were vpon	1147
Come fellow, follow vs for thy Reward. | *Sound a flourish. Exeunt.*	1167
Elianor. Come you, my Lord, to see my open shame?	1195
Come *Stanley,* shall we goe?	1284
King. I muse my Lord of Gloster is not come:	1295
That he should come about your Royall Person,	1320
Suff. Nay *Gloster,* know that thou art come too soone,	1393
And yet, good *Humfrey,* is the houre to come,	1505
Post. Great Lords, from Ireland am I come amaine,	1585
And vndiscouer'd, come to me againe,	1675
Why then from Ireland come I with my strength,	1686
Yet doe not goe away: come Basiliske,	1752
Warw. Come hither gracious Soueraigne, view this | body.	1852
Come *Warwicke,* come good *Warwicke,* goe with mee,	2012
Lieu. Water: W. Come Suffolke, I must waft thee | to thy death.	2283
Come Souldiers, shew what cruelty ye can.	2300
Therefore come you with vs, and let him go. | *Exit Lieutenant, and the rest.*	2310
Beuis. Come and get thee a sword, though made of a	2320
Hol. Come, come, let's fall in with them.	2349
Come hither sirrah, I must examine thee: What is thy | name?| Clearke. Emanuell.	2414
Ouer whom (in time to come) I hope to raigne:	2450
of order. Come, march forward.	2510
*shall be dragg'd at my horse heeles, till I do come to	2523
Cade. Feare not that I warrant thee. Come, let's march | towards London. *Exeunt.*	2528
King. Come *Margaret,* God our hope will succor vs.	2592
Cade. Come, then let's go fight with them:	2629
Come, let's away. *Exeunt omnes.*	2632
But. Onely that the Lawes of England may come out | of your mouth.	2640
Geo. O monstrous Coward! What, to come behinde | Folkes?	2716
Know *Cade,* we come Ambassadors from the King	2783
The Duke of Yorke is newly come from Ireland,	2877
King. Come wife, let's in, and learne to gouern better,	2902
Cade. Heere's the Lord of the soile come to seize me	2929
And like a Theefe to come to rob my grounds:	2938
*eate no meate these fiue dayes, yet come thou and thy	2943
*thousand diuelles come against me, and giue me but the	2966
Art thou a Messenger, or come of pleasure.	3008
Qu. Call hither *Clifford,* bid him come amaine,	3109
See where they come, Ile warrant they'l make it good.	3118
Bid Salsbury and Warwicke come to me.	3144
Clifford I say, come forth and fight with me,	3223
War. Of one or both of vs the time is come.	3233
Come thou new ruine of olde Cliffords house:	3283
Shall be eterniz'd in all Age to come.	3353

COMES = 6*4

Peter. Here a comes me thinkes, and the Queene with | him: Ile be the first sure.	392
Card. Here comes the Townes-men, on Procession,	797
But soft, I thinke she comes, and Ile prepare	1186
*Faster the(n) Spring-time showres, comes thoght on thoght,	1643
1. Here comes my Lord.	1696
And still proclaimeth as he comes along,	2881
Yor. From Ireland thus comes York to claim his right,	2992

55

COMES *cont.*
  *K. See Buckingham, Somerset comes with th'Queene,   3078
  Qu. And here comes *Clifford* to deny their baile.   3120
  But Noble as he is, looke where he comes.   3335
COMFORT = 7*2
  Warwicke my sonne, the comfort of my age,   198
  Giues Light in Darknesse, Comfort in Despaire.   794
  King. Great is his comfort in this Earthly Vale,   799
  Elianor. Art thou gone to? all comfort goe with thee,   1267
  *Suff. Comfort my Soueraigne, gracious *Henry* com-|fort.   1737
  King. What, doth my Lord of Suffolke comfort me?   1739
  By crying comfort from a hollow breast,   1743
  Is all thy comfort shut in Glosters Tombe?   1778
COMMAND = 8*3
  Hast thou not worldly pleasure at command,   319
  The *Neuills* are thy Subiects to command.   967
  Vs'd to command, vntaught to pleade for fauour.   2290
  *with the spirit of putting down Kings and Princes. Com-|mand silence.   2356
  Scales. Such ayd as I can spare you shall command,   2606
  I charge and command, that of the Cities cost   2617
  *Cade. Away with him, and do as I command ye: the   2751
  *And we charge and command, that their wiues be as free   2756
  When I command them kill?   2780
  And could command no more content then I?   2851
  Command my eldest sonne, nay all my sonnes,   3041
COMMANDED = 2
  Onely conuey me where thou art commanded.   1273
  We haue dispatcht the Duke, as he commanded.   1693
COMMANDEMENTS = 1
  I could set my ten Commandements in your face.   534
COMMENCD = 1
  His Fathers Acts, commenc'd in burning Troy.   1818
COMMEND = 1
  Buc. Yorke, I commend this kinde submission,   3046
COMMENT = 1
  And comment then vpon his sodaine death.   1835
COMMENTARIES = 1
  Kent, in the Commentaries *Caesar* writ,   2694
COMMING = 4*1
  Wee'le see your Trinkets here all forth-comming. | All away. *Exit.*   683
  Your Lady is forth-comming, yet at London.   931
  To watch the comming of my punisht Duchesse: 1178
  *Now get thee hence, the King thou know'st is comming,   2103
  And duly wayted for my comming forth?   2230
COMMISSION = 1*1
  Let not her Penance exceed the Kings Commission.   1252
  *Sh. And't please your Grace, here my Commission stayes: 1253
COMMIT = 3
  Did neuer Traytor in the Land commit.   569
  And here commit you to my Lord Cardinall   1437
  And *Somerset* we will commit thee thither,   2893
COMMODITIES = *1
  *When shall we go to Cheapside, and take vp commodi-|ties vpon our
  billes?   2759
COMMON = 3*2
  Your greefe, the common greefe of all the Land.   84
  What though the common people fauour him,   165

COMMON *cont.*

And common profit of his Countrey.	214
*small Beere. All the Realme shall be in Common, and in	2386
Cade. And hence-forward all things shall be in Com-|mon. *Enter a*	
Messenger.	2651

COMMONS = 12*3

Hath wonne the greatest fauour of the Commons,	200
*Suffolke, for enclosing the Commons of Melforde. How | now, Sir	
Knaue?	406
Card. The Commons hast thou rackt, the Clergies Bags	518
By flatterie hath he wonne the Commons hearts:	1322
Because I would not taxe the needie Commons,	1416
The Commons haply rise, to saue his Life;	1542
By this, I shall perceiue the Commons minde,	1680
Noyse within. Enter Warwicke, and many | Commons.	1822
The Commons like an angry Hiue of Bees	1827
Dread Lord, the Commons send you word by me,	1955
Commons within. An answer from the King, my Lord | of Salisbury.	1982
Suff. 'Tis like the Commons, rude vnpolisht Hindes,	1984
The Commons heere in Kent are vp in armes,	2268
Cade. And you that loue the Commons, follow me:	2502
Vnto the Commons, whom thou hast misled,	2784

COMMONWEALE = *1

*What Madame, are you there? the King & Commonweale	673

COMMONWEALTH = *1

* gelded the Commonwealth, and made it an Eunuch: &	2485

COMMON-WEALE = 3

Vnlike the Ruler of a Common-weale.	197
That smooth'st it so with King and Common-weale.	739
How I haue lou'd my King, and Common-weale:	943

COMMON-WEALTH = 2*1

The Common-wealth hath dayly run to wrack,	514
I come to talke of Common-wealth Affayres.	549
*dresse the Common-wealth and turne it, and set a new | nap vpon it.	2324

COMMOTION = 2

And when he please to make Commotion,	1323
To make Commotion, as full well he can,	1664

COMPANIE = 2

I banish her my Bed, and Companie,	949
Be play-fellowes to keepe you companie:	2016

COMPANION = 1

Iden. Why rude Companion, whatsoere thou be,	2935

COMPANY = 3

In Courtly company, or at my Beades,	34
So Suffolke had thy heauenly company:	2076
Alarums. Mathew Goffe is slain, and all the rest. | Then enter Iacke	
Cade, with his Company.	2633

COMPARED = 1

Thy legge a sticke compared with this Truncheon,	2953

COMPASSE = 1

Aboue the reach or compasse of thy thought?	320

COMPLAINT = 1

As for the Duke of Yorke, this late Complaint	483

COMPLEATE = *1

Cade. By my Valour: the most compleate Champi-|on	2959

COMPLICES = 1

To quell the Rebels, and their Complices.	3212

COMPLOT = 1
I know, their Complot is to haue my Life: 1447
COMPOUND = 1
I pray my Lords let me compound this strife.   783
COMST = *1
*King. How now? What newes? Why com'st thou in | such haste?   2561
CONCEIUED = 1
Can chase away the first-conceiued sound?   1744
CONCLUDE = 3
Or else conclude my words effectuall.   1335
Will not conclude their plotted Tragedie.   1453
And to conclude, Reproach and Beggerie, | Is crept into the Pallace of
our King,   2269
CONCLUDED = 2
For eighteene moneths concluded by consent.   49
Suffolke concluded on the Articles,   229
CONDEMND = 2
'Tis meet he be condemn'd by course of Law.   1539
Oh go not yet. Euen thus, two Friends condemn'd,   2068
CONDEMNE = 2
I shall not want false Witnesse, to condemne me,   1468
That faultlesse may condemne a Noble man: 1718
CONDEMNES = 1
I cannot iustifie whom the Law condemnes: 1070
CONDIGNE = 1
I neuer gaue them condigne punishment.   1430
CONDITION = 1
Iden. If one so rude, and of so meane condition   3058
CONDUCT = 2
Although thou hast beene Conduct of my shame.   1281
Will he conduct you through the heart of France,   2813
CONDUIT = 1
The pissing Conduit run nothing but Clarret Wine   2618
CONFEDERACIE = 1
Vnder the Countenance and Confederacie   920
CONFEDERATES = 1
With thy Confederates in this weightie cause. | *Exit Elianor.*   361
CONFERD = 1
Elia. What saist thou man? Hast thou as yet confer'd   349
CONFERENCE = 1
The mutuall conference that my minde hath had,   32
CONFESSE = 1*2
Armorer. Hold *Peter*, hold, I confesse, I confesse Trea-|son.   1156
Oh torture me no more, I will confesse.   2145
CONFEST = *1
All. He hath confest: away with him: he's a Villaine | and a Traitor.   2424
CONFIRMES = 1
And what we doe establish, he confirmes: 1622
CONFLICT = 1
Who in the Conflict that it holds with death,   1868
CONFUSION = 2
Heaping confusion on their owne heads thereby.   939
Clif. Shame and Confusion all is on the rout,   3253
CONIURATIONS = 1
And buzze these Coniurations in her brayne.   375
CONIURE = 1
Then any thou canst coniure vp to day: 3199

CONIURER = 2
With *Roger Bollingbrooke* the Coniurer?	351
Cade. Nay then he is a Coniurer.	2409

CONIURERS = 1
Dealing with Witches and with Coniurers,	924

CONIURO = 1
Bullingbrooke or Southwell reades, Coniuro | te, &c. *It Thunders and Lightens*	644

CONQUER = 3
To conquer France, his true inheritance?	89
For were there hope to conquer them againe,	124
Those Prouinces, these Armes of mine did conquer,	127

CONQUERD = 1
Defacing Monuments of Conquer'd France, | Vndoing all as all had neuer bin.	109

CONQUEST = 1
Shall *Henries* Conquest, *Bedfords* vigilance,	103

CONSCIENCE = 4
Is worthy prayse: but shall I speake my conscience,	1362
My Conscience tells me you are innocent.	1441
Whose Conscience with Iniustice is corrupted.	1941
And in my conscience, do repute his grace	3177

CONSENT = 4
For eighteene moneths concluded by consent.	49
Glost. And my consent ne're ask'd herein before?	1249
Say you consent, and censure well the deed,	1577
Suff. Why, our Authoritie is his consent,	1621

CONSIDER = 1
Consider Lords, he is the next of blood,	158

CONSIDERED = 1
Sal. My Lord, I haue considered with my selfe	3175

CONSORT = 1
And boading Screech-Owles, make the Consort full.	2042

CONSULT = 1
Least they consult about the giuing vp	2767

CONSUMING = 1
Or blood-consuming sighes recall his Life;	1761

CONTAGIOUS = 1
Breath foule contagious darknesse in the ayre:	2176

CONTAINE = 1
That euer did containe a thing of worth,	2128

CONTEMPT = 2
Who in contempt shall hisse at thee againe.	2246
And tread it vnder foot with all contempt,	3209

CONTEMPTUOUS = 1
Contemptuous base-borne Callot as she is,	469

CONTEND = 1
And with the Southerne clouds, contend in teares?	2101

CONTENT = 4*2
Such is the Fulnesse of my hearts content.	42
In England worke your Graces full content.	453
Yorke. I am content: Prouide me Souldiers, Lords,	1624
King. I thanke thee *Nell*, these wordes content mee | much.	1720
*for French Crownes) I am content he shall raigne, but Ile | be Protector ouer him.	2478
And could command no more content then I?	2851

CONTENTETH = 1
Contenteth me, and worth a Monarchy. 2924
CONTINUE = 1
Continue still in this so good a minde, 2869
CONTRACTED = 1
Heere are the Articles of contracted peace, 47
CONTRADICT = 1
As being thought to contradict your liking, 1964
CONTRARY = 1*1
Card. Did he not, contrary to forme of Law, 1352
*and contrary to the King, his Crowne, and Dignity, thou 2670
CONTROLLER = 1
Nor cease to be an arrogant Controller, 1910
CONTROLLING = 1
And with the same to acte controlling Lawes: 3098
CONTUMELIOUS = 1
Qu. He dares not calme his contumelious Spirit, 1909
CONTUSIONS = 1
That Winter Lyon, who in rage forgets | Aged contusions, and all brush
of Time: 3322
CONUENIENT = 1*1
For single Combat, in conuenient place, 605
*an inuincible spirit: but it shall be conuenient, Master 626
CONUENTICLES = 1
My selfe had notice of your Conuenticles, 1466
CONUERSED = 1
Hath he conuersed with the Enemie, 1674
CONUERST = 1
Noble shee is: but if shee haue forgot | Honor and Vertue, and conuers't
with such, 946
CONUEY = 3
Onely conuey me where thou art commanded. 1273
Lieu. Conuey him hence, and on our long boats side, 2236
And all by thee: away, conuey him hence. 2271
COOLE = 1*1
'Twill make them coole in zeale vnto your Grace. 1477
*picke a Sallet another while, which is not amisse to coole 2913
COOLES = 1
Which with the heart there cooles, and ne're returneth, 1870
COPE = 1
Vnworthy though thou art, Ile cope with thee, 1935
COPIES = 1
Cade. O monstrous. | *Wea.* We tooke him setting of boyes Copies. 2405
CORN = *1
Elia. Why droopes my Lord like ouer-ripen'd Corn, 274
CORNE = 1
Like to the Summers Corne by Tempest lodged: 1880
CORNER = 1*1
Will we ride through the streets, & at euery Corner 2771
Cade. Vp Fish-streete, downe Saint Magnes corner, 2775
CORONATION = 1
Come, let vs in, and with all speede prouide | To see her Coronation be
perform'd. 78
COROSIUE = *1
Queen. Away: Though parting be a fretfull corosiue, 2120
CORPES = 1
Enter his Chamber, view his breathlesse Corpes, 1834

CORRECT = *1
*words: my accuser is my Prentice, and when I did cor-|rect 595
CORRONE = 1
   Clif. La fin Corrone les eumenes. 3249
CORRUPTED = 1*1
   Whose Conscience with Iniustice is corrupted. 1941
   *art: Thou hast most traiterously corrupted the youth of 2666
COSIN = 3
   And girt thee with the Sword. Cosin of Yorke, 70
   Cosin of Somerset, ioyne you with me, 174
   Som. Cosin of Buckingham, though *Humfries* pride 179
COST = 2*1
   Englands owne proper Cost and Charges, without hauing any | Dowry. 66
   Haue cost a masse of publique Treasurie. 521
   I charge and command, that of the Cities cost 2617
COSTLY = 1
   I tooke a costly Iewell from my necke, 1806
COSTS = 1
   For Costs and Charges in transporting her: 141
COTTAGES = 1
   Home to your Cottages: forsake this Groome. 2444
COUCHT = 1
   With ignominious words, though Clarkely coucht? 1479
COULD *l.*533 534 734 880 881 1238 1728 1801 1985 2050 2058 2108 2549
   *2677 2702 2851 *2911 3016 3019 = 17*2
COULDST *l.*810 = *1
COUNCELL = 3*1
   Studied so long, sat in the Councell house, 97
   And other of your Highnesse Priuie Councell, 928
   Or be admitted to your Highnesse Councell. 1321
   Beuis. Nay more, the Kings Councell are no good | Workemen. 2333
COUNCELLOUR = *1
   *with the tongue of an enemy, be a good Councellour, or | no? 2491
COUNSAILE = 2
   For I am bold to counsaile you in this; 479
   What counsaile giue you in this weightie cause? 1592
COUNSELL = 2
   With all the Learned Counsell of the Realme, 96
   Your Deeds of Warre, and all our Counsell dye? 104
COUNT = 1
   Or count them happy, that enioyes the Sunne? 1215
COUNTENANCE = 3
   Vnder the Countenance and Confederacie 920
   The strangenesse of his alter'd Countenance? 1299
   Nor change my Countenance for this Arrest: 1397
COUNTER = *1
   *the fift, (in whose time, boyes went to Span-counter 2477
COUNTER-POYSD = 1
   Be counter-poys'd with such a pettie summe. 2191
COUNTIE = 1
   Collected choycely, from each Countie some, 1618
COUNTIES = 1
   These Counties were the Keyes of *Normandie*: 121
COUNTREY = 5*1
   And common profit of his Countrey. 214
   As I in dutie loue my King and Countrey. 553
   Liue in your Countrey here, in Banishment, 1065

COUNTREY *cont.*
Fight for your King, your Countrey, and your Liues, | 2611
*And shew'd how well you loue your Prince & Countrey: | 2868
Or vnto death, to do my Countrey good. | 2897
COUNTRIES = 1
I do dismisse you to your seuerall Countries. | 2873
COUNTRIMEN = 1*1
*Say. Ah Countrimen: If when you make your prair's, | 2747
Clif. What say ye Countrimen, will ye relent | 2787
COUNTRY = 1*1
Sweet is the Country, because full of Riches, | 2696
*the Country is laid for me: but now am I so hungry, that | 2909
COUNTY = *1
*Item, *That the Dutchy of Aniou, and the County of Main,* | 56
COURAGE = 3
In Courage, Courtship, and Proportion: | 440
Hume. I, what else? feare you not her courage. | 624
Hath giuen them heart and courage to proceede: | 2571
COURSE = 1
'Tis meet he be condemn'd by course of Law. | 1539
COURT = 9*4
Hum. Me thought this staffe mine Office-badge in | Court | 298
Is this the Fashions in the Court of England? | 429
*She sweepes it through the Court with troups of Ladies, | 463
Strangers in Court, doe take her for the Queene: | 465
Left I the Court, to see this Quarrell try'de. | 1109
That all the Court admir'd him for submission. | 1306
But. Nay, he can make Obligations, and write Court | hand. | 2410
To spoyle the City, and your Royall Court. | 2590
Others to'th Innes of Court, downe with them all. | 2636
*that must sweepe the Court cleane of such filth as thou | 2665
Iden. Lord, who would liue turmoyled in the Court, | 2921
Or dare to bring thy Force so neere the Court? | 3014
To call a present Court of Parliament: | 3347
COURTIERS = 1
All Schollers, Lawyers, Courtiers, Gentlemen, | 2572
COURTLY = 1
In Courtly company, or at my Beades, | 34
COURTS = 1
And Princes Courts be fill'd with my reproach: | 1769
COURTSHIP = 1
In Courage, Courtship, and Proportion: | 440
COUSIN = 2
Card. Beleeue me, Cousin *Gloster,* | 765
King. What Tidings with our Cousin *Buckingham?* | 917
COWARD = 2*2
I would, false murd'rous Coward, on thy Knee | 1925
Queen. Fye Coward woman, and soft harted wretch, | 2021
And I proclaim'd a Coward through the world. | 2212
Geo. O monstrous Coward! What, to come behinde | Folkes? | 2716
COWARDS = *1
*the World to be Cowards: For I that neuer feared any, | 2979
COWRD = 1
The splitting Rockes cowr'd in the sinking sands, | 1797
CRAB-TREE = 1
Was graft with Crab-tree slippe, whose Fruit thou art, | 1919

CRADLE = 1
No sooner was I crept out of my Cradle,   2852
CRADLE-BABE = 1
As milde and gentle as the Cradle-babe,   2109
CRAFTIE = 4
They say, A craftie Knaue do's need no Broker,   376
To call them both a payre of craftie Knaues.   379
Who being accus'd a craftie Murtherer,   1556
Full often, like a shag-hayr'd craftie Kerne,   1673
CRAFTS = 1
*Beuis. O miserable Age: Vertue is not regarded in | Handy-crafts men.   2329
CRAUES = *2
*Card. A Breach that craues a quick expedient stoppe.   1591
*The L.(ord) Maior craues ayd of your Honor from the Tower   2604
CRAUING = 1
In crauing your opinion of my Title,   963
CREATE = 1
We heere create thee the first Duke of Suffolke,   69
CREATED = 2
He were created Knight for his good seruice.   3071
O're him, whom heauen created for thy Ruler.   3100
CREATURES = 1
To see how God in all his Creatures workes,   723
CREDIT = 1*1
Fight for credit of the Prentices.   1132
*Staf. And will you credit this base Drudges Wordes,   2471
CREPT = 3
Is crept into the bosome of the Sea: 2171
And to conclude, Reproach and Beggerie, | Is crept into the Pallace of
our King,   2269
No sooner was I crept out of my Cradle,   2852
CREST = 1
War. Now by my Fathers badge, old Neuils Crest,   3202
CREST-FALNE = 1
Remember it, and let it make thee Crest-falne,   2227
CREW = 1
At Buckingham, and all the Crew of them,   1038
CRIDE = 1
Hath clapt his taile, betweene his legges and cride,   3153
CRIES = 2
That euen now he cries alowd for him.   2095
And dead mens cries do fill the emptie ayre,   3222
CRIMELESSE = 1
So long as I am loyall, true, and crimelesse.   1239
CRIMES = 1
But mightier Crimes are lay'd vnto your charge,   1434
CRIMSON = 2
Before his Chaps be stayn'd with Crimson blood,   1561
That slanders me with Murthers Crimson Badge.   1904
CRIPPLE = 1
That could restore this Cripple to his Legges againe.   880
CROCODILE = 1
Beguiles him, as the mournefull Crocodile   1528
CROMER = *1
*breake into his Sonne in Lawes house, Sir Iames Cromer,   2743
CROOKED = 1
As crooked in thy manners, as thy shape.   3157

CROSSE = 1
I charge thee waft me safely crosse the Channell.   2282
CROWES = 2
Leauing thy trunke for Crowes to feed vpon. *Exit.*   2989
And made a prey for Carrion Kytes and Crowes   3230
CROWN = *1
* *War.* Then nobly Yorke, 'tis for a Crown thou fightst: 3236
CROWND = 3*1
*And in that Chaire where Kings & Queens wer crownd,   312
Crown'd by the Name of *Henry* the fourth,   982
But I am not your King, till I be Crown'd,   1030
To be a Queene, and Crown'd with infamie.   1771
CROWNE = 23*2
* *Naples, Sicillia, and Ierusalem, and Crowne her Queene of*   54
And heyre apparant to the English Crowne: 159
And when I spy aduantage, claime the Crowne,   .   254
Whose Church-like humors fits not for a Crowne.   259
And force perforce Ile make him yeeld the Crowne,   270
*That the Duke of Yorke was rightfull Heire to the | Crowne.   411
say, hee was rightfull Heire to the Crowne?   414
And set the Triple Crowne vpon his Head;   449
Was rightfull Heire vnto the English Crowne,   581
Beat on a Crowne, the Treasure of thy Heart,   737
Ile shaue your Crowne for this,   775
Which is infallible, to Englands Crowne.   964
Thus got the House of *Lancaster* the Crowne.   988
From whose Line I clayme the Crowne,   995
As I haue read, layd clayme vnto the Crowne,   1001
Yorke. His eldest Sister, *Anne,* | My Mọther, being Heire vnto the
Crowne,   1005
Henry doth clayme the Crowne from *Iohn* of Gaunt,   1018
With honor of his Birth-right to the Crowne.   1026
And now the House of Yorke thrust from the Crowne,   2262
For I am rightfull heyre vnto the Crowne.   2451
And vowes to Crowne himselfe in Westminster.   2567
*and contrary to the King, his Crowne, and Dignity, thou   2670
And plucke the Crowne from feeble *Henries* head.   2993
That Head of thine doth not become a Crowne: 3091
Of Capitall Treason 'gainst the King and Crowne: 3102
CROWNED = 1
Crowned in Paris in despight of foes,   101
CROWNES = 1*4
* *Ma.* A thousand Crownes, or else lay down your head   2185
* *Lieu.* What thinke you much to pay 2000. Crownes,   2187
*for French Crownes) I am content he shall raigne, but Ile | be
Protector ouer him.   2478
Shall haue a thousand Crownes for his reward. | *Exeunt some of them.*   2844
*Villaine, thou wilt betray me, and get a 1000. Crownes   2931
CRUELTIE = 1
Buck. Thy Crueltie in execution | Vpon Offendors, hath exceeded Law,   522
CRUELTY = 2
Come Souldiers, shew what cruelty ye can.   2300
In cruelty, will I seeke out my Fame.   3282
CRUTCH = *1
* *Glost.* Ah, thus King *Henry* throwes away his Crutch,   1489
CRY = 5
I cry you mercy, Madame: was it you?   531

CRY *cont.*
The time when Screech-owles cry, and Bandogs howle,	638
the Stoole, and runnes away: and they | follow, and cry, A Miracle.	903
And therefore doe they cry, though you forbid,	1976
And cry out for thee to close vp mine eyes:	2112

CRYING = 4
Clapping their hands, and crying with loud voyce,	167
Enter one crying a Miracle.	784
By crying comfort from a hollow breast,	1743
Crying *Villiago* vnto all they meete.	2823

CULLIONS = 1
Away, base Cullions: *Suffolke* let them goe.	426

CULPABLE = 1
He be approu'd in practise culpable.	1716

CUMBERLAND = 1*1
War. Clifford of Cumberland, 'tis Warwicke calles:	3219
Proud Northerne Lord, Clifford of Cumberland,	3224

CUNNING = 3
With *Margerie Iordane* the cunning Witch,	350
And would ye not thinke it, Cunning to be great,	879
A cunning man did calculate my birth,	2203

CUP = 1*1
*in a Cup of Sack; and feare not Neighbor, you shall doe | well enough.	1121
How often hast thou waited at my cup,	2224

CUPPE = *1
*2.*Neighbor.* And here Neighbour, here's a Cuppe of | Charneco.	1123

CURE = 1
Is able with the change, to kill and cure.	3096

CURRE = 1
Rich. Oft haue I seene a hot ore-weening Curre,	3150

CURRES = 2
Small Curres are not regarded when they grynne,	1312
They may astonish these fell-lurking Curres,	3143

CURSE = 8
To free vs from his Fathers wrathfull curse,	1859
Hast thou not spirit to curse thine enemy.	2022
I, euery ioynt should seeme to curse and ban,	2034
Should I not curse them. Poyson be their drinke.	2036
Well could I curse away a Winters night,	2050
And seeing Ignorance is the curse of God,	2707
For yet may England curse my wretched raigne. | *Flourish. Exeunt.*	2903
Die damned Wretch, the curse of her that bare thee:	2982

CURSES = 2
Would curses kill, as doth the Mandrakes grone,	2025
And these dread curses like the Sunne 'gainst glasse,	2045

CURSING = 1
Blaspheming God, and cursing men on earth.	2089

CURSSE = *2
Suf. A plague vpon them: wherefore should I cursse | them?	2023
*make shift for one, and so Gods Cursse light vppon you | all.	2807

CURST = 2
What did I then? But curst the gentle gusts,	1788
As curst, as harsh, and horrible to heare,	2027

CURTAINE = 1
Close vp his eyes, and draw the Curtaine close,	2166

CURTEZANS = 1
And purchase Friends, and giue to Curtezans,	235

CUSTOMD = 1
To wring the Widdow from her custom'd right,   3188
CUT = 6*1
The ruthlesse Flint doth cut my tender feet,   1210
Cut both the Villaines throats, for dy you shall: 2189
*Beuis. Then is sin strucke downe like an Oxe, and ini-|quities throate
cut like a Calfe.   2345
Rather then bloody Warre shall cut them short,   2544
*cut not out the burly bon'd Clowne in chines of Beefe,   2961
And there cut off thy most vngracious head,   2987
Into as many gobbits will I cut it   3280
CUTTING = 1
Hangs on the cutting short that fraudfull man.   1375
CYPRESSE = 1
Their sweetest shade, a groue of Cypresse Trees: 2038
DAIES = *1
*sword, and yet am ready to famish. These fiue daies haue   2907
DAINTIEST = 1
Gall, worse then Gall, the daintiest that they taste: 2037
DAM = 1
Now will I dam vp this thy yawning mouth,   2241
DAME = 8
Where *Henrie* and Dame *Margaret* kneel'd to me,   313
Presumptuous Dame, ill-nurter'd *Elianor*,   316
Dame *Elianor* giues Gold, to bring the Witch: 367
They (knowing Dame *Elianors* aspiring humor)   373
As that prowd Dame, the Lord Protectors Wife: 462
She shall not strike Dame *Elianor* vnreueng'd. | *Exit Elianor.*   539
King. Stand forth Dame *Elianor Cobham,* | *Glosters* Wife: 1053
Why then Dame *Elianor* was neere thy ioy.   1779
DAMME = 1
And as the Damme runnes lowing vp and downe,   1515
DAMNED = 1
Die damned Wretch, the curse of her that bare thee: 2982
DAMSONS = *1
*Damsons, and made me climbe, with danger of my | Life.   843
DANCE = 1
And sooner dance vpon a bloody pole,   2295
DANCT = 1
Last time I danc't attendance on his will,   566
DANDLE = 1
Shee'le hamper thee, and dandle thee like a Baby: 537
DANGER = 3*1
*Damsons, and made me climbe, with danger of my | Life.   843
But I in danger for the breach of Law.   1242
Say. So might your Graces person be in danger.   2581
But still where danger was, still there I met him,   3332
DANGEROUS = 4*1
He will be found a dangerous Protector.   171
Pernitious Protector, dangerous Peere,   738
Doe you as I doe in these dangerous dayes,   1035
* *Qu.* Ah what's more dangerous, then this fond affiance?   1368
Glost. Ah gracious Lord, these dayes are dangerous: 1442
DANGEROUSLY = 1
Haue practis'd dangerously against your State,   923
DANGERS = 1
Made me collect these dangers in the Duke.   1329

DANTED = 1
What, are ye danted now? Now will ye stoope.   2287
DARE = 9*1
Ready to sterue, and dare not touch his owne.   241
I dare not say, from the rich Cardinall,   370
*Warw. What dares not Warwick, if false Suffolke dare | him?   1907
Though Suffolke dare him twentie thousand times.   1911
Here in our presence? Dare you be so bold?   1948
More can I beare, then you dare execute.   2298
As would (but that they dare not) take our parts.   2507
Dare any be so bold to sound Retreat or Parley   2779
Buc. I heere they be, that dare and will disturb thee: 2782
Or dare to bring thy Force so neere the Court?   3014
DARES = 1*1
*Warw. What dares not Warwick, if false Suffolke dare | him?   1907
Qu. He dares not calme his contumelious Spirit,   1909
DARING = 1
For daring to affye a mighty Lord   2248
DARKE = 3
Deepe Night, darke Night, the silent of the Night,   636
No: Darke shall be my Light, and Night my Day.   1216
All the foule terrors in darke seated hell -- -   2043
DARKNESSE = 2*1
*Bulling. Discend to Darknesse, and the burning Lake: 666
Giues Light in Darknesse, Comfort in Despaire.   794
Breath foule contagious darknesse in the ayre: 2176
DARLINGS = 1
And can doe naught but wayle her Darlings losse;   1517
DARST = 8
Card. Marry, when thou dar'st.   758
Card. I, where thou dar'st not peepe: 761
And if thou dar'st, this Euening,   762
Say, if thou dar'st, prowd Lord of Warwickshire,   1905
If from this presence thou dar'st goe with me.   1933
Strike off his head. Suf. Thou dar'st not for thy owne.   2237
Which dar'st not, no nor canst not rule a Traitor.   3090
If thou dar'st bring them to the bayting place.   3149
DARTS = 2
And fought so long, till that his thighes with Darts   1668
Shaking the bloody Darts, as he his Bells.   1672
DASH = 1
And would not dash me with their ragged sides,   1798
DASTARDS = *1
*all Recreants and Dastards, and delight to liue in slauerie   2803
DAUGHTER = 5*3
*espouse the Lady Margaret, daughter vnto Reignier King of   53
*To change two Dukedomes for a Dukes faire daughter.   231
Till Suffolke gaue two Dukedomes for his Daughter.   473
Had Issue Phillip, a Daughter, | Who marryed Edmond Mortimer, Earle
of March: 996
Who marryed Phillip, sole Daughter | Vnto Lionel, Duke of Clarence. 1013
Vnto the daughter of a worthlesse King,   2249
*But. She was indeed a Pedlers daughter, & sold many | Laces.   2364
married the Duke of Clarence daughter, did he not? | Staf. I sir.   2457
DAUGHTERS = *1
*Wiues and Daughters before your faces. For me, I will   2806

DAUNTED = 1

A Heart vnspotted, is not easily daunted. 1398

DAUPHIN *see* Dolphin

DAY = 29*7

By day, by night; waking, and in my dreames,	33
A day will come, when Yorke shall claime his owne,	251
She vaunted 'mongst her Minions t'other day,	470
*him for his fault the other day, he did vow vpon his	596
And let these haue a day appointed them	604
*King. Away with them to Prison: and the day of	615
I saw not better sport these seuen yeeres day:	718
Let neuer Day nor Night vnhallowed passe,	817
*Simpc. Yes Master, cleare as day, I thanke God and | Saint *Albones.*	848
*Glost. But Cloakes and Gownes, before this day, a | many.	859
Wife. Neuer before this day, in all his life.	861
Card. Duke *Humfrey* ha's done a Miracle to day.	912
You made in a day, my Lord, whole Townes to flye.	915
Shall one day make the Duke of Yorke a King.	1046
This is the day appointed for the Combat,	1104
*Glost. Thus sometimes hath the brightest day a Cloud:	1171
No: Darke shall be my Light, and Night my Day.	1216
When euery one will giue the time of day,	1308
By meanes whereof, the Townes each day reuolted.	1357
Be brought against me at my Tryall day.	1414
Buck. Hee'le wrest the sence, and hold vs here all day.	1486
And so breake off, the day is almost spent,	1630
Say, we intend to try his Grace to day,	1710
Lieu. The gaudy blabbing and remorsefull day,	2170
*the brickes are aliue at this day to testifie it: therefore | deny it not.	2469
Souldiers, this day haue you redeem'd your liues,	2867
Then any thou canst coniure vp to day:	3199
This day Ile weare aloft my Burgonet,	3204
As I intend Clifford to thriue to day,	3237
And the premised Flames of the Last day,	3263
To see their day, and them our Fortune giue.	3317
Repaires him with Occasion. This happy day	3325
Rich. My Noble Father: | Three times to day I holpe him to his horse,	3328
*Sal. Now by my Sword, well hast thou fought to day:	3337
And it hath pleas'd him that three times to day	3340
Now by my hand (Lords) 'twas a glorious day.	3351

DAYES = 11*2

Doe you as I doe in these dangerous dayes,	1035
Shall, after three dayes open Penance done,	1064
Thus *Elianors* Pride dyes in her youngest dayes.	1102
These few dayes wonder will be quickly worne.	1245
Glost. Ah gracious Lord, these dayes are dangerous:	1442
Yorke. My Lord of Suffolke, within foureteene dayes	1632
But three dayes longer, on the paine of death.	2002
If after three dayes space thou here bee'st found,	2009
Lath, they haue bene vp these two dayes.	2321
But. No question of that: for I haue seene him whipt | three Market	
dayes together.	2375
*eate no meate these fiue dayes, yet come thou and thy	2943
And in thy Reuerence, and thy Chaire-dayes, thus	3270
And more such dayes as these, to vs befall. *Exeunt.*	3355

DAYLY = 1

The Common-wealth hath dayly run to wrack, 514

DE *l.**51 304 2214 3002 = 3*1
DEAD = 19*3

For *Richard*, the first Sonnes Heire, being dead,	990
Farewell good King: when I am dead, and gone,	1092
So he be dead; for that is good deceit,	1566
**Card.* But I would haue him dead, my Lord of Suffolke,	1575
For that *Iohn Mortimer*, which now is dead,	1678
For *Humfrey*; being dead, as he shall be,	1688
1. I, my good Lord, hee's dead.	1698
Suff. Dead in his Bed, my Lord: *Gloster* is dead. | *Queene.* Marry God forfend.	1725
**Qu.* How fares my Lord? Helpe Lords, the King is | dead.	1730
In life, but double death, now *Gloster's* dead.	1755
King. That he is dead good Warwick, 'tis too true,	1832
And to suruey his dead and earthy Image:	1850
**Warw.* Who finds the Heyfer dead, and bleeding fresh,	1892
But may imagine how the Bird was dead,	1896
If thou be found by me, thou art but dead.	2104
I feare me (Loue) if that I had beene dead,	2556
Those that I neuer saw, and strucke them dead.	2715
*fiue men, and if I doe not leaue you all as dead as a doore	2944
And hang thee o're my Tombe, when I am dead.	2973
Oh let me view his Visage being dead,	3063
And dead mens cries do fill the emptie ayre,	3222

DEADLY = 2

With full as many signes of deadly hate,	2029
Yor. The deadly handed Clifford slew my Steed:	3228

DEAD-MENS = 1

Cleape dead-mens graues, and from their misty Iawes,	2175

DEAFE = 2

What? Art thou like the Adder waxen deafe?	1776
To tell my loue vnto his dumbe deafe trunke,	1846

DEALE = 3*1

But God in mercie so deale with my Soule,	552
*God, for I am neuer able to deale with my Master, hee	1138
Card. No more of him: for I will deale with him,	1628
Buc. I will my Lord, and doubt not so to deale,	2900

DEALING = 2*1

Dealing with Witches and with Coniurers,	924
This is close dealing. Well, I will be there.	1250
*Or hast thou a marke to thy selfe, like a honest plain dea-|ling man?	2420

DEARE = 1

Wife. Too true, and bought his climbing very deare.	839

DEATH = 51*6

Sal. Now by the death of him that dyed for all,	120
But him out-liue, and dye a violent death.	658
But him out-liue, and dye a violent death.	690
Demanding of King *Henries* Life and Death,	927
Who after *Edward* the third's death, raign'd as King,	979
Such as by Gods Booke are adiudg'd to death.	1057
**Elianor.* Welcome is Banishment, welcome were my | Death.	1067
*take my death, I neuer meant him any ill, nor the King,	1150
For by his death we doe perceiue his guilt,	1163
Nor stirre at nothing, till the Axe of Death	1225
For none abides with me: my Ioy, is Death;	1268
Death, at whose Name I oft haue beene afear'd,	1269
And if my death might make this Iland happy,	1448

DEATH   *cont.*

But yet we want a Colour for his death:	1538
More then mistrust, that shewes him worthy death.	1544
Yorke. 'Tis *Yorke* that hath more reason for his death.	1547
Queene. So the poore Chicken should be sure of death.	1553
Resigne to death, it is not worth th'enioying:	1640
For in the shade of death, I shall finde ioy;	1754
In life, but double death, now *Gloster*'s dead.	1755
Yet he most Christian-like laments his death:	1758
This get I by his death: Aye me vnhappie,,	1770
Vntill they heare the order of his death.	1831
And comment then vpon his sodaine death.	1835
For seeing him, I see my life in death.	1856
Who in the Conflict that it holds with death,	1868
Suf. Why Warwicke, who should do the D.(uke) to death?	1883
As guilty of Duke *Humfries* timelesse death.	1891
That I am faultie in Duke *Humfreyes* death.	1906
Vnlesse Lord *Suffolke* straight be done to death,	1956
And torture him with grieuous lingring death.	1959
They say, in him they feare your Highnesse death;	1961
In paine of your dislike, or paine of death;	1969
But three dayes longer, on the paine of death.	2002
That Cardinall *Beauford* is at point of death:	2086
From thee to dye, were torture more then death:	2118
This way fall I to death.	2130
Ca. If thou beest death, Ile giue thee Englands Treasure,	2136
War. See how the pangs of death do make him grin.	2158
War. So bad a death, argues a monstrous life.	2164
How now? why starts thou? What doth death affright?	2201
Suf. Thy name affrights me, in whose sound is death:	2202
And thou that smil'dst at good Duke *Humfries* death,	2244
Lieu. Water: W. Come Suffolke, I must waft thee | to thy death.	2283
Suf. That this my death may neuer be forgot.	2301
King. How now Madam? | Still lamenting and mourning for Suffolkes	
death?	2554
Sir *Humfrey Stafford*, and his Brothers death,	2570
They call false Catterpillers, and intend their death.	2573
Whom haue I iniur'd, that ye seeke my death?	2734
Expect your Highnesse doome of life, or death.	2864
Or vnto death, to do my Countrey good.	2897
Clif. Are these thy Beares? Wee'l bate thy Bears to death,	3147
I am resolu'd for death and dignitie.	3194
For I my selfe must hunt this Deere to death.	3235
Hath made the Wizard famous in his death:	3292
You haue defended me from imminent death.	3341
with the death of the Good Duke | HVMFREY.	3358

DEATHFULL = 1

It is applyed to a deathfull wound.	2121

DEATHS = 4

Shall finde their deaths, if *Yorke* can prophecie.	1042
Deuise strange deaths, for small offences done?	1353
Where death's approach is seene so terrible.	2140
Or let a rabble leade you to your deaths.	2789

DEATHS-MAN = 1

And I should rob the Deaths-man of his Fee,	1922

DEATH-BED = 1

What wilt thou on thy death-bed play the Ruffian?	3164

DEBATING = 1
Early and late, debating too and fro   98
DECAY = 1
For good King *Henry*, thy decay I feare. *Exit Gloster.*   1494
DECEASE = 1
And his aduantage following your decease,   1319
DECEAST = 1
Qu. My hope is gone, now Suffolke is deceast.   2593
DECEIT = 4
Vnsounded yet, and full of deepe deceit.   1351
Who cannot steale a shape, that meanes deceit?   1373
So he be dead; for that is good deceit,   1566
Which mates him first, that first intends deceit.   1567
DECEITFULL = 1
This breast from harbouring foule deceitfull thoughts.   2736
DEDICATE = 1
He that is truly dedicate to Warre,   3259
DEED = 4
Seeing the deed is meritorious,   1572
Say you consent, and censure well the deed,   1577
Suff. Here is my Hand, the deed is worthy doing. | *Queene.* And so say
I.   1580
I will reward you for this venturous deed: 1700
DEEDE = 2
Sword, I will hallow thee for this thy deede,   2972
To do a murd'rous deede, to rob a man,   3185
DEEDS = 3
Your Deeds of Warre, and all our Counsell dye?   104
Thy deeds, thy plainnesse, and thy house-keeping,   199
And as we may, cherish Duke Humfries deeds,   211
DEEME = 1
What know I how the world may deeme of me?   1765
DEEPE = 6
Receiud deepe scarres in France and Normandie: 94
Deepe Night, darke Night, the silent of the Night,   636
Smooth runnes the Water, where the Brooke is deepe,   1347
Vnsounded yet, and full of deepe deceit.   1351
King. That is to see how deepe my graue is made,   1854
My minde was troubled with deepe Melancholly.   3026
DEEPELY = 1
Are deeply indebted for this peece of paines;   674
DEEPE-FET = 1
To see my teares, and heare my deepe-fet groanes.   1209
DEERE = 4*1
*With his new Bride, & Englands deere bought Queen,   264
So will the Queene, that liuing, held him deere.   2318
Ah *Sancta Maiestas*! who would not buy thee deere?   2996
For I my selfe must hunt this Deere to death.   3235
Particularities, and pettie sounds | To cease. Was't thou ordain'd (deere
Father)   3266
DEFACD = 1
Broke be my sword, my Armes torne and defac'd,   2211
DEFACING = 1
Defacing Monuments of Conquer'd France, | Vndoing all as all had
neuer bin.   109
DEFAMD = 1
That England was defam'd by Tyrannie.   1423

DEFENCE = 1
Now is it manhood, wisedome, and defence,   3301
DEFEND = 2
Here let them end it, and God defend the right.   1111
To defend the City from the Rebels.   2605
DEFENDANT = 1
And ready are the Appellant and Defendant,   1105
DEFENDED = 1
You haue defended me from imminent death.   3341
DEFERRE = 1
Deferre the spoile of the Citie vntill night: 2769
DEFIE = *1
*ten meales I haue lost, and I'de defie them all. Wither   2967
DEFILE = 1
As like to Pytch, defile Nobilitie;   948
DEGENERATE = 1
And makes it fearefull and degenerate,   2534
DEGREE = 1
King. How art thou call'd? And what is thy degree?   3067
DELAY = 1
Car. This weighty businesse will not brooke delay,   177
DELIGHT = *1
*all Recreants and Dastards, and delight to liue in slauerie   2803
DELIUER = 2
Deliuer vp my Title in the Queene   19
deliuer our Supplications in the Quill.   388
DELIUERD = 2
Deliuer'd vp againe with peacefull words? | *Mort Dieu.*   129
Deliuer'd strongly through my fixed teeth,   2028
DELIUERED = 1*1
shall be released and deliuered to the King her father.   57
* *Dutchesse of Aniou and Maine, shall be released and deliuered*   64
DEMAND = 2
That Suffolke should demand a whole Fifteenth,   140
The King hath yeelded vnto thy demand: 3032
DEMANDING = 1
Demanding of King *Henries* Life and Death,   927
DEMEAND = 1
Yorke. If *Yorke* haue ill demean'd himselfe in France,   493
DEMEANE = 1
Sweare like a Ruffian, and demeane himselfe   196
DEMEANOR = 1
Suff. Blunt-witted Lord, ignoble in demeanor,   1915
DENAYD = 1
Then let him be denay'd the Regent-ship.   494
DENY = 3
His sonne am I, deny it if you can.   2466
*the brickes are aliue at this day to testifie it: therefore | deny it not.   2469
Qu. And here comes *Clifford* to deny their baile.   3120
DEPART = 3
I had in charge at my depart for France,   9
Suf. If I depart from thee, I cannot liue,   2105
It is our pleasure one of them depart: 2309
DEPARTED = 1
How would it fare with your departed soules,   2749
DEPOSD = 1
Seiz'd on the Realme, depos'd the rightfull King,   983

DEPOSE = 2
 Spirit. The Duke yet liues, that *Henry* shall depose: 657
 The Duke yet liues, that Henry *shall depose*:   689
DEPTH = 1
 A Spirit rais'd from depth of vnder ground,   354
DEPUTIE = 1
 Whose farre-vnworthie Deputie I am,   2000
DESCENDED = 3
 Being all descended to the labouring heart,   1867
 Cade. My wife descended of the *Lacies*.   2363
 Descended from the Duke of *Clarence* house,   2565
DESCENT *see* discent
DESERTS = 1
 See you well guerdon'd for these good deserts.   676
DESERUST = 1
 Cade. And to speake truth, thou deseru'st no lesse.   2521
DESIRE = 1
 But. I desire no more.   2520
DESIRED = *1
 Simpc. Alas, good Master, my Wife desired some   842
DESOLATE = *1
 *to an hundred mischiefes, and makes them leaue mee de-|solate. 2834
DESOLATION = 1
 And where thou art not, Desolation.   2079
DESPAIRE *see also* dispaire = 1
 Giues Light in Darknesse, Comfort in Despaire.   794
DESPIGHT = 2*1
 Crowned in Paris in despight of foes,   101
 *in despight of the diuels and hell, haue through the verie 2837
 Despight the Bearard, that protects the Beare.   3210
DESPITE = 1
 Despite Duke *Humfrey*, or the Cardinall.| *Exit Buckingham, and*
 Somerset.   186
DESPOYLED = 1
 Despoyled of your Honor in your Life,   1063
DESTRUCTION = 1
 Shee'le gallop farre enough to her destruction. | *Exit Buckingham*. 544
DETERMINE = 1
 Say. Long sitting tc determine poore mens causes,   2721
DEUILL = 3
 Gold cannot come amisse, were she a Deuill.   368
 This Deuill here shall be my substitute;   1677
 There's two of you, the Deuill make a third,   2017
DEUILLISH *see* diuellish
DEUILLS *see* diuelles, diuels
DEUILS = 1
 Now pray my Lord, let's see the Deuils Writ.   687
DEUISE = 3
 Deuise strange deaths, for small offences done?   1353
 Yorke. In your Protectorship, you did deuise   1421
 Follow me souldiers, wee'l deuise a meane,   2846
DEUOTION = 2
 Cam'st thou here by Chance, or of Deuotion, | To this holy Shrine? 820
 Simpc. God knowes of pure Deuotion,   822
DEW = 2
 That I may dew it with my mournfull teares: 2055
 Shall be to me, euen as the Dew to Fire,   3275

DIADEM = 4
Nor weare the Diadem vpon his head,   258
What seest thou there? King *Henries* Diadem,   280
And on my head did set the Diadem.   314
Hauing neyther Subiect, Wealth, nor Diadem: 2250
DIAMONDS = 1
A Hart it was bound in with Diamonds,   1807
DIC = 1
DICKE see also Dic. = 2*1
Hol. And Dicke the Butcher.   2344
*Drumme. Enter Cade, Dicke Butcher, Smith the Weauer, | and a
Sawyer, with infinite numbers.*   2350
Cade. Where's Dicke, the Butcher of Ashford? | *But.* Heere sir.   2513
DICKE = 2*2
DID *l.*21 39 85 87 90 126 127 192 *221 222 246 314 *413 569 *587 *595
*596 858 908 1184 1304 1345 1352 1354 1421 *1727 1786 1788 1816
1996 2128 2203 2208 *2399 2457 3088 3281 3284 3338 = 32*7
DIDO = 1
When he to madding *Dido* would vnfold   1817
DIDST = 3
When thou didst ride in triumph through the streets.   1185
Thou neuer didst them wrong, nor no man wrong: 1510
Didst euer heare a man so penitent? *Enter Suffolke.*   1695
DIE *see also* dy, dye = 3*1
*mine Honour: vnlesse I finde him guilty he shall not die.   2413
Die damned Wretch, the curse of her that bare thee: 2982
Is his to vse, so Somerset may die.   3045
To die in Ruffian battell? Euen at this sight,   3271
DIED *see* dy'de, dyed
DIES *see also* dyes = 1
He dies and makes no signe: Oh God forgiue him.   2163
DIEU = 1
Deliuer'd vp againe with peacefull words? | *Mort Dieu.*   129
DIGGD = 1
Thy graue is digg'd already in the earth: 2956
DIGGE = 1
Wilt thou go digge a graue to finde out Warre,   3169
DIGNITIE = 3
And not a thought, but thinkes on Dignitie.   1644
Is slander to your Royall Dignitie.   1914
I am resolu'd for death and dignitie.   3194
DIGNITY = *1
*and contrary to the King, his Crowne, and Dignity, thou   2670
DIMD = 1
And dim'd mine eyes, that I can reade no further.   61
DIMME = 1
Gazing on that which seemes to dimme thy sight?   279
DIMND = 1
With sad vnhelpefull teares, and with dimn'd eyes;   1519
DIMS = 1
That dims the Honor of this Warlike Isle: 132
DIRECTIONS = 1
According as I gaue directions? | 1. 'Tis, my good Lord.   1703
DIRT = 1
Lieu. Poole, Sir *Poole*? Lord, | I kennell, puddle, sinke, whose filth and
dirt   2238

DISCEND = *1
  Bulling. Discend to Darknesse, and the burning Lake: 666
DISCENT = 2
  First note, that he is neere you in discent,   1315
  Yet by reputing of his high discent,   1342
DISCHARGD = 1
  Elianor. I, I, farewell, thy Office is discharg'd: 1283
DISCHARGE = 2
  We heere discharge your Grace from being Regent   71
  Without Discharge, Money, or Furniture,   564
DISCIPLINE = 1
  In bringing them to ciuill Discipline: 203
DISCOLOURED = 1
  Or with their blood staine this discoloured shore.   2180
DISCOMFITE = 1
  But flye you must: Vncureable discomfite   3314
DISCOMFITED = 1
  Who since I heard to be discomfited.   3056
DISCONTENT = 2
  For what's more miserable then Discontent?   1502
  Hearts Discontent, and sowre Affliction,   2015
DISCOURSE = *1
  Car. Nephew, what meanes this passionate discourse?   111
DISDAINE = 1
  Disdaine to call vs Lord, and *Piccardie*   2256
DISDAINING = 1
  Disdaining dutie that to vs belongs.   1311
DISEASES = 1
  Hath made me full of sicknesse and diseases.   2722
DISGRACE = 1
  Till we haue brought Duke *Humphrey* in disgrace.   482
DISGRACES = 2
  From top of Honor, to Disgraces feete?   323
  Causelesse haue lay'd disgraces on my head,   1462
DISHONOR = 1
  Ah *Humfrey*, this dishonor in thine age,   1072
DISHONORED *see* dis-honored
DISHONOUR *see also* dis-honour = 1
  Neuer yet did base dishonour blurre our name,   2208
DISLIKE = 1
  In paine of your dislike, or paine of death;   1969
DISMALL = 1
  Whose dismall tune bereft my Vitall powres: 1741
DISMISSE = 2
  I do dismisse you to your seuerall Countries.   2873
  Yorke. Then Buckingham I do dismisse my Powres.   3036
DISMIST = 1
  Vntill his Army be dismist from him.   2894
DISORDER = 2
  Feare frames disorder, and disorder wounds   3254
DISPAIRE = 1
  And from his bosome purge this blacke dispaire.   2157
DISPATCH = *1
  Yorke. Dispatch, this Knaues tongue begins to double.   1153
DISPATCHT = 2
  We haue dispatcht the Duke, as he commanded.   1693
  Suff. Now Sirs, haue you dispatcht this thing?   1697

DISPENSE = *1
*Ki. Canst thou dispense with heauen for such an oath? 3181
DISPERSE = 1
Souldiers, I thanke you all: disperse your selues: 3037
DISPIERCD = 1
But now is Cade driuen backe, his men dispierc'd, 2888
DISPLACD = 1
If Gloster be displac'd, hee'l be Protector. 184
DISPLAYD = 1
His hands abroad display'd, as one that graspt 1876
DISPLEASD = 1
There's reason he should be displeas'd at it: 162
DISPOSED = 1
For hee's disposed as the hatefull Rauen. 1370
DISPURSED see dis-pursed
DISPUTE = 1
Dispute not that, Yorke is the worthyer. 498
DISSEMBLE = 1
The king hath sent him sure: I must dissemble. 3005
DISTINGUISH = 1
Sight may distinguish of Colours: 875
DISTRACT = 1
Mine haire be fixt an end, as one distract: 2033
DISTREST = 1
*King. Thus stands my state, 'twixt Cade and Yorke | distrest, 2884
DISTURB = 1
Buc. I heere they be, that dare and will disturb thee: 2782
DISTURBE = 3
And charge, that no man should disturbe your rest, 1968
Sal. Disturbe him not, let him passe peaceably. 2159
Whom haue we heere? Buckingham to disturbe me? 3004
DIS-HONORED = 1
That hath dis-honored Glosters honest Name. 951
DIS-HONOUR = 1
Then bring a burthen of dis-honour home, 1601
DIS-PURSED = 1
Haue I dis-pursed to the Garrisons, 1417
DIUELLES = *1
*thousand diuelles come against me, and giue me but the 2966
DIUELLISH = 3
Vpon my Life began her diuellish practises: 1340
By diuellish policy art thou growne great, 2251
Vnlesse you be possest with diuellish spirits, 2709
DIUELS = *1
*in despight of the diuels and hell, haue through the verie 2837
DO l.147 189 212 260 332 333 352 461 1756 1836 1860 *1883 2158 2394
*2395 *2523 *2526 *2574 *2751 *2797 2812 2855 *2862 2873 2897 *2915
*2968 3036 3123 3126 3127 3154 3177 3185 3222 3256 3278 = 27*10
DOE l.358 372 457 458 459 465 592 *598 643 726 744 780 874 *900 *942
1035 1047 1088 *1121 1163 1197 1227 1261 1395 1436 1496 1509 1517
1520 1563 1589 1604 1622 1660 1694 1752 1936 1976 1996 1997
*2944 = 38*5
DOEST l.3172 = 1
DOGGE = 1
A Staffe is quickly found to beat a Dogge. 1471
DOGGED = 1
And dogged Yorke, that reaches at the Moone, 1458

DOGGES = 1
*Beuis. Hee shall haue the skinnes of our enemies, to | make Dogges
Leather of.   2342
DOING = 1
  Suff. Here is my Hand, the deed is worthy doing. | Queene. And so say
I.   1580
DOLPHIN = 1
  The Dolphin hath preuayl'd beyond the Seas,   515
DOLPHINE = *1
  *Normandie vnto Mounsieur Basimecu, the Dolphine of   2662
DOLPHINS = 1
  Till France be wonne into the Dolphins hands: 565
DONE l.76 204 654 665 818 878 912 914 1064 1285 1353 1383 1569 1599
  *1635 1647 1694 1929 1956 2701 2746 = 20*1
DOOME = 4
  Humf. This doome, my Lord, if I may iudge: 601
  This is the Law, and this Duke Humfreyes doome.   607
  It skills not greatly who impugnes our doome.   1583
  Expect your Highnesse doome of life, or death.   2864
DOORE = *3
  *Enter at one Doore the Armorer and his Neighbors, drinking   1115
  *fastened to it: and at the other Doore his Man, with a   1118
  *fiue men, and if I doe not leaue you all as dead as a doore   2944
DOORES = 1
  Be hang'd vp for example at their doores: 2500
DOS l.376 = 1
DOST l.*290 786 1196 1774 1821 2005 *2419 2680 2725 *3053 3220
  3240 = 10*3
DOTH l.38 148 276 295 305 575 579 918 1018 1210 1460 1531 1679 1734
  1739 1842 2025 2201 *3049 3052 3091 = 20*1
DOUBLE = 1*1
  *Yorke. Dispatch, this Knaues tongue begins to double.   1153
  In life, but double death, now Gloster's dead.   1755
DOUBLET = 1
  Come on Sirrha, off with your Doublet, quickly.   899
DOUBLETS = 1
  *a Cloake, when honester men then thou go in their Hose | and
  Doublets.   2683
DOUBLE-BEERE = *1
  *3. Neighbor. And here's a Pot of good Double-Beere   1125
DOUBT = 3
  My Lord Protector will, I doubt it not,   675
  God on our side, doubt not of Victorie.   2829
  Buc. I will my Lord, and doubt not so to deale,   2900
DOUE = 2
  As is the sucking Lambe, or harmelesse Doue: 1365
  Seemes he a Doue? his feathers are but borrow'd,   1369 .
DOWN = *4
  *King. They please vs well. Lord Marques kneel down,   68
  *Ma. A thousand Crownes, or else lay down your head   2185
  *with the spirit of putting down Kings and Princes. Com-|mand silence.   2356
  *Cade. So sirs: now go some and pull down the Sauoy: 2635
DOWNE = 14*4
  Whose bookish Rule, hath pull'd faire England downe. | Exit Yorke.   271
  To tumble downe thy husband, and thy selfe,   322
  They fight, and Peter strikes him downe.   1155
  To mowe downe Thornes that would annoy our Foot,   1361

DOWNE *cont.*

And as the Damme runnes lowing vp and downe,	1515
That want their Leader, scatter vp and downe,	1828
*Combe downe his haire; looke, looke, it stands vpright,	2149
Fed from my Trencher, kneel'd downe at the boord,	2225
Beuis. Then is sin strucke downe like an Oxe, and ini-|quities throate	
cut like a Calfe.	2345
Cade. Stand villaine, stand, or Ile fell thee downe: he	2434
Mark'd for the Gallowes: Lay your Weapons downe,	2443
Vntill a power be rais'd to put them downe.	2576
Soul. Iacke Cade, Iacke Cade.| Cade. Knocke him downe there. *They*	
kill him.	2623
And if you can, burne downe the Tower too.	2631
Others to'th Innes of Court, downe with them all.	2636
Cade. Vp Fish-streete, downe Saint Magnes corner,	2775
kill and knocke downe, throw them into Thames:	2776
King. Iden, kneele downe, rise vp a Knight:	3072

DOWNEFALL = 1

To dreame on euill, or to worke my downefall.	1367

DOWNES = 1

For whilst our Pinnace Anchors in the Downes,	2178

DOWNE-RIGHT = 1

*nor the Queene: and therefore *Peter* haue at thee with a | downe-right	
blow.	1151

DOWRIES = 1

Large summes of Gold, and Dowries with their wiues,	136

DOWRY = 1

Englands owne proper Cost and Charges, without hauing any | Dowry.	66

DOYT = 1

That Doyt that ere I wrested from the King,	1412

DRAB = 1

Glost. Follow the Knaue, and take this Drab away.	907

DRAG = 1

Warw. Away euen now, or I will drag thee hence:	1934

DRAGGD = *1

*shall be dragg'd at my horse heeles, till I do come to	2523

DRAGGE = 2

That dragge the Tragicke melancholy night:	2173
Hence will I dragge thee headlong by the heeles	2985

DRAINE = 1

With twenty thousand kisses, and to draine	1844

DRAUGHT = *1

*you, for I thinke I haue taken my last Draught in this	1134

DRAW = 1

Close vp his eyes, and draw the Curtaine close,	2166

DRAWNE = 3

Enter Suffolke and Warwicke, with their | Weapons drawne.	1944
Your wrathfull Weapons drawne,	1947
Whose dreadfull swords were neuer drawne in vaine,	2260

DREAD = 4

With that dread King that tooke our state vpon him,	1858
Dread Lord, the Commons send you word by me,	1955
And these dread curses like the Sunne 'gainst glasse,	2045
Buc. A Messenger from *Henry,* our dread Liege,	3009

DREADFULL = 3*1

Or turne our Sterne vpon a dreadfull Rocke:	1791
Suf. A dreadfull Oath, sworne with a solemn tongue:	1862

DREADFULL *cont.*
Whose dreadfull swords were neuer drawne in vaine,	2260
Yor. A dreadfull lay, addresse thee instantly.	3248

DREAMD = *1
Eli. What dream'd my Lord, tell me, and Ile requite it	296

DREAME = 4*2
With sweet rehearsall of my mornings dreame?	297
This was my dreame, what it doth bode God knowes.	305
With *Elianor*, for telling but her dreame?	326
To dreame on euill, or to worke my downefall.	1367
Card. Gods secret Iudgement: I did dreame to Night,	1727
War. You were best to go to bed, and dreame againe,	3196

DREAMES = 3*1
By day, by night; waking, and in my dreames,	33
My troublous dreames this night, doth make me sad.	295
Next time Ile keepe my dreames vnto my selfe, | And not be check'd.	327
Old Clif. The first I warrant thee, if dreames proue true	3195

DRESSE = *1
*dresse the Common-wealth and turne it, and set a new | nap vpon it.	2324

DRINK = *1
*shall haue ten hoopes, and I wil make it Fellony to drink	2385

DRINKE = 3*5
*1.*Neighbor.* Here Neighbour *Horner*, I drinke to you	1120
Neighbor: drinke, and feare not your Man.	1126
*1.*Prent.* Here *Peter*, I drinke to thee, and be not a-|fraid.	1129
Peter. I thanke you all: drinke, and pray for me, I pray	1133
Should I not curse them. Poyson be their drinke.	2036
Giue me some drinke, and bid the Apothecarie	2151
*mony, all shall eate and drinke on my score, and I will	2391
*it hath seru'd me insteede of a quart pot to drinke	2918

DRINKES = 1
Troubles the siluer Spring, where England drinkes:	2240

DRINKING = 2*2
Enter at one Doore the Armorer and his Neighbors, drinking	1115
Drumme and Sand-bagge, and Prentices drinking to him.	1119
Salisb. Come, leaue your drinking, and fall to blowes.	1140
Looke pale as Prim-rose with blood-drinking sighes,	1763

DRIUEN = 1
But now is Cade driuen backe, his men dispierc'd,	2888

DRONES = 1
Drones sucke not Eagles blood, but rob Bee-hiues:	2277

DROOPES = *1
Elia. Why droopes my Lord like ouer-ripen'd Corn,	274

DROUE = 1
Droue backe againe vnto my Natiue Clime.	1784

DROUPES = *1
Suff. Thus droupes this loftie Pyne, & hangs his sprayes,	1101

DROWND = 2
King. I *Margaret*: my heart is drown'd with griefe,	1499
Knowing that thou wouldst haue me drown'd on shore	1795

DROWNE = 1
The pretty vaulting Sea refus'd to drowne me,	1794

DROWSIE = 1
Who with their drowsie, slow, and flagging wings	2174

DRUDGES = 1*1
Vpon these paltry, seruile, abiect Drudges:	2273
Staf. And will you credit this base Drudges Wordes,	2471

DRUM = 3
  Enter Sir Humfrey Stafford, and his Brother, | with Drum and Soldiers.   2440
  Enter Yorke, and his Army of Irish, with | Drum and Colours.   2990
  Alarum. Retreat. Enter Yorke, Richard, Warwicke, | and Soldiers, with
  Drum & Colours.   3319
DRUMME = 2*2
  * *Drumme before him, and his Staffe, with a Sand-bagge*   1117
  Drumme and Sand-bagge, and Prentices drinking to him.   1119
  * *Drumme. Enter Cade, Dicke Butcher, Smith the Weauer, | and a*
  Sawyer, with infinite numbers.   2350
  Sound Drumme and Trumpets, and to London all,   3354
DRUNKE = *1
  * *to him so much, that hee is drunke; and he enters with a*   1116
DRY = *1
  * *and many a time when I haue beene dry, & brauely mar- | ching,*   2917
DUCH = 1*1
DUCHESSE see also Duch., Dutchesse = 10*3
  * *Hume. Hume* must make merry with the Duchesse Gold: 363
  Haue hyred me to vnder-mine the Duchesse,   374
  Humes Knauerie will be the Duchesse Wracke,   381
  Yorke, Salisbury, Warwicke, | and the Duchesse.   489
  Giue me my Fanne: what, Mynion, can ye not? | *She giues the Duchesse*
  a box on the eare.   529
  * *Hume. Come my Masters, the Duchesse I tell you ex- | pects*
  performance of your promises.   620
  Sound Trumpets. Enter the King and State, | with Guard, to banish the
  Duchesse.   1051
  To watch the comming of my punisht Duchesse: 1178
  Enter the Duchesse in a white Sheet, and a Taper   1188
  As he stood by, whilest I, his forlorne Duchesse,   1221
  * *Stanley. Like to a Duchesse, and Duke *Humfreyes* Lady,   1278
  The Duchesse, by his subornation,   1339
  Did instigate the Bedlam braine-sick Duchesse,   1345
DUE = 2
  Ere you can take due Orders for a Priest: 1576
  I cannot giue due action to my words,   2999
DUGGE = 1
  Dying with mothers dugge betweene it's lips.   2110
DUKE = 90*11
  * *Enter King, Duke Humfrey, Salisbury, Warwicke, and Beau- | ford on*
  the one side.   3
  We heere create thee the first Duke of Suffolke,   69
  To you Duke *Humfrey* must vnload his greefe: 83
  Suffolke, the new made Duke that rules the rost,   116
  Yorke. For Suffolkes Duke, may he be suffocate,   131
  Calling him, *Humfrey the good Duke of Gloster,*   166
  With God preserue the good Duke *Humfrey*:   169
  And altogether with the Duke of Suffolke,   175
  Wee'l quickly hoyse Duke *Humfrey* from his seat.   176
  Ile to the Duke of Suffolke presently. *Exit Cardinall.*   178
  Despite Duke *Humfrey*, or the Cardinall. | *Exit Buckingham, and*
  Somerset.   186
  I neuer saw but Humfrey Duke of Gloster,   191
  Excepting none but good Duke Humfrey.   201
  And as we may, cherish Duke Humfries deeds,   211
  And make a shew of loue to proud Duke *Humfrey*,   253
  Enter Duke Humfrey and his wife Elianor.   273

DUKE *cont.*

Why doth the Great Duke *Humfrey* knit his browes,	276
Were plac'd the heads of *Edmond* Duke of Somerset,	303
And *William de la Pole* first Duke of Suffolke.	304
But list to me my *Humfrey*, my sweete Duke:	309
Were I a Man, a Duke, and next of blood,	338
And from the great and new-made Duke of Suffolke;	371
2. Pet. Come backe foole, this is the Duke of Suffolk, | and not my	
Lord Protector.	394
*What's yours? What's heere? Against the Duke of	405
*That the Duke of Yorke was rightfull Heire to the | Crowne.	411
* *Queene.* What say'st thou? Did the Duke of Yorke	413
And must be made a Subiect to a Duke?	435
More like an Empresse, then Duke *Humphreyes* Wife:	464
Till we haue brought Duke *Humphrey* in disgrace.	482
As for the Duke of Yorke, this late Complaint	483
Enter the King, Duke Humfrey, Cardinall, Bucking-|ham,	488
Pray God the Duke of Yorke excuse himselfe.	574
His words were these: That *Richard*, Duke of Yorke,	580
This is the Law, and this Duke *Humfreyes* doome.	607
Spirit. The Duke yet liues, that *Henry* shall depose:	657
Bulling. What fates await the Duke of Suffolke?	659
Bulling. What shall befall the Duke of Somerset?	661
Enter the Duke of Yorke and the Duke of Buckingham | with their Guard,	
and breake in.	669
Iniurious Duke, that threatest where's no cause.	678
The Duke yet liues, that Henry *shall depose:*	689
Well, to the rest: | Tell me what fate awaits the Duke of Suffolke?	692
What shall betide the Duke of Somerset?	695
Card. Duke *Humfrey* ha's done a Miracle to day.	912
Lionel, Duke of Clarence; next to whom,	972
Was *Iohn* of Gaunt, the Duke of Lancaster;	973
The fift, was *Edmond Langley*, Duke of Yorke;	974
The sixt, was *Thomas* of Woodstock, Duke of Gloster;	975
Till *Henry Bullingbrooke*, Duke of Lancaster,	980
Warw. Father, the Duke hath told the truth;	987
Yorke. The third Sonne, Duke of Clarence,	994
Who marryed *Phillip*, sole Daughter | Vnto *Lionel*, Duke of Clarence.	1013
Winke at the Duke of Suffolkes insolence,	1036
That vertuous Prince, the good Duke *Humfrey*:	1040
Shall one day make the Duke of Yorke a King.	1046
King. Stay *Humfrey*, Duke of Gloster,	1076
And *Humfrey*, Duke of Gloster, scarce himselfe,	1096
*an honest man: and touching the Duke of Yorke, I will	1149
Enter Duke Humfrey and his Men in | Mourning Cloakes.	1169
Sometime Ile say, I am Duke *Humfreyes* Wife,	1218
* *Stanley.* Like to a Duchesse, and Duke *Humfreyes* Lady,	1278
Made me collect these dangers in the Duke.	1329
I will subscribe, and say I wrong'd the Duke.	1332
Suff. Well hath your Highnesse seene into this Duke:	1336
*Which time will bring to light in smooth Duke *Humfrey*.	1359
The Duke is vertuous, milde, and too well giuen,	1366
Card. Sirs, take away the Duke, and guard him sure.	1488
As place Duke *Humfrey* for the Kings Protector?	1552
But now returne we to the false Duke *Humfrey*.	1627
Enter two or three running ouer the Stage, from the | Murther of Duke	
Humfrey.	1690

DUKE *cont.*

We haue dispatcht the Duke, as he commanded.	1693
The Duke was dumbe, and could not speake a word. | *King sounds.*	1728
Although the Duke was enemie to him,	1757
And all to haue the Noble Duke aliue.	1764
It may be iudg'd I made the Duke away,	1767
That good Duke *Humfrey* Traiterously is murdred	1825
Vpon the life of this thrice-famed Duke.	1861
*Suf. Why Warwicke, who should do the D.(uke) to death?	1883
*War. But both of you were vowed D.(uke) Humfries foes,	1886
And you (forsooth) had the good Duke to keepe:	1887
As guilty of Duke *Humfries* timelesse death.	1891
That I am faultie in Duke *Humfreyes* death.	1906
And doe some seruice to Duke *Humfreyes* Ghost. | *Exeunt.*	1936
They say, by him the good Duke *Humfrey* dy'de:	1960
Sometime he talkes, as if Duke *Humfries* Ghost	2090
Suf. Stay *Whitmore*, for thy Prisoner is a Prince, | The Duke of Suffolke, *William de la Pole.*	2213
Whit. The Duke of Suffolke, muffled vp in ragges?	2215
Suf. I, but these ragges are no part of the Duke.	2216
And thou that smil'dst at good Duke *Humfries* death,	2244
married the Duke of *Clarence* daughter, did he not? | *Staf.* I sir.	2457
*Bro. Iacke Cade, the D.(uke) of York hath taught you this.	2474
head, the Duke of Buckingham, and the | *Lord Say.*	2531
Descended from the Duke of *Clarence* house,	2565
Qu. Ah were the Duke of Suffolke now aliue,	2577
The Duke of Yorke is newly come from Ireland,	2877
The Duke of Somerset, whom he tearmes a Traitor.	2883
Tell him, Ile send Duke *Edmund* to the Tower,	2892
The Duke of Somerset is in the Tower.	3033
Go bid her hide him quickly from the Duke.	3079
The Title of this most renowned Duke,	3176
with the death of the Good Duke | HVMFREY.	3358

DUKEDOME = 1

head, for selling the Dukedome of *Maine.*	2481

DUKEDOMES = 1*1

*To change two Dukedomes for a Dukes faire daughter.	231
Till *Suffolke* gaue two Dukedomes for his Daughter.	473

DUKES = 2*2

*The Dukes of *Orleance, Calaber, Britaigne*, and *Alanson*,	14
*To change two Dukedomes for a Dukes faire daughter.	231
She beares a Dukes Reuenewes on her backe,	466
And make the meanest of you Earles and Dukes?	2814

DULY = 1

And duly wayted for my comming forth?	2230

DUMBE = 2

The Duke was dumbe, and could not speake a word. | *King sounds.*	1728
To tell my loue vnto his dumbe deafe trunke,	1846

DUNGHILL = 2

Yorke. Base Dunghill Villaine, and Mechanicall,	590
Vnto a dunghill, which shall be thy graue,	2986

DURST = *1

*I hid me in these Woods, and durst not peepe out, for all	2908

DUSKIE = 2

And when the duskie sky, began to rob	1804
And call'd them blinde and duskie Spectacles,	1812

DUST = 1
He hath no eyes, the dust hath blinded them 2148
DUTCHESSE = *1
*Dutchesse of Aniou and Maine, shall be released and deliuered 64
DUTCHY = 1*1
*Item, That the Dutchy of Aniou, and the County of Main, 56
Hath giuen the Dutchy of Aniou and Mayne, 117
DUTIE = 3
As I in dutie loue my King and Countrey. 553
Disdaining dutie that to vs belongs. 1311
For shame in dutie bend thy knee to me, 3173
DWELL = *1
*dwell in this house, because the vnconquered soule of | Cade is fled. 2969
DY = 1
Cut both the Villaines throats, for dy you shall: 2189
DYDE = 2
They say, by him the good Duke Humfrey dy'de: 1960
Dy'de he not in his bed? Where should he dye? 2143
DYE = 21*3
And shall these Labours, and these Honours dye? 102
Your Deeds of Warre, and all our Counsell dye? 104
But him out-liue, and dye a violent death. 658
Spirit. By Water shall he dye, and take his end. 660
But him out-liue, and dye a violent death. 690
By Water shall he dye, and take his end. 694
*World. Here Robin, and if I dye, I giue thee my Aporne; 1135
Card. That he should dye, is worthie pollicie, 1537
Yorke. So that by this, you would not haue him dye. 1545
No: let him dye, in that he is a Fox, 1559
Aye me, I can no more: Dye Elinor, 1820
Loather a hundred times to part then dye; 2070
And in thy sight to dye, what were it else, 2106
To dye by thee, were but to dye in iest, 2117
From thee to dye, were torture more then death: 2118
Dy'de he not in his bed? Where should he dye? 2143
And therefore to reuenge it, shalt thou dye, 2195
And told me that by Water I should dye: 2204
It is impossible that I should dye 2278
Great men oft dye by vilde Bezonions. 2302
If you go forward: therefore yeeld, or dye. 2447
*Qu. No my Loue, I should not mourne, but dye for | thee. 2558
*Ile bridle it: he shall dye, and it bee but for pleading so 2739
DYED = 4*1
Sal. Now by the death of him that dyed for all, 120
Edward the Black-Prince dyed before his Father, 977
*Salisb. But William of Hatfield dyed without an | Heire. 992
Who kept him in Captiuitie, till he dyed. | But, to the rest. 1003
But how he dyed, God knowes, not Henry: 1833
DYES = 3
Thus Elianors Pride dyes in her youngest dayes. 1102
Pompey the Great, and Suffolke dyes by Pyrats. | Exit Water with
Suffolke. 2306
am vanquished by Famine, not by Valour. Dyes. 2980
DYING = 1
Dying with mothers dugge betweene it's lips. 2110
EACH = 4
And each of them had twentie times their power, 1237

EACH *cont.*

By meanes whereof, the Townes each day reuolted. 1357
His fortunes I will weepe, and 'twixt each groane, 1522
Collected choycely, from each Countie some, 1618

EAGLE = 1

Wer't not all one, an emptie Eagle were set, 1550

EAGLES = 1

Drones sucke not Eagles blood, but rob Bee-hiues: 2277

EARE = 1*2

Giue me my Fanne: what, Mynion, can ye not? | *She giues the Duchesse*
a box on the eare. 529
*no Christian eare can endure to heare. Thou hast appoin-|ted 2674
Cade. Giue him a box o'th'eare, and that wil make'em | red againe. 2719

EARLE = 5*2

Had Issue *Phillip*, a Daughter, | Who marryed *Edmond Mortimer*, Earle
of March: 996
Edmond had Issue, *Roger*, Earle of March; 998
Marryed *Richard*, Earle of Cambridge, 1007
She was Heire to *Roger*, Earle of March, 1011
Warw. My heart assures me, that the Earle of Warwick 1045
Richard shall liue to make the Earle of Warwick 1048
Cade. Marry, this *Edmund Mortimer* Earle of March, 2456

EARLES = 2*1

*Seuen Earles, twelue Barons, & twenty reuerend Bishops 15
And make the meanest of you Earles and Dukes? 2814
Enter the Earles of Warwicke, and | *Salisbury.* 3145

EARLY = 1

Early and late, debating too and fro 98

EARNEST = 1

My tongue should stumble in mine earnest words, 2031

EARNEST-GAPING-SIGHT = 1

My earnest-gaping-sight of thy Lands view, 1805

EARTH = 6*2

Why are thine eyes fixt to the sullen earth, 278
*Earth; *Iohn Southwell* reade you, and let vs to our worke. 631
Card. Thy Heauen is on Earth, thine Eyes & Thoughts 736
For blessed are the Peace-makers on Earth. 754
Blaspheming God, and cursing men on earth. 2089
Thy graue is digg'd already in the earth: 2956
Where shall it finde a harbour in the earth? 3168
Knit earth and heauen together. 3264

EARTHLY = 3

A world of earthly blessings to my soule, 29
King. Great is his comfort in this Earthly Vale, 799
King. Was euer King that ioy'd an earthly Throne, 2850

EARTHS = 1

Theirs for the earths encrease, mine for my sorrowes. 2102

EARTHY = 1

And to suruey his dead and earthy Image: 1850

EASE = 2

Sorrow would sollace, and mine Age would ease. 1075
But here's a vengefull Sword, rusted with ease, 1902

EASIE = *1

Suff. My Lord, these faults are easie, quickly answer'd: 1433

EASILY = 2

A Heart vnspotted, is not easily daunted. 1398
Whereof you cannot easily purge your selfe. 1435

EAST – 2
On the East side of the Groue.	763
The East side of the Groue: | Cardinall, I am with you.	770

EATE = 2*4
And Caterpillers eate my Leaues away:	1387
*mony, all shall eate and drinke on my score, and I will	2391
*I climb'd into this Garden, to see if I can eate Grasse, or	2912
*thee eate Iron like an Ostridge, and swallow my Sword	2933
*eate no meate these fiue dayes, yet come thou and thy	2943
naile, I pray God I may neuer eate grasse more.	2945

EATING = 1
*Smith. Nay Iohn, it wil be stinking Law, for his breath | stinkes with	
eating toasted cheese.	2644

EDGE = 1*1
This Newes I thinke hath turn'd your Weapons edge;	932
*that euer I heard. Steele, if thou turne the edge, or	2960

EDICT = 1
Yet not withstanding such a strait Edict,	1970

EDMOND = 8
Were plac'd the heads of *Edmond* Duke of Somerset,	303
The fift, was *Edmond Langley*, Duke of Yorke;	974
Had Issue *Phillip*, a Daughter, | Who marryed *Edmond Mortimer*, Earle	
of March:	996
Edmond had Issue, *Roger*, Earle of March;	998
Roger had Issue, *Edmond, Anne*, and *Elianor*.	999
Salisb. This *Edmond*, in the Reigne of *Bullingbrooke*,	1000
Who was to *Edmond Langley*, | *Edward* the thirds fift Sonnes Sonne;	1008
Who was the Sonne of *Edmond Mortimer*,	1012

EDMUND = 1*1
*Cade. Marry, this *Edmund Mortimer* Earle of March,	2456
Tell him, Ile send Duke *Edmund* to the Tower,	2892

EDW = 1
EDWARD see also Edw. = 6
Yorke. Then thus: | *Edward* the third, my Lords, had seuen Sonnes:	968
The first, *Edward* the Black-Prince, Prince of Wales;	970
Edward the Black-Prince dyed before his Father,	977
Who after *Edward* the third's death, raign'd as King,	979
Who was to *Edmond Langley*, | *Edward* the thirds fift Sonnes Sonne;	1008
Enter Edward and Richard.	3117

EFFECTED = 2
Wee'le see these things effected to the full.	359
The ancient Prouerbe will be well effected,	1470

EFFECTUALL = 1
Or else conclude my words effectuall.	1335

EIGHTEENE = 2
For eighteene moneths concluded by consent.	49
I'th parts of France, till terme of eighteene Moneths	72

EITHER *see* eyther
ELDER = 2
So, if the Issue of the elder Sonne	1015
The elder of them being put to nurse,	2462

ELDEST = 3
The eldest Sonne and Heire of *Iohn* of Gaunt,	981
Yorke. His eldest Sister, *Anne*, | My Mother, being Heire vnto the	
Crowne,	1005
Command my eldest sonne, nay all my sonnes,	3041

ELECTION = 1
Suff. Before we make election, giue me leaue   557
ELI = 2*1
ELIA = 3*1
ELIANOR see also Eli., Elia. = 15
  Enter Duke Humfrey and his wife Elianor.   273
  Presumptuous Dame, ill-nurter'd *Elianor,*   316
  With *Elianor,* for telling but her dreame?   326
  With thy Confederates in this weightie cause. | *Exit Elianor.*   361
  Dame *Elianor* giues Gold, to bring the Witch: 367
  She shall not strike Dame *Elianor* vnreueng'd. | *Exit Elianor.* 539
  Buck. Lord Cardinall, I will follow *Elianor,*   541
  Enter Elianor aloft.   632
  Of Lady *Elianor,* the Protectors Wife,   921
  Roger had Issue, *Edmond, Anne,* and *Elianor.*   999
  King. Stand forth Dame *Elianor Cobham,* | *Glosters* Wife: 1053
  Glost. Elianor, the Law thou seest hath iudged thee,   1069
  Why then Dame *Elianor* was neere thy ioy.   1779
  Might in thy Pallace, perish *Elianor.*   1800
ELIANOR = 9*3
ELIANORS = 2
  They (knowing Dame *Elianors* aspiring humor)   373
  Thus *Elianors* Pride dyes in her youngest dayes.   1102
ELINOR = 2
  Hum. Nay *Elinor,* then must I chide outright: 315
  Aye me, I can no more: Dye *Elinor,*   1820
ELIZIUM = 1
  And then it liu'd in sweete Elizium.   2116
ELSE = 7*1
  Which I will win from France, or else be slaine.   224
  Humf. Sirrha, or you must fight, or else be hang'd.   614
  Hume. I, what else? feare you not her courage.   624
  Glost. Talking of Hawking; nothing else, my Lord.   773
  Or else conclude my words effectuall.   1335
  Murther indeede, that bloodie sinne, I tortur'd | Aboue the Felon, or
  what Trespas else.   1431
  And in thy sight to dye, what were it else,   2106
  Ma. A thousand Crownes, or else lay down your head   2185
EM = *1
  Cade. Giue him a box o'th'eare, and that wil make'em | red againe. 2719
EMANUELL = 1
  *Come hither sirrah, I must examine thee: What is thy | name? |
  Clearke. Emanuell.   2414
EMBASSADOR = 1
  Is, that he was the Lord Embassador,   1989
EMBLAZE = 1
  To emblaze the Honor that thy Master got.   2976
EMBRACE *see also* imbrace = 1
  Embrace, and kisse, and take ten thousand leaues,   2069
EMPIRE = 1
  Had *Henrie* got an Empire by his marriage,   160
EMPLOYD *see* imploy'd
EMPRESSE = 1
  More like an Empresse, then Duke *Humphreyes* Wife: 464

EMPTIE = 2
Wer't not all one, an emptie Eagle were set,   1550
And dead mens cries do fill the emptie ayre,   3222
ENCHACD *see* inchac'd
ENCITED *see* cited
ENCLIND = 1
For hee's enclin'd as is the rauenous Wolues.   1372
ENCLOSING = *1
*Suffolke, for enclosing the Commons of Melforde. How | now, Sir
Knaue?   406
ENCOUNTRED = 1*1
*shall be encountred with a man as good as himselfe. He   2435
But match to match I haue encountred him,   3229
ENCREASE = 2
Thou wilt but adde encrease vnto my Wrath.   2006
Theirs for the earths encrease, mine for my sorrowes.   2102
ENCROACHING *see* incroaching
END = 7
Spirit. By Water shall he dye, and take his end.   660
By Water shall he dye, and take his end.   694
Here let them end it, and God defend the right.   1111
And in the end being rescued, I haue seene   1670
Mine haire be fixt an end, as one distract: 2033
But if thy Armes be to no other end,   3031
The name of Valour. O let the vile world end,   3262
ENDED = 1
Our simple Supper ended, giue me leaue,   961
ENDEUOUR = 1
And with your best endeuour haue stirr'd vp   1463
ENDS = 1
That those which flye before the battell ends,   2498
ENDURE = 4*1
Haue done, for more I hardly can endure.   665
Vnneath may shee endure the Flintie Streets,   1179
Cade. I am able to endure much.   2374
*no Christian eare can endure to heare. Thou hast appoin-|ted   2674
Shall I endure the sight of Somerset?   3085
ENEMIE = 5
My liefest Liege to be mine Enemie: 1464
By nature prou'd an Enemie to the Flock,   1560
Hath he conuersed with the Enemie,   1674
Although the Duke was enemie to him,   1757
But that thou art so fast mine enemie.   3242
ENEMIES = 4*4
Peter. O God, haue I ouercome mine Enemies in this   1160
And banne thine Enemies, both mine and thine.   1201
So mightie are his vowed Enemies.   1521
Weaues tedious Snares to trap mine Enemies.   1646
Beuis. Hee shall haue the skinnes of our enemies, to | make Dogges
Leather of.   2342
Cade. For our enemies shall faile before vs, inspired   2355
*enemies: go too then, I ask but this: Can he that speaks   2490
Priests pray for enemies, but Princes kill. | *Fight. Excursions.* 3294
ENEMY = 6*1
'Tis knowne to you he is mine enemy: 155

ENEMY *cont.*

Nay more, an enemy vnto you all,	156
Attracts the same for aydance 'gainst the enemy,	1869
And 'tis well seene, he found an enemy.	1889
Hast thou not spirit to curse thine enemy.	2022
*with the tongue of an enemy, be a good Councellour, or | no?	2491
To giue the enemy way, and to secure vs	3302

ENFORCE *see* inforce

ENFRANCHISEMENT *see* infranchisement

ENGIRT = 1

That Gold, must round engirt these browes of mine,	3094

ENGLAND = 21*8

In sight of England, and her Lordly Peeres,	18
* *Queen.* Great King of England, & my gracious Lord,	31
* *for Henry King of England, That the said Henry shal*	52
England, ere the thirtieth of May next ensuing.	55
Glo. Braue Peeres of England, Pillars of the State,	82
O Peeres of England, shamefull is this League,	105
Me thinkes the Realmes of England, France, & Ireland,	244
Whose bookish Rule, hath pull'd faire England downe. | *Exit Yorke.*	271
Is this the Fashions in the Court of England?	429
Your Highnesse came to England, so will I	452
In England worke your Graces full content.	453
But can doe more in England then the King.	457
Cannot doe more in England then the *Neuils:*	459
* *Glost.* Why *Suffolke,* England knowes thine insolence.	750
The greatest man in England, but the King. | *Exeunt.*	1049
And *Humfrey* is no little Man in England.	1314
As firmely as I hope for fertile England.	1385
I, Night by Night, in studying good for England.	1411
That England was defam'd by Tyrannie.	1423
I will stirre vp in England some black Storme,	1655
Troubles the siluer Spring, where England drinkes:	2240
*it was neuer merrie world in England, since Gentlemen | came vp.	2327
*Vowes Reformation. There shall be in England, seuen	2383
* *Cade* And good reason: for thereby is England main'd	2482
* *But.* Onely that the Lawes of England may come out | of your mouth.	2640
*burne all the Records of the Realme, my mouth shall be | the	
Parliament of England.	2647
Spare England, for it is your Natiue Coast:	2827
For yet may England curse my wretched raigne. | *Flourish. Exeunt.*	2903
* *Iden.* Nay, it shall nere be said, while England stands,	2946

ENGLANDS = 12*5

* *All kneel.* Long liue Qu.(eene) *Margaret,* Englands happines.	44
* *Englands owne proper Cost and Charges, without hauing any | Dowry.*	66
I neuer read but Englands Kings haue had	135
Euen as I haue of fertile Englands soile.	250
*With this new Bride, & Englands deere bought Queen,	264
Elianor. Not halfe so bad as thine to Englands King,	677
Which is infallible, to Englands Crowne.	964
* *Both.* Long liue our Soueraigne *Richard,* Englands | King.	1027
God and King *Henry* gouerne Englands Realme:	1085
And twice by aukward winde from Englands banke	1783
And bid them blow towards Englands blessed shore,	1790
And euen with this, I lost faire Englands view,	1810
Or banished faire Englands Territories,	1957
* *Ca.* If thou beest death, Ile giue thee Englands Treasure,	2136

ENGLANDS *cont.*
To entertaine great Englands lawfull King.	2995
Out-cast of *Naples*, Englands bloody Scourge,	3113
The rightfull heyre to Englands Royall seate.	3178

ENGLISH = 2
And heyre apparant to the English Crowne:	159
Was rightfull Heire vnto the English Crowne,	581

ENGLISHMEN = 2
And put the Englishmen vnto the Sword.	1587
And temper Clay with blood of Englishmen.	1616

ENGYRT = 1
My Body round engyrt with miserie:	1501

ENIOY *see also* ioy = 1
And may enioy such quiet walkes as these?	2922

ENIOYD *see* ioy'd
ENIOYES = 1
Or count them happy, that enioyes the Sunne?	1215

ENIOYING = 1
Resigne to death, it is not worth th'enioying:	1640

ENOUGH = 10*1
Elianor. It is enough, Ile thinke vpon the Questions:	357
Humf. Madame, the King is old enough himselfe	506
Queene. If he be old enough, what needs your Grace	508
Shee'le gallop farre enough to her destruction. | *Exit Buckingham.*	544
*in a Cup of Sack; and feare not Neighbor, you shall doe | well enough.	1121
Elianor. That's bad enough, for I am but reproach:	1276
Q. Enough sweet Suffolke, thou torment'st thy selfe,	2044
A Wildernesse is populous enough,	2075
Enough to purchase such another Island,	2137
Is't not enough to breake into my Garden,	2937
'Tis not enough our foes are this time fled,	3343

ENSUING = 1
England, ere the thirtieth of May next ensuing.	55

ENTER = 79*4
Enter King, Duke Humfrey, Salisbury, Warwicke, and Beau-|ford on the one side.	3
Enter Duke Humfrey and his wife Elianor.	273
Enter Messenger.	330
We are alone, here's none but thee, & I. *Enter Hume.*	344
Enter three or foure Petitioners, the Armorers | Man being one.	384
Enter Suffolke, and Queene.	391
Enter Seruant.	418
Enter the King, Duke Humfrey, Cardinall, Bucking-|ham,	488
Enter Humfrey.	546
Enter Armorer and his Man.	572
Enter the Witch, the two Priests, and Bullingbrooke.	619
Enter Elianor aloft.	632
Enter the Duke of Yorke and the Duke of Buckingham | with their Guard, and breake in.	669
Enter a Seruingman.	711
Enter the King, Queene, Protector, Cardinall, and| Suffolke, with Faulkners hallowing.	715
Enter one crying a Miracle.	784
Enter the Maior of Saint Albones, and his Brethren, | bearing the man betweene two in a Chayre.	795
Enter a Beadle with Whippes.	894
Enter Buckingham.	916

ENTER *cont.*

Enter Yorke, Salisbury, and Warwick.	959
Sound Trumpets. Enter the King and State, | with Guard, to banish the	
Duchesse.	1051
The Armorer and his Man, to enter the Lists,	1106
*Enter at one Doore the Armorer and his Neighbors, drinking	1115
Enter Duke Humfrey and his Men in | Mourning Cloakes.	1169
Enter the Duchesse in a white Sheet, and a Taper	1188
Enter a Herald.	1246
Sound a Senet. Enter King, Queene, Cardinall, Suffolke,	1292
Enter Somerset.	1376
Enter Gloucester.	1390
Enter a Poste.	1584
Enter two or three running ouer the Stage, from the | Murther of Duke	
Humfrey.	1690
Didst euer heare a man so penitent? *Enter Suffolke.*	1695
Sound Trumpets. Enter the King, the Queene, | Cardinall, Suffolke,	
Somerset, with | Attendants.	1706
Enter Suffolke.	1722
Noyse within. Enter Warwicke, and many | Commons.	1822
Enter his Chamber, view his breathlesse Corpes,	1834
Enter Suffolke and Warwicke, with their | Weapons drawne.	1944
Enter Salisbury.	1952
Enter Vaux.	2082
Enter the King, Salisbury, and Warwicke, to the | Cardinal in bed.	2132
Enter Lieutenant, Suffolke, and others.	2169
Manet the first Gent. Enter Walter with the body.	2312
Enter Beuis, and Iohn Holland.	2319
*Drumme. Enter Cade, Dicke Butcher, Smith the Weauer, | and a	
Sawyer, with infinite numbers.	2350
Enter a Clearke.	2402
Enter Michael.	2429
Enter Sir Humfrey Stafford, and his Brother, | with Drum and Soldiers.	2440
Alarums to the fight, wherein both the Staffords are slaine. | Enter Cade	
and the rest.	2511
*Enter the King with a Supplication, and the Queene with Suf-|folkes	2530
Enter a Messenger.	2560
Enter another Messenger.	2585
Enter Lord Scales vpon the Tower walking. Then enters | two or three	
Citizens below.	2598
Enter Iacke Cade and the rest, and strikes his | staffe on London stone.	2613
Enter a Soldier running.	2622
Alarums. Mathew Goffe is slain, and all the rest. | Then enter Iacke	
Cade, with his Company.	2633
*Cade. And hence-forward all things shall be in Com-|mon. *Enter a*	
Messenger.	2651
Enter George, with the Lord Say.	2657
Enter one with the heads.	2763
Alarum, and Retreat. Enter againe Cade, | and all his rabblement.	2773
Enter Buckingham, and old Clifford.	2781
Sound Trumpets. Enter King, Queene, and | Somerset on the Tarras.	2848
Enter Buckingham and Clifford.	2856
Enter Multitudes with Halters about their | Neckes.	2860
Enter a Messenger.	2875
Enter Cade.	2905
Enter Iden.	2920
Enter Yorke, and his Army of Irish, with | Drum and Colours.	2990

ENTER *cont.*
 Enter Buckingham.   3003
 Enter King and Attendants.   3048
 Enter Iden with Cades head.   3057
 Enter Queene and Somerset.   · 3077
 Enter Edward and Richard.   3117
 Enter Clifford.   3119
 Enter the Earles of Warwicke, and | Salisbury.   3145
 Enter Warwicke.   .   3218
 Enter Yorke.   3226
 Enter Clifford.   3232
 Enter yong Clifford.   3252
 Enter Richard, and Somerset to fight.   3288
 Enter King, Queene, and others.   3296
 Enter Clifford.   3311
 Alarum. Retreat. Enter Yorke, Richard, Warwicke, | and Soldiers, with
 Drum & Colours.   3319
 Enter Salisbury.   3336
ENTERING = *1
 *for a stray, for entering his Fee-simple without leaue. A   2930
ENTERS = 1*1
 to him so much, that hee is drunke; and he enters with a   1116
 Enter Lord Scales vpon the Tower walking. Then enters | two or three
 Citizens below.   2598
ENTERTAINE = 2
 To entertaine my vowes of thankes and praise.   2866
 To entertaine great Englands lawfull King.   2995
ENTERTAINMENT = 1
 In entertainment to my Princely Queene.   77
ENTICING = 1
 And plac't a Quier of such enticing Birds,   475
ENTREAT *see also* intreat = 2
 Glost. Entreat her not the worse, in that I pray   . 1259
 Yet did I purpose as they doe entreat: 1996
ENUENOMED *see* inuenomed
ENUIES = 1
 What lowring Starre now enuies thy estate?   1507
ENUIOUS = 3
 With enuious Lookes laughing at thy shame,   1183
 And when I start, the enuious people laugh,   1211
 The enuious Load that lyes vpon his heart: 1457
ENUY = 2
 As leane-fac'd enuy in her loathsome caue.   2030
 Or gather wealth I care not with what enuy: 2926
EQUALL = 2*1
 And poyse the Cause in Iustice equall Scales,   956
 Cade. To equall him I will make my selfe a knight, pre- | sently;   2438
 And let thy tongue be equall with thy heart.   3084
EQUITIE = 1
 And Equitie exil'd your Highnesse Land.   1446
ERE = 14*2
 England, ere the thirtieth of May next ensuing.   55
 I prophesied, France will be lost ere long. *Exit Humfrey.*   153
 Ere thou goe, giue vp thy Staffe,   1077
 As ere thy Father *Henry* made it mine;   1089
 Trowest thou, that ere Ile looke vpon the World,   1214
 What e're occasion keepes him from vs now.   1297

ERE *cont.*

But I will remedie this geare ere long,	1388
That Doyt that ere I wrested from the King,	1412
That ere I prou'd thee false, or fear'd thy faith.	1506
Ere you can take due Orders for a Priest:	1576
*ere they haue it: Men shall hold of mee in Capite.	2755
like a great pin ere thou and I part.	2934
*ere thou sleepe in thy Sheath, I beseech Ioue on my knees	2962
I know ere they will haue me go to Ward,	3107
I would speake blasphemy ere bid you flye:	3313
Let vs pursue him ere the Writs go forth.	3348

ERECT = 1

Erect his Statue, and worship it,	1780

ERECTING = *1

*the Realme, in erecting a Grammar Schoole: and where-|as	2667

ERGO *see* argo

ERST = 1

That erst did follow thy prowd Chariot-Wheeles,	1184

ESCAPD *see* scap'd

ESCAPE *see* scape

ESPOUSD = 1

I haue perform'd my Taske, and was espous'd,	16

ESPOUSE = *1

*espouse the Lady Margaret, daughter vnto Reignier King of	53

ESQUIRE = 2

That *Alexander Iden* an Esquire of Kent,	2947
A poore Esquire of Kent, that loues his King.	3069

ESSENTIALLY = 1

Hath not essentially, but by circumstance	3261

ESTABLISH = 1

And what we doe establish, he confirmes:	1622

ESTATE = 1

What lowring Starre now enuies thy estate?	1507

ESTEEME = 1*1

Then from true euidence, of good esteeme,	1715
*Clif. Nor should thy prowesse want praise & esteeme,	3243

ETCETERA *see* &c.

ETERNALL = 3

Spirit. Ad sum. | *Witch. Asmath*, by the eternall God,	648
The mortall Worme might make the sleepe eternall.	1975
King. Oh thou eternall mouer of the heauens,	2153

ETERNITIE = 1

Because I wish'd this Worlds eternitie.	1270

ETERNIZD = 1

Shall be eterniz'd in all Age to come.	3353

EUEN = 17*3

Euen as I haue of fertile Englands soile.	250
*knees he would be euen with me: I haue good witnesse	597
And euen as willingly at thy feete I leaue it,	1090
Euen so remorselesse haue they borne him hence:	1514
Euen so my selfe bewayles good *Glosters* case	1518
And euen with this, I lost faire Englands view,	1810
Euen so suspitious is this Tragedie.	1898
Warw. Away euen now, or I will drag thee hence:	1934
And euen now my burthen'd heart would breake	2035
Go, speake not to me; euen now be gone.	2067
Oh go not yet. Euen thus, two Friends condemn'd,	2068

EUEN *cont.*

That euen now he cries alowd for him.	2095
Euen as a splitted Barke, so sunder we:	2129
May euen in their Wiues and Childrens sight,	2499
*France? Be it knowne vnto thee by these presence, euen	2663
*euen with you. Ile see if his head will stand steddier on	2728
Euen to affright thee with the view thereof.	3207
Euen of the bonnie beast he loued so well.	3231
To die in Ruffian battell? Euen at this sight,	3271
Shall be to me, euen as the Dew to Fire,	3275

EUENING = 1

And if thou dar'st, this Euening,	762

EUENT = 1

Lord *Suffolke*, you and I must talke of that euent.	1631

EUER = 7*4

The happiest Gift, that euer Marquesse gaue,	22
The Fairest Queene, that euer King receiu'd.	23
Armorer. Alas, my Lord, hang me if euer I spake the	594
Nor euer had one penny Bribe from France.	1409
Didst euer heare a man so penitent? *Enter Suffolke.*	1695
If euer Lady wrong'd her Lord so much,	1916
That euer did containe a thing of worth,	2128
Cade. Was euer Feather so lightly blowne too & fro,	2832
King. Was euer King that ioy'd an earthly Throne,	2850
Cade. Braue thee? I by the best blood that euer was	2941
*that euer I heard. Steele, if thou turne the edge, or	2960

EUERLASTING = 2

King. The Treasurie of euerlasting Ioy.	735
King. Then heauen set ope thy euerlasting gates,	2865

EUERMORE = 1

And after Summer, euermore succeedes	1172

EUERY = 9

Glost. Let the(m) be whipt through euery Market Towne,	909
Was made a wonder, and a pointing stock | To euery idle Rascall	
follower.	1222
When euery one will giue the time of day,	1308
For euery word you speake in his behalfe,	1913
I, euery ioynt should seeme to curse and ban,	2034
With euery seuerall pleasure in the World:	2078
Staf. Herald away, and throughout euery Towne,	2496
Will we ride through the streets, & at euery Corner	2771
You shall haue pay, and euery thing you wish.	3039

EUERYONE *see* euery
EUERYTHING *see* euery
EUIDENCE = 1

Then from true euidence, of good esteeme,	1715

EUILL = 2

To dreame on euill, or to worke my downefall.	1367
King. Ah, what a signe it is of euill life,	2139

EUMENES = 1

Clif. La fin Corrone les eumenes.	3249

EUNUCH = *1

*gelded the Commonwealth, and made it an Eunuch: &	2485

EX = *1

Hu. I go. Come *Nel* thou wilt ride with vs? *Ex. Hum*	334

EXACTED = 1

When haue I ought exacted at your hands?	2703

EXAMINE = *1
*Come hither sirrah, I must examine thee: What is thy | name? |
Clearke. Emanuell.   2414
EXAMPLE = 1*1
Be hang'd vp for example at their doores: 2500
**Dicke.* And worke in their shirt to, as my selfe for ex- | ample, that am
a butcher.   2685
EXCEEDE = 1
Let not her Penance exceede the Kings Commission.   1252
EXCEEDED = 1
Buck. Thy Crueltie in execution | Vpon Offendors, hath exceeded Law,   522
EXCEEDING = 1
That liuing wrought me such exceeding trouble.   3064
EXCELLENCE = 3
As Procurator to your Excellence, | To marry Princes *Margaret* for your
Grace;   10
Iesu maintaine your Royall Excellence,   168
To be Protector of his Excellence?   509
EXCELLENT = 1
That for the beautie thinkes it excellent.   1532
EXCEPT = 2
Suff. Not resolute, except so much were done,   1569
Except a Sword or Scepter ballance it.   3000
EXCEPTING = 1
Excepting none but good Duke Humfrey.   201
EXCLAIME = 1
That thus you do exclaime you'l go with him.   2812
EXCURSIONS = 1
Priests pray for enemies, but Princes kill. | *Fight. Excursions.*   3294
EXCUSE = 1
Pray God the Duke of Yorke excuse himselfe.   574
EXECRATIONS = 1
Suff. Cease, gentle Queene, these Execrations,   2019
EXECUTE = 1
More can I beare, then you dare execute.   2298
EXECUTED = 1
Because his purpose is not executed.   1558
EXECUTION = 2
Buck. Thy Crueltie in execution | Vpon Offendors, hath exceeded Law,   522
From thence, vnto the place of Execution: 1059
EXECUTIONER = 1
And Ile prouide his Executioner,   1578
EXEMPT = 1
True Nobility, is exempt from feare: 2297
EXEUNT = 20*1
Somerset, wee'le see thee sent away. | *Flourish. Exeunt.*   617
To suppe with me to morrow Night. Away. | *Exeunt.*   713
*Whose Beame stands sure, whose rightful cause preuailes. | *Flourish.
Exeunt.*   957
The greatest man in England, but the King. | *Exeunt.*   1049
Come fellow, follow vs for thy Reward. | *Sound a flourish. Exeunt.*   1167
Goe, leade the way, I long to see my Prison. *Exeunt.*   1291
**Suff.* Ile see it truly done, my Lord of Yorke. *Exeunt.*   1635
Suff. Away, be gone. *Exeunt.*   1705
And doe some seruice to Duke *Humfreyes* Ghost. | *Exeunt.*   1936
Qu. This way for me. *Exeunt*   2131
And let vs all to Meditation. *Exeunt.*   2167

EXEUNT *cont.*
*Cade. Feare not that I warrant thee. Come, let's march | towards
London. *Exeunt.* 2528
And therefore am I bold and resolute. *Exeunt.* 2597
And so farwell, for I must hence againe. *Exeunt* 2612
Come, let's away. *Exeunt omnes.* 2632
Shall haue a thousand Crownes for his reward. | *Exeunt some of them.* 2844
To reconcile you all vnto the King. *Exeunt omnes.* 2847
For yet may England curse my wretched raigne. | *Flourish. Exeunt.* 2903
Ric. If not in heauen, you'l surely sup in hell. *Exeunt* 3217
Away my Lord, away. *Exeunt* 3318
And more such dayes as these, to vs befall. *Exeunt.* 3355

EXHORT = *1
**Kent from me, she hath lost her best man, and exhort all 2978

EXILD = 1
And Equitie exil'd your Highnesse Land. 1446

EXILE = 1
Omitting Suffolkes exile, my soules Treasure? 2099

EXIT see also Ex. = 36
Exit King, Queene, and Suffolke. | *Manet the rest.* 80
I prophesied, France will be lost ere long. *Exit Humfrey.* 153
Ile to the Duke of Suffolke presently. *Exit Cardinall.* 178
Despite Duke *Humfrey,* or the Cardinall. | *Exit Buckingham, and
Somerset.* 186
Exit Warwicke, and Salisbury. Manet Yorke. 225
Whose bookish Rule, hath pull'd faire England downe. | *Exit Yorke.* 271
With thy Confederates in this weightie cause. | *Exit Elianor.* 361
Sort how it will, I shall haue Gold for all. *Exit.* 383
**presently: wee'le heare more of your matter before | the King. *Exit.* 420
All. Come, let's be gone. *Exit.* 427
And you your selfe shall steere the happy Helme. *Exit.* 486
Would make thee quickly hop without thy Head. | *Exit Humfrey.* 527
She shall not strike Dame *Elianor* vnreueng'd. | *Exit Elianor.* 539
Shee'le gallop farre enough to her destruction. | *Exit Buckingham.* 544
**and so I pray you goe in Gods Name, and leaue vs. | *Exit Hume.* 628
False Fiend auoide. | *Thunder and Lightning. Exit Spirit.* 667
Wee'le see your Trinkets here all forth-comming. | All away. *Exit.* 683
Maior. Sirrha, goe fetch the Beadle hither straight. | *Exit.* 887
Till they come to Barwick, from whence they came. | *Exit.* 910
Exit Gloster. 1094
Glost. Witnesse my teares, I cannot stay to speake. | *Exit Gloster.* 1265
For good King *Henry,* thy decay I feare. *Exit Gloster.* 1494
Say, who's a Traytor? *Gloster* he is none. *Exit.* 1523
And *Henry* put apart: the next for me. *Exit.* 1689
Suff. Ile call him presently, my Noble Lord. *Exit.* 1712
I haue great matters to impart to thee. *Exit.* 2013
Qu. Go tell this heauy Message to the King. *Exit* 2096
Pompey the Great, and *Suffolke* dyes by Pyrats. | *Exit Water with
Suffolke.* 2306
Therefore come you with vs, and let him go. | *Exit Lieutenant, and the
rest.* 2310
Vntill the Queene his Mistris bury it. *Exit Walter.* 2314
and Inke-horne about his necke. [*Exit one with the Clearke* 2427
And you that be the Kings Friends follow me. *Exit.* 2501
Haue them kisse. Away. *Exit* 2772
**base and ignominious treasons, makes me betake mee to | my heeles.
Exit* 2840

EXIT cont.
Leauing thy trunke for Crowes to feed vpon. *Exit.*	2989
It greeues my soule to leaue thee vnassail'd. *Exit War.*	3238

EXORCISMES = 1
her Ladyship behold and heare our Exorcismes?	623

EXPECT = 2
At Bristow I expect my Souldiers,	1633
Expect your Highnesse doome of life, or death.	2864

EXPECTS = *1
Hume. Come my Masters, the Duchesse I tell you ex-|pects performance of your promises.	620

EXPEDIENT = *1
Card. A Breach that craues a quick expedient stoppe.	1591

EXPEND = 1
I would expend it with all willingnesse.	1450

EXPERIENCE = 1
Why art thou old, and want'st experience?	3171

EXPLOITS = 1
Thy late exploits done in the heart of France,	204

EXPRESSE = 2
I can expresse no kinder signe of Loue	25
As I in iustice, and true right expresse it.	3246

EXPYRD = 1
Be full expyr'd. Thankes Vncle Winchester,	73

EXTORTED = 1
Are my Chests fill'd vp with extorted Gold?	2732

EXTORTIONS = 1
Are lanke and leane with thy Extortions.	519

EYE = 3
He, knits his Brow, and shewes an angry Eye,	1309
Looke with a gentle eye vpon this Wretch,	2154
Whitm. I lost mine eye in laying the prize aboord,	2194

EYES = 18*2
And dim'd mine eyes, that I can reade no further.	61
My sword should shed hot blood, mine eyes no teares.	125
Why are thine eyes fixt to the sullen earth,	278
Card. Thy Heauen is on Earth, thine Eyes & Thoughts	736
Let me see thine Eyes; winck now, now open them,	846
Mine eyes are full of teares, my heart of griefe.	1071
My teare-stayn'd eyes, to see her Miseries.	1187
And nodde their heads, and throw their eyes on thee.	1198
Beaufords red sparkling eyes blab his hearts mallice,	1454
Whose floud begins to flowe within mine eyes;	1500
With sad vnhelpefull teares, and with dimn'd eyes;	1519
Qu. Runne, goe, helpe, helpe: Oh *Henry* ope thine eyes.	1733
Looke not vpon me, for thine eyes are wounding;	1751
And bid mine eyes be packing with my Heart,	1811
Mine eyes should sparkle like the beaten Flint,	2032
And cry out for thee to close vp mine eyes:	2112
He hath no eyes, the dust hath blinded them.	2148
Close vp his eyes, and draw the Curtaine close,	2166
The sight of me is odious in their eyes:	2582
Oppose thy stedfast gazing eyes to mine,	2949

EYE-BALLES = 1
His eye-balles further out, than when he liued,	1873

EYE-BALLS = 1
Vpon thy eye-balls, murderous Tyrannie	1749

EYTHER = 1
So should'st thou eyther turne my flying soule, 2114
FACD = 2
As leane-fac'd enuy in her loathsome caue. 2030
Aduance our halfe-fac'd Sunne, striuing to shine; 2266
FACE = 14*1
For thou hast giuen me in this beauteous Face 28
Rancour will out, proud Prelate, in thy face 149
If so, Gaze on, and grouell on thy face, 282
I could set my ten Commandements in your face. 534
The abiect People, gazing on thy face, 1182
Ah Vnckle *Humfrey*, in thy face I see 1503
In face, in gate, in speech he doth resemble. 1679
What, Dost thou turne away, and hide thy face? 1774
Vpon his face an Ocean of salt teares, 1845
War. See how the blood is setled in his face. 1864
But see, his face is blacke, and full of blood: 1872
Qu. Ah barbarous villaines: Hath this louely face, 2547
*hast built a Paper-Mill. It will be prooued to thy Face, 2671
See if thou canst out-face me with thy lookes: 2950
But boldly stand, and front him to his face. 3081
FACES = *1
*Wiues and Daughters before your faces. For me, I will '2806
FACT = 3
Warw. That can I witnesse, and a fouler fact 568
Whom we haue apprehended in the Fact, 925
Let pale-fac't feare keepe with the meane-borne man, 1641
FACTIOUS = 2
Glost. Make vp no factious numbers for the matter, 759
And chop away that factious pate of his. 3132
FAILE = *1
Cade. For our enemies shall faile before vs, inspired 2355
FAINE = 2*1
Suff. Ah *Yorke*, no man aliue, so faine as I. 1546
Faine would I go to chafe his palie lips, 1843
*And faine to go with a staffe, but that my puissance holds 2483
FAIR = *1
*1.*Gent.* My gracious Lord intreat him, speak him fair. 2288
FAIRE = 7*1
*To change two Dukedomes for a Dukes faire daughter. 231
Whose bookish Rule, hath pull'd faire England downe. | *Exit Yorke.* 271
And in thy Sonnes, faire slippes of such a Stock. 1022
Haue you layd faire the Bed? Is all things well, 1702
And euen with this, I lost faire Englands view, 1810
Or banished faire Englands Territories, 1957
Cade more, I thinke he hath a very faire warning. 2626
But I must make faire weather yet a while, 3022
FAIREST = 1
The Fairest Queene, that euer King receiu'd. 23
FAITH = 3*2
Glost. Faith holy Vnckle, would't were come to that. 757
That ere I prou'd thee false, or fear'd thy faith. 1506
But. I by my faith, the field is honourable, and there 2369
False King, why hast thou broken faith with me, 3086
Oh where is Faith? Oh, where is Loyalty? 3166
FALL = 7*1
Makes me from Wondring, fall to Weeping ioyes, 41

FALL *cont.*

And her Attainture, will be *Humphreyes* fall:	382
Suff. How cam'st thou so? | *Simpc.* A fall off of a Tree.	832
Salisb. Come, leaue your drinking, and fall to blowes.	1140
And should you fall, he is the next will mount.	1316
By wicked meanes to frame our Soueraignes fall.	1346
This way fall I to death.	2130
Hol. Come, come, let's fall in with them.	2349

FALNE = 2

And *Humfrey* with the Peeres be falne at iarres:	265
Remember it, and let it make thee Crest-falne,	2227

FALSE = 18*1

As for your spightfull false Obiections,	550
False Fiend auoide. | *Thunder and Lightning. Exit Spirit.*	667
And *Yorke*, and impious *Beauford*, that false Priest,	1229
By false accuse doth leuell at my Life.	1460
I shall not want false Witnesse, to condemne me,	1468
False allegations, to o'rethrow his state.	1481
Beshrew the winners, for they play'd me false,	1484
Ah that my feare were false, ah that it were;	1493
That ere I prou'd thee false, or fear'd thy faith.	1506
But now returne we to the false Duke *Humfrey.*	1627
Am I not witcht like her? Or thou not false like him?	1819
If my suspect be false, forgiue me God,	1841
Warw. What dares not *Warwick*, if false *Suffolke* dare | him?	1907
I would, false murd'rous Coward, on thy Knee	1925
From such fell Serpents as false *Suffolke* is;	1978
The false reuolting Normans thorough thee,	2255
Cade. By her he had two children at one birth. | *Bro.* That's false.	2459
They call false Catterpillers, and intend their death.	2573
False King, why hast thou broken faith with me,	3086

FALSELY = 1

falsely accus'd by the Villaine.	586

FALSE-HEART = 1

I am thy King, and thou a false-heart Traitor:	3140

FAME = 2

Fatall this Marriage, cancelling your Fame,	106
In cruelty, will I seeke out my Fame.	3282

FAMED = 1

Vpon the life of this thrice-famed Duke.	1861

FAMILIAR = *1

*well for his life. Away with him, he ha's a Familiar vn-|der	2740

FAMINE = 1*1

*O I am slaine, Famine and no other hath slaine me, let ten	2965
am vanquished by Famine, not by Valour. *Dyes.*	2980

FAMISH = *1

*sword, and yet am ready to famish. These fiue daies haue	2907

FAMISHT = 2

Till Paris was besieg'd, famisht, and lost.	567
Tooke oddes to combate a poore famisht man.	2948

FAMOUS = 3

So in the Famous Ancient City, *Toures*,	12
Hath made the Wizard famous in his death:	3292
Saint Albons battell wonne by famous Yorke,	3352

FANCIE = 1

Although we fancie not the Cardinall,	480

FANNE = 1
Giue me my Fanne: what, Mynion, can ye not? | *She giues the Duchesse
a box on the eare.*   529
FARE = 2
Elianor. Sherife farewell, and better then I fare,   1280
How would it fare with your departed soules,   2749
FARES = 1*2
Qu. How fares my Lord? Helpe Lords, the King is | dead.   1730
King. Oh Heauenly God. | *Qu.* How fares my gracious Lord?   1735
King. How fare's my Lord? Speake *Beauford* to thy | Soueraigne.   2134
FAREWELL = 7*3
Lordings farewell, and say when I am gone,   152
Farewell good King: when I am dead, and gone,   1092
And so Sir *Iohn*, farewell.   1262
Elianor. What, gone my Lord, and bid me not fare-|well?   1263
Elianor. Sherife farewell, and better then I fare,   1280
Elianor. I, I, farewell, thy Office is discharg'd: 1283
Yet now farewell, and farewell Life with thee.   2071
King. Farewell my Lord, trust not the Kentish Rebels   2594
Cade. Iden farewell, and be proud of thy victory: Tell   2977
FARRE = 8
Shee'le gallop farre enough to her destruction. | *Exit Buckingham.*   544
Glost. Farre truer spoke then meant: I lose indeede,   1483
Might happily haue prou'd farre worse then his.   1609
As farre as I could ken thy Chalky Cliffes,   1801
Farre be it, we should honor such as these   2291
Set limbe to limbe, and thou art farre the lesser: 2951
I am farre better borne then is the king: 3020
By what we can, which can no more but flye. | *Alarum a farre off.*   3303
FARRE-FET = 1
Som. If *Yorke*, with all his farre-fet pollicie,   1596
FARRE-OFF = 1
And if we did but glance a farre-off Looke,   1304
FARRE-VNWORTHIE = 1
Whose farre-vnworthie Deputie I am,   2000
FARWELL = 1
And so farwell, for I must hence againe. *Exeunt*   2612
FASHIONS = 1
Is this the Fashions in the Court of England?   429
FAST = 3*1
Wee will make fast within a hallow'd Verge.   642
Thither goes these Newes, | As fast as Horse can carry them: 704
Queene. Whether goes *Vaux* so fast? What newes I | prethee?   2083
But that thou art so fast mine enemie.   3242
FASTENED = *1
fastened to it: and at the other Doore his Man, with a   1118
FASTER = *1
*Faster the(n) Spring-time showres, comes thoght on thoght,   1643
FAST-BY = 1
And sees fast-by, a Butcher with an Axe,   1893
FATALL = 3
Fatall this Marriage, cancelling your Fame,   106
As did the fatall brand *Althaea* burnt,   246
With whose inuenomed and fatall sting,   1979
FATE = 1
Well, to the rest: | Tell me what fate awaits the Duke of Suffolke?   692

99

FATES = 1
Bulling. What fates await the Duke of Suffolke?   659
FATHER = 16*3
shall be released and deliuered to the King her father.   57
*ouer to the King her Father, and shee sent ouer of the King of   65
Oh Father, *Maine* is lost,   220
Main-chance father you meant, but I meant *Maine*,   223
Edward the Black-Prince dyed before his Father,   977
Warw. Father, the Duke hath told the truth;   987
Then Father *Salisbury*, kneele we together,   1023
As ere thy Father *Henry* made it mine;   1089
**Cade.* Wee *Iohn Cade*, so tearm'd of our supposed Fa-|ther.   2352
Cade. My Father was a *Mortimer.*   2359
*was he borne, vnder a hedge: for his Father had neuer a | house but
the Cage.   2370
Staff. Villaine, thy Father was a Playsterer,   2452
Who hateth him, and honors not his Father,   2792
This small inheritance my Father left me,   2923
Shall be the Surety for their Traitor Father.   3111
Yor. Will you not Sonnes? | *Edw.* I Noble Father, if our words will
serue.   3135
Yo.Clif. And so to Armes victorious Father,   3211
Particularities, and pettie sounds | To cease. Was't thou ordain'd (deere
Father)   3266
Rich. My Noble Father: | Three times to day I holpe him to his horse,   3328
FATHERS = 5*3
Was better worth then all my Fathers Lands,   472
His Fathers Acts, commenc'd in burning Troy.   1818
To free vs from his Fathers wrathfull curse,   1859
* *Wea.* Sir, he made a Chimney in my Fathers house, &   2468
*tell the King from me, that for his Fathers sake *Hen-* | *ry*   2476
*before, our Fore-fathers had no other Bookes but the   2668
Shall be their Fathers baile, and bane to those   3115
War. Now by my Fathers badge, old *Neuils* Crest,   3202
FAULCON = 1
King. But what a point, my Lord, your Faulcon made,   721
FAULCONS = 1
And beares his thoughts aboue his Faulcons Pitch.   728
FAULKNERS = 1
*Enter the King, Queene, Protector, Cardinall, and | Suffolke, with
Faulkners hallowing.*   715
FAULT = 2*1
*him for his fault the other day, he did vow vpon his   596
Pittie was all the fault that was in me: 1425
And lowly words were Ransome for their fault: 1427
FAULTIE = 1
That I am faultie in Duke *Humfreyes* death.   1906
FAULTLESSE = 2
And looke thy selfe be faultlesse, thou wert best.   941
That faultlesse may condemne a Noble man: 1718
FAULTS = 3*1
Or if he were not priuie to those Faults,   1341
Buck. Tut, these are petty faults to faults vnknowne,   1358
**Suff.* My Lord, these faults are easie, quickly answer'd: 1433
FAUOR = 1
I care not whither, for I begge no fauor;   1272

FAUOUR = 5
  We thanke you all for this great fauour done,   76
  What though the common people fauour him,   165
  Hath wonne the greatest fauour of the Commons,   200
  Vs'd to command, vntaught to pleade for fauour.   2290
  Iustice with fauour haue I alwayes done,   2701
FAUOURS = 1
  As frowning at the Fauours of the world?   277
FAYLE = 1
  Or all my Fence shall fayle.   776
FAYLES = 2
  Till *Lionels* Issue fayles, his should not reigne.   1020
  It fayles not yet, but flourishes in thee,   1021
FAYNE = 1
  Yea Man and Birds are fayne of climbing high.   724
FEALTIE = 1
  As pledges of my Fealtie and Loue,   3042
FEARD = 3
  Haue made thee fear'd and honor'd of the people,   206
  'Tis to be fear'd they all will follow him.   1324
  That ere I prou'd thee false, or fear'd thy faith.   1506
FEARE = 24*5
  And no great friend, I feare me to the King;   157
  I feare me Lords, for all this flattering glosse,   170
  Where are you there? Sir *Iohn*; nay feare not man,   343
  Well, so it stands: and thus I feare at last,   380
  Hume. I, what else? feare you not her courage.   624
  Madame, sit you, and feare not: whom wee rayse,   641
  *in a Cup of Sack; and feare not Neighbor, you shall doe | well enough.   1121
  Neighbor: drinke, and feare not your Man.   1126
  2.*Prent.* Be merry *Peter*, and feare not thy Master,   1131
  But feare not thou, vntill thy foot be snar'd,   1232
  If it be fond, call it a Womans feare: 1330
  Which feare, if better Reasons can supplant,   1331
  Ah that my feare were false, ah that it were;   1493
  For good King *Henry*, thy decay I feare. *Exit Gloster.*   1494
  To rid vs from the feare we haue of him.   1536
  Let pale-fac't feare keepe with the meane-borne man,   1641
  I feare me, you but warme the starued Snake,   1649
  They say, in him they feare your Highnesse death;   1961
  Suf. Pine gelidus timor occupat artus, it is thee I feare.   2285
  * *Wal.* Thou shalt haue cause to feare before I leaue thee.   2286
  True Nobility, is exempt from feare: 2297
  Cade. I feare neither sword, nor fire.   2377
  * *Wea.* He neede not feare the sword, for his Coate is of | proofe.   2378
  * *But.* But me thinks he should stand in feare of fire, be-|ing   2380
  * *Cade.* Feare not that I warrant thee. Come, let's march | towards
London. *Exeunt.*   2528
  I feare me (Loue) if that I had beene dead,   2556
  Buc. Trust no body for feare you betraid.   2595
  Dicke. Why dost thou quiuer man? | *Say.* The Palsie, and not feare
prouokes me.   2725
  Feare frames disorder, and disorder wounds   3254
FEARED = *1
  *the World to be Cowards: For I that neuer feared any,   2979
FEAREFULL = 2
  And after all this fearefull Homage done,   1929

FEAREFULL *cont.*
    And makes it fearefull and degenerate,   2534
FEARFULL = 1*1
    Yorke. Now *Yorke,* or neuer, steele thy fearfull thoughts,   1637
    The fearfull French, whom you late vanquished   2819
FEAST = 1
    Tis like you would not feast him like a friend,   1888
FEASTED = 1
    When I haue feasted with Queene *Margaret?*   2226
FEATHER = *1
    Cade. Was euer Feather so lightly blowne too & fro,   2832
FEATHERS = 1
    Seemes he a Doue? his feathers are but borrow'd,   1369
FED = 1
    Fed from my Trencher, kneel'd downe at the boord,   2225
FEE = 1
    And I should rob the Deaths-man of his Fee,   1922
FEEBLE = 2
    And plucke the Crowne from feeble *Henries* head.   2993
    So was his Will, in his old feeble body,   3334
FEED = 3
    If Wind and Fuell be brought, to feed it with: 1606
    in: and now the word Sallet must serue me to feed on.   2919
    Leauing thy trunke for Crowes to feed vpon. *Exit.*   2989
FEELE = 2*1
    And with my fingers feele his hand, vnfeeling: 1847
    So thou wilt let me liue, and feele no paine.   2138
    O let me liue. | *Cade.* I feele remorse in my selfe with his words: but 2737
FEELING = 1
    To treade them with her tender-feeling feet.   1180
FEET = 2
    To treade them with her tender-feeling feet.   1180
    The ruthlesse Flint doth cut my tender feet,   1210
FEETE = 3
    From top of Honor, to Disgraces feete?   323
    And God shall be my hope, my stay, my guide, | And Lanthorne to my
    feete: 1079
    And euen as willingly at thy feete I leaue it,   1090
FEE-SIMPLE = *1
    *for a stray, for entering his Fee-simple without leaue. A   2930
FELL = 3*2
    And this fell Tempest shall not cease to rage,   1657
    From such fell Serpents as false *Suffolke* is;   1978
    Cade. Stand villaine, stand, or Ile fell thee downe: he   2434
    Cade. They fell before thee like Sheepe and Oxen, &   2515
    Who being suffer'd with the Beares fell paw,   3152
FELLONY = *1
    *shall haue ten hoopes, and I wil make it Fellony to drink   2385
FELLOW = 9*2
    Suff. How now fellow: would'st any thing with me?   396
    *Take this fellow in, and send for his Master with a Purse-|uant   419
    Fellow, what Miracle do'st thou proclayme?   786
    King. Good-fellow, tell vs here the circumstance,   803
    Queene. Tell me, good-fellow,   819
    Yorke. I neuer saw a fellow worse bestead,   1112
    Yorke. Take away his Weapon: Fellow thanke God,   1158
    The truth and innocence of this poore fellow,   1165

FELLOW *cont.*

Come fellow, follow vs for thy Reward. | *Sound a flourish. Exeunt.*	1167
Cade. Heere I am thou particular fellow.	2431
But. If this Fellow be wise, hee'l neuer call yee *Iacke*	2625

FELLOWES = 1

Be play-fellowes to keepe you companie:	2016

FELLOW-KINGS = *1

*it vp. Fellow-Kings, I tell you, that that Lord *Say* hath	2484

FELL-LURKING = 1

They may astonish these fell-lurking Curres,	3143

FELON = 1

Murther indeede, that bloodie sinne, I tortur'd | Aboue the Felon, or what Trespas else.	1431

FELONIOUS = 1

Or foule felonious Theefe, that fleec'd poore passengers,	1429

FENCE = 2

Or all my Fence shall fayle.	776
hath learnt so much fence already.	1139

FERTILE = 2

Euen as I haue of fertile Englands soile.	250
As firmely as I hope for fertile England.	1385

FET = 2

To see my teares, and heare my deepe-fet groanes.	1209
Som. If *Yorke*, with all his farre-fet pollicie,	1596

FETCH = 2

Maior. Sirrha, goe fetch the Beadle hither straight. | *Exit.*	887
Glost. Now fetch me a Stoole hither by and by.	889

FEW = 1

These few dayes wonder will be quickly worne.	1245

FIE *see also* fye = 1*1

Cade. Fye on Ambitions: fie on my selfe, that haue a	2906
Rich. Fie, Charitie for shame, speake not in spight,	3213

FIELD = 4*2

Did he so often lodge in open field:	87
Warw. The Cardinall's not my better in the field.	500
But. I by my faith, the field is honourable, and there	2369
Cade. Tut, when struck'st thou one blow in the field?	2713
Meet me to morrow in S.(aint) Georges Field,	3038
To keepe thee from the Tempest of the field.	3197

FIEND = 2

False Fiend auoide. | *Thunder and Lightning. Exit Spirit.*	667
Oh beate away the busie medling Fiend,	2155

FIERCE = 1

For he is fierce, and cannot brooke hard Language.	2899

FIFT = 4*2

The fift, was *Edmond Langley*, Duke of Yorke;	974
Who was to *Edmond Langley*, | *Edward* the thirds fift Sonnes Sonne;	1008
*the fift, (in whose time, boyes went to Span-counter	2477
Henry the fift, that made all France to quake,	2793
Clif. Is *Cade* the sonne of *Henry* the fift,	2811
*as this multitude? The name of Henry the fift, hales them	2833

FIFTEENES = *1

*one and twenty Fifteenes, and one shilling to the pound, | the last Subsidie.	2655

FIFTEENTH = 1

That Suffolke should demand a whole Fifteenth,	140

FIGGE = 1
*Armorer. Let it come yfaith, and Ile pledge you all, | and a figge for
Peter.   1127
FIGHT = 18*2
*Peter. Alas, my Lord, I cannot fight; for Gods sake   610
*O Lord haue mercy vpon me, I shall neuer be able to | fight a blow: O
Lord my heart.   612
Humf. Sirrha, or you must fight, or else be hang'd.   614
So please your Highnesse to behold the fight.   1107
Or more afraid to fight, then is the Appellant,   1113
Fight for credit of the Prentices.   1132
They fight, and Peter strikes him downe.   1155
Alarum. Fight at Sea. Ordnance goes off.   2168
The liues of those which we haue lost in fight,   2190
Alarums to the fight, wherein both the Staffords are slaine. | Enter Cade
and the rest.   2511
Fight for your King, your Countrey, and your Liues,   2611
Cade. Come, then let's go fight with them: 2629
My foote shall fight with all the strength thou hast,   2954
thou mayst be turn'd to Hobnailes. | Heere they Fight.   2963
Oh I could hew vp Rockes, and fight with Flint,   3016
And fight against that monstrous Rebell Cade,   3055
Clifford I say, come forth and fight with me,   3223
Enter Richard, and Somerset to fight.   3288
Priests pray for enemies, but Princes kill. | Fight. Excursions.   3294
*Qu. What are you made of? You'l nor fight nor fly: 3300
FIGHTST = *1
*War. Then nobly Yorke, 'tis for a Crown thou fightst: 3236
FILL = 1
And dead mens cries do fill the emptie ayre,   3222
FILLD = 2
And Princes Courts be fill'd with my reproach: 1769
Are my Chests fill'd vp with extorted Gold?   2732
FILTH = 2*1
Lieu. Poole, Sir Poole? Lord, | I kennell, puddle, sinke, whose filth and
dirt   2238
Staf. Rebellious Hinds, the filth and scum of Kent,   2442
*that must sweepe the Court cleane of such filth as thou   2665
FIN = 1
Clif. La fin Corrone les eumenes.   3249
FINDE = 7*2
Yet I doe finde it so: for to be plaine,   372
*Glost. Well Sir, we must haue you finde your Legges.   895
Shall finde their deaths, if Yorke can prophecie.   1042
And finde no harbor in a Royall heart.   1642
For in the shade of death, I shall finde ioy;   1754
Ile haue an Iris that shall finde thee out.   2124
*mine Honour: vnlesse I finde him guilty he shall not die.   2413
Where shall it finde a harbour in the earth?   3168
Wilt thou go digge a graue to finde out Warre,   3169
FINDS = 1*1
*Warw. Who finds the Heyfer dead, and bleeding fresh,   1892
Who finds the Partridge in the Puttocks Nest,   1895
FINGER = 1
Thy hand is but a finger to my fist,   2952
FINGERS = 1
And with my fingers feele his hand, vnfeeling: 1847

FINIS *l.*3356 = 1
FIRE = 6*1

The time of Night when Troy was set on fire,	637
Qu. Nay then, this sparke will proue a raging fire,	1605
Burnes with reuenging fire, whose hopefull colours	2265
Cade. I feare neither sword, nor fire.	2377
But. But me thinks he should stand in feare of fire, be-|ing	2380
But first, go and set London Bridge on fire,	2630
Shall be to me, euen as the Dew to Fire,	3275

FIRME = 1

Before his Legges be firme to beare his Body.	1490

FIRMELY = 1

As firmely as I hope for fertile England.	1385

FIRST = 18*3

We heere create thee the first Duke of Suffolke,	69
And *William de la Pole* first Duke of Suffolke.	304
Peter. Here a comes me thinkes, and the Queene with | him : Ile be the	
first sure.	392
First, for I cannot flatter thee in Pride:	561
Bulling. First of the King: What shall of him be-|come?	655
The first, *Edward* the Black-Prince, Prince of Wales;	970
For *Richard,* the first Sonnes Heire, being dead,	990
And in this priuate Plot be we the first,	1024
Holden at Bury, the first of this next Moneth.	1248
First note, that he is neere you in discent,	1315
And had I first beene put to speake my minde,	1337
And Wolues are gnarling, who shall gnaw thee first.	1492
Which mates him first, that first intends deceit.	1567
Lieu. First let my words stab him, as he hath me.	2234
Manet the first Gent. Enter Walter with the body.	2312
But. The first thing we do, let's kill all the Lawyers.	2394
This first yeare of our raigne.	2619
But first, go and set London Bridge on fire,	2630
York. Wold'st haue me kneele? First let me ask of thee,	3104
Old Clif. The first I warrant thee, if dreames proue true	3195

FIRST-CONCEIUED = 1

Can chase away the first-conceiued sound?	1744

FISH-STREETE = *1

Cade. Vp Fish-streete, downe Saint Magnes corner,	2775

FIST = 2

Nor hold the Scepter in his childish Fist,	257
Thy hand is but a finger to my fist,	2952

FIT = 3

That were a State fit for his Holinesse.	450
King. A Gods Name see the Lysts and all things fit,	1110
Not fit to gouerne and rule multitudes,	3089

FITS = 3

Whose Church-like humors fits not for a Crowne.	259
That time best fits the worke we haue in hand.	640
Where it best fits to be, in *Henries* hand.	1100

FIUE = *3

*sword, and yet am ready to famish. These fiue daies haue	2907
*eate no meate these fiue dayes, yet come thou and thy	2943
*fiue men, and if I doe not leaue you all as dead as a doore	2944

FIXED = 1

Deliuer'd strongly through my fixed teeth,	2028

FIXT = 2
  Why are thine eyes fixt to the sullen earth, 278
  Mine haire be fixt an end, as one distract: 2033
FLAGGING = 1
  Who with their drowsie, slow, and flagging wings 2174
FLAMES = 1
  And the premised Flames of the Last day, 3263
FLAMING = 1
  Shall to my flaming wrath, be Oyle and Flax: 3277
FLATTER = 1
  First, for I cannot flatter thee in Pride: 561
FLATTERIE = 1
  By flatterie hath he wonne the Commons hearts: 1322
FLATTERING = 1
  I feare me Lords, for all this flattering glosse, 170
FLAWE = 1
  Doe calme the furie of this mad-bred Flawe. 1660
FLAX = 1
  Shall to my flaming wrath, be Oyle and Flax: 3277
FLED = 5*1
  For with his soule fled all my worldly solace: 1855
  Buck. What, is he fled? Go some and follow him, 2842
  Clif. He is fled my Lord, and all his powers do yeeld, 2862
  *dwell in this house, because the vnconquered soule of | *Cade* is fled. 2969
  'Tis not enough our foes are this time fled, 3343
  For (as I heare) the King is fled to London, 3346
FLEECD = 1
  Or foule felonious Theefe, that fleec'd poore passengers, 1429
FLEET = 1
  So Cares and Ioyes abound, as Seasons fleet. 1174
FLESH = 2
  Beare that proportion to my flesh and blood, 245
  Mens flesh preseru'd so whole, doe seldome winne. 1604
FLEURE-DE-LUCE = 1
  On which Ile tosse the Fleure-de-Luce of France. 3002
FLEW = 1
  And what a pytch she flew aboue the rest: 722
FLING = 1
  Fling vp his cap, and say, God saue his Maiesty. 2791
FLINT = 3
  The ruthlesse Flint doth cut my tender feet, 1210
  Mine eyes should sparkle like the beaten Flint, 2032
  Oh I could hew vp Rockes, and fight with Flint, 3016
FLINTIE = 1
  Vnneath may shee endure the Flintie Streets, 1179
FLINTY = 1
  Because thy flinty heart more hard then they, 1799
FLOCK = 2
  Till they haue snar'd the Shepheard of the Flock, 1039
  By nature prou'd an Enemie to the Flock, 1560
FLORISH = 1
  Queene. We thanke you all. *Florish* 45
FLOUD = 1
  Whose floud begins to flowe within mine eyes; 1500
FLOURISH = 5
  Flourish of Trumpets: Then Hoboyes. 2
  Somerset, wee'le see thee sent away. | *Flourish. Exeunt.* 617

FLOURISH *cont.*

*Whose Beame stands sure, whose rightful cause preuailes. | *Flourish.*
Exeunt.   957
Come fellow, follow vs for thy Reward. | *Sound a flourish. Exeunt.*   1167
For yet may England curse my wretched raigne. | *Flourish. Exeunt.*   2903
FLOURISHES = 1
It fayles not yet, but flourishes in thee,   1021
FLOWE = 1
Whose floud begins to flowe within mine eyes;   1500
FLOWRING = 1
Or as the Snake, roll'd in a flowring Banke,   1530
FLY = 1*4
**Mich.* Fly, fly, fly, Sir *Humfrey Stafford* and his brother   2432
Mes. The Rebels are in Southwarke: Fly my Lord: 2563
**Qu.* What are you made of? You'l nor fight nor fly: 3300
FLYE = 12
Were it not good your Grace could flye to Heauen?   734
Suff. True: made the Lame to leape and flye away.   913
You made in a day, my Lord, whole Townes to flye.   915
And flye thou how thou canst, they'le tangle thee.   1231
That those which flye before the battell ends,   2498
The Citizens flye and forsake their houses: 2587
Knowledge the Wing wherewith we flye to heauen.   2708
Alas, he hath no home, no place to flye too: 2815
Hot Coales of Vengeance. Let no Souldier flye.   3258
By what we can, which can no more but flye. | *Alarum a farre off.*   3303
I would speake blasphemy ere bid you flye: 3313
But flye you must: Vncureable discomfite   3314
FLYES = 1
Yet haue I Gold flyes from another Coast: 369
FLYING = 2
Queene. Beleeue me Lords, for flying at the Brooke,   717
So should'st thou eyther turne my flying soule,   2114
FOE = 2
And to preserue my Soueraigne from his Foe,   1573
And for my selfe, Foe as he was to me,   1759
FOES = 4*1
Crowned in Paris in despight of foes,   101
Nor neuer seeke preuention of thy foes.   1233
And had I twentie times so many foes,   1236
**War.* But both of you were vowed D.(uke) Humfries foes,   1886
'Tis not enough our foes are this time fled,   3343
FOLD = 2
To make the Fox surueyor of the Fold?   1555
And three-fold Vengeance tend vpon your steps.   2018
FOLKES = 1
**Geo.* O monstrous Coward! What, to come behinde | Folkes?   2716
FOLLOW = 16
Eli. Yes my good Lord, Ile follow presently.   335
Follow I must, I cannot go before,   336
Buck. Lord Cardinall, I will follow *Elianor*,   541
the Stoole, and runnes away: and they | follow, and cry, A Miracle.   903
Glost. Follow the Knaue, and take this Drab away.   907
Come fellow, follow vs for thy Reward. | *Sound a flourish. Exeunt.*   1167
That erst did follow thy prowd Chariot-Wheeles,   1184
'Tis to be fear'd they all will follow him.   1324
And you that be the Kings Friends follow me. *Exit.*   2501

FOLLOW *cont.*

Cade. And you that loue the Commons, follow me:	2502
All. Wee'l follow *Cade,*	2809
Wee'l follow *Cade.*	2810
Wee'l follow the King, and Clifford.	2831
Buck. What, is he fled? Go some and follow him,	2842
Follow me souldiers, wee'l deuise a meane,	2846
Yorke. I know our safety is to follow them,	3345

FOLLOWD = 1

And follow'd with a Rabble, that reioyce	1208

FOLLOWER = 1

Was made a wonder, and a pointing stock | To euery idle Rascall follower.	1222

FOLLOWERS = *1

*no want of resolution in mee, but onely my Followers	2839

FOLLOWES = 1

Sal. Pride went before, Ambition followes him.	188

FOLLOWING = 1

And his aduantage following your decease,	1319

FOND = 1 *1

If it be fond, call it a Womans feare:	1330
* *Qu.* Ah what's more dangerous, then this fond affiance?	1368

FOOLE = *1

*2. *Pet.* Come backe foole, this is the Duke of Suffolk, | and not my Lord Protector.	394

FOOLISH = 1

Too full of foolish pittie: and *Glosters* shew	1527

FOOT = 5

But feare not thou, vntill thy foot be snar'd,	1232
To mowe downe Thornes that would annoy our Foot,	1361
And tread it vnder foot with all contempt,	3209
War. How now my Noble Lord? What all a-foot.	3227
Is not it selfe, nor haue we wonne one foot, | If Salsbury be lost.	3326

FOOTE = 1

My foote shall fight with all the strength thou hast,	2954

FOOTING = 1

Nor set no footing on this vnkinde Shore.	1787

FOOT-CLOTH = 2

Bare-headed plodded by my foot-cloth Mule,	2222
dost ride in a foot-cloth, dost thou not? | *Say.* What of that?	2680

FOR *l.*9 11 28 49 *52 76 113 120 123 124 131 141 170 189 190 205 207 216
*231 243 249 255 259 308 326 372 383 *389 *397 *402 *406 *410 *419
422 450 465 473 474 479 483 484 491 550 561 562 575 591 *596 599 605
606 *610 651 665 674 676 706 717 754 755 759 775 804 886 908 *942
944 952 990 1002 1056 1062 1104 1108 1128 1132 *1133 *1134 *1138
1163 1167 *1193 1204 1227 1242 1268 1272 1276 1287 1306 1327 1353
1356 1370 1372 1384 1385 1389 1397 1411 1418 1422 1426 1427 1452
1484 1494 1502 1532 1538 1547 1552 1566 1570 1576 1590 1625 1628
1634 1661 1678 1688 1689 1700 1751 1754 1759 1766 1772 1773 1782
1813 1821 1842 1855 1856 1863 1869 1877 1913 1926 1994 1997 2003
2005 2011 *2060 2074 2077 2087 2095 2100 2102 2112 2123 2131 2165
2178 2189 2193 2213 2230 2237 2242 2248 2290 2308 *2326 *2338 *2355
*2370 2373 *2375 *2378 2381 *2382 *2384 *2399 2443 2448 2451 *2475
*2476 *2478 2481 *2482 2500 2503 2506 2519 2542 2555 591 *2558
2595 2602 2611 2612 2620 *2638 *2642 *2644 *2658 *2661 *2678 *2685
2712 *2718 *2739 *2740 2765 2770 *2806 *2807 2827 *2836 2844 2899
2903 *2908 *2909 *2910 *2915 *2930 2957 2972 *2979 2989 3071 3073

FOR *cont.*
3080 3100 3103 3111 3116 3125 3134 3165 3173 *3181 3189 3194 3213
3214 3230 3235 *3236 *3250 3290 3294 *3297 3316 3346 = 204*57
FORBEARE = 4

Glost. Ah *Nell,* forbeare: thou aymest all awry.	1234
Lay not thy hands on me: forbeare I say,	1746
King. Forbeare to iudge, for we are sinners all.	2165
You cannot but forbeare to murther me:	2710

FORBEARES = 1

Let this my sword report what speech forbeares.	2958

FORBID = 3

Queene. God forbid any Malice should preuayle,	1717
And therefore doe they cry, though you forbid,	1976
For God forbid, so many simple soules	2542

FORCE = 5*2

*That *Maine,* which by maine force Warwicke did winne,	221
And force perforce Ile make him yeeld the Crowne,	270
To shew some reason, of no little force,	558
Yorke. Which now they hold by force, and not by right:	989
And turnes the force of them vpon thy selfe.	2047
Or dare to bring thy Force so neere the Court?	3014
To force a spotlesse Virgins Chastitie,	3186

FORCES = 1*1

are hard by, with the Kings Forces.	2433
K. Then what intends these Forces thou dost bring?	3053

FORE-FATHERS = *1

*before, our Fore-fathers had no other Bookes but the	2668

FORE-WARNING = 1

What boaded this? but well fore-warning winde	1785

FORFEND = 1

Suff. Dead in his Bed, my Lord: *Gloster* is dead.	*Queene.* Marry God forfend.	1725

FORGET = 2

Glost. Be patient, gentle *Nell,* forget this griefe.	1202
Elianor. Ah *Gloster,* teach me to forget my selfe:	1203

FORGETS = 1

That Winter Lyon, who in rage forgets	Aged contusions, and all brush of Time:	3322

FORGIUE = 2

If my suspect be false, forgiue me God,	1841
He dies and makes no signe: Oh God forgiue him.	2163

FORGOT = 3*1

Was broke in twaine: by whom, I haue forgot,	300
Noble shee is: but if shee haue forgot	Honor and Vertue, and conuers't with such,	946
Suf. That this my death may neuer be forgot.	2301
King. Why Warwicke, hath thy knee forgot to bow?	3161

FORKED = 1

Were there a Serpent seene, with forked Tongue,	1971

FORLORN = *1

Whit. Speak Captaine, shall I stab the forlorn Swain.	2233

FORLORNE = 2

As he stood by, whilest I, his forlorne Duchesse,	1221
Be poysonous too, and kill thy forlorne Queene.	1777

FORME = 1

Card. Did he not, contrary to forme of Law,	1352

FORRAIGNE = 1
This Tongue hath parlied vnto Forraigne Kings | For your behoofe.   2711
FORSAKE = 3
Home to your Cottages: forsake this Groome.   2444
The Citizens flye and forsake their houses: 2587
That will forsake thee, and go home in peace.   2786
FORSOOTH = 6*1
  *Peter. That my Mistresse was? No forsooth: my Master   415
  Queene. Because the King forsooth will haue it so.   505
  One. Forsooth, a blinde man at Saint Albones Shrine,   790
  And I will helpe thee. | Wife. Most true, forsooth: 826
  Simpc. Black forsooth, Coale-Black, as Iet.   855
  Sirrha, what's thy Name? | Peter. Peter forsooth.   1141
  And you (forsooth) had the good Duke to keepe: 1887
FORT = *1
  *Cade. I am sorry for't: The man is a proper man of   2412
FORTH = 9
Put forth thy hand, reach at the glorious Gold.   284
King. Stand forth Dame Elianor Cobham, | Glosters Wife: 1053
And he that loos'd them forth their Brazen Caues,   1789
But all in vaine are these meane Obsequies, | Bed put forth.   1848
Therefore bring forth the Souldiers of our prize,   2177
And duly wayted for my comming forth?   2230
Suf. O that I were a God, to shoot forth Thunder   2272
Clifford I say, come forth and fight with me,   3223
Let vs pursue him ere the Writs go forth.   3348
FORTH-COMMING = 2
Wee'le see your Trinkets here all forth-comming. | All away. Exit.   683
Your Lady is forth-comming, yet at London.   931
FORTS = 1
Hath slaine their Gouernors, surpriz'd our Forts,   2257
FORTUNE = 4
Witnesse the fortune he hath had in France.   1595
Thy fortune, Yorke, hadst thou beene Regent there,   1608
Card. My Lord of Yorke, trie what your fortune is: 1614
To see their day, and them our Fortune giue.   3317
FORTUNES = 4
To play my part in Fortunes Pageant.   342
His fortunes I will weepe, and 'twixt each groane,   1522
Of all our Fortunes: but if we haply scape,   3306
And where this breach now in our Fortunes made | May readily be
stopt.   3309
FORWARD = 3*1
Makes them thus forward in his Banishment.   1965
If you go forward: therefore yeeld, or dye.   2447
of order. Come, march forward.   2510
  *Cade. And hence-forward all things shall be in Com-|mon. Enter a
Messenger.   2651
FOUGHT = 1*1
And fought so long, till that his thighes with Darts   1668
  *Sal. Now by my Sword, well hast thou fought to day: 3337
FOULE = 10
And call these foule Offendors to their Answeres;   955
Or foule felonious Theefe, that fleec'd poore passengers,   1429
Vertue is choakt with foule Ambition,   1443
Foule Subornation is predominant,   1445
(The agent of thy foule inconstancie)   1815

FOULE *cont.*

All the foule terrors in darke seated hell -- -	2043
Breath foule contagious darknesse in the ayre:	2176
This breast from harbouring foule deceitfull thoughts.	2736
Clif. Hence heape of wrath, foule indigested lumpe,	3156
Yo.Clif. Foule stygmaticke that's more then thou	canst tell.	3215

FOULER = 1

Warw. That can I witnesse, and a fouler fact	568

FOUND = 5

He will be found a dangerous Protector.	171
A Staffe is quickly found to beat a Dogge.	1471
And 'tis well seene, he found an enemy.	1889
If after three dayes space thou here bee'st found,	2009
If thou be found by me, thou art but dead.	2104

FOURE = 2

Enter three or foure Petitioners, the Armorers	*Man being one.*	384
You foure from hence to Prison, back againe;	1058

FOURETEENE = *1

Yorke. My Lord of Suffolke, within foureteene dayes	1632

FOURTH = 2

Crown'd by the Name of *Henry* the fourth,	982
The fourth Sonne, *Yorke* claymes it from the third:	1019

FOWLE = 1

Had not your man put vp the Fowle so suddenly,	We had had more sport.	766

FOX = 3

The Fox barkes not, when he would steale the Lambe.	1349
To make the Fox surueyor of the Fold?	1555
No: let him dye, in that he is a Fox,	1559

FRAME = 1

By wicked meanes to frame our Soueraignes fall.	1346

FRAMES = 1

Feare frames disorder, and disorder wounds	3254

FRANCE = 38*3

I had in charge at my depart for France,	9
In presence of the Kings of *France,* and *Sicill,*	13
I'th parts of France, till terme of eighteene Moneths	72
To conquer France, his true inheritance?	89
Receiud deepe scarres in France and Normandie:	94
How France and Frenchmen might be kept in awe,	99
Defacing Monuments of Conquer'd France,	Vndoing all as all had neuer bin.	109
For France, 'tis ours; and we will keepe it still.	113
France should haue torne and rent my very hart,	133
She should haue staid in France, and steru'd in France	Before ---	142
I prophesied, France will be lost ere long. *Exit Humfrey.*	153
Thy late exploits done in the heart of France,	204
Which I will win from France, or else be slaine.	224
Me thinkes the Realmes of England, France, & Ireland,	244
Cold newes for me: for I had hope of France,	249
And stol'st away the Ladies hearts of France;	438
Yorke. If *Yorke* haue ill demean'd himselfe in France,	493
Queene. Thy sale of Offices and Townes in France,	525
To be your Regent in the Realme of France.	556
Till France be wonne into the Dolphins hands:	565
*Sent his poore Queene to France, from whence she came,	984
For Souldiers pay in France, and neuer sent it?	1356

FRANCE *cont.*

 *_King._ Welcome Lord _Somerset_: What Newes from | France? 1378
 Yorke. Cold Newes for me: for I had hope of France, 1384
 Yorke. 'Tis thought, my Lord, | That you tooke Bribes of France, 1402
 By meanes whereof, his Highnesse hath lost France. 1405
 Nor euer had one penny Bribe from France. 1409
 Witnesse the fortune he hath had in France. 1595
 He neuer would haue stay'd in France so long. 1598
 To France sweet Suffolke: Let me heare from thee: 2122
 By thee _Aniou_ and _Maine_ were sold to France. 2254
 I go of Message from the Queene to France: 2281
 *which sold the Townes in France. He that made vs pay 2654
 *France? Be it knowne vnto thee by these presence, euen 2663
 Of some more Townes in France. Soldiers, 2768
 Henry the fift, that made all France to quake, 2793
 Will he conduct you through the heart of France, 2813
 To France, to France, and get what you haue lost: 2826
 On which Ile tosse the Fleure-de-Luce of France. 3002
FRAUDFULL = 1
 Hangs on the cutting short that fraudfull man. 1375
FREE = 6*1
 The purest Spring is not so free from mudde, 1399
 Queene. Free Lords: | Cold Snow melts with the Sunnes hot Beames: 1524
 To free vs from his Fathers wrathfull curse, 1859
 Free from a stubborne opposite intent, 1963
 These hands are free from guiltlesse bloodshedding, 2735
 *And we charge and command, that their wiues be as free 2756
 And heere pronounce free pardon to them all, 2785
FREEDOME = *1
 *you had recouered your ancient Freedome. But you are 2802
FREELY = 1
 Maister, this Prisoner freely giue I thee, 2181
FRENCH = 4*4
 *Betweene our Soueraigne, and the French King _Charles_, 48
 *_Glo. Reads._ Inprimis, _It is agreed betweene the French K.(ing)_ 50
 Yorke. Aniou and _Maine_ are giuen to the French, 226
 Aniou and _Maine_ both giuen vnto the French? 248
 Let _Somerset_ be Regent o're the French, 602
 *for French Crownes) I am content he shall raigne, but Ile | be
 Protector ouer him. 2478
 *more then that, he can speake French, and therefore hee is | a Traitor. 2486
 The fearfull French, whom you late vanquished 2819
FRENCHMANS = 1
 Then you should stoope vnto a Frenchmans mercy. 2825
FRENCHMEN = 1*1
 How France and Frenchmen might be kept in awe, 99
 *_Cade._ Nay answer if you can: The Frenchmen are our 2489
FRENCH-WOMAN = 1
 Duch. Was't I? yea, I it was, prowd French-woman: 532
FRESH = *1
 *_Warw._ Who finds the Heyfer dead, and bleeding fresh, 1892
FRET = 1
 So Yorke must sit, and fret, and bite his tongue, 242
FRETFULL = *1
 *_Queen._ Away: Though parting be a fretfull corosiue, 2120
FRIEND = 3
 And no great friend, I feare me to the King; 157

FRIEND *cont.*
Tis like you would not feast him like a friend, 1888
Tell me my Friend, art thou the man that slew him? 3065
FRIENDS = 6*1
And purchase Friends, and giue to Curtezans, 235
For it is knowne we were but hollow Friends: 1766
Oh go not yet. Euen thus, two Friends condemn'd, 2068
If he reuenge it not, yet will his Friends, 2317
And you that be the Kings Friends follow me. *Exit.* 2501
Vnlesse by robbing of your Friends, and vs. 2817
Yorke. Call Buckingham, and all the friends thou hast, 3193
FRIGHT = 2
Sits in grim Maiestie, to fright the World. 1750
Nay, do not fright vs with an angry looke: 3123
FRIGHTFULL = 1
Their Musicke, frightfull as the Serpents' hisse, 2041
FRO = 1*1
Early and late, debating too and fro 98
Cade. Was euer Feather so lightly blowne too & fro, 2832
FROM *l.*41 71 107 176 224 323 324 354 358 369 370 371 403 652 *890 910
926 *984 995 1018 1019 1058 1059 1162 *1191 1199 1240 1297 1364
*1378 1399 1400 1412 1440 1474 1491 1536 1549 1551 1573 1585
1618 1686 1690 1715 1743 1783 1802 1806 1859 1933 1958 1963 1978
*1982 1990 *1991 1993 2049 2066 2105 2111 2118 2122 2157 2175 2225
2262 2281 2297 *2476 2565 *2604 2605 2735 2736 2783 2877 2882 2894
2928 2974 *2978 *2992 2993 3009 3028 3054 3079 3167 3188 3197 *3208
3220 3331 3341 = 86*11
FRONT = 1
But boldly stand, and front him to his face. 3081
FROSTIE = 1
If it be banisht from the frostie head, 3167
FROWNE = 1
Whose Smile and Frowne, like to *Achilles* Speare 3095
FROWNING = 1
As frowning at the Fauours of the world? 277
FROZEN = 1
Throw in the frozen bosomes of our part, 3257
FRUIT = 1
Was graft with Crab-tree slippe, whose Fruit thou art, 1919
FUELL = 1
If Wind and Fuell be brought, to feed it with: 1606
FULL = 16
Be full expyr'd. Thankes Vncle Winchester, 73
Wee'le see these things effected to the full. 359
In England worke your Graces full content. 453
Salisb. My Lord, I long to heare it at full. 965
Salisb. My Lord, breake we off; we know your minde | at full. 1043
Mine eyes are full of teares, my heart of griefe. 1071
Vnsounded yet, and full of deepe deceit. 1351
Too full of foolish pittie: and *Glosters* shew 1527
To make Commotion, as full well he can, 1664
Full often, like a shag-hayr'd craftie Kerne, 1673
But see, his face is blacke, and full of blood: 1872
Staring full gastly, like a strangled man: 1874
With full as many signes of deadly hate, 2029
And boading Screech-Owles, make the Consort full. 2042
Sweet is the Country, because full of Riches, 2696

FULL *cont.*
Hath made me full of sicknesse and diseases.   2722
FULNESSE = 1
Such is the Fulnesse of my hearts content.   42
FUME = 1
Shee's tickled now, her Fume needs no spurres,   543
FURIE = 3
I see thy furie: If I longer stay,   150
Doe calme the furie of this mad-bred Flawe.   1660
On Sheepe or Oxen could I spend my furie.   3019
FURIOUS = 1
And whet not on these furious Peeres,   753
FURNITURE = 1
Without Discharge, Money, or Furniture,   564
FURRD = 1
furr'd Packe, she washes buckes here at home.   2367
FURTHER = 4*1
And dim'd mine eyes, that I can reade no further.   61
Win. Item, *It is further agreed betweene them, That the*   63
To keepe, vntill your further time of Tryall.   1438
His eye-balles further out, than when he liued,   1873
Perswaded him from any further act: 3331
FURTHERMORE = *1
Butcher. And furthermore, wee'l haue the Lord *Sayes*   2480
FUTURE = 1
Clif. But that my hearts on future mischeefe set,   3312
FYE = *2
Queen. Fye Coward woman, and soft harted wretch,   2021
Cade. Fye on Ambitions: fie on my selfe, that haue a   2906
GAINST = 4
Proceed no straiter 'gainst our Vnckle *Gloster,*   1714
Attracts the same for aydance 'gainst the enemy,   1869
And these dread curses like the Sunne 'gainst glasse,   2045
Of Capitall Treason 'gainst the King and Crowne: 3102
GAIT *see* gate
GALL = 2
Gall, worse then Gall, the daintiest that they taste: 2037
GALLANT = 1
And like a Gallant, in the brow of youth,   3324
GALLOP = 1
Shee'le gallop farre enough to her destruction. | *Exit Buckingham.*   544
GALLOWES = 2
And you three shall be strangled on the Gallowes.   1061
Mark'd for the Gallowes: Lay your Weapons downe,   2443
GALLOW-GLASSES = 1
And with a puissant and a mighty power | Of Gallow-glasses and stout
Kernes,   2878
GAOLES = 1
the Gaoles, and let out the Prisoners.   2527
GAPING = 1
My earnest-gaping-sight of thy Lands view,   1805
GARDEN = 2*2
Suffer them now, and they'le o're-grow the Garden,   1326
*I climb'd into this Garden, to see if I can eate Grasse, or   2912
Is't not enough to breake into my Garden,   2937
*Garden, and be henceforth a burying place to all that do   2968

GARDINER = 1
Cade. And *Adam* was a Gardiner. | *Bro*. And what of that?   2454
GARRET = *1
  *them to me in the Garret one Night, as wee were scow-|ring my Lord
  of Yorkes Armor.   588
GARRISONS = 1
  Haue I dis-pursed to the Garrisons,   1417
GASPE = 1
  That makes him gaspe, and stare, and catch the aire,   2088
GASTLY = 1
  Staring full gastly, like a strangled man: 1874
GATE = 2
  In face, in gate, in speech he doth resemble.   1679
  And sends the poore well pleased from my gate.   2928
GATES = 1 *1
  *my sword therefore broke through London gates, that   2799
  King. Then heauen set ope thy euerlasting gates,   2865
GATHER = 2
  But get you to Smithfield, and gather head,   2609
  Or gather wealth I care not with what enuy: 2926
GATHERED = *1
  **Dicke*. My Lord, there's an Army gathered together | in Smithfield.   2627
GAUDY = 1
  Lieu. The gaudy blabbing and remorsefull day,   2170
GAUE = 4
  The happiest Gift, that euer Marquesse gaue,   22
  Till *Suffolke* gaue two Dukedomes for his Daughter.   473
  I neuer gaue them condigne punishment.   1430
  According as I gaue directions? | 1. 'Tis, my good Lord.   1703
GAUNT = 3
  Was *Iohn* of Gaunt, the Duke of Lancaster;   973
  The eldest Sonne and Heire of *Iohn* of Gaunt,   981
  Henry doth clayme the Crowne from *Iohn* of Gaunt,   1018
GAZE = 2
  If so, Gaze on, and grouell on thy face,   282
  Now thou do'st Penance too. Looke how they gaze,   1196
GAZER = 1
  And kill the innocent gazer with thy sight: 1753
GAZING = 3
  Gazing on that which seemes to dimme thy sight?   279
  The abiect People, gazing on thy face,   1182
  Oppose thy stedfast gazing eyes to mine,   2949
GEARE = 1
  But I will remedie this geare ere long,   1388
GEERE = 1
  this geere, the sooner the better.   634
GELDED = *1
  * gelded the Commonwealth, and made it an Eunuch: &   2485
GELIDUS = 1
  Suf. Pine gelidus timor occupat artus, it is thee I feare.   2285
GENERALL = 3
  Mich. Where's our Generall?   2430
  Will parley with *Iacke Cade* their Generall.   2545
  Now let the generall Trumpet blow his blast,   3265
GENS = 1
  Dic. What say you of Kent. | *Say*. Nothing but this: 'Tis *bona terra*,
  mala gens.   2688

GENT = 1
Manet the first Gent. Enter Walter with the body. 2312
GENTLE = 9
Glost. Be patient, gentle *Nell*, forget this griefe. 1202
Thy greatest helpe is quiet, gentle *Nell*: 1243
What did I then? But curst the gentle gusts, 1788
Qu. Oh *Henry*, let me pleade for gentle *Suffolke*. 2003
King. Vngentle Queene, to call him gentle *Suffolke*. 2004
Suff. Cease, gentle Queene, these Execrations, 2019
As milde and gentle as the Cradle-babe, 2109
Looke with a gentle eye vpon this Wretch, 2154
Bro. Well, seeing gentle words will not preuayle, 2494
GENTLEMAN *see also* 1.*Gent.*, 2.*Gent.* = 3
Did beare him like a Noble Gentleman: 192
Suf. Looke on my George, I am a Gentleman, 2198
We will not leaue one Lord, one Gentleman: 2504
GENTLEMEN = 2*1
And beare the name and port of Gentlemen? 2188
*it was neuer merrie world in England, since Gentlemen | came vp. 2327
All Schollers, Lawyers, Courtiers, Gentlemen, 2572
GEO = *1
GEORGE see also Geo. = 2
Suf. Looke on my George, I am a Gentleman, 2198
Enter George, with the Lord Say. 2657
GEORGES = 1
Meet me to morrow in S.(aint) Georges Field, 3038
GET = 6*4
**Suff.* Why that's well said. Goe, get you to my House, 1699
This get I by his death: Aye me vnhappie, 1770
So get thee gone, that I may know my greefe, 2061
*Now get thee hence, the King thou know'st is comming, 2103
* *Beuis.* Come and get thee a sword, though made of a 2320
All. I marry will we: therefore get ye gone. 2473
But get you to Smithfield, and gather head, 2609
To France, to France, and get what you haue lost: 2826
*Villaine, thou wilt betray me, and get a 1000. Crownes 2931
We shall to London get, where you are lou'd, 3308
GHOST = 3
Oft haue I seene a timely-parted Ghost, 1865
And doe some seruice to Duke *Humfreyes* Ghost. | *Exeunt.* 1936
Sometime he talkes, as if Duke *Humfries* Ghost 2090
GHOSTS = 1
And Spirits walke, and Ghosts breake vp their Graues; 639
GIDDY = 1
See how the giddy multitude doe point, 1197
GIFT = 1
The happiest Gift, that euer Marquesse gaue, 22
GIFTS = 2
Prayres and Teares haue mou'd me, Gifts could neuer. 2702
Large gifts haue I bestow'd on learned Clearkes, 2705
GINNES *see* gynnes
GIRT = 1
And girt thee with the Sword. Cosin of Yorke, 70
GIUE = 27*6
'Tis thine they giue away, and not their owne. 233
And purchase Friends, and giue to Curtezans, 235
Seale vp your Lips, and giue no words but Mum, 365

GIUE *cont.*

To giue his Censure: These are no Womens matters.	507
Giue me my Fanne: what, Mynion, can ye not?	*She giues the Duchesse*	
a box on the eare.	529
Suff. Before we make election, giue me leaue	557
*Buck. Your Grace shal giue me leaue, my Lord of York,	707
And giue her as a Prey to Law and Shame,	950
Our simple Supper ended, giue me leaue,	961
I beseech your Maiestie giue me leaue to goe;	1074
Ere thou goe, giue vp thy Staffe,	1077
Giue vp your Staffe, Sir, and the King his Realme.	1086
*World. Here *Robin,* and if I dye, I giue thee my Aporne;	1135
When euery one will giue the time of day,	1308
Qu. But I can giue the loser leaue to chide.	1482
What counsaile giue you in this weightie cause?	1592
'Twas men I lackt, and you will giue them me;	1651
Giue thee thy hyre, and send thy Soule to Hell,	1930
Qu. Oh, let me intreat thee cease, giue me thy hand,	2054
*Ca. If thou beest death, Ile giue thee Englands Treasure,	2136
Ile giue a thousand pound to looke vpon him.	2147
Giue me some drinke, and bid the Apothecarie	2151
Maister, this Prisoner freely giue I thee,	2181
*Mate. And so much shall you giue, or off goes yours.	2186
1.*Gent.* Ile giue it sir, and therefore spare my life.	2192
*Cade. Giue him a box o'th'eare, and that wil make'em	red againe.	2719
**thousand diuelles come against me, and giue me but the	2966
I cannot giue due action to my words,	2999
We giue thee for reward a thousand Markes,	3073
Giue place: by heauen thou shalt rule no more	3099
His sonnes (he sayes) shall giue their words for him.	3134
To giue the enemy way, and to secure vs	3302
To see their day, and them our Fortune giue.	3317

GIUEN = 8*3

For thou hast giuen me in this beauteous Face	28
Hath giuen the Dutchy of *Aniou* and *Mayne,*	117
Yorke. Aniou and *Maine* are giuen to the French,	226
Aniou and *Maine* both giuen vnto the French?	248
*Stanly. So am I giuen in charge, may't please your	Grace.	1257
The Duke is vertuous, milde, and too well giuen,	1366
And giuen me notice of their Villanies.	1676
Hath giuen them heart and courage to proceede:	2571
**I thought ye would neuer haue giuen out these Armes til	2801
That I haue giuen no answer all this while:	3025
*Yor. Thus Warre hath giuen thee peace, for y art still,	3250

GIUES = 5

And our King *Henry* giues away his owne,	137
Dame *Elianor* giues Gold, to bring the Witch:	367
Giue me my Fanne: what, Mynion, can ye not?	*She giues the Duchesse*	
a box on the eare.	529
Giues Light in Darknesse, Comfort in Despaire.	794
What instance giues Lord Warwicke for his vow.	1863

GIUING = 1*1

**What canst thou answer to my Maiesty, for giuing vp of	2661
Least they consult about the giuing vp	2767

GLAD = 2

But you, my Lord, were glad to be imploy'd,	1986
Buc. Health and glad tydings to your Maiesty.	2857

GLANCE = 2
As to vouchsafe one glance vnto the ground.   289
And if we did but glance a farre-off Looke,   1304
GLASSE = 2
And these dread curses like the Sunne 'gainst glasse,   2045
Yorke. Looke in a Glasse, and call thy Image so.   3139
GLASSES = 1
And with a puissant and a mighty power | Of Gallow-glasses and stout
Kernes,   2878
GLENDOUR = 1
And but for *Owen Glendour*, had beene King;   1002
GLO = 3*1
GLOBE = 1
For wheresoere thou art in this worlds Globe,   2123
GLORIFIE = 1
That we for thee may glorifie the Lord.   804
GLORIOUS = 4
Put forth thy hand, reach at the glorious Gold.   284
Or sell my Title for a glorious Graue.   1389
Like to the glorious Sunnes transparant Beames,   1659
Now by my hand (Lords) 'twas a glorious day.   3351
GLOSSE = 1
I feare me Lords, for all this flattering glosse,   170
GLOST = 37*14
GLOSTER see also Glo., Glost. = 26*1
Gloster, Yorke, Buckingham, Somerset, | Salisburie, and Warwicke.   74
Car. My Lord of Gloster, now ye grow too hot,   144
Calling him, *Humfrey the good Duke of Gloster,*   166
If Gloster be displac'd, hee'l be Protector.   184
I neuer saw but Humfrey Duke of Gloster,   191
While Gloster beares this base and humble minde.   337
Queene. And thy Ambition, *Gloster.*   751
Card. Beleeue me, Cousin *Gloster,*   765
King. Why how now, Vnckle *Gloster?*   772
Queene. Gloster, see here the Taincture of thy Nest,   940
The sixt, was *Thomas* of Woodstock, Duke of Gloster;   975
King. Stay *Humfrey,* Duke of Gloster,   1076
Exit Gloster.   1094
And *Humfrey,* Duke of Gloster, scarce himselfe,   1096
Ah *Gloster,* hide thee from their hatefull lookes,   1199
Elianor. Ah *Gloster,* teach me to forget my selfe: 1203
Glost. Witnesse my teares, I cannot stay to speake. | *Exit Gloster.* 1265
King. I muse my Lord of Gloster is not come: 1295
Our Kinsman *Gloster* is as innocent,   1363
* *Suff.* Nay *Gloster,* know that thou art come too soone,   1393
King. My Lord of Gloster, 'tis my speciall hope,   1439
For good King *Henry,* thy decay I feare. *Exit Gloster.*   1494
Say, who's a Traytor? *Gloster* he is none. *Exit.*   1523
This *Gloster* should be quickly rid the World,   1535
Proceed no straiter 'gainst our Vnckle *Gloster,*   1714
Suff. Dead in his Bed, my Lord: *Gloster* is dead. | *Queene.* Marry God
forfend.   1725
King. Ah woe is me for Gloster, wretched man.   1772
GLOSTER = *1
GLOSTERS = 8
That he that breakes a sticke of Glosters groue,   307
Vnder the surly *Glosters* Gouernance?   433

GLOSTERS *cont.*
 That hath dis-honored *Glosters* honest Name.   951
 King. Stand forth Dame *Elianor Cobham,* | *Glosters* Wife: 1053
 Euen so my selfe bewayles good *Glosters* case   1518
 Too full of foolish pittie: and *Glosters* shew   1527
 In life, but double death, now *Gloster*'s dead.   1755
 Is all thy comfort shut in Glosters Tombe?   1778
GLOUCESTER = 1
 Enter Gloucester.   1390
GLOUSTER = 1
 No, no, my Soueraigne, *Glouster* is a man   1350
GLYDED = 1
 That slyly glyded towards your Maiestie,   1972
GNARLING = 1
 And Wolues are gnarling, who shall gnaw thee first.   1492
GNAW = 1
 And Wolues are gnarling, who shall gnaw thee first.   1492
GO = 22*9
 **Hu.* I go. Come *Nel* thou wilt ride with vs? *Ex. Hum*   334
 Follow I must, I cannot go before,   336
 Faine would I go to chafe his palie lips,   1843
 Go, speake not to me; euen now be gone.   2067
 Oh go not yet. Euen thus, two Friends condemn'd,   2068
 Qu. Go tell this heauy Message to the King. *Exit*   2096
 Suf. I go. | *Qu.* And take my heart with thee.   2125
 I go of Message from the Queene to France: 2281
 Therefore come you with vs, and let him go. | *Exit Lieutenant, and the*
 rest.   2310
 *Cheapside shall my Palfrey go to grasse: and when I am | King, as
 King I will be.   2387
 * *But.* They vse to writ it on the top of Letters: 'Twill | go hard with
 you.   2417
 If you go forward: therefore yeeld, or dye.   2447
 * *Cade.* He lyes, for I inuented it my selfe. Go too Sir-|rah,   2475
 *And faine to go with a staffe, but that my puissance holds   2483
 *enemies: go too then, I ask but this: Can he that speaks   2490
 Spare none, but such as go in clouted shooen,   2505
 Cade. Come, then let's go fight with them: 2629
 But first, go and set London Bridge on fire,   2630
 * *Cade.* So sirs: now go some and pull downe the Sauoy: 2635
 *a Cloake, when honester men then thou go in their Hose | and
 Doublets.   2683
 *When shall we go to Cheapside, and take vp commodi-|ties vpon our
 billes?   2759
 That will forsake thee, and go home in peace.   2786
 That thus you do exclaime you'l go with him.   2812
 Buck. What, is he fled? Go some and follow him,   2842
 I pray thee Buckingham go and meete him,   2890
 We twaine will go into his Highnesse Tent.   3047
 Go bid her hide him quickly from the Duke.   3079
 I know ere they will haue me go to Ward,   3107
 Wilt thou go digge a graue to finde out Warre,   3169
 * *War.* You were best to go to bed, and dreame againe,   3196
 Let vs pursue him ere the Writs go forth.   3348
GOBBETS = 1
 With gobbets of thy Mother-bleeding heart.   2253

GOBBITS = 1
Into as many gobbits will I cut it   3280
GOD = 41*9
With God preserue the good Duke *Humfrey*:   169
**War*. So God helpe Warwicke, as he loues the Land,   213
This was my dreame, what it doth bode God knowes.   305
Hume. But by the grace of God, and *Humes* aduice,   347
But God in mercie so deale with my Soule,   552
Pray God the Duke of Yorke excuse himselfe.   574
*nor thought any such matter: God is my witnesse, I am   585
Spirit. Ad sum. | *Witch. Asmath*, by the eternall God,   648
To see how God in all his Creatures workes,   723
King. Now God be prays'd, that to beleeuing Soules   793
Simpc. God knowes of pure Deuotion,   822
Card. What, art thou lame? | *Simpc*. I, God Almightie helpe me.   830
**Simpc*. Yes Master, cleare as day, I thanke God and | Saint *Albones*.   848
King. O God, seest thou this, and bearest so long?   905
**King*. O God, what mischiefes work the wicked ones?   938
In sight of God, and vs, your guilt is great,   1055
And God shall be my hope, my stay, my guide, | And Lanthorne to my
feete: 1079
God and King *Henry* gouerne Englands Realme: 1085
Here let them end it, and God defend the right.   1111
*God, for I am neuer able to deale with my Master, hee   1138
Yorke. Take away his Weapon: Fellow thanke God,   1158
**Peter*. O God, haue I ouercome mine Enemies in this   1160
And God in Iustice hath reueal'd to vs   1164
So helpe me God, as I haue watcht the Night,   1410
Glost. I say no more then truth, so helpe me God.   1420
Queene. God forbid any Malice should preuayle,   1717
Pray God he may acquit him of suspition.   1719
Suff. Dead in his Bed, my Lord: *Gloster* is dead. | *Queene*. Marry God
forfend.   1725
King. Oh Heauenly God. | *Qu*. How fares my gracious Lord?   1735
But how he dyed, God knowes, not *Henry*:   1833
If my suspect be false, forgiue me God,   1841
Blaspheming God, and cursing men on earth.   2089
He dies and makes no signe: Oh God forgiue him.   2163
Suf. O that I were a God, to shoot forth Thunder   2272
Saue to the God of heauen, and to my King: 2294
All. God saue your Maiesty. | **Cade*. I thanke you good people. There
shall bee no   2389
**Clearke*. Sir I thanke God, I haue bin so well brought | vp, that I can
write my name.   2422
For God forbid, so many simple soules   2542
**King*. Come *Margaret*, God our hope will succor vs.   2592
And seeing Ignorance is the curse of God,   2707
God should be so obdurate as your selues: 2748
Fling vp his cap, and say, God saue his Maiesty.   2791
All. God saue the King, God saue the King.   2795
God on our side, doubt not of Victorie.   2829
All. God saue the King, God saue the King.   2874
naile, I pray God I may neuer eate grasse more.   2945
**King*. The head of *Cade*? Great God, how iust art thou?   3062
God knowes how long it is I haue to liue: 3339
GODS = 5*6
**Peter*. Alas, my Lord, I cannot fight; for Gods sake   610

GODS *cont.*

*and so I pray you goe in Gods Name, and leaue vs. | *Exit Hume.*	628
Now by Gods Mother, Priest,	774
King. Poore Soule, | Gods goodnesse hath beene great to thee:	815
Such as by Gods Booke are adiudg'd to death.	1057
King. A Gods Name see the Lysts and all things fit,	1110
**King.* Cold Newes, Lord *Somerset*: but Gods will be | done.	1382
**Card.* Gods secret Iudgement: I did dreame to Night,	1727
King. Peace to his soule, if Gods good pleasure be.	2160
*his Tongue, he speakes not a Gods name. Goe, take	2741
*make shift for one, and so Gods Cursse light vppon you | all.	2807

GOE = 20*5

Hume, if you take not heed, you shall goe neere	378
Away, base Cullions: *Suffolke* let them goe.	426
*and so I pray you goe in Gods Name, and leaue vs. | *Exit Hume.*	628
Maior. Sirrha, goe fetch the Beadle hither straight. | *Exit.*	887
You goe about to torture me in vaine.	893
I beseech your Maiestie giue me leaue to goe;	1074
Ere thou goe, giue vp thy Staffe,	1077
And goe in peace, *Humfrey*, no lesse belou'd,	1081
Yorke. Lords, let him goe. Please it your Maiestie,	1103
King. Goe, take hence that Traytor from our sight,	1162
Elianor. Art thou gone to? all comfort goe with thee,	1267
Stanley, I prethee goe, and take me hence,	1271
Come *Stanley*, shall we goe?	1284
And goe we to attyre you for our Iourney.	1287
Goe, leade the way, I long to see my Prison. *Exeunt.*	1291
**Suff.* Why that's well said. Goe, get you to my House,	1699
King. Goe call our Vnckle to our presence straight:	1709
**Qu.* Runne, goe, helpe, helpe: Oh *Henry* ope thine eyes.	1733
Yet doe not goe away: come Basiliske,	1752
If from this presence thou dar'st goe with me.	1933
King. Goe *Salisbury*, and tell them all from me,	1993
Come *Warwicke*, come good *Warwicke*, goe with mee,	2012
Qu. Mischance and Sorrow goe along with you,	2014
**Hol.* The Nobilitie thinke scorne to goe in Leather | Aprons.	2331
*his Tongue, he speakes not a Gods name. Goe, take	2741

GOES = 3*2

Car. So, there goes our Protector in a rage:	154
Thither goes these Newes, | As fast as Horse can carry them:	704
**Queene.* Whether goes *Vaux* so fast? What newes I | prethee?	2083
Alarum. Fight at Sea. Ordnance goes off.	2168
**Mate.* And so much shall you giue, or off goes yours.	2186

GOFFE = 2

And thither I will send you *Mathew Goffe*.	2610
Alarums. Mathew Goffe is slain, and all the rest. | Then enter Iacke	
Cade, with his Company.	2633

GOLD = 9*1

Large summes of Gold, and Dowries with their wiues,	136
Put forth thy hand, reach at the glorious Gold.	284
**Hume.* Hume must make merry with the Duchesse Gold:	363
Dame *Elianor* giues Gold, to bring the Witch:	367
Gold cannot come amisse, were she a Deuill.	368
Yet haue I Gold flyes from another Coast:	369
Sort how it will, I shall haue Gold for all. *Exit.*	383
Are my Chests fill'd vp with extorted Gold?	2732
This hand was made to handle nought but Gold.	2998

GOLD *cont.*
That Gold, must round engirt these browes of mine,   3094
GOLDEN = 2
For that's the Golden marke I seeke to hit: 255
Vntill the Golden Circuit on my Head,   1658
GONE *see also* begone = 12*1
Lordings farewell, and say when I am gone,   152
Paris is lost, the state of *Normandie* | Stands on a tickle point, now they
are gone: 227
Still reuelling like Lords till all be gone,   236
All. Come, let's be gone. *Exit.*   427
And ten to one, old *Ioane* had not gone out.   720
Farewell good King: when I am dead, and gone,   1092
Elianor. What, gone my Lord, and bid me not fare-|well?   1263
Elianor. Art thou gone to? all comfort goe with thee,   1267
Suff. Away, be gone. *Exeunt.*   1705
So get thee gone, that I may know my greefe,   2061
Go, speake not to me; euen now be gone.   2067
All. I marry will we: therefore get ye gone.   2473
Qu. My hope is gone, now Suffolke is deceast.   2593
GOOD = 43*17
Calling him, *Humfrey the good Duke of Gloster,*   166
With God preserue the good Duke *Humfrey:*   169
Excepting none but good Duke Humfrey.   201
Ioyne we together for the publike good,   207
Eli. Yes my good Lord, Ile follow presently.   335
And will they vndertake to do me good?   352
2.Pet. Marry the Lord protect him, for hee's a good | man, Iesu blesse
him.   389
Duch. Against her will, good King? looke to't in time,   536
*knees he would be euen with me: I haue good witnesse   597
Bullin. Patience, good Lady, Wizards know their times: 635
See you well guerdon'd for these good deserts.   676
Yorke. At your pleasure, my good Lord.   709
Were it not good your Grace could flye to Heauen?   734
Good Vnckle hide such mallice: 743
So good a Quarrell, and so bad a Peere.   746
King. I prythee peace, good Queene,   752
In my sleepe, by good Saint *Albon:*   824
Simpc. Alas, good Master, my Wife desired some   842
Yorke. Now my good Lords of Salisbury & Warwick,   960
Warw. Sweet *Yorke* begin: and if thy clayme be good,   966
That vertuous Prince, the good Duke *Humfrey:*   1040
Farewell good King: when I am dead, and gone,   1092
Queene. I, good my Lord: for purposely therefore   1108
3.Neighbor. And here's a Pot of good Double-Beere   1125
and the good Wine in thy Masters way.   1159
I, Night by Night, in studying good for England.   1411
For good King *Henry,* thy decay I feare. *Exit Gloster.*   1494
And yet, good *Humfrey,* is the houre to come,   1505
Euen so my selfe bewayles good *Glosters* case   1518
Looke after him, and cannot doe him good: 1520
And yet herein I iudge mine owne Wit good;   1534
So he be dead; for that is good deceit,   1566
No more, good *Yorke;* sweet *Somerset* be still.   1607
1. I, my good Lord, hee's dead.   1698
According as I gaue directions? | 1. 'Tis, my good Lord.   1703

GOOD *cont.*

Then from true euidence, of good esteeme,	1715
That good Duke *Humfrey* Traiterously is murdred	1825
King. That he is dead good Warwick, 'tis too true,	1832
And you (forsooth) had the good Duke to keepe:	1887
They say, by him the good Duke *Humfrey* dy'de:	1960
Come *Warwicke*, come good *Warwicke*, goe with mee,	2012
King. Peace to his soule, if Gods good pleasure be.	2160
And thou that smil'dst at good Duke *Humfries* death,	2244
*Beuis. Nay more, the Kings Councell are no good | Workemen.	2333
But. He was an honest man, and a good Bricklayer.	2360
All. God saue your Maiesty. | **Cade.* I thanke you good people. There shall bee no	2389
**shall be encountred with a man as good as himselfe. He	2435
It is to you good people, that I speake,	2449
*Cade And good reason: for thereby is England main'd	2482
**with the tongue of an enemy, be a good Councellour, or | no?	2491
*But. If we meane to thriue, and do good, breake open	2526
*Say. These cheekes are pale for watching for your good	2718
Continue still in this so good a minde,	2869
Or vnto death, to do my Countrey good.	2897
As all things shall redound vnto your good.	2901
**Sallet was borne to do me good: for many a time but for	2915
He were created Knight for his good seruice.	3071
See where they come, Ile warrant they'l make it good.	3118
*King. Can we outrun the Heauens? Good *Margaret* | stay.	3298
with the death of the Good Duke | HVMFREY.	3358

GOODMAN = *1

*Goodman, my Lord Cardinals Man, for keeping my House,	402

GOODNESSE = 1

King. Poore Soule, | Gods goodnesse hath beene great to thee:	815

GOODS = 2

While as the silly Owner of the goods	237
Lands, Goods, Horse, Armor, any thing I haue	3044

GOOD-FELLOW = 2

King. Good-fellow, tell vs here the circumstance,	803
Queene. Tell me, good-fellow,	819

GORGD = 1

And like ambitious Sylla ouer-gorg'd,	2252

GOT = 6

To keepe by policy what *Henrie* got:	91
And are the Cities that I got with wounds,	128
Had *Henrie* got an Empire by his marriage,	160
Thus got the House of *Lancaster* the Crowne.	988
To emblaze the Honor that thy Master got.	2976
Well Lords, we haue not got that which we haue,	3342

GOTTEN = 1

Mess. Iacke Cade hath gotten London-bridge.	2586

GOUERN = *1

*King. Come wife, let's in, and learne to gouern better,	2902

GOUERNANCE = 1

Vnder the surly *Glosters* Gouernance?	433

GOUERNE = 3

He being of age to gouerne of himselfe.	173
God and King *Henry* gouerne Englands Realme:	1085
Not fit to gouerne and rule multitudes,	3089

GOUERNMENT = 1
  Is this the Gouernment of Britaines Ile? 430
GOUERNORS = 1
  Hath slaine their Gouernors, surpriz'd our Forts, 2257
GOWNE = 2
  The very trayne of her worst wearing Gowne, 471
  *Glost. Why that's well said: What Colour is my | Gowne of? 853
GOWNES = *1
  *Glost. But Cloakes and Gownes, before this day, a | many. 859
GRACE = 25*6
  As Procurator to your Excellence, | To marry Princes *Margaret* for your
    Grace; 10
  King. Her sight did rauish, but her grace in Speech, 39
  Suf. My Lord Protector, so it please your Grace, 46
  We heere discharge your Grace from being Regent 71
  Elia. What saist thou? Maiesty: I am but Grace. 346
  Hume. But by the grace of God, and *Humes* aduice, 347
  As by your Grace shall be propounded him. 356
  1.Pet. Mine is, and't please your Grace, against *Iohn* 401
  Vnder the Wings of our Protectors Grace, 423
  Warw. Whether your Grace be worthy, yea or no, 497
  Queene. If he be old enough, what needs your Grace 508
  Buck. Your Grace shal giue me leaue, my Lord of York, 707
  Were it not good your Grace could flye to Heauen? 734
  Simpc. Borne blinde, and't please your Grace. | *Wife.* I indeede was he. 806
  Simpc. At Barwick in the North, and't like your | Grace. 813
  Maior. Yes, my Lord, if it please your Grace. 885
  As more at large your Grace shall vnderstand. 929
  Seru. So please your Grace, wee'le take her from the | Sherife. 1191
  Her. I summon your Grace to his Maiesties Parliament, 1247
  Sh. And't please your Grace, here my Commission stayes: 1253
  Stanly. So am I giuen in charge, may't please your | Grace. 1257
  'Twill make them coole in zeale vnto your Grace. 1477
  Say, we intend to try his Grace to day, 1710
  Buc. What answer makes your Grace to the Rebells | Supplication? 2539
  And calles your Grace Vsurper, openly, 2566
  Mes. Please it your Grace to be aduertised, 2876
  Seditious to his Grace, and to the State. 3029
  Loe, I present your Grace a Traitors head, 3060
  And not to grace an awefull Princely Scepter. 3093
  Obey audacious Traitor, kneele for Grace. 3103
  And in my conscience, do repute his grace 3177
GRACELESSE = *1
  Kin. Oh gracelesse men: they know not what they do. 2574
GRACES = 4
  Your Graces Title shall be multiplied. 348
  In England worke your Graces full content. 453
  I thinke I should haue told your Graces Tale. 1338
  Say. So might your Graces person be in danger. 2581
GRACIOUS = 6*4
  To your most gracious hands, that are the Substance 20
  Queen. Great King of England, & my gracious Lord, 31
  King. Vnkle, how now? | *Glo.* Pardon me gracious Lord, 58
  Som. All health vnto my gracious Soueraigne. 1377
  Glost. Ah gracious Lord, these dayes are dangerous: 1442
  King. Oh Heauenly God. | *Qu.* How fares my gracious Lord? 1735
  Suff. Comfort my Soueraigne, gracious *Henry* com-|fort. 1737

GRACIOUS *cont.*
  * *Warw.* Come hither gracious Soueraigne, view this | body.   1852
  *1.*Gent.* My gracious Lord intreat him, speak him fair.   2288
  Buck. My gracious Lord, retire to Killingworth,   2575
GRAFT = 1
  Was graft with Crab-tree slippe, whose Fruit thou art,   1919
GRAMMAR = *1
  *the Realme, in erecting a Grammar Schoole: and where-|as   2667
GRAPPLE = 1
  To grapple with the house of Lancaster,   269
GRASPE = 1
  Thy Hand is made to graspe a Palmers staffe,   3092
GRASPT = 1
  His hands abroad display'd, as one that graspt   1876
GRASSE = 2*2
  Where byting cold would neuer let grasse grow,   2052
  *Cheapside shall my Palfrey go to grasse: and when I am | King, as
    King I will be.   2387
  *I climb'd into this Garden, to see if I can eate Grasse, or   2912
  naile, I pray God I may neuer eate grasse more.   2945
GRAUE = 6
  Or sell my Title for a glorious Graue.   1389
  King. That is to see how deepe my graue is made,   1854
  Thy graue is digg'd already in the earth: 2956
  Vnto a dunghill, which shall be thy graue,   2986
  Wilt thou go digge a graue to finde out Warre,   3169
  That bowes vnto the graue with mickle age.   3174
GRAUES = 2
  And Spirits walke, and Ghosts breake vp their Graues;   639
  Cleape dead-mens graues, and from their misty Iawes,   2175
GRAUNTED = 1
  And the Offendor graunted scope of speech,   1476
GREAT = 27*3
  Of that great Shadow I did represent: 21
  * *Queen.* Great King of England, & my gracious Lord,   31
  We thanke you all for this great fauour done,   76
  And no great friend, I feare me to the King;   157
  Why doth the Great Duke *Humfrey* knit his browes,   276
  And from the great and new-made Duke of Suffolke;   371
  If they were knowne, as the suspect is great,   526
  King. Great is his comfort in this Earthly Vale,   799
  King. Poore Soule, | Gods goodnesse hath beene great to thee: 815
  And would ye not thinke it, Cunning to be great,   879
  In sight of God, and vs, your guilt is great,   1055
  But great men tremble when the Lyon rores,   1313
  Leuie great summes of Money through the Realme,   1355
  That these great Lords, and *Margaret* our Queene,   1508
  Henry, my Lord, is cold in great Affaires,   1526
  Post. Great Lords, from Ireland am I come amaine,   1585
  For being greene, there is great hope of helpe.   1590
  Say that he thriue, as 'tis great like he will,   1685
  I haue great matters to impart to thee. *Exit.*   2013
  By diuellish policy art thou growne great,   2251
  Great men oft dye by vilde Bezonions.   2302
  Pompey the Great, and *Suffolke* dyes by Pyrats. | *Exit Water with*
  Suffolke.   2306
  * *Say.* Great men haue reaching hands: oft haue I struck   2714

GREAT *cont.*

I seeke not to waxe great by others warning,	2925
like a great pin ere thou and I part.	2934
To entertaine great Englands lawfull King.	2995
Should raise so great a power without his leaue?	3013
Yor. Scarse can I speake, my Choller is so great.	3015
King. The head of *Cade*? Great God, how iust art thou?	3062
Sal. It is great sinne, to sweare vnto a sinne:	3182

GREATER = 3

What were it but to make my sorrow greater?	1851
But greater sinne to keepe a sinfull oath:	3183
Old Clif. I am resolu'd to beare a greater storme,	3198

GREATEST = 4

Hath wonne the greatest fauour of the Commons,	200
Yor. And so sayes Yorke, | For he hath greatest cause.	215
The greatest man in England, but the King. | *Exeunt.*	1049
Thy greatest helpe is quiet, gentle *Nell*:	1243

GREATLY = 1

It skills not greatly who impugnes our doome.	1583

GREATNESSE = 2

And greatnesse of his place be greefe to vs,	180
As for words, whose greatnesse answer's words,	2957

GREEFE = 6*1

To you Duke *Humfrey* must vnload his greefe:	83
Your greefe, the common greefe of all the Land.	84
War. For greefe that they are past recouerie.	123
And greatnesse of his place be greefe to vs,	180
So get thee gone, that I may know my greefe,	2061
Queene. Oft haue I heard that greefe softens the mind,	2533

GREENE = 1

For being greene, there is great hope of helpe.	1590

GREET = 1

Buc. Yorke, if thou meanest wel, I greet thee well.	3006

GREETING = *1

Yor. Humfrey of Buckingham, I accept thy greeting.	3007

GREEUE = 1

But wherefore greeue I at an houres poore losse,	2098

GREEUES = 1

It greeues my soule to leaue thee vnassail'd. *Exit War.*	3238

GREEUOUS = 1

For sodainly a greeuous sicknesse tooke him,	2087

GRIEFE = 4

Sorrow and griefe haue vanquisht all my powers;	935
Mine eyes are full of teares, my heart of griefe.	1071
Glost. Be patient, gentle *Nell*, forget this griefe.	1202
King. I *Margaret*: my heart is drown'd with griefe,	1499

GRIEUOUS = 1

And torture him with grieuous lingring death.	1959

GRIM = 1

Sits in grim Maiestie, to fright the World.	1750

GRIN = 2

War. See how the pangs of death do make him grin.	2158
Against the senselesse windes shall grin in vaine,	2245

GROANE = 1

His fortunes I will weepe, and 'twixt each groane,	1522

GROANES = 2

To see my teares, and heare my deepe-fet groanes.	1209

GROANES *cont.*
Might liquid teares, or heart-offending groanes,   1760
GROAT = 1
Or any Groat I hoorded to my vse,   1413
GRONE = 1
Would curses kill, as doth the Mandrakes grone,   2025
GRONES = 1
I would be blinde with weeping, sicke with grones,   1762
GROOME = 4
And vanquisht as I am, I yeeld to thee, | Or to the meanest Groome.   936
Must not be shed by such a iaded Groome: 2220
Then stand vncouer'd to the Vulgar Groome.   2296
Home to your Cottages: forsake this Groome.   2444
GROSSE = 1
Staf. O grosse and miserable ignorance.   2488
GROUE = 4
That he that breakes a sticke of Glosters groue,   307
On the East side of the Groue.   763
The East side of the Groue: | Cardinall, I am with you.   770
Their sweetest shade, a groue of Cypresse Trees: 2038
GROUELL = 1*1
If so, Gaze on, and grouell on thy face,   282
*Mother *Iordan*, be you prostrate, and grouell on the   630
GROUND = 6*1
As to vouchsafe one glance vnto the ground.   289
A Spirit rais'd from depth of vnder ground,   354
Raysing vp wicked Spirits from vnder ground,   926
Will bring thy head with sorrow to the ground.   1073
On any ground that I am Ruler of,   2010
Now by the ground that I am banish'd from,   2049
*Thy lips that kist the Queene, shall sweepe the ground: 2243
GROUNDS = 1
And like a Theefe to come to rob my grounds: 2938
GROW = 5
Car. My Lord of Gloster, now ye grow too hot,   144
King. The Windes grow high,   779
Suffer them now, and they'le o're-grow the Garden,   1326
Before the Wound doe grow vncurable;   1589
Where byting cold would neuer let grasse grow,   2052
GROWNE = 3
Glost. What, Cardinall? | Is your Priest-hood growne peremptorie?   740
By diuellish policy art thou growne great,   2251
To Bedlem with him, is the man growne mad.   3128
GRUMBLING = 1
And grumbling *Yorke*: and not the least of these,   456
GRYNNE = 1
Small Curres are not regarded when they grynne,   1312
GUALTIER = 2
Thy name is *Gualtier*, being rightly sounded.   2206
Whit. Gualtier or *Walter*, which it is I care not,   2207
GUARD = 6
*Enter the Duke of Yorke and the Duke of Buckingham | with their Guard,
and breake in.*   669
*Sound Trumpets. Enter the King and State, | with Guard, to banish the
Duchesse.*   1051
Card. Sirs, take away the Duke, and guard him sure.   1488
To guard the Chicken from a hungry Kyte,   1551

GUARD *cont.*
That they will guard you, where you will, or no, 1977
Where it should guard. O Warre, thou sonne of hell, 3255
GUERDOND = 1
See you well guerdon'd for these good deserts. 676
GUIDE = 1
And God shall be my hope, my stay, my guide, | And Lanthorne to my
feete: 1079
GUILT = 5
In sight of God, and vs, your guilt is great, 1055
For by his death we doe perceiue his guilt, 1163
Nor store of Treasons, to augment my guilt: 1469
His guilt should be but idly posted ouer, 1557
Warw. But that the guilt of Murther bucklers thee, 1921
GUILTIE = 2
Who can accuse me? wherein am I guiltie? 1401
If he be guiltie, as 'tis published. 1711
GUILTLESSE = 3
And all to make away my guiltlesse Life. 1467
By shamefull murther of a guiltlesse King, 2263
These hands are free from guiltlesse bloodshedding, 2735
GUILTY = 1*1
As guilty of Duke *Humfries* timelesse death. 1891
*mine Honour: vnlesse I finde him guilty he shall not die. 2413
GUISE = 1
Queene. My Lord of Suffolke, say, is this the guise? 428
GUN = 1
Or like an ouer-charged Gun, recoile, 2046
GUSTS = 1
What did I then? But curst the gentle gusts, 1788
GYNNES = 1
Be it by Gynnes, by Snares, by Subtletie, 1564
HAD *l.*9 32 110 135 160 249 439 *653 720 766 767 969 996 998 999 1002
1166 1236 1237 1337 1384 1409 1466 1480 1595 1597 1884 1887 1995
2007 2076 *2326 *2370 2459 2556 *2668 *2802 *2916 = 33*6
HADST *l.*810 872 1608 *2516 = 2*2
HAGGES = 1
And wedded be thou to the Hagges of hell, 2247
HAIRE = 3*1
Looke on the sheets his haire (you see) is sticking, 1878
Mine haire be fixt an end, as one distract: 2033
*Combe downe his haire; looke, looke, it stands vpright, 2149
Old Salsbury, shame to thy siluer haire, 3162
HALE = 1
Lieu. Hale him away, and let him talke no more: 2299
HALES = *1
*as this multitude? The name of Henry the fift, hales them 2833
HALFE = 3*1
Queene. Not all these Lords do vex me halfe so much, 461
Elianor. Not halfe so bad as thine to Englands King, 677
Within this halfe houre hath receiu'd his sight, 791
*halfe peny Loaues sold for a peny: the three hoop'd pot, 2384
HALFE-FACD = 1
Aduance our halfe-fac'd Sunne, striuing to shine; 2266
HALLOW = 1
Sword, I will hallow thee for this thy deede, 2972

HALLOWD = 1
Wee will make fast within a hallow'd Verge.   642
HALLOWING = 1
Enter the King, Queene, Protector, Cardinall, and | Suffolke, with
Faulkners hallowing.   715
HALTERS = 2
Enter Multitudes with Halters about their | Neckes.   2860
And humbly thus with halters on their neckes,   2863
HAMMER = *1
*and *Will*, thou shalt haue my Hammer: and here *Tom*,   1136
HAMMERING = 1
And wilt thou still be hammering Treachery,   321
HAMPER = 1
Shee'le hamper thee, and dandle thee like a Baby: 537
HAND = 25
Put forth thy hand, reach at the glorious Gold.   284
But to the matter that we haue in hand: 554
That time best fits the worke we haue in hand.   640
Come with thy two-hand Sword.   768
Where it best fits to be, in *Henries* hand.   1100
burning in her hand, with the Sherife | and Officers.   1189
And Charitie chas'd hence by Rancours hand;   1444
Suff. Here is my Hand, the deed is worthy doing. | *Queene.* And so say
I.   1580
Then, Noble *Yorke*, take thou this Taske in hand.   1623
The King and all the Peeres are here at hand.   1701
And with my fingers feele his hand, vnfeeling: 1847
Qu. Oh, let me intreat thee cease, giue me thy hand,   2054
Oh, could this kisse be printed in thy hand,   2058
Hold vp thy hand, make signall of thy hope.   2162
Hast thou not kist thy hand, and held my stirrop?   2221
This hand of mine hath writ in thy behalfe,   2231
A Romane Sworder, and Bandetto slaue | Murder'd sweet *Tully. Brutus*
Bastard hand   2303
Beuis. Thou hast hit it: for there's no better signe of a | braue minde,
then a hard hand.   2338
burnt i'th hand for stealing of Sheepe.   2381
But. Nay, he can make Obligations, and write Court | hand.   2410
Thy hand is but a finger to my fist,   2952
This hand was made to handle nought but Gold.   2998
Thy Hand is made to graspe a Palmers staffe,   3092
Heere is hand to hold a Scepter vp,   3097
Now by my hand (Lords) 'twas a glorious day.   3351
HANDED = 1
Yor. The deadly handed Clifford slew my Steed: 3228
HANDLE = 1
This hand was made to handle nought but Gold.   2998
HANDS = 11*2
To your most gracious hands, that are the Substance   20
Clapping their hands, and crying with loud voyce,   167
Weepes ouer them, and wrings his haplesse hands,   238
Till France be wonne into the Dolphins hands: 565
Yorke. Lay hands vpon these Traytors, and their trash: 671
You put sharpe Weapons in a mad-mans hands.   1653
Lay not thy hands on me: forbeare I say,   1746
Some violent hands were laid on *Humfries* life: 1840
I do beleeue that violent hands were laid   1860

HANDS *cont.*

His hands abroad display'd, as one that graspt	1876
When haue I ought exacted at your hands?	2703
Say. Great men haue reaching hands: oft haue I struck	2714
These hands are free from guiltlesse bloodshedding,	2735

HANDY-CRAFTS = 1

Beuis. O miserable Age: Vertue is not regarded in | Handy-crafts men.	2329

HANG = 3*2

Armorer. Alas, my Lord, hang me if euer I spake the	594
Hang ouer thee, as sure it shortly will.	1226
No, it will hang vpon my richest Robes,	1289
Cade. Away with him I say: Hang him with his Pen	2426
And hang thee o're my Tombe, when I am dead.	2973

HANGD = 2*2

Humf. Sirrha, or you must fight, or else be hang'd.	614
Be hang'd vp for example at their doores:	2500
*reade, thou hast hang'd them, when (indeede) onely for	2678
*be hang'd with your Pardons about your neckes? Hath	2798

HANGING = 1

Hanging the head at Ceres plenteous load?	275

HANGINGS = 1

And like rich hangings in a homely house,	3333

HANGS = 1*1

Suff. Thus droupes this loftie Pyne, & hangs his sprayes,	1101
Hangs on the cutting short that fraudfull man.	1375

HAP = 1

And trie your hap against the Irishmen?	1619

HAPLESSE = 1

Weepes ouer them, and wrings his haplesse hands,	238

HAPLY = 2

The Commons haply rise, to saue his Life;	1542
Of all our Fortunes: but if we haply scape,	3306

HAPPIEST = 1

The happiest Gift, that euer Marquesse gaue,	22

HAPPILY = 1

Might happily haue prou'd farre worse then his.	1609

HAPPINES = *1

All kneel. Long liue Qu.(eene) *Margaret,* Englands happines.	44

HAPPINESSE = 1*1

Glost. All happinesse vnto my Lord the King:	1391
Clif. Health, and all happinesse to my Lord the King.	3121

HAPPY = 5

And you your selfe shall steere the happy Helme. *Exit.*	486
Or count them happy, that enioyes the Sunne?	1215
And if my death might make this Iland happy,	1448
And thought thee happy when I shooke my head.	2223
Repaires him with Occasion. This happy day	3325

HARBOR = 1

And finde no harbor in a Royall heart.	1642

HARBOUR = 1

Where shall it finde a harbour in the earth?	3168

HARBOURING = 1

This breast from harbouring foule deceitfull thoughts.	2736

HARBOURS = 1

And in his simple shew he harbours Treason.	1348

HARD = 5

Because thy flinty heart more hard then they,	1799

HARD *cont.*
  Beuis. Thou hast hit it: for there's no better signe of a | braue minde,
    then a hard hand.   2338
  But. They vse to writ it on the top of Letters: 'Twill | go hard with
    you.   2417
  are hard by, with the Kings Forces.   2433
  For he is fierce, and cannot brooke hard Language.   2899
HARDLY = 4
  Haue done, for more I hardly can endure.   665
  These Oracles are hardly attain'd, | And hardly vnderstood.   700
  Knowing how hardly I can brooke abuse?   3087
HARME = *1
  King. Buckingham, doth Yorke intend no harme to vs   3049
HARMEFULL = 1
  Least being suffer'd in that harmefull slumber,   1974
HARMELESSE = 4
  Harmelesse *Richard* was murthered traiterously.   986
  As is the sucking Lambe, or harmelesse Doue: 1365
  Doe seeke subuersion of thy harmelesse Life.   1509
  Looking the way her harmelesse young one went,   1516
HARMONY = 1
  When such Strings iarre, what hope of Harmony?   782
HARSH = 1
  As curst, as harsh, and horrible to heare,   2027
HART = 2
  France should haue torne and rent my very hart,   133
  A Hart it was bound in with Diamonds,   1807
HARTED = *1
  Queen. Fye Coward woman, and soft harted wretch,   2021
HARUEST = 1
  And reape the Haruest which that Rascall sow'd.   1687
HAS *l.*912 *2740 = 1*1, *1
  Wea. Ha's a Booke in his pocket with red Letters in't   2408
HAST *l.*28 319 349 *518 805 835 1161 1281 1599 2022 2221 2224 2229
  *2338 *2420 *2666 *2669 *2671 *2672 *2674 *2677 *2678 2784 2954
  3086 3172 3179 *3193 *3337 = 17*12, 1
  Salisbury. Then lets make hast away,   217
HASTE *see also* hast = 1
  King. How now? What newes? Why com'st thou in | such haste?   2561
HATCHES = 1
  I stood vpon the Hatches in the storme: 1803
HATCHET = 1
  Cade. Ye shall haue a hempen Candle then, & the help | of hatchet.   2723
HATE = 2
  And *Suffolks* cloudie Brow his stormie hate;   1455
  With full as many signes of deadly hate,   2029
HATEFULL = 3
  Ah *Gloster*, hide thee from their hatefull lookes,   1199
  For hee's disposed as the hatefull Rauen.   1370
  But left that hatefull office vnto thee.   1793
HATES = 1
  With her, that hateth thee and hates vs all,   1228
HATETH = 3
  With her, that hateth thee and hates vs all,   1228
  King. Lord *Say*, the Traitors hateth thee,   2579
  Who hateth him, and honors not his Father,   2792

HATFIELD = 1 *1
The second, *William* of Hatfield; and the third,   971
Salisb. But *William* of Hatfield dyed without an | Heire.   992
HATH *l*.32 60 95 100 117 200 216 271 514 515 523 606 791 816 818 878
902 932 951 987 1069 1139 1164 *1171 1322 1336 1405 1478 1547 1595
1674 1939 1988 2148 2231 2234 2257 *2424 *2474 *2484 2547 2551 2571
2586 2626 2711 2722 *2798 2815 2828 *2918 *2965 *2978 3005 3032
3153 *3161 *3250 3260 3261 3292 3340 = 53*10
HATING = 1
As hating thee, and rising vp in armes.   2261
HAUE *l*.16 92 133 134 135 142 193 206 222 250 300 *353 369 374 383
*454 474 482 493 505 517 521 554 591 593 *597 604 *612 *625 640 665
688 *810 828 873 883 *895 914 923 925 935 943 945 946 991 1001 1039
*1134 *1136 *1137 *1151 *1160 1166 1230 1240 1269 1338 1360 1392
1410 1417 1447 1459 1462 1463 1465 1485 1514 1536 1543 1545 *1575
1582 1598 1600 1609 1662 1666 1670 1693 1694 1697 1702 1764 1795
1814 1830 1865 1949 2007 2013 2113 2124 2190 2196 2226 *2286 2308
2321 2322 *2342 *2375 *2385 *2422 2439 *2480 2493 2519 *2524 *2533
2551 2553 2557 2596 2602 2608 2637 *2638 *2646 2649 *2679 2701 2702
2703 2705 *2714 *2723 2730 2731 2734 *2755 2772 *2801 2826 *2837
2844 2867 *2906 *2907 *2910 *2911 *2917 2927 *2942 *2967 *2971 3001
3004 3025 3027 3039 3044 *3104 3107 3138 3150 3175 3180 3189 3229
3278 3326 3339 3341 3342 = 129*39
HAUGHTIE = 1 *1
Yet let vs watch the haughtie Cardinall,   181
Queene. Beside the haughtie Protector, haue we *Beauford*   454
HAUGHTY = 1
Oft haue I seene the haughty Cardinall,   193
HAUING = 3 *1
Englands owne proper Cost and Charges, without hauing any | *Dowry*.   66
And hauing both together heau'd it vp,   286
Hauing neyther Subiect, Wealth, nor Diadem: 2250
Like to a Ship, that hauing scap'd a Tempest,   2886
HAWKE = 1
Where as the King and Queene do meane to Hawke.   333
HAWKES = 1
My Lord Protectors Hawkes doe towre so well,   726
HAWKING = 1
Glost. Talking of Hawking; nothing else, my Lord.   773
HAYRD = 1
Full often, like a shag-hayr'd craftie Kerne,   1673
HAYRE = 1
His hayre vprear'd, his nostrils stretcht with strugling: 1875
HE *see also* a = 135*28
HEAD = 32*7
And shakes his head, and trembling stands aloofe,   239
Nor weare the Diadem vpon his head,   258
Hanging the head at Ceres plenteous load?   275
Vntill thy head be circled with the same.   283
Shall loose his head for his presumption.   308
And on my head did set the Diadem.   314
And set the Triple Crowne vpon his Head;   449
Would make thee quickly hop without thy Head. | *Exit Humfrey*.   527
Ile haue thy Head for this thy Traytors speech: 591
The Ring-leader and Head of all this Rout,   922
Will bring thy head with sorrow to the ground.   1073
Causelesse haue lay'd disgraces on my head,   1462

HEAD *cont.*
Vntill the Golden Circuit on my Head,	1658
Ma. A thousand Crownes, or else lay down your head	2185
And thought thee happy when I shooke my head.	2223
Strike off his head. *Suf.* Thou dar'st not for thy owne.	2237
With humble suite: no, rather let my head	2292
Wal. There let his head, and liuelesse bodie lye,	2313
head, for selling the Dukedome of *Maine*.	2481
All. No, no, and therefore wee'l haue his head.	2493
head, the Duke of Buckingham, and the | *Lord Say.*	2531
Heere may his head lye on my throbbing brest:	2537
King. Lord *Say, Iacke Cade* hath sworne to haue thy | head.	2551
But get you to Smithfield, and gather head,	2609
*euen with you. Ile see if his head will stand steddier on	2728
*him away I say, and strike off his head presently, and then	2742
*and strike off his head, and bring them both vppon two | poles hither.	2744
*proudest Peere in the Realme, shall not weare a head on	2752
And he that brings his head vnto the King,	2843
*of the King by carrying my head to him, but Ile make	2932
And there cut off thy most vngracious head,	2987
And plucke the Crowne from feeble *Henries* head.	2993
Enter Iden with Cades head.	3057
Loe, I present your Grace a Traitors head,	3060
The head of *Cade*, whom I in combat slew.	3061
King. The head of *Cade*? Great God, how iust art thou?	3062
Qu. For thousand Yorkes he shall not hide his head,	3080
That Head of thine doth not become a Crowne:	3091
If it be banisht from the frostie head,	3167

HEADED = 1
Bare-headed plodded by my foot-cloth Mule,	2222

HEADES = *1
*I see them lay their heades together to surprize	2835

HEADLESSE = 1
And smooth my way vpon their headlesse neckes.	340

HEADLONG = 1
Hence will I dragge thee headlong by the heeles	2985

HEADS = 6*1
Wee'l both together lift our heads to heauen,	287
Were plac'd the heads of *Edmond* Duke of Somerset,	303
Heaping confusion on their owne heads thereby.	939
And nodde their heads, and throw their eyes on thee.	1198
I, all of you haue lay'd your heads together,	1465
Enter one with the heads.	2763
*take your houses ouer your heads, rauish your	2805

HEAD-STRONG = 2
Suff. Peace head-strong *Warwicke.*	570
I haue seduc'd a head-strong Kentishman, | *Iohn Cade* of Ashford,	1662

HEALTH = 2*1
Som. All health vnto my gracious Soueraigne.	1377
Buc. Health and glad tydings to your Maiesty.	2857
Clif. Health, and all happinesse to my Lord the King.	3121

HEAPE = 1
Clif. Hence heape of wrath, foule indigested lumpe,	3156

HEAPING = 1
Heaping confusion on their owne heads thereby.	939

HEARD = 5*3
Hum. A proper iest, and neuer heard before,	139

HEARD *cont.*

Bulling. I haue heard her reported to be a Woman of   625
And many time and oft my selfe haue heard a Voyce, | To call him so.   828
Sorry I am to heare what I haue heard,   945
Strange Tortures for Offendors, neuer heard of,   1422
Queene. Oft haue I heard that greefe softens the mind,   2533
*that euer I heard. Steele, if thou turne the edge, or   2960
Who since I heard to be discomfited.   3056

HEARE = 11*3
Away from me, and let me heare no more.   324
*presently: wee'le heare more of your matter before | the King. *Exit.* 420
her Ladyship behold and heare our Exorcismes?   623
Sorry I am to heare what I haue heard,   945
Salisb. My Lord, I long to heare it at full.   965
To see my teares, and heare my deepe-fet groanes.   1209
Didst euer heare a man so penitent? *Enter Suffolke.*   1695
Vntill they heare the order of his death.   1831
As curst, as harsh, and horrible to heare,   2027
To France sweet Suffolke: Let me heare from thee: 2122
*no Christian eare can endure to heare. Thou hast appoin-|ted   2674
Say. Heare me but speake, and beare mee wher'e you | will: 2692
Sound a parley. | What noise is this I heare?   2777
For (as I heare) the King is fled to London,   3346

HEART *see also* hart = 33*4
Lend me a heart repleate with thankfulnesse: 27
And ouer ioy of heart doth minister.   38
Some sodaine qualme hath strucke me at the heart,   60
Thy late exploits done in the heart of France,   204
Vnto the Princes heart of *Calidon*:   247
And in her heart she scornes our Pouertie: 467
*O Lord haue mercy vpon me, I shall neuer be able to | fight a blow: O
Lord my heart.   612
Beat on a Crowne, the Treasure of thy Heart,   737
How irkesome is this Musick to my heart?   781
Buck. Such as my heart doth tremble to vnfold: 918
Glost. Ambitious Church-man, leaue to afflict my heart: 934
Warw. My heart assures me, that the Earle of Warwick   1045
Mine eyes are full of teares, my heart of griefe.   1071
I pray thee sort thy heart to patience,   1244
A Heart vnspotted, is not easily daunted.   1398
The enuious Load that lyes vpon his heart: 1457
King. I *Margaret*: my heart is drown'd with griefe,   1499
But that my heart accordeth with my tongue,   1571
And finde no harbor in a Royall heart.   1642
Because thy flinty heart more hard then they,   1799
And so I wish'd thy body might my Heart: 1809
And bid mine eyes be packing with my Heart,   1811
Being all descended to the labouring heart,   1867
Which with the heart there cooles, and ne're returneth,   1870
That shall be scowred in his rancorous heart,   1903
King. What stronger Brest-plate then a heart vntainted?   1938
And euen now my burthen'd heart would breake   2035
Suf. I go. | *Qu.* And take my heart with thee.   2125
With gobbets of thy Mother-bleeding heart.   2253
Hath giuen them heart and courage to proceede: 2571
as heart can wish, or tongue can tell. | *Dicke.* My Lord,   2757
*you should leaue me at the White-heart in Southwarke.   2800

HEART *cont.*

Will he conduct you through the heart of France,	2813
And let thy tongue be equall with thy heart.	3084
I am thy King, and thou a false-heart Traitor:	3140
My heart is turn'd to stone: and while 'tis mine,	3272
Sword, hold thy temper; Heart, be wrathfull still:	3293

HEARTED *see* harted

HEARTS = 9

Such is the Fulnesse of my hearts content.	42
Bewitch your hearts, be wise and circumspect.	164
And stol'st away the Ladies hearts of France;	438
By flatterie hath he wonne the Commons hearts:	1322
Beaufords red sparkling eyes blab his hearts mallice,	1454
Who cherisht in your breasts, will sting your hearts.	1650
Hearts Discontent, and sowre Affliction,	2015
Clif. But that my hearts on future mischeefe set,	3312
Reignes in the hearts of all our present parts.	3315

HEART-BLOOD = 1

With heart-blood of the House of *Lancaster*:	1032

HEART-OFFENDING = 1

Might liquid teares, or heart-offending groanes,	1760

HEATE = 3

In Winters cold, and Summers parching heate,	88
Yor. Nay we shall heate you thorowly anon.	3158
Clif. Take heede least by your heate you burne your | selues:	3159

HEAUD = 1

And hauing both together heau'd it vp,	286

HEAUE = 1

Yor. To heaue the Traitor Somerset from hence,	3054

HEAUED = 1

And if mine arme be heaued in the Ayre,	2955

HEAUEN = 12*4

Wee'l both together lift our heads to heauen,	287
Were it not good your Grace could flye to Heauen?	734
Card. Thy Heauen is on Earth, thine Eyes & Thoughts	736
Glost. Madame, for my selfe, to Heauen I doe appeale,	942
Shall blowe ten thousand Soules to Heauen, or Hell:	1656
Nor let the raine of heauen wet this place,	2056
Saue to the God of heauen, and to my King:	2294
Knowledge the Wing wherewith we flye to heauen.	2708
King. Then heauen set ope thy euerlasting gates,	2865
Id. How much thou wrong'st me, heauen be my iudge;	2981
Giue place: by heauen thou shalt rule no more	3099
O're him, whom heauen created for thy Ruler.	3100
Ki. Canst thou dispense with heauen for such an oath?	3181
Ric. If not in heauen, you'l surely sup in hell. *Exeunt*	3217
Peace with his soule, heauen if it be thy will.	3251
Knit earth and heauen together.	3264

HEAUENLY = 2

King. Oh Heauenly God. | *Qu.* How fares my gracious Lord?	1735
So Suffolke had thy heauenly company:	2076

HEAUENS = 3*2

King. Oh thou eternall mouer of the heauens,	2153
Lord Card'nall, if thou think'st on heauens blisse,	2161
*middest of you, and heauens and honor be witnesse, that	2838
Whom angry heauens do make their minister,	3256
King. Can we outrun the Heauens? Good *Margaret* | stay.	3298

HEAUIE = 1
  And let thy *Suffolke* take his heauie leaue.   2020
HEAUY = 2
  Qu. Go tell this heauy Message to the King. *Exit*   2096
  Nothing so heauy as these woes of mine.   3287
HEDGE = *1
  *was he borne, vnder a hedge: for his Father had neuer a | house but
  the Cage.   2370
HEE *l.*414 *587 *731 *1116 *1138 *2342 *2403 *2486 *2658 = 1*8
HEED = 2
  Hume, if you take not heed, you shall goe neere   378
  Take heed, my Lord, the welfare of vs all,   1374
HEEDE = 1
  Clif. Take heede least by your heate you burne your | selues: 3159
HEEL *l.*184 *2625 = 1*1
HEELE *l.*1486 = 1
HEELES = 2*1
  *shall be dragg'd at my horse heeles, till I do come to   2523
  *base and ignominious treasons, makes me betake mee to | my heeles.
  Exit   2840
  Hence will I dragge thee headlong by the heeles   2985
HEERE = 18*3
  Heere are the Articles of contracted peace,   47
  We heere create thee the first Duke of Suffolke,   69
  We heere discharge your Grace from being Regent   71
  *What's yours? What's heere? Against the Duke of   405
  It cannot be but he was murdred heere,   1881
  Heere could I breath my soule into the ayre,   2108
  Heere shall they make their ransome on the sand,   2179
  The Commons heere in Kent are vp in armes,   2268
  *Small things make base men proud. This Villaine heere,   2274
  Cade. Heere I am thou particular fellow.   2431
  Cade. Where's Dicke, the Butcher of Ashford? | *But.* Heere sir.   2513
  Heere may his head lye on my throbbing brest: 2537
  But I am troubled heere with them my selfe,   2607
  And heere sitting vpon London Stone,   2616
  Buc. I heere they be, that dare and will disturb thee: 2782
  And heere pronounce free pardon to them all,   2785
  *me. My sword make way for me, for heere is no staying: 2836
  thou mayst be turn'd to Hobnailes. | *Heere they Fight.*   2963
  Whom haue we heere? Buckingham to disturbe me?   3004
  Heere is hand to hold a Scepter vp,   3097
  Clif. Why what a brood of Traitors haue we heere?   3138
HEERES = *2
  Mes. My Lord, a prize, a prize, heeres the Lord *Say*,   2653
  Cade. Heere's the Lord of the soile come to seize me   2929
HEES = 3*1
  2.Pet. Marry the Lord protect him, for hee's a good | man, Iesu blesse
  him.   389
  For hee's disposed as the hatefull Rauen.   1370
  For hee's enclin'd as is the rauenous Wolues.   1372
  1. I, my good Lord, hee's dead.   1698
HEIRE = 8*1
  *That the Duke of Yorke was rightfull Heire to the | Crowne.   411
  say, hee was rightfull Heire to the Crowne?   414
  Was rightfull Heire vnto the English Crowne,   581
  The eldest Sonne and Heire of *Iohn* of Gaunt,   981

HEIRE *cont.*
For *Richard*, the first Sonnes Heire, being dead,	990
Salisb. But *William* of Hatfield dyed without an | Heire.	992
Yorke. His eldest Sister, *Anne*, | My Mother, being Heire vnto the Crowne,	1005
She was Heire to *Roger*, Earle of March,	1011
As next the King, he was successiue Heire,	1343

HELD = 3
Hast thou not kist thy hand, and held my stirrop?	2221
So will the Queene, that liuing, held him deere.	2318
Run backe and bite, because he was with-held,	3151

HELL = 8*1
To thinke vpon my Pompe, shall be my Hell.	1217
Shall blowe ten thousand Soules to Heauen, or Hell:	1656
Giue thee thy hyre, and send thy Soule to Hell,	1930
All the foule terrors in darke seated hell -- -	2043
And wedded be thou to the Hagges of hell,	2247
*in despight of the diuels and hell, haue through the verie	2837
So wish I, I might thrust thy soule to hell.	2984
Ric. If not in heauen, you'l surely sup in hell. *Exeunt*	3217
Where it should guard. O Warre, thou sonne of hell,	3255

HELME = 1
And you your selfe shall steere the happy Helme. *Exit*.	486

HELP = *1
Cade. Ye shall haue a hempen Candle then, & the help | of hatchet.	2723

HELPE = 7*4
War. So God helpe Warwicke, as he loues the Land,	213
And I will helpe thee. | *Wife*. Most true, forsooth:	826
Card. What, art thou lame? | *Simpc*. I, God Almightie helpe me.	830
Thy greatest helpe is quiet, gentle *Nell*:	1243
So helpe me God, as I haue watcht the Night,	1410
Glost. I say no more then truth, so helpe me God.	1420
For being greene, there is great hope of helpe.	1590
Qu. How fares my Lord? Helpe Lords, the King is | dead.	1730
Qu. Runne, goe, helpe, helpe: Oh *Henry* ope thine eyes.	1733
Yorke. So let it helpe me now against thy sword,	3245

HEMPEN = *1
Cade. Ye shall haue a hempen Candle then, & the help | of hatchet.	2723

HENCE = 13*1
Thou shalt not passe from hence.	652
You foure from hence to Prison, back againe;	1058
King. Goe, take hence that Traytor from our sight,	1162
Stanley, I prethee goe, and take me hence,	1271
And Charitie chas'd hence by Rancours hand;	1444
Euen so remorselesse haue they borne him hence:	1514
Warw. Away euen now, or I will drag thee hence:	1934
*Now get thee hence, the King thou know'st is comming,	2103
Lieu. Conuey him hence, and on our long boats side,	2236
And all by thee: away, conuey him hence.	2271
And so farwell, for I must hence againe. *Exeunt*	2612
Hence will I dragge thee headlong by the heeles	2985
Yor. To heaue the Traitor Somerset from hence,	3054
Clif. Hence heape of wrath, foule indigested lumpe,	3156

HENCEFORTH = 3*1
That henceforth he shall trouble vs no more:	1629
*Garden, and be henceforth a burying place to all that do	2968
And will, that thou henceforth attend on vs.	3074

HENCEFORTH *cont.*
Henceforth, I will not haue to do with pitty.   3278
HENCEFORWARD = 1
And now henceforward it shall be Treason for any,   2620
HENCE-FORWARD = *1
 Cade. And hence-forward all things shall be in Com-|mon. *Enter a*
Messenger.   2651
HENRIE = 4
To keepe by policy what *Henrie* got: 91
Had *Henrie* got an Empire by his marriage,   160
Till *Henrie* surfetting in ioyes of loue,   263
Where *Henrie* and Dame *Margaret* kneel'd to me,   313
HENRIES = 6
Shall *Henries* Conquest, *Bedfords* vigilance,   103
What seest thou there? King *Henries* Diadem,   280
Demanding of King *Henries* Life and Death,   927
Where it best fits to be, in *Henries* hand.   1100
Obscure and lowsie Swaine, King *Henries* blood.   2218
And plucke the Crowne from feeble *Henries* head.   2993
HENRY = 29*8
 for Henry King of England, That the said Henry shal   52
What? did my brother *Henry* spend his youth,   85
And our King *Henry* giues away his owne,   137
The Peeres agreed, and *Henry* was well pleas'd,   230
Against my King and Nephew, vertuous *Henry*,   293
What, shall King *Henry* be a Pupill still,   432
I thought King *Henry* had resembled thee,   439
Spirit. The Duke yet liues, that *Henry* shall depose: 657
The Duke yet liues, that Henry *shall depose*:   689
Till *Henry Bullingbrooke*, Duke of Lancaster,   980
Crown'd by the Name of *Henry* the fourth,   982
Henry doth clayme the Crowne from *Iohn* of Gaunt,   1018
Henry will to himselfe Protector be,   1078
God and King *Henry* gouerne Englands Realme: 1085
Glost. My Staffe? Here, Noble *Henry*, is my Staffe: 1087
As ere thy Father *Henry* made it mine;   1089
 Queene. Why now is *Henry* King, and *Margaret* Queen,   1095
 Glost. Ah, thus King *Henry* throwes away his Crutch,   1489
For good King *Henry*, thy decay I feare. *Exit Gloster.*   1494
Henry, my Lord, is cold in great Affaires,   1526
And *Henry* put apart: the next for me. *Exit.*   1689
 Qu. Runne, goe, helpe, helpe: Oh *Henry* ope thine eyes.   1733
 Suff. Comfort my Soueraigne, gracious *Henry* com-|fort.   1737
For *Henry* weepes, that thou dost liue so long.   1821
But how he dyed, God knowes, not *Henry*:   1833
Qu. Oh *Henry*, let me pleade for gentle *Suffolke*.   2003
*tell the King from me, that for his Fathers sake *Hen-|ry*   2476
Henry the fift, that made all France to quake,   2793
Clif. Is *Cade* the sonne of *Henry* the fift,   2811
Henry hath mony, you are strong and manly: 2828
*as this multitude? The name of Henry the fift, hales them   2833
And *Henry* though he be infortunate,   2870
Buc. A Messenger from *Henry*, our dread Liege,   3009
Till *Henry* be more weake, and I more strong.   3023
And let my Soueraigne, vertuous *Henry*,   3040
The second Part of Henry the Sixt,   3357

HER *l.*18 39 40 *54 57 *65 79 138 141 326 375 382 465 466 467 468 470
471 474 478 535 *536 543 544 623 624 *625 *627 682 *685 949 950 1010
1102 1180 1187 1189 *1191 *1193 1228 1252 1255 1259 1260 1261 1340
1516 1517 1819 1916 1917 2030 2362 *2366 2459 *2754 *2978 2982 3079
3188 = 50*11

HER = *1

HERALD see also Her. = 2

Enter a Herald.	1246
Staf. Herald away, and throughout euery Towne,	2496

HERALDS = 1

But thou shalt weare it as a Heralds coate,	2975

HERBES = 1

And choake the Herbes for want of Husbandry.	1327

HERE = 30*7

Here *Hume,* take this reward, make merry man	360
* *Peter.* Here a comes me thinkes, and the Queene with | him: Ile be the first sure.	392
My Lord of Somerset will keepe me here,	563
Suff. Because here is a man accused of Treason,	573
Here doe the Ceremonies belonging, and make the Circle,	643
Wee'le see your Trinkets here all forth-comming. | All away. *Exit.*	683
What haue we here? *Reades.*	688
Card. Here comes the Townes-men, on Procession,	797
King. Good-fellow, tell vs here the circumstance,	803
Cam'st thou here by Chance, or of Deuotion, | To this holy Shrine?	820
My Lords, Saint *Albone* here hath done a Miracle:	878
Queene. Gloster, see here the Taincture of thy Nest,	940
King. Well, for this Night we will repose vs here:	952
Liue in your Countrey here, in Banishment,	1065
Glost. My Staffe? Here, Noble *Henry,* is my Staffe:	1087
Here let them end it, and God defend the right.	1111
1.Neighbor. Here Neighbour *Horner,* I drinke to you	1120
2.Neighbor. And here Neighbour, here's a Cuppe of | Charneco.	1123
1.Prent. Here *Peter,* I drinke to thee, and be not a-|fraid.	1129
World. Here *Robin,* and if I dye, I giue thee my Aporne;	1135
and Will, thou shalt haue my Hammer: and here *Tom,*	1136
* *Sh.* And't please your Grace, here my Commission stayes:	1253
Glost. Must you, Sir *Iohn,* protect my Lady here?	1256
I doe arrest thee of High Treason here.	1395
And here commit you to my Lord Cardinall	1437
Suff. Hath he not twit our Soueraigne Lady here	1478
Buck. Hee'le wrest the sence, and hold vs here all day.	1486
Doe, or vndoe, as if our selfe were here.	1496
Suff. Here is my Hand, the deed is worthy doing. | *Queene.* And so say I.	1580
This Deuill here shall be my substitute;	1677
1. Here comes my Lord.	1696
The King and all the Peeres are here at hand.	1701
Here in our presence? Dare you be so bold?	1948
Why what tumultuous clamor haue we here?	1949
If after three dayes space thou here bee'st found,	2009
furr'd Packe, she washes buckes here at home.	2367
Qu. And here comes *Clifford* to deny their baile.	3120

HEREIN = 2

Glost. And my consent ne're ask'd herein before?	1249
And yet herein I iudge mine owne Wit good;	1534

HERES = 3*2

We are alone, here's none but thee, & I. *Enter Hume.*   344
*2.*Neighbor.* And here Neighbour, here's a Cuppe of | Charneco.   1123
*3.*Neighbor.* And here's a Pot of good Double-Beere   1125
But here's a vengefull Sword, rusted with ease,   1902
Cade. Here's a Villaine.   2407

HERRINGS = 1

But. Or rather of stealing a Cade of Herrings.   2354

HES = *1

**All.* He hath confest: away with him: he's a Villaine | and a Traitor.   2424

HEW = 1

Oh I could hew vp Rockes, and fight with Flint,   3016

HEYFER = *1

* *Warw.* Who finds the Heyfer dead, and bleeding fresh,   1892

HEYRE = 3

And heyre apparant to the English Crowne: 159
For I am rightfull heyre vnto the Crowne.   2451
The rightfull heyre to Englands Royall seate.   3178

HID = *1

*I hid me in these Woods, and durst not peepe out, for all   2908

HIDE = 7

Good Vnckle hide such mallice: 743
Ah *Gloster*, hide thee from their hatefull lookes,   1199
Hide not thy poyson with such sugred words,   1745
What, Dost thou turne away, and hide thy face?   1774
Go bid her hide him quickly from the Duke.   3079
Qu. For thousand Yorkes he shall not hide his head,   3080
And if thou dost not hide thee from the Beare,   3220

HIGH = 8

Suffolke. | As by your high Imperiall Maiesty,   7
That doth accuse his Master of High Treason;   579
Yet by your leaue, the Winde was very high,   719
Yea Man and Birds are fayne of climbing high.   724
King. The Windes grow high,   779
Yet by reputing of his high discent,   1342
And such high vaunts of his Nobilitie,   1344
I doe arrest thee of High Treason here.   1395

HIGHER = 1

That mounts no higher then a Bird can sore: 730

HIGHNES = *2

* *Mess.* My Lord Protector, 'tis his Highnes pleasure,   331
* *Hume.* This they haue promised to shew your Highnes   353

HIGHNESSE = 17*1

And hath his Highnesse in his infancie,   100
Your Highnesse came to England, so will I   452
To present your Highnesse with the man.   798
His Highnesse pleasure is to talke with him.   802
And other of your Highnesse Priuie Councell,   928
So please your Highnesse to behold the fight.   1107
Or be admitted to your Highnesse Councell.   1321
Suff. Well hath your Highnesse seene into this Duke: 1336
By meanes whereof, his Highnesse hath lost France.   1405
I doe arrest you in his Highnesse Name,   1436
And Equitie exil'd your Highnesse Land.   1446
* *Queene.* What, will your Highnesse leaue the Parlia-|ment?   1497
They say, in him they feare your Highnesse death;   1961
That if your Highnesse should intend to sleepe,   1967

HIGHNESSE *cont.*
Say. I, but I hope your Highnesse shall haue his.	2553
Expect your Highnesse doome of life, or death.	2864
We twaine will go into his Highnesse Tent.	3047
Yorke doth present himselfe vnto your Highnesse.	3052

HIM *l.*120 165 166 188 192 270 318 356 *389 390 393 424 448 481 494 496
593 *596 *655 658 662 690 696 703 *788 *801 802 829 *896 902 978 985
1003 1103 *1116 *1117 1119 *1148 *1150 1155 1255 1297 1306 1307
1324 1371 1488 1514 1520 1528 1536 1544 1545 1559 1563 1567 *1575
1628 1671 1683 1684 1692 1712 1719 1732 1757 1819 1856 1858 1884
1888 1908 1911 1958 1959 1960 1961 2004 2005 2087 2088 2092 2095
2147 2152 2158 2159 2163 2197 2234 2236 2271 *2288 2299 2310 2318
*2375 2406 *2413 *2424 *2426 *2438 2439 2479 2624 *2690 *2719 2729
*2740 *2742 *2751 2792 *2797 2812 2842 2859 2889 2890 2891 2892
2894 *2932 3005 3065 3079 3081 3100 3109 3128 3130 3131 3134 3192
3229 3321 3325 3329 3330 3331 3332 3340 3348 = 127*27

HIMSELFE = 16*1
He being of age to gouerne of himselfe.	173
Sweare like a Ruffian, and demeane himselfe	196
Yorke. If *Yorke* haue ill demean'd himselfe in France,	493
Humf. Madame, the King is old enough himselfe	506
Pray God the Duke of Yorke excuse himselfe.	574
Henry will to himselfe Protector be,	1078
And *Humfrey*, Duke of Gloster, scarce himselfe,	1096
With what a Maiestie he beares himselfe,	1300
How prowd, how peremptorie, and vnlike himselfe.	1302
Oppose himselfe against a Troupe of Kernes,	1667
*shall be encountred with a man as good as himselfe. He	2435
Iacke Cade proclaimes himselfe Lord *Mortimer*,	2564
And vowes to Crowne himselfe in Westminster.	2567
Yorke doth present himselfe vnto your Highnesse.	3052
Makes him oppose himselfe against his King.	3130
King. Call Buckingham, and bid him arme himselfe.	3192
Hath no selfe-loue: nor he that loues himself,	3260

HINDES = 2
Suff. 'Tis like the Commons, rude vnpolisht Hindes,	1984
Of Hindes and Pezants, rude and mercilesse:	2569

HINDMOST = 1
'Tis not his wont to be the hindmost man,	1296

HINDS = 1
Staf. Rebellious Hinds, the filth and scum of Kent,	2442

HIRE *see* hyre
HIRED *see* hyred
HIS *l.*83 85 86 89 90 100 119 137 160 163 176 180 182 214 238 239 241 242
243 251 257 258 *264 273 276 308 *331 400 *419 441 442 443 444 445
449 450 473 484 507 509 511 566 572 579 580 *596 606 660 694 708 723
728 791 792 795 799 800 802 809 *810 839 861 864 866 880 977 978
*984 1005 1020 1026 1086 1098 *1101 1106 *1115 *1117 *1118 1158
1163 1169 1173 1221 *1247 1296 1299 1305 1309 1319 1339 1342 1344
1348 1354 1369 1371 1405 1436 1454 1455 1456 1457 1472 1481 *1489
1490 1521 1522 1538 1541 1542 1547 1557 1558 1561 1573 1574 1578
1596 1609 1620 1621 1668 1672 1710 1725 1732 1758 1761 1770 1780
1818 1829 1831 1834 1835 1843 1845 1846 1847 1850 1855 1859 1863
1864 1872 1873 1875 1876 1878 1879 1900 1903 1909 1913 1922 1939
1965 1980 1999 2020 2085 2091 2092 2093 2094 2143 *2149 2157 2160
2166 2182 2237 2313 2314 2316 2317 *2370 *2378 *2408 *2426 2427
*2432 2440 2464 2466 *2476 2493 2537 2553 2568 2570 2613 2634 *2644

HIS *cont.*
2650 *2670 *2728 *2738 *2740 *2741 *2742 *2743 *2744 *2753 2774
2790 2791 2792 2794 2843 2844 *2862 2882 2888 2894 *2930 2990 *2992
3013 3029 3045 3047 3063 3069 3071 3076 3080 3081 3130 3132 3134
3153 3177 3187 3206 3251 3265 3292 3329 3334 = 222*33
HISSE = 2

Their Musicke, frightfull as the Serpents hisse,	2041
Who in contempt shall hisse at thee againe.	2246

HIT = 2*1

For that's the Golden marke I seeke to hit:	255
After the Beadle hath hit him once, he leapes ouer	902
Beuis. Thou hast hit it: for there's no better signe of a | braue minde,	
then a hard hand.	2338

HITHER = 6*3

Maior. Sirrha, goe fetch the Beadle hither straight. | *Exit.*	887
Glost. Now fetch me a Stoole hither by and by.	889
Armorer. Masters, I am come hither as it were vpon	1147
Warw. Come hither gracious Soueraigne, view this | body.	1852
*Come hither sirrah, I must examine thee: What is thy | name?|	
Clearke. Emanuell.	2414
*and strike off his head, and bring them both vppon two | poles hither.	2744
The cause why I haue brought this Armie hither,	3027
Qu. Call hither *Clifford,* bid him come amaine,	3109
Call hither to the stake my two braue Beares,	3141

HITHERWARD = 1

Is marching hitherward in proud array,	2880

HIUE = 1

The Commons like an angry Hiue of Bees	1827

HIUES = 1

Drones sucke not Eagles blood, but rob Bee-hiues:	2277

HOARSE = 1

Warwicke is hoarse with calling thee to armes.	3225

HOAST = 1

To send me packing with an Hoast of men:	1648

HOBNAILES = 1

thou mayst be turn'd to Hobnailes. | *Heere they Fight.*	2963

HOBOYES = 1

Flourish of Trumpets: Then Hoboyes.	2

HOE = 1

Who's within there, hoe?	710

HOL = 4*4
HOLD = 5*6

Nor hold the Scepter in his childish Fist,	257
Warw. Image of Pride, why should I hold my peace?	571
Yorke. Which now they hold by force, and not by right:	989
Armorer. Hold *Peter,* hold, I confesse, I confesse Trea-|son.	1156
Buck. Hee'le wrest the sence, and hold vs here all day.	1486
Hold vp thy hand, make signall of thy hope.	2162
*ere they haue it: Men shall hold of mee in Capite.	2755
Heere is hand to hold a Scepter vp,	3097
Yor. Hold Warwick: seek thee out some other chace	3234
Sword, hold thy temper; Heart, be wrathfull still:	3293

HOLDEN = 1

Holden at Bury, the first of this next Moneth.	1248

HOLDS = 1*1

Who in the Conflict that it holds with death,	1868
⸪And faine to go with a staffe, but that my puissance holds	2483

HOLINESSE = 2
But all his minde is bent to Holinesse, 441
That were a State fit for his Holinesse. 450
HOLLAND see also Hol. = 1
Enter Beuis, and Iohn Holland. 2319
HOLLOW = 2
By crying comfort from a hollow breast, 1743
For it is knowne we were but hollow Friends: 1766
HOLPE = 1
Rich. My Noble Father: | Three times to day I holpe him to his horse, 3328
HOLY = 3*1
His Weapons, holy Sawes of sacred Writ, 444
**Glost.* Faith holy Vnckle, would't were come to that. 757
Cam'st thou here by Chance, or of Deuotion, | To this holy Shrine? 820
King. Ile send some holy Bishop to intreat: 2541
HOLYNESSE = 1
With such Holynesse can you doe it? 744
HOMAGE = 1
And after all this fearefull Homage done, 1929
HOME = 7
Then bring a burthen of dis-honour home, 1601
2.*Gent.* And so will I, and write home for it straight. 2193
And sent the ragged Souldiers wounded home. 2258
furr'd Packe, she washes buckes here at home. 2367
Home to your Cottages: forsake this Groome. 2444
That will forsake thee, and go home in peace. 2786
Alas, he hath no home, no place to flye too: 2815
HOMELY = 1
And like rich hangings in a homely house, 3333
HONEST = 4*2
away an honest man for a Villaines accusation. 599
That hath dis-honored *Glosters* honest Name. 951
*an honest man: and touching the Duke of Yorke, I will 1149
But. He was an honest man, and a good Bricklayer. 2360
*Or hast thou a marke to thy selfe, like a honest plain dea-|ling man? 2420
For they are thrifty honest men, and such 2506
HONESTER = *1
*a Cloake, when honester men then thou go in their Hose | and
Doublets. 2683
HONOR = 14*2
That dims the Honor of this Warlike Isle: 132
From top of Honor, to Disgraces feete? 323
Thou ran'st a-tilt in honor of my Loue, 437
Noble shee is: but if shee haue forgot | Honor and Vertue, and conuers't
with such, 946
With honor of his Birth-right to the Crowne. 1026
Despoyled of your Honor in your Life, 1063
This Staffe of Honor raught, there let it stand, 1099
The Map of Honor, Truth, and Loyaltie: 1504
But all the Honor *Salisbury* hath wonne, 1988
Farre be it, we should honor such as these 2291
*The L.(ord) Maior craues ayd of your Honor from the Tower 2604
Haue I affected wealth, or honor? Speake. 2731
*middest of you, and heauens and honor be witnesse, that 2838
To emblaze the Honor that thy Master got. 2976
Yorke. Vpon thine Honor is he Prisoner? 3034
Buck. Vpon mine Honor he is Prisoner. 3035

HONORABLE = 2

May honorable Peace attend thy Throne.	1093
Cade. Therefore am I of an honorable house.	2368

HONORD = 1

Haue made thee fear'd and honor'd of the people,	206

HONORED = 1

That hath dis-honored *Glosters* honest Name.	951

HONORS = 2

Inchac'd with all the Honors of the world?	281
Who hateth him, and honors not his Father,	2792

HONOUR = 1*1

Then bring a burthen of dis-honour home,	1601
*mine Honour: vnlesse I finde him guilty he shall not die.	2413

HONOURABLE = 2*1

Suf. The honourable blood of Lancaster	2219
* *But.* I by my faith, the field is honourable, and there	2369
And shame thine honourable Age with blood?	3170

HONOURS = 1

And shall these Labours, and these Honours dye?	102

HOOD = 1

Glost. What, Cardinall?	Is your Priest-hood growne peremptorie?	740

HOOPD = *1

*halfe peny Loaues sold for a peny: the three hoop'd pot,	2384

HOOPES = *1

*shall haue ten hoopes, and I wil make it Fellony to drink	2385

HOORDED = 1

Or any Groat I hoorded to my vse,	1413

HOP = 1

Would make thee quickly hop without thy Head.	*Exit Humfrey.*	527

HOPE = 15*1

For were there hope to conquer them againe,	124
Cold newes for me: for I had hope of France,	249
To be the Poste, in hope of his reward.	708
When such Strings iarre, what hope of Harmony?	782
And God shall be my hope, my stay, my guide,	And Lanthorne to my feete:	1079
Yorke. Cold Newes for me: for I had hope of France,	1384
As firmely as I hope for fertile England.	1385
King. My Lord of Gloster, 'tis my speciall hope,	1439
For being greene, there is great hope of helpe.	1590
And we I hope sir, are no murtherers.	1885
Hold vp thy hand, make signall of thy hope.	2162
Ouer whom (in time to come) I hope to raigne:	2450
Say. I, but I hope your Highnesse shall haue his.	2553
* *King.* Come *Margaret*, God our hope will succor vs.	2592
Qu. My hope is gone, now Suffolke is deceast.	2593
Which makes me hope you are not void of pitty.	2698

HOPEFULL = 1

Burnes with reuenging fire, whose hopefull colours	2265

HOPST = 1

Be that thou hop'st to be, or what thou art;	1639

HORNE = 1

and Inke-horne about his necke.	*Exit one with the Clearke*	2427

HORNER = *2

* *Peter.* Against my Master *Thomas Horner*, for saying,	410
*1.*Neighbor.* Here Neighbour *Horner*, I drinke to you	1120

HORRIBLE = 1
As curst, as harsh, and horrible to heare, 2027
HORSE = 4*2
Thither goes these Newes, | As fast as Horse can carry them: 704
*shall be dragg'd at my horse heeles, till I do come to 2523
Buc. Then linger not my Lord, away, take horse. 2591
*Cade. Marry, thou ought'st not to let thy horse weare 2682
Lands, Goods, Horse, Armor, any thing I haue 3044
Rich. My Noble Father: | Three times to day I holpe him to his horse, 3328
HOSE = *1
*a Cloake, when honester men then thou go in their Hose | and
Doublets. 2683
HOT = 6*1
My sword should shed hot blood, mine eyes no teares. 125
Car. My Lord of Gloster, now ye grow too hot, 144
Tantaene animis Coelestibus irae, Church-men so hot? 742
Queene. Free Lords: | Cold Snow melts with the Sunnes hot Beames: 1524
*a mans stomacke this hot weather: and I think this word 2914
Rich. Oft haue I seene a hot ore-weening Curre, 3150
Hot Coales of Vengeance. Let no Souldier flye. 3258
HOULING = 1
And now loud houling Wolues arouse the Iades 2172
HOURE = 4
Within this halfe houre hath receiu'd his sight, 791
'Tis like, my Lord, you will not keepe your houre. 933
Glost. Tenne is the houre that was appointed me, 1177
And yet, good Humfrey, is the houre to come, 1505
HOURELY = 1
For sure, my thoughts doe hourely prophecie, 1997.
HOURES = 1
But wherefore greeue I at an houres poore losse, 2098
HOUSE = 15*6
Studied so long, sat in the Councell house, 97
To grapple with the house of Lancaster, 269
*Goodman, my Lord Cardinals Man, for keeping my House, 402
Thus got the House of Lancaster the Crowne. 988
With heart-blood of the House of Lancaster: 1032
Bearing it to the bloody Slaughter-house; 1513
How they affect the House and Clayme of Yorke. 1681
*Suff. Why that's well said. Goe, get you to my House, 1699
And make my Image but an Ale-house signe. 1781
And now the House of Yorke thrust from the Crowne, 2262
Cade. Therefore am I of an honorable house. 2368
*was he borne, vnder a hedge: for his Father had neuer a | house but
the Cage. 2370
* Wea. Sir, he made a Chimney in my Fathers house, & 2468
*owne Slaughter-house: Therfore thus will I reward thee, 2517
Descended from the Duke of Clarence house, 2565
*breake into his Sonne in Lawes house, Sir Iames Cromer, 2743
*dwell in this house, because the vnconquered soule of | Cade is fled. 2969
Meet I an infant of the house of Yorke, 3279
Come thou new ruine of olde Cliffords house: 3283
For vnderneath an Ale-house paltry signe, 3290
And like rich hangings in a homely house, 3333
HOUSED = 1
Might I but know thee by thy housed Badge. 3201

HOUSES = 1*1

  The Citizens flye and forsake their houses: 2587
  *take your houses ouer your heads, rauish your 2805

HOUSE-KEEPING = 1

  Thy deeds, thy plainnesse, and thy house-keeping, 199

HOW = 50*8

  King. Vnkle, how now? | *Glo*. Pardon me gracious Lord, 58
  How France and Frenchmen might be kept in awe, 99
  Marry and shall: but how now, Sir *Iohn Hume*? 364
  Sort how it will, I shall haue Gold for all. *Exit*. 383
  Suff. How now fellow: would'st any thing with me? 396
  *Suffolke, for enclosing the Commons of Melforde. How | now, Sir
  Knaue? 406
  And listen after *Humfrey*, how he proceedes: 542
  To see how God in all his Creatures workes, 723
  Glost. I my Lord Cardinall, how thinke you by that? 733
  King. How now, my Lords? 764
  King. Why how now, Vnckle *Gloster*? 772
  How irkesome is this Musick to my heart? 781
  Suff. How cam'st thou so? | *Simpc*. A fall off of a Tree. 832
  Glost. How long hast thou beene blinde? | *Simpc*. O borne so, Master. 835
  How I haue lou'd my King, and Common-weale: 943
  And for my Wife, I know not how it stands, 944
  Now thou do'st Penance too. Looke how they gaze, 1196
  See how the giddy multitude doe point, 1197
  And bid me be aduised how I treade. 1212
  And flye thou how thou canst, they'le tangle thee. 1231
  And shew it selfe, attyre me how I can. 1290
  How insolent of late he is become, 1301
  How prowd, how peremptorie, and vnlike himselfe. 1302
  And doe not stand on Quillets how to slay him: 1563
  Sleeping, or Waking, 'tis no matter how, 1565
  How they affect the House and Clayme of *Yorke*. 1681
  How now? why look'st thou pale? why tremblest thou? 1723
  Qu. How fares my Lord? Helpe Lords, the King is | dead. 1730
  King. Oh Heauenly God. | *Qu*. How fares my gracious Lord? 1735
  What know I how the world may deeme of me? 1765
  How often haue I tempted Suffolkes tongue 1814
  But how he dyed, God knowes, not *Henry*: 1833
  King. That is to see how deepe my graue is made, 1854
  War. See how the blood is setled in his face. 1864
  But may imagine how the Bird was dead, 1896
  King. Why how now Lords? 1946
  To shew how queint an Orator you are. 1987
  King. How fare's my Lord? Speake *Beauford* to thy | Soueraigne. 2134
  War. See how the pangs of death do make him grin. 2158
  How now? why starts thou? What doth death affright? 2201
  How often hast thou waited at my cup, 2224
  How in our voyding Lobby hast thou stood, 2229
  *I was neuer mine owne man since. How now? Who's | there? 2400
  King. How now Madam? | Still lamenting and mourning for Suffolkes
  death? 2554
  King. How now? What newes? Why com'st thou in | such haste? 2561
  Scales. How now? Is *Iacke Cade* slaine? 2600
  How would it fare with your departed soules, 2749
  Nor knowes he how to liue, but by the spoile, 2816
  *And shew'd how well you loue your Prince & Countrey: 2868

HOW *cont.*

Id. How much thou wrong'st me, heauen be my iudge;	2981
Let them obey, that knowes not how to Rule.	2997
King. The head of *Cade*? Great God, how iust art thou?	3062
King. How art thou call'd? And what is thy degree?	3067
Yor. How now? is Somerset at libertie?	3082
Knowing how hardly I can brooke abuse?	3087
War. How now my Noble Lord? What all a-foot.	3227
God knowes how long it is I haue to liue:	3339

HOWLE = 1

The time when Screech-owles cry, and Bandogs howle,	638

HOYSE = 1

Wee'l quickly hoyse Duke *Humfrey* from his seat.	176

HU = *1

HUM = *1

Hu. I go. Come *Nel* thou wilt ride with vs? *Ex. Hum*	334

HUM = 4*2

HUMBLE = 2

While Gloster beares this base and humble minde.	337
With humble suite: no, rather let my head	2292

HUMBLY = 3

And humbly now vpon my bended knee,	17
Som. I humbly thanke your Royall Maiestie.	608
And humbly thus with halters on their neckes,	2863

HUME = 5*3

We are alone, here's none but thee, & I. *Enter Hume.*	344
Here *Hume*, take this reward, make merry man	360
Hume. *Hume* must make merry with the Duchesse Gold:	363
Marry and shall: but how now, Sir *Iohn Hume*?	364
Hume, if you take not heed, you shall goe neere	378
Bulling. Master *Hume*, we are therefore prouided: will	622
Hume, that you be by her aloft, while wee be busie be-|low;	627
*and so I pray you goe in Gods Name, and leaue vs.| *Exit Hume.*	628

HUME = 3*3

HUMES = 2

Hume. But by the grace of God, and *Humes* aduice,	347
Humes Knauerie will be the Duchesse Wracke,	381

HUMF = 5

HUMFREY see also Hu., Hum., Humf. = 38*4

Enter King, Duke Humfrey, Salisbury, Warwicke, and Beau-|ford on the one side.	3
To you Duke *Humfrey* must vnload his greefe:	83
I prophesied, France will be lost ere long. *Exit Humfrey.*	153
Calling him, *Humfrey the good Duke of Gloster,*	166
With God preserue the good Duke *Humfrey:*	169
Wee'l quickly hoyse Duke *Humfrey* from his seat.	176
Despite Duke *Humfrey*, or the Cardinall.| *Exit Buckingham, and Somerset.*	186
I neuer saw but Humfrey Duke of Gloster,	191
Excepting none but good Duke Humfrey.	201
And make a shew of loue to proud Duke *Humfrey,*	253
And *Humfrey* with the Peeres be falne at iarres:	265
Enter Duke Humfrey and his wife Elianor.	273
Why doth the Great Duke *Humfrey* knit his browes,	276
But list to me my *Humfrey*, my sweete Duke:	309
Enter the King, Duke Humfrey, Cardinall, Bucking-|ham,	488
Would make thee quickly hop without thy Head.| *Exit Humfrey.*	527

HUMFREY cont.

And listen after *Humfrey*, how he proceedes:	542
Enter Humfrey.	546
Card. Duke *Humfrey* ha's done a Miracle to day.	912
That vertuous Prince, the good Duke *Humfrey*:	1040
Ah *Humfrey*, this dishonor in thine age,	1072
King. Stay *Humfrey*, Duke of Gloster,	1076
And goe in peace, *Humfrey*, no lesse belou'd,	1081
And *Humfrey*, Duke of Gloster, scarce himselfe,	1096
Enter Duke Humfrey and his Men in | Mourning Cloakes.	1169
Ah *Humfrey*, can I beare this shamefull yoake?	1213
And *Humfrey* is no little Man in England.	1314
*Which time will bring to light in smooth Duke *Humfrey*.	1359
Ah Vnckle *Humfrey*, in thy face I see	1503
And yet, good *Humfrey*, is the houre to come,	1505
As place Duke *Humfrey* for the Kings Protector?	1552
As *Humfrey* prou'd by Reasons to my Liege.	1562
But now returne we to the false Duke *Humfrey*.	1627
For *Humfrey*; being dead, as he shall be,	1688
Enter two or three running ouer the Stage, from the | Murther of Duke Humfrey.	1690
That good Duke *Humfrey* Traiterously is murdred	1825
They say, by him the good Duke *Humfrey* dy'de:	1960
* *Mich.* Fly, fly, fly, Sir *Humfrey Stafford* and his brother	2432
Enter Sir Humfrey Stafford, and his Brother, | with Drum and Soldiers.	2440
Sir *Humfrey Stafford*, and his Brothers death,	2570
* *Yor.* *Humfrey* of Buckingham, I accept thy greeting.	3007
with the death of the Good Duke | HVMFREY.	3358

HUMFREYES = 4*1

This is the Law, and this Duke *Humfreyes* doome.	607
Sometime Ile say, I am Duke *Humfreyes* Wife,	1218
* *Stanley.* Like to a Duchesse, and Duke *Humfreyes* Lady,	1278
That I am faultie in Duke *Humfreyes* death.	1906
And doe some seruice to Duke *Humfreyes* Ghost. | *Exeunt.*	1936

HUMFRIES = 6*1

Som. Cosin of Buckingham, though *Humfries* pride	179
And as we may, cherish Duke Humfries deeds,	211
Some violent hands were laid on *Humfries* life:	1840
* *War.* But both of you were vowed D.(uke) Humfries foes,	1886
As guilty of Duke *Humfries* timelesse death.	1891
Sometime he talkes, as if Duke *Humfries* Ghost	2090
And thou that smil'dst at good Duke *Humfries* death,	2244

HUMILITY = 1

Yorke. In all submission and humility,	3051

HUMOR = 2

They (knowing Dame *Elianors* aspiring humor)	373
King. I Clifford, a Bedlem and ambitious humor	3129

HUMORS = 1

Whose Church-like humors fits not for a Crowne.	259

HUMPHREY = 1

Till we haue brought Duke *Humphrey* in disgrace.	482

HUMPHREYES = 2

And her Attainture, will be *Humphreyes* fall:	382
More like an Empresse, then Duke *Humphreyes* Wife:	464

HUNDRED = 3*1

Being call'd a hundred times, and oftner,	823
Loather a hundred times to part then dye;	2070

148

HUNDRED *cont.*
haue a License to kill for a hundred lacking one.   2519
*to an hundred mischiefes, and makes them leaue mee de-|solate.   2834
HUNGRY = 1*1
  To guard the Chicken from a hungry Kyte,   1551
*the Country is laid for me: but now am I so hungry, that   2909
HUNT = 1
For I my selfe must hunt this Deere to death.   3235
HUSBAND = 2
To tumble downe thy husband, and thy selfe,   322
With him, the Husband of this louely Lady: 703
HUSBANDRY = 1
And choake the Herbes for want of Husbandry.   1327
HYRE = 1
Giue thee thy hyre, and send thy Soule to Hell,   1930
HYRED = 1
Haue hyred me to vnder-mine the Duchesse,   374
I = 425*108, 24*2
Glo. I Vnckle, we will keepe it, if we can: 114
Hume. I, what else? feare you not her courage.   624
Glost. I my Lord Cardinall, how thinke you by that?   733
Card. I, where thou dar'st not peepe: 761
Simpc. Borne blinde, and't please your Grace. | *Wife.* I indeede was he.   806
Card. What, art thou lame? | *Simpc.* I, God Almightie helpe me.   830
Queene. I, good my Lord: for purposely therefore   1108
Elianor. I, I, farewell, thy Office is discharg'd: 1283
I, Night by Night, in studying good for England.   1411
I, all of you haue lay'd your heads together,   1465
King. I *Margaret*: my heart is drown'd with griefe,   1499
1. I, my good Lord, hee's dead.   1698
I, euery ioynt should seeme to curse and ban,   2034
Suf. I, but these ragges are no part of the Duke.   2216
I, and alay this thy abortiue Pride: 2228
Lieu. Poole, Sir *Poole*? Lord, | I kennell, puddle, sinke, whose filth and
dirt   2238
But. I by my faith, the field is honourable, and there   2369
married the Duke of *Clarence* daughter, did he not? | *Staf.* I sir.   2457
Cade. I, there's the question; But I say, 'tis true: 2461
All. I marry will we: therefore get ye gone.   2473
Say. I, but I hope your Highnesse shall haue his.   2553
Buc. I heere they be, that dare and will disturb thee: 2782
Cade. Braue thee? I by the best blood that euer was   2941
King. I Clifford, a Bedlem and ambitious humor   3129
Yor. Will you not Sonnes? | *Edw.* I Noble Father, if our words will
serue.   3135
IACKE = 9*3
Beuis. I tell thee, *Iacke Cade* the Cloathier, meanes to   2323
Bro. Iacke Cade, the D.(uke) of York hath taught you this.   2474
Will parley with *Iacke Cade* their Generall.   2545
King. Lord *Say, Iacke Cade* hath sworne to haue thy | head.   2551
Iacke Cade proclaimes himselfe Lord *Mortimer*,   2564
Mess. Iacke Cade hath gotten London-bridge.   2586
Scales. How now? Is *Iacke Cade* slaine?   2600
Enter Iacke Cade and the rest, and strikes his | staffe on London stone.   2613
Soul. Iacke Cade, Iacke Cade. | *Cade.* Knocke him downe there. *They
kill him.*   2623
But. If this Fellow be wise, hee'l neuer call yee *Iacke*   2625

IACKE *cont.*
    Alarums. Mathew Goffe is slain, and all the rest. | Then enter Iacke
    Cade, with his Company.   2633
IADED = 1
    Must not be shed by such a iaded Groome: 2220
IADES = 1
    And now loud houling Wolues arouse the Iades   2172
IAMES = *1
    *breake into his Sonne in Lawes house, Sir *Iames Cromer*,   2743
IARRE = 2
    When such Strings iarre, what hope of Harmony?   782
    Wer't not a shame, that whilst you liue at iarre,   2818
IARRES = 1
    And *Humfrey* with the Peeres be falne at iarres: 265
IAWES = 1
    Cleape dead-mens graues, and from their misty Iawes,   2175
ID = *1
IDE = *1
    *ten meales I haue lost, and I'de defie them all. Wither   2967
*IDEN see also Id. = 6*1*
    Enter Iden.   2920
    That *Alexander Iden* an Esquire of Kent,   2947
    Cade. Iden farewell, and be proud of thy victory: Tell   2977
    Enter Iden with Cades head.   3057
    Iden. Alexander Iden, that's my name,   3068
    King. Iden, kneele downe, rise vp a Knight: 3072
    Iden. May *Iden* liue to merit such a bountie,   3075
IDEN = 5*3
IDLE = 1
    Was made a wonder, and a pointing stock | To euery idle Rascall
    follower.   1222
IDLY = 1
    His guilt should be but idly posted ouer,   1557
IERUSALEM = *1
    Naples, Sicillia, and Ierusalem, and Crowne her Queene of   54
IEST = 2
    Hum. A proper iest, and neuer heard before,   139
    To dye by thee, were but to dye in iest,   2117
IESU = 3
    Iesu maintaine your Royall Excellence,   168
    2.Pet. Marry the Lord protect him, for hee's a good | man, Iesu blesse
    him.   389
    For you shall sup with Iesu Christ to night.   3214
IESUS = 1
    Hume. Iesus preserue your Royall Maiesty.   345
IET = 2*1
    Simpc. Black forsooth, Coale-Black, as Iet.   855
    King. Why then, thou know'st what Colour Iet is | of?   856
    Suff. And yet I thinke, Iet did he neuer see.   858
IEWELL = 2
    I tooke a costly Iewell from my necke,   1806
    Suf. A Iewell lockt into the wofulst Caske,   2127
IF *1.*30 114 150 184 282 *290 378 493 495 508 526 562 *594 601 762 869
    872 885 *890 946 *966 1015 1042 *1135 1261 1304 1330 1331 1334 1341
    1448 1473 1480 1496 1596 1606 1711 1841 1905 *1907 1916 1933 1967
    2005 2009 2066 2090 2104 2105 *2136 2160 2161 2196 2317 2445 2447
    2466 *2489 *2516 *2526 2556 *2625 2631 *2728 *2747 *2910 *2912

IF *cont.*
  *2944 2950 2955 *2960 3006 3031 3058 3105 3110 3136 *3137 3149 3155
  3167 3172 *3195 3217 3220 3251 3305 3306 3307 3327 3350 = 72*19
IFAITH *see* yfaith
IGNOBLE = 2

Glost. My Lord, 'tis but a base ignoble minde,	729
Suff. Blunt-witted Lord, ignoble in demeanor,	1915

IGNOBLY = 1

But that 'tis shewne ignobly, and in Treason.	3244

IGNOMINIOUS = 1*1

With ignominious words, though Clarkely coucht?	1479
*base and ignominious treasons, makes me betake mee to | my heeles. *Exit*	2840

IGNORANCE = 2

Staf. O grosse and miserable ignorance.	2488
And seeing Ignorance is the curse of God,	2707

IGNORANT = 1

And ignorant of his birth and parentage,	2464

ILAND = 1

And if my death might make this Iland happy,	1448

ILE *l.*178 270 285 *296 327 335 357 393 560 591 775 *1127 1186 1214 1218
  1578 1634 *1635 1712 1935 2124 *2136 2147 2192 *2434 *2478 2541
  2546 *2727 *2728 *2739 2892 2896 *2932 3002 3043 3118 3200 3204
  *3208 = 29*11, 4

Is this the Gouernment of Britaines Ile?	430
With Sir *Iohn Stanly*, in the Ile of Man.	1066
To take her with him to the Ile of Man.	1255
Stanley. Why, Madame, that is to the Ile of Man,	1274

ILL = 3*1

And may that thought, when I imagine ill	292
Yorke. If *Yorke* haue ill demean'd himselfe in France,	493
*take my death, I neuer meant him any ill, nor the King,	1150
Sweet *Nell*, ill can thy Noble Minde abrooke	1181

ILLYRIAN = 1

Then *Bargulus* the strong Illyrian Pyrate.	2276

ILL-NURTERD = 1

Presumptuous Dame, ill-nurter'd *Elianor*,	316

IMAGE = 3*1

* *Warw.* Image of Pride, why should I hold my peace?	571
And make my Image but an Ale-house signe.	1781
And to suruey his dead and earthy Image:	1850
Yorke. Looke in a Glasse, and call thy Image so.	3139

IMAGES = 1

Are brazen Images of Canonized Saints.	446

IMAGINE = 2

And may that thought, when I imagine ill	292
But may imagine how the Bird was dead,	1896

IMBRACE = 2

But where's the body that I should imbrace?	2538
Who loues the King, and will imbrace his pardon,	2790

IMMEDIATELY = 1

Immediately he was vpon his Knee,	1305

IMMINENT = 1

You haue defended me from imminent death.	3341

IMPART = 1

I haue great matters to impart to thee. *Exit.*	2013

IMPERIALL = 2
Suffolke. | As by your high Imperiall Maiesty,   7
Suf. Suffolkes Imperiall tongue is sterne and rough: 2289
IMPERIOUS = 1
The imperious Churchman; *Somerset, Buckingham,*   455
IMPIOUS = 1
And *Yorke*, and impious *Beauford*, that false Priest,   1229
IMPLOYD = 2
'Tis meet that luckie Ruler be imploy'd,   1594
But you, my Lord, were glad to be imploy'd,   1986
IMPOSSIBLE = 3
But now it is impossible we should.   115
But suddenly to nominate them all, | It is impossible.   876
It is impossible that I should dye   2278
IMPRIMIS *see* inprimis
IMPRISONED = 1
Then Yorke vnloose thy long imprisoned thoughts,   3083
IMPUGNES = 1
It skills not greatly who impugnes our doome.   1583
IN *see also* i' = 287*50
INCH *see* ynch
INCHACD = 1
Inchac'd with all the Honors of the world?   281
INCLIND *see also* enclin'd = 1
Bro. But angry, wrathfull, and inclin'd to blood,   2446
INCONSTANCIE = 1
(The agent of thy foule inconstancie)   1815
INCREASE *see* encrease
INCROACHING = 1
And lofty proud incroaching tyranny,   2264
INDEBTED = 1
Are deepely indebted for this peece of paines;   674
INDEED = *1
But. She was indeed a Pedlers daughter, & sold many | Laces.   2364
INDEEDE = 4*2
Suff. Thy Wife too? that's some Wrong indeede.   404
Simpc. Borne blinde, and't please your Grace. | *Wife.* I indeede was he. 806
Glost. Nor his? | *Simpc.* No indeede, Master.   866
Murther indeede, that bloodie sinne, I tortur'd | Aboue the Felon, or
what Trespas else.   1431
Glost. Farre truer spoke then meant: I lose indeede,   1483
*reade, thou hast hang'd them, when (indeede) only for   2678
INDIGESTED = 1
Clif. Hence heape of wrath, foule indigested lumpe,   3156
INFALLIBLE = 1
Which is infallible, to Englands Crowne.   964
INFAMIE = 1
To be a Queene, and Crown'd with infamie.   1771
INFANCIE = 1
And hath his Highnesse in his infancie,   100
INFANT = 1
Meet I an infant of the house of Yorke,   3279
INFECTION = 1
He shall not breathe infection in this ayre,   2001
INFINITE = 1
Drumme. Enter Cade, Dicke Butcher, Smith the Weauer, | *and a*
Sawyer, with infinite numbers.   2350

INFLICT = 1
I know, no paine they can inflict vpon him,   1683
INFORCE = 1
And could it not inforce them to relent,   2549
INFORTUNATE = 1
And *Henry* though he be infortunate,   2870
INFRANCHISEMENT = 1
They'l pawne their swords of my infranchisement.   3108
INHERITANCE = 2
To conquer France, his true inheritance?   89
This small inheritance my Father left me,   2923
INIQUITIES = *1
Beuis. Then is sin strucke downe like an Oxe, and ini-|quities throate
cut like a Calfe.   2345
INIURD = 1
Whom haue I iniur'd, that ye seeke my death?   2734
INIURIOUS = 1
Iniurious Duke, that threatest where's no cause.   678
INIUSTICE = 1
Whose Conscience with Iniustice is corrupted.   1941
INKE-HORNE = 1
and Inke-horne about his necke. | *Exit one with the Clearke*   2427
INNES = 1
Others to'th Innes of Court, downe with them all.   2636
INNOCENCE = 2
The truth and innocence of this poore fellow,   1165
Say. The trust I haue, is in mine innocence,   2596
INNOCENT = 3*1
Our Kinsman *Gloster* is as innocent,   1363
My Conscience tells me you are innocent.   1441
And kill the innocent gazer with thy sight: 1753
*thing, that of the skin of an innocent Lambe should   2396
INPRIMIS = *1
Glo. Reads. Inprimis, *It is agreed betweene the French K.(ing)*   50
INSOLENCE = 3*1
His insolence is more intollerable   182
Suff. Resigne it then, and leaue thine insolence.   512
Glost. Why *Suffolke*, England knowes thine insolence.   750
Winke at the Duke of Suffolkes insolence,   1036
INSOLENT = 1
How insolent of late he is become,   1301
INSPIGHT = 2
Climbing my walles inspight of me the Owner,   2939
That keepes his leaues inspight of any storme,   3206
INSPIRED = *1
Cade. For our enemies shall faile before vs, inspired   2355
INSTANCE = 1
What instance giues Lord Warwicke for his vow.   1863
INSTANTLY = 1
Yor. A dreadfull lay, addresse thee instantly.   3248
INSTEEDE *see also* stead, steed = *1
*it hath seru'd me insteede of a quart pot to drinke   2918
INSTIGATE = 1
Did instigate the Bedlam braine-sick Duchesse,   1345
INSTIGATION = *1
*my Mans instigation, to proue him a Knaue, and my selfe   1148

INSTINCT = 1
| And meere instinct of Loue and Loyaltie, | 1962 |
INT = *1
| *Wea. Ha's a Booke in his pocket with red Letters in't | 2408 |
INTEND = 4*1
Say, we intend to try his Grace to day,	1710
That if your Highnesse should intend to sleepe,	1967
They call.false Catterpillers, and intend their death.	2573
*King. Buckingham, doth Yorke intend no harme to vs	3049
As I intend Clifford to thriue to day,	3237
INTENDS = 2*1
Which mates him first, that first intends deceit.	1567
War. As surely as my soule intends to liue	1857
*K. Then what intends these Forces thou dost bring?	3053
INTENT = 2
And for a minister of my intent,	1661
Free from a stubborne opposite intent,	1963
INTEREST = 1
Som. That all your Interest in those Territories,	1380
INTO l.262 565 954 1336 1917 2108 2115 2127 2171 2270 *2743 2776
*2912 2937 3047 3059 3280 = 15*2
INTOLLERABLE = 2
| His insolence is more intollerable | 182 |
| Card. My Liege, his rayling is intollerable. | 1472 |
INTREAT = 2*1
Qu. Oh, let me intreat thee cease, giue me thy hand,	2054
*1.Gent. My gracious Lord intreat him, speak him fair.	2288
King. Ile send some holy Bishop to intreat:	2541
INUENOMED = 1
With whose inuenomed and fatall sting,	1979
INUENT = 1
I would inuent as bitter searching termes,	2026
INUENTED = *1
*Cade. He lyes, for I inuented it my selfe. Go too Sir-|rah,	2475
INUINCIBLE = *1
*an inuincible spirit: but it shall be conuenient, Master	626
INUITE = 1
Inuite my Lords of Salisbury and Warwick	712
INUITIS = 1
Vnder the which is writ, Inuitis nubibus.	2267
IOANE = 1
And ten to one, old Ioane had not gone out.	720
IOHN = 14*4
Where are you there? Sir Iohn; nay feare not man,	343
Marry and shall: but how now, Sir Iohn Hume?	364
*1.Pet. Mine is, and't please your Grace, against Iohn	401
*Earth; Iohn Southwell reade you, and let vs to our worke.	631
Was Iohn of Gaunt, the Duke of Lancaster;	973
The eldest Sonne and Heire of Iohn of Gaunt,	981
Henry doth clayme the Crowne from Iohn of Gaunt,	1018
With Sir Iohn Stanly, in the Ile of Man.	1066
And Sir Iohn Stanly is appointed now,	1254
Glost. Must you, Sir Iohn, protect my Lady here?	1256
And so Sir Iohn, farewell.	1262
I haue seduc'd a head-strong Kentishman,	Iohn Cade of Ashford,	1662
Vnder the Title of Iohn Mortimer.	1665
For that Iohn Mortimer, which now is dead,	1678

IOHN *cont.*
  Enter Beuis, and Iohn Holland.   2319
  Cade. Wee *Iohn Cade*, so tearm'd of our supposed Fa-|ther.   2352
  Rise vp Sir *Iohn Mortimer.* Now haue at him.   2439
  Smith. Nay *Iohn*, it wil be stinking Law, for his breath | stinkes with
  eating toasted cheese.   2644
IOHN = 1*1
IORDAN = *1
  *Mother *Iordan*, be you prostrate, and grouell on the   630
IORDANE = 1
  With *Margerie Iordane* the cunning Witch,   350
IOUE = 1*1
  Lieu. But Ioue was neuer slaine as thou shalt be,   2217
  *ere thou sleepe in thy Sheath, I beseech Ioue on my knees   2962
IOURNEY = 1
  And goe we to attyre you for our Iourney.   1287
IOY = 7
  And ouer ioy of heart doth minister.   38
  King. The Treasurie of euerlasting Ioy.   735
  For none abides with me: my Ioy, is Death;   1268
  For in the shade of death, I shall finde ioy;   1754
  Why then Dame *Elianor* was neere thy ioy.   1779
  I can no more: Liue thou to ioy thy life;   2080
  My selfe no ioy in nought, but that thou liu'st.   2081
IOYD = 1
  King. Was euer King that ioy'd an earthly Throne,   2850
IOYES = 3
  Makes me from Wondring, fall to Weeping ioyes,   41
  Till *Henrie* surfetting in ioyes of loue,   263
  So Cares and Ioyes abound, as Seasons fleet.   1174
IOYNE = 4
  Cosin of Somerset, ioyne you with me,   174
  Ioyne we together for the publike good,   207
  Yet must we ioyne with him and with the Lords,   481
  Ioyne with the Traitor, and they ioyntly sweare   2589
IOYNT = 1
  I, euery ioynt should seeme to curse and ban,   2034
IOYNTLY = 1
  Ioyne with the Traitor, and they ioyntly sweare   2589
IRAE = 1
  Tantaene animis Coelestibus irae, Church-men so hot?   742
IRELAND = 10*1
  And Brother Yorke, thy Acts in Ireland,   202
  Me thinkes the Realmes of England, France, & Ireland,   244
  Post. Great Lords, from Ireland am I come amaine,   1585
  Th'vnciuill Kernes of Ireland are in Armes,   1615
  To Ireland will you leade a Band of men,   1617
  For there Ile shippe them all for Ireland.   1634
  Whiles I in Ireland nourish a mightie Band,   1654
  In Ireland haue I seene this stubborne *Cade*   1666
  Why then from Ireland come I with my strength,   1686
  The Duke of Yorke is newly come from Ireland,   2877
  Yor. From Ireland thus comes York to claim his right,   2992
IRIS = 1
  Ile haue an *Iris* that shall finde thee out.   2124
IRISH = 1
  Enter Yorke, and his Army of Irish, with | Drum and Colours.   2990

IRISHMEN = 1
  And trie your hap against the Irishmen?   1619
IRKESOME = 1
  How irkesome is this Musick to my heart?   781
IRON = *1
  *thee eate Iron like an Ostridge, and swallow my Sword   2933
IRREUOCABLE = 1
  But when I sweare, it is irreuocable: 2008
IS *see also* all's, Cardinall's, *Glocester*'s, hearts, hee's, here's, he's, shee's,
  that's, there's, 'tis, what's, where's, who's = 211*34
ISLAND *see also* iland = 1
  Enough to purchase such another Island,   2137
ISLANDERS = 1
  Stab'd *Iulius Caesar.* Sauage Islanders   2305
ISLE *see also* ile = 2
  That dims the Honor of this Warlike Isle: 132
  Is term'd the ciuel'st place of all this Isle: 2695
ISSUE = 6
  The Issue of the next Sonne should haue reign'd.   991
  Had Issue *Phillip*, a Daughter, | Who marryed *Edmond Mortimer*, Earle
  of March: 996
  Edmond had Issue, *Roger*, Earle of March;   998
  Roger had Issue, *Edmond*, *Anne*, and *Elianor*.   999
  So, if the Issue of the elder Sonne   1015
  Till *Lionels* Issue fayles, his should not reigne.   1020
IST = 3*1
  I cannot blame them all, what is't to them?   232
  What, is't too short? Ile lengthen it with mine,   285
  Is't not enough to breake into my Garden,   2937
  Iden. Is't *Cade* that I haue slain, that monstrous traitor?   2971
IT *see also* and't, an't, for't, in't, is't, may't, 't, to't, was't, wer't,
  would't = 144*34
ITEM = *2
  *Item, *That the Dutchy of Aniou, and the County of Main,*   56
  Win. Item, *It is further agreed betweene them, That the*   63
ITH = 2
  I'th parts of France, till terme of eighteene Moneths   72
  burnt i'th hand for stealing of Sheepe.   2381
ITS = 1
  Dying with mothers dugge betweene it's lips.   2110
ITSELFE *see* selfe
IUDGD = 1
  It may be iudg'd I made the Duke away,   1767
IUDGE = 3*1
  Humf. This doome, my Lord, if I may iudge: 601
  And yet herein I iudge mine owne Wit good;   1534
  King. Forbeare to iudge, for we are sinners all.   2165
  Id. How much thou wrong'st me, heauen be my iudge;   2981
IUDGED = 1
  Glost. Elianor, the Law thou seest hath iudged thee,   1069
IUDGEMENT = 1*1
  Card. Gods secret Iudgement: I did dreame to Night,   1727
  For iudgement onely doth belong to thee: 1842
IUDGEST = *1
  King. O thou that iudgest all things, stay my thoghts: 1838
IULIUS = 1
  Stab'd *Iulius Caesar.* Sauage Islanders   2305

IURISDICTION = *1
    *art thou within point-blanke of our Iurisdiction Regall.   2660
IUST = 2*1
    Why this is iust, *Aio Aeacida Romanos vincere posso.*   691
    Thrice is he arm'd, that hath his Quarrell iust;   1939
    King. The head of *Cade*? Great God, how iust art thou?   3062
IUSTICE = 4
    And poyse the Cause in Iustice equall Scales,   956
    And God in Iustice hath reueal'd to vs   1164
    Iustice with fauour haue I alwayes done,   2701
    As I in iustice, and true right expresse it.   3246
IUSTICES = *1
    *Iustices of Peace, to call poore men before them, a-|bout   2675
IUSTIFIE = 1
    I cannot iustifie whom the Law condemnes: 1070
K = *2
KEEPE = 13
    To keepe by policy what *Henrie* got: 91
    For France, 'tis ours; and we will keepe it still.   113
    Glo. I Vnckle, we will keepe it, if we can: 114
    Next time Ile keepe my dreames vnto my selfe, | And not be check'd.   327
    My Lord of Somerset will keepe me here,   563
    'Tis like, my Lord, you will not keepe your houre.   933
    To keepe, vntill your further time of Tryall.   1438
    If those that care to keepe your Royall Person   1473
    Let pale-fac't feare keepe with the meane-borne man,   1641
    And you (forsooth) had the good Duke to keepe: 1887
    Be play-fellowes to keepe you companie: 2016
    But greater sinne to keepe a sinfull oath: 3183
    To keepe thee from the Tempest of the field.   3197
KEEPES = 2
    What e're occasion keepes him from vs now.   1297
    That keepes his leaues inspight of any storme,   3206
KEEPING = 1*1
    Thy deeds, thy plainnesse, and thy house-keeping,   199
    Goodman, my Lord Cardinals Man, for keeping my House,   402
KEN = 2
    As farre as I could ken thy Chalky Cliffes,   1801
    For loosing ken of *Albions* wished Coast.   1813
KENNELL = 1
    Lieu. Poole, Sir *Poole*? Lord, | I kennell, puddle, sinke, whose filth and
    dirt   2238
KENT = 8*1
    The Commons heere in Kent are vp in armes,   2268
    Staf. Rebellious Hinds, the filth and scum of Kent,   2442
    Say. You men of Kent.   2687
    Dic. What say you of Kent. | *Say*. Nothing but this: 'Tis *bona terra,*
    mala gens.   2688
    Kent, in the Commentaries *Caesar* writ,   2694
    Kent to maintaine, the King, the Realme and you,   2704
    That *Alexander Iden* an Esquire of Kent,   2947
    *Kent from me, she hath lost her best man, and exhort all   2978
    A poore Esquire of Kent, that loues his King.   3069
KENTISH = 1*1
    These Kentish Rebels would be soone appeas'd.   2578
    King. Farewell my Lord, trust not the Kentish Rebels   2594

KENTISHMAN = 1
   I haue seduc'd a head-strong Kentishman, | *Iohn Cade* of Ashford,   1662
KEPT = 5
   How France and Frenchmen might be kept in awe,   99
   And would haue kept, so long as breath did last: 222
   And kept asunder: you Madame shall with vs.   681
   Who kept him in Captiuitie, till he dyed. | But, to the rest.   1003
   Had I but sayd, I would haue kept my Word;   2007
KERNE = 1
   Full often, like a shag-hayr'd craftie Kerne,   1673
KERNES = 3
   Th'vnciuill Kernes of Ireland are in Armes,   1615
   Oppose himselfe against a Troupe of Kernes,   1667
   And with a puissant and a mighty power | Of Gallow-glasses and stout
   Kernes,   2878
KEYES = 1
   These Counties were the Keyes of *Normandie*:   121
KI = *1
KILL = 10
   And kill the innocent gazer with thy sight: 1753
   Be poysonous too, and kill thy forlorne Queene.   1777
   Would curses kill, as doth the Mandrakes grone,   2025
   But. The first thing we do, let's kill all the Lawyers.   2394
   haue a License to kill for a hundred lacking one.   2519
   Soul. Iacke Cade, Iacke Cade. | Cade، Knocke him downe there. *They*
   kill him.   2623
   kill and knocke downe, throw them into Thames: 2776
   When I command them kill?   2780
   Is able with the change, to kill and cure.   3096
   Priests pray for enemies, but Princes kill. | *Fight. Excursions.*   3294
KILLING = 1
   Killing all those that withstand them: 2603
KILLINGWORTH = 2
   Buck. My gracious Lord, retire to Killingworth,   2575
   Therefore away with vs to Killingworth.   2580
KIN = *2
KINDE = 2
   Then this kinde kisse: O Lord, that lends me life,   26
   Buc. Yorke, I commend this kinde submission,   3046
KINDER = 1
   I can expresse no kinder signe of Loue   25
KINDLY = 1
   I take it kindly: yet be well assur'd,   1652
KINDNESSE = 1
   And I may liue to doe you kindnesse, if you doe it her.   1261
KING see also K., Ki., Kin. = 104*26
   Enter King, Duke Humfrey, Salisbury, Warwicke, and Beau-|ford on
   the one side.   3
   The Fairest Queene, that euer King receiu'd.   23
   Queen. Great King of England, & my gracious Lord,   31
   Makes me the bolder to salute my King,   36
   Betweene our Soueraigne, and the French King Charles,   48
   Glo. Reads. Inprimis, *It is agreed betweene the French K.(ing)*   50
   for Henry King of England, That the said Henry shal   52
   espouse the Lady Margaret, daughter vnto Reignier King of   53
   shall be released and deliuered to the King her father.   57
   ouer to the King her Father, and shee sent ouer of the King of   65

KING cont.

Exit King, Queene, and Suffolke. | *Manet the rest.*	80
Vnto the poore King *Reignier,* whose large style	118
And our King *Henry* giues away his owne,	137
It was the pleasure of my Lord the King.	145
And no great friend, I feare me to the King;	157
What seest thou there? King *Henries* Diadem,	280
Against my King and Nephew, vertuous *Henry,*	293
Where as the King and Queene do meane to Hawke.	333
said, That he was, and that the King was an Vsurper.	416
*presently: wee'le heare more of your matter before | the King. *Exit.*	420
And this the Royaltie of *Albions* King?	431
What, shall King *Henry* be a Pupill still,	432
I thought King *Henry* had resembled thee,	439
But can doe more in England then the King.	457
Enter the King, Duke Humfrey, Cardinall, Bucking-|*ham,*	488
Queene. Because the King forsooth will haue it so.	505
Humf. Madame, the King is old enough himselfe	506
Since thou wert King; as who is King, but thou?	513
Duch. Against her will, good King? looke to't in time,	536
As I in dutie loue my King and Countrey.	553
Bulling. First of the King: What shall of him be-|come?	655
*What Madame, are you there? the King & Commonweale	673
Elianor. Not halfe so bad as thine to Englands King,	677
The King is now in progresse towards Saint *Albones,*	702
Enter the King, Queene, Protector, Cardinall, and | *Suffolke, with Faulkners hallowing.*	715
That smooth'st it so with King and Common-weale.	739
Suffolke. Come to the King, and tell him what Mi-|racle.	788
Glost. Stand by, my Masters, bring him neere the King,	801
Demanding of King *Henries* Life and Death,	927
How I haue lou'd my King, and Common-weale:	943
Who after *Edward* the third's death, raign'd as King,	979
Seiz'd on the Realme, depos'd the rightfull King,	983
And but for *Owen Glendour,* had beene King;	1002
Succeed before the younger, I am King.	1016
Both. Long liue our Soueraigne *Richard,* Englands | King.	1027
But I am not your King, till I be Crown'd,	1030
Shall one day make the Duke of Yorke a King.	1046
The greatest man in England, but the King. | *Exeunt.*	1049
Sound Trumpets. Enter the King and State, | *with Guard, to banish the Duchesse.*	1051
Then when thou wert Protector to thy King.	1082
Queene. I see no reason, why a King of yeeres	1083
God and King *Henry* gouerne Englands Realme:	1085
Giue vp your Staffe, Sir, and the King his Realme.	1086
Farewell good King: when I am dead, and gone,	1092
Queene. Why now is *Henry* King, and *Margaret* Queen,	1095
*take my death, I neuer meant him any ill, nor the King,	1150
Sound a Senet. Enter King, Queene, Cardinall, Suffolke,	1292
As next the King, he was successiue Heire,	1343
Glost. All happinesse vnto my Lord the King:	1391
That Doyt that ere I wrested from the King,	1412
Glost. Ah, thus King *Henry* throwes away his Crutch,	1489
For good King *Henry,* thy decay I feare. *Exit Gloster.*	1494
The King will labour still to saue his Life,	1541
The King and all the Peeres are here at hand.	1701

KING cont.

Sound Trumpets. Enter the King, the Queene, | Cardinall, Suffolke,
Somerset, with | Attendants.   1706
The Duke was dumbe, and could not speake a word. | *King sounds.*   1728
* *Qu.* How fares my Lord? Helpe Lords, the King is | dead.   1730
With that dread King that tooke our state vpon him,   1858
* *Salisb.* Sirs stand apart, the King shall know your | minde.   1953
* *Commons within.* An answer from the King, my Lord | of Salisbury.   1982
Sent from a sort of Tinkers to the King.   1990
* *Within.* An answer from the King, or wee will all | breake in.   1991
Once by the King, and three times thrice by thee.   2073
Were by his side: Sometime, he calles the King,   2091
Qu. Go tell this heauy Message to the King. *Exit*   2096
*Now get thee hence, the King thou know'st is comming,   2103
Enter the King, Salisbury, and Warwicke, to the | Cardinal in bed.   2132
Obscure and lowsie Swaine, King *Henries* blood.   2218
Vnto the daughter of a worthlesse King,   2249
By shamefull murther of a guiltlesse King,   2263
And to conclude, Reproach and Beggerie, | Is crept into the Pallace of
our King,   2269
Saue to the God of heauen, and to my King: 2294
His body will I beare vnto the King: 2316
*Cheapside shall my Palfrey go to grasse: and when I am | King, as
King I will be.   2387
The King is mercifull, if you reuolt.   2445
But. Nay, 'tis too true, therefore he shall be King.   2467
*tell the King from me, that for his Fathers sake *Hen-| ry*   2476
Assaile them with the Army of the King.   2495
* *Enter the King with a Supplication, and the Queene with Suf-| folkes*   2530
Fight for your King, your Countrey, and your Liues,   2611
*and contrary to the King, his Crowne, and Dignity, thou   2670
Kent to maintaine, the King, the Realme and you,   2704
Because my Booke preferr'd me to the King.   2706
Know *Cade*, we come Ambassadors from the King   2783
Who loues the King, and will imbrace his pardon,   2790
All. God saue the King, God saue the King.   2795
Wee'l follow the King, and Clifford.   2831
And he that brings his head vnto the King,   2843
To reconcile you all vnto the King. *Exeunt omnes.*   2847
Sound Trumpets. Enter King, Queene, and | Somerset on the Tarras.   2848
King. Was euer King that ioy'd an earthly Throne,   2850
But I was made a King, at nine months olde.   2853
Was neuer Subiect long'd to be a King,   2854
All. God saue the King, God saue the King.   2874
*of the King by carrying my head to him, but Ile make   2932
Which I will beare in triumph to the King,   2988
To entertaine great Englands lawfull King.   2995
The king hath sent him sure: I must dissemble.   3005
I am farre better borne then is the king: 3020
More like a King, more Kingly in my thoughts.   3021
Is to remoue proud Somerset from the King,   3028
The King hath yeelded vnto thy demand: 3032
Enter King and Attendants.   3048
May passe into the presence of a King: 3059
A poore Esquire of Kent, that loues his King.   3069
False King, why hast thou broken faith with me,   3086
King did I call thee? No: thou art not King: 3088

KING *cont.*
Of Capitall Treason 'gainst the King and Crowne:	3102
Clif. Health, and all happinesse to my Lord the King.	3121
Clif. This is my King Yorke, I do not mistake,	3126
Makes him oppose himselfe against his King.	3130
I am thy King, and thou a false-heart Traitor:	3140
Enter King, Queene, and others.	3296
For (as I heare) the King is fled to London,	3346

KING = 56*21
KINGDOME = 1
By her I clayme the Kingdome:	1010

KINGDOMES = 1
And all the wealthy Kingdomes of the West,	161

KINGLY = 1
More like a King, more Kingly in my thoughts.	3021

KINGS = 7*4
In presence of the Kings of *France*, and *Sicill*,	13
I neuer read but Englands Kings haue had	135
*And in that Chaire where Kings & Queens wer crownd,	312
Let not her Penance exceede the Kings Commission.	1252
As place Duke *Humfrey* for the Kings Protector?	1552
Beuis. Nay more, the Kings Councell are no good | Workemen.	2333
*with the spirit of putting down Kings and Princes. Com-|mand silence.	2356
are hard by, with the Kings Forces.	2433
*it vp. Fellow-Kings, I tell you, that that Lord *Say* hath	2484
And you that be the Kings Friends follow me. *Exit.*	2501
This Tongue hath parlied vnto Forraigne Kings | For your behoofe.	2711

KINSMAN = 1
Our Kinsman *Gloster* is as innocent,	1363

KISSE = 5
Then this kinde kisse: O Lord, that lends me life,	26
Oh, could this kisse be printed in thy hand,	2058
Embrace, and kisse, and take ten thousand leaues,	2069
Let them kisse one another: For they lou'd well	2765
Haue them kisse. Away. *Exit*	2772

KISSES = 1
With twenty thousand kisses, and to draine	1844

KIST = 1*1
Hast thou not kist thy hand, and held my stirrop?	2221
*Thy lips that kist the Queene, shall sweepe the ground:	2243

KITE *see* kyte
KITES *see* kytes
KNAUE = 5*1
They say, A craftie Knaue do's need no Broker,	376
*Suffolke, for enclosing the Commons of Melforde. How | now, Sir Knaue?	406
Glost. A subtill Knaue, but yet it shall not serue:	845
The lying'st Knaue in Christendome.	871
Glost. Follow the Knaue, and take this Drab away.	907
*my Mans instigation, to proue him a Knaue, and my selfe	1148

KNAUERIE = 1
Humes Knauerie will be the Duchesse Wracke,	381

KNAUES = 1*1
To call them both a payre of craftie Knaues.	379
Yorke. Dispatch, this Knaues tongue begins to double.	1153

KNEE = 6*1
And humbly now vpon my bended knee,	17

KNEE *cont.*

Immediately he was vpon his Knee, 1305
And passeth by with stiffe vnbowed Knee, 1310
I would, false murd'rous Coward, on thy Knee 1925
If they can brooke I bow a knee to man: 3105
King. Why Warwicke, hath thy knee forgot to bow? 3161
For shame in dutie bend thy knee to me, 3173
KNEEL = *2

All kneel. Long liue Qu.(eene) *Margaret*, Englands happines. 44
King. They please vs well. Lord Marques kneel down, 68
KNEELD = 2

Where *Henrie* and Dame *Margaret* kneel'd to me, 313
Fed from my Trencher, kneel'd downe at the boord, 2225
KNEELE = 4*1

Then Father *Salisbury*, kneele we together, 1023
King. Iden, kneele downe, rise vp a Knight: 3072
Obey audacious Traitor, kneele for Grace. 3103
York. Wold'st haue me kneele? First let me ask of thee, 3104
We are thy Soueraigne *Clifford*, kneele againe; 3124
KNEES = 1*2

*knees he would be euen with me: I haue good witnesse 597
Stoope to the blocke, then these knees bow to any, 2293
*ere thou sleepe in thy Sheath, I beseech Ioue on my knees 2962
KNEW = 1

Butch. I knew her well, she was a Midwife. 2362
KNIFE = 2*1

From Treasons secret Knife, and Traytors Rage, 1474
Qu. Are you the Butcher, *Suffolk?* where's your Knife? 1899
Suff. I weare no Knife, to slaughter sleeping men, 1901
KNIGHT = 3*1

is but a Knight, is a? | *Mich.* No. 2436
Cade. To equall him I will make my selfe a knight, pre-|sently; 2438
He were created Knight for his good seruice. 3071
King. Iden, kneele downe, rise vp a Knight: 3072
KNIT = 2

Why doth the Great Duke *Humfrey* knit his browes, 276
Knit earth and heauen together. 3264
KNITS = 1

He knits his Brow, and shewes an angry Eye, 1309
KNOCKE = 2

Soul. Iacke Cade, Iacke Cade. | *Cade.* Knocke him downe there. *They*
kill him. 2623
kill and knocke downe, throw them into Thames: 2776
KNOW = 19*5

Hum. My Lord of Winchester I know your minde. 146
Bullin. Patience, good Lady, Wizards know their times: 635
They know their Master loues to be aloft, 727
Glost. Tell me Sirrha, what's my Name? | *Simpc.* Alas Master, I know
not. 862
Glost. What's his Name? | *Simpc.* I know not. 864
And for my Wife, I know not how it stands, 944
And him to Pumfret; where, as all you know, 985
Salisb. My Lord, breake we off; we know your minde | at full. 1043
We know the time since he was milde and affable, 1303
Suff. Nay *Gloster*, know that thou art come too soone, 1393
I know, their Complot is to haue my Life: 1447
I know, no paine they can inflict vpon him, 1683

KNOW *cont.*
  1. Runne to my Lord of Suffolke: let him know   1692
  What know I how the world may deeme of me?   1765
  Salisb. Sirs stand apart, the King shall know your | minde.   1953
  So get thee gone, that I may know my greefe,   2061
  1.*Gent.* What is my ransome Master, let me know.   2184
  Kin. Oh gracelesse men: they know not what they do.   2574
  Know *Cade*, we come Ambassadors from the King   2783
  I know thee not, why then should I betray thee?   2936
  To know the reason of these Armes in peace.   3010
  I know ere they will haue me go to Ward,   3107
  Might I but know thee by thy housed Badge.   3201
  Yorke. I know our safety is to follow them,   3345
KNOWES = 7*1
  This was my dreame, what it doth bode God knowes.   305
  Glost. Why *Suffolke*, England knowes thine insolence.   750
  Simpc. God knowes of pure Deuotion,   822
  But how he dyed, God knowes, not *Henry*:   1833
  that speakes he knowes not what.   2472
  Nor knowes he how to liue, but by the spoile,   2816
  Let them obey, that knowes not how to Rule.   2997
  God knowes how long it is I haue to liue: ,3339
KNOWING = 3
  They (knowing Dame *Elianors* aspiring humor)   373
  Knowing that thou wouldst haue me drown'd on shore   1795
  Knowing how hardly I can brooke abuse?   3087
KNOWLEDGE = 1
  Knowledge the Wing wherewith we flye to heauen.   2708
KNOWN = *1
  Glost. Why 'tis well known, that whiles I was Protector,   1424
KNOWNE = 4*1
  'Tis knowne to you he is mine enemy: 155
  If they were knowne, as the suspect is great,   526
  Thou might'st as well haue knowne all our Names,   873
  For it is knowne we were but hollow Friends: 1766
  France? Be it knowne vnto thee by these presence, euen   2663
KNOWST = *2
  King. Why then, thou know'st what Colour Iet is | of?   856
  *Now get thee hence, the King thou know'st is comming,   2103
KYTE = 3
  To guard the Chicken from a hungry Kyte,   1551
  Although the Kyte soare with vnbloudied Beake?   1897
  Is *Beauford* tearm'd a Kyte? where are his Tallons?   1900
KYTES = 1
  And made a prey for Carrion Kytes and Crowes   3230
LA *l.**51 304 2214 3249 = 3*1
LABOR = 1
  Behooues it vs to labor for the Realme.   190
LABORING = 1
  My Brayne, more busie then the laboring Spider,   1645
LABOUR = 3*1
  While these do labour for their owne preferment,   189
  The King will labour still to saue his Life,   1541
  My thoughts, that labour to perswade my soule,   1839
  Hol. True: and yet it is said, Labour in thy Vocati-|on: 2335
LABOURING = 1*1
  Being all descended to the labouring heart,   1867

LABOURING   *cont.*
*which is as much to say, as let the Magistrates be la-|bouring   2336
LABOURS = 1
And shall these Labours, and these Honours dye?   102
LACES = 1
But. She was indeed a Pedlers daughter, & sold many | Laces.   2364
LACIES = 1
Cade. My wife descended of the *Lacies.*   2363
LACKING = 1
haue a License to kill for a hundred lacking one.   2519
LACKT = 1
'Twas men I lackt, and you will giue them me;   1651
LADIES = 1*1
And stol'st away the Ladies hearts of France;   438
*She sweepes it through the Court with troups of Ladies,   463
LADY = 8*3
espouse the Lady Margaret, daughter vnto Reignier King of   53
Bullin. Patience, good Lady, Wizards know their times: 635
With him, the Husband of this louely Lady: 703
Of Lady *Elianor*, the Protectors Wife,   921
Your Lady is forth-comming, yet at London.   931
His Lady banisht, and a Limbe lopt off.   1098
Glost. Must you, Sir *Iohn*, protect my Lady here?   1256
Stanley. Like to a Duchesse, and Duke *Humfreyes* Lady,   1278
And you, my Soueraigne Lady, with the rest,   1461
Suff. Hath he not twit our Soueraigne Lady here   1478
If euer Lady wrong'd her Lord so much,   1916
LADYSHIP = 1
her Ladyship behold and heare our Exorcismes?   623
LAID = 2*1
Some violent hands were laid on *Humfries* life: 1840
I do beleeue that violent hands were laid   1860
*the Country is laid for me: but now am I so hungry, that   2909
LAKE = *1
Bulling. Discend to Darknesse, and the burning Lake: 666
LAMBE = 3*1
The Fox barkes not, when he would steale the Lambe.   1349
As is the sucking Lambe, or harmelesse Doue: 1365
Is he a Lambe? his Skinne is surely lent him,   1371
*thing, that of the skin of an innocent Lambe should   2396
LAME = 2
Card. What, art thou lame? | *Simpc.* I, God Almightie helpe me.   830
Suff. True: made the Lame to leape and flye away.   913
LAMENTABLE = *1
Cade. Nay, that I meane to do. Is not this a lamenta-|ble   2395
LAMENTING = 1
King. How now Madam? | Still lamenting and mourning for Suffolkes
death?   2554
LAMENTS = 1
Yet he most Christian-like laments his death: 1758
LANCASTER = 7
Nor shall proud Lancaster vsurpe my right,   256
To grapple with the house of Lancaster,   269
Was *Iohn* of Gaunt, the Duke of Lancaster;   973
Till *Henry Bullingbrooke*, Duke of Lancaster,   980
Thus got the House of *Lancaster* the Crowne.   988
With heart-blood of the House of *Lancaster*:   1032

LANCASTER *cont.*
  Suf. The honourable blood of Lancaster   2219
LAND = 9*1
  Your greefe, the common greefe of all the Land.   84
  Then all the Princes in the Land beside,   183
  While they do tend the profit of the Land.   212
  War. So God helpe Warwicke, as he loues the Land,   213
  Did neuer Traytor in the Land commit.   569
  And thou a Prince, Protector of this Land;   1205
  And he a Prince, and Ruler of the Land: 1219
  And Equitie exil'd your Highnesse Land.   1446
  And threw it towards thy Land: The Sea receiu'd it,   1808
  'Tis not the Land I care for, wer't thou thence,   2074
LANDS = 5
  While his owne Lands are bargain'd for, and sold: 243
  and Lands, and Wife and all, from me.   403
  Was better worth then all my Fathers Lands,   472
  My earnest-gaping-sight of thy Lands view,   1805
  Lands, Goods, Horse, Armor, any thing I haue   3044
LANGLEY = 2
  The fift, was *Edmond Langley*, Duke of Yorke;   974
  Who was to *Edmond Langley*, | *Edward* the thirds fift Sonnes Sonne;   1008
LANGUAGE = 1
  For he is fierce, and cannot brooke hard Language.   2899
LANKE = 1
  Are lanke and leane with thy Extortions.   519
LANTHORNE = 1
  And God shall be my hope, my stay, my guide, | And Lanthorne to my
  feete: 1079
LAP = 1
  But like a pleasant slumber in thy lap?   2107
LARGE = 4
  Vnto the poore King *Reignier*, whose large style   118
  Large summes of Gold, and Dowries with their wiues,   136
  As more at large your Grace shall vnderstand.   929
  Large gifts haue I bestow'd on learned Clearkes,   2705
LAST = 8*2
  And would haue kept, so long as breath did last: 222
  Be my last breathing in this mortall world.   294
  Well, so it stands: and thus I feare at last,   380
  So one by one wee'le weed them all at last,   485
  Last time I danc't attendance on his will,   566
  *Combat, shall be the last of the next moneth. Come   616
  William of Windsor was the seuenth, and last.   976
  *you, for I thinke I haue taken my last Draught in this   1134
  *one and twenty Fifteenes, and one shilling to the pound, | the last
  Subsidie.   2655
  And the premised Flames of the Last day,   3263
LATE = 5*1
  Early and late, debating too and fro   98
  Thy late exploits done in the heart of France,   204
  As for the Duke of Yorke, this late Complaint   483
  How insolent of late he is become,   1301
  Weauer. But now of late, not able to trauell with her   2366
  The fearfull French, whom you late vanquished   2819
LATH = 1
  Lath, they haue bene vp these two dayes.   2321

LATINE = *1
*Cade. Away with him, away with him, he speaks La-|tine. 2690
LAUGH = 3
Queene. It made me laugh, to see the Villaine runne. 906
And when I start, the enuious people laugh, 1211
You vse her well: the World may laugh againe, 1260
LAUGHING = 1
With enuious Lookes laughing at thy shame, 1183
LAW = 13*2
Buck. Thy Crueltie in execution | Vpon Offendors, hath exceeded Law, 522
And left thee to the mercy of the Law. 524
Proue them, and I lye open to the Law: 551
Let him haue all the rigor of the Law. 593
King. Vnckle, what shall we say to this in law? 600
This is the Law, and this Duke Humfreyes doome. 607
And giue her as a Prey to Law and Shame, 950
Receiue the Sentence of the Law for sinne, 1056
Glost. Elianor, the Law thou seest hath iudged thee, 1069
I cannot iustifie whom the Law condemnes: 1070
But I in danger for the breach of Law. 1242
Card. Did he not, contrary to forme of Law, 1352
'Tis meet he be condemn'd by course of Law. 1539
*Iohn. Masse 'twill be sore Law then, for he was thrust 2642
*Smith. Nay Iohn, it wil be stinking Law, for his breath | stinkes with
eating toasted cheese. 2644
LAWES = 1*2
*But. Onely that the Lawes of England may come out | of your mouth. 2640
*breake into his Sonne in Lawes house, Sir Iames Cromer, 2743
And with the same to acte controlling Lawes: 3098
LAWFULL = 1
To entertaine great Englands lawfull King. 2995
LAWYERS = 2
But. The first thing we do, let's kill all the Lawyers. 2394
All Schollers, Lawyers, Courtiers, Gentlemen, 2572
LAY = 3*3
*Yorke. Lay hands vpon these Traytors, and their trash: 671
Lay not thy hands on me: forbeare I say, 1746
*Ma. A thousand Crownes, or else lay down your head 2185
Mark'd for the Gallowes: Lay your Weapons downe, 2443
*I see them lay their heades together to surprize 2835
Yor. A dreadfull lay, addresse thee instantly. 3248
LAYD = 5
As I haue read, layd clayme vnto the Crowne, 1001
But mightier Crimes are lay'd vnto your charge, 1434
Causelesse haue lay'd disgraces on my head, 1462
I, all of you haue lay'd your heads together, 1465
Haue you layd faire the Bed? Is all things well, 1702
LAYES = 2
That she will light to listen to the Layes, 476
That layes strong siege vnto this wretches soule, 2156
LAYING = 1
Whitm. I lost mine eye in laying the prize aboord, 2194
LEADE = 3
Goe, leade the way, I long to see my Prison. Exeunt. 1291
To Ireland will you leade a Band of men, 1617
Or let a rabble leade you to your deaths. 2789

LEADER = 2
The Ring-leader and Head of all this Rout, 922
That want their Leader, scatter vp and downe, 1828
LEAGUE = 2
O Peeres of England, shamefull is this League, 105
Before I would haue yeelded to this League. 134
LEANE = 1
Are lanke and leane with thy Extortions. 519
LEANE-FACD = 1
As leane-fac'd enuy in her loathsome caue. 2030
LEANNESSE = 1
Agrees not with the leannesse of his purse. 119
LEAPE = 1*2
*leape me ouer this Stoole, and runne away. 891
*Sirrha Beadle, whippe him till he leape ouer that same | Stoole. 896
Suff. True: made the Lame to leape and flye away. 913
LEAPER = 1
I am no loathsome Leaper, looke on me. 1775
LEAPES = 1
After the Beadle hath hit him once, he leapes ouer 902
LEARNE = *1
**King*. Come wife, let's in, and learne to gouern better, 2902
LEARNED = 2
With all the Learned Counsell of the Realme, 96
Large gifts haue I bestow'd on learned Clearkes, 2705
LEARNT = 1
hath learnt so much fence already. 1139
LEASE = *1
*if I might haue a Lease of my life for a thousand yeares, I 2910
LEAST = 5
And grumbling *Yorke*: and not the least of these, 456
The least of all these signes were probable. 1882
Least being suffer'd in that harmefull slumber, 1974
Least they consult about the giuing vp 2767
Clif. Take heede least by your heate you burne your | selues: 3159
LEATHER = 1*1
**Hol*. The Nobilitie thinke scorne to goe in Leather | Aprons. 2331
**Beuis*. Hee shall haue the skinnes of our enemies, to | make Dogges
Leather of. 2342
LEAUE = 14*10
Suff. Resigne it then, and leaue thine insolence. 512
Suff. Before we make election, giue me leaue 557
*and so I pray you goe in Gods Name, and leaue vs. | *Exit Hume*. 628
**Buck*. Your Grace shal giue me leaue, my Lord of York, 707
Yet by your leaue, the Winde was very high, 719
**Glost*. Ambitious Church-man, leaue to afflict my heart: 934
Our simple Supper ended, giue me leaue, 961
I beseech your Maiestie giue me leaue to goe; 1074
And euen as willingly at thy feete I leaue it, 1090
**Salisb*. Come, leaue your drinking, and fall to blowes. 1140
My *Nell*, I take my leaue: and Master Sherife, 1251
Qu. But I can giue the loser leaue to chide. 1482
And well such losers may haue leaue to speake. 1485
**Queene*. What, will your Highnesse leaue the Parlia-|ment? 1497
And let thy *Suffolke* take his heauie leaue. 2020
Suf. You bad me ban, and will you bid me leaue? 2048
**Wal*. Thou shalt haue cause to feare before I leaue thee. 2286

LEAVE *cont.*
We will not leaue one Lord, one Gentleman:	2504
*you should leaue me at the White-heart in Southwarke.	2800
*to an hundred mischiefes, and makes them leaue mee de-|solate.	2834
*for a stray, for entering his Fee-simple without leaue. A	2930
*fiue men, and if I doe not leaue you all as dead as a doore	2944
Should raise so great a power without his leaue?	3013
It greeues my soule to leaue thee vnassail'd. *Exit War.*	3238

LEAVES = 3
And Caterpillers eate my Leaues away:	1387
Embrace, and kisse, and take ten thousand leaues,	2069
That keepes his leaues inspight of any storme,	3206

LEAVING = 1
Leauing thy trunke for Crowes to feed vpon. *Exit.*	2989

LED = 2
Me thinkes I should not thus be led along,	1206
Three times bestrid him: Thrice I led him off,	3330

LEFT = 5
And left thee to the mercy of the Law.	524
And left behinde him *Richard*, his onely Sonne,	978
Left I the Court, to see this Quarrell try'de.	1109
But left that hatefull office vnto thee.	1793
This small inheritance my Father left me,	2923

LEGGE = 1
Thy legge a sticke compared with this Truncheon,	2953

LEGGES = 3*1
That could restore this Cripple to his Legges againe.	880
Glost. Well Sir, we must haue you finde your Legges.	895
Before his Legges be firme to beare his Body.	1490
Hath clapt his taile, betweene his legges and cride,	3153

LEND = 1
Lend me a heart repleate with thankfulnesse:	27

LENDS = 1
Then this kinde kisse: O Lord, that lends me life,	26

LENGTHEN = 1
What, is't too short? Ile lengthen it with mine,	285

LENT = 1*1
Is he a Lambe? his Skinne is surely lent him,	1371
*the Lent shall bee as long againe as it is, and thou shalt	2518

LES *l*.3249 = 1

LESSE = 2
And goe in peace, *Humfrey*, no lesse belou'd,	1081
Cade. And to speake truth, thou deseru'st no lesse.	2521

LESSER = 1
Set limbe to limbe, and thou art farre the lesser:	2951

LEST *see* least

LET = 62*9
Come, let vs in, and with all speede prouide | To see her Coronation be perform'd.	78
Looke to it Lords, let not his smoothing words	163
Yet let vs watch the haughtie Cardinall,	181
Away from me, and let me heare no more.	324
to his Lordship? Let me see them: what is thine?	400
Away, base Cullions: *Suffolke* let them goe.	426
So let her rest: and Madame list to me,	478
Then let him be deny'd the Regent-ship.	494
Let *Yorke* be Regent, I will yeeld to him.	496

LET *cont.*

Card. Ambitious *Warwicke*, let thy betters speake.	499
Let him haue all the rigor of the Law.	593
Let *Somerset* be Regent o're the French,	602
And let these haue a day appointed them	604
*Earth; *Iohn Southwell* reade you, and let vs to our worke.	631
Spirit. Let him shun Castles,	662
Away with them, let them be clapt vp close,	680
Let him shunne Castles,	696
Card. Let me be blessed for the Peace I make	755
I pray my Lords let me compound this strife.	783
Let neuer Day nor Night vnhallowed passe,	817
Let me see thine Eyes; winck now, now open them,	846
Glost. Let the(m) be whipt through euery Market Towne,	909
This Staffe of Honor raught, there let it stand,	1099
Yorke. Lords, let him goe. Please it your Maiestie,	1103
Here let them end it, and God defend the right.	1111
Armorer. Let it come yfaith, and Ile pledge you all, | and a figge for	
Peter.	1127
Gloster. No, stirre not for your liues, let her passe | by.	1193
Let not her Penance exceede the Kings Commission.	1252
No: let him dye, in that he is a Fox,	1559
Let pale-fac't feare keepe with the meane-borne man,	1641
1. Runne to my Lord of Suffolke: let him know	1692
Qu. Oh *Henry*, let me pleade for gentle *Suffolke.*	2003
And let thy *Suffolke* take his heauie leaue.	2020
Where byting cold would neuer let grasse grow,	2052
Qu. Oh, let me intreat thee cease, giue me thy hand,	2054
Nor let the raine of heauen wet this place,	2056
Oh let me stay, befall what may befall.	2119
To France sweet Suffolke: Let me heare from thee:	2122
So thou wilt let me liue, and feele no paine.	2138
Sal. Disturbe him not, let him passe peaceably.	2159
And let vs all to Meditation. *Exeunt.*	2167
1.*Gent.* What is my ransome Master, let me know.	2184
Lieu. Be not so rash, take ransome, let him liue.	2197
Yet let not this make thee be bloody-minded,	2205
Remember it, and let it make thee Crest-falne,	2227
Lieu. First let my words stab him, as he hath me.	2234
With humble suite: no, rather let my head	2292
Lieu. Hale him away, and let him talke no more:	2299
Therefore come you with vs, and let him go. | *Exit Lieutenant, and the*	
rest.	2310
Wal. There let his head, and liuelesse bodie lye,	2313
*which is as much to say, as let the Magistrates be la-|bouring	2336
Cade. Let me alone: Dost thou vse to write thy name?	2419
the Gaoles, and let out the Prisoners.	2527
Cade. Marry, thou ought'st not to let thy horse weare	2682
O let me liue. | *Cade.* I feele remorse in my selfe with his words: but	2737
Let them kisse one another: For they lou'd well	2765
Or let a rabble leade you to your deaths.	2789
*to the Nobility. Let them breake your backes with bur-|thens,	2804
Let this my sword report what speech forbeares.	2958
*O I am slaine, Famine and no other hath slaine me, let ten	2965
Let them obey, that knowes not how to Rule.	2997
And let my Soueraigne, vertuous *Henry*,	3040
Oh let me view his Visage being dead,	3063

LET *cont.*

And let thy tongue be equall with thy heart.	3084
York. Wold'st haue me kneele? First let me ask of thee,	3104
Clif. He is a Traitor, let him to the Tower,	3131
Yorke. So let it helpe me now against thy sword,	3245
Hot Coales of Vengeance. Let no Souldier flye.	3258
The name of Valour. O let the vile world end,	3262
Now let the generall Trumpet blow his blast,	3265
Let vs pursue him ere the Writs go forth.	3348

LETS = 7*3

Salisbury. Then lets make hast away,	217
1.Pet. My Masters, let's stand close, my Lord Pro-|tector	386
All. Come, let's be gone. *Exit.*	427
Now pray my Lord, let's see the Deuils Writ.	687
Hol. Come, come, let's fall in with them.	2349
But. The first thing we do, let's kill all the Lawyers.	2394
Cade. Feare not that I warrant thee. Come, let's .march | towards London. *Exeunt.*	2528
Cade. Come, then let's go fight with them:	2629
Come, let's away. *Exeunt omnes.*	2632
King. Come wife, let's in, and learne to gouern better,	2902

LETTERS = *2

Wea. Ha's a Booke in his pocket with red Letters in't	2408
But. They vse to writ it on the top of Letters: 'Twill | go hard with you.	2417

LEUELL = 1

By false accuse doth leuell at my Life.	1460

LEUIE = 1

Leuie great summes of Money through the Realme,	1355

LEWDLY = 1

A sort of naughtie persons, lewdly bent,	919

LIBERALL = 1

The People Liberall, Valiant, Actiue, Wealthy,	2697

LIBERTIE = 1

Yor. How now? is Somerset at libertie?	3082

LIBERTY = 1

Now shew your selues men, 'tis for Liberty.	2503

LICENSE = 1

haue a License to kill for a hundred lacking one.	2519

LIE *see* lye

LIEFEST = 2

With you mine *Alder liefest* Soueraigne,	35
My liefest Liege to be mine Enemie:	1464

LIEGE = 8

Pardon, my Liege, that I haue stay'd so long.	1392
My liefest Liege to be mine Enemie:	1464
Card. My Liege, his rayling is intollerable.	1472
As *Humfrey* prou'd by Reasons to my Liege.	1562
I tender so the safetie of my Liege.	1579
War. That shall I do my Liege; Stay Salsburie	1836
Buc. A Messenger from *Henry*, our dread Liege,	3009
And neuer liue but true vnto his Liege.	3076

LIES *see* lyes

LIEU = 8*2

LIEUTENANT *see also Lieu.* = 2

Enter Lieutenant, Suffolke, and others.	2169

LIEUTENANT cont.
   Therefore come you with vs, and let him go. | *Exit Lieutenant, and the*
   rest.   2310

LIFE = 32*2
   Then this kinde kisse: O Lord, that lends me life,   26
   A man that ne're saw in his life before.   792
   Simpc. But that in all my life, when I was a youth.   838
   *Damsons, and made me climbe, with danger of my | Life.   843
   Wife. Neuer before this day, in all his life.   861
   Demanding of King *Henries* Life and Death,   927
   Despoyled of your Honor in your Life,   1063
   Vpon my Life began her diuellish practises: 1340
   I know, their Complot is to haue my Life: 1447
   By false accuse doth leuell at my Life.   1460
   And all to make away my guiltlesse Life.   1467
   Doe seeke subuersion of thy harmelesse Life.   1509
   The King will labour still to saue his Life,   1541
   The Commons haply rise, to saue his Life;   1542
   I rather would haue lost my Life betimes,   1600
   In life, but double death, now *Gloster's* dead.   1755
   Or blood-consuming sighes recall his Life;   1761
   Some violent hands were laid on *Humfries* life: 1840
   For seeing him, I see my life in death.   1856
   Vpon the life of this thrice-famed Duke.   1861
   And tugg'd for Life, and was by strength subdude.   1877
   They say is shamefully bereft of life.   1981
   The World shall not be Ransome for thy Life.   2011
   Yet now farewell, and farewell Life with thee.   2071
   I can no more: Liue thou to ioy thy life;   2080
   King. Ah, what a signe it is of euill life,   2139
   War. So bad a death, argues a monstrous life.   2164
   1.*Gent.* Ile giue it sir, and therefore spare my life.   2192
   Hol. And Smith the Weauer. | *Beu.* Argo, their thred of life is spun. 2347
   Yet to recouer them would loose my life: 2700
   *well for his life. Away with him, he ha's a Familiar vn-|der 2740
   And therefore yet relent, and saue my life.   2750
   Expect your Highnesse doome of life, or death.   2864
   *if I might haue a Lease of my life for a thousand yeares, I 2910

LIFT = 1
   Wee'l both together lift our heads to heauen,   287

LIGHT = 3*2
   That she will light to listen to the Layes,   476
   Giues Light in Darknesse, Comfort in Despaire.   794
   No: Darke shall be my Light, and Night my Day.   1216
   *Which time will bring to light in smooth Duke *Humfrey.* 1359
   *make shift for one, and so Gods Cursse light vppon you | all. 2807

LIGHTENS = 1
   Bullingbrooke or Southwell reades, Coniuro | te, &c. *It Thunders and*
   Lightens   644

LIGHTLY = *1
   Cade. Was euer Feather so lightly blowne too & fro,   2832

LIGHTNING = 1
   False Fiend auoide. | *Thunder and Lightning. Exit Spirit.* 667

LIKE = 47*8
   Did beare him like a Noble Gentleman: 192
   More like a Souldier then a man o'th'Church,   194
   Sweare like a Ruffian, and demeane himselfe   196

LIKE *cont.*

Still reuelling like Lords till all be gone,	236
Whose Church-like humors fits not for a Crowne.	259
Elia. Why droopes my Lord like ouer-ripen'd Corn,	274
More like an Empresse, then Duke *Humphreyes* Wife:	464
Shee'le hamper thee, and dandle thee like a Baby:	537
Suff. No maruell, and it like your Maiestie,	725
An't like your Lordly Lords Protectorship.	749
Suff. What Woman is this? | *Wife.* His Wife, and't like your Worship.	808
Simpc. At Barwick in the North, and't like your | Grace.	813
'Tis like, my Lord, you will not keepe your houre.	933
As like to Pytch, defile Nobilitie;	948
Should be to be protected like a Child,	1084
Stanley. Like to a Duchesse, and Duke *Humfreyes* Lady,	1278
Like to the glorious Sunnes transparant Beames,	1659
Were almost like a sharpe-quill'd Porpentine:	1669
Him capre vpright, like a wilde Morisco,	1671
Full often, like a shag-hayr'd craftie Kerne,	1673
Say that he thriue, as 'tis great like he will,	1685
Yet he most Christian-like laments his death:	1758
What? Art thou like the Adder waxen deafe?	1776
Am I not witcht like her? Or thou not false like him?	1819
The Commons like an angry Hiue of Bees	1827
Staring full gastly, like a strangled man:	1874
Like to the Summers Corne by Tempest lodged:	1880
Tis like you would not feast him like a friend,	1888
Suff. 'Tis like the Commons, rude vnpolisht Hindes,	1984
Mine eyes should sparkle like the beaten Flint,	2032
And these dread curses like the Sunne 'gainst glasse,	2045
Or like an ouer-charged Gun, recoile,	2046
But like a pleasant slumber in thy lap?	2107
Like Lime-twigs set to catch my winged soule:	2150
Therefore, when Merchant-like I sell reuenge,	2210
And like ambitious Sylla ouer-gorg'd,	2252
Beuis. Then is sin strucke downe like an Oxe, and ini-|quities throate cut like a Calfe.	2345
*apparrell them all in one Liuery, that they may agree like	2392
*Or hast thou a marke to thy selfe, like a honest plain dea-|ling man?	2420
Cade. They fell before thee like Sheepe and Oxen, &	2515
Rul'd like a wandering Plannet ouer me,	2548
Iohn. Then we are like to haue biting Statutes	2649
Like to a Ship, that hauing scap'd a Tempest,	2886
*thee eate Iron like an Ostridge, and swallow my Sword	2933
like a great pin ere thou and I part.	2934
And like a Theefe to come to rob my grounds:	2938
And now like *Aiax Telamonius,*	3018
More like a King, more Kingly in my thoughts.	3021
Iden. I was, an't like your Maiesty.	3066
Whose Smile and Frowne, like to *Achilles* Speare	3095
And like a Gallant, in the brow of youth,	3324
And like rich hangings in a homely house,	3333

LIKELY = 1

1.*Cit.* No my Lord, nor likely to be slaine:	2601

LIKING = 1

As being thought to contradict your liking,	1964

LIMBE = 3

His Lady banisht, and a Limbe lopt off.	1098

LIMBE *cont.*

Set limbe to limbe, and thou art farre the lesser: 2951
LIMD *see* lym'd
LIME-TWIGS = 1

Like Lime-twigs set to catch my winged soule: 2150
LINE = 1

From whose Line I clayme the Crowne,   995
LINGER = 1

Buc. Then linger not my Lord, away, take horse.   2591
LINGRING = 1

And torture him with grieuous lingring death.   1959
LION *see* lyon
LIONEL = 2

Lionel, Duke of Clarence; next to whom,   972
Who marryed *Phillip*, sole Daughter | Vnto *Lionel*, Duke of Clarence.   1013
LIONELS = 1

Till *Lionels* Issue fayles, his should not reigne.   1020
LIPPES = 1

To haue thee with thy lippes to stop my mouth: 2113
LIPS = 3*1

Seale vp your Lips, and giue no words but Mum,   365
Faine would I go to chafe his palie lips,   1843
Dying with mothers dugge betweene it's lips.   2110
*Thy lips that kist the Queene, shall sweepe the ground: 2243
LIQUID = 1

Might liquid teares, or heart-offending groanes,   1760
LIST = 2

But list to me my *Humfrey*, my sweete Duke: 309
So let her rest: and Madame list to me,   478
LISTEN = 2

That she will light to listen to the Layes,   476
And listen after *Humfrey*, how he proceedes: 542
LISTS *see also* lysts = 1

The Armorer and his Man, to enter the Lists,   1106
LITTLE = 3

Will make but little for his benefit: 484
To shew some reason, of no little force,   558
And *Humfrey* is no little Man in England.   1314
LIUD = 1

And then it liu'd in sweete Elizium.   2116
LIUE = 23*5

All kneel. Long liue Qu.(eene) *Margaret*, Englands happines.   44
Shall I not liue to be aueng'd on her?   468
Warw. Warwicke may liue to be the best of all.   502
But him out-liue, and dye a violent death.   658
But him out-liue, and dye a violent death.   690
Both. Long liue our Soueraigne *Richard*, Englands | King.   1027
Richard shall liue to make the Earle of Warwick   1048
Liue in your Countrey here, in Banishment,   1065
And I may liue to doe you kindnesse, if you doe it her.   1261
For *Henry* weepes, that thou dost liue so long.   1821
War. As surely as my soule intends to liue   1857
I can no more: Liue thou to ioy thy life;   2080
Suf. If I depart from thee, I cannot liue,   2105
So thou wilt let me liue, and feele no paine.   2138
Can I make men liue where they will or no?   2144
Lieu. Be not so rash, take ransome, let him liue.   2197

LIUE *cont.*

And liue alone as secret as I may.	2584
*that cause they haue beene most worthy to liue. Thou	2679
O let me liue. | *Cade. I feele remorse in my selfe with his words: but	2737
*all Recreants and Dastards, and delight to liue in slauerie	2803
Nor knowes he how to liue, but by the spoile,	2816
Wer't not a shame, that whilst you liue at iarre,	2818
*Iden. Lord, who would liue turmoyled in the Court,	2921
Ile send them all as willing as I liue:	3043
Iden. May Iden liue to merit such a bountie,	3075
And neuer liue but true vnto his Liege.	3076
Away for your releefe, and we will liue	3316
God knowes how long it is I haue to liue:	3339

LIUED = 1

His eye-balles further out, than when he liued,	1873

LIUELESSE = 1

Wal. There let his head, and liuelesse bodie lye,	2313

LIUERY = 1*1

*apparrell them all in one Liuery, that they may agree like	2392
To loose thy youth in peace, and to atcheeue | The Siluer Liuery of	
aduised Age,	3268

LIUES = 5*1

Spirit. The Duke yet liues, that Henry shall depose:	657
The Duke yet liues, that Henry shall depose:	689
*Gloster. No, stirre not for your liues, let her passe | by.	1193
The liues of those which we haue lost in fight,	2190
Fight for your King, your Countrey, and your Liues,	2611
Souldiers, this day haue you redeem'd your liues,	2867

LIUING = 3

So will the Queene, that liuing, held him deere.	2318
That liuing wrought me such exceeding trouble.	3064
But then, Aeneas bare a liuing loade;	3286

LIUST = 1

My selfe no ioy in nought, but that thou liu'st.	2081

LIZARDS *see also* lyzards

LOAD = 2

Hanging the head at Ceres plenteous load?	275
The enuious Load that lyes vpon his heart:	1457

LOADE = 1

But then, Aeneas bare a liuing loade;	3286

LOATHER = 1

Loather a hundred times to part then dye;	2070

LOATHSOME = 2

I am no loathsome Leaper, looke on me.	1775
As leane-fac'd enuy in her loathsome caue.	2030

LOAUES = *1

*halfe peny Loaues sold for a peny: the three hoop'd pot,	2384

LOBBY = 1

How in our voyding Lobby hast thou stood,	2229

LOCKT = 2

And he but naked, though lockt vp in Steele,	1940
Suf. A Iewell lockt into the wofulst Caske,	2127

LODGE = 1

Did he so often lodge in open field:	87

LODGED = 1

Like to the Summers Corne by Tempest lodged:	1880

LOE = 1
Loe, I present your Grace a Traitors head,   3060
LOFTIE = *1
*Suff. Thus droupes this loftie Pyne, & hangs his sprayes,   1101
LOFTY = 1
And lofty proud incroaching tyranny,   2264
LONDON = 10*2
Your Lady is forth-comming, yet at London.   931
To morrow toward London, back againe,   953
*London, where we will haue the Maiors sword born be-|fore vs.   2524
*Cade. Feare not that I warrant thee. Come, let's march | towards
London. Exeunt.   2528
Enter Iacke Cade and the rest, and strikes his | staffe on London stone.   2613
And heere sitting vpon London Stone,   2616
But first, go and set London Bridge on fire,   2630
*my sword therefore broke through London gates, that   2799
I see them Lording it in London streets,   2822
We shall to London get, where you are lou'd,   3308
For (as I heare) the King is fled to London,   3346
Sound Drumme and Trumpets, and to London all,   3354
LONDON-BRIDGE = 1
Mess. Iacke Cade hath gotten London-bridge.   2586
LONG = 20*3
*All kneel. Long liue Qu.(eene) Margaret, Englands happines.   44
Studied so long, sat in the Councell house,   97
I prophesied, France will be lost ere long. Exit Humfrey.   153
And would haue kept, so long as breath did last: 222
What, hast thou beene long blinde, and now restor'd?   805
Glost. How long hast thou beene blinde? | Simpc. O borne so, Master.   835
King. O God, seest thou this, and bearest so long?   905
Salisb. My Lord, I long to heare it at full.   965
*Both. Long liue our Soueraigne Richard, Englands | King.   1027
So long as I am loyall, true, and crimelesse.   1239
Goe, leade the way, I long to see my Prison. Exeunt.   1291
But I will remedie this geare ere long,   1388
Pardon, my Liege, that I haue stay'd so long.   1392
He neuer would haue stay'd in France so long.   1598
By staying there so long, till all were lost.   1602
And fought so long, till that his thighes with Darts   1668
For Henry weepes, that thou dost liue so long.   1821
Lieu. Conuey him hence, and on our long boats side,   2236
*the Lent shall bee as long againe as it is, and thou shalt   2518
Say. Long sitting to determine poore mens causes,   2721
As I do long and wish to be a Subiect.   2855
Then Yorke vnloose thy long imprisoned thoughts,   3083
God knowes how long it is I haue to liue: 3339
LONGD = 1
Was neuer Subiect long'd to be a King,   2854
LONGER = 2*1
I see thy furie: If I longer stay,   150
But three dayes longer, on the paine of death.   2002
*could stay no longer. Wherefore on a Bricke wall haue   2911
LOOKE = 19*4
Looke to it Lords, let not his smoothing words   163
And looke vnto the maine.   218
*Duch. Against her will, good King? looke to't in time,   536
And looke thy selfe be faultlesse, thou wert best.   941

LOOKE *cont.*

To looke into this Businesse thorowly,	954
Now thou do'st Penance too. Looke how they gaze,	1196
Trowest thou, that ere Ile looke vpon the World,	1214
And if we did but glance a farre-off Looke,	1304
Looke after him, and cannot doe him good:	1520
Looke not vpon me, for thine eyes are wounding;	1751
Looke pale as Prim-rose with blood-drinking sighes,	1763
I am no loathsome Leaper, looke on me.	1775
Looke on the sheets his haire (you see) is sticking,	1878
Ile giue a thousand pound to looke vpon him.	2147
*Combe downe his haire; looke, looke, it stands vpright,	2149
Looke with a gentle eye vpon this Wretch,	2154
Suf. Looke on my George, I am a Gentleman,	2198
But who can cease to weepe, and looke on this.	2536
*broach'd, and beard thee to. Looke on mee well, I haue	2942
Nay, do not fright vs with an angry looke:	3123
Yorke. Looke in a Glasse, and call thy Image so.	3139
But Noble as he is, looke where he comes.	3335

LOOKES = 3

With enuious Lookes laughing at thy shame,	1183
Ah *Gloster*, hide thee from their hatefull lookes,	1199
See if thou canst out-face me with thy lookes:	2950

LOOKING = 1

Looking the way her harmelesse young one went,	1516

LOOKST = 1

How now? why look'st thou pale? why tremblest thou?	1723

LOOSD = 1

And he that loos'd them forth their Brazen Caues,	1789

LOOSE = 3

Shall loose his head for his presumption.	308
Yet to recouer them would loose my life:	2700
To loose thy youth in peace, and to atcheeue | The Siluer Liuery of	
aduised Age, •	3268

LOOSING = 1

For loosing ken of *Albions* wished Coast.	1813

LOPT = 1

His Lady banisht, and a Limbe lopt off.	1098

LORD = 103*43

Then this kinde kisse: O Lord, that lends me life,	26
Queen. Great King of England, & my gracious Lord,	31
Suf. My Lord Protector, so it please your Grace,	46
King. Vnkle, how now? | *Glo.* Pardon me gracious Lord,	58
King. They please vs well. Lord Marques kneel down,	68
Car. My Lord of Gloster, now ye grow too hot,	144
It was the pleasure of my Lord the King.	145
Hum. My Lord of Winchester I know your minde.	146
As stout and proud as he were Lord of all,	195
Elia. Why droopes my Lord like ouer-ripen'd Corn,	274
Hum. O *Nell*, sweet *Nell*, if thou dost loue thy Lord,	290
Eli. What dream'd my Lord, tell me, and Ile requite it	296
Elia. What, what, my Lord? Are you so chollericke	325
Mess. My Lord Protector, 'tis his Highnes pleasure,	331
Eli. Yes my good Lord, Ile follow presently.	335
*1.*Pet.* My Masters, let's stand close, my Lord Pro-|tector	386
*2.*Pet.* Marry the Lord protect him, for hee's a good | man, Iesu blesse	
him.	389

LORD *cont.*

*2.*Pet.* Come backe foole, this is the Duke of Suffolk, | and not my
Lord Protector.   394
*1.*Pet.* I pray my Lord pardon me, I tooke ye for my | Lord Protector.   397
* *Queene.* To my Lord Protector? Are your Supplica-|tions   399
* *Goodman,* my Lord Cardinals Man, for keeping my House,   402
Queene. My Lord of Suffolke, say, is this the guise?   428
As that prowd Dame, the Lord Protectors Wife: 462
Buck. Lord Cardinall, I will follow *Elianor,*   541
My Lord of Somerset will keepe me here,   563
*them to me in the Garret one Night, as wee were scow-|ring my Lord
of Yorkes Armor.   588
* *Armorer.* Alas, my Lord, hang me if euer I spake the   594
Humf. This doome, my Lord, if I may iudge: 601
* *Peter.* Alas, my Lord, I cannot fight; for Gods sake   610
*O Lord haue mercy vpon me, I shall neuer be able to | fight a blow: O
Lord my heart.   612
My Lord Protector will, I doubt it not,   675
* *Yorke.* Lord *Buckingham,* me thinks you watcht her well: 685
Now pray my Lord, let's see the Deuils Writ.   687
A sorry Breakfast for my Lord Protector.   706
* *Buck.* Your Grace shal giue me leaue, my Lord of York,   707
Yorke. At your pleasure, my good Lord.   709
King. But what a point, my Lord, your Faulcon made,   721
My Lord Protectors Hawkes doe towre so well,   726
Glost. My Lord, 'tis but a base ignoble minde,   729
Glost. I my Lord Cardinall, how thinke you by that?   733
Glost. As who, my Lord? | *Suff.* Why, as you, my Lord,   747
Glost. Talking of Hawking; nothing else, my Lord.   773
That we for thee may glorifie the Lord.   804
But still remember what the Lord hath done.   818
Maior. Yes, my Lord, if it please your Grace.   885
Beadle. I will, my Lord.   898
You made in a day, my Lord, whole Townes to flye.   915
Card. And so my Lord Protector, by this meanes   930
'Tis like, my Lord, you will not keepe your houre.   933
Salisb. My Lord, I long to heare it at full.   965
* *Salisb.* My Lord, breake we off; we know your minde | at full.   1043
Queene. I, good my Lord: for purposely therefore   1108
*take all the Money that I haue. O Lord blesse me, I pray   1137
Sirs, what's a Clock? | *Seru.* Tenne, my Lord.   1175
Elianor. Come you, my Lord, to see my open shame?   1195
* *Elianor.* What, gone my Lord, and bid me not fare-|well?   1263
King. I muse my Lord of Gloster is not come: 1295
The reuerent care I beare vnto my Lord,   1328
My Lord of Suffolke, Buckingham, and Yorke, | Reproue my
allegation, if you can,   1333
Take heed, my Lord, the welfare of vs all,   1374
* *King.* Welcome Lord *Somerset:* What Newes from | France?   1378
* *King.* Cold Newes, Lord *Somerset:* but Gods will be | done.   1382
Glost. All happinesse vnto my Lord the King: 1391
Yorke. 'Tis thought, my Lord, | That you tooke Bribes of France,   1402
Card. It serues you well, my Lord, to say so much.   1419
* *Suff.* My Lord, these faults are easie, quickly answer'd: 1433
And here commit you to my Lord Cardinall   1437
King. My Lord of Gloster, 'tis my speciall hope,   1439
Glost. Ah gracious Lord, these dayes are dangerous: 1442

LORD *cont.*

Lord Cardinall, he is your Prisoner.	1487
Henry, my Lord, is cold in great Affaires,	1526
But my Lord Cardinall, and you my Lord of Suffolke,	1548
Card. But I would haue him dead, my Lord of Suffolke,	1575
Card. My Lord of Yorke, trie what your fortune is:	1614
Yorke. I will, my Lord, so please his Maiestie.	1620
Suff. A charge, Lord *Yorke,* that I will see perform'd.	1626
Lord *Suffolke,* you and I must talke of that euent.	1631
Yorke. My Lord of Suffolke, within fourteene dayes	1632
Suff. Ile see it truly done, my Lord of Yorke. *Exeunt.*	1635
1. Runne to my Lord of Suffolke: let him know	1692
1. Here comes my Lord.	1696
1. I, my good Lord, hee's dead.	1698
According as I gaue directions? | 1. 'Tis, my good Lord.	1703
Suff. Ile call him presently, my Noble Lord. *Exit.*	1712
Suff. Dead in his Bed, my Lord: *Gloster* is dead. | *Queene.* Marry God forfend.	1725
Qu. How fares my Lord? Helpe Lords, the King is | dead.	1730
King. Oh Heauenly God. | *Qu.* How fares my gracious Lord?	1735
King. What, doth my Lord of Suffolke comfort me?	1739
Queene. Why do you rate my Lord of Suffolke thus?	1756
What instance giues Lord Warwicke for his vow.	1863
Say, if thou dar'st, prowd Lord of Warwickshire,	1905
Suff. Blunt-witted Lord, ignoble in demeanor,	1915
If euer Lady wrong'd her Lord so much,	1916
Dread Lord, the Commons send you word by me,	1955
Vnlesse Lord *Suffolke* straight be done to death,	1956
Commons within. An answer from the King, my Lord | of Salisbury.	1982
But you, my Lord, were glad to be imploy'd,	1986
Is, that he was the Lord Embassador,	1989
King. How fare's my Lord? Speake *Beauford* to thy | Soueraigne.	2134
Lord Card'nall, if thou think'st on heauens blisse,	2161
Lieu. Poole, Sir *Poole?* Lord, | I kennell, puddle, sinke, whose filth and dirt	2238
For daring to affye a mighty Lord	2248
Disdaine to call vs Lord, and *Piccardie*	2256
1. Gent. My gracious Lord intreat him, speak him fair.	2288
Brothers, and worship me their Lord.	2393
Butcher. And furthermore, wee'l haue the Lord *Sayes*	2480
it vp. Fellow-Kings, I tell you, that that Lord *Say* hath	2484
We will not leaue one Lord, one Gentleman:	2504
head, the Duke of Buckingham, and the | Lord Say.	2531
King. Lord *Say, Iacke Cade* hath sworne to haue thy | head.	2551
Mes. The Rebels are in Southwarke: Fly my Lord:	2563
Iacke Cade proclaimes himselfe Lord *Mortimer,*	2564
Buck. My gracious Lord, retire to Killingworth,	2575
King. Lord *Say,* the Traitors hateth thee,	2579
Buc. Then linger not my Lord, away, take horse.	2591
King. Farewell my Lord, trust not the Kentish Rebels	2594
Enter Lord Scales vpon the Tower walking. Then enters | two or three Citizens below.	2598
1. Cit. No my Lord, nor likely to be slaine:	2601
*The L.(ord) Maior craues ayd of your Honor from the Tower	2604
Cade. Now is *Mortimer* Lord of this City,	2615
That calles me other then Lord *Mortimer.*	2621
Dicke. My Lord, there's an Army gathered together | in Smithfield.	2627

LORD *cont.*

Mes. My Lord, a prize, a prize, heeres the Lord *Say*,	2653
Enter George, with the Lord Say.	2657
*Ah thou Say, thou Surge, nay thou Buckram Lord, now	2659
*the presence of Lord *Mortimer*, that I am the Beesome	2664
as heart can wish, or tongue can tell.	*Dicke.* My Lord,	2757
Clif. He is fled my Lord, and all his powers do yeeld,	2862
Somerset. My Lord,	Ile yeelde my selfe to prison willingly,	2895
Buc. I will my Lord, and doubt not so to deale,	2900
Iden. Lord, who would liue turmoyled in the Court,	2921
Cade. Heere's the Lord of the soile come to seize me	2929
Buc. So please it you my Lord, 'twere not amisse	3070
Clif. Health, and all happinesse to my Lord the King.	3121
If you oppose your selues to match Lord Warwicke.	3155
Sal. My Lord, I haue considered with my selfe	3175
Proud Northerne Lord, Clifford of Cumberland,	3224
War. How now my Noble Lord? What all a-foot.	3227
Qu. Away my Lord, you are slow, for shame away.	3297
Away my Lord, away. *Exeunt*	3318
What sayes Lord Warwicke, shall we after them?	3349

LORDING = 1

I see them Lording it in London streets,	2822

LORDINGS = 1

Lordings farewell, and say when I am gone,	152

LORDLY = 2

In sight of England, and her Lordly Peeres,	18
An't like your Lordly Lords Protectorship.	749

LORDS = 32*4

Lords, with one cheerefull voice, Welcome my Loue.	43
Consider Lords, he is the next of blood,	158
Looke to it Lords, let not his smoothing words	163
I feare me Lords, for all this flattering glosse,	170
Still reuelling like Lords till all be gone,	236
Queene. Not all these Lords do vex me halfe so much,	461
Yet must we ioyne with him and with the Lords,	481
King. For my part, Noble Lords, I care not which,	491
Humf. Now Lords, my Choller being ouer-blowne,	547
Peter. By these tenne bones, my Lords, hee did speake	587
Come, come, my Lords,	699
Inuite my Lords of Salisbury and Warwick	712
Queene. Beleeue me Lords, for flying at the Brooke,	717
An't like your Lordly Lords Protectorship.	749
King. How now, my Lords?	764
So doe your Stomacks, Lords:	780
I pray my Lords let me compound this strife.	783
My Lords, Saint *Albone* here hath done a Miracle:	878
Yorke. Now my good Lords of Salisbury & Warwick,	960
Yorke. Then thus:	*Edward* the third, my Lords, had seuen Sonnes:	968
Yorke. We thanke you Lords:	1029
Yorke. Lords, let him goe. Please it your Maiestie,	1103
The seruant of this Armorer, my Lords.	1114
King. My Lords at once: the care you haue of vs,	1360
King. My Lords, what to your wisdomes seemeth best,	1495
That these great Lords, and *Margaret* our Queene,	1508
Queene. Free Lords:	Cold Snow melts with the Sunnes hot Beames:	1524
Beleeue me Lords, were none more wise then I,	1533
Post. Great Lords, from Ireland am I come amaine,	1585

LORDS *cont.*

Send Succours (Lords) and stop the Rage betime,	1588
Yorke. I am content: Prouide me Souldiers, Lords,	1624
King. Lords take your places: and I pray you all	1713
Qu. How fares my Lord? Helpe Lords, the King is | dead.	1730
King. Why how now Lords?	1946
Well Lords, we haue not got that which we haue,	3342
Now by my hand (Lords) 'twas a glorious day.	3351

LORDSHIP = 2

to his Lordship? Let me see them: what is thine?	400
But. I haue a suite vnto your Lordship.	2637

LORDSHIPPE = *1

Cade. Bee it a Lordshippe, thou shalt haue it for that | word.	2638

LOSE *see also* loose = 2

Glost. Farre truer spoke then meant: I lose indeede,	1483
Yorke. No, not to lose it all, as thou hast done.	1599

LOSER = 1

Qu. But I can giue the loser leaue to chide.	1482

LOSERS = 1

And well such losers may haue leaue to speake.	1485

LOSSE = 2

And can doe naught but wayle her Darlings losse;	1517
But wherefore greeue I at an houres poore losse,	2098

LOST = 14*2

I prophesied, France will be lost ere long. *Exit Humfrey.*	153
Oh Father, *Maine* is lost,	220
Paris is lost, the state of *Normandie* | Stands on a tickle point, now they	
are gone:	227
Till Paris was besieg'd, famisht, and lost.	567
Is vtterly bereft you: all is lost.	1381
By meanes whereof, his Highnesse hath lost France.	1405
I rather would haue lost my Life betimes,	1600
By staying there so long, till all were lost.	1602
And euen with this, I lost faire Englands view,	1810
The liues of those which we haue lost in fight,	2190
Whitm. I lost mine eye in laying the prize aboord,	2194
I sold not *Maine,* I lost not *Normandie,*	2699
To France, to France, and get what you haue lost:	2826
*ten meales I haue lost, and I'de defie them all. Wither	2967
*Kent from me, she hath lost her best man, and exhort all	2978
Is not it selfe, nor haue we wonne one foot, | If Salsbury be lost.	3326

LOUD = 5

Clapping their hands, and crying with loud voyce,	167
How I haue lou'd my King, and Common-weale:	943
And now loud houling Wolues arouse the Iades	2172
Let them kisse one another: For they lou'd well	2765
We shall to London get, where you are lou'd,	3308

LOUDST = *1

Glost. 'Masse, thou lou'dst Plummes well, that would'st | venture so.	840

LOUE = 15*3

I can expresse no kinder signe of Loue	25
If Simpathy of Loue vnite our thoughts.	30
Lords, with one cheerefull voice, Welcome my Loue.	43
And make a shew of loue to proud Duke *Humfrey,*	253
Till *Henrie* surfetting in ioyes of loue,	263
Hum. O *Nell,* sweet *Nell,* if thou dost loue thy Lord,	290
Queene. And as for you that loue to be protected	422

LOUE *cont.*

Thou ran'st a-tilt in honor of my Loue,	437
As I in dutie loue my King and Countrey.	553
To tell my loue vnto his dumbe deafe trunke,	1846
And meere instinct of Loue and Loyaltie,	1962
Cade. And you that loue the Commons, follow me:	2502
I feare me (Loue) if that I had beene dead,	2556
* *Qu.* No my Loue, I should not mourne, but dye for | thee.	2558
*And shew'd how well you loue your Prince & Countrey:	2868
As pledges of my Fealtie and Loue,	3042
Yorke. With thy braue bearing should I be in loue,	3241
Hath no selfe-loue: nor he that loues himselfe,	3260

LOUED = 1

Euen of the bonnie beast he loued so well.	3231

LOUELY = 2

With him, the Husband of this louely Lady:	703
Qu. Ah barbarous villaines: Hath this louely face,	2547

LOUES = 5*1

* *War.* So God helpe Warwicke, as he loues the Land,	213
His Studie is his Tilt-yard, and his Loues	445
They know their Master loues to be aloft,	727
Who loues the King, and will imbrace his pardon,	2790
A poore Esquire of Kent, that loues his King.	3069
Hath no selfe-loue: nor he that loues himselfe,	3260

LOUING = 2

Your louing Vnckle, twentie times his worth,	1980
I thanke them for their tender louing care;	1994

LOW = 1

And neuer more abase our sight so low,	288

LOWING = 1

And as the Damme runnes lowing vp and downe,	1515

LOWLY = 2

And lowly words were Ransome for their fault:	1427
By such a lowly Vassall as thy selfe.	2279

LOWRING = 1

What lowring Starre now enuies thy estate?	1507

LOWSIE = 1

Obscure and lowsie Swaine, King *Henries* blood.	2218

LOYALL = 2

So long as I am loyall, true, and crimelesse.	1239
Vnlesse thou wert more loyall then thou art:	1394

LOYALTIE = 2

The Map of Honor, Truth, and Loyaltie:	1504
And meere instinct of Loue and Loyaltie,	1962

LOYALTY = 1

Oh where is Faith? Oh, where is Loyalty?	3166

LUCE = 1

On which Ile tosse the Fleure-de-Luce of France.	3002

LUCKIE = 1

'Tis meet that luckie Ruler be imploy'd,	1594

LUMPE = 1

Clif. Hence heape of wrath, foule indigested lumpe,	3156

LURKING = 1

They may astonish these fell-lurking Curres,	3143

LYE = 4

Proue them, and I lye open to the Law:	551
Wal. There let his head, and liuelesse bodie lye,	2313

LYE *cont.*

Heere may his head lye on my throbbing brest:	2537
Rich. So lye thou there:	3289

LYES = 1*1

The enuious Load that lyes vpon his heart:	1457
Cade. He lyes, for I inuented it my selfe. Go too Sir-|rah,	2475

LYINGST = 1

The lying'st Knaue in Christendome.	871

LYMD = 2

Suff. Madame, my selfe haue lym'd a Bush for her,	474
Haue all lym'd Bushes to betray thy Wings,	1230

LYON = 2

But great men tremble when the Lyon rores,	1313
That Winter Lyon, who in rage forgets | Aged contusions, and all brush of Time:	3322

LYSTS = 1

King. A Gods Name see the Lysts and all things fit,	1110

LYZARDS = 1

Their softest Touch, as smart as Lyzards stings:	2040

MA = *1

MACES = 1

For with these borne before vs, in steed of Maces,	2770

MAD = 3

Where from thy sight, I should be raging mad,	2111
To Bedlem with him, is the man growne mad.	3128
Thou mad misleader of thy brain-sicke sonne,	3163

MADAM = 1

King. How now Madam? | Still lamenting and mourning for Suffolkes death?	2554

MADAME = 15*3

Suff. Madame be patient: as I was cause	451
Suff. Madame, my selfe haue lym'd a Bush for her,	474
So let her rest: and Madame list to me,	478
Humf. Madame, the King is old enough himselfe	506
Humf. Madame, I am Protector of the Realme,	510
I cry you mercy, Madame: was it you?	531
Madame, sit you, and feare not: whom wee rayse,	641
*What Madame, are you there? the King & Commonweale	673
Buck. True Madame, none at all: what call you this?	679
And kept asunder: you Madame shall with vs.	681
Glost. Madame, for my selfe, to Heauen I doe appeale,	942
You Madame, for you are more Nobly borne,	1062
Stanley. Why, Madame, that is to the Ile of Man,	1274
Sherife. It is my Office, and Madame pardon me.	1282
Stanley. Madame, your Penance done, | Throw off this Sheet,	1285
Suff. Madame 'tis true: and wer't not madnesse then,	1554
Suff. He doth reuiue againe, Madame be patient.	1734
Warw. Madame be still: with reuerence may I say,	1912

MADDING = 1

When he to madding *Dido* would vnfold	1817

MADE = 24*7

Suffolke, the new made Duke that rules the rost,	116
Haue made thee fear'd and honor'd of the people,	206
And from the great and new-made Duke of Suffolke;	371
And must be made a Subiect to a Duke?	435
King. But what a point, my Lord, your Faulcon made,	721
*Damsons, and made me climbe, with danger of my | Life.	843

MADE *cont.*

Queene. It made me laugh, to see the Villaine runne.	906
Suff. True: made the Lame to leape and flye away.	913
You made in a day, my Lord, whole Townes to flye.	915
As ere thy Father *Henry* made it mine;	1089
Was made a wonder, and a pointing stock	To euery idle Rascall	
follower.	1222
Made me collect these dangers in the Duke.	1329
But mine is made the Prologue to their Play:	1451
It may be iudg'd I made the Duke away,	1767
King. That is to see how deepe my graue is made,	1854
His well proportion'd Beard, made ruffe and rugged,	1879
But will suspect, 'twas he that made the slaughter?	1894
*Beuis. Come and get thee a sword, though made of a	2320
*be made Parchment; that Parchment being scribeld ore,	2397
* Wea. Sir, he made a Chimney in my Fathers house, z	2468
*gelded the Commonwealth, and made it an Eunuch: &	2485
*which sold the Townes in France. He that made vs pay	2654
Hath made me full of sicknesse and diseases.	2722
Henry the fift, that made all France to quake,	2793
But I was made a King, at nine months olde.	2853
This hand was made to handle nought but Gold.	2998
Thy Hand is made to graspe a Palmers staffe,	3092
And made a prey for Carrion Kytes and Crowes	3230
Hath made the Wizard famous in his death:	3292
* Qu. What are you made of? You'l nor fight nor fly:	3300
And where this breach now in our Fortunes made	May readily be	
stopt.	3309

MADNESSE = *1

*Suff. Madame 'tis true: and wer't not madnesse then,	1554

MAD-BRED = 1

Doe calme the furie of this mad-bred Flawe.	1660

MAD-MANS = 1

You put sharpe Weapons in a mad-mans hands.	1653

MAGISTRATES = 1*1

*which is as much to say, as let the Magistrates be la-|bouring	2336
men, and therefore should we be Magistrates.	2337

MAGNES = *1

*Cade. Vp Fish-streete, downe Saint Magnes corner,	2775

MAID = *1

*a maid be married, but she shall pay to me her Mayden-|head	2754

MAIESTAS = 1

Ah *Sancta Maiestas*! who would not buy thee deere?	2996

MAIESTIE = 13*2

Suff. Please it your Maiestie, this is the man	578
And that your Maiestie was an Vsurper.	582
*Armorer. And't shall please your Maiestie, I neuer sayd	584
I doe beseech your Royall Maiestie,	592
*of this; therefore I beseech your Maiestie, doe not cast	598
Som. I humbly thanke your Royall Maiestie.	608
Suff. No maruell, and it like your Maiestie,	725
I beseech your Maiestie giue me leaue to goe;	1074
Yorke. Lords, let him goe. Please it your Maiestie,	1103
With what a Maiestie he beares himselfe,	1300
Yorke. I will, my Lord, so please his Maiestie.	1620
Sits in grim Maiestie, to fright the World.	1750
That slyly glyded towards your Maiestie,	1972

MAIESTIE *cont.*
And therefore by his Maiestie I sweare,   1999
And I am sent to tell his Maiestie,   2094
MAIESTIES = *1
Her. I summon your Grace to his Maiesties Parliament,   1247
MAIESTY = 10*1
Suffolke. | As by your high Imperiall Maiesty,   7
Her words yclad with wisedomes Maiesty,   40
Me thought I sate in Seate of Maiesty,   310
Hume. Iesus preserue your Royall Maiesty.   345
Elia. What saist thou? Maiesty: I am but Grace.   346
Vaux. To signifie vnto his Maiesty,   2085
All. God saue your Maiesty. | *Cade.* I thanke you good people. There
shall bee no   2389
*What canst thou answer to my Maiesty, for giuing vp of   2661
Fling vp his cap, and say, God saue his Maiesty.   2791
Buc. Health and glad tydings to your Maiesty.   2857
Iden. I was, an't like your Maiesty.   3066
MAIN = *1
*Item, *That the Dutchy of Aniou, and the County of Main,*   56
MAIND = *1
Cade And good reason: for thereby is England main'd   2482
MAINE = 10*3
Dutchesse of Aniou and Maine, shall be released and deliuered   64
Aniou and *Maine?* My selfe did win them both: 126
And looke vnto the maine.   218
Warwicke. Vnto the maine?   219
Oh Father, *Maine* is lost,   220
*That *Maine,* which by maine force Warwicke did winne,   221
Main-chance father you meant, but I meant *Maine,*   223
Yorke. Aniou and *Maine* are giuen to the French,   226
Aniou and *Maine* both giuen vnto the French?   248
By thee *Aniou* and *Maine* were sold to France.   2254
head, for selling the Dukedome of *Maine.*   2481
I sold not *Maine,* I lost not *Normandie,*   2699
MAINTAINE = 2
Iesu maintaine your Royall Excellence,   168
Kent to maintaine, the King, the Realme and you,   2704
MAINTAINES = 1
Sufficeth, that I haue maintaines my state,   2927
MAIN-CHANCE = 1
Main-chance father you meant, but I meant *Maine,*   223
MAIOR = 1*1
Enter the Maior of Saint Albones, and his Brethren, | *bearing the man
betweene two in a Chayre.*   795
*The L.(ord) Maior craues ayd of your Honor from the Tower   2604
MAIOR = 2
MAIORS = *1
*London, where we will haue the Maiors sword born be-| fore vs.   2524
MAISTER = 1
Maister, this Prisoner freely giue I thee,   2181
MAKE = 44*10
Salisbury. Then lets make hast away,   217
Pirates may make cheape penyworths of their pillage,   234
And make a shew of loue to proud Duke *Humfrey,*   253
And force perforce Ile make him yeeld the Crowne,   270
My troublous dreames this night, doth make me sad.   295

MAKE *cont.*

That shall make answere to such Questions,	355
When from Saint *Albones* we doe make returne,	358
Here *Hume*, take this reward, make merry man	360
*Hume. Hume must make merry with the Duchesse Gold:	363
Will make but little for his benefit:	484
Would make thee quickly hop without thy Head. | *Exit Humfrey.*	527
Suff. Before we make election, giue me leaue	557
Wee will make fast within a hallow'd Verge.	642
Here doe the Ceremonies belonging, and make the Circle,	643
Card. Let me be blessed for the Peace I make	755
Glost. Make vp no factious numbers for the matter,	759
Shall one day make the Duke of Yorke a King.	1046
Richard shall liue to make the Earle of Warwick	1048
And when he please to make Commotion,	1323
And if my death might make this Iland happy,	1448
And all to make away my guiltlesse Life.	1467
'Twill make them coole in zeale vnto your Grace.	1477
To make the Fox surueyor of the Fold?	1555
To make Commotion, as full well he can,	1664
Will make him say, I mou'd him to those Armes.	1684
And make my Image but an Ale-house signe.	1781
What were it but to make my sorrow greater?	1851
Make thee begge pardon for thy passed speech,	1926
The mortall Worme might make the sleepe eternall.	1975
There's two of you, the Deuill make a third,	2017
And boading Screech-Owles, make the Consort full.	2042
Can I make men liue where they will or no?	2144
War. See how the pangs of death do make him grin.	2158
Hold vp thy hand, make signall of thy hope.	2162
Heere shall make their ransome on the sand,	2179
And thou that art his Mate, make boote of this:	2182
Yet let not this make thee be bloody-minded,	2205
Remember it, and let it make thee Crest-falne,	2227
**Small things make base men proud. This Villaine heere,	2274
*Beuis. Hee shall haue the skinnes of our enemies, to | make Dogges	
Leather of.	2342
**shall haue ten hoopes, and I wil make it Fellony to drink	2385
*But. Nay, he can make Obligations, and write Court | hand.	2410
*Cade. To equall him I will make my selfe a knight, pre-|sently;	2438
*Cade. Giue him a box o'th'eare, and that wil make'em | red againe.	2719
*Say. Ah Countrimen: If when you make your prair's,	2747
**make shift for one, and so Gods Cursse light vppon you | all.	2807
And make the meanest of you Earles and Dukes?	2814
Should make a start ore-seas, and vanquish you?	2820
**me. My sword make way for me, for heere is no staying:	2836
Or is he but retir'd to make him strong?	2859
**of the King by carrying my head to him, but Ile make	2932
But I must make faire weather yet a while,	3022
See where they come, Ile warrant they'l make it good.	3118
Whom angry heauens do make their minister,	3256

MAKERS = 1

For blessed are the Peace-makers on Earth.	754

MAKES = 9*3

Makes me the bolder to salute my King,	36
Makes me from Wondring, fall to Weeping ioyes,	41
And that my Soueraignes presence makes me milde,	1924

MAKES *cont.*

Makes them thus forward in his Banishment.	1965
That makes him gaspe, and stare, and catch the aire,	2088
He dies and makes no signe: Oh God forgiue him.	2163
And makes it fearefull and degenerate,	2534
Buc. What answer makes your Grace to the Rebells | Supplication?	2539
Which makes me hope you are not void of pitty.	2698
*to an hundred mischiefes, and makes them leaue mee de-|solate.	2834
*base and ignominious treasons, makes me betake mee to | my heeles.	
Exit	2840
Makes him oppose himselfe against his King.	3130

MALA = 1

Dic. What say you of Kent. | *Say.* Nothing but this: 'Tis *bona terra,*	
mala gens.	2688

MALICE = 2

For he hath witnesse of his seruants malice:	606
Queene. God forbid any Malice should preuayle,	1717

MALLICE = 3

Good Vnckle hide such mallice:	743
Suff. No mallice Sir, no more then well becomes	745
Beaufords red sparkling eyes blab his hearts mallice,	1454

MAN = 48*11

More like a Souldier then a man o'th'Church,	194
Were I a Man, a Duke, and next of blood,	338
Where are you there? Sir *Iohn*; nay feare not man,	343
Elia. What saist thou man? Hast thou as yet confer'd	349
Here *Hume*, take this reward, make merry man	360
Enter three or foure Petitioners, the Armorers | Man being one.	384
2. Pet. Marry the Lord protect him, for hee's a good | man, Iesu blesse	
him.	389
Goodman, my Lord Cardinals Man, for keeping my House,	402
I say, my Soueraigne, *Yorke* is meetest man	555
That *Yorke* is most vnmeet of any man.	559
Enter Armorer and his Man.	572
Suff. Because here is a man accused of Treason,	573
Suff. Please it your Maiestie, this is the man	578
King. Say man, were these thy words?	583
away an honest man for a Villaines accusation.	599
*pitty my case: the spight of man preuayleth against me.	611
Yea Man and Birds are fayne of climbing high.	724
Had not your man put vp the Fowle so suddenly, | We had had more	
sport.	766
One. Forsooth, a blinde man at Saint *Albones* Shrine,	790
A man that ne're saw in his life before.	792
Enter the Maior of Saint Albones, and his Brethren, | bearing the man	
betweene two in a Chayre.	795
To present your Highnesse with the man.	798
Glost. Ambitious Church-man, leaue to afflict my heart:	934
The greatest man in England, but the King. | *Exeunt.*	1049
With Sir *Iohn Stanly*, in the Ile of Man.	1066
The Armorer and his Man, to enter the Lists,	1106
fastened to it: and at the other Doore his Man, with a	1118
Neighbor: drinke, and feare not your Man.	1126
*an honest man: and touching the Duke of Yorke, I will	1149
To take her with him to the Ile of Man.	1255
Stanley. Why, Madame, that is to the Ile of Man,	1274
'Tis not his wont to be the hindmost man,	1296

MAN *cont.*
And *Humfrey* is no little Man in England.	1314
No, no, my Soueraigne, *Glouster* is a man	1350
Hangs on the cutting short that fraudfull man.	1375
Thou neuer didst them wrong, nor no man wrong:	1510
Suff. Ah *Yorke*, no man aliue, so faine as I.	1546
Let pale-fac't feare keepe with the meane-borne man,	1641
Didst euer heare a man so penitent? *Enter Suffolke.*	1695
That faultlesse may condemne a Noble man:	1718
King. Ah woe is me for Gloster, wretched man.	1772
Staring full gastly, like a strangled man:	1874
And I should rob the Deaths-man of his Fee,	1922
And charge, that no man should disturbe your rest,	1968
A cunning man did calculate my birth,	2203
But. He was an honest man, and a good Bricklayer.	2360
*should vndoe a man. Some say the Bee stings, but I say,	2398
*I was neuer mine owne man since. How now? Who's | there?	2400
Cade. I am sorry for't: The man is a proper man of	2412
*Or hast thou a marke to thy selfe, like a honest plain dea-|ling man?	2420
*shall be encountred with a man as good as himselfe. He	2435
Dicke. Why dost thou quiuer man? | *Say.* The Palsie, and not feare	
prouokes me.	2725
Tooke oddes to combate a poore famisht man.	2948
*Kent from me, she hath lost her best man, and exhort all	2978
Tell me my Friend, art thou the man that slew him?	3065
If they can brooke I bow a knee to man:	3105
To Bedlem with him, is the man growne mad.	3128
To do a murd'rous deede, to rob a man,	3185

MANACLE = 1
And manacle the Berard in their Chaines,	3148

MANDRAKES = 1
Would curses kill, as doth the Mandrakes grone,	2025

MANET = 4
Exit King, Queene, and Suffolke. | *Manet the rest.*	80
Exit Warwicke, and Salisbury. Manet Yorke.	225
Manet Yorke.	1636
Manet the first Gent. Enter Walter with the body.	2312

MANHOOD = 1
Now is it manhood, wisedome, and defence,	3301

MANLY = 2
Henry hath mony, you are strong and manly:	2828
So beare I thee vpon my manly shoulders:	3285

MANNERS = 1
As crooked in thy manners, as thy shape.	3157

MANS = 1 *2
*my Mans instigation, to proue him a Knaue, and my selfe	1148
You put sharpe Weapons in a mad-mans hands.	1653
*a mans stomacke this hot weather: and I think this word	2914

MANY = 8 *3
And many time and oft my selfe haue heard a Voyce, | To call him so.	828
Glost. But Cloakes and Gownes, before this day, a | many.	859
And had I twentie times so many foes,	1236
No: many a Pound of mine owne proper store,	1415
Noyse within. Enter Warwicke, and many | *Commons.*	1822
With full as many signes of deadly hate,	2029
But. She was indeed a Pedlers daughter, & sold many | Laces.	2364
For God forbid, so many simple soules	2542

MANY *cont.*

*Sallet was borne to do me good: for many a time but for	2915
*and many a time when I haue beene dry, & brauely mar-|ching,	2917
Into as many gobbits will I cut it	3280

MAP = 1

The Map of Honor, Truth, and Loyaltie:	1504

MARCH = 5*2

Had Issue *Phillip*, a Daughter, | Who marryed *Edmond Mortimer*, Earle of March:	996
Edmond had Issue, *Roger*, Earle of March;	998
She was Heire to *Roger*, Earle of March,	1011
Cade. Marry, this *Edmund Mortimer* Earle of March,	2456
But. They are all in order, and march toward vs.	2508
of order. Come, march forward.	2510
*Cade. Feare not that I warrant thee. Come, let's march | towards London. *Exeunt.*	2528

MARCHETH = 1

That thus he marcheth with thee arme in arme?	3050

MARCHING = 1*1

Is marching hitherward in proud array,	2880
*and many a time when I haue beene dry, & brauely mar-|ching,	2917

MARGARET = 6*5

As Procurator to your Excellence, | To marry Princes *Margaret* for your Grace;	10
King. Suffolke arise. Welcome Queene *Margaret*,	24
*All kneel. Long liue Qu.(eene) *Margaret*, Englands happines.	44
espouse the Lady Margaret, daughter vnto Reignier King of	53
Where *Henrie* and Dame *Margaret* kneel'd to me,	313
Queene. Why now is *Henry* King, and *Margaret* Queen,	1095
King. I *Margaret*: my heart is drown'd with griefe,	1499
That these great Lords, and *Margaret* our Queene,	1508
When I haue feasted with Queene *Margaret*?	2226
King. Come *Margaret*, God our hope will succor vs.	2592
King. Can we outrun the Heauens? Good *Margaret* | stay.	3298

MARGERIE = 1

With *Margerie Iordane* the cunning Witch,	350

MARIES = 1

To number *Aue-Maries* on his Beades:	442

MARKD = 1

Mark'd for the Gallowes: Lay your Weapons downe,	2443

MARKE = 1*1

For that's the Golden marke I seeke to hit:	255
*Or hast thou a marke to thy selfe, like a honest plain dea-|ling man?	2420

MARKES = 1

We giue thee for reward a thousand Markes,	3073

MARKET = 2

Glost. Let the(m) be whipt through euery Market Towne,	909
But. No question of that: for I haue seene him whipt | three Market dayes together.	2375

MARQUES = *1

King. They please vs well. Lord Marques kneel down,	68

MARQUESSE = 1*1

The happiest Gift, that euer Marquesse gaue,	22
Charles, and William de la Pole Marquesse of Suffolke, Am-|bassador	51

MARRIAGE = 2

Fatall this Marriage, cancelling your Fame,	106
Had *Henrie* got an Empire by his marriage,	160

MARRIED = 2*1
For whilest I thinke I am thy married Wife,	1204
married the Duke of *Clarence* daughter, did he not? | *Staf.* I sir.	2457
*a maid be married, but she shall pay to me her Mayden-|head	2754

MARRY = 6*3
As Procurator to your Excellence, | To marry Princes *Margaret* for your Grace;	10
Marry and shall: but how now, Sir *Iohn Hume*?	364
*2.*Pet.* Marry the Lord protect him, for hee's a good | man, Iesu blesse him.	389
Card. Marry, when thou dar'st.	758
Suff. Dead in his Bed, my Lord: *Gloster* is dead. | *Queene.* Marry God forfend.	1725
Cade. Marry, this *Edmund Mortimer* Earle of March,	2456
All. I marry will we: therefore get ye gone.	2473
Cade. Marry, thou ought'st not to let thy horse weare	2682
Cade. Marry presently. | *All.* O braue.	2761

MARRYED = 3
Had Issue *Phillip*, a Daughter, | Who married *Edmond Mortimer*, Earle of March:	996
Marryed *Richard*, Earle of Cambridge,	1007
Who marryed *Phillip*, sole Daughter | Vnto *Lionel*, Duke of Clarence.	1013

MARUELL = 1
Suff. No maruell, and it like your Maiestie,	725

MASSE = 2*2
Haue cost a masse of publique Treasurie.	521
Glost. 'Masse, thou lou'dst Plummes well, that would'st | venture so.	840
Iohn. Masse 'twill be sore Law then, for he was thrust	2642
By'th'Masse so did we all. I thanke you *Richard*.	3338

MASTER = 15*10
Peter. Against my Master *Thomas Horner*, for saying,	410
Peter. That my Mistresse was? No forsooth: my Master	415
*Take this fellow in, and send for his Master with a Purse-|uant	419
Though in this place most Master weare no Breeches,	538
That doth accuse his Master of High Treason;	579
Bulling. Master *Hume*, we are therefore prouided: will	622
*an inuincible spirit: but it shall be conuenient, Master	626
They know their Master loues to be aloft,	727
Wife. A Plum-tree, Master.	834
Glost. How long hast thou beene blinde? | *Simpc.* O borne so, Master.	835
Simpc. Alas, good Master, my Wife desired some	842
Simpc. Yes Master, cleare as day, I thanke God and | Saint *Albones*.	848
Simpc. Red Master, Red as Blood.	852
Glost. Tell me Sirrha, what's my Name? | *Simpc.* Alas Master, I know not.	862
Glost. Nor his? | *Simpc.* No indeede, Master.	866
Glost. What's thine owne Name? | *Simpc. Saunder Simpcoxe*, and if it please you, Master.	868
Simpc. O Master, that you could?	881
Simpc. Alas Master, I am not able to stand alone:	892
Simpc. Alas Master, what shall I doe? I am not able to | stand.	900
*2.*Prent.* Be merry *Peter*, and feare not thy Master,	1131
*God, for I am neuer able to deale with my Master, hee	1138
Salisb. Thumpe? Then see thou thumpe thy Master | well.	1145
My *Nell*, I take my leaue: and Master Sherife,	1251
*1.*Gent.* What is my ransome Master, let me know.	2184
To emblaze the Honor that thy Master got.	2976

MASTERS = 3*4
*1. *Pet.* My Masters, let's stand close, my Lord Pro-|tector   386
* *Hume.* Come my Masters, the Duchesse I tell you ex-|pects
performance of your promises.   620
Elianor. Well said my Masters, and welcome all: To   633
* *Glost.* Stand by, my Masters, bring him neere the King,   801
Glost. My Masters of Saint *Albones,*   882
* *Armorer.* Masters, I am come hither as it were vpon   1147
and the good Wine in thy Masters way.   1159
MATCH = 4
To match with her that brings no vantages.   138
If you oppose your selues to match Lord Warwicke.   3155
But match to match I haue encountred him,   3229
MATE *see also Ma.* = 1
And thou that art his Mate, make boote of this: 2182
MATE = *1
MATES = 1
Which mates him first, that first intends deceit.   1567
MATHEW = 2
And thither I will send you *Mathew Goffe.*   2610
Alarums. Mathew Goffe is slain, and all the rest. | *Then enter Iacke*
Cade, with his Company.   2633
MATTER = 4*2
*presently: wee'le heare more of your matter before | the King. *Exit.*   420
But to the matter that we haue in hand: 554
*nor thought any such matter: God is my witnesse, I am   585
Glost. Make vp no factious numbers for the matter,   759
Sleeping, or Waking, 'tis no matter how,   1565
Where is our Vnckle? what's the matter, *Suffolke?*   1724
MATTERS = 2*1
To giue his Censure: These are no Womens matters.   507
I haue great matters to impart to thee. *Exit.*   2013
*matters they were not able to answer. Moreouer,   2676
MAY *l.*131 211 234 292 *387 502 601 804 875 1093 1179 1260 1261 1485
1718 1719 1765 1767 1896 1912 2055 2061 2119 2301 *2392 2499 2537
2584 *2640 2903 2922 2945 3045 3059 3075 3143 3307 3310 = 35*3, 1
England, ere the thirtieth of May next ensuing.   55
MAYDENHEAD = *1
*a maid be married, but she shall pay to me her Mayden-|head   2754
MAYLD = 1
Mayl'd vp in shame, with Papers on my back,   1207
MAYME = 1
That beares so shrewd a mayme: two Pulls at once;   1097
MAYNE = 1
Hath giuen the Dutchy of *Aniou* and *Mayne,*   117
MAYST = 1
thou mayst be turn'd to Hobnailes. | *Heere they Fight.*   2963
MAYT = *1
* *Stanly.* So am I giuen in charge, may't please your | Grace.   1257
ME *l.*26 27 28 36 41 59 60 157 170 174 244 249 295 *296 *298 309 310 313
324 352 374 *392 396 *397 400 403 461 478 492 529 557 563 *576 *588
*594 *597 *611 *612 *685 693 *707 713 717 755 765 783 819 831 *843
846 *850 862 889 *891 893 906 961 *1045 1074 *1133 *1137 1177 1203
1206 1212 1238 1240 *1263 1268 1271 1273 1282 1290 1317 1329 1384
1396 1401 1410 1414 1420 1425 1441 1468 1484 1533 1597 1603 1624
1648 1649 1651 1675 1676 1689 1739 1746 1747 1751 1759 1765 1770
1772 1773 1775 1794 1795 1798 1816 1820 1841 1904 1924 1933 1951

ME *cont.*
  1955 1993 2003 2048 2054 2067 2097 2104 2119 2122 2131 2138 2142
  2145 2146 2151 2184 2199 *2202 2204 2234 2280 2282 *2380 2393 *2419
  *2476 2501 2502 2548 2556 2557 2582 2621 *2692 2698 2702 2706 2710
  2722 2726 2730 2737 *2753 *2754 *2800 *2806 2821 *2836 *2840 2846
  *2908 *2909 *2915 *2918 2919 2923 2924 *2929 *2931 2939 2940 2950
  *2965 *2966 *2978 *2981 3004 3024 3038 3063 3064 3065 3086 *3104
  3107 3127 3144 3173 3179 3223 3239 3245 3275 3341 = 162*44

MEAGER = 1
  Of ashy semblance, meager, pale, and bloodlesse,   1866
MEALES = *1
  *ten meales I haue lost, and I'de defie them all. Wither   2967
MEANE = 4*3
  Where as the King and Queene do meane to Hawke.   333
  *Now Sirrha, if you meane to saue your selfe from Whip-|ping,   890
  But all in vaine are these meane Obsequies, | *Bed put forth.*   1848
  Cade. Nay, that I meane to do. Is not this a lamenta-|ble   2395
  But. If we meane to thriue, and do good, breake open   2526
  Follow me souldiers, wee'l deuise a meane,   2846
  Iden. If one so rude, and of so meane condition   3058
MEANES = 8*2
  Car. Nephew, what meanes this passionate discourse?   111
  Glost. What meanes this noyse?   785
  Card. And so my Lord Protector, by this meanes   930
  By wicked meanes to frame our Soueraignes fall.   1346
  By meanes whereof, the Townes each day reuolted,   1357
  Who cannot steale a shape, that meanes deceit?   1373
  By meanes whereof, his Highnesse hath lost France.   1405
  By Suffolke, and the Cardinall *Beaufords* meanes: 1826
  Mischance vnto my State by *Suffolkes* meanes.   1998
  Beuis. I tell thee, *Iacke Cade* the Cloathier, meanes to   2323
MEANEST = 3
  And vanquisht as I am, I yeeld to thee, | Or to the meanest Groome.   936
  And make the meanest of you Earles and Dukes?   2814
  Buc. Yorke, if thou meanest wel, I greet thee well.   3006
MEANE-BORNE = 1
  Let pale-fac't feare keepe with the meane-borne man,   1641
MEANING = 1
  From meaning Treason to our Royall Person,   1364
MEANST = *1
  King. What mean'st thou, *Suffolke*? tell me, what are | these?   576
MEANT = 4*1
  Main-chance father you meant, but I meant *Maine*,   223
  *take my death, I neuer meant him any ill, nor the King,   1150
  Glost. Farre truer spoke then meant: I lose indeede,   1483
  For things are often spoke, and seldome meant,   1570
MEANTST = 1
  And say, it was thy Mother that thou meant'st,   1927
MEATE = *1
  *eate no meate these fiue dayes, yet come thou and thy   2943
MECHANICALL = 1
  Yorke. Base Dunghill Villaine, and Mechanicall,   590
MEDEA = 1
  As wilde *Medea* yong *Absirtis* did.   3281
MEDICE = *1
  Card. *Medice teipsum*, Protector see to't well, protect | your selfe.   777

MEDITATION = 1
And let vs all to Meditation. *Exeunt.*   2167
MEDLING = 1
Oh beate away the busie medling Fiend,   2155
MEE *l.**1720 2012 *2692 *2755 *2834 *2839 *2840 *2942 = 1*7
MEERE = 1
And meere instinct of Loue and Loyaltie,   1962
MEET = 5
But meet him now, and be it in the Morne,   1307
'Tis meet he be condemn'd by course of Law.   1539
'Tis meet that luckie Ruler he imploy'd,   1594
Meet me to morrow in S.(aint) Georges Field,   3038
Meet I an infant of the house of Yorke,   3279
MEETE = 2
Crying *Villiago* vnto all they meete.   2823
I pray thee Buckingham go and meete him,   2890
MEETEST = 1
I say, my Soueraigne, *Yorke* is meetest man   555
MELANCHOLLY = 1
My minde was troubled with deepe Melancholly.   3026
MELANCHOLY = 1
That dragge the Tragicke melancholy night: 2173
MELFORDE = *1
*Suffolke, for enclosing the Commons of Melforde. How | now, Sir
Knaue?   406
MELT = 1
For I should melt at an Offendors teares,   1426
MELTS = 1
Queene. Free Lords: | Cold Snow melts with the Sunnes hot Beames: 1524
MEMORY = 1
Blotting your names from Bookes of memory,   107
MEN = 21*8
Haue beene as Bond-men to thy Soueraigntie.   517
Tantaene animis Coelestibus irae, Church-men so hot?   742
Card. Here comes the Townes-men, on Procession,   797
Enter Duke Humfrey and his Men in | Mourning Cloakes.   1169
But great men tremble when the Lyon rores,   1313
To Ireland will you leade a Band of men,   1617
To send me packing with an Hoast of men: 1648
'Twas men I lackt, and you will giue them me;   1651
Suff. I weare no Knife, to slaughter sleeping men,   1901
Pernicious blood-sucker of sleeping men.   1931
Suff. The trayt'rous *Warwick*, with the men of Bury,   1950
Blaspheming God, and cursing men on earth.   2089
Can I make men liue where they will or no?   2144
*Small things make base men proud. This Villaine heere,   2274
Great men oft dye by vilde Bezonions.   2302
**Beuis.* O miserable Age: Vertue is not regarded in | Handy-crafts men. 2329
men, and therefore should we be Magistrates.   2337
Now shew your selues men, 'tis for Liberty.   2503
For they are thrifty honest men, and such   2506
**Kin.* Oh gracelesse men: they know not what they do.   2574
*that thou hast men about thee, that vsually talke of a   2672
*Iustices of Peace, to call poore men before them, a-|bout   2675
*a Cloake, when honester men then thou go in their Hose | and
Doublets.   2683
Say. You men of Kent.   2687

MEN *cont.*
Say. Great men haue reaching hands: oft haue I struck	2714
*ere they haue it: Men shall hold of mee in Capite.	2755
But now is Cade driuen backe, his men dispierc'd,	2888
*fiue men, and if I doe not leaue you all as dead as a doore	2944
It shall be stony. Yorke, not our old men spares:	3273

MENS = 4
Mens flesh preseru'd so whole, doe seldome winne.	1604
Cleape dead-mens graues, and from their misty Iawes,	2175
Say. Long sitting to determine poore mens causes,	2721
And dead mens cries do fill the emptie ayre,	3222

MERCHANT-LIKE = 1
Therefore, when Merchant-like I sell reuenge,	2210

MERCIE = 1
But God in mercie so deale with my Soule,	552

MERCIFULL = 1
The King is mercifull, if you reuolt.	2445

MERCILESSE = 1
Of Hindes and Pezants, rude and mercilesse:	2569

MERCY = 4*1
And left thee to the mercy of the Law.	524
I cry you mercy, Madame: was it you?	531
*O Lord haue mercy vpon me, I shall neuer be able to | fight a blow: O	
Lord my heart.	612
And yeeld to mercy, whil'st 'tis offered you,	2788
Then you should stoope vnto a Frenchmans mercy.	2825

MERIT = 1
Iden. May *Iden* liue to merit such a bountie,	3075

MERITORIOUS = 1
Seeing the deed is meritorious,	1572

MERRIE = *1
*it was neuer merrie world in England, since Gentlemen | came vp.	2327

MERRY = 2*1
Here *Hume,* take this reward, make merry man	360
Hume. Hume must make merry with the Duchesse Gold:	363
2.Prent. Be merry *Peter,* and feare not thy Master,	1131

MES = 2*1
MESS = 1*1
MESSAGE = 3
Could send such Message to their Soueraigne:	1985
Qu. Go tell this heauy Message to the King. *Exit*	2096
I go of Message from the Queene to France:	2281

MESSENGER see also Mes., Mess. = 8
Enter Messenger.	330
Thou balefull Messenger, out of my sight:	1748
Enter a Messenger.	2560
Enter another Messenger.	2585
Cade. And hence-forward all things shall be in Com-|mon. *Enter a*	
Messenger.	2651
Enter a Messenger.	2875
Art thou a Messenger, or come of pleasure.	3008
Buc. A Messenger from *Henry,* our dread Liege,	3009

MET = 1
But still where danger was, still there I met him,	3332

METHINKES *see* thinkes, thinks
METHOUGHT *see* thought

MICH = 2*1
MICHAEL see also Mich. = 1
  Enter Michael.   2429
MICKLE = 1
  That bowes vnto the graue with mickle age.   3174
MIDDEST = *1
  *middest of you, and heauens and honor be witnesse, that   2838
MIDWIFE = 1
  Butch. I knew her well, she was a Midwife.   2362
MIGHT *l*.99 1448 1609 1760 1800 1809 1975 2196 2581 *2910 2984
  3201 = 11*1
MIGHTIE = 3
  So mightie are his vowed Enemies.   1521
  Whiles I in Ireland nourish a mightie Band,   1654
  Set all vpon me, mightie Soueraigne.   1951
MIGHTIER = 1
  But mightier Crimes are lay'd vnto your charge,   1434
MIGHTST *l*.873 2059 = 2
MIGHTY = 3
  War. It is reported, mighty Soueraigne,   1824
  For daring to affye a mighty Lord   2248
  And with a puissant and a mighty power | Of Gallow-glasses and stout
  Kernes,   2878
MILDE = 5
  But be thou milde, and blush not at my shame,   1224
  We know the time since he was milde and affable,   1303
  The Duke is vertuous, milde, and too well giuen,   1366
  And that my Soueraignes presence makes me milde,   1924
  As milde and gentle as the Cradle-babe,   2109
MILKE-WHITE-ROSE = 1
  Then will I raise aloft the Milke-white-Rose,   266
MILL = *1
  *hast built a Paper-Mill. It will be prooued to thy Face, 2671
MIND = *1
  **Queene.* Oft haue I heard that greefe softens the mind, 2533
MINDE = 14*1
  The mutuall conference that my minde hath had,   32
  Hum. My Lord of Winchester I know your minde.   146
  While Gloster beares this base and humble minde.   337
  But all his minde is bent to Holinesse,   441
  Glost. My Lord, 'tis but a base ignoble minde,   729
  **Salisb.* My Lord, breake we off; we know your minde | at full. 1043
  Sweet *Nell,* ill can thy Noble Minde abrooke   1181
  Respecting what a rancorous minde he beares,   1318
  And had I first beene put to speake my minde,   1337
  Suff. But in my minde, that were no pollicie: 1540
  By this, I shall perceiue the Commons minde,   1680
  **Salisb.* Sirs stand apart, the King shall know your | minde. 1953
  **Beuis.* Thou hast hit it: for there's no better signe of a | braue minde,
  then a hard hand.   2338
  Continue still in this so good a minde,   2869
  My minde was troubled with deepe Melancholly.   3026
MINDED = 1
  Yet let not this make thee be bloody-minded,   2205
MINE *l*.35 61 95 125 127 155 285 *298 374 *401 1071 1075 1089 *1160
  1201 1415 1451 1464 1500 1534 1625 1646 1811 2031 2032 2033 2102

MINE *cont.*
2112 2194 2231 *2400 *2413 2596 2949 2955 3035 3094 3242 3272
3287 = 35*5
MINION *see* mynion
MINIONS = 1
She vaunted 'mongst her Minions t'other day,   470
MINISTER = 3
And ouer ioy of heart doth minister.   38
And for a minister of my intent,   1661
Whom angry heauens do make their minister,   3256
MINUTE = 1
And thinke it but a minute spent in sport.   2053
MIRACLE = 7*1
Enter one crying a Miracle.   784
Fellow, what Miracle do'st thou proclayme?   786
One. A Miracle, a Miracle.   787
Suffolke. Come to the King, and tell him what Mi-|racle.   788
My Lords, Saint *Albone* here hath done a Miracle: 878
the Stoole, and runnes away: and they | follow, and cry, A Miracle.   903
Card. Duke *Humfrey* ha's done a Miracle to day.   912
MIRACLES = 1
Glost. But you haue done more Miracles then I: 914
MISCARRY = 1
Better ten thousand base-borne *Cades* miscarry,   2824
MISCHANCE = 2
Mischance vnto my State by *Suffolkes* meanes.   1998
Qu. Mischance and Sorrow goe along with you,   2014
MISCHEEFE = 1
Clif. But that my hearts on future mischeefe set,   3312
MISCHIEFES = *2
King. O God, what mischiefes work the wicked ones?   938
*to an hundred mischiefes, and makes them leaue mee de-|solate.   2834
MISDOUBT = 1
And change misdoubt to resolution;   1638
MISERABLE = 2*1
For what's more miserable then Discontent?   1502
Beuis. O miserable Age: Vertue is not regarded in | Handy-crafts men.   2329
Staf. O grosse and miserable ignorance.   2488
MISERIE = 1
My Body round engyrt with miserie: 1501
MISERIES = 1
My teare-stayn'd eyes, to see her Miseries.   1187
MISLEADER = 1
Thou mad misleader of thy brain-sicke sonne,   3163
MISLED = 1
Vnto the Commons, whom thou hast misled,   2784
MISLIKE = 1
'Tis not my speeches that you do mislike: 147
MISTAKE = 1
Clif. This is my King Yorke, I do not mistake,   3126
MISTAKES = 1
But thou mistakes me much to thinke I do,   3127
MISTAKING = 1
For thy mistaking so, We pardon thee.   3125
MISTRESSE = *1
Peter. That my Mistresse was? No forsooth: my Master   415

MISTRIS = 1
Vntill the Queene his Mistris bury it. *Exit Walter.*   2314
MISTRUST = 1
More then mistrust, that shewes him worthy death.   1544
MISTY = 1
Cleape dead-mens graues, and from their misty Iawes,   2175
MONARCHY = 1
Contenteth me, and worth a Monarchy.   2924
MONETH = 1*1
*Combat, shall be the last of the next moneth. Come   616
Holden at Bury, the first of this next Moneth.   1248
MONETHS = 2
For eighteene moneths concluded by consent.   49
I'th parts of France, till terme of eighteene Moneths   72
MONEY = 2*1
Without Discharge, Money, or Furniture,   564
*take all the Money that I haue. O Lord blesse me, I pray   1137
Leuie great summes of Money through the Realme,   1355
MONGST = 1
She vaunted 'mongst her Minions t'other day,   470
MONSTROUS = 4*2
War. So bad a death, argues a monstrous life.   2164
Cade. O monstrous. | *Wea.* We tooke him setting of boyes Copies.   2405
**Geo.* O monstrous Coward! What, to come behinde | Folkes?   2716
**Iden.* Is't *Cade* that I haue slain, that monstrous traitor?   2971
And fight against that monstrous Rebell *Cade,*   3055
Som. O monstrous Traitor! I arrest thee Yorke   3101
MONTHS = 1
But I was made a King, at nine months olde.   2853
MONUMENT = *1
*This Monument of the victory will I beare, and the bo-|dies   2522
MONUMENTS = 2
Defacing Monuments of Conquer'd France, | Vndoing all as all had
neuer bin.   109
To wash away my wofull Monuments.   2057
MONY = 1*1
*mony, all shall eate and drinke on my score, and I will   2391
Henry hath mony, you are strong and manly: 2828
MOONE = 1
And dogged *Yorke,* that reaches at the Moone,   1458
MORE = 53*4
Nay more, an enemy vnto you all,   156
His insolence is more intollerable   182
More like a Souldier then a man o'th'Church,   194
And neuer more abase our sight so low,   288
Away from me, and let me heare no more.   324
*presently: wee'le heare more of your matter before | the King. *Exit.*   420
But can doe more in England then the King.   457
Cannot doe more in England then the *Neuils*:   459
More like an Empresse, then Duke *Humphreyes* Wife: 464
Haue done, for more I hardly can endure.   665
Suff. No mallice Sir, no more then well becomes   745
Had not your man put vp the Fowle so suddenly, | We had had more
sport.   766
Glost. But you haue done more Miracles then I: 914
As more at large your Grace shall vnderstand.   929
Warw. What plaine proceedings is more plain then this?   1017

MORE *cont.*

You Madame, for you are more Nobly borne,	1062
Or more afraid to fight, then is the Appellant,	1113
Salisb. Peter? what more? | *Peter. Thumpe.*	1143
*Qu. Ah what's more dangerous, then this fond affiance?	1368
Vnlesse thou wert more loyall then thou art:	1394
Glost. I say no more then truth, so helpe me God.	1420
For thousands more, that yet suspect no perill,	1452
For what's more miserable then Discontent?	1502
Beleeue me Lords, were none more wise then I,	1533
More then mistrust, that shewes him worthy death.	1544
Yorke. 'Tis *Yorke* that hath more reason for his death.	1547
No more, good *Yorke*; sweet *Somerset* be still.	1607
Card. No more of him: for I will deale with him,	1628
That henceforth he shall trouble vs no more:	1629
My Brayne, more busie then the laboring Spider,	1645
Queen. Be woe for me, more wretched then he is.	1773
Because thy flinty heart more hard then they,	1799
Aye me, I can no more: Dye *Elinor,*	1820
No more I say: if thou do'st pleade for him,	2005
I can no more: Liue thou to ioy thy life;	2080
From thee to dye, were torture more then death:	2118
Oh torture me no more, I will confesse.	2145
Being Captaine of a Pinnace, threatens more	2275
More can I beare, then you dare execute.	2298
Lieu. Hale him away, and let him talke no more:	2299
Hol. They haue the more neede to sleepe now then.	2322
*Beuis. Nay more, the Kings Councell are no good | Workemen.	2333
**more then that, he can speake French, and therefore hee is | a Traitor.	2486
But. I desire no more.	2520
Cade more, I thinke he hath a very faire warning.	2626
Of some more Townes in France. Soldiers,	2768
And could command no more content then I?	2851
naile, I pray God I may neuer eate grasse more.	2945
More like a King, more Kingly in my thoughts.	3021
Till *Henry* be more weake, and I more strong.	3023
Giue place: by heauen thou shalt rule no more	3099
Yo.Clif. Foule stygmaticke that's more then thou | canst tell.	3215
No more will I their Babes, Teares Virginall,	3274
By what we can, which can no more but flye. | *Alarum a farre off.*	3303
And more such dayes as these, to vs befall. *Exeunt.*	3355

MOREOUER = **1

*matters they were not able to answer. Moreouer,	2676

MORISCO = 1

Him capre vpright, like a wilde Morisco,	1671

MORNE = 1

But meet him now, and be it in the Morne,	1307

MORNINGS = 1

With sweet rehearsall of my mornings dreame?	297

MORROW = 3

To suppe with me to morrow Night. Away. | *Exeunt.*	713
To morrow toward London, back againe,	953
Meet me to morrow in S.(aint) Georges Field,	3038

MORT = 1

Deliuer'd vp againe with peacefull words? | *Mort Dieu.*	129

MORTALL = 2

Be my last breathing in this mortall world.	294

MORTALL *cont.*
The mortall Worme might make the sleepe eternall.   1975
MORTIMER = 9*2
Had Issue *Phillip*, a Daughter, | Who marryed *Edmond Mortimer*, Earle
of March: 996
Who was the Sonne of *Edmond Mortimer*,   1012
Vnder the Title of *Iohn Mortimer*.   1665
For that *Iohn Mortimer*, which now is dead,   1678
Cade. My Father was a *Mortimer*.   2359
Rise vp Sir *Iohn Mortimer*. Now haue at him.   2439
Cade. Marry, this *Edmund Mortimer* Earle of March,   2456
Iacke Cade proclaimes himselfe Lord *Mortimer*,   2564
Cade. Now is *Mortimer* Lord of this City,   2615
That calles me other then Lord *Mortimer*.   2621
*the presence of Lord *Mortimer*, that I am the Beesome   2664
MOST = 10*4
To your most gracious hands, that are the Substance   20
Suff. And he of these, that can doe most of all,   458
Though in this place most Master weare no Breeches,   538
That *Yorke* is most vnmeet of any man.   559
And I will helpe thee. | *Wife.* Most true, forsooth: 826
Yet he most Christian-like laments his death: 1758
They say, in care of your most Royall Person,   1966
Cade. But then are we in order, when we are most out   2509
*art: Thou hast most traiterously corrupted the youth of   2666
*that cause they haue beene most worthy to liue. Thou   2679
Say. Tell me: wherein haue I offended most?   2730
Cade. By my Valour: the most compleate Champi-|on   2959
And there cut off thy most vngracious head,   2987
The Title of this most renowned Duke,   3176
MOTHER = 5*2
*Mother *Iordan*, be you prostrate, and grouell on the   630
Now by Gods Mother, Priest,   774
Glost. Hadst thou been his Mother, thou could'st haue | better told. 810
Yorke. His eldest Sister, *Anne*, | My Mother, being Heire vnto the
Crowne,   1005
Thy Mother tooke into her blamefull Bed   1917
And say, it was thy Mother that thou meant'st,   1927
Cade. My mother a *Plantagenet*.   2361
MOTHERS = 1
Dying with mothers dugge betweene it's lips.   2110
MOTHER-BLEEDING = 1
With gobbets of thy Mother-bleeding heart.   2253
MOUD = 2
Will make him say, I mou'd him to those Armes.   1684
Prayres and Teares haue mou'd me, Gifts could neuer.   2702
MOUE = 1
Thy words moue Rage, and not remorse in me: 2280
MOUER = 1
King. Oh thou eternall mouer of the heauens,   2153
MOUNSIEUR = *1
*Normandie vnto Mounsieur *Basimecu*, the Dolphine of   2662
MOUNT = 2
And neuer mount to trouble you againe.   477
And should you fall, he is the next will mount.   1316
MOUNTAINE = 2
Though standing naked on a Mountaine top,   2051

MOUNTAINE *cont.*
As on a Mountaine top, the Cedar shewes,   3205
MOUNTED = 2
Then where Castles mounted stand.   664
Then where Castles mounted stand.   698
MOUNTS = 1
That mounts no higher then a Bird can sore: 730
MOURND = 1
Thou would'st not haue mourn'd so much for me.   2557
MOURNE = 1*1
Why onely Suffolke mourne I not for thee?   2100
Qu. No my Loue, I should not mourne, but dye for | thee.   2558
MOURNEFULL = 1
Beguiles him, as the mournefull Crocodile   1528
MOURNFULL = 1
That I may dew it with my mournfull teares: 2055
MOURNING = 2
Enter Duke Humfrey and his Men in | Mourning Cloakes.   1169
King. How now Madam? | Still lamenting and mourning for Suffolkes
death?   2554
MOUTH = 4*1
To haue thee with thy lippes to stop my mouth: 2113
Now will I dam vp this thy yawning mouth,   2241
But. Onely that the Lawes of England may come out | of your mouth. 2640
in the mouth with a Speare, and 'tis not whole yet.   2643
*burne all the Records of the Realme, my mouth shall be | the
Parliament of England.   2647
MOWE = 1
To mowe downe Thornes that would annoy our Foot,   1361
MUCH = 10*6
Queene. Not all these Lords do vex me halfe so much,   461
Card. I thought as much, hee would be aboue the | Clouds.   731
to him so much, that hee is drunke; and he enters with a   1116
hath learnt so much fence already.   1139
Card. It serues you well, my Lord, to say so much.   1419
Suff. Not resolute, except so much were done,   1569
King. I thanke thee *Nell*, these wordes content mee | much. 1720
If euer Lady wrong'd her Lord so much,   1916
Mate. And so much shall you giue, or off goes yours.   2186
Lieu. What thinke you much to pay 2000. Crownes,   2187
*which is as much to say, as let the Magistrates be la-|bouring 2336
Cade. I am able to endure much.   2374
Thou would'st not haue mourn'd so much for me.   2557
Id. How much thou wrong'st me, heauen be my iudge;   2981
Buc. That is too much presumption on thy part: 3030
But thou mistakes me much to thinke I do,   3127
MUDDE = 1
The purest Spring is not so free from mudde,   1399
MUFFLED = 1
Whit. The Duke of Suffolke, muffled vp in ragges?   2215
MULE = 1
Bare-headed plodded by my foot-cloth Mule,   2222
MULTIPLIED = 1
Your Graces Title shall be multiplied.   348
MULTIPLYED = 1
Although by his sight his sinne be multiplyed.   800

199

MULTITUDE = 3*1
See how the giddy multitude doe point,	1197
With the rude multitude, till I returne.	1837
His Army is a ragged multitude	2568
*as this multitude? The name of Henry the fift, hales them	2833

MULTITUDES = 2
*Enter Multitudes with Halters about their	Neckes.*	2860
Not fit to gouerne and rule multitudes,	3089

MUM = 1
Seale vp your Lips, and giue no words but Mum,	365

MURDERD = 1
A Romane Sworder, and Bandetto slaue	Murder'd sweet *Tully. Brutus*	
Bastard hand	2303

MURDEROUS = 1
Vpon thy eye-balls, murderous Tyrannie	1749

MURDRED = 2
That good Duke *Humfrey* Traiterously is murdred	1825
It cannot be but he was murdred heere,	1881

MURDRING = 1
Their cheefest Prospect, murd'ring Basiliskes:	2039

MURDROUS = 2
I would, false murd'rous Coward, on thy Knee	1925
To do a murd'rous deede, to rob a man,	3185

MURTHER = 5
Murther indeede, that bloodie sinne, I tortur'd	Aboue the Felon, or	
what Trespas else.	1431
*Enter two or three running ouer the Stage, from the	Murther of Duke*	
Humfrey.	1690
Warw. But that the guilt of Murther bucklers thee,	1921
By shamefull murther of a guiltlesse King,	2263
You cannot but forbeare to murther me:	2710

MURTHERD = 1
Which he had thought to haue murther'd wrongfully.	1166

MURTHERED = 1
Harmelesse *Richard* was murthered traiterously.	986

MURTHERER = 3
Vnlesse it were a bloody Murtherer,	1428
Who being accus'd a craftie Murtherer,	1556
Yet Aeolus would not be a murtherer,	1792

MURTHERERS = 1
And we I hope sir, are no murtherers.	1885

MURTHERS = 1
That slanders me with Murthers Crimson Badge.	1904

MUSE = 1
King. I muse my Lord of Gloster is not come:	1295

MUSICK = 1
How irkesome is this Musick to my heart?	781

MUSICKE = 1
Their Musicke, frightfull as the Serpents hisse,	2041

MUST = 19*5
To you Duke *Humfrey* must vnload his greefe:	83
So Yorke must sit, and fret, and bite his tongue,	242
Hum. Nay *Elinor*, then must I chide outright:	315
Follow I must, I cannot go before,	336
**Hume. Hume* must make merry with the Duchesse Gold:	363
And must be made a Subiect to a Duke?	435
Yet must we ioyne with him and with the Lords,	481
Humf. Sirrha, or you must fight, or else be hang'd.	614

MUST *cont.*
Glost. Well Sir, we must haue you finde your Legges.	895
I must offend, before I be attainted:	1235
Glost. Must you, Sir *Iohn*, protect my Lady here?	1256
Lord *Suffolke*, you and I must talke of that euent.	1631
Must not be shed by such a iaded Groome:	2220
Lieu. Water: W. Come Suffolke, I must waft thee | to thy death.	2283
Weauer. A must needs, for beggery is valiant.	2373
*Come hither sirrah, I must examine thee: What is thy | name? |	
Clearke. Emanuell.	2414
And so farwell, for I must hence againe. *Exeunt*	2612
*that must sweepe the Court cleane of such filth as thou	2665
in: and now the word Sallet must serue me to feed on.	2919
The king hath sent him sure: I must dissemble.	3005
But I must make faire weather yet a while,	3022
That Gold, must round engirt these browes of mine,	3094
For I my selfe must hunt this Deere to death.	3235
But flye you must: Vncureable discomfite	3314

MUTINIE = 1
My selfe haue calm'd their spleenfull mutinie,	1830

MUTUALL = 1
The mutuall conference that my minde hath had,	32

MY *l.9* 16 17 19 29 *31 32 33 34 36 37 42 43 46 77 85 90 95 122 125 126
133 144 145 146 147 148 198 245 256 268 *274 293 294 295 *296 297
305 309 314 325 327 *331 335 340 342 *386 395 *397 *399 *402 *410
*415 428 437 472 474 491 500 511 529 533 534 547 552 553 555 563
*571 *585 *587 590 *594 *595 601 *610 *611 613 *620 633 675 687 699
706 *707 709 712 721 726 729 733 747 748 756 764 773 776 781 783
*801 824 825 828 838 *842 *843 847 *853 862 878 882 885 898 915 918
930 933 *934 935 *942 943 944 949 *960 962 963 965 969 1006 1031
*1043 *1045 1047 *1067 1071 1079 1080 1087 1108 1114 *1134 *1135
*1136 *1138 *1148 *1150 1176 1178 1187 1195 1200 1203 1207 1209
1210 1216 1217 1224 1249 1251 *1253 1256 *1263 1265 1268 1281 1282
*1288 1289 1291 1295 1328 1333 1334 1335 1337 1340 1350 1360 1362
1367 1374 1377 1386 1387 1389 1391 1392 1397 1400 1402 1413 1414
1419 *1433 1437 1439 1441 1447 1448 1460 1461 1462 1464 1466 1467
1469 1472 1493 *1495 1499 1501 1518 1526 1540 1548 1562 1571 1573
*1575 1579 1580 1600 1614 1620 *1632 1633 *1635 1645 1658 1661 1677
1686 1692 1696 1698 *1699 1704 1712 1725 *1730 1736 *1737 1739 1741
1748 1756 1759 1768 1769 1781 1784 1805 1806 1809 1811 1830 1836
*1838 1839 1841 1846 1847 1851 1855 1856 1857 1884 1924 *1982
1986 1997 1998 2006 2007 2028 2031 2035 2055 2057 2061 2065 2081
2099 2102 2108 2113 2114 2126 *2134 2142 2150 2184 2192 2196 2198
2200 2203 2211 2221 2222 2223 2224 2225 2230 2234 *2288 2292 2294
2301 2359 2361 2363 *2369 *2387 2391 2423 *2438 *2468 *2475 *2483
*2523 2537 2543 *2558 2563 2575 2591 2593 *2594 2601 2607 *2627
*2647 *2653 *2661 *2685 2700 2706 2732 2733 2734 *2738 2750 2758
*2799 *2836 *2839 2841 2852 *2862 2866 *2884 2895 2896 2897 2900
2903 *2906 *2910 *2916 2923 2927 2928 *2932 *2933 2937 2938 2939
2952 2954 2958 *2959 *2962 2973 *2981 2983 2999 3015 3019 3021 3026
3036 3040 3041 3042 3065 3068 3070 3106 3108 3116 *3121 3126 3141
3175 3177 3202 3204 3227 3228 3235 3238 3247 3272 3277 3282 3285
*3297 3312 3318 3328 *3337 3351 = 352*89

MYNION = 1
Giue me my Fanne: what, Mynion, can ye not? | *She giues the Duchesse*	
a box on the eare.	529

MYSELFE *see* selfe

NAILE = 1
naile, I pray God I may neuer eate grasse more.	2945

NAKED = 2
| And he but naked, though lockt vp in Steele, | 1940 |
| Though standing naked on a Mountaine top, | 2051 |

NAME = 20*5
*and so I pray you goe in Gods Name, and leaue vs.	*Exit Hume.*	628
Whose name and power thou tremblest at,	650
Glost. Tell me Sirrha, what's my Name?	*Simpc.* Alas Master, I know not.	862
Glost. What's his Name?	*Simpc.* I know not.	864
Glost. What's thine owne Name?	*Simpc. Saunder Simpcoxe,* and if it please you, Master.	868
As thus to name the seuerall Colours we doe weare.	874
That hath dis-honored *Glosters* honest Name.	951
Crown'd by the Name of *Henry* the fourth,	982
King. A Gods Name see the Lysts and all things fit,	1110
Sirrha, what's thy Name?	*Peter. Peter* forsooth.	1141
Death, at whose Name I oft haue beene afear'd,	1269
I doe arrest you in his Highnesse Name,	1436
So shall my name with Slanders tongue be wounded,	1768
And beare the name and port of Gentlemen?	2188
Whit. And so am I: my name is *Walter Whitmore.*	2200
Suf. Thy name affrights me, in whose sound is death:	2202
Thy name is *Gualtier,* being rightly sounded.	2206
Neuer yet did base dishonour blurre our name,	2208
*Come hither sirrah, I must examine thee: What is thy	name?	*Clearke. Emanuell.*	2414
Cade. Let me alone: Dost thou vse to write thy name?	2419
Clearke. Sir I thanke God, I haue bin so well brought	vp, that I can write my name.	2422
*his Tongue, he speakes not a Gods name. Goe, take	2741
*as this multitude? The name of Henry the fift, hales them	2833
Iden. Alexander Iden, that's my name,	3068
The name of Valour. O let the vile world end,	3262

NAMES = 2
| Blotting your names from Bookes of memory, | 107 |
| Thou might'st as well haue knowne all our Names, | 873 |

NAP = 1
| *dresse the Common-wealth and turne it, and set a new | nap vpon it. | 2324 |

NAPLES = 1*1
| *Naples, Sicillia, and Ierusalem, and Crowne her Queene of* | 54 |
| Out-cast of *Naples,* Englands bloody Scourge, | 3113 |

NATIUE = 2
| Droue backe againe vnto my Natiue Clime. | 1784 |
| Spare England, for it is your Natiue Coast: | 2827 |

NATURE = 2
| By nature prou'd an Enemie to the Flock, | 1560 |
| Being opposites of such repayring Nature. | 3344 |

NAUGHT *see also* nought = 1*1
| And can doe naught but wayle her Darlings losse; | 1517 |
| *Yorke.* What, worse then naught? nay, then a shame | take all. | 1610 |

NAUGHTIE = 1
| A sort of naughtie persons, lewdly bent, | 919 |

NAY = 11*10
Nay more, an enemy vnto you all,	156
Hum. Nay *Elinor,* then must I chide outright:	315
Hum. Nay be not angry, I am pleas'd againe.	329
Where are you there? Sir *Iohn*; nay feare not man,	343

NAY *cont.*
Suff. Nay *Gloster*, know that thou art come too soone,	1393
Qu. Nay then, this sparke will proue a raging fire,	1605
Yorke. What, worse then naught? nay, then a shame | take all.	1610
Beuis. Nay more, the Kings Councell are no good | Workemen.	2333
Cade. Nay, that I meane to do. Is not this a lamenta-|ble	2395
Cade. Nay then he is a Coniurer.	2409
But. Nay, he can make Obligations, and write Court | hand.	2410
But. Nay, 'tis too true, therefore he shall be King.	2467
Cade. Nay answer if you can: The Frenchmen are our	2489
Smith. Nay *Iohn*, it wil be stinking Law, for his breath | stinkes with	
eating toasted cheese.	2644
*Ah thou Say, thou Surge, nay thou Buckram Lord, now	2659
Cade. Nay, he noddes at vs, as who should say, Ile be	2727
Iden. Nay, it shall nere be said, while England stands,	2946
Command my eldest sonne, nay all my sonnes,	3041
Nay, do not fright vs with an angry looke:	3123
Yor. Nay we shall heate you thorowly anon.	3158
War. After them: nay before them if we can:	3350

NAYLES = 1
Could I come neere your Beautie with my Nayles,	533

NECESSARIE = 1
It were but necessarie you were wak't:	1973

NECKE = 2
I tooke a costly Iewell from my necke,	1806
and Inke-horne about his necke. | *Exit one with the Clearke*	2427

NECKES = 3*1
And smooth my way vpon their headlesse neckes.	340
*be hang'd with your Pardons about your neckes? Hath	2798
Enter Multitudes with Halters about their | *Neckes.*	2860
And humbly thus with halters on their neckes,	2863

NEED = 2*1
They say, A craftie Knaue do's need no Broker,	376
Wife. Alas Sir, we did it for pure need.	908
Hol. So he had need, for 'tis thred-bare. Well, I say,	2326

NEEDE = 1*1
Hol. They haue the more neede to sleepe now then.	2322
Wea. He neede not feare the sword, for his Coate is of | proofe.	2378

NEEDIE = 1
Because I would not taxe the needie Commons,	1416

NEEDS = 4*1
Queene. If he be old enough, what needs your Grace	508
Shee's tickled now, her Fume needs no spurres,	543
Weauer. A must needs, for beggery is valiant.	2373
*And you base Pezants, do ye beleeue him, will you needs	2797
Qu. A subtle Traitor needs no Sophister.	3191

NEERE = 5*1
Hume, if you take not heed, you shall goe neere	378
Could I come neere your Beautie with my Nayles,	533
Glost. Stand by, my Masters, bring him neere the King,	801
First note, that he is neere you in discent,	1315
Why then Dame *Elianor* was neere thy ioy.	1779
Or dare to bring thy Force so neere the Court?	3014

NEGLECT = 1
(As well we may, if not through your neglect)	3307

NEIGHBOR = 1*1
*in a Cup of Sack; and feare not Neighbor, you shall doe | well enough.	1121

NEIGHBOR *cont.*
  Neighbor: drinke, and feare not your Man.   1126
NEIGHBORS = *1
  Enter at one Doore the Armorer and his Neighbors, drinking   1115
NEIGHBOUR *see also* 1.*Neighbor*, 2.*Neighbor*, 3.*Neighbor* = *2
  1.Neighbor. Here Neighbour *Horner*, I drinke to you   1120
  2.Neighbor. And here Neighbour, here's a Cuppe of | Charneco. 1123
NEITHER = 1
  Cade. I feare neither sword, nor fire.   2377
NEL = *1
  Hu. I go. Come *Nel* thou wilt ride with vs? *Ex. Hum*   334
NELL = 5*3
  Hum. O *Nell*, sweet *Nell*, if thou dost loue thy Lord,   290
  Sweet *Nell*, ill can thy Noble Minde abrooke   1181
  Glost. Be patient, gentle *Nell*, forget this griefe.   1202
  Glost. Ah *Nell*, forbeare: thou aymest all awry.   1234
  Thy greatest helpe is quiet, gentle *Nell*:   1243
  My *Nell*, I take my leaue: and Master Sherife,   1251
  King. I thanke thee *Nell*, these wordes content mee | much. 1720
NEOPOLITAN = 1
  Yorke. O blood-bespotted Neopolitan,   3112
NEPHEW = 1*1
  Car. Nephew, what meanes this passionate discourse?   111
  Against my King and Nephew, vertuous *Henry*,   293
NERE = 4*1
  A man that ne're saw in his life before.   792
  Glost. And my consent ne're ask'd herein before?   1249
  Which with the heart there cooles, and ne're returneth,   1870
  Iden. Nay, it shall nere be said, while England stands,   2946
  Ne're shall this blood be wiped from thy point,   2974
NEST = 3
  Queene. Gloster, see here the Taincture of thy Nest,   940
  Did seeme to say, seeke not a Scorpions Nest,   1786
  Who finds the Partridge in the Puttocks Nest,   1895
NEUER *see also* ne're = 31*11
  Defacing Monuments of Conquer'd France, | Vndoing all as all had
  neuer bin.   109
  I neuer read but Englands Kings haue had   135
  Hum. A proper iest, and neuer heard before,   139
  I neuer saw but Humfrey Duke of Gloster,   191
  And neuer more abase our sight so low,   288
  And neuer mount to trouble you againe.   477
  Did neuer Traytor in the Land commit.   569
  Armorer. And't shall please your Maiestie, I neuer sayd   584
  *O Lord haue mercy vpon me, I shall neuer be able to ⌈ fight a blow: O
  Lord my heart.   612
  Let neuer Day nor Night vnhallowed passe,   817
  Suff. And yet I thinke, Iet did he neuer see.   858
  Wife. Neuer before this day, in all his life.   861
  Yorke. I neuer saw a fellow worse bestead,   1112
  *God, for I am neuer able to deale with my Master, hee   1138
  *take my death, I neuer meant him any ill, nor the King,   1150
  Nor neuer seeke preuention of thy foes.   1233
  For Souldiers pay in France, and neuer sent it?   1356
  I neuer rob'd the Souldiers of their pay,   1408
  And neuer ask'd for restitution.   1418
  Strange Tortures for Offendors, neuer heard of,   1422

NEUER *cont.*

I neuer gaue them condigne punishment.	1430
Thou neuer didst them wrong, nor no man wrong:	1510
He neuer would haue stay'd in France so long.	1598
Yorke. Now *Yorke,* or neuer, steele thy fearfull thoughts,	1637
And neuer of the *Neuils* Noble Race.	1920
Where byting cold would neuer let grasse grow,	2052
Neuer yet did base dishonour blurre our name,	2208
Lieu. But Ioue was neuer slaine as thou shalt be,	2217
Whose dreadfull swords were neuer drawne in vaine,	2260
Suf. That this my death may neuer be forgot.	2301
*it was neuer merrie world in England, since Gentlemen | came vp.	2327
*was he borne, vnder a hedge: for his Father had neuer a | house but	
the Cage.	2370
*I was neuer mine owne man since. How now? Who's | there?	2400
But. If this Fellow be wise, hee'l neuer call yee *Iacke*	2625
Prayres and Teares haue mou'd me, Gifts could neuer.	2702
Those that I neuer saw, and strucke them dead.	2715
*I thought ye would neuer haue giuen out these Armes til	2801
Was neuer Subiect long'd to be a King,	2854
Assure your selues will neuer be vnkinde:	2871
naile, I pray God I may neuer eate grasse more.	2945
*the World to be Cowards: For I that neuer feared any,	2979
And neuer liue but true vnto his Liege.	3076

NEUILL = 1

Yorke. And *Neuill,* this I doe assure my selfe,	1047

NEUILLS = 1

The *Neuills* are thy Subiects to command.	967

NEUILS = 5

And therefore I will take the *Neuils* parts,	252
Cannot doe more in England then the *Neuils*:	459
And neuer of the *Neuils* Noble Race.	1920
The Princely Warwicke, and the *Neuils* all,	2259
War. Now by my Fathers badge, old *Neuils* Crest,	3202

NEW = 2*2

Suffolke, the new made Duke that rules the rost,	116
*With his new Bride, & Englands deere bought Queen,	264
*dresse the Common-wealth and turne it, and set a new | nap vpon it.	2324
Come thou new ruine of olde Cliffords house:	3283

NEWES = 5*5

Cold newes for me: for I had hope of France,	249
Thither goes these Newes, | As fast as Horse can carry them:	704
This Newes I thinke hath turn'd your Weapons edge;	932
King. Welcome Lord *Somerset:* What Newes from | France?	1378
King. Cold Newes, Lord *Somerset:* but Gods will be | done.	1382
Yorke. Cold Newes for me: for I had hope of France,	1384
Queene. Whether goes *Vaux* so fast? What newes I | prethee?	2083
Aye me! What is this World? What newes are these?	2097
King. How now? What newes? Why com'st thou in | such haste?	2561
Yor. I thanke thee *Clifford:* Say, what newes with thee?	3122

NEWLY = 1

The Duke of Yorke is newly come from Ireland,	2877

NEW-MADE = 1

And from the great and new-made Duke of Suffolke;	371

NEXT = 11*1

England, ere the thirtieth of May next ensuing.	55
Consider Lords, he is the next of blood,	158

NEXT *cont.*

Next time Ile keepe my dreames vnto my selfe, | And not be check'd.	327
Were I a Man, a Duke, and next of blood,	338
Next, if I be appointed for the Place,	562
*Combat, shall be the last of the next moneth. Come	616
Lionel, Duke of Clarence; next to whom,	972
The Issue of the next Sonne should haue reign'd.	991
Holden at Bury, the first of this next Moneth.	1248
And should you fall, he is the next will mount.	1316
As next the King, he was successiue Heire,	1343
And *Henry* put apart: the next for me. *Exit.*	1689

NEYTHER = 1

Hauing neyther Subiect, Wealth, nor Diadem:	2250

NIGH *see* nye

NIGHT = 17*2

By day, by night; waking, and in my dreames,	33
My troublous dreames this night, doth make me sad.	295
*them to me in the Garret one Night, as wee were scow-|ring my Lord of Yorkes Armor.	588
Deepe Night, darke Night, the silent of the Night,	636
The time of Night when Troy was set on fire,	637
To suppe with me to morrow Night. Away. | *Exeunt.*	713
Let neuer Day nor Night vnhallowed passe,	817
King. Well, for this Night we will repose vs here:	952
No: Darke shall be my Light, and Night my Day.	1216
So helpe me God, as I haue watcht the Night,	1410
I, Night by Night, in studying good for England.	1411
Card. Gods secret Iudgement: I did dreame to Night,	1727
Well could I curse away a Winters night,	2050
That dragge the Tragicke melancholy night:	2173
Deferre the spoile of the Citie vntill night:	2769
For you shall sup with Iesu Christ to night.	3214

NINE = 1

But I was made a King, at nine months olde.	2853

NIPPING = 1

Barren Winter, with his wrathfull nipping Cold;	1173

NO *1*.25 61 125 138 157 324 365 376 *415 460 497 507 538 543 558 678 725 730 745 759 867 1081 1083 *1193 1216 1272 1289 1314 1317 1350 1415 1420 1452 1510 1540 1546 1559 1565 1599 1607 1628 1629 1642 1683 1714 1775 1787 1820 1885 1901 1968 1977 2005 2080 2081 2138 2144 2145 2148 2163 2216 2292 2299 *2333 *2338 *2375 *2390 2437 2492 2493 2520 2521 *2558 2595 2601 *2668 *2674 2729 2815 *2836 *2839 2851 2852 *2911 *2943 *2965 3025 3031 *3049 3088 3090 3099 3189 3191 3258 3260 3274 3303 = 87*15

NOBILITIE = 2*1

As like to Pytch, defile Nobilitie;	948
And such high vaunts of his Nobilitie,	1344
Hol. The Nobilitie thinke scorne to goe in Leather | Aprons.	2331

NOBILITY = 1*1

True Nobility, is exempt from feare:	2297
*to the Nobility. Let them breake your backes with bur-|thens,	2804

NOBLE = 16

Did beare him like a Noble Gentleman:	192
King. For my part, Noble Lords, I care not which,	491
Noble shee is: but if shee haue forgot | Honor and Vertue, and conuers't with such,	946
Glost. My Staffe? Here, Noble *Henry*, is my Staffe:	1087

NOBLE *cont.*

Sweet *Nell*, ill can thy Noble Minde abrooke	1181
Queene. Thrice Noble *Suffolke*, 'tis resolutely spoke.	1568
Then, Noble *Yorke*, take thou this Taske in hand.	1623
Suff. Ile call him presently, my Noble Lord. *Exit.*	1712
That faultlesse may condemne a Noble man:	1718
And all to haue the Noble Duke aliue.	1764
Some sterne vntutur'd Churle; and Noble Stock	1918
And neuer of the *Neuils* Noble Race.	1920
Yor. Will you not Sonnes? | *Edw.* I Noble Father, if our words will serue.	3135
War. How now my Noble Lord? What all a-foot.	3227
Rich. My Noble Father: | Three times to day I holpe him to his horse,	3328
But Noble as he is, looke where he comes.	3335

NOBLEMEN = 1

Queen. Than you belike suspect these Noblemen,	1890

NOBLES = 2

And all the Peeres and Nobles of the Realme	516
Well Nobles, well: 'tis politikely done,	1647

NOBLY = 1*1

You Madame, for you are more Nobly borne,	1062
War. Then nobly Yorke, 'tis for a Crown thou fightst:	3236

NOBODY *see* body

NODDE = 1

And nodde their heads, and throw their eyes on thee.	1198

NODDES = *1

Cade. Nay, he noddes at vs, as who should say, Ile be	2727

NOISE = 1

Sound a parley. | What noise is this I heare?	2777

NOMINATE = 1

But suddenly to nominate them all, | It is impossible.	876

NONE = 7

Excepting none but good Duke Humfrey.	201
We are alone, here's none but thee, & I. *Enter Hume.*	344
Buck. True Madame, none at all: what call you this?	679
For none abides with me: my Ioy, is Death;	1268
Say, who's a Traytor? *Gloster* he is none. *Exit.*	1523
Beleeue me Lords, were none more wise then I,	1533
Spare none, but such as go in clouted shooen,	2505

NOR *l.*256 257 258 *585 817 866 *1150 *1151 1225 1233 1397 1409 1469 1510 1787 1910 2056 2250 2377 2601 2816 3090 *3243 3260 *3300 3326 = 21*6

NORMANDIE = 4*1

Receiud deepe scarres in France and Normandie:	94
These Counties were the Keyes of *Normandie*:	121
Paris is lost, the state of *Normandie* | Stands on a tickle point, now they are gone:	227
Normandie vnto Mounsieur *Basimecu*, the Dolphine of	2662
I sold not *Maine*, I lost not *Normandie*,	2699

NORMANS = 1

The false reuolting Normans thorough thee,	2255

NORTH = *1

Simpc. At Barwick in the North, and't like your | Grace.	813

NORTHERNE = 1

Proud Northerne Lord, Clifford of Cumberland,	3224

NOSE = 1

Som. Rere vp his Body, wring him by the Nose.	1732

NOSTRILS = 1
His hayre vprear'd, his nostrils stretcht with strugling: 1875
NOT *l.*119 147 163 177 233 241 259 317 319 328 329 341 343 370 378 395
    456 461 468 480 491 498 500 529 539 *598 624 641 652 675 677 718 720
    734 753 761 766 845 847 863 865 879 883 892 *900 933 944 *989 1020
    1021 1030 1033 *1121 1126 *1129 1131 *1193 1206 1224 1232 1238 1241
    1252 1259 *1263 1272 *1288 1295 1296 1298 1312 1341 1349 1352 1354
    1396 1398 1399 1416 1453 1468 1478 1545 1550 *1554 1558 1563 1569
    1583 1599 1640 1644 1657 1728 1745 1746 1751 1752 1786 1792 1798
    1819 1829 1833 1888 *1907 1909 1970 1995 2001 2011 2022 2036 2067
    2068 2074 2079 2100 2143 2159 2197 2205 2207 2220 2221 2237 2277
    2280 2317 *2329 *2366 *2378 *2395 *2413 2448 2453 2457 2470 2472
    2494 2504 2507 *2528 2549 2557 *2558 *2574 2591 *2594 2643 *2676
    *2677 2680 *2682 2698 2699 2726 *2741 *2752 *2753 2764 2792 2818
    2829 2898 2900 *2908 *2913 2925 2926 2936 2937 *2944 *2961 2980
    2996 2997 3070 3080 3088 3089 3090 3091 3093 3123 3126 3133 3135
    *3137 3179 3213 3217 3220 3261 3273 3278 3307 3326 3342
    3343 = 174*30
NOTE = 2
First note, that he is neere you in discent,   1315
Came he right now to sing a Rauens Note,   1740
NOTHING = 6
Eli. Tut, this was nothing but an argument,   306
Glost. Talking of Hawking; nothing else, my Lord.   773
Nor stirre at nothing, till the Axe of Death   1225
The pissing Conduit run nothing but Clarret Wine   2618
Dic. What say you of Kent. | *Say.* Nothing but this: 'Tis *bona terra,*
mala gens.   2688
Nothing so heauy as these woes of mine.   3287
NOTICE = 2
My selfe had notice of your Conuenticles,   1466
And giuen me notice of their Villanies.   1676
NOUGHT = 2
My selfe no ioy in nought, but that thou liu'st.   2081
This hand was made to handle nought but Gold.   2998
NOURISH = 1
Whiles I in Ireland nourish a mightie Band,   1654
NOW = 71*13
And humbly now vpon my bended knee,   17
King. Vnkle, how now? | *Glo.* Pardon me gracious Lord,   58
But now it is impossible we should.   115
Sal. Now by the death of him that dyed for all,   120
Car. My Lord of Gloster, now ye grow too hot,   144
Paris is lost, the state of *Normandie* | Stands on a tickle point, now they
are gone: 227
Marry and shall: but how now, Sir *Iohn Hume?*   364
Suff. How now fellow: would'st any thing with me?   396
·*Suffolke, for enclosing the Commons of Melforde. How | now, Sir
Knaue?   406
Shee's tickled now, her Fume needs no spurres,   543
Humf. Now Lords, my Choller being ouer-blowne,   547
Now pray my Lord, let's see the Deuils Writ.   687
The King is now in progresse towards Saint *Albones,*   702
King. How now, my Lords?   764
King. Why how now, Vnckle *Gloster?*   772
Now by Gods Mother, Priest,   774
King. Now God be prays'd, that to beleeuing Soules   793

NOW *cont.*

What, hast thou beene long blinde, and now restor'd?	805
Let me see thine Eyes; winck now, now open them,	846
Glost. Now fetch me a Stoole hither by and by.	889
*Now Sirrha, if you meane to saue your selfe from Whip-|ping,	890
Yorke. Now my good Lords of Salisbury & Warwick,	960
Yorke. Which now they hold by force, and not by right:	989
Queene. Why now is *Henry* King, and *Margaret* Queen,	1095
Now thou do'st Penance too. Looke how they gaze,	1196
And Sir *Iohn Stanly* is appointed now,	1254
What e're occasion keepes him from vs now.	1297
But meet him now, and be it in the Morne,	1307
Now 'tis the Spring, and Weeds are shallow-rooted,	1325
Suffer them now, and they'le o're-grow the Garden,	1326
What lowring Starre now enuies thy estate?	1507
Yorke. And I: and now we three haue spoke it,	1582
But now returne we to the false Duke *Humfrey.*	1627
Yorke. Now *Yorke*, or neuer, steele thy fearfull thoughts,	1637
For that *Iohn Mortimer*, which now is dead,	1678
Suff. Now Sirs, haue you dispatcht this thing?	1697
How now? why look'st thou pale? why tremblest thou?	1723
Came he right now to sing a Rauens Note,	1740
In life, but double death, now *Gloster*'s dead.	1755
Warw. Away euen now, or I will drag thee hence:	1934
King. Why how now Lords?	1946
And euen now my burthen'd heart would breake	2035
Now by the ground that I am banish'd from,	2049
Go, speake not to me; euen now be gone.	2067
Yet now farewell, and farewell Life with thee.	2071
That euen now he cries alowd for him.	2095
*Now get thee hence, the King thou know'st is comming,	2103
And now loud houling Wolues arouse the Iades	2172
How now? why starts thou? What doth death affright?	2201
Now will I dam vp this thy yawning mouth,	2241
And now the House of Yorke thrust from the Crowne,	2262
What, are ye danted now? Now will ye stoope.	2287
Hol. They haue the more neede to sleepe now then.	2322
Weauer. But now of late, not able to trauell with her	2366
*I was neuer mine owne man since. How now? Who's | there?	2400
Rise vp Sir *Iohn Mortimer.* Now haue at him.	2439
Now shew your selues men, 'tis for Liberty.	2503
King. How now Madam? | Still lamenting and mourning for Suffolkes	
death?	2554
King. How now? What newes? Why com'st thou in | such haste?	2561
Qu. Ah were the Duke of Suffolke now aliue,	2577
Qu. My hope is gone, now Suffolke is deceast.	2593
Scales. How now? Is *Iacke Cade* slaine?	2600
Cade. Now is *Mortimer* Lord of this City,	2615
And now henceforward it shall be Treason for any,	2620
Cade. So sirs: now go some and pull down the Sauoy:	2635
*Ah thou Say, thou Surge, nay thou Buckram Lord, now	2659
When they were aliue. Now part them againe,	2766
But now is Cade driuen backe, his men dispierc'd,	2888
And now is Yorke in Armes, to second him.	2889
*the Country is laid for me: but now am I so hungry, that	2909
in: and now the word Sallet must serue me to feed on.	2919
And now like *Aiax Telamonius,*	3018

NOW *cont.*

Yor. How now? is Somerset at libertie?	3082
War. Now by my Fathers badge, old *Neuils* Crest,	3202
Now when the angrie Trumpet sounds alarum,	3221
War. How now my Noble Lord? What all a-foot.	3227
Yorke. So let it helpe me now against thy sword,	3245
Now let the generall Trumpet blow his blast,	3265
Now is it manhood, wisedome, and defence,	3301
And where this breach now in our Fortunes made	May readily be stopt.	3309
Sal. Now by my Sword, well hast thou fought to day:	3337
Now by my hand (Lords) 'twas a glorious day.	3351

NOWNE = *1

*Nowne and a Verbe, and such abhominable wordes, as	2673

NOYSE = 4

Glost. What meanes this noyse?	785
Noyse within. Enter Warwicke, and many	*Commons.*	1822
A noyse within.	*Queene.* What noyse is this?	1942

NUBIBUS = 1

Vnder the which is writ, *Inuitis nubibus.*	2267

NUMBER = 1*1

To number *Aue-Maries* on his Beades:	442
Somerset. And in the number, thee, that wishest	shame.	1612

NUMBERS = 2

Glost. Make vp no factious numbers for the matter,	759
Drumme. Enter Cade, Dicke Butcher, Smith the Weauer,	*and a Sawyer, with infinite numbers.*	2350

NURSE = 1

The elder of them being put to nurse,	2462

NURTERD = 1

Presumptuous Dame, ill-nurter'd *Elianor,*	316

NYE = 1

Was I for this nye wrack'd vpon the Sea,	1782

O *l.*26 105 *290 *612 613 836 881 905 *938 *1137 *1160 1161 *1838 2272 2315 *2329 2405 2488 *2716 2737 2762 *2965 3101 3112 3255 3262 = 17*9

OATH = 3*2

Suf. A dreadfull Oath, sworne with a solemn tongue:	1862
Against thy Oath, and true Allegeance sworne,	3012
Ki. Canst thou dispense with heauen for such an oath?	3181
But greater sinne to keepe a sinfull oath:	3183
But that he was bound by a solemne Oath?	3190

OBDURATE = 1

God should be so obdurate as your selues:	2748

OBEY = 3

Let them obey, that knowes not how to Rule.	2997
Obey audacious Traitor, kneele for Grace.	3103
Qu. He is arrested, but will not obey:	3133

OBIECTIONS = 1

As for your spightfull false Obiections,	550

OBLIGATIONS = *1

But. Nay, he can make Obligations, and write Court	hand.	2410

OBSCURE = 1

Obscure and lowsie Swaine, King *Henries* blood.	2218

OBSEQUIES = 1

But all in vaine are these meane Obsequies,	*Bed put forth.*	1848

OBSERUE = 1
Queene. Can you not see? or will ye not obserue   1298
OCCASION = 2
What e're occasion keepes him from vs now.   1297
Repaires him with Occasion. This happy day   3325
OCCUPAT = 1
Suf. Pine gelidus timor occupat artus, it is thee I feare.   2285
OCEAN = 1
Vpon his face an Ocean of salt teares,   1845
ODDES = 1
Tooke oddes to combate a poore famisht man.   2948
ODIOUS = 1
The sight of me is odious in their eyes: 2582
OF *see also* o' = 451*87
OFF *see also* farre-off *l*.833 899 *1043 1098 1286 1304 1630 2168 *2186
2237 *2742 *2744 2987 3304 3330 = 11*4
OFFENCES = 1
Deuise strange deaths, for small offences done?   1353
OFFEND = 1
I must offend, before I be attainted: .   1235
OFFENDED = 1
Say. Tell me: wherein haue I offended most?   2730
OFFENDING = 1
Might liquid teares, or heart-offending groanes,   1760
OFFENDOR = 1
And the Offendor graunted scope of speech,   1476
OFFENDORS = 4
Buck. Thy Crueltie in execution | Vpon Offendors, hath exceeded Law,   522
And call these foule Offendors to their Answeres;   955
Strange Tortures for Offendors, neuer heard of,   1422
For I should melt at an Offendors teares,   1426
OFFER = 1
Who said; *Symon*, come; come offer at my Shrine,   825
OFFERED = 1
And yeeld to mercy, whil'st 'tis offered you,   2788
OFFICE = 3
Sherife. It is my Office, and Madame pardon me.   1282
Elianor. I, I, farewell, thy Office is discharg'd: 1283
But left that hatefull office vnto thee.   1793
OFFICERS = 1
burning in her hand, with the Sherife | and Officers.   1189
OFFICES = 1
Queene. Thy sale of Offices and Townes in France,   525
OFFICE-BADGE = *1
**Hum.* Me thought this staffe mine Office-badge in | Court   298
OFT = 7*2
Oft haue I seene the haughty Cardinall,   193
And many time and oft my selfe haue heard a Voyce, | To call him so.   828
Death, at whose Name I oft haue beene afear'd,   1269
Oft haue I seene a timely-parted Ghost,   1865
Great men oft dye by vilde Bezonions.   2302
**Queene.* Oft haue I heard that greefe softens the mind,   2533
**Say.* Great men haue reaching hands: oft haue I struck   2714
Rich. Oft haue I seene a hot ore-weening Curre,   3150
And Beautie, that the Tyrant oft reclaimes,   3276
OFTEN = 5
Did he so often lodge in open field: 87

OFTEN *cont.*

For things are often spoke, and seldome meant,	1570
Full often, like a shag-hayr'd craftie Kerne,	1673
How often haue I tempted Suffolkes tongue	1814
How often hast thou waited at my cup,	2224

OFTNER = 1

Being call'd a hundred times, and oftner,	823

OH *see also* O *l.*220 1694 *1733 1735 2003 2054 2058 2068 2119 2145 2153 2155 2163 *2574 3016 3063 3166 = 16*2

OILE *see* oyle

OLD = 11*2

Humf. Madame, the King is old enough himselfe	506
Queene. If he be old enough, what needs your Grace	508
And ten to one, old *Ioane* had not gone out.	720
Enter Buckingham, and old Clifford.	2781
Old Salsbury, shame to thy siluer haire,	3162
Why art thou old, and want'st experience?	3171
Old Clif. The first I warrant thee, if dreames proue true	3195
Old Clif. I am resolu'd to beare a greater storme,	3198
War. Now by my Fathers badge, old *Neuils* Crest,	3202
Old Clif. And from thy Burgonet Ile rend thy Beare,	3208
It shall be stony. Yorke, not our old men spares:	3273
As did *Aeneas* old *Anchyses* beare,	3284
So was his Will, in his old feeble body,	3334

OLDE = 2

But I was made a King, at nine months olde.	2853
Come thou new ruine of olde Cliffords house:	3283

OMITTING = 1

Omitting Suffolkes exile, my soules Treasure?	2099

OMNES = 2

Come, let's away. *Exeunt omnes.*	2632
To reconcile you all vnto the King. *Exeunt omnes.*	2847

ON *see also* a, an = 70*12

ONCE = 6*1

With walking once about the Quadrangle,	548
After the Beadle hath hit him once, he leapes ouer	902
That beares so shrewd a mayme: two Pulls at once;	1097
King. My Lords at once: the care you haue of vs,	1360
Once by the King, and three times thrice by thee.	2073
*'tis the Bees waxe: for I did but seale once to a thing, and	2399
But stay, Ile read it ouer once againe.	2546

ONE *see also* 1. = 31*7

Enter King, Duke Humfrey, Salisbury, Warwicke, and Beau-|ford on the one side.	3
Lords, with one cheerefull voice, Welcome my Loue.	43
As to vouchsafe one glance vnto the ground.	289
Enter three or foure Petitioners, the Armorers | Man being one.	384
So one by one wee'le weed them all at last,	485
Or *Somerset*, or *Yorke*, all's one to me.	492
Yorke. Doth any one accuse *Yorke* for a Traytor?	575
*them to me in the Garret one Night, as wee were scow-|ring my Lord of Yorkes Armor.	588
And ten to one, old *Ioane* had not gone out.	720
Enter one crying a Miracle.	784
Glost. Then send for one presently.	886
Shall one day make the Duke of Yorke a King.	1046
*Enter at one Doore the Armorer and his Neighbors, drinking	1115

ONE *cont.*

When euery one will giue the time of day,	1308
Nor euer had one penny Bribe from France.	1409
Looking the way her harmelesse young one went,	1516
Wer't not all one, an emptie Eagle were set,	1550
Shew me one skarre, character'd on thy Skinne,	1603
His hands abroad display'd, as one that graspt	1876
Mine haire be fixt an end, as one distract:	2033
As one that surfets, thinking on a want:	2063
It is our pleasure one of them depart:	2309
*apparrell them all in one Liuery, that they may agree like	2392
and Inke-horne about his necke. | *Exit one with the Clearke*	2427
Cade. By her he had two children at one birth. | *Bro.* That's false.	2459
We will not leaue one Lord, one Gentleman:	2504
haue a License to kill for a hundred lacking one.	2519
*one and twenty Fifteenes, and one shilling to the pound, | the last	
Subsidie.	2655
Cade. Tut, when struck'st thou one blow in the field?	2713
Enter one with the heads.	2763
Let them kisse one another: For they lou'd well	2765
*make shift for one, and so Gods Cursse light vppon you | all.	2807
Iden. If one so rude, and of so meane condition	3058
War. Of one or both of vs the time is come.	3233
Is not it selfe, nor haue we wonne one foot, | If Salsbury be lost.	3326

ONE = 2

ONELY = 5*3

And left behinde him *Richard,* his onely Sonne,	978
Onely conuey me where thou art commanded.	1273
For iudgement onely doth belong to thee:	1842
Why onely Suffolke mourne I not for thee?	2100
But. Onely that the Lawes of England may come out | of your mouth.	2640
*reade, thou hast hang'd them, when (indeede) onely for	2678
*no want of resolution in mee, but onely my Followers	2839
His Armes are onely to remoue from thee	2882

ONES = *1

King. O God, what mischiefes work the wicked ones?	938

OPE = 1*1

Qu. Runne, goe, helpe, helpe: Oh *Henry* ope thine eyes.	1733
King. Then heauen set ope thy euerlasting gates,	2865

OPEN = 5*1

Did he so often lodge in open field:	87
Proue them, and I lye open to the Law:	551
Let me see thine Eyes; winck now, now open them,	846
Shall, after three dayes open Penance done,	1064
Elianor. Come you, my Lord, to see my open shame?	1195
But. If we meane to thriue, and do good, breake open	2526

OPENLY = 1

And calles your Grace Vsurper, openly,	2566

OPINION = 2

In my opinion, yet thou seest not well.	847
In crauing your opinion of my Title,	963

OPPOSE = 4

Oppose himselfe against a Troupe of Kernes,	1667
Oppose thy stedfast gazing eyes to mine,	2949
Makes him oppose himselfe against his King.	3130
If you oppose your selues to match Lord Warwicke.	3155

OPPOSITE = 1
Free from a stubborne opposite intent, 1963
OPPOSITES = 1
Being opposites of such repayring Nature. 3344
OR *l.*34 95 185 186 224 320 384 492 497 564 614 644 776 820 937 1113
1215 1298 1321 1335 1341 1365 1367 1389 1413 1429 1432 1496 1506
1530 1565 *1637 1639 1656 1690 1760 1761 1791 1819 1934 1957 1969
1977 *1991 2046 2064 2115 2144 2180 *2185 *2186 2207 2354 *2420
*2434 2447 *2491 2599 2729 2731 2757 2779 2789 2859 2864 2897 *2912
2926 *2960 3000 3008 3011 3014 3019 3172 3233 = 70*9
ORACLES = 1
These Oracles are hardly attain'd, | And hardly vnderstood. 700
ORATOR = 1
To shew how queint an Orator you are. 1987
ORDAIND = 1
Particularities, and pettie sounds | To cease. Was't thou ordain'd (deere
Father) 3266
ORDER = 4*1
Whiles I take order for mine owne affaires. 1625
Vntill they heare the order of his death. 1831
But. They are all in order, and march toward vs. 2508
Cade. But then are we in order, when we are most out 2509
of order. Come, march forward. 2510
ORDERS = 1
Ere you can take due Orders for a Priest: 1576
ORDNANCE = 1
Alarum. Fight at Sea. Ordnance goes off. 2168
ORE = 3*1
Let *Somerset* be Regent o're the French, 602
*be made Parchment; that Parchment being scribeld ore, 2397
And hang thee o're my Tombe, when I am dead. 2973
O're him, whom heauen created for thy Ruler. 3100
ORETHROW = 1
False allegations, to o'rethrow his state. 1481
ORE-GROW = 1
Suffer them now, and they'le o're-grow the Garden, 1326
ORE-SEAS = 1
Should make a start ore-seas, and vanquish you? 2820
ORE-WEENING = 1
Rich. Oft haue I seene a hot ore-weening Curre, 3150
ORLEANCE = *1
*The Dukes of *Orleance, Calaber, Britaigne,* and *Alanson,* 14
ORPHAN = 1
To reaue the Orphan of his Patrimonie, 3187
OSTRIDGE = *1
*thee eate Iron like an Ostridge, and swallow my Sword 2933
OTH = 1*1
More like a Souldier then a man o'th'Church, 194
Cade. Giue him a box o'th'eare, and that wil make'em | red againe. 2719
OTHER = 7*5
The Queene, Suffolke, Yorke, Somerset, and Buckingham, | on the other. 5
She vaunted 'mongst her Minions t'other day, 470
*him for his fault the other day, he did vow vpon his 596
And other of your Highnesse Priuie Councell, 928
fastened to it: and at the other Doore his Man, with a 1118
The other *Walter Whitmore* is thy share. 2183
That calles me other then Lord *Mortimer.* 2621

OTHER   *cont.*
*before, our Fore-fathers had no other Bookes but the   2668
*O I am slaine, Famine and no other hath slaine me, let ten   2965
But if thy Armes be to no other end,   3031
And haue no other reason for this wrong,   3189
Yor. Hold Warwick: seek thee out some other chace   3234
OTHERS = 6
Watch thou, and wake when others be asleepe,   261
As others would ambitiously receiue it.   1091
Enter Lieutenant, Suffolke, and others.   2169
Others to'th Innes of Court, downe with them all.   2636
I seeke not to waxe great by others warning,   2925
Enter King, Queene, and others.   3296
OUER *see also* o're = 10*5
And ouer ioy of heart doth minister.   38
ouer to the King her Father, and shee sent ouer of the King of   65
Weepes ouer them, and wrings his haplesse hands,   238
*leape me ouer this Stoole, and runne away.   891
*Sirrha Beadle, whippe him till he leape ouer that same | Stoole.   896
After the Beadle hath hit him once, he leapes ouer   902
Hang ouer thee, as sure it shortly will.   1226
His guilt should be but idly posted ouer,   1557
*Enter two or three running ouer the Stage, from the | Murther of Duke
Humfrey.*   1690
Ouer whom (in time to come) I hope to raigne: 2450
*for French Crownes) I am content he shall raigne, but Ile | be
Protector ouer him.   2478
But stay, Ile read it ouer once againe.   2546
Rul'd like a wandering Plannet ouer me,   2548
*take your houses ouer your heads, rauish your   2805
OUERCOME = *1
Peter. O God, haue I ouercome mine Enemies in this   1160
OUER-BLOWNE = 1
Humf. Now Lords, my Choller being ouer-blowne,   547
OUER-CHARGED = 2
Or like an ouer-charged Gun, recoile,   2046
The secrets of his ouer-charged soule,   2093
OUER-GORGD = 1
And like ambitious Sylla ouer-gorg'd,   2252
OUER-RIPEND = *1
Elia. Why droopes my Lord like ouer-ripen'd Corn,   274
OUER-WEENING = 1
Whose ouer-weening Arme I haue pluckt back,   1459
OUGHT = 1
When haue I ought exacted at your hands?   2703
OUGHTST = *1
Cade. Marry, thou ought'st not to let thy horse weare   2682
OUR *l.*30 *48 104 137 151 154 172 205 287 288 388 *408 423 467 623 *631
873 917 961 1025 *1027 1162 1287 1346 1361 1363 1364 1478 1496 1508
1583 1621 1709 1714 1724 1791 1858 1948 2177 2178 2208 2209 2229
2236 2257 2266 2270 2309 *2342 *2352 *2355 2430 *2489 2507 *2592
2619 *2660 *2668 2761 2829 3009 3136 *3137 3257 3273 3306 3309 3315
3317 3343 3345 = 60*12
OURS = 1
For France, 'tis ours; and we will keepe it still.   113
OURSELFE *see* selfe

OUT *l.*149 720 1748 1873 2112 2124 *2509 2527 *2640 2650 *2801 2852
*2908 *2961 3169 *3234 3282 = 11*6
OUTRIGHT = 1
 Hum. Nay *Elinor*, then must I chide outright: 315
OUTRUN = *1
 King. Can we outrun the Heauens? Good *Margaret* | stay. 3298
OUT-CAST = 1
 ⁾Out-cast of *Naples*, Englands bloody Scourge,   3113
OUT-FACE = 1
 See if thou canst out-face me with thy lookes: 2950
OUT-LIUE = 2
 But him out-liue, and dye a violent death.   658
 But him out-liue, and dye a violent death.   690
OWEN = 1
 And but for *Owen Glendour*, had beene King;   1002
OWLES = 2
 The time when Screech-owles cry, and Bandogs howle, 638
 And boading Screech-Owles, make the Consort full.   2042
OWNE = 13*3
 Englands owne proper Cost and Charges, without hauing any | Dowry. 66
 And our King *Henry* giues away his owne,   137
 While these do labour for their owne preferment,   189
 'Tis thine they giue away, and not their owne.   233
 Ready to sterue, and dare not touch his owne.   241
 While his owne·Lands are bargain'd for, and sold: 243
 A day will come, when Yorke shall claime his owne, 251
 In thine owne person answere thy abuse.   760
 Glost. What's thine owne Name? | *Simpc. Saunder Simpcoxe*, and if it
 please you, Master.   868
 Heaping confusion on their owne heads thereby.   939
 No: many a Pound of mine owne proper store,   1415
 And yet herein I iudge mine owne Wit good;   1534
 Whiles I take order for mine owne affaires.   1625
 Strike off his head. *Suf.* Thou dar'st not for thy owne. 2237
 *I was neuer mine owne man since. How now? Who's | there? 2400
 *owne Slaughter-house: Therfore thus will I reward thee, 2517
OWNER = 2
 While as the silly Owner of the goods   237
 Climbing my walles inspight of me the Owner,   2939
OXE = *1
 Beuis. Then is sin strucke downe like an Oxe, and ini-|quities throate
 cut like a Calfe.   2345
OXEN = 1*1
 Cade. They fell before thee like Sheepe and Oxen, & 2515
 On Sheepe or Oxen could I spend my furie.   3019
OYLE = 1
 Shall to my flaming wrath, be Oyle and Flax: 3277
PACKE = 1
 furr'd Packe, she washes buckes here at home.   2367
PACKING = 2
 To send me packing with an Hoast of men: 1648
 And bid mine eyes be packing with my Heart,   1811
PAGEANT = 1
 To play my part in Fortunes Pageant.   342
PAINE = 5
 I know, no paine they can inflict vpon him,   1683
 In paine of your dislike, or paine of death;   1969

PAINE *cont.*
But three dayes longer, on the paine of death. 2002
So thou wilt let me liue, and feele no paine. 2138
PAINES = 1
Are deepely indebted for this peece of paines; 674
PALE = 3*1
How now? why look'st thou pale? why tremblest thou? 1723
Looke pale as Prim-rose with blood-drinking sighes, 1763
Of ashy semblance, meager, pale, and bloodlesse, 1866
*Say. These cheekes are pale for watching for your good 2718
PALE-FACT = 1
Let pale-fac't feare keepe with the meane-borne man, 1641
PALFREY = *1
*Cheapside shall my Palfrey go to grasse: and when I am | King, as
King I will be. 2387
PALIE = 1
Faine would I go to chafe his palie lips, 1843
PALLACE = 3
Might in thy Pallace, perish *Elianor.* 1800
They will by violence teare him from your Pallace, 1958
And to conclude, Reproach and Beggerie, | Is crept into the Pallace of
our King, 2269
PALMERS = 1
Thy Hand is made to graspe a Palmers staffe, 3092
PALSIE = 1
Dicke. Why dost thou quiuer man? | *Say.* The Palsie, and not feare
prouokes me. 2725
PALTRY = 2
Vpon these paltry, seruile, abiect Drudges: 2273
For vnderneath an Ale-house paltry signe, 3290
PAN = *1
*a Sallet, my brain-pan had bene cleft with a brown Bill; 2916
PANGS = 1
War. See how the pangs of death do make him grin. 2158
PAPERS = 1
Mayl'd vp in shame, with Papers on my back, 1207
PAPER-MILL = *1
*hast built a Paper-Mill. It will be prooued to thy Face, 2671
PARCHING = 1
In Winters cold, and Summers parching heate, 88
PARCHMENT = *2
*be made Parchment; that Parchment being scribeld ore, 2397
PARDON = 9*1
King. Vnkle, how now? | *Glo.* Pardon me gracious Lord, 58
*1.*Pet.* I pray my Lord pardon me, I tooke ye for my | Lord Protector. 397
Sherife. It is my Office, and Madame pardon me. 1282
Pardon, my Liege, that I haue stay'd so long. 1392
Make thee begge pardon for thy passed speech, 1926
And heere pronounce free pardon to them all, 2785
Who loues the King, and will imbrace his pardon, 2790
And so with thankes, and pardon to you all, 2872
Buckingham, I prethee pardon me, 3024
For thy mistaking so, We pardon thee. 3125
PARDONS = *1
*be hang'd with your Pardons about your neckes? Hath 2798
PARENTAGE = 1
And ignorant of his birth and parentage, 2464

PARIS = 3
Crowned in Paris in despight of foes,   101
Paris is lost, the state of *Normandie* | Stands on a tickle point, now they
are gone: 227
Till Paris was besieg'd, famisht, and lost.   567
PARLEY = 3
Will parley with *Iacke Cade* their Generall.   2545
Sound a parley. | What noise is this I heare?   2777
Dare any be so bold to sound Retreat or Parley   2779
PARLIAMENT = 3*2
Her. I summon your Grace to his Maiesties Parliament,   1247
Yorke, Buckingham, Salisbury, and Warwicke, | *to the Parliament.*   1293
Queene. What, will your Highnesse leaue the Parlia-|ment?   1497
*burne all the Records of the Realme, my mouth shall be | the
Parliament of England.   2647
To call a present Court of Parliament: 3347
PARLIED = 1
This Tongue hath parlied vnto Forraigne Kings | For your behoofe.   2711
PART = 9
To play my part in Fortunes Pageant.   342
King. For my part, Noble Lords, I care not which,   491
Loather a hundred times to part then dye;   2070
Suf. I, but these ragges are no part of the Duke.   2216
When they were aliue. Now part them againe,   2766
like a great pin ere thou and I part.   2934
Buc. That is too much presumption on thy part: 3030
Throw in the frozen bosomes of our part,   3257
The second Part of Henry the Sixt,   3357
PARTED = 1
Oft haue I seene a timely-parted Ghost,   1865
PARTICULAR = 1
Cade. Heere I am thou particular fellow.   2431
PARTICULARITIES = 1
Particularities, and pettie sounds | To cease. Was't thou ordain'd (deere
Father)   3266
PARTING = *1
Queen. Away: Though parting be a fretfull corosiue,   2120
PARTRIDGE = 1
Who finds the Partridge in the Puttocks Nest,   1895
PARTS = 4
I'th parts of France, till terme of eighteene Moneths   72
And therefore I will take the *Neuils* parts,   252
As would (but that they dare not) take our parts.   2507
Reignes in the hearts of all our present parts.   3315
PASSE = 6*1
Thou shalt not passe from hence.   652
Let neuer Day nor Night vnhallowed passe,   817
Gloster. No, stirre not for your liues, let her passe | by.   1193
Sal. Disturbe him not, let him passe peaceably.   2159
Cade. As for these silken-coated slaues I passe not,   2448
Shake he his weapon at vs, and passe by.   2794
May passe into the presence of a King: 3059
PASSED = 1
Make thee begge pardon for thy passed speech,   1926
PASSENGERS = 2
Or foule felonious Theefe, that fleec'd poore passengers,   1429
With sorrow snares relenting passengers;   1529

PASSETH = 1
And passeth by with stiffe vnbowed Knee,   1310
PASSIONATE = *1
*Car. Nephew, what meanes this passionate discourse?   111
PAST = 1
War. For greefe that they are past recouerie.   123
PATE = 1
And chop away that factious pate of his.   3132
PATIENCE = 1*1
*Bullin. Patience, good Lady, Wizards know their times: 635
I pray thee sort thy heart to patience,   1244
PATIENT = 3
Suff. Madame be patient: as I was cause   451
Glost. Be patient, gentle Nell, forget this griefe.   1202
Suff. He doth reuiue againe, Madame be patient.   1734
PATRIMONIE = 1
To reaue the Orphan of his Patrimonie,   3187
PAUSE = 1
Why dost thou pause?   3240
PAW = 1
Who being suffer'd with the Beares fell paw,   3152
PAWNE = 1
They'l pawne their swords of my infranchisement.   3108
PAY = 4*4
For Souldiers pay in France, and neuer sent it?   1356
And being Protector, stay'd the Souldiers pay,   1404
I neuer rob'd the Souldiers of their pay,   1408
*Lieu. What thinke you much to pay 2000. Crownes,   2187
*which sold the Townes in France. He that made vs pay   2654
*his shoulders, vnlesse he pay me tribute: there shall not   2753
*a maid be married, but she shall pay to me her Mayden-|head   2754
You shall haue pay, and euery thing you wish.   3039
PAYED = 1
Rate me at what thou wilt, thou shalt be payed.   2199
PAYRE = 1
To call them both a payre of craftie Knaues.   379
PEACE = 11*4
Heere are the Articles of contracted peace,   47
*Salisb. Peace Sonne, and shew some reason Buckingham   503
Suff. Peace head-strong Warwicke.   570
*Warw. Image of Pride, why should I hold my peace?   571
King. I prythee peace, good Queene,   752
Card. Let me be blessed for the Peace I make   755
And goe in peace, Humfrey, no lesse belou'd,   1081
May honorable Peace attend thy Throne.   1093
King. Peace to his soule, if Gods good pleasure be.   2160
*Iustices of Peace, to call poore men before them, a-|bout   2675
That will forsake thee, and go home in peace.   2786
To know the reason of these Armes in peace.   3010
*Yor. Thus Warre hath giuen thee peace, for y art still,   3250
Peace with his soule, heauen if it be thy will.   3251
To loose thy youth in peace, and to atcheeue | The Siluer Liuery of
aduised Age,   3268
PEACEABLY = 1
Sal. Disturbe him not, let him passe peaceably.   2159
PEACEFULL = 1
Deliuer'd vp againe with peacefull words? | Mort Dieu.   129

PEACE-MAKERS = 1
For blessed are the Peace-makers on Earth. 754
PEDLERS = *1
*But. She was indeed a Pedlers daughter, & sold many | Laces. 2364
PEECE = 2
Are deepely indebted for this peece of paines; 674
And such a peece of seruice will you do, 3154
PEECES = 1
And on the peeces of the broken Wand 302
PEEPE = 1*1
Card. I, where thou dar'st not peepe: 761
*I hid me in these Woods, and durst not peepe out, for all 2908
PEERE = 2*1
Pernitious Protector, dangerous Peere, 738
So good a Quarrell, and so bad a Peere. 746
*proudest Peere in the Realme, shall not weare a head on 2752
PEERES = 9
In sight of England, and her Lordly Peeres, 18,
Glo. Braue Peeres of England, Pillars of the State, 82
O Peeres of England, shamefull is this League, 105
The Peeres agreed, and Henry was well pleas'd, 230
And Humfrey with the Peeres be falne at iarres: 265
Salisbury and Warwick are no simple Peeres. 460
And all the Peeres and Nobles of the Realme 516
And whet not on these furious Peeres, 753
The King and all the Peeres are here at hand. 1701
PEN = *1
*Cade. Away with him I say: Hang him with his Pen 2426
PENANCE = 4
Shall, after three dayes open Penance done, 1064
Now thou do'st Penance too. Looke how they gaze, 1196
Let not her Penance exceede the Kings Commission. 1252
Stanley. Madame, your Penance done, | Throw off this Sheet, 1285
PENITENT = 1
Didst euer heare a man so penitent? Enter Suffolke. 1695
PENNY = 1
Nor euer had one penny Bribe from France. 1409
PENT = 1
And in thy Closet pent vp, rue my shame, 1200
PENY = *2
*halfe peny Loaues sold for a peny: the three hoop'd pot, 2384
PENYWORTHS = 1
Pirates may make cheape penyworths of their pillage, 234
PEOPLE = 8*1
His valour, coine, and people in the warres? 86
What though the common people fauour him, 165
Haue made thee fear'd and honor'd of the people, 206
The abiect People, gazing on thy face, 1182
And when I start, the enuious people laugh, 1211
All. God saue your Maiesty. | *Cade. I thanke you good people. There
shall bee no 2389
It is to you good people, that I speake, 2449
The Rascall people, thirsting after prey, 2588
The People Liberall, Valiant, Actiue, Wealthy, 2697
PERCEIUE = 2
For by his death we doe perceiue his guilt, 1163
By this, I shall perceiue the Commons minde, 1680

PEREMPTORIE = 2
Glost. What, Cardinall? | Is your Priest-hood growne peremptorie?   740
How prowd, how peremptorie, and vnlike himselfe.   1302
PERFORCE = 1
And force perforce Ile make him yeeld the Crowne,   270
PERFORMANCE = 1
Hume. Come my Masters, the Duchesse I tell you ex-|pects
performance of your promises.   620
PERFORMD = 4
I haue perform'd my Taske, and was espous'd,   16
Come, let vs in, and with all speede prouide | To see her Coronation be
perform'd.   78
And that's not suddenly to be perform'd,   1033
Suff. A charge, Lord *Yorke*, that I will see perform'd.   1626
PERFUMD = 1
With whose sweet smell the Ayre shall be perfum'd,   267
PERILL = 1
For thousands more, that yet suspect no perill,   1452
PERIOD = 1
And proue the Period of their Tyrannie,   1449
PERISH = 2
Might in thy Pallace, perish *Elianor.*   1800
Should perish by the Sword. And I my selfe,   2543
PERNICIOUS = 1
Pernicious blood-sucker of sleeping men.   1931
PERNITIOUS = 1
Pernitious Protector, dangerous Peere,   738
PERSON = 6
In thine owne person answere thy abuse.   760
That he should come about your Royall Person,   1320
From meaning Treason to our Royall Person,   1364
If those that care to keepe your Royall Person   1473
They say, in care of your most Royall Person,   1966
Say. So might your Graces person be in danger.   2581
PERSONS = 1
A sort of naughtie persons, lewdly bent,   919
PERSWADE = 1
My thoughts, that labour to perswade my soule,   1839
PERSWADED = 1
Perswaded him from any further act: 3331
PETER = 6*3
Armorer. Let it come yfaith, and Ile pledge you all, | and a figge for
Peter.   1127
1.Prent. Here *Peter*, I drinke to thee, and be not a-|fraid.   1129
2.Prent. Be merry *Peter*, and feare not thy Master,   1131
Sirrha, what's thy Name? | *Peter. Peter* forsooth.   1141
Salisb. Peter? what more? | *Peter.* Thumpe.   1143
*nor the Queene: and therefore *Peter* haue at thee with a | downe-right
blow.   1151
They fight, and Peter strikes him downe.   1155
Armorer. Hold *Peter*, hold, I confesse, I confesse Trea-|son.   1156
presence? O *Peter*, thou hast preuayl'd in right.   1161
PETER = 2*7
PETITIONER see also 1.Pet., 2.Pet. = *1
2.Pet. Alas Sir, I am but a poore Petitioner of our | whole Towneship.   408
PETITIONERS = 1
Enter three or foure Petitioners, the Armorers | Man being one.   384

PETTIE = 2
   Be counter-poys'd with such a pettie summe.   2191
   Particularities, and pettie sounds | To cease. Was't thou ordain'd (deere
     Father)   3266
PETTY = 1
   Buck. Tut, these are petty faults to faults vnknowne,   1358
PEZANTS = 1*1
   Of Hindes and Pezants, rude and mercilesse: 2569
   *And you base Pezants, do ye beleeue him, will you needs   2797
PHILLIP = 2
   Had Issue *Phillip*, a Daughter, | Who marryed *Edmond Mortimer*, Earle
    of March: 996
   Who marryed *Phillip*, sole Daughter | Vnto *Lionel*, Duke of Clarence.   1013
PICCARDIE = 1
   Disdaine to call vs Lord, and *Piccardie*   2256
PICKE = *1
   *picke a Sallet another while, which is not amisse to coole   2913
PIECE *see* peece
PIECES *see* peeces
PILLAGE = 1
   Pirates may make cheape penyworths of their pillage,   234
PILLARS = 1
   Glo. Braue Peeres of England, Pillars of the State,   82
PILLOW = 1
   And whispers to his pillow, as to him,   2092
PIN = 1
   like a great pin ere thou and I part.   2934
PINE *see also* pyne = 1
   Suf. Pine gelidus timor occupat artus, it is thee I feare.   2285
PINNACE = 2
   For whilst our Pinnace Anchors in the Downes,   2178
   Being Captaine of a Pinnace, threatens more   2275
PIRATE *see* pyrate
PIRATES *see also* pyrats = 1
   Pirates may make cheape penyworths of their pillage,   234
PISSING = 1
   The pissing Conduit run nothing but Clarret Wine   2618
PITCH *see also* pytch = 1
   And beares his thoughts aboue his Faulcons Pitch.   728
PITTIE = 2
   Pittie was all the fault that was in me: 1425
   Too full of foolish pittie: and *Glosters* shew   1527
PITTY = 2*1
   *pitty my case: the spight of man preuayleth against me.   611
   Which makes me hope you are not void of pitty.   2698
   Henceforth, I will not haue to do with pitty.   3278
PLACD = 1
   Were plac'd the heads of *Edmond* Duke of Somerset,   303
PLACE = 13*1
   And greatnesse of his place be greefe to vs,   180
   Som. If *Somerset* be vnworthy of the Place,   495
   And at his pleasure will resigne my Place.   511
   Though in this place most Master weare no Breeches,   538
   Next, if I be appointed for the Place,   562
   For single Combat, in conuenient place,   605
   From thence, vnto the place of Execution: 1059
   As place Duke *Humfrey* for the Kings Protector?   1552

PLACE *cont.*
Nor let the raine of heauen wet this place,	2056
Is term'd the ciuel'st place of all this Isle:	2695
Alas, he hath no home, no place to flye too:	2815
*Garden, and be henceforth a burying place to all that do	2968
Giue place: by heauen thou shalt rule no more	3099
If thou dar'st bring them to the bayting place.	3149

PLACES = 1
King. Lords take your places: and I pray you all	1713

PLACT = 1
And plac't a Quier of such enticing Birds,	475

PLAGUE = *1
Suf. A plague vpon them: wherefore should I cursse | them?	2023

PLAIN = 1*1
Warw. What plaine proceedings is more plain then this?	1017
*Or hast thou a marke to thy selfe, like a honest plain dea-|ling man?	2420

PLAINE = 2
Yet I doe finde it so: for to be plaine,	372
Warw. What plaine proceedings is more plaine then this?	1017

PLAINES = 2
Safer shall he be vpon the sandie Plaines,	663
Safer shall he be vpon the sandie Plaines,	697

PLAINNESSE = 1
Thy deeds, thy plainnesse, and thy house-keeping,	199

PLANNET = 1
Rul'd like a wandering Plannet ouer me,	2548

PLANTAGENET = 1
Cade. My mother a *Plantagenet.*	2361

PLATE = *1
King. What stronger Brest-plate then a heart vntainted?	1938

PLAY = 3
To play my part in Fortunes Pageant.	342
But mine is made the Prologue to their Play:	1451
What wilt thou on thy death-bed play the Ruffian?	3164

PLAYD = 1
Beshrew the winners, for they play'd me false,	1484

PLAYSTERER = 1
Staff. Villaine, thy Father was a Playsterer,	2452

PLAY-FELLOWES = 1
Be play-fellowes to keepe you companie:	2016

PLEADE = 3
Qu. Oh *Henry*, let me pleade for gentle *Suffolke.*	2003
No more I say: if thou do'st pleade for him,	2005
Vs'd to command, vntaught to pleade for fauour.	2290

PLEADING = *1
*Ile bridle it: he shall dye, and it bee but for pleading so	2739

PLEASANT = 1
But like a pleasant slumber in thy lap?	2107

PLEASD = 3
The Peeres agreed, and *Henry* was well pleas'd,	230
Hum. Nay be not angry, I am pleas'd againe.	329
And it hath pleas'd him that three times to day	3340

PLEASE = 11*6
Suf. My Lord Protector, so it please your Grace,	46
King. They please vs well. Lord Marques kneel down,	68
1.Pet. Mine is, and't please your Grace, against *Iohn*	401
Suff. Please it your Maiestie, this is the man	578

PLEASE *cont.*
Armorer. And't shall please your Maiestie, I neuer sayd	584
Simpc. Borne blinde, and't please your Grace. | *Wife.* I indeede was he.	806
Glost. What's thine owne Name? | *Simpc. Saunder Simpcoxe,* and if it	
please you, Master.	868
Maior. Yes, my Lord, if it please your Grace.	885
Yorke. Lords, let him goe. Please it your Maiestie,	1103
So please your Highnesse to behold the fight.	1107
Seru. So please your Grace, wee'le take her from the | Sherife.	1191
Sh. And't please your Grace, here my Commission stayes:	1253
Stanly. So am I giuen in charge, may't please your | Grace.	1257
And when he please to make Commotion,	1323
Yorke. I will, my Lord, so please his Maiestie.	1620
Mes. Please it your Grace to be aduertised,	2876
Buc. So please it you my Lord, 'twere not amisse	3070

PLEASED = 1
And sends the poore well pleased from my gate.	2928

PLEASURE = 9*1
It was the pleasure of my Lord the King.	145
Hast thou not worldly pleasure at command,	319
Mess. My Lord Protector, 'tis his Highnes pleasure,	331
And at his pleasure will resigne my Place.	511
Yorke. At your pleasure, my good Lord.	709
His Highnesse pleasure is to talke with him.	802
With euery seuerall pleasure in the World:	2078
King. Peace to his soule, if Gods good pleasure be.	2160
It is our pleasure one of them depart:	2309
Art thou a Messenger, or come of pleasure.	3008

PLEDGE = *1
Armorer. Let it come yfaith, and Ile pledge you all, | and a figge for	
Peter.	1127

PLEDGES = 1
As pledges of my Fealtie and Loue,	3042

PLENTEOUS = 1
Hanging the head at Ceres plenteous load?	275

PLODDED = 1
Bare-headed plodded by my foot-cloth Mule,	2222

PLOT = 2
A pretty Plot, well chosen to build vpon.	686
And in this priuate Plot be we the first,	1024

PLOTTED = 1
Will not conclude their plotted Tragedie.	1453

PLUCKE = 1
And plucke the Crowne from feeble *Henries* head.	2993

PLUCKT = 1
Whose ouer-weening Arme I haue pluckt back,	1459

PLUMMES = *1
Glost. 'Masse, thou lou'dst Plummes well, that would'st | venture so.	840

PLUM-TREE = 1
Wife. A Plum-tree, Master.	834

POCKET = *1
Wea. Ha's a Booke in his pocket with red Letters in't	2408

POINT = 5
Paris is lost, the state of *Normandie* | Stands on a tickle point, now they	
are gone:	227
King. But what a point, my Lord, your Faulcon made,	721
See how the giddy multitude doe point,	1197

POINT *cont.*
That Cardinall *Beauford* is at point of death: 2086
Ne're shall this blood be wiped from thy point,   2974
POINTING = 1
Was made a wonder, and a pointing stock | To euery idle Rascall
follower.   1222
POINT-BLANKE = *1
*art thou within point-blanke of our Iurisdiction Regall.   2660
POLE = 4*1
*Charles, and William de la Pole Marquesse of Suffolke, Am-|bassador   51
And *William de la Pole* first Duke of Suffolke.   304
Suf. Stay *Whitmore,* for thy Prisoner is a Prince, | The Duke of
Suffolke, *William de la Pole.*   2213
And sooner dance vpon a bloody pole,   2295
a pole, or no: Take him away, and behead him.   2729
POLES = 1
*and strike off his head, and bring them both vppon two | poles hither.   2744
POLICY = 2
To keepe by policy what *Henrie* got: 91
By diuellish policy art thou growne great,   2251
POLITIKELY = 1
Well Nobles, well: 'tis politikely done,   1647
POLLICIE = 4
Me seemeth then, it is no Pollicie,   1317
Card. That he should dye, is worthie pollicie,   1537
Suff. But in my minde, that were no pollicie: 1540
Som. If *Yorke,* with all his farre-fet pollicie,   1596
POMFRET *see* Pumfret
POMPE = 1
To thinke vpon my Pompe, shall be my Hell.   1217
POMPEY = 1
Pompey the Great, and *Suffolke* dyes by Pyrats. | *Exit Water with*
Suffolke.   2306
POOLE = 3
I tell thee *Poole,* when in the Citie *Tours*   436
Lieu. Poole, Sir *Poole?* Lord, | I kennell, puddle, sinke, whose filth and
dirt   2238
POORE = 10*4
Vnto the poore King *Reignier,* whose large style   118
2. Pet. Alas Sir, I am but a poore Petitioner of our | whole Towneship.   408
King. Poore Soule, | Gods goodnesse hath beene great to thee: 815
*Sent his poore Queene to France, from whence she came,   984
The truth and innocence of this poore fellow,   1165
Or foule felonious Theefe, that fleec'd poore passengers,   1429
* *Queene.* So the poore Chicken should be sure of death.   1553
Suf. Thus is poore Suffolke ten times banished,   2072
But wherefore greeue I at an houres poore losse,   2098
*Iustices of Peace, to call poore men before them, a-|bout   2675
Say. Long sitting to determine poore mens causes,   2721
And sends the poore well pleased from my gate.   2928
Tooke oddes to combate a poore famisht man.   2948
A poore Esquire of Kent, that loues his King.   3069
POPE = 1
Would chuse him Pope, and carry him to Rome,   448
POPULOUS = 1
A Wildernesse is populous enough,   2075

PORPENTINE = 1
Were almost like a sharpe-quill'd Porpentine: 1669
PORT = 1
And beare the name and port of Gentlemen?   2188
POSSEST = 1
Vnlesse you be possest with diuellish spirits,   2709
POSSO = 1
Why this is iust, *Aio Aeacida Romanos vincere posso.*   691
POST = 1
POSTE = 2
To be the Poste, in hope of his reward.   708
Enter a Poste.   1584
POSTED = 1
His guilt should be but idly posted ouer,   1557
POT = *3
*3. *Neighbor.* And here's a Pot of good Double-Beere   1125
*halfe peny Loaues sold for a peny: the three hoop'd pot,   2384
*it hath seru'd me insteede of a quart pot to drinke   2918
POUERTIE = 1
And in her heart she scornes our Pouertie: 467
POUND = 2*1
No: many a Pound of mine owne proper store,   1415
Ile giue a thousand pound to looke vpon him.   2147
*one and twenty Fifteenes, and one shilling to the pound, | the last
Subsidie.   2655
POWER = 5
Whose name and power thou tremblest at,   650
And each of them had twentie times their power,   1237
Vntill a power be rais'd to put them downe.   2576
And with a puissant and a mighty power | Of Gallow-glasses and stout
Kernes,   2878
Should raise so great a power without his leaue?   3013
POWERS = 1*1
Sorrow and griefe haue vanquisht all my powers;   935
Clif. He is fled my Lord, and all his powers do yeeld,   2862
POWRES = 2
Whose dismall tune bereft my Vitall powres: 1741
Yorke. Then Buckingham I do dismisse my Powres.   3036
POYSD = 1
Be counter-poys'd with such a pettie summe.   2191
POYSE = 1
And poyse the Cause in Iustice equall Scales,   956
POYSON = 3
Hide not thy poyson with such sugred words,   1745
Should I not curse them. Poyson be their drinke.   2036
Bring the strong poyson that I bought of him.   2152
POYSONOUS = 1
Be poysonous too, and kill thy forlorne Queene.   1777
PRACTISD = 1
Haue practis'd dangerously against your State,   923
PRACTISE = 1
He be approu'd in practise culpable.   1716
PRACTISES = 1
Vpon my Life began her diuellish practises: 1340
PRAIRS = *1
Say. Ah Countrimen: If when you make your prair's,   2747

PRAISE = 1*1
To entertaine my vowes of thankes and praise.   2866
*Clif. Nor should thy prowesse want praise & esteeme,   3243
PRAY = 11*5
    King. Vnckle of Winchester, I pray read on.   62
    *1.Pet. I pray my Lord pardon me, I tooke ye for my | Lord Protector.   397
    Pray God the Duke of Yorke excuse himselfe.   574
    *and so I pray you goe in Gods Name, and leaue vs. | Exit Hume.   628
    Now pray my Lord, let's see the Deuils Writ.   687
    I pray my Lords let me compound this strife.   783
    *Peter. I thanke you all: drinke, and pray for me, I pray   1133
    *take all the Money that I haue. O Lord blesse me, I pray   1137
    I pray thee sort thy heart to patience,   1244
    Glost. Entreat her not the worse, in that I pray   1259
    King. Lords take your places: and I pray you all   1713
    Pray God he may acquit him of suspition.   1719
    I pray thee Buckingham go and meete him,   2890
    naile, I pray God I may neuer eate grasse more.   2945
    Priests pray for enemies, but Princes kill. | Fight. Excursions.   3294
PRAYRES = 1
    Prayres and Teares haue mou'd me, Gifts could neuer.   2702
PRAYSD = 1
    King. Now God be prays'd, that to beleeuing Soules   793
PRAYSE = 1
    Is worthy prayse: but shall I speake my conscience,   1362
PREDOMINANT = 1
    Foule Subornation is predominant,   1445
PREFERMENT = 1
    While these do labour for their owne preferment,   189
PREFERRD = 2
    Why Somerset should be preferr'd in this?   504
    Because my Booke preferr'd me to the King.   2706
PRELATE = 1
    Rancour will out, proud Prelate, in thy face   149
PREMISED = 1
    And the premised Flames of the Last day,   3263
PRENTICE see also 1.Prent., 2.Prent. = *1
    *words: my accuser is my Prentice, and when I did cor-|rect   595
PRENTICES = 2
    Drumme and Sand-bagge, and Prentices drinking to him.   1119
    Fight for credit of the Prentices.   1132
PREPARE = 2
    You do prepare to ride vnto S.(aint) Albons,   332
    But soft, I thinke she comes, and Ile prepare   1186
PRERORATION = 1
    This preroration with such circumstance: 112
PRESENCE = 9*2
    In presence of the Kings of France, and Sicill,   13
    But 'tis my presence that doth trouble ye,   148
    Buck. All in this presence are thy betters, Warwicke.   501
    presence? O Peter, thou hast preuayl'd in right.   1161
    King. Goe call our Vnckle to our presence straight: 1709
    And that my Soueraignes presence makes me milde,   1924
    If from this presence thou dar'st goe with me.   1933
    Here in our presence? Dare you be so bold?   1948
    *France? Be it knowne vnto thee by these presence, euen   2663
    *the presence of Lord Mortimer, that I am the Beesome   2664

PRESENCE *cont.*
May passe into the presence of a King: 3059
PRESENT = 5
To present your Highnesse with the man.   798
Yorke doth present himselfe vnto your Highnesse.   3052
Loe, I present your Grace a Traitors head,   3060
Reignes in the hearts of all our present parts.   3315
To call a present Court of Parliament: 3347
PRESENTLY = 5*3
Ile to the Duke of Suffolke presently. *Exit Cardinall.*   178
Eli. Yes my good Lord, Ile follow presently.   335
*presently: wee'le heare more of your matter before | the King. *Exit.*   420
Glost. Then send for one presently.   886
Suff. Ile call him presently, my Noble Lord. *Exit.*   1712
* *Cade.* To equall him I will make my selfe a knight, pre-|sently;   2438
*him away I say, and strike off his head presently, and then   2742
Cade. Marry presently. | *All.* O braue.   2761
PRESERUD = 1
Mens flesh preseru'd so whole, doe seldome winne.   1604
PRESERUE = 3
With God preserue the good Duke *Humfrey*:   169
Hume. Iesus preserue your Royall Maiesty.   345
And to preserue my Soueraigne from his Foe,   1573
PRESUMPTION = 2
Shall loose his head for his presumption.   308
Buc. That is too much presumption on thy part: 3030
PRESUMPTUOUS = 1
Presumptuous Dame, ill-nurter'd *Elianor*,   316
PRETHEE = 3
Stanley, I prethee goe, and take me hence,   1271
* *Queene.* Whether goes *Vaux* so fast? What newes I | prethee?   2083
Buckingham, I prethee pardon me,   3024
PRETTY = 2
A pretty Plot, well chosen to build vpon.   686
The pretty vaulting Sea refus'd to drowne me,   1794
PREUAILES = *1
*Whose Beame stands sure, whose rightful cause preuailes. | *Flourish.*
Exeunt.   957
PREUAYLD = 2
The Dolphin hath preuayl'd beyond the Seas,   515
presence? O *Peter*, thou hast preuayl'd in right.   1161
PREUAYLE = 2
Queene. God forbid any Malice should preuayle,   1717
Bro. Well, seeing gentle words will not preuayle,   2494
PREUAYLETH = *1
*pitty my case: the spight of man preuayleth against me.   611
PREUENTION = 1
Nor neuer seeke preuention of thy foes.   1233
PREY = 3
And giue her as a Prey to Law and Shame,   950
The Rascall people, thirsting after prey,   2588
And made a prey for Carrion Kytes and Crowes   3230
PRIDE = 7*1
Som. Cosin of Buckingham, though *Humfries* pride   179
Sal. Pride went before, Ambition followes him.   188
The pride of Suffolke, and the Cardinall, | With Somersets and
Buckinghams Ambition,   209

PRIDE *cont.*
First, for I cannot flatter thee in Pride:	561
Warw. Image of Pride, why should I hold my peace?	571
At *Beaufords* Pride, at *Somersets* Ambition,	1037
Thus *Elianors* Pride dyes in her youngest dayes.	1102
I, and alay this thy abortiue Pride:	2228

PRIE = 1
To prie into the secrets of the State,	262

PRIEST = 4
Now by Gods Mother, Priest,	774
And *Yorke*, and impious *Beauford*, that false Priest,	1229
Say but the word, and I will be his Priest.	1574
Ere you can take due Orders for a Priest:	1576

PRIESTS = 2
Enter the Witch, the two Priests, and Bullingbrooke.	619
Priests pray for enemies, but Princes kill. | *Fight. Excursions.*	3294

PRIEST-HOOD = 1
Glost. What, Cardinall? | Is your Priest-hood growne peremptorie?	740

PRIMA *l*.1 = 1
PRIMUS *l*.1 = 1
PRIM-ROSE = 1
Looke pale as Prim-rose with blood-drinking sighes,	1763

PRINCE = 8*1
The first, *Edward* the Black-Prince, Prince of Wales;	970
Edward the Black-Prince dyed before his Father,	977
That vertuous Prince, the good Duke *Humfrey*:	1040
And thou a Prince, Protector of this Land;	1205
And he a Prince, and Ruler of the Land:	1219
Yet so he rul'd, and such a Prince he was,	1220
Suf. Stay *Whitmore*, for thy Prisoner is a Prince, | The Duke of Suffolke, *William de la Pole.*	2213
*And shew'd how well you loue your Prince & Countrey:	2868

PRINCELY = 3
In entertainment to my Princely Queene.	77
The Princely Warwicke, and the *Neuils* all,	2259
And not to grace an awefull Princely Scepter.	3093

PRINCES = 5*1
As Procurator to your Excellence, | To marry Princes *Margaret* for your Grace;	10
Then all the Princes in the Land beside,	183
Vnto the Princes heart of *Calidon*:	247
And Princes Courts be fill'd with my reproach:	1769
*with the spirit of putting down Kings and Princes. Com-|mand silence.	2356
Priests pray for enemies, but Princes kill. | *Fight. Excursions.*	3294

PRINTED = 1
Oh, could this kisse be printed in thy hand,	2058

PRINTING = *1
*Score and the Tally, thou hast caused printing to be vs'd,	2669

PRISON = 3*2
King. Away with them to Prison: and the day of	615
You foure from hence to Prison, back againe;	1058
Goe, leade the way, I long to see my Prison. *Exeunt.*	1291
*thou hast put them in prison, and because they could not	2677
Somerset. My Lord, | Ile yeelde my selfe to prison willingly,	2895

PRISONER = 5
Lord Cardinall, he is your Prisoner.	1487
Maister, this Prisoner freely giue I thee,	2181

PRISONER *cont.*

Suf. Stay *Whitmore*, for thy Prisoner is a Prince, | The Duke of
Suffolke, *William de la Pole*,   2213

Yorke. Vpon thine Honor is he Prisoner?   3034

Buck. Vpon mine Honor he is Prisoner.   3035

PRISONERS = 1

the Gaoles, and let out the Prisoners.   2527

PRIUATE = 1

And in this priuate Plot be we the first,   1024

PRIUIE = 2

And other of your Highnesse Priuie Councell,   928

Or if he were not priuie to those Faults,   1341

PRIZE = 2*2

Therefore bring forth the Souldiers of our prize,   2177

Whitm. I lost mine eye in laying the prize aboord,   2194

Mes. My Lord, a prize, a prize, heeres the Lord *Say*,   2653

PROBABLE = 1

The least of all these signes were probable.   1882

PROCEED = 1

Proceed no straiter 'gainst our Vnckle *Gloster*,   1714

PROCEEDE = 1

Hath giuen them heart and courage to proceede: 2571

PROCEEDES = 1

And listen after *Humfrey*, how he proceedes: 542

PROCEEDINGS = 1

Warw. What plaine proceedings is more plain then this?   1017

PROCESSION = 1

Card. Here comes the Townes-men, on Procession,   797

PROCLAIMD = 1

And I proclaim'd a Coward through the world.   2212

PROCLAIME = 1

Proclaime them Traitors that are vp with *Cade*,   2497

PROCLAIMES = 1

Iacke Cade proclaimes himselfe Lord *Mortimer*,   2564

PROCLAIMETH = 1

And still proclaimeth as he comes along,   2881

PROCLAYME = 1

Fellow, what Miracle do'st thou proclayme?   786

PROCURATOR = 1

As Procurator to your Excellence, | To marry Princes *Margaret* for your
Grace;   10

PROCURE = 1

All these could not procure me any scathe,   1238

PROFIT = 2

While they do tend the profit of the Land.   212

And common profit of his Countrey.   214

PROGRESSE = 1

The King is now in progresse towards Saint *Albones*,   702

PROLOGUE = 1

But mine is made the Prologue to their Play: 1451

PROMISED = *1

Hume. This they haue promised to shew your Highnes   353

PROMISES = 1

Hume. Come my Masters, the Duchesse I tell you ex-|pects
performance of your promises.   620

PRONOUNCE = 1

And heere pronounce free pardon to them all,   2785

PROOFE = 1
  *_Wea._ He neede not feare the sword, for his Coate is of | proofe.   2378
PROOUED = *1
  *hast built a Paper-Mill. It will be prooued to thy Face,   2671
PROPER = 2*2
  *_Englands owne proper Cost and Charges, without hauing any_ | _Dowry._   66
  Hum. A proper iest, and neuer heard before,   139
  No: many a Pound of mine owne proper store,   1415
  *_Cade._ I am sorry for't: The man is a proper man of   2412
PROPHECIE = 2
  Shall finde their deaths, if _Yorke_ can prophecie.   1042
  For sure, my thoughts doe hourely prophecie,   1997
PROPHESIED = 1
  I prophesied, France will be lost ere long. _Exit Humfrey._   153
PROPHETS = 1
  His Champions, are the Prophets and Apostles,   443
PROPORTION = 2
  Beare that proportion to my flesh and blood,   245
  In Courage, Courtship, and Proportion: 440
PROPORTIOND = 1
  His well proportion'd Beard, made ruffe and rugged,   1879
PROPOUNDED = 1
  As by your Grace shall be propounded him.   356
PROSPECT = 1
  Their cheefest Prospect, murd'ring Basiliskes: 2039
PROSTRATE = *1
  *Mother _Iordan_, be you prostrate, and grouell on the   630
PROTECT = 2*2
  Buc. Why should he then protect our Soueraigne?   172
  *2._Pet._ Marry the Lord protect him, for hee's a good | man, Iesu blesse
    him.   389
  *_Card. Medice teipsum_, Protector see to't well, protect | your selfe.   777
  Glost. Must you, Sir _Iohn_, protect my Lady here?   1256
PROTECTED = 2
  Queene. And as for you that loue to be protected   422
  Should be to be protected like a Child,   1084
PROTECTION = 1
  My selfe and _Beauford_ had him in protection,   1884
PROTECTOR = 20*6
  Suf. My Lord Protector, so it please your Grace,   46
  Car. So, there goes our Protector in a rage: 154
  He will be found a dangerous Protector.   171
  If Gloster be displac'd, hee'l be Protector.   184
  *_Mess._ My Lord Protector, 'tis his Highnes pleasure,   331
  *1._Pet._ My Masters, let's stand close, my Lord Pro-|tector.   386
  *2._Pet._ Come backe foole, this is the Duke of Suffolk, | and not my
    Lord Protector.   394
  *1._Pet._ I pray my Lord pardon me, I tooke ye for my | Lord Protector.   397
  *_Queene._ To my Lord Protector? Are your Supplica-|tions   399
  *_Queene._ Beside the haughtie Protector, haue we _Beauford_   454
  To be Protector of his Excellence?   509
  Humf. Madame, I am Protector of the Realme,   510
  My Lord Protector will, I doubt it not,   675
  A sorry Breakfast for my Lord Protector.   706
  Enter the King, Queene, Protector, Cardinall, and | _Suffolke, with_
    Faulkners hallowing.   715
  Pernitious Protector, dangerous Peere,   738

PROTECTOR *cont.*

Against this prowd Protector with my Sword.	756
Card. Medice teipsum, Protector see to't well, protect | your selfe.	777
Card. And so my Lord Protector, by this meanes	930
Henry will to himselfe Protector be,	1078
Then when thou wert Protector to thy King.	1082
And thou a Prince, Protector of this Land;	1205
And being Protector, stay'd the Souldiers pay,	1404
Glost. Why 'tis well known, that whiles I was Protector,	1424
As place Duke *Humfrey* for the Kings Protector?	1552
*for French Crownes) I am content he shall raigne, but Ile | be Protector ouer him.	2478

PROTECTORS = 6

Buc. Or thou, or I Somerset will be Protectors,	185
And the Protectors wife belou'd of him?	318
Vnder the Wings of our Protectors Grace,	423
As that prowd Dame, the Lord Protectors Wife:	462
My Lord Protectors Hawkes doe towre so well,	726
Of Lady *Elianor,* the Protectors Wife,	921

PROTECTORSHIP = 3

An't like your Lordly Lords Protectorship.	749
Yorke. And did he not, in his Protectorship,	1354
Yorke. In your Protectorship, you did deuise	1421

PROTECTS = 1

Despight the Bearard, that protects the Beare.	3210

PROUD = 12*2

Rancour will out, proud Prelate, in thy face	149
As stout and proud as he were Lord of all,	195
And make a shew of loue to proud Duke *Humfrey,*	253
Nor shall proud Lancaster vsurpe my right,	256
That ere I prou'd thee false, or fear'd thy faith.	1506
By nature prou'd an Enemie to the Flock,	1560
As *Humfrey* prou'd by Reasons to my Liege.	1562
Might happily haue prou'd farre worse then his.	1609
And lofty proud incroaching tyranny,	2264
*Small things make base men proud. This Villaine heere,	2274
Is marching hitherward in proud array,	2880
Cade. Iden farewell, and be proud of thy victory: Tell	2977
Is to remoue proud Somerset from the King,	3028
Proud Northerne Lord, Clifford of Cumberland,	3224

PROUDEST = *1

*proudest Peere in the Realme, shall not weare a head on	2752

PROUE = 3*2

Proue them, and I lye open to the Law:	551
*my Mans instigation, to proue him a Knaue, and my selfe	1148
And proue the Period of their Tyrannie,	1449
Qu. Nay then, this sparke will proue a raging fire,	1605
Old Clif. The first I warrant thee, if dreames proue true	3195

PROUERBE = 1

The ancient Prouerbe will be well effected,	1470

PROUIDE = 3

Come, let vs in, and with all speede prouide | To see her Coronation be perform'd.	78
And Ile prouide his Executioner,	1578
Yorke. I am content: Prouide me Souldiers, Lords,	1624

PROUIDED = *1

Bulling. Master *Hume,* we are therefore prouided: will	622

PROUINCES = 1
   Those Prouinces, these Armes of mine did conquer,   127
PROUOKES = 1
   Dicke. Why dost thou quiuer man? | *Say.* The Palsie, and not feare
   prouokes me.   2725
PROWD = 6
   As that prowd Dame, the Lord Protectors Wife: 462
   Duch. Was't I? yea, I it was, prowd French-woman: 532
   Against this prowd Protector with my Sword.   756
   That erst did follow thy prowd Chariot-Wheeles,   1184
   How prowd, how peremptorie, and vnlike himselfe.   1302
   Say, if thou dar'st, prowd Lord of Warwickshire,   1905
PROWESSE = *1
   **Clif.* Nor should thy prowesse want praise & esteeme,   3243
PRYTHEE = 1
   King. I prythee peace, good Queene,   752
PUBLIKE = 1
   Ioyne we together for the publike good,   207
PUBLIQUE = 1
   Haue cost a masse of publique Treasurie.   521
PUBLISHED = 1
   If he be guiltie, as 'tis published.   1711
PUDDLE = 1
   Lieu. Poole, Sir *Poole?* Lord, | I kennell, puddle, sinke, whose filth and
   dirt   2238
PUISSANCE = *1
   *And faine to go with a staffe, but that my puissance holds   2483
PUISSANT = 1
   And with a puissant and a mighty power | Of Gallow-glasses and stout
   Kernes,   2878
PULL = *1
   **Cade.* So sirs: now go some and pull down the Sauoy: 2635
PULLD = 2
   Whose bookish Rule, hath pull'd faire England downe. | *Exit Yorke.*   271
   Vnlesse his teeth be pull'd out.   2650
PULLS = 1
   That beares so shrewd a mayme: two Pulls at once;   1097
PUMFRET = 1
   And him to Pumfret; where, as all you know,   985
PUNISHMENT = 1
   I neuer gaue them condigne punishment.   1430
PUNISHT = 1
   To watch the comming of my punisht Duchesse: 1178
PUPILL = 1
   What, shall King *Henry* be a Pupill still,   432
PURCHASE = 2
   And purchase Friends, and giue to Curtezans,   235
   Enough to purchase such another Island,   2137
PURE = 2
   Simpc. God knowes of pure Deuotion,   822
   Wife. Alas Sir, we did it for pure need.   908
PUREST = 1
   The purest Spring is not so free from mudde,   1399
PURGE = 2
   Whereof you cannot easily purge your selfe.   1435
   And from his bosome purge this blacke dispaire.   2157

PURPOSE = 2
Because his purpose is not executed. 1558
Yet did I purpose as they doe entreat: 1996
PURPOSELY = 1
Queene. I, good my Lord: for purposely therefore 1108
PURSE = 1
Agrees not with the leannesse of his purse. 119
PURSED = 1
Haue I dis-pursed to the Garrisons, 1417
PURSEUANT = *1
*Take this fellow in, and send for his Master with a Purse-|uant 419
PURSUE = 1
Let vs pursue him ere the Writs go forth. 3348
PUT = 9*1
Put forth thy hand, reach at the glorious Gold. 284
Had not your man put vp the Fowle so suddenly, | We had had more
sport. 766
And had I first beene put to speake my minde, 1337
And put the Englishmen vnto the Sword. 1587
You put sharpe Weapons in a mad-mans hands. 1653
And *Henry* put apart: the next for me. *Exit.* 1689
But all in vaine are these meane Obsequies, | *Bed put forth.* 1848
The elder of them being put to nurse, 2462
Vntill a power be rais'd to put them downe. 2576
*thou hast put them in prison, and because they could not 2677
PUTTING = *1
*with the spirit of putting down Kings and Princes. Com-|mand silence. 2356
PUTTOCKS = 1
Who finds the Partridge in the Puttocks Nest, 1895
PYNE = *1
Suff. Thus droupes this loftie Pyne, & hangs his sprayes, 1101
PYRATE = 2
Then *Bargulus* the strong Illyrian Pyrate. 2276
Is straight way calme, and boorded with a Pyrate. 2887
PYRATS = 1
Pompey the Great, and *Suffolke* dyes by Pyrats. | *Exit Water with
Suffolke.* 2306
PYTCH = 2
And what a pytch she flew aboue the rest: 722
As like to Pytch, defile Nobilitie; 948
Q = *1
QU = 18*7
QUADRANGLE = 1
With walking once about the Quadrangle, 548
QUAKE = 1
Henry the fift, that made all France to quake, 2793
QUALME = 1
Some sodaine qualme hath strucke me at the heart, 60
QUARRELL = 3
So good a Quarrell, and so bad a Peere. 746
Left I the Court, to see this Quarrell try'de. 1109
Thrice is he arm'd, that hath his Quarrell iust; 1939
QUART = *1
*it hath seru'd me insteede of a quart pot to drinke 2918
QUEEN = *2
*With his new Bride, & Englands deere bought Queen, 264
Queene. Why now is *Henry* King, and *Margaret* Queen, 1095

QUEEN = 2*3
QUEENE see also Q., Qu., Queen. = 26*8
   The Queene, Suffolke, Yorke, Somerset, and Buckingham, | on the other.   5
   Deliuer vp my Title in the Queene   19
   The Fairest Queene, that euer King receiu'd.   23
   King. Suffolke arise. Welcome Queene *Margaret,*   24
   **All kneel.* Long liue Qu.(eene) *Margaret,* Englands happines.   44
   **Naples, Sicillia, and Ierusalem, and Crowne her Queene of*   54
   In entertainment to my Princely Queene.   77
   Exit King, Queene, and Suffolke. | Manet the rest.   80
   Where as the King and Queene do meane to Hawke.   333
   Enter Suffolke, and Queene.   391
   **Peter.* Here a comes me thinkes, and the Queene with | him: Ile be the
   first sure.   392
   Am I a Queene in Title and in Stile,   434
   Strangers in Court, doe take her for the Queene: 465
   Enter the King, Queene, Protector, Cardinall, and | Suffolke, with
   Faulkners hallowing.   715
   King. I prythee peace, good Queene,   752
   *Sent his poore Queene to France, from whence she came,   984
   *nor the Queene: and therefore *Peter* haue at thee with a | downe-right
   blow.   1151
   Sound a Senet. Enter King, Queene, Cardinall, Suffolke,   1292
   That these great Lords, and *Margaret* our Queene,   1508
   Sound Trumpets. Enter the King, the Queene, | Cardinall, Suffolke,
   Somerset, with | Attendants.   1706
   To be a Queene, and Crown'd with infamie.   1771
   Be poysonous too, and kill thy forlorne Queene.   1777
   King. Vngentle Queene, to call him gentle *Suffolke.*   2004
   Suff. Cease, gentle Queene, these Execrations,   2019
   When I haue feasted with Queene *Margaret*?   2226
   *Thy lips that kist the Queene, shall sweepe the ground: 2243
   I go of Message from the Queene to France: 2281
   Vntill the Queene his Mistris bury it. *Exit Walter.*   2314
   So will the Queene, that liuing, held him deere.   2318
   **Enter the King with a Supplication, and the Queene with Suf-|folkes*   2530
   Sound Trumpets. Enter King, Queene, and | Somerset on the Tarras.   2848
   Enter Queene and Somerset.   3077
   **K.* See Buckingham, Somerset comes with th'Queene,   3078
   Enter King, Queene, and others.   3296
QUEENE = 22*8
QUEENS = *1
   *And in that Chaire where Kings & Queens wer crownd,   312
QUEINT = 1
   To shew how queint an Orator you are.   1987
QUELL = 1
   To quell the Rebels, and their Complices.   3212
QUESTION = 1*1
   **But.* No question of that: for I haue seene him whipt | three Market
   dayes together.   2375
   Cade. I, there's the question; But I say, 'tis true: 2461
QUESTIONS = 2
   That shall make answere to such Questions,   355
   Elianor. It is enough, Ile thinke vpon the Questions: 357
QUICK = *1
   **Card.* A Breach that craues a quick expedient stoppe.   1591

QUICKLY = 7*1
Wee'l quickly hoyse Duke *Humfrey* from his seat.	176
Would make thee quickly hop without thy Head. | *Exit Humfrey.*	527
Come on Sirrha, off with your Doublet, quickly.	899
These few dayes wonder will be quickly worne.	1245
Suff. My Lord, these faults are easie, quickly answer'd:	1433
A Staffe is quickly found to beat a Dogge.	1471
This *Gloster* should be quickly rid the World,	1535
Go bid her hide him quickly from the Duke.	3079

QUIER = 1
And plac't a Quier of such enticing Birds,	475

QUIET = 3
King. Sweet Aunt be quiet, 'twas against her will.	535
Thy greatest helpe is quiet, gentle *Nell*:	1243
And may enioy such quiet walkes as these?	2922

QUILL = 1
deliuer our Supplications in the Quill.	388

QUILLD = 1
Were almost like a sharpe-quill'd Porpentine:	1669

QUILLETS = 1
And doe not stand on Quillets how to slay him:	1563

QUITTING = 1
Quitting thee thereby of ten thousand shames,	1923

QUIUER = 1
Dicke. Why dost thou quiuer man? | *Say.* The Palsie, and not feare prouokes me.	2725

RABBLE = 2
And follow'd with a Rabble, that reioyce	1208
Or let a rabble leade you to your deaths.	2789

RABBLEMENT = 1
Alarum, and Retreat. Enter againe Cade, | *and all his rabblement.*	2773

RACE = 1
And neuer of the *Neuils* Noble Race.	1920

RACING = 1
Racing the Charracters of your Renowne,	108

RACKT = 1*1
Card. The Commons hast thou rackt, the Clergies Bags	518
Say he be taken, rackt, and tortured;	1682

RAGE = 6
Car. So, there goes our Protector in a rage:	154
From Treasons secret Knife, and Traytors Rage,	1474
Send Succours (Lords) and stop the Rage betime,	1588
And this fell Tempest shall not cease to rage,	1657
Thy words moue Rage, and not remorse in me:	2280
That Winter Lyon, who in rage forgets | Aged contusions, and all brush of Time:	3322

RAGGED = 4
And would not dash me with their ragged sides,	1798
And sent the ragged Souldiers wounded home.	2258
His Army is a ragged multitude	2568
The rampant Beare chain'd to the ragged staffe,	3203

RAGGES = 2
Whit. The Duke of Suffolke, muffled vp in ragges?	2215
Suf. I, but these ragges are no part of the Duke.	2216

RAGING = 2
Qu. Nay then, this sparke will proue a raging fire,	1605
Where from thy sight, I should be raging mad,	2111

RAIGND = 1
Who after *Edward* the third's death, raign'd as King,   979
RAIGNE = 3*1
Ouer whom (in time to come) I hope to raigne: 2450
*for French Crownes) I am content he shall raigne, but Ile | be
Protector ouer him.   2478
This first yeare of our raigne.   2619
For yet may England curse my wretched raigne. | *Flourish. Exeunt.*   2903
RAINE = 1
Nor let the raine of heauen wet this place,   2056
RAISD = 2
A Spirit rais'd from depth of vnder ground,   354
Vntill a power be rais'd to put them downe.   2576
RAISE = 2
Then will I raise aloft the Milke-white-Rose,   266
Should raise so great a power without his leaue?   3013
RAMPANT = 1
The rampant Beare chain'd to the ragged staffe,   3203
RANCOROUS = 2
Respecting what a rancorous minde he beares,   1318
That shall be scowred in his rancorous heart,   1903
RANCOUR = 1
Rancour will out, proud Prelate, in thy face   149
RANCOURS = 1
And Charitie chas'd hence by Rancours hand;   1444
RANSOME = 6
And lowly words were Ransome for their fault: 1427
The World shall not be Ransome for thy Life.   2011
Heere shall they make their ransome on the sand,   2179
1.*Gent.* What is my ransome Master, let me know.   2184
Lieu. Be not so rash, take ransome, let him liue.   2197
Lieu. And as for these whose ransome we haue set,   2308
RANST = 1
Thou ran'st a-tilt in honor of my Loue,   437
RASCALL = 3
Was made a wonder, and a pointing stock | To euery idle Rascall
follower.   1222
And reape the Haruest which that Rascall sow'd.   1687
The Rascall people, thirsting after prey,   2588
RASH = 1
Lieu. Be not so rash, take ransome, let him liue.   2197
RATE = 2
Queene. Why do you rate my Lord of Suffolke thus?   1756
Rate me at what thou wilt, thou shalt be payed.   2199
RATED = 1
Be thus vpbrayded, chid, and rated at,   1475
RATHER = 4
I rather would haue lost my Life betimes,   1600
With humble suite: no, rather let my head   2292
But. Or rather of stealing a Cade of Herrings.   2354
Rather then bloody Warre shall cut them short,   2544
RAUEN = 1
For hee's disposed as the hatefull Rauen.   1370
RAUENOUS = 1
For hee's enclin'd as is the rauenous Wolues.   1372
RAUENS = 1
Came he right now to sing a Rauens Note,   1740

RAUGHT = 1
This Staffe of Honor raught, there let it stand,   1099
RAUISH = 1*1
  King. Her sight did rauish, but her grace in Speech,   39
  *take your houses ouer your heads, rauish your   2805
RAYLING = 1
  Card. My Liege, his rayling is intollerable.   1472
RAYSE = 1
Madame, sit you, and feare not: whom wee rayse,   641
RAYSING = 1
Raysing vp wicked Spirits from vnder ground,   926
RAZING *see* racing
REACH = 2
Put forth thy hand, reach at the glorious Gold.   284
Aboue the reach or compasse of thy thought?   320
REACHES = 1
And dogged *Yorke*, that reaches at the Moone,   1458
REACHING = *1
  **Say*. Great men haue reaching hands: oft haue I struck   2714
READ = 4
  King. Vnckle of Winchester, I pray read on.   62
I neuer read but Englands Kings haue had   135
As I haue read, layd clayme vnto the Crowne,   1001
But stay, Ile read it ouer once againe.   2546
READE = 2*2
And dim'd mine eyes, that I can reade no further.   61
  *Earth; *Iohn Southwell* reade you, and let vs to our worke.   631
  * *Weauer*. The Clearke of Chartam: hee can write and | reade, and cast
accompt.   2403
  *reade, thou hast hang'd them, when (indeede) onely for   2678
READES = 2
Bullingbrooke or Southwell reades, Coniuro | te, &c. *It Thunders and*
Lightens   644
What haue we here? *Reades*.   688
READILY = 1
And where this breach now in our Fortunes made | May readily be
stopt.   3309
READS = *1
  **Glo. Reads*. Inprimis, *It is agreed betweene the French K.(ing)*   50
READY = 2*1
Ready to sterue, and dare not touch his owne.   241
And ready are the Appellant and Defendant,   1105
  *sword, and yet am ready to famish. These fiue daies haue   2907
REALME = 12*4
With all the Learned Counsell of the Realme,   96
Behooues it vs to labor for the Realme.   190
Art thou not second Woman in the Realme?   317
  Humf. Madame, I am Protector of the Realme,   510
And all the Peeres and Nobles of the Realme   516
To be your Regent in the Realme of France.   556
Seiz'd on the Realme, depos'd the rightfull King,   983
God and King *Henry* gouerne Englands Realme: 1085
Giue vp your Staffe, Sir, and the King his Realme.   1086
Leuie great summes of Money through the Realme,   1355
For swallowing the Treasure of the Realme.   2242
  *small Beere. All the Realme shall be in Common, and in   2386

REALME *cont.*

*burne all the Records of the Realme, my mouth shall be | the
Parliament of England.   2647
*the Realme, in erecting a Grammar Schoole: and where-|as   2667
Kent to maintaine, the King, the Realme and you,   2704
*proudest Peere in the Realme, shall not weare a head on   2752
REALMES = 1
Me thinkes the Realmes of England, France, & Ireland,   244
REAPE = 1
And reape the Haruest which that Rascall sow'd.   1687
REASON = 7*2
There's reason he should be displeas'd at it: 162
*Salisb. Peace Sonne, and shew some reason *Buckingham*   503
To shew some reason, of no little force,   558
Queene. I see no reason, why a King of yeeres   1083
Yorke. 'Tis *Yorke* that hath more reason for his death.   1547
*Cade And good reason: for thereby is England main'd   2482
And aske him what's the reason of these Armes: 2891
To know the reason of these Armes in peace.   3010
And haue no other reason for this wrong,   3189
REASONS = 2
Which feare, if better Reasons can supplant,   1331
As *Humfrey* prou'd by Reasons to my Liege.   1562
REAUE = 1
To reaue the Orphan of his Patrimonie,   3187
REBELL = 1
And fight against that monstrous Rebell *Cade*,   3055
REBELLIOUS = 1
Staf. Rebellious Hinds, the filth and scum of Kent,   2442
REBELLS = *1
*Buc. What answer makes your Grace to the Rebells | Supplication?   2539
REBELS = 6*1
To signifie, that Rebels there are vp,   1586
Mes. The Rebels are in Southwarke: Fly my Lord: 2563
These Kentish Rebels would be soone appeas'd.   2578
King. Farewell my Lord, trust not the Kentish Rebels   2594
To defend the City from the Rebels.   2605
The Rebels haue assay'd to win the Tower.   2608
To quell the Rebels, and their Complices.   3212
RECALL = 1
Or blood-consuming sighes recall his Life;   1761
RECEIUD = 4
The Fairest Queene, that euer King receiu'd.   23
Receiud deepe scarres in France and Normandie: 94
Within this halfe houre hath receiu'd his sight,   791
And threw it towards thy Land: The Sea receiu'd it,   1808
RECEIUE = 2
Receiue the Sentence of the Law for sinne,   1056
As others would ambitiously receiue it.   1091
RECLAIMES = 1
And Beautie, that the Tyrant oft reclaimes,   3276
RECOILE = 1
Or like an ouer-charged Gun, recoile,   2046
RECONCILE = 1
To reconcile you all vnto the King. *Exeunt omnes.*   2847

RECORDS = *1
*burne all the Records of the Realme, my mouth shall be | the
Parliament of England.   2647
RECOUER = 1
Yet to recouer them would loose my life: 2700
RECOUERED = *1
*you had recouered your ancient Freedome. But you are   2802
RECOUERIE = 1
War. For greefe that they are past recouerie.   123
RECREANTS = *1
*all Recreants and Dastards, and delight to liue in slauerie   2803
RED = 4*1
Simpc. Red Master, Red as Blood.   852
Beaufords red sparkling eyes blab his hearts mallice,   1454
* *Wea.* Ha's a Booke in his pocket with red Letters in't   2408
* *Cade.* Giue him a box o'th'eare, and that wil make'em | red againe. 2719
REDEEMD = 1
Souldiers, this day haue you redeem'd your liues,   2867
REDOUND = 1
As all things shall redound vnto your good.   .   2901
REFORMATION = *1
*Vowes Reformation. There shall be in England, seuen   2383
REFUSD = 1
The pretty vaulting Sea refus'd to drowne me,   1794
REFUSE = 1
That for my Surety will refuse the Boyes.   3116
REGALL = *1
*art thou within point-blanke of our Iurisdiction Regall.   2660
REGARDED = 1*1
Small Curres are not regarded when they grynne,   1312
* *Beuis.* O miserable Age: Vertue is not regarded in | Handy-crafts men. 2329
REGENT = 8
We heere discharge your Grace from being Regent   71
When thou wert Regent for our Soueraigne,   205
Let *Yorke* be Regent, I will yeeld to him.   496
To be your Regent in the Realme of France.   556
Let *Somerset* be Regent o're the French,   602
Yorke. That *Somerset* be sent as Regent thither: 1593
Had beene the Regent there, in stead of me,   1597
Thy fortune, *Yorke*, hadst thou beene Regent there,   1608
REGENT-SHIP = 1
Then let him be denay'd the Regent-ship.   494
REHEARSALL = 1
With sweet rehearsall of my mornings dreame?   297
REIGND *see also* raign'd = 1
The Issue of the next Sonne should haue reign'd.   991
REIGNE *see also* raigne = 2
Salisb. This *Edmond*, in the Reigne of *Bullingbrooke*,   1000
Till *Lionels* Issue fayles, his should not reigne.   1020
REIGNES = 1
Reignes in the hearts of all our present parts.   3315
REIGNIER = 1*1
espouse the Lady Margaret, daughter vnto Reignier King of   53
Vnto the poore King *Reignier*, whose large style   118
REIOYCE = 1
And follow'd with a Rabble, that reioyce   1208

240

RELEASED = 1 *1
   shall be released and deliuered to the King her father.   57
   **Dutchesse of Aniou and Maine, shall be released and deliuered*   64
RELEEFE = 1
   Away for your releefe, and we will liue   3316
RELENT = 3
   And could it not inforce them to relent,   2549
   And therefore yet relent, and saue my life.   2750
   Clif. What say ye Countrimen, will ye relent   2787
RELENTING = 1
   With sorrow snares relenting passengers;   1529
REMEDIE = 1
   But I will remedie this geare ere long,   1388
REMEMBER = 2
   But still remember what the Lord hath done.   818
   Remember it, and let it make thee Crest-falne,   2227
REMORSE = 1 *1
   Thy words moue Rage, and not remorse in me: 2280
   O let me liue. | **Cade.* I feele remorse in my selfe with his words: but   2737
REMORSEFULL = 1
   Lieu. The gaudy blabbing and remorsefull day,   2170
REMORSELESSE = 1
   Euen so remorselesse haue they borne him hence: 1514
REMOUE = 3
   I would remoue these tedious stumbling blockes,   339
   His Armes are onely to remoue from thee.   2882
   Is to remoue proud Somerset from the King,   3028
REND = *1
   **Old Clif.* And from thy Burgonet Ile rend thy Beare,   3208
RENOWNE = 1
   Racing the Charracters of your Renowne,   108
RENOWNED = 1
   The Title of this most renowned Duke,   3176
RENT = 1
   France should haue torne and rent my very hart,   133
REPAIRES = 1
   Repaires him with Occasion. This happy day   3325
REPAYRING = 1
   Being opposites of such repayring Nature.   3344
REPEALE = 1
   I will repeale thee, or be well assur'd,   2064
REPLEATE = 1
   Lend me a heart repleate with thankfulnesse: 27
REPORT = 2
   Let this my sword report what speech forbeares.   2958
   Yorke. Of Salsbury, who can report of him,   3321
REPORTED = 1 *1
   **Bulling.* I haue heard her reported to be a Woman of   625
   War. It is reported, mighty Soueraigne,   1824
REPOSE = 1
   King. Well, for this Night we will repose vs here: 952
REPRESENT = 1
   Of that great Shadow I did represent: 21
REPROACH = 4
   Would'st haue me rescue thee from this reproach?   1240
   Elianor. That's bad enough, for I am but reproach: 1276
   And Princes Courts be fill'd with my reproach: 1769

REPROACH *cont.*

And to conclude, Reproach and Beggerie, | Is crept into the Pallace of
our King,   2269
REPROACHFULLY = 1

And shall I then be vs'd reproachfully?   1277
REPROUE = 1

My Lord of Suffolke, Buckingham, and Yorke, | Reproue my
allegation, if you can,   1333
REPUTE = 1

And in my conscience, do repute his grace   3177
REPUTING = 1

Yet by reputing of his high discent,   1342
REQUITE = *1

Eli. What dream'd my Lord, tell me, and Ile requite it   296
RERE = 1

Som. Rere vp his Body, wring him by the Nose.   1732
RESCUE = 1

Would'st haue me rescue thee from this reproach?   1240
RESCUED = 1

And in the end being rescued, I haue seene   1670
RESEMBLE = 1

In face, in gate, in speech he doth resemble.   1679
RESEMBLED = 1

I thought King *Henry* had resembled thee,   439
RESIGNE = 4

And at his pleasure will resigne my Place.   511
Suff. Resigne it then, and leaue thine insolence.   512
As willingly doe I the same resigne,   1088
Resigne to death, it is not worth th'enioying: 1640
RESOLUD = 2

I am resolu'd for death and dignitie.   3194
Old Clif. I am resolu'd to beare a greater storme,   3198
RESOLUTE = 2

Suff. Not resolute, except so much were done,   1569
And therefore am I bold and resolute. *Exeunt.*   2597
RESOLUTELY = 1

Queene. Thrice Noble *Suffolke*, 'tis resolutely spoke.   1568
RESOLUTION = 1*1

And change misdoubt to resolution;   1638
*no want of resolution in mee, but onely my Followers   2839
RESPECTING = 1

Respecting what a rancorous minde he beares,   1318
REST = 11

Exit King, Queene, and Suffolke. | *Manet the rest.*   80
So let her rest: and Madame list to me,   478
Well, to the rest: | Tell me what fate awaits the Duke of Suffolke?   692
And what a pytch she flew aboue the rest: 722
Who kept him in Captiuitie, till he dyed. | But, to the rest.   1003
And you, my Soueraigne Lady, with the rest,   1461
And charge, that no man should disturbe your rest,   1968
Therefore come you with vs, and let him go. | *Exit Lieutenant, and the
rest.*   2310
Alarums to the fight, wherein both the Staffords are slaine. | *Enter Cade
and the rest.*   2511
Enter Iacke Cade and the rest, and strikes his | *staffe on London stone.*   2613
Alarums. Mathew Goffe is slain, and all the rest. | *Then enter Iacke
Cade, with his Company.*   2633

RESTITUTION = 1
And neuer ask'd for restitution.   1418
RESTORD = 1
What, hast thou beene long blinde, and now restor'd?   805
RESTORE = 1
That could restore this Cripple to his Legges againe.   880
RETIRD = 1
Or is he but retir'd to make him strong?   2859
RETIRE = 1
Buck. My gracious Lord, retire to Killingworth,   2575
RETREAT = 3
Alarum, and Retreat. Enter againe Cade, | and all his rabblement.   2773
Dare any be so bold to sound Retreat or Parley   2779
Alarum. Retreat. Enter Yorke, Richard, Warwicke, | and Soldiers, with
Drum & Colours.   3319
RETURNE = 3
When from Saint *Albones* we doe make returne,   358
But now returne we to the false Duke *Humfrey.*   1627
With the rude multitude, till I returne.   1837
RETURNETH = 1
Which with the heart there cooles, and ne're returneth,   1870
REUEALD = 1
And God in Iustice hath reueal'd to vs   1164
REUELLING = 1
Still reuelling like Lords till all be gone,   236
REUENEWES = 1
She beares a Dukes Reuenewes on her backe,   466
REUENGE = 5
And care not who they sting in his reuenge.   1829
And therefore to reuenge it, shalt thou dye,   2195
Therefore, when Merchant-like I sell reuenge,   2210
If he reuenge it not, yet will his Friends,   2317
Thinke therefore on reuenge, and cease to weepe.   2535
REUENGING = 1
Burnes with reuenging fire, whose hopefull colours   2265
REUERENCE = 2
Warw. Madame be still: with reuerence may I say,   1912
And in thy Reuerence, and thy Chaire-dayes, thus   3270
REUEREND = *1
*Seuen Earles, twelue Barons, & twenty reuerend Bishops   15
REUERENT = 1
The reuerent care I beare vnto my Lord,   1328
REUIUE = 1
Suff. He doth reuiue againe, Madame be patient.   1734
REUOLT = 1
The King is mercifull, if you reuolt.   2445
REUOLTED = 1
By meanes whereof, the Townes each day reuolted.   1357
REUOLTING = 1
The false reuolting Normans thorough thee,   2255
REWARD = 6*1
Here *Hume*, take this reward, make merry man   360
To be the Poste, in hope of his reward.   708
Come fellow, follow vs for thy Reward. | *Sound a flourish. Exeunt.*   1167
I will reward you for this venturous deed: 1700
*owne Slaughter-house: Therfore thus will I reward thee,   2517
Shall haue a thousand Crownes for his reward. | *Exeunt some of them.*   2844

REWARD *cont.*
We giue thee for reward a thousand Markes,   3073
RIC = 1
RICH = 2
I dare not say, from the rich Cardinall,   370
And like rich hangings in a homely house,   3333
RICH = 4*1
RICHARD see also Ric., Rich. = 10*1
His words were these: That *Richard*, Duke of Yorke,   580
And left behinde him *Richard*, his onely Sonne,   978
Harmelesse *Richard* was murthered traiterously.   986
For *Richard*, the first Sonnes Heire, being dead,   990
Marryed *Richard*, Earle of Cambridge,   1007
Both. Long liue our Soueraigne *Richard*, Englands | King.   1027
Richard shall liue to make the Earle of Warwick   1048
Enter Edward and Richard.   3117
Enter Richard, and Somerset to fight.   3288
Alarum. Retreat. Enter Yorke, Richard, Warwicke, | and Soldiers, with
Drum & Colours.   3319
By 'th'Masse so did we all. I thanke you *Richard*.   3338
RICHES = 1
Sweet is the Country, because full of Riches,   2696
RICHEST = 1
No, it will hang vpon my richest Robes,   1289
RID = 2
This *Gloster* should be quickly rid the World,   1535
To rid vs from the feare we haue of him.   1536
RIDE = 4*1
You do prepare to ride vnto S.(aint) *Albons*,   332
Hu. I go. Come *Nel* thou wilt ride with vs? *Ex. Hum*   334
When thou didst ride in triumph through the streets.   1185
dost ride in a foot-cloth, dost thou not? | *Say.* What of that?   2680
Will we ride through the streets, & at euery Corner   2771
RIGHT = 8*2
Nor shall proud Lancaster vsurpe my right,   256
Yorke. Which now they hold by force, and not by right: 989
With honor of his Birth-right to the Crowne.   1026
Here let them end it, and God defend the right.   1111
*nor the Queene: and therefore *Peter* haue at thee with a | downe-right
blow.   1151
presence? O *Peter*, thou hast preuayl'd in right.   1161
Came he right now to sing a Rauens Note,   1740
Yor. From Ireland thus comes York to claim his right,   2992
To wring the Widdow from her custom'd right,   3188
As I in iustice, and true right expresse it.   3246
RIGHTFUL = *1
*Whose Beame stands sure, whose rightful cause preuailes. | *Flourish.*
Exeunt.   957
RIGHTFULL = 6*1
*That the Duke of Yorke was rightfull Heire to the | Crowne.   411
say, hee was rightfull Heire to the Crowne?   414
Was rightfull Heire vnto the English Crowne,   581
Seiz'd on the Realme, depos'd the rightfull King,   983
That shall salute our rightfull Soueraigne   1025
For I am rightfull heyre vnto the Crowne.   2451
The rightfull heyre to Englands Royall seate.   3178

RIGHTLY = 1
Thy name is *Gualtier*, being rightly sounded.   2206
RIGOR = 1
Let him haue all the rigor of the Law.   593
RING = 1
Ring Belles alowd, burne Bonfires cleare and bright   2994
RING-LEADER = 1
The Ring-leader and Head of all this Rout,   922
RIOTOUS = 1
And therefore shall it charme thy riotous tongue.   2232
RIPEND = *1
Elia. Why droopes my Lord like ouer-ripen'd Corn,   274
RISE = 3
The Commons haply rise, to saue his Life;   1542
Rise vp Sir *Iohn Mortimer*. Now haue at him.   2439
King. *Iden*, kneele downe, rise vp a Knight: 3072
RISETH = 1
terribly: then the Spirit | riseth.   646
RISING = 1
As hating thee, and rising vp in armes.   2261
ROB = 5
And when the duskie sky, began to rob   1804
And I should rob the Deaths-man of his Fee,   1922
Drones sucke not Eagles blood, but rob Bee-hiues: 2277
And like a Theefe to come to rob my grounds: 2938
To do a murd'rous deede, to rob a man,   3185
ROBBING = 1
Vnlesse by robbing of your Friends, and vs.   2817
ROBD = 1
I neuer rob'd the Souldiers of their pay,   1408
ROBES = 1
No, it will hang vpon my richest Robes,   1289
ROBIN = *1
*World. Here *Robin*, and if I dye, I giue thee my Aporne;   1135
ROCKE = 1
Or turne our Sterne vpon a dreadfull Rocke: 1791
ROCKES = 2
The splitting Rockes cowr'd in the sinking sands,   1797
Oh I could hew vp Rockes, and fight with Flint,   3016
ROGER = 4
With *Roger Bollingbrooke* the Coniurer?   351
Edmond had Issue, *Roger*, Earle of March;   998
Roger had Issue, *Edmond, Anne,* and *Elianor*.   999
She was Heire to *Roger*, Earle of March,   1011
ROLLD = 1
Or as the Snake, roll'd in a flowring Banke,   1530
ROMANE = 1
A Romane Sworder, and Bandetto slaue | Murder'd sweet *Tully. Brutus*
Bastard hand   2303
ROMANOS = 1
Why this is iust, *Aio Aeacida Romanos vincere posso.*   691
ROME = 1
Would chuse him Pope, and carry him to Rome,   448
ROOTED = 1
Now 'tis the Spring, and Weeds are shallow-rooted,   1325
RORES = 1
But great men tremble when the Lyon rores,   1313

245

ROSE = 2
| Then will I raise aloft the Milke-white-Rose, | 266 |
| Looke pale as Prim-rose with blood-drinking sighes, | 1763 |

ROST = 1
| Suffolke, the new made Duke that rules the rost, | 116 |

ROUGH = 2
| *Suf.* Suffolkes Imperiall tongue is sterne and rough: | 2289 |
| *King.* In any case, be not to rough in termes, | 2898 |

ROUND = 2
| My Body round engyrt with miserie: | 1501 |
| That Gold, must round engirt these browes of mine, | 3094 |

ROUT = 2
| The Ring-leader and Head of all this Rout, | 922 |
| *Clif.* Shame and Confusion all is on the rout, | 3253 |

ROYALL = 12
Iesu maintaine your Royall Excellence,	168
Hume. Iesus preserue your Royall Maiesty.	345
I doe beseech your Royall Maiestie,	592
Som. I humbly thanke your Royall Maiestie.	608
That he should come about your Royall Person,	1320
From meaning Treason to our Royall Person,	1364
If those that care to keepe your Royall Person	1473
And finde no harbor in a Royall heart.	1642
Is slander to your Royall Dignitie.	1914
They say, in care of your most Royall Person,	1966
To spoyle the City, and your Royall Court.	2590
The rightfull heyre to Englands Royall seate.	3178

ROYALTIE = 1
| And this the Royaltie of *Albions* King? | 431 |

RUDE = 5
With the rude multitude, till I returne.	1837
Suff. 'Tis like the Commons, rude vnpolisht Hindes,	1984
Of Hindes and Pezants, rude and mercilesse:	2569
Iden. Why rude Companion, whatsoere thou be,	2935
Iden. If one so rude, and of so meane condition	3058

RUDER = 1
| With ruder termes, such as my wit affoords, | 37 |

RUE = 1
| And in thy Closet pent vp, rue my shame, | 1200 |

RUFFE = 1
| His well proportion'd Beard, made ruffe and rugged, | 1879 |

RUFFIAN = 3
Sweare like a Ruffian, and demeane himselfe	196
What wilt thou on thy death-bed play the Ruffian?	3164
To die in Ruffian battell? Euen at this sight,	3271

RUGGED = 1
| His well proportion'd Beard, made ruffe and rugged, | 1879 |

RUINE = 1
| Come thou new ruine of olde Cliffords house: | 3283 |

RULD = 2
| Yet so he rul'd, and such a Prince he was, | 1220 |
| Rul'd like a wandering Plannet ouer me, | 2548 |

RULE = 5
Whose bookish Rule, hath pull'd faire England downe. | *Exit Yorke.*	271
Let them obey, that knowes not how to Rule.	2997
Not fit to gouerne and rule multitudes,	3089
Which dar'st not, no nor canst not rule a Traitor.	3090

RULE *cont.*
Giue place: by heauen thou shalt rule no more   3099
RULER = 5
Vnlike the Ruler of a Common-weale.   197
And he a Prince, and Ruler of the Land: 1219
'Tis meet that luckie Ruler be imploy'd,   1594
On any ground that I am Ruler of,   2010
O're him, whom heauen created for thy Ruler.   3100
RULES = 1
Suffolke, the new made Duke that rules the rost,   116
RUN = 3
The Common-wealth hath dayly run to wrack,   514
The pissing Conduit run nothing but Clarret Wine   2618
Run backe and bite, because he was with-held,   3151
RUNNE = 2*2
*leape me ouer this Stoole, and runne away.   891
Queene. It made me laugh, to see the Villaine runne.   906
1. Runne to my Lord of Suffolke: let him know   1692
Qu. Runne, goe, helpe, helpe: Oh *Henry* ope thine eyes.   1733
RUNNES = 3
the Stoole, and runnes away: and they | follow, and cry, A Miracle.   903
Smooth runnes the Water, where the Brooke is deepe,   1347
And as the Damme runnes lowing vp and downe,   1515
RUNNING = 2
Enter two or three running ouer the Stage, from the | Murther of Duke
Humfrey.   1690
Enter a Soldier running.   2622
RUSTED = 1
But here's a vengefull Sword, rusted with ease,   1902
RUTHLESSE = 1
The ruthlesse Flint doth cut my tender feet,   1210
SACK = *1
*in a Cup of Sack; and feare not Neighbor, you shall doe | well enough.   1121
SACRED = 1
His Weapons, holy Sawes of sacred Writ,   444
SAD = 2
My troublous dreames this night, doth make me sad.   295
With sad vnhelpefull teares, and with dimn'd eyes;   1519
SAFELY = 1
I charge thee waft me safely crosse the Channell.   2282
SAFER = 2
Safer shall he be vpon the sandie Plaines,   663
Safer shall he be vpon the sandie Plaines,   697
SAFETIE = 1
I tender so the safetie of my Liege.   1579
SAFETY = 1
Yorke. I know our safety is to follow them,   3345
SAID = 3*5
for Henry King of England, That the said Henry shal   52
said, That he was, and that the King was an Vsurper.   416
Elianor. Well said my Masters, and welcome all: To   633
Who said; *Symon,* come; come offer at my Shrine,   825
**Glost.* Why that's well said: What Colour is my | Gowne of?   853
**Suff.* Why that's well said. Goe, get you to my House,   1699
**Hol.* True: and yet it is said, Labour in thy Vocati-|on: 2335
**Iden.* Nay, it shall nere be said, while England stands,   2946

SAINT = 12*1
You do prepare to ride vnto S.(aint) *Albons,*	332
When from Saint *Albones* we doe make returne,	358
The King is now in progresse towards Saint *Albones,*	702
One. Forsooth, a blinde man at Saint *Albones* Shrine,	790
Enter the Maior of Saint Albones, and his Brethren, | *bearing the man*	
betweene two in a Chayre.	795
In my sleepe, by good Saint *Albon:*	824
Simpc. Yes Master, cleare as day, I thanke God and | Saint *Albones.*	848
My Lords, Saint *Albone* here hath done a Miracle:	878
Glost. My Masters of Saint *Albones,*	882
Cade. Vp Fish-streete, downe Saint Magnes corner,	2775
Meet me to morrow in S.(aint) Georges Field,	3038
The Castle in S.(aint) *Albons,* Somerset	3291
Saint Albons battell wonne by famous Yorke,	3352

SAINTS = 1
Are brazen Images of Canonized Saints.	446

SAIST = 2
Elia. What saist thou? Maiesty: I am but Grace.	346
Elia. What saist thou man? Hast thou as yet confer'd	349

SAKE = *2
Peter. Alas, my Lord, I cannot fight; for Gods sake	610
*tell the King from me, that for his Fathers sake *Hen-*|*ry*	2476

SAL = 6*1

SALE = 1
Queene. Thy sale of Offices and Townes in France,	525

SALISB = 3*6

SALISBURIE = 1
Gloster, Yorke, Buckingham, Somerset, | Salisburie, and Warwicke.	74

SALISBURY see also Sal., Salisb. = 14*2
Enter King, Duke Humfrey, Salisbury, Warwicke, and Beau-|*ford on*	
the one side.	3
Braue *Yorke, Salisbury,* and victorious *Warwicke,*	93
Exit Warwicke, and Salisbury. Manet Yorke.	225
Salisbury and *Warwick* are no simple Peeres.	460
Yorke, Salisbury, Warwicke, | *and the Duchesse.*	489
Inuite my Lords of Salisbury and Warwick	712
Enter Yorke, Salisbury, and Warwick.	959
Yorke. Now my good Lords of Salisbury & Warwick,	960
Then Father *Salisbury,* kneele we together,	1023
Yorke, Buckingham, Salisbury, and Warwicke, | *to the Parliament.*	1293
Enter Salisbury.	1952
Commons within. An answer from the King, my Lord | of Salisbury.	1982
But all the Honor *Salisbury* hath wonne,	1988
King. Goe *Salisbury,* and tell them all from me,	1993
Enter the King, Salisbury, and Warwicke, to the | *Cardinal in bed.*	2132
Enter Salisbury.	3336

SALISBURY = 2

SALLET = 1*3
*picke a Sallet another while, which is not amisse to coole	2913
*Sallet was borne to do me good: for many a time but for	2915
*a Sallet, my brain-pan had bene cleft with a brown Bill;	2916
in: and now the word Sallet must serue me to feed on.	2919

SALSBURIE = 1
War. That shall I do my Liege; Stay Salsburie	1836

SALSBURY = 4
Bid Salsbury and Warwicke come to me.	3144

SALSBURY *cont.*
Old Salsbury, shame to thy siluer haire,	3162
Yorke. Of Salsbury, who can report of him,	3321
Is not it selfe, nor haue we wonne one foot, | If Salsbury be lost.	3326

SALT = 2
With teares as salt as Sea, through thy vnkindnesse.	1796
Vpon his face an Ocean of salt teares,	1845

SALUTE = 2
Makes me the bolder to salute my King,	36
That shall salute our rightfull Soueraigne	1025

SAME = 5*1
Vntill thy head be circled with the same.	283
*Sirrha Beadle, whippe him till he leape ouer that same | Stoole.	896
As willingly doe I the same resigne,	1088
Attracts the same for aydance 'gainst the enemy,	1869
That were vnworthy to behold the same.	2550
And with the same to acte controlling Lawes:	3098

SANCTA = 1
Ah *Sancta Maiestas!* who would not buy thee deere?	2996

SAND = 1
Heere shall they make their ransome on the sand,	2179

SANDIE = 2
Safer shall he be vpon the sandie Plaines,	663
Safer shall he be vpon the sandie Plaines,	697

SANDS = 1
The splitting Rockes cowr'd in the sinking sands,	1797

SAND-BAGGE = 1*1
Drumme before him, and his Staffe, with a Sand-bagge	1117
Drumme and Sand-bagge, and Prentices drinking to him.	1119

SAT = 1
Studied so long, sat in the Councell house,	97

SATE = 1
Me thought I sate in Seate of Maiesty,	310

SATISFIE = 1
In this close Walke, to satisfie my selfe,	962

SAUAGE = 1
Stab'd *Iulius Caesar.* Sauage Islanders	2305

SAUE = 10*1
*Now Sirrha, if you meane to saue your selfe from Whip-|ping,	890
The King will labour still to saue his Life,	1541
The Commons haply rise, to saue his Life;	1542
Saue to the God of heauen, and to my King:	2294
All. God saue your Maiesty. | *Cade.* I thanke you good people. There shall bee no	2389
And therefore yet relent, and saue my life.	2750
Fling vp his cap, and say, God saue his Maiesty.	2791
All. God saue the King, God saue the King.	2795
All. God saue the King, God saue the King.	2874

SAUNDER = 2
Glost. What's thine owne Name? | *Simpc. Saunder Simpcoxe,* and if it please you, Master.	868
Glost. Then *Saunder,* sit there,	870

SAUOY = *1
*Cade. So sirs: now go some and pull down the Sauoy:	2635

SAW = 5
I neuer saw but Humfrey Duke of Gloster,	191
I saw not better sport these seuen yeeres day:	718

SAW *cont.*

A man that ne're saw in his life before.	792
Yorke. I neuer saw a fellow worse bestead,	1112
Those that I neuer saw, and strucke them dead.	2715

SAWCIE = 1

But thou wilt braue me with these sawcie termes?	2940

SAWES = 1

His Weapons, holy Sawes of sacred Writ,	444

SAWYER = 1

Drumme. Enter Cade, Dicke Butcher, Smith the Weauer, | and a Sawyer, with infinite numbers.	2350

SAY = 41*11

Lordings farewell, and say when I am gone,	152
I dare not say, from the rich Cardinall,	370
They say, A craftie Knaue do's need no Broker,	376
say, hee was rightfull Heire to the Crowne?	414
Queene. My Lord of Suffolke, say, is this the guise?	428
I say, my Soueraigne, *Yorke* is meetest man	555
King. Say man, were these thy words?	583
King. Vnckle, what shall we say to this in law?	600
Sometime Ile say, I am Duke *Humfreyes* Wife,	1218
I will subscribe, and say I wrong'd the Duke.	1332
Card. It serues you well, my Lord, to say so much.	1419
Glost. I say no more then truth, so helpe me God.	1420
Say, who's a Traytor? *Gloster* he is none. *Exit.*	1523
Say as you thinke, and speake it from your Soules:	1549
Say but the word, and I will be his Priest.	1574
Say you consent, and censure well the deed,	1577
Suff. Here is my Hand, the deed is worthy doing. | *Queene.* And so say I.	1580
Say he be taken, rackt, and tortured;	1682
Will make him say, I mou'd him to those Armes.	1684
Say that he thriue, as 'tis great like he will,	1685
Say, we intend to try his Grace to day,	1710
Lay not thy hands on me: forbeare I say,	1746
Did seeme to say, seeke not a Scorpions Nest,	1786
Say, if thou dar'st, prowd Lord of Warwickshire,	1905
Warw. Madame be still: with reuerence may I say,	1912
And say, it was thy Mother that thou meant'st,	1927
They say, by him the good Duke *Humfrey* dy'de:	1960
They say, in him they feare your Highnesse death;	1961
They say, in care of your most Royall Person,	1966
They say is shamefully bereft of life.	1981
No more I say: if thou do'st pleade for him,	2005
Hol. So he had need, for 'tis thred-bare. Well, I say,	2326
*which is as much to say, as let the Magistrates be la-|bouring	2336
*should vndoe a man. Some say the Bee stings, but I say,	2398
Cade. Away with him I say: Hang him with his Pen	2426
Cade. I, there's the question; But I say, 'tis true:	2461
*it vp. Fellow-Kings, I tell you, that that Lord *Say* hath	2484
head, the Duke of Buckingham, and the | Lord Say.	2531
King. Lord *Say, Iacke Cade* hath sworne to haue thy | head.	2551
King. Lord *Say,* the Traitors hateth thee,	2579
Mes. My Lord, a prize, a prize, heeres the Lord *Say,*	2653
Enter George, with the Lord Say.	2657
*Ah thou Say, thou Surge, nay thou Buckram Lord, now	2659

SAY *cont.*

   Dic. What say you of Kent. | *Say.* Nothing but this: 'Tis *bona terra,*
mala gens.   2688
   *Cade. Nay, he noddes at vs, as who should say, Ile be   2727
   *him away I say, and strike off his head presently, and then   2742
   Clif. What say ye Countrimen, will ye relent   2787
   Fling vp his cap, and say, God saue his Maiesty.   2791
   To say, if that the Bastard boyes of Yorke   3110
   * Yor. I thanke thee *Clifford*: Say, what newes with thee?   3122
   Clifford I say, come forth and fight with me,   3223

SAY = 9*4
SAYD = 1*2

   *Armorer. And't shall please your Maiestie, I neuer sayd   584
   *Spirit. Aske what thou wilt; that I had sayd, and | done.   653
   Had I but sayd, I would haue kept my Word;   2007

SAYES = 3*1

   Yor. And so sayes Yorke, | For he hath greatest cause.   215
   *Butcher. And furthermore, wee'l haue the Lord *Sayes*   2480
   His sonnes (he sayes) shall giue their words for him.   3134
   What sayes Lord Warwicke, shall we after them?   3349

SAYING = *1

   * Peter. Against my Master *Thomas Horner,* for saying,   410

SAYST = *2

   *Queene. What say'st thou? Did the Duke of Yorke   413
   *Glost. Say'st thou me so: what Colour is this Cloake | of?   850

SCALES = 2

   And poyse the Cause in Iustice equall Scales,   956
   Enter Lord Scales vpon the Tower walking. Then enters | two or three
Citizens below.   2598

SCALES = 2
SCANDALL = 1

   Why yet thy scandall were not wipt away,   1241

SCAPD = 1

   Like to a Ship, that hauing scap'd a Tempest,   2886

SCAPE = 1

   Of all our Fortunes: but if we haply scape,   3306

SCARCE = 1

   And *Humfrey,* Duke of Gloster, scarce himselfe,   1096

SCARRE *see* skarre
SCARRES = 1

   Receiud deepe scarres in France and Normandie: 94

SCARSE = 1

   Yor. Scarse can I speake, my Choller is so great.   3015

SCATHE = 1

   All these could not procure me any scathe,   1238

SCATTER = 1

   That want their Leader, scatter vp and downe,   1828

SCEPTER = 5

   Nor hold the Scepter in his childish Fist,   257
   Except a Sword or Scepter ballance it.   3000
   A Scepter shall it haue, haue I a soule,   3001
   And not to grace an awefull Princely Scepter.   3093
   Heere is hand to hold a Scepter vp,   3097

SCHOLLERS = 1

   All Schollers, Lawyers, Courtiers, Gentlemen,   2572

SCHOOLE = *1

   *the Realme, in erecting a Grammar Schoole: and where-|as   2667

SCOENA *l.*1 = 1
SCOPE = 1
    And the Offendor graunted scope of speech,   1476
SCORE = *2
    *mony, all shall eate and drinke on my score, and I will   2391
    *Score and the Tally, thou hast caused printing to be vs'd,   2669
SCORNE = *1
    Hol. The Nobilitie thinke scorne to goe in Leather | Aprons.   2331
SCORNES = 1
    And in her heart she scornes our Pouertie: 467
SCORPIONS = 1
    Did seeme to say, seeke not a Scorpions Nest,   1786
SCOURGE = 1
    Out-cast of *Naples,* Englands bloody Scourge,   3113
SCOWRED = 1
    That shall be scowred in his rancorous heart,   1903
SCOWRING = *1
    *them to me in the Garret one Night, as wee were scow-|ring my Lord
    of Yorkes Armor.   588
SCREECH-OWLES = 2
    The time when Screech-owles cry, and Bandogs howle,   638
    And boading Screech-Owles, make the Consort full.   2042
SCRIBELD = *1
    *be made Parchment; that Parchment being scribeld ore,   2397
SCUM = 1
    Staf. Rebellious Hinds, the filth and scum of Kent,   2442
SEA = 6
    Was I for this nye wrack'd vpon the Sea,   1782
    The pretty vaulting Sea refus'd to drowne me,   1794
    With teares as salt as Sea, through thy vnkindnesse.   1796
    And threw it towards thy Land: The Sea receiu'd it,   1808
    Alarum. Fight at Sea. Ordnance goes off.   2168
    Is crept into the bosome of the Sea: 2171
SEALE = 2*1
    Seale vp your Lips, and giue no words but Mum,   365
    That thou might'st thinke vpon these by the Seale,   2059
    *'tis the Bees waxe: for I did but seale once to a thing, and   2399
SEARCHING = 1
    I would inuent as bitter searching termes,   2026
SEAS = 2
    The Dolphin hath preuayl'd beyond the Seas,   515
    Should make a start ore-seas, and vanquish you?   2820
SEASONS = 1
    So Cares and Ioyes abound, as Seasons fleet.   1174
SEAT = 1
    Wee'l quickly hoyse Duke *Humfrey* from his seat.   176
SEATE = 2
    Me thought I sate in Seate of Maiesty,   310
    The rightfull heyre to Englands Royall seate.   3178
SEATED = 1
    All the foule terrors in darke seated hell -- -   2043
SECOND = 4
    Art thou not second Woman in the Realme?   317
    The second, *William* of Hatfield; and the third,   971
    And now is Yorke in Armes, to second him.   2889
    The second Part of Henry the Sixt,   3357

SECRECIE = 2
The businesse asketh silent secrecie. 366
But with aduice and silent secrecie. 1034
SECRET = 2*1
From Treasons secret Knife, and Traytors Rage, 1474
*Card. Gods secret Iudgement: I did dreame to Night, 1727
And liue alone as secret as I may. 2584
SECRETS = 2
To prie into the secrets of the State, 262
The secrets of his ouer-charged soule, 2093
SECURE = 1
To giue the enemy way, and to secure vs 3302
SEDITIOUS = 1
Seditious to his Grace, and to the State. 3029
SEDUCD = 1
I haue seduc'd a head-strong Kentishman, | Iohn Cade of Ashford, 1662
SEE = 36*9
Come, let vs in, and with all speede prouide | To see her Coronation be
perform'd. 78
I see thy furie: If I longer stay, 150
Wee'le see these things effected to the full. 359
to his Lordship? Let me see them: what is thine? 400
Somerset, wee'le see thee sent away. | Flourish. Exeunt. 617
See you well guerdon'd for these good deserts. 676
Wee'le see your Trinkets here all forth-comming. | All away. Exit. 683
Now pray my Lord, let's see the Deuils Writ. 687
To see how God in all his Creatures workes, 723
*Card. Medice teipsum, Protector see to't well, protect | your selfe. 777
Let me see thine Eyes; winck now, now open them, 846
Suff. And yet I thinke, Iet did he neuer see. 858
Queene. It made me laugh, to see the Villaine runne. 906
Queene. Gloster, see here the Taincture of thy Nest, 940
Queene. I see no reason, why a King of yeeres 1083
Left I the Court, to see this Quarrell try'de. 1109
King. A Gods Name see the Lysts and all things fit, 1110
*Salisb. Thumpe? Then see thou thumpe thy Master | well. 1145
My teare-stayn'd eyes, to see her Miseries. 1187
Elianor. Come you, my Lord, to see my open shame? 1195
See how the giddy multitude doe point, 1197
To see my teares, and heare my deepe-fet groanes. 1209
Goe, leade the way, I long to see my Prison. Exeunt. 1291
Queene. Can you not see? or will ye not obserue 1298
Glost. Well Suffolke, thou shalt not see me blush, 1396
Ah Vnckle Humfrey, in thy face I see 1503
Suff. A charge, Lord Yorke, that I will see perform'd. 1626
*Suff. Ile see it truly done, my Lord of Yorke. Exeunt. 1635
King. That is to see how deepe my graue is made, 1854
For seeing him, I see my life in death. 1856
War. See how the blood is setled in his face. 1864
But see, his face is blacke, and full of blood: 1872
Looke on the sheets his haire (you see) is sticking, 1878
War. See how the pangs of death do make him grin. 2158
*Hol. I see them, I see them: There's Bests Sonne, the | Tanner of
Wingham. 2340
*euen with you. Ile see if his head will stand steddier on 2728
I see them Lording it in London streets, 2822
*I see them lay their heades together to surprize 2835

SEE *cont.*

*I climb'd into this Garden, to see if I can eate Grasse, or	2912
See if thou canst out-face me with thy lookes:	2950
*K. See Buckingham, Somerset comes with th'Queene,	3078
See where they come, Ile warrant they'l make it good.	3118
If you be tane, we then should see the bottome	3305
To see their day, and them our Fortune giue.	3317

SEEING = 4

Seeing the deed is meritorious,	1572
For seeing him, I see my life in death.	1856
Bro. Well, seeing gentle words will not preuayle,	2494
And seeing Ignorance is the curse of God,	2707

SEEK = *1

Yor. Hold Warwick: seek thee out some other chace	3234

SEEKE = 9

For that's the Golden marke I seeke to hit:	255
'Tis that they seeke; and they, in seeking that,	1041
Nor neuer seeke preuention of thy foes.	1233
Doe seeke subuersion of thy harmelesse Life.	1509
Did seeme to say, seeke not a Scorpions Nest,	1786
Whom haue I iniur'd, that ye seeke my death?	2734
I seeke not to waxe great by others warning,	2925
And seeke for sorrow with thy Spectacles?	3165
In cruelty, will I seeke out my Fame.	3282

SEEKING = 1

'Tis that they seeke; and they, in seeking that,	1041

SEEME = 2

Did seeme to say, seeke not a Scorpions Nest,	1786
I, euery ioynt should seeme to curse and ban,	2034

SEEMES = 2

Gazing on that which seemes to dimme thy sight?	279
Seemes he a Doue? his feathers are but borrow'd,	1369

SEEMETH = 1*1

Me seemeth then, it is no Pollicie,	1317
King. My Lords, what to your wisdomes seemeth best,	1495

SEENE = 9*1

Oft haue I seene the haughty Cardinall,	193
Suff. Well hath your Highnesse seene into this Duke:	1336
In Ireland haue I seene this stubborne *Cade*	1666
And in the end being rescued, I haue seene	1670
Oft haue I seene a timely-parted Ghost,	1865
And 'tis well seene, he found an enemy.	1889
Were there a Serpent seene, with forked Tongue,	1971
Where death's approach is seene so terrible.	2140
But. No question of that: for I haue seene him whipt | three Market	
dayes together.	2375
Rich. Oft haue I seene a hot ore-weening Curre,	3150

SEES = 1

And sees fast-by, a Butcher with an Axe,	1893

SEEST = 5

What seest thou there? King *Henries* Diadem,	280
In my opinion, yet thou seest not well.	847
King. O God, seest thou this, and bearest so long?	905
Glost. Elianor, the Law thou seest hath iudged thee,	1069
Clif. What seest thou in me Yorke?	3239

SEIZD = 1

Seiz'd on the Realme, depos'd the rightfull King,	983

SEIZE = *1
   Cade. Heere's the Lord of the soile come to seize me   2929
SELDOME = 2
   For things are often spoke, and seldome meant,   1570
   Mens flesh preseru'd so whole, doe seldome winne.   1604
SELFE = 34*11
   Or hath mine Vnckle *Beauford*, and my selfe,   95
   Aniou and *Maine*? My selfe did win them both: 126
   To tumble downe thy husband, and thy selfe,   322
   Next time Ile keepe my dreames vnto my selfe, | And not be check'd.   327
   Suff. Madame, my selfe haue lym'd a Bush for her,   474
   And you your selfe shall steere the happy Helme. *Exit*.   486
   Card. *Medice teipsum*, Protector see to't well, protect | your selfe.   777
   And many time and oft my selfe haue heard a Voyce, | To call him so.   828
   *Now Sirrha, if you meane to saue your selfe from Whip-|ping,   890
   And looke thy selfe be faultlesse, thou wert best.   941
   Glost. Madame, for my selfe, to Heauen I doe appeale,   942
   In this close Walke, to satisfie my selfe,   962
   Yorke. And *Neuill*, this I doe assure my selfe,   1047
   *my Mans instigation, to proue him a Knaue, and my selfe   1148
   Elianor. Ah *Gloster*, teach me to forget my selfe: 1203
   And shew it selfe, attyre me how I can.   1290
   Whereof you cannot easily purge your selfe.   1435
   That you will cleare your selfe from all suspence,   1440
   My selfe had notice of your Conuenticles,   1466
   Doe, or vndoe, as if our selfe were here.   1496
   Euen so my selfe bewayles good *Glosters* case   1518
   And for my selfe, Foe as he was to me,   1759
   My selfe haue calm'd their spleenfull mutinie,   1830
   My selfe and *Beauford* had him in protection,   1884
   That thou thy selfe wast borne in Bastardie;   1928
   Q. Enough sweet Suffolke, thou torment'st thy selfe,   2044
   And turnes the force of them vpon thy selfe.   2047
   Aduenture to be banished my selfe: 2065
   For where thou art, there is the World it selfe,   2077
   My selfe no ioy in nought, but that thou liu'st.   2081
   By such a lowly Vassall as thy selfe.   2279
   *Or hast thou a marke to thy selfe, like a honest plain dea-|ling man?   2420
   Cade. To equall him I will make my selfe a knight, pre-|sently;   2438
   And thou thy selfe a Sheareman, art thou not?   2453
   Cade. He lyes, for I inuented it my selfe. Go too Sir-|rah,   2475
   *thou behaued'st thy selfe, as if thou hadst beene in thine   2516
   Should perish by the Sword. And I my selfe,   2543
   But I am troubled here with them my selfe,   2607
   Dicke. And worke in their shirt to, as my selfe for ex-|ample, that am
a butcher.   2685
   O let me liue. | *Cade*. I feele remorse in my selfe with his words: but   2737
   Somerset. My Lord, | Ile yeelde my selfe to prison willingly,   2895
   Cade. Fye on Ambitions: fie on my selfe, that haue a   2906
   Sal. My Lord, I haue considered with my selfe   3175
   For I my selfe must hunt this Deere to death.   3235
   Is not it selfe, nor haue we wonne one foot, | If Salsbury be lost.   3326
SELFE-LOUE = 1
   Hath no selfe-loue: nor he that loues himselfe,   3260
SELL = 2
   Or sell my Title for a glorious Graue.   1389
   Therefore, when Merchant-like I sell reuenge,   2210

SELLING = 1
head, for selling the Dukedome of *Maine.* 2481
SELUES = 7
Haue you your selues, *Somerset, Buckingham,* 92
Now shew your selues men, 'tis for Liberty. 2503
God should be so obdurate as your selues: 2748
Assure your selues will neuer be vnkinde: 2871
Souldiers, I thanke you all: disperse your selues: 3037
If you oppose your selues to match Lord Warwicke. 3155
Clif. Take heede least by your heate you burne your | selues: 3159
SEMBLANCE = 1
Of ashy semblance, meager, pale, and bloodlesse, 1866
SENCE = 1
Buck. Hee'le wrest the sence, and hold vs here all day. 1486
SEND = 10*1
*Take this fellow in, and send for his Master with a Purse-|uant 419
Glost. Then send for one presently. 886
Send Succours (Lords) and stop the Rage betime, 1588
To send me packing with an Hoast of men: 1648
Giue thee thy hyre, and send thy Soule to Hell, 1930
Dread Lord, the Commons send you word by me, 1955
Could send such Message to their Soueraigne: 1985
King. Ile send some holy Bishop to intreat: 2541
And thither I will send you *Mathew Goffe.* 2610
Tell him, Ile send Duke *Edmund* to the Tower, 2892
Ile send them all as willing as I liue: 3043
SENDS = 1
And sends the poore well pleased from my gate. 2928
SENET = 1
Sound a Senet. Enter King, Queene, Cardinall, Suffolke, 1292
SENNET = 1
Sound a Sennet. 487
SENSELESSE = 1
Against the senselesse windes shall grin in vaine, 2245
SENT = 7*2
**ouer to the King her Father, and shee sent ouer of the King of* 65
Somerset, wee'le see thee sent away. | *Flourish. Exeunt.* 617
*Sent his poore Queene to France, from whence she came, 984
For Souldiers pay in France, and neuer sent it? 1356
Yorke. That *Somerset* be sent as Regent thither: 1593
Sent from a sort of Tinkers to the King. 1990
And I am sent to tell his Maiestie, 2094
And sent the ragged Souldiers wounded home. 2258
The king hath sent him sure: I must dissemble. 3005
SENTENCE = 1
Receiue the Sentence of the Law for sinne, 1056
SERPENT = 1
Were there a Serpent seene, with forked Tongue, 1971
SERPENTS = 3
Their touch affrights me as a Serpents sting. 1747
From such fell Serpents as false *Suffolke* is; 1978
Their Musicke, frightfull as the Serpents hisse, 2041
SERU = 1*1
SERUANT = 2
Enter Seruant. 418
The seruant of this Armorer, my Lords. 1114

SERUANTS = 1
For he hath witnesse of his seruants malice: 606
SERUD = *1
*it hath seru'd me insteede of a quart pot to drinke   2918
SERUE = 4
Then Yorke be still a-while, till time do serue: 260
Glost. A subtill Knaue, but yet it shall not serue: 845
in: and now the word Sallet must serue me to feed on.   2919
Yor. Will you not Sonnes? | *Edw.* I Noble Father, if our words will
serue.   3135
SERUES = 1
Card. It serues you well, my Lord, to say so much.   1419
SERUICE = 3
And doe some seruice to Duke *Humfreyes* Ghost. | *Exeunt.*   1936
He were created Knight for his good seruice.   3071
And such a peece of seruice will you do,   3154
SERUILE = 1
Vpon these paltry, seruile, abiect Drudges: 2273
SERUINGMAN see also Seru. = 1
Enter a Seruingman.   711
SET = 13*1
And on my head did set the Diadem.   314
And set the Triple Crowne vpon his Head;   449
I could set my ten Commandements in your face.   534
The time of Night when Troy was set on fire,   637
Wer't not all one, an emptie Eagle were set,   1550
Nor set no footing on this vnkinde Shore.   1787
Set all vpon me, mightie Soueraigne.   1951
Like Lime-twigs set to catch my winged soule: 2150
Lieu. And as for these whose ransome we haue set,   2308
*dresse the Common-wealth and turne it, and set a new | nap vpon it.   2324
But first, go and set London Bridge on fire,   2630
King. Then heauen set ope thy euerlasting gates,   2865
Set limbe to limbe, and thou art farre the lesser: 2951
Clif. But that my hearts on future mischeefe set,   3312
SETLED = 1
War. See how the blood is setled in his face.   1864
SETTING = 1
Cade. O monstrous. | *Wea.* We tooke him setting of boyes Copies.   2405
SEUEN = 2*2
*Seuen Earles, twelue Barons, & twenty reuerend Bishops   15
I saw not better sport these seuen yeeres day: 718
Yorke. Then thus: | *Edward* the third, my Lords, had seuen Sonnes: 968
*Vowes Reformation. There shall be in England, seuen   2383
SEUENTH = 1
William of Windsor was the seuenth, and last.   976
SEUERALL = 3
As thus to name the seuerall Colours we doe weare.   874
With euery seuerall pleasure in the World: 2078
I do dismisse you to your seuerall Countries.   2873
SH = *1
SHADE = 2
For in the shade of death, I shall finde ioy;   1754
Their sweetest shade, a groue of Cypresse Trees: 2038
SHADOW = 1
Of that great Shadow I did represent: 21

SHAG-HAYRD = 1
Full often, like a shag-hayr'd craftie Kerne,   1673
SHAKE = 1
Shake he his weapon at vs, and passe by.   2794
SHAKES = 1
And shakes his head, and trembling stands aloofe,   239
SHAKING = 2
Shaking the bloody Darts, as he his Bells.   1672
That with the very shaking of their Chaines,   3142
SHAL *l.*52 *707 *3137 = *3
SHALL *l.*57 *64 102 103 151 251 256 267 308 348 355 356 364 378 383
    432 468 486 539 *584 600 *612 *616 *626 651 *655 657 660 661 663 681
    689 694 695 697 776 845 *900 929 1025 1042 1046 1048 1060 1061 1064
    1079 *1121 1216 1217 1277 1279 1284 1362 1468 1492 1629 1656 1657
    1677 1680 1688 1754 1768 1836 1903 *1953 2001 2011 2124 2179 *2186
    2189 2232 *2233 *2243 2245 2246 *2342 *2355 *2383 *2385 *2386 *2387
    *2390 *2391 *2413 *2435 2467 *2478 *2518 *2523 2544 2553 2606 2620
    *2646 *2647 *2651 *2658 *2723 *2739 2746 *2752 *2753 *2754 *2755
    *2759 2844 2901 *2946 2954 2974 2986 3001 3039 3080 3085 3111 3115
    3134 3158 3168 3214 3273 3275 3277 3308 3349 3353 = 93*37
SHALLOW-ROOTED = 1
Now 'tis the Spring, and Weeds are shallow-rooted,   1325
SHALT *l.*652 *1136 1396 1932 2195 2199 2217 *2286 *2518 *2638 2975
    3099 = 8*4
SHAME = 14*3
And giue her as a Prey to Law and Shame,   950
With enuious Lookes laughing at thy shame,   1183
Elianor. Come you, my Lord, to see my open shame?   1195
And in thy Closet pent vp, rue my shame,   1200
Mayl'd vp in shame, with Papers on my back,   1207
But be thou milde, and blush not at my shame,   1224
Although thou hast beene Conduct of my shame.   1281
Elianor. My shame will not be shifted with my Sheet: 1288
Yorke. What, worse then naught? nay, then a shame | take all.   1610
Somerset. And in the number, thee, that wishest | shame.   1612
Wer't not a shame, that whilst you liue at iarre,   2818
Old Salsbury, shame to thy siluer haire,   3162
And shame thine honourable Age with blood?   3170
For shame in dutie bend thy knee to me,   3173
Rich. Fie, Charitie for shame, speake not in spight,   3213
Clif. Shame and Confusion all is on the rout,   3253
Qu. Away my Lord, you are slow, for shame away.   3297
SHAMEFULL = 3
O Peeres of England, shamefull is this League,   105
Ah *Humfrey,* can I beare this shamefull yoake?   1213
By shamefull murther of a guiltlesse King,   2263
SHAMEFULLY = 1
They say is shamefully bereft of life.   1981
SHAMES = 1
Quitting thee thereby of ten thousand shames,   1923
SHAPE = 2
Who cannot steale a shape, that meanes deceit?   1373
As crooked in thy manners, as thy shape.   3157
SHARD = 1
While all is shar'd, and all is borne away,   240
SHARE = 1
The other *Walter Whitmore* is thy share.   2183

SHARPE = 2
Sharpe *Buckingham* vnburthens with his tongue,   1456
You put sharpe Weapons in a mad-mans hands.   1653
SHARPE-QUILLD = 1
Were almost like a sharpe-quill'd Porpentine: 1669
SHAUE = 1
Ile shaue your Crowne for this,   775
SHE = 15*5
SHEAREMAN = 1
And thou thy selfe a Sheareman, art thou not?   2453
SHEATH = *1
*ere thou sleepe in thy Sheath, I beseech Ioue on my knees   2962
SHED = 3
My sword should shed hot blood, mine eyes no teares.   125
Suff. Thou shalt be waking, while I shed thy blood,   1932
Must not be shed by such a iaded Groome: 2220
SHEE *l.*65 946 1179 = 3*1
SHEELE = 2
Shee'le hamper thee, and dandle thee like a Baby: 537
Shee'le gallop farre enough to her destruction. | *Exit Buckingham.* 544
SHEEPE = 2*1
burnt i'th hand for stealing of Sheepe.   2381
* *Cade.* They fell before thee like Sheepe and Oxen, &   2515
On Sheepe or Oxen could I spend my furie.   3019
SHEES = 1
Shee's tickled now, her Fume needs no spurres.   543
SHEET = 2*1
Enter the Duchesse in a white Sheet, and a Taper   1188
Stanley. Madame, your Penance done, | Throw off this Sheet,   1285
* *Elianor.* My shame will not be shifted with my Sheet: 1288
SHEETS = 1
Looke on the sheets his haire (you see) is sticking,   1878
SHEPHEARD = 2
Till they haue snar'd the Shepheard of the Flock,   1039
Thus is the Shepheard beaten from thy side,   1491
SHERIFE see also Sh. = 4
burning in her hand, with the Sherife | and Officers.   1189
* *Seru.* So please your Grace, wee'le take her from the | Sherife. 1191
My *Nell*, I take my leaue: and Master Sherife,   1251
Elianor. Sherife farewell, and better then I fare,   1280
SHERIFE = 1
SHEW = 10*2
And make a shew of loue to proud Duke *Humfrey*,   253
* *Hume.* This they haue promised to shew your Highnes   353
* *Salisb.* Peace Sonne, and shew some reason *Buckingham*   503
To shew some reason, of no little force,   558
And shew it selfe, attyre me how I can.   1290
And in his simple shew he harbours Treason.   1348
Too full of foolish pittie: and *Glosters* shew   1527
Shew me one skarre, character'd on thy Skinne,   1603
To shew how queint an Orator you are.   1987
Aliue againe? Then shew me where he is,   2146
Come Souldiers, shew what cruelty ye can.   2300
Now shew your selues men, 'tis for Liberty.   2503
SHEWD = *1
*And shew'd how well you loue your Prince & Countrey: 2868

SHEWES = 3
He knits his Brow, and shewes an angry Eye,	1309
More then mistrust, that shewes him worthy death.	1544
As on a Mountaine top, the Cedar shewes,	3205

SHEWNE = 1
But that 'tis shewne ignobly, and in Treason.	3244

SHIFT = *1
*make shift for one, and so Gods Cursse light vppon you | all.	2807

SHIFTED = *1
*Elianor. My shame will not be shifted with my Sheet:	1288

SHILLING = *1
*one and twenty Fifteenes, and one shilling to the pound, | the last Subsidie.	2655

SHINE = 1
Aduance our halfe-fac'd Sunne, striuing to shine;	2266

SHINING = 1
With shining checker'd slough doth sting a Child,	1531

SHIP = 1
Like to a Ship, that hauing scap'd a Tempest,	2886

SHIPPE = 1
For there Ile shippe them all for Ireland.	1634

SHIRT = *1
*Dicke. And worke in their shirt to, as my selfe for ex-|ample, that am a butcher.	2685

SHOOEN = 1
Spare none, but such as go in clouted shooen,	2505

SHOOKE = 1
And thought thee happy when I shooke my head.	2223

SHOOT = 1
Suf. O that I were a God, to shoot forth Thunder	2272

SHORE = 5
Nor set no footing on this vnkinde Shore.	1787
And bid them blow towards Englands blessed shore,	1790
Knowing that thou wouldst haue me drown'd on shore	1795
When from thy Shore, the Tempest beáte vs backe,	1802
Or with their blood staine this discoloured shore.	2180

SHORT = 3
What, is't too short? Ile lengthen it with mine,	285
Hangs on the cutting short that fraudfull man.	1375
Rather then bloody Warre shall cut them short,	2544

SHORTLY = 1
Hang ouer thee, as sure it shortly will.	1226

SHOULD *l.*115 125 133 140 142 162 172 504 *571 991 1020 1084 1206
1316 1320 1338 1426 1535 1537 *1553 1557 1717 *1883 1922 1967 1968
*2023 2031 2032 2034 2036 2111 2115 2143 2196 2204 2278 2291 2337
*2380 *2396 *2398 2538 2543 *2558 *2727 2748 *2800 2820 2825 2936
3013 3241 *3243 3255 3305 = 45*11

SHOULDERS = 1*1
*his shoulders, vnlesse he pay me tribute: there shall not	2753
So beare I thee vpon my manly shoulders:	3285

SHOULDST *l.*2114 = 1
SHOW *see* shew
SHOWD *see* shew'd
SHOWES *see* shewes
SHOWRES = *1
*Faster the(n) Spring-time showres, comes thoght on thoght,	1643

SHREWD = 1
That beares so shrewd a mayme: two Pulls at once;   1097
SHRINE = 3
One. Forsooth, a blinde man at Saint *Albones* Shrine,   790
Cam'st thou here by Chance, or of Deuotion, | To this holy Shrine?   820
Who said; *Symon,* come; come offer at my Shrine,   825
SHUN = 1
Spirit. Let him shun Castles,   662
SHUNNE = 1
Let him shunne Castles,   696
SHUT = 1
Is all thy comfort shut in Glosters Tombe?   1778
SICILL = 1
In presence of the Kings of *France,* and *Sicill,*   13
SICILLIA = *1
Naples, Sicillia, and Ierusalem, and Crowne her Queene of   54
SICK = 1
Did instigate the Bedlam braine-sick Duchesse,   1345
SICKE = 2
I would be blinde with weeping, sicke with grones,   1762
Thou mad misleader of thy brain-sicke sonne,   3163
SICKNESSE = 2
For sodainly a greeuous sicknesse tooke him,   2087
Hath made me full of sicknesse and diseases.   2722
SIDE = 7
Enter King, Duke Humfrey, Salisbury, Warwicke, and Beau-|ford on
the one side.   3
On the East side of the Groue.   763
The East side of the Groue: | Cardinall, I am with you.   770
Thus is the Shepheard beaten from thy side,   1491
Were by his side: Sometime, he calles the King,   2091
Lieu. Conuey him hence, and on our long boats side,   2236
God on our side, doubt not of Victorie.   2829
SIDES = 1
And would not dash me with their ragged sides,   1798
SIEGE = 1
That layes strong siege vnto this wretches soule,   2156
SIGHES = 2*1
Or blood-consuming sighes recall his Life;   1761
Looke pale as Prim-rose with blood-drinking sighes,   1763
*Through whom a thousand sighes are breath'd for thee.   2060
SIGHT = 18
In sight of England, and her Lordly Peeres,   18
King. Her sight did rauish, but her grace in Speech,   39
Gazing on that which seemes to dimme thy sight?   279
And neuer more abase our sight so low,   288
Within this halfe houre hath receiu'd his sight,   791
Although by his sight his sinne be multiplyed.   800
Sight may distinguish of Colours: 875
In sight of God, and vs, your guilt is great,   1055
King. Goe, take hence that Traytor from our sight,   1162
Thou balefull Messenger, out of my sight: 1748
And kill the innocent gazer with thy sight: 1753
My earnest-gaping-sight of thy Lands view,   1805
And in thy sight to dye, what were it else,   2106
Where from thy sight, I should be raging mad,   2111
May euen in their Wiues and Childrens sight,   2499

SIGHT *cont.*
The sight of me is odious in their eyes: 2582
Shall I endure the sight of Somerset?   3085
To die in Ruffian battell? Euen at this sight,   3271
SIGNALL = 1
Hold vp thy hand, make signall of thy hope.   2162
SIGNE = 5*1
I can expresse no kinder signe of Loue   25
And make my Image but an Ale-house signe.   1781
King. Ah, what a signe it is of euill life,   2139
He dies and makes no signe: Oh God forgiue him.   2163
Beuis. Thou hast hit it: for there's no better signe of a | braue minde,
then a hard hand.   2338
For vnderneath an Ale-house paltry signe,   3290
SIGNES = 2
The least of all these signes were probable.   1882
With full as many signes of deadly hate,   2029
SIGNIFIE = 2
To signifie, that Rebels there are vp,   1586
Vaux. To signifie vnto his Maiesty,   2085
SILENCE = 2
*with the spirit of putting down Kings and Princes. Com-|mand silence.   2356
But. Silence.   2358
SILENT = 3
The businesse asketh silent secrecie.   366
Deepe Night, darke Night, the silent of the Night,   636
But with aduice and silent secrecie.   1034
SILKEN-COATED = 1
Cade. As for these silken-coated slaues I passe not,   2448
SILLY = 1
While as the silly Owner of the goods   237
SILUER = 3
Troubles the siluer Spring, where England drinkes: 2240
Old Salsbury, shame to thy siluer haire,   3162
To loose thy youth in peace, and to atcheeue | The Siluer Liuery of
aduised Age,   3268
SIMPATHY = 1
If Simpathy of Loue vnite our thoughts.   30
SIMPC = 14*4
SIMPCOXE see also Simpc. = 1
Glost. What's thine owne Name? | *Simpc.* Saunder Simpcoxe, and if it
please you, Master.   868
SIMPLE = 4*1
Salisbury and *Warwick* are no simple Peeres.   460
Our simple Supper ended, giue me leaue,   961
And in his simple shew he harbours Treason.   1348
For God forbid, so many simple soules   2542
*for a stray, for entering his Fee-simple without leaue. A   2930
SIN = *1
Beuis. Then is sin strucke downe like an Oxe, and ini-|quities throate
cut like a Calfe.   2345
SINCE = 3*2
Since thou wert King; as who is King, but thou?   513
We know the time since he was milde and affable,   1303
*it was neuer merrie world in England, since Gentlemen | came vp.   2327
*I was neuer mine owne man since. How now? Who's | there?   2400
Who since I heard to be discomfited.   3056

SINFULL = 1
But greater sinne to keepe a sinfull oath: 3183
SING = 1
Came he right now to sing a Rauens Note,   1740
SINGLE = 1
For single Combat, in conuenient place,   605
SINKE = 1
Lieu. Poole, Sir *Poole*? Lord, | I kennell, puddle, sinke, whose filth and
dirt   2238
SINKING = 1
The splitting Rockes cowr'd in the sinking sands,   1797
SINNE = 6
Although by his sight his sinne be multiplyed.   800
Receiue the Sentence of the Law for sinne,   1056
Murther indeede, that bloodie sinne, I tortur'd | Aboue the Felon, or
what Trespas else.   1431
Sal. It is great sinne, to sweare vnto a sinne: 3182
But greater sinne to keepe a sinfull oath: 3183
SINNERS = 1
King. Forbeare to iudge, for we are sinners all.   2165
SIR *l.*343 364 407 *408 745 *895 908 1066 1086 1254 1256 1262 1885 2192
2238 *2422 *2432 2439 2440 2458 *2468 2514 2570 *2743 = 18*6
SIRRAH = 1*2
*Come hither sirrah, I must examine thee: What is thy | name? |
Clearke. Emanuell.   2414
Cade. He lyes, for I inuented it my selfe. Go too Sir-|rah,   2475
Sirrah, call in my sonne to be my bale: 3106
SIRRHA = 5*2
Humf. Sirrha, or you must fight, or else be hang'd.   614
Glost. Tell me Sirrha, what's my Name? | *Simpc.* Alas Master, I know
not.   862
Maior. Sirrha, goe fetch the Beadle hither straight. | *Exit.*   887
*Now Sirrha, if you meane to saue your selfe from Whip-|ping,   890
*Sirrha Beadle, whippe him till he leape ouer that same | Stoole.   896
Come on Sirrha, off with your Doublet, quickly.   899
Sirrha, what's thy Name? | *Peter. Peter* forsooth.   1141
SIRS = 3*2
Sirs, what's a Clock? | *Seru.* Tenne, my Lord.   1175
Card. Sirs, take away the Duke, and guard him sure.   1488
Suff. Now Sirs, haue you dispatcht this thing?   1697
Salisb. Sirs stand apart, the King shall know your | minde.   1953
Cade. So sirs: now go some and pull down the Sauoy: 2635
SISTER = 1
Yorke. His eldest Sister, *Anne,* | My Mother, being Heire vnto the
Crowne,   1005
SIT = 4
So Yorke must sit, and fret, and bite his tongue,   242
Madame, sit you, and feare not: whom wee rayse,   641
Glost. Then *Saunder*, sit there,   870
To sit and watch me as *Ascanius* did,   1816
SITS = 1
Sits in grim Maiestie, to fright the World.   1750
SITTING = 2
And heere sitting vpon London Stone,   2616
Say. Long sitting to determine poore mens causes,   2721
SIXT = 2
The sixt, was *Thomas* of Woodstock, Duke of Gloster;   975

263

SIXT *cont.*
 The second Part of Henry the Sixt,   3357
SKARRE = 1
 Shew me one skarre, character'd on thy Skinne,   1603
SKILLS = 1
 It skills not greatly who impugnes our doome.   1583
SKIN = *1
 *thing, that of the skin of an innocent Lambe should   2396
SKINNE = 2
 Is he a Lambe? his Skinne is surely lent him,   1371
 Shew me one skarre, character'd on thy Skinne,   1603
SKINNES = *1
 Beuis. Hee shall haue the skinnes of our enemies, to | make Dogges
 Leather of.   2342
SKY = 1
 And when the duskie sky, began to rob   1804
SLACKE = 1
 And being a woman, I will not be slacke   341
SLAIN = 1*1
 Alarums. Mathew Goffe is slain, and all the rest. | *Then enter Iacke*
 Cade, with his Company.   2633
 Iden. Is't *Cade* that I haue slain, that monstrous traitor?   2971
SLAINE = 6*2
 Which I will win from France, or else be slaine.   224
 Lieu. But Ioue was neuer slaine as thou shalt be,   2217
 Hath slaine their Gouernors, surpriz'd our Forts,   2257
 Alarums to the fight, wherein both the Staffords are slaine. | *Enter Cade*
 and the rest.   2511
 Scales. How now? Is *Iacke Cade* slaine?   2600
 1.*Cit.* No my Lord, nor likely to be slaine: 2601
 *O I am slaine, Famine and no other hath slaine me, let ten   2965
SLANDER = 1
 Is slander to your Royall Dignitie.   1914
SLANDERS = 2
 So shall my name with Slanders tongue be wounded,   1768
 That slanders me with Murthers Crimson Badge.   1904
SLAUE = 2
 Suf. Base slaue, thy words are blunt, and so art thou.   2235
 A Romane Sworder, and Bandetto slaue | Murder'd sweet *Tully. Brutus*
 Bastard hand   2303
SLAUERIE = *1
 *all Recreants and Dastards, and delight to liue in slauerie   2803
SLAUES = 1
 Cade. As for these silken-coated slaues I passe not,   2448
SLAUGHTER = 2
 But will suspect, 'twas he that made the slaughter?   1894
 Suff. I weare no Knife, to slaughter sleeping men,   1901
SLAUGHTER-HOUSE = 1*1
 Bearing it to the bloody Slaughter-house;   1513
 *owne Slaughter-house: Therfore thus will I reward thee,   2517
SLAY = 1
 And doe not stand on Quillets how to slay him: 1563
SLEEPE = 4*1
 In my sleepe, by good Saint *Albon*:   824
 That if your Highnesse should intend to sleepe,   1967
 The mortall Worme might make the sleepe eternall.   1975
 Hol. They haue the more neede to sleepe now then.   2322

SLEEPE *cont.*
*ere thou sleepe in thy Sheath, I beseech Ioue on my knees   2962
SLEEPING = 3
Sleeping, or Waking, 'tis no matter how,   1565
Suff. I weare no Knife, to slaughter sleeping men,   1901
Pernicious blood-sucker of sleeping men.   1931
SLEW = 3
The head of *Cade*, whom I in combat slew.   3061
Tell me my Friend, art thou the man that slew him?   3065
Yor. The deadly handed Clifford slew my Steed: 3228
SLIPPE = 1
Was graft with Crab-tree slippe, whose Fruit thou art,   1919
SLIPPES = 1
And in thy Sonnes, faire slippes of such a Stock.   1022
SLOUGH = 1
With shining checker'd slough doth sting a Child,   1531
SLOW = 1*1
Who with their drowsie, slow, and flagging wings   2174
**Qu.* Away my Lord, you are slow, for shame away.   3297
SLUMBER = 2
Least being suffer'd in that harmefull slumber,   1974
But like a pleasant slumber in thy lap?   2107
SLYLY = 1
That slyly glyded towards your Maiestie,   1972
SMALL = 3*2
Small Curres are not regarded when they grynne,   1312
Deuise strange deaths, for small offences done?   1353
*Small things make base men proud. This Villaine heere,   2274
*small Beere. All the Realme shall be in Common, and in   2386
This small inheritance my Father left me,   2923
SMART = 1
Their softest Touch, as smart as Lyzards stings: 2040
SMELL = 1
With whose sweet smell the Ayre shall be perfum'd,   267
SMILDST = 1
And thou that smil'dst at good Duke *Humfries* death,   2244
SMILE = 1
Whose Smile and Frowne, like to *Achilles* Speare   3095
SMITH = 1*2
Hol. And Smith the Weauer. | *Beu.* Argo, their thred of life is spun.   2347
**Drumme. Enter Cade, Dicke Butcher, Smith the Weauer, | and a
Sawyer, with infinite numbers.*   2350
**Smith.* Nay *Iohn*, it wil be stinking Law, for his breath | stinkes with
eating toasted cheese.   2644
SMITHFIELD = 3
The Witch in Smithfield shall be burnt to ashes,   1060
But get you to Smithfield, and gather head,   2609
**Dicke.* My Lord, there's an Army gathered together | in Smithfield.   2627
SMOOTH = 2*1
And smooth my way vpon their headlesse neckes.   340
Smooth runnes the Water, where the Brooke is deepe,   1347
*Which time will bring to light in smooth Duke *Humfrey.*   1359
SMOOTHING = 1
Looke to it Lords, let not his smoothing words   163
SMOOTHST = 1
That smooth'st it so with King and Common-weale.   739

265

SNAKE = 2
Or as the Snake, roll'd in a flowring Banke,   1530
I feare me, you but warme the starued Snake,   1649
SNARD = 2
Till they haue snar'd the Shepheard of the Flock,   1039
But feare not thou, vntill thy foot be snar'd,   1232
SNARES = 3
With sorrow snares relenting passengers;   1529
Be it by Gynnes, by Snares, by Subtletie,   1564
Weaues tedious Snares to trap mine Enemies.   1646
SNOW = 1
Queene. Free Lords: | Cold Snow melts with the Sunnes hot Beames: 1524
SO *l.*12 46 87 97 154 *213 215 222 242 282 288 325 372 380 452 461 478
485 505 552 *628 677 726 739 742 746 766 780 829 832 836 841 *850
905 930 1015 1097 1107 *1116 1139 1174 *1191 1220 1236 1239 *1257
1262 1392 1399 1406 1410 1419 1420 1514 1518 1521 1545 1546 *1553
1566 1569 1579 1581 1598 1602 1604 1620 1630 1668 1695 1768 1809
1821 1898 1916 1948 1995 2061 2076 *2083 2114 2115 2129 2138 2140
2164 *2186 2193 2196 2197 2200 2235 2318 *2326 *2352 *2422 2542
2557 2581 2612 *2635 *2646 *2739 2748 2779 *2796 *2807 *2832 2869
2872 2900 *2909 2984 3013 3014 3015 3017 3045 3058 3070 3125 3139
3211 3231 3242 3245 3285 3287 3289 3334 3338 = 114*19
SOARE *see also* sore = 1
Although the Kyte soare with vnbloudied Beake?   1897
SODAINE = 2
Some sodaine qualme hath strucke me at the heart,   60
And comment then vpon his sodaine death.   1835
SODAINLY = 1
For sodainly a greeuous sicknesse tooke him,   2087
SOFT = 1*1
But soft, I thinke she comes, and Ile prepare   1186
Queen. Fye Coward woman, and soft harted wretch,   2021
SOFTENS = *1
Queene. Oft haue I heard that greefe softens the mind,   2533
SOFTEST = 1
Their softest Touch, as smart as Lyzards stings: 2040
SOILE = 1*1
Euen as I haue of fertile Englands soile.   250
Cade. Heere's the Lord of the soile come to seize me   2929
SOLACE = 1
For with his soule fled all my worldly solace: 1855
SOLD = 3*3
While his owne Lands are bargain'd for, and sold: 243
By thee *Aniou* and *Maine* were sold to France.   2254
But. She was indeed a Pedlers daughter, & sold many | Laces.   2364
*halfe peny Loaues sold for a peny: the three hoop'd pot,   2384
*which sold the Townes in France. He that made vs pay   2654
I sold not *Maine*, I lost not *Normandie*,   2699
SOLDIER *see also Soul.* = 1
Enter a Soldier running.   2622
SOLDIERS = 3
Enter Sir Humfrey Stafford, and his Brother, | with Drum and Soldiers.   2440
Of some more Townes in France. Soldiers,   2768
Alarum. Retreat. Enter Yorke, Richard, Warwicke, | and Soldiers, with
Drum & Colours.   3319
SOLE = 1
Who marryed *Phillip*, sole Daughter | Vnto *Lionel*, Duke of Clarence.   1013

SOLEMN = *1
  Suf. A dreadfull Oath, sworne with a solemn tongue: 1862
SOLEMNE = 2
  Who can be bound by any solemne Vow   3184
  But that he was bound by a solemne Oath?   3190
SOLLACE = 1
  Sorrow would sollace, and mine Age would ease.   1075
SOM = 8*1
SOME = 13*6
  Some sodaine qualme hath strucke me at the heart,   60
  Suff. Thy Wife too? that's some Wrong indeede.   404
  Salisb. Peace Sonne, and shew some reason *Buckingham*   503
  To shew some reason, of no little force,   558
  Simpc. Alas, good Master, my Wife desired some   842
  As if she had suborned some to sweare   1480
  Collected choycely, from each Countie some,   1618
  I will stirre vp in England some black Storme,   1655
  Some violent hands were laid on *Humfries* life: 1840
  Some sterne vntutur'd Churle; and Noble Stock   1918
  And doe some seruice to Duke *Humfreyes* Ghost. | *Exeunt.*   1936
  Giue me some drinke, and bid the Apothecarie   2151
  *should vndoe a man. Some say the Bee stings, but I say,   2398
  King. Ile send some holy Bishop to intreat: 2541
  Cade. So sirs: now go some and pull down the Sauoy: 2635
  Of some more Townes in France. Soldiers,   2768
  Buck. What, is he fled? Go some and follow him,   2842
  Shall haue a thousand Crownes for his reward. | *Exeunt some of them.*   2844
  Yor. Hold Warwick: seek thee out some other chace   3234
SOMERSET see also Som. = 32*3
  The Queene, Suffolke, Yorke, Somerset, and Buckingham, | *on the other.*   5
  Gloster, Yorke, Buckingham, Somerset, | Salisburie, and Warwicke.   74
  Haue you your selues, *Somerset, Buckingham,*   92
  Cosin of Somerset, ioyne you with me,   174
  Buc. Or thou, or I Somerset will be Protectors,   185
  Despite Duke *Humfrey*, or the Cardinall. | *Exit Buckingham, and*
  Somerset.   186
  Were plac'd the heads of *Edmond* Duke of Somerset,   303
  The imperious Churchman; *Somerset, Buckingham,*   455
  Or *Somerset*, or *Yorke*, all's one to me.   492
  Som. If *Somerset* be vnworthy of the Place,   495
  Why *Somerset* should be preferr'd in this?   504
  My Lord of Somerset will keepe me here,   563
  Let *Somerset* be Regent o're the French,   602
  Somerset, wee'le see thee sent away. | *Flourish. Exeunt.*   617
  Bulling. What shall befall the Duke of Somerset?   661
  What shall betide the Duke of Somerset?   695
  Enter Somerset.   1376
  King. Welcome Lord *Somerset*: What Newes from | France? 1378
  King. Cold Newes, Lord *Somerset*: but Gods will be | done. 1382
  Yorke. That *Somerset* be sent as Regent thither: 1593
  No more, good *Yorke*; sweet *Somerset* be still.   1607
  Sound Trumpets. Enter the King, the Queene, | *Cardinall, Suffolke,*
  Somerset, with | *Attendants.*   1706
  Sound Trumpets. Enter King, Queene, and | *Somerset on the Tarras.* 2848
  The Duke of Somerset, whom he tearmes a Traitor.   2883
  And *Somerset* we will commit thee thither,   2893
  Is to remoue proud Somerset from the King,   3028

SOMERSET cont.
The Duke of Somerset is in the Tower.	3033
Is his to vse, so Somerset may die.	3045
Yor. To heaue the Traitor Somerset from hence,	3054
Enter Queene and Somerset.	3077
*K. See Buckingham, Somerset comes with th'Queene,	3078
Yor. How now? is Somerset at libertie?	3082
Shall I endure the sight of Somerset?	3085
Enter Richard, and Somerset to fight.	3288
The Castle in S.(aint) *Albons,* Somerset	3291

SOMERSET = 1*1
SOMERSETS = 2
The pride of Suffolke, and the Cardinall, | With Somersets and Buckinghams Ambition,	209
At *Beaufords* Pride, at *Somersets* Ambition,	1037

SOMETIME = 3
Sometime Ile say, I am Duke *Humfreyes* Wife,	1218
Sometime he talkes, as if Duke *Humfries* Ghost	2090
Were by his side: Sometime, he calles the King,	2091

SOMETIMES = *1
*Glost. Thus sometimes hath the brightest day a Cloud:	1171

SONNE = 16*3
But wherefore weepes *Warwicke,* my valiant sonne?	122
Warwicke my sonne, the comfort of my age,	198
*Salisb. Peace Sonne, and shew some reason *Buckingham*	503
And left behinde him *Richard,* his onely Sonne,	978
The eldest Sonne and Heire of *Iohn* of Gaunt,	981
The Issue of the next Sonne should haue reign'd.	991
Yorke. The third Sonne, Duke of Clarence,	994
Who was to *Edmond Langley,* | *Edward* the thirds fift Sonnes Sonne;	1008
Who was the Sonne of *Edmond Mortimer,*	1012
So, if the Issue of the elder Sonne	1015
The fourth Sonne, *Yorke* claymes it from the third:	1019
*Hol. I see them, I see them: There's *Bests* Sonne, the | Tanner of Wingham.	2340
His sonne am I, deny it if you can.	2466
*breake into his Sonne in Lawes house, Sir *Iames Cromer,*	2743
Clif. Is *Cade* the sonne of *Henry* the fift,	2811
Command my eldest sonne, nay all my sonnes,	3041
Sirrah, call in my sonne to be my bale:	3106
Thou mad misleader of thy brain-sicke sonne,	3163
Where it should guard. O Warre, thou sonne of hell,	3255

SONNES = 8
Yorke. Then thus: | *Edward* the third, my Lords, had seuen Sonnes:	968
For *Richard,* the first Sonnes Heire, being dead,	990
Who was to *Edmond Langley,* | *Edward* the thirds fift Sonnes Sonne;	1008
And in thy Sonnes, faire slippes of such a Stock.	1022
Command my eldest sonne, nay all my sonnes,	3041
The sonnes of Yorke, thy betters in their birth,	3114
His sonnes (he sayes) shall giue their words for him.	3134
Yor. Will you not Sonnes? | *Edw.* I Noble Father, if our words will serue.	3135

SOONE = 1*1
*Suff. Nay *Gloster,* know that thou art come too soone,	1393
These Kentish Rebels would be soone appeas'd.	2578

SOONER = 3
this geere, the sooner the better.	634

SOONER *cont.*

And sooner dance vpon a bloody pole,	2295
No sooner was I crept out of my Cradle,	2852

SOPHISTER = 1

Qu. A subtle Traitor needs no Sophister.	3191

SORE = 1*1

That mounts no higher then a Bird can sore:	730
Iohn. Masse 'twill be sore Law then, for he was thrust	2642

SORROW = 7

Sorrow and griefe haue vanquisht all my powers;	935
Will bring thy head with sorrow to the ground.	1073
Sorrow would sollace, and mine Age would ease.	1075
With sorrow snares relenting passengers;	1529
What were it but to make my sorrow greater?	1851
Qu. Mischance and Sorrow goe along with you,	2014
And seeke for sorrow with thy Spectacles?	3165

SORROWES = 1

Theirs for the earths encrease, mine for my sorrowes.	2102

SORRY = 2*1

A sorry Breakfast for my Lord Protector.	706
Sorry I am to heare what I haue heard,	945
Cade. I am sorry for't: The man is a proper man of	2412

SORT = 4

Sort how it will, I shall haue Gold for all. *Exit.*	383
A sort of naughtie persons, lewdly bent,	919
I pray thee sort thy heart to patience,	1244
Sent from a sort of Tinkers to the King.	1990

SOUERAIGNE = 18*4

With you mine *Alder liefest* Soueraigne,	35
*Betweene our Soueraigne, and the French King *Charles*,	48
Buc. Why should he then protect our Soueraigne?	172
When thou wert Regent for our Soueraigne,	205
I say, my Soueraigne, *Yorke* is meetest man	555
That shall salute our rightfull Soueraigne	1025
Both. Long liue our Soueraigne *Richard*, Englands | King.	1027
No, no, my Soueraigne, *Glouster* is a man	1350
Som. All health vnto my gracious Soueraigne.	1377
As I am cleare from Treason to my Soueraigne.	1400
And you, my Soueraigne Lady, with the rest,	1461
Suff. Hath he not twit our Soueraigne Lady here	1478
And to preserue my Soueraigne from his Foe,	1573
Suff. Comfort my Soueraigne, gracious *Henry* com-|fort.	1737
War. It is reported, mighty Soueraigne,	1824
Warw. Come hither gracious Soueraigne, view this | body.	1852
Set all vpon me, mightie Soueraigne.	1951
Could send such Message to their Soueraigne:	1985
King. How fare's my Lord? Speake *Beauford* to thy | Soueraigne.	2134
War. Beauford, it is thy Soueraigne speakes to thee.	2141
And let my Soueraigne, vertuous *Henry*,	3040
We are thy Soueraigne *Clifford*, kneele againe;	3124

SOUERAIGNES = 2

By wicked meanes to frame our Soueraignes fall.	1346
And that my Soueraignes presence makes me milde,	1924

SOUERAIGNTIE = 1

Haue beene as Bond-men to thy Soueraigntie.	517

SOUL = 1

SOULDIER = 2
| More like a Souldier then a man o'th'Church, | 194 |
| Hot Coales of Vengeance. Let no Souldier flye. | 3258 |

SOULDIERS = 11
For Souldiers pay in France, and neuer sent it?	1356
And being Protector, stay'd the Souldiers pay,	1404
I neuer rob'd the Souldiers of their pay,	1408
Yorke. I am content: Prouide me Souldiers, Lords,	1624
At Bristow I expect my Souldiers,	1633
Therefore bring forth the Souldiers of our prize,	2177
And sent the ragged Souldiers wounded home.	2258
Come Souldiers, shew what cruelty ye can.	2300
Follow me souldiers, wee'l deuise a meane,	2846
Souldiers, this day haue you redeem'd your liues,	2867
Souldiers, I thanke you all: disperse your selues:	3037

SOULE = 18*1
A world of earthly blessings to my soule,	29
But God in mercie so deale with my Soule,	552
King. Poore Soule, | Gods goodnesse hath beene great to thee:	815
My thoughts, that labour to perswade my soule,	1839
For with his soule fled all my worldly solace:	1855
War. As surely as my soule intends to liue	1857
Giue thee thy hyre, and send thy Soule to Hell,	1930
The secrets of his ouer-charged soule,	2093
Heere could I breath my soule into the ayre,	2108
So should'st thou eyther turne my flying soule,	2114
Like Lime-twigs set to catch my winged soule,	2150
That layes strong siege vnto this wretches soule,	2156
King. Peace to his soule, if Gods good pleasure be.	2160
*dwell in this house, because the vnconquered soule of | *Cade* is fled.	2969
So wish I, I might thrust thy soule to hell.	2984
A Scepter shall it haue, haue I a soule,	3001
It greeues my soule to leaue thee vnassail'd. *Exit War*.	3238
Clif. My soule and bodie on the action both.	3247
Peace with his soule, heauen if it be thy will.	3251

SOULES = 6
King. Now God be prays'd, that to beleeuing Soules	793
Say as you thinke, and speake it from your Soules:	1549
Shall blowe ten thousand Soules to Heauen, or Hell:	1656
Omitting Suffolkes exile, my soules Treasure?	2099
For God forbid, so many simple soules	2542
How would it fare with your departed soules,	2749

SOUND = 11*1
Sound a Sennet.	487
Sound Trumpets. Enter the King and State, | *with Guard, to banish the*	
Duchesse.	1051
Sound Trumpets, Alarum to the Combattants.	1154
Come fellow, follow vs for thy Reward. | *Sound a flourish. Exeunt*.	1167
Sound a Senet. Enter King, Queene, Cardinall, Suffolke,	1292
Sound Trumpets. Enter the King, the Queene, | *Cardinall, Suffolke,*	
Somerset, with | *Attendants*.	1706
Can chase away the first-conceiued sound?	1744
**Suf*. Thy name affrights me, in whose sound is death:	2202
Sound a parley. | What noise is this I heare?	2777
Dare any be so bold to sound Retreat or Parley	2779
Sound Trumpets. Enter King, Queene, and | *Somerset on the Tarras*.	2848
Sound Drumme and Trumpets, and to London all,	3354

SOUNDED = 1
Thy name is *Gualtier*, being rightly sounded.   2206
SOUNDS = 3
The Duke was dumbe, and could not speake a word. | *King sounds.*   1728
Now when the angrie Trumpet sounds alarum,   3221
Particularities, and pettie sounds | To cease. Was't thou ordain'd (deere
Father)   3266
SOUTHERNE = 1
And with the Southerne clouds, contend in teares?   2101
SOUTHWARKE = 1*1
Mes. The Rebels are in Southwarke: Fly my Lord: 2563
*you should leaue me at the White-heart in Southwarke.   2800
SOUTHWELL = 1*1
*Earth; *Iohn Southwell* reade you, and let vs to our worke.   631
Bullingbrooke or Southwell reades, Coniuro | te, &c. *It Thunders and
Lightens*   644
SOWD = 1
And reape the Haruest which that Rascall sow'd.   1687
SOWRE = 1
Hearts Discontent, and sowre Affliction,   2015
SPACE = 1
If after three dayes space thou here bee'st found,   2009
SPAKE = *1
**Armorer.* Alas, my Lord, hang me if euer I spake the   594
SPAN-COUNTER = *1
*the fift, (in whose time, boyes went to Span-counter   2477
SPARE = 4
1.*Gent.* Ile giue it sir, and therefore spare my life.   2192
Spare none, but such as go in clouted shooen,   2505
Scales. Such ayd as I can spare you shall command,   2606
Spare England, for it is your Natiue Coast: 2827
SPARES = 1
It shall be stony. Yorke, not our old men spares: 3273
SPARKE = 1
Qu. Nay then, this sparke will proue a raging fire,   1605
SPARKLE = 1
Mine eyes should sparkle like the beaten Flint,   2032
SPARKLING = 1
Beaufords red sparkling eyes blab his hearts mallice,   1454
SPEAK = *2
* *Whit.* Speak Captaine, shall I stab the forlorn Swain.   2233
*1.*Gent.* My gracious Lord intreat him, speak him fair.   2288
SPEAKE = 16*4
Card. Ambitious *Warwicke*, let thy betters speake.   499
* *Peter.* By these tenne bones, my Lords, hee did speake   587
Answere that I shall aske: for till thou speake,   651
Glost. Witnesse my teares, I cannot stay to speake. | *Exit Gloster.*   1265
And had I first beene put to speake my minde,   1337
Is worthy prayse: but shall I speake my conscience,   1362
And well such losers may haue leaue to speake.   1485
Say as you thinke, and speake it from your Soules: 1549
The Duke was dumbe, and could not speake a word. | *King sounds.*   1728
For euery word you speake in his behalfe,   1913
Go, speake not to me; euen now be gone.   2067
* *King.* How fare's my Lord? Speake *Beauford* to thy | Soueraigne.   2134
It is to you good people, that I speake,   2449
*more then that, he can speake French, and therefore hee is | a Traitor.   2486

SPEAKE *cont.*

Cade. And to speake truth, thou deseru'st no lesse.	2521
*Say. Heare me but speake, and beare mee wher'e you | will:	2692
Haue I affected wealth, or honor? Speake.	2731
Yor. Scarse can I speake, my Choller is so great.	3015
Rich. Fie, Charitie for shame, speake not in spight,	3213
I would speake blasphemy ere bid you flye:	3313

SPEAKES = 2*1

War. Beauford, it is thy Soueraigne speakes to thee.	2141
that speakes he knowes not what.	2472
*his Tongue, he speakes not a Gods name. Goe, take	2741

SPEAKS = *2

*enemies: go too then, I ask but this: Can he that speaks	2490
**Cade.* Away with him, away with him, he speaks La-|tine.	2690

SPEARE = 2

in the mouth with a Speare, and 'tis not whole yet.	2643
Whose Smile and Frowne, like to *Achilles* Speare	3095

SPECIALL = 1

King. My Lord of Gloster, 'tis my speciall hope,	1439

SPECTACLE = 1

1.Gent. O barbarous and bloudy spectacle,	2315

SPECTACLES = 2

And call'd them blinde and duskie Spectacles,	1812
And seeke for sorrow with thy Spectacles?	3165

SPEECH = 6

King. Her sight did rauish, but her grace in Speech,	39
Ile haue thy Head for this thy Traytors speech:	591
And the Offendor graunted scope of speech,	1476
In face, in gate, in speech he doth resemble.	1679
Make thee begge pardon for thy passed speech,	1926
Let this my sword report what speech forbeares.	2958

SPEECHES = 1

'Tis not my speeches that you do mislike:	147

SPEEDE = 1

Come, let vs in, and with all speede prouide | To see her Coronation be perform'd.	78

SPEND = 2

What? did my brother *Henry* spend his youth,	85
On Sheepe or Oxen could I spend my furie.	3019

SPENT = 2

And so breake off, the day is almost spent,	1630
And thinke it but a minute spent in sport.	2053

SPIDER = 1

My Brayne, more busie then the laboring Spider,	1645

SPIGHT *see also* inspight = 1*1

*pitty my case: the spight of man preuayleth against me.	611
Rich. Fie, Charitie for shame, speake not in spight,	3213

SPIGHTFULL = 1

As for your spightfull false Obiections,	550

SPIRIT = 5*2

A Spirit rais'd from depth of vnder ground,	354
*an inuincible spirit: but it shall be conuenient, Master	626
terribly: then the Spirit | riseth.	646
False Fiend auoide. | *Thunder and Lightning. Exit Spirit.*	667
Qu. He dares not calme his contumelious Spirit,	1909
Hast thou not spirit to curse thine enemy.	2022
*with the spirit of putting down Kings and Princes. Com-|mand silence.	2356

SPIRIT = 4*1
SPIRITS = 3
  And Spirits walke, and Ghosts breake vp their Graues;   639
  Raysing vp wicked Spirits from vnder ground,   926
  Vnlesse you be possest with diuellish spirits,   2709
SPLEENFULL = 1
  My selfe haue calm'd their spleenfull mutinie,   1830
SPLITTED = 1
  Euen as a splitted Barke, so sunder we: 2129
SPLITTING = 1
  The splitting Rockes cowr'd in the sinking sands,   1797
SPOILE = 2
  Deferre the spoile of the Citie vntill night: 2769
  Nor knowes he how to liue, but by the spoile,   2816
SPOKE = 4
  Glost. Farre truer spoke then meant: I lose indeede,   1483
  Queene. Thrice Noble *Suffolke*, 'tis resolutely spoke.   1568
  For things are often spoke, and seldome meant,   1570
  Yorke. And I: and now we three haue spoke it,   1582
SPORT = 3
  I saw not better sport these seuen yeeres day: 718
  Had not your man put vp the Fowle so suddenly, | We had had more
  sport.   766
  And thinke it but a minute spent in sport.   2053
SPOTLESSE = 1
  To force a spotlesse Virgins Chastitie,   3186
SPOYLE = 1
  To spoyle the City, and your Royall Court.   2590
SPRAYES = *1
  Suff. Thus droupes this loftie Pyne, & hangs his sprayes,   1101
SPRING = 3
  Now 'tis the Spring, and Weeds are shallow-rooted,   1325
  The purest Spring is not so free from mudde,   1399
  Troubles the siluer Spring, where England drinkes: 2240
SPRING-TIME = *1
  *Faster the(n) Spring-time showres, comes thoght on thoght,   1643
SPUN = 1
  Hol. And Smith the Weauer. | *Beu.* Argo, their thred of life is spun.   2347
SPURRES = 1
  Shee's tickled now, her Fume needs no spurres,   543
SPY = 1
  And when I spy aduantage, claime the Crowne,   254
STAB = 1*1
  Whit. Speak Captaine, shall I stab the forlorn Swain.   2233
  Lieu. First let my words stab him, as he hath me.   2234
STABD = 1
  Stab'd *Iulius Caesar*. Sauage Islanders   2305
STAF = 4*1
STAFF = 1
STAFFE = 9*3
  Hum. Me thought this staffe mine Office-badge in | Court   298
  Ere thou goe, giue vp thy Staffe,   1077
  Giue vp your Staffe, Sir, and the King his Realme.   1086
  Glost. My Staffe? Here, Noble *Henry*, is my Staffe: 1087
  This Staffe of Honor raught, there let it stand,   1099
  Drumme before him, and his Staffe, with a Sand-bagge   1117
  A Staffe is quickly found to beat a Dogge.   1471

STAFFE *cont.*
*And faine to go with a staffe, but that my puissance holds   2483
Enter Iacke Cade and the rest, and strikes his | staffe on London stone.   2613
Thy Hand is made to graspe a Palmers staffe,   3092
The rampant Beare chain'd to the ragged staffe,   3203
STAFFORD *see also Staf., Staff.* = 3*1
Stafford take her to thee.   682
Mich. Fly, fly, fly, Sir *Humfrey Stafford* and his brother   2432
Enter Sir Humfrey Stafford, and his Brother, | *with Drum and Soldiers.*   2440
Sir *Humfrey Stafford*, and his Brothers death,   2570
STAFFORDS = 1
Alarums to the fight, wherein both the Staffords are slaine. | *Enter Cade and the rest.*   2511
STAGE = 1
Enter two or three running ouer the Stage, from the | *Murther of Duke Humfrey.*   1690
STAID = 1
She should haue staid in France, and steru'd in France | Before ---   142
STAINE = 1
Or with their blood staine this discoloured shore.   2180
STAKE = 1
Call hither to the stake my two braue Beares,   3141
STAND = 9*7
*1.*Pet.* My Masters, let's stand close, my Lord Pro-|tector   386
Then where Castles mounted stand.   664
Then where Castles mounted stand.   698
Glost. Stand by, my Masters, bring him neere the King,   801
Simpc. Alas Master, I am not able to stand alone: 892
Simpc. Alas Master, what shall I doe? I am not able to | stand.   900
King. Stand forth Dame *Elianor Cobham,* | *Glosters* Wife: 1053
This Staffe of Honor raught, there let it stand,   1099
And doe not stand on Quillets how to slay him: 1563
Salisb. Sirs stand apart, the King shall know your | minde.   1953
Then stand vncouer'd to the Vulgar Groome.   2296
But. But me thinks he should stand in feare of fire, be-|ing   2380
Cade. Stand villaine, stand, or Ile fell thee downe: he   2434
*euen with you. Ile see if his head will stand steddier on   2728
But boldly stand, and front him to his face.   3081
STANDARD = 1
And in my Standard beare the Armes of Yorke,   268
STANDING = 2
Though standing naked on a Mountaine top,   2051
'Tis but surmiz'd, whiles thou art standing by,   2062
STANDS = 4*4
Paris is lost, the state of *Normandie* | Stands on a tickle point, now they are gone: 227
And shakes his head, and trembling stands aloofe,   239
Well, so it stands: and thus I feare at last,   380
And for my Wife, I know not how it stands,   944
*Whose Beame stands sure, whose rightful cause preuailes. | *Flourish. Exeunt.*   957
*Combe downe his haire; looke, looke, it stands vpright,   2149
King. Thus stands my state, 'twixt Cade and Yorke | distrest,   2884
Iden. Nay, it shall nere be said, while England stands,   2946
STANLEY *see also Stanly.* = 2
Stanley, I prethee goe, and take me hence,   1271
Come *Stanley,* shall we goe?   1284

STANLEY = 2*1
STANLY = 2
    With Sir *Iohn Stanly*, in the Ile of Man.   1066
    And Sir *Iohn Stanly* is appointed now,   1254
STANLY = *1
STARE = 1
    That makes him gaspe, and stare, and catch the aire,   2088
STARING = 1
    Staring full gastly, like a strangled man: 1874
STARRE = 1
    What lowring Starre now enuies thy estate?   1507
START = 2
    And when I start, the enuious people laugh,   1211
    Should make a start ore-seas, and vanquish you?   2820
STARTS = 1
    How now? why starts thou? What doth death affright?   2201
STARUED = 1
    I feare me, you but warme the starued Snake,   1649
STATE = 13*1
    Glo. Braue Peeres of England, Pillars of the State,   82
    Paris is lost, the state of *Normandie* | Stands on a tickle point, now they
    are gone: 227
    To prie into the secrets of the State,   262
    That were a State fit for his Holinesse.   450
    Haue practis'd dangerously against your State,   923
    Sound Trumpets. Enter the King and State, | *with Guard, to banish the*
    Duchesse.   1051
    There to be vs'd according to your State.   1275
    According to that State you shall be vs'd.   1279
    False allegations, to o'rethrow his state.   1481
    With that dread King that tooke our state vpon him,   1858
    Mischance vnto my State by *Suffolkes* meanes.   1998
    King. Thus stands my state, 'twixt Cade and Yorke | distrest, 2884
    Sufficeth, that I haue maintaines my state,   2927
    Seditious to his Grace, and to the State.   3029
STATUE = 1
    Erect his Statue, and worship it,   1780
STATUTES = 1
    Iohn. Then we are like to haue biting Statutes   2649
STAY = 10*2
    I see thy furie: If I longer stay,   150
    King. Stay *Humfrey*, Duke of Gloster,   1076
    And God shall be my hope, my stay, my guide, | And Lanthorne to my
    feete: 1079
    Glost. Witnesse my teares, I cannot stay to speake. | *Exit Gloster.* 1265
    War. That shall I do my Liege; Stay Salsburie   1836
    King. O thou that iudgest all things, stay my thoghts: 1838
    Oh let me stay, befall what may befall.   2119
    Suf. Stay *Whitmore*, for thy Prisoner is a Prince, | The Duke of
    Suffolke, *William de la Pole.*   2213
    But stay, Ile read it ouer once againe.   2546
    And therefore in this Citty will I stay,   2583
    *could stay no longer. Wherefore on a Bricke wall haue   2911
    King. Can we outrun the Heauens? Good *Margaret* | stay. 3298
STAYD = 3
    Pardon, my Liege, that I haue stay'd so long.   1392
    And being Protector, stay'd the Souldiers pay,   1404

STAYD *cont.*
He neuer would haue stay'd in France so long.   1598
STAYES = *1
*Sh. And't please your Grace, here my Commission stayes: 1253
STAYING = 1*1
By staying there so long, till all were lost.   1602
*me. My sword make way for me, for heere is no staying: 2836
STAYND = 3
And that my Sword be stayn'd   1031
My teare-stayn'd eyes, to see her Miseries.   1187
Before his Chaps be stayn'd with Crimson blood,   1561
STEAD = 1
Had beene the Regent there, in stead of me,   1597
STEALE = 2
The Fox barkes not, when he would steale the Lambe.   1349
Who cannot steale a shape, that meanes deceit?   1373
STEALING = 2
But. Or rather of stealing a Cade of Herrings.   2354
burnt i'th hand for stealing of Sheepe.   2381
STEDDIER = *1
*euen with you. Ile see if his head will stand steddier on   2728
STEDFAST = 1
Oppose thy stedfast gazing eyes to mine,   2949
STEED = 2
For with these borne before vs, in steed of Maces,   2770
Yor. The deadly handed Clifford slew my Steed: 3228
STEELE = 1*2
Yorke. Now *Yorke*, or neuer, steele thy fearfull thoughts,   1637
And he but naked, though lockt vp in Steele,   1940
*that euer I heard. Steele, if thou turne the edge, or   2960
STEERE = 1
And you your selfe shall steere the happy Helme. *Exit.*   486
STEPS = 1
And three-fold Vengeance tend vpon your steps.   2018
STERNE = 3
Or turne our Sterne vpon a dreadfull Rocke: 1791
Some sterne vntutur'd Churle; and Noble Stock   1918
Suf. Suffolkes Imperiall tongue is sterne and rough: 2289
STERUD = 1
She should haue staid in France, and steru'd in France | Before ---   142
STERUE = 1
Ready to sterue, and dare not touch his owne.   241
STICKE = 2
That he that breakes a sticke of Glosters groue,   307
Thy legge a sticke compared with this Truncheon,   2953
STICKING = 1
Looke on the sheets his haire (you see) is sticking,   1878
STIFFE = 1
And passeth by with stiffe vnbowed Knee,   1310
STILE = 1
Am I a Queene in Title and in Stile,   434
STILL = 15*1
For France, 'tis ours; and we will keepe it still.   113
Still reuelling like Lords till all be gone,   236
Then Yorke be still a-while, till time do serue: 260
And wilt thou still be hammering Treachery,   321
What, shall King *Henry* be a Pupill still,   432

STILL *cont.*

But still remember what the Lord hath done.	818
The King will labour still to saue his Life,	1541
No more, good *Yorke*; sweet *Somerset* be still.	1607
Warw. Madame be still: with reuerence may I say,	1912
King. How now Madam?	Still lamenting and mourning for Suffolkes death?	2554
Continue still in this so good a minde,	2869
And still proclaimeth as he comes along,	2881
* *Yor.* Thus Warre hath giuen thee peace, for y art still,	3250
Sword, hold thy temper; Heart, be wrathfull still:	3293
But still where danger was, still there I met him,	3332

STING = 5

With shining checker'd slough doth sting a Child,	1531
Who cherisht in your breasts, will sting your hearts.	1650
Their touch affrights me as a Serpents sting.	1747
And care not who they sting in his reuenge.	1829
With whose inuenomed and fatall sting,	1979

STINGS = 1 *1

Their softest Touch, as smart as Lyzards stings:	2040
*should vndoe a man. Some say the Bee stings, but I say,	2398

STINKES = 1

* *Smith.* Nay *Iohn*, it wil be stinking Law, for his breath	stinkes with eating toasted cheese.	2644

STINKING = *1

* *Smith.* Nay *Iohn*, it wil be stinking Law, for his breath	stinkes with eating toasted cheese.	2644

STIRR'D = 1

And with your best endeuour haue stirr'd vp	1463

STIRRE = 2 *1

* *Gloster.* No, stirre not for your liues, let her passe	by.	1193
Nor stirre at nothing, till the Axe of Death	1225
I will stirre vp in England some black Storme,	1655

STIRROP = 1

Hast thou not kist thy hand, and held my stirrop?	2221

STOCK = 3

And in thy Sonnes, faire slippes of such a Stock.	1022
Was made a wonder, and a pointing stock	To euery idle Rascall follower.	1222
Some sterne vntutur'd Churle; and Noble Stock	1918

STOLNE = 1

Was by a begger-woman stolne away,	2463

STOLST = 1

And stol'st away the Ladies hearts of France;	438

STOMACKE = *1

*a mans stomacke this hot weather: and I think this word	2914

STOMACKS = 1

So doe your Stomacks, Lords:	780

STONE = 3

Enter Iacke Cade and the rest, and strikes his	*staffe on London stone.*	2613
And heere sitting vpon London Stone,	2616
My heart is turn'd to stone: and while 'tis mine,	3272

STONY = 1

It shall be stony. Yorke, not our old men spares:	3273

STOOD = 3

As he stood by, whilest I, his forlorne Duchesse,	1221
I stood vpon the Hatches in the storme:	1803

STOOD *cont.*
How in our voyding Lobby hast thou stood,   2229
STOOLE = 3*1
  Glost. Now fetch me a Stoole hither by and by.   889
  *leape me ouer this Stoole, and runne away.   891
  *Sirrha Beadle, whippe him till he leape ouer that same | Stoole.   896
  the Stoole, and runnes away: and they | follow, and cry, A Miracle.   903
STOOPE = 3
  What, are ye danted now? Now will ye stoope.   2287
  Stoope to the blocke, then these knees bow to any,   2293
  Then you should stoope vnto a Frenchmans mercy.   2825
STOP = 2
  Send Succours (Lords) and stop the Rage betime,   1588
  To haue thee with thy lippes to stop my mouth: 2113
STOPPE = *1
  Card. A Breach that craues a quick expedient stoppe.   1591
STOPT = 1
  And where this breach now in our Fortunes made | May readily be
  stopt.   3309
STORE = 2
  No: many a Pound of mine owne proper store,   1415
  Nor store of Treasons, to augment my guilt: 1469
STORME = 4
  I will stirre vp in England some black Storme,   1655
  I stood vpon the Hatches in the storme: 1803
  Old Clif. I am resolu'd to beare a greater storme,   3198
  That keepes his leaues inspight of any storme,   3206
STORMIE = 1
  And *Suffolks* cloudie Brow his stormie hate;   1455
STOUT = 2
  As stout and proud as he were Lord of all,   195
  And with a puissant and a mighty power | Of Gallow-glasses and stout
  Kernes,   2878
STRAIGHT = 5
  Maior. Sirrha, goe fetch the Beadle hither straight. | *Exit.*   887
  King. Goe call our Vnckle to our presence straight: 1709
  Vnlesse Lord *Suffolke* straight be done to death,   1956
  2.Gent. And so will I, and write home for it straight.   2193
  Is straight way calme, and boorded with a Pyrate.   2887
STRAIT = 1
  Yet not withstanding such a strait Edict,   1970
STRAITER = 1
  Proceed no straiter 'gainst our Vnckle *Gloster,*   1714
STRANGE = 2
  Deuise strange deaths, for small offences done?   1353
  Strange Tortures for Offendors, neuer heard of,   1422
STRANGENESSE = 1
  The strangenesse of his alter'd Countenance?   1299
STRANGERS = 1
  Strangers in Court, doe take her for the Queene: 465
STRANGLED = 2
  And you three shall be strangled on the Gallowes.   1061
  Staring full gastly, like a strangled man: 1874
STRAY = *1
  *for a stray, for entering his Fee-simple without leaue. A   2930
STRAYES = 1
  And binds the Wretch, and beats it when it strayes,   1512

STREETE = *1
    Cade. Vp Fish-streete, downe Saint Magnes corner,   2775
STREETS = 4
    Vnneath may shee endure the Flintie Streets,   1179
    When thou didst ride in triumph through the streets.   1185
    Will we ride through the streets, & at euery Corner   2771
    I see them Lording it in London streets,   2822
STRENGTH = 3
    Why then from Ireland come I with my strength,   1686
    And tugg'd for Life, and was by strength subdude.   1877
    My foote shall fight with all the strength thou hast,   2954
STRETCHT = 1
    His hayre vprear'd, his nostrils stretcht with strugling: 1875
STRIFE = 1
    I pray my Lords let me compound this strife.   783
STRIKE = 2*2
    She shall not strike Dame *Elianor* vnreueng'd. | *Exit Elianor.*   539
    Strike off his head. *Suf.* Thou dar'st not for thy owne.   2237
    *him away I say, and strike off his head presently, and then   2742
    *and strike off his head, and bring them both vppon two | poles hither.   2744
STRIKES = 2
    They fight, and Peter strikes him downe.   1155
    Enter Iacke Cade and the rest, and strikes his | staffe on London stone.   2613
STRINGS = 1
    When such Strings iarre, what hope of Harmony?   782
STRIUING = 1
    Aduance our halfe-fac'd Sunne, striuing to shine;   2266
STRONG = 8
    Suff. Peace head-strong *Warwicke.*   570
    I haue seduc'd a head-strong Kentishman, | *Iohn Cade* of Ashford,   1662
    Bring the strong poyson that I bought of him.   2152
    That layes strong siege vnto this wretches soule,   2156
    Then *Bargulus* the strong Illyrian Pyrate.   2276
    Henry hath mony, you are strong and manly: 2828
    Or is he but retir'd to make him strong?   2859
    Till *Henry* be more weake, and I more strong.   3023
STRONGER = *1
    King. What stronger Brest-plate then a heart vntainted?   1938
STRONGLY = 1
    Deliuer'd strongly through my fixed teeth,   2028
STRUCK = *1
    Say. Great men haue reaching hands: oft haue I struck   2714
STRUCKE = 2*1
    Some sodaine qualme hath strucke me at the heart,   60
    Beuis. Then is sin strucke downe like an Oxe, and ini-|quities throate
    cut like a Calfe.   2345
    Those that I neuer saw, and strucke them dead.   2715
STRUCKST = *1
    Cade. Tut, when struck'st thou one blow in the field?   2713
STRUGLING = 1
    His hayre vprear'd, his nostrils stretcht with strugling: 1875
STUBBORNE = 2
    In Ireland haue I seene this stubborne *Cade*   1666
    Free from a stubborne opposite intent,   1963
STUDIE = 1
    His Studie is his Tilt-yard, and his Loues   445

STUDIED = 1
Studied so long, sat in the Councell house,   97
STUDYING = 1
I, Night by Night, in studying good for England.   1411
STUMBLE = 1
My tongue should stumble in mine earnest words,   2031
STUMBLING = 1
I would remoue these tedious stumbling blockes,   339
STYGMATICKE = 1
Yo.Clif. Foule stygmaticke that's more then thou | canst tell.   3215
STYLE = 1
Vnto the poore King *Reignier*, whose large style   118
SUBDUDE = 1
And tugg'd for Life, and was by strength subdude.   1877
SUBIECT = 5
And must be made a Subiect to a Duke?   435
Hauing neyther Subiect, Wealth, nor Diadem: 2250
Was neuer Subiect long'd to be a King,   2854
As I do long and wish to be a Subiect.   2855
Or why, thou being a Subiect, as I am,   3011
SUBIECTS = 1
The *Neuills* are thy Subiects to command.   967
SUBMISSION = 3
That all the Court admir'd him for submission.   1306
Buc. Yorke, I commend this kinde submission,   3046
Yorke. In all submission and humility,   3051
SUBORNATION = 2
The Duchesse, by his subornation,   1339
Foule Subornation is predominant,   1445
SUBORNED = 1
As if she had suborned some to sweare   1480
SUBSCRIBE = 1
I will subscribe, and say I wrong'd the Duke.   1332
SUBSIDIE = 1
*one and twenty Fifteenes, and one shilling to the pound, | the last
Subsidie.   2655
SUBSTANCE = 1
To your most gracious hands, that are the Substance   20
SUBSTITUTE = 1
This Deuill here shall be my substitute;   1677
SUBTILL = 1
Glost. A subtill Knaue, but yet it shall not serue: 845
SUBTLE = 1
Qu. A subtle Traitor needs no Sophister.   3191
SUBTLETIE = 1
Be it by Gynnes, by Snares, by Subtletie,   1564
SUBUERSION = 1
Doe seeke subuersion of thy harmelesse Life.   1509
SUCCEED = 1
Succeed before the younger, I am King.   1016
SUCCEEDES = 1
And after Summer, euermore succeedes   1172
SUCCESSIUE = 1
As next the King, he was successiue Heire,   1343
SUCCOR = *1
King. Come *Margaret*, God our hope will succor vs.   2592

SUCCOURS = 1
Send Succours (Lords) and stop the Rage betime,   1588
SUCH = 34*4
With ruder termes, such as my wit affoords,   37
Such is the Fulnesse of my hearts content.   42
This preroration with such circumstance: 112
That shall make answere to such Questions,   355
And plac't a Quier of such enticing Birds,   475
*nor thought any such matter: God is my witnesse, I am   585
Good Vnckle hide such mallice: 743
With such Holynesse can you doe it?   744
When such Strings iarre, what hope of Harmony?   782
Buck. Such as my heart doth tremble to vnfold: 918
Noble shee is: but if shee haue forgot | Honor and Vertue, and conuers't
with such,   946
And in thy Sonnes, faire slippes of such a Stock.   1022
Such as by Gods Booke are adiudg'd to death.   1057
Yet so he rul'd, and such a Prince he was,   1220
And such high vaunts of his Nobilitie,   1344
And well such losers may haue leaue to speake.   1485
Hide not thy poyson with such sugred words,   1745
Yet not withstanding such a strait Edict,   1970
From such fell Serpents as false *Suffolke* is;   1978
Could send such Message to their Soueraigne: 1985
Enough to purchase such another Island,   2137
Be counter-poys'd with such a pettie summe.   2191
Must not be shed by such a iaded Groome: 2220
By such a lowly Vassall as thy selfe.   2279
Farre be it, we should honor such as these   2291
Spare none, but such as go in clouted shooen,   2505
For they are thrifty honest men, and such   2506
King. How now? What newes? Why com'st thou in | such haste?   2561
Scales. Such ayd as I can spare you shall command,   2606
*that must sweepe the Court cleane of such filth as thou   2665
*Nowne and a Verbe, and such abhominable wordes, as   2673
And may enioy such quiet walkes as these?   2922
That liuing wrought me such exceeding trouble.   3064
Iden. May *Iden* liue to merit such a bountie,   3075
And such a peece of seruice will you do,   3154
Ki. Canst thou dispense with heauen for such an oath?   3181
Being opposites of such repayring Nature.   3344
And more such dayes as these, to vs befall. *Exeunt.*   3355
SUCKE = 1
Drones sucke not Eagles blood, but rob Bee-hiues: 2277
SUCKER = 1
Pernicious blood-sucker of sleeping men.   1931
SUCKING = 1
As is the sucking Lambe, or harmelesse Doue: 1365
SUDDEN *see* sodaine
SUDDENLY *see also* sodainly = 3
Had not your man put vp the Fowle so suddenly, | We had had more
sport.   766
But suddenly to nominate them all, | It is impossible.   876
And that's not suddenly to be perform'd,   1033
SUE = 1
Begin your Suites anew, and sue to him. | *Teare the Supplication.*   424

SUF = 16*4
SUFF = 36*8
SUFFER = 1
Suffer them now, and they'le o're-grow the Garden,   1326
SUFFERD = 2
Least being suffer'd in that harmefull slumber,   1974
Who being suffer'd with the Beares fell paw,   3152
SUFFICETH = 1
Sufficeth, that I haue maintaines my state,   2927
SUFFOCATE = 1
Yorke. For Suffolkes Duke, may he be suffocate,   131
SUFFOLK = *2
*2. *Pet.* Come backe foole, this is the Duke of Suffolk, | and not my
Lord Protector.   394
* *Qu.* Are you the Butcher, *Suffolk?* where's your Knife?   1899
SUFFOLKE see also *Suf., Suff.* = 54*9
The Queene, Suffolke, Yorke, Somerset, and Buckingham, | on the other.   5
. King. Suffolke arise. Welcome Queene *Margaret,*   24
* *Charles, and William de la Pole Marquesse of Suffolke, Am-* | bassador   51
We heere create thee the first Duke of Suffolke,   69
Exit King, Queene, and Suffolke. | *Manet the rest.*   80
Suffolke, the new made Duke that rules the rost,   116
That Suffolke should demand a whole Fifteenth,   140
And altogether with the Duke of Suffolke,   175
Ile to the Duke of Suffolke presently. *Exit Cardinall.*   178
The pride of Suffolke, and the Cardinall, | With Somersets and
Buckinghams Ambition,   209
Suffolke concluded on the Articles,   229
And *William de la Pole* first Duke of Suffolke.   304
And from the great and new-made Duke of Suffolke;   371
Yet am I *Suffolke* and the Cardinalls Broker.   377
Enter Suffolke, and Queene.   391
*Suffolke, for enclosing the Commons of Melforde. How | now, Sir
Knaue?   406
Away, base Cullions: *Suffolke* let them goe.   426
Queene. My Lord of Suffolke, say, is this the guise?   428
Till *Suffolke* gaue two Dukedomes for his Daughter.   473
Yorke. Ile tell thee, *Suffolke,* why I am vnmeet.   560
* *King.* What mean'st thou, *Suffolke?* tell me, what are | these?   576
Bulling. What fates await the Duke of Suffolke?   659
Well, to the rest: | Tell me what fate awaits the Duke of Suffolke?   692
*Enter the King, Queene, Protector, Cardinall, and | Suffolke, with
Faulkners hallowing.*   715
* *Glost.* Why *Suffolke,* England knowes thine insolence.   750
For *Suffolke,* he that can doe all in all   1227
Sound a Senet. Enter King, Queene, Cardinall, Suffolke,   1292
My Lord of Suffolke, Buckingham, and Yorke, | Reproue my
allegation, if you can,   1333
Glost. Well *Suffolke,* thou shalt not see me blush,   1396
But my Lord Cardinall, and you my Lord of Suffolke,   1548
Queene. Thrice Noble *Suffolke,* 'tis resolutely spoke.   1568
* *Card.* But I would haue him dead, my Lord of Suffolke,   1575
Lord *Suffolke,* you and I must talke of that euent.   1631
* *Yorke.* My Lord of Suffolke, within foureteene dayes   1632
1. Runne to my Lord of Suffolke: let him know   1692
Didst euer heare a man so penitent? *Enter Suffolke.*   1695

SUFFOLKE cont.

Sound Trumpets. Enter the King, the Queene, | Cardinall, Suffolke,
Somerset, with | Attendants.   1706
Enter Suffolke.   1722
Where is our Vnckle? what's the matter, Suffolke?   1724
King. What, doth my Lord of Suffolke comfort me?   1739
Queene. Why do you rate my Lord of Suffolke thus?   1756
By Suffolke, and the Cardinall Beaufords meanes: 1826
*Warw. What dares not Warwick, if false Suffolke dare | him?   1907
Though Suffolke dare him twentie thousand times.   1911
Enter Suffolke and Warwicke, with their | Weapons drawne.   1944
Vnlesse Lord Suffolke straight be done to death,   1956
From such fell Serpents as false Suffolke is;   1978
Qu. Oh Henry, let me pleade for gentle Suffolke.   2003
King. Vngentle Queene, to call him gentle Suffolke.   2004
And let thy Suffolke take his heauie leaue.   2020
*Q. Enough sweet Suffolke, thou torment'st thy selfe,   2044
Suf. Thus is poore Suffolke ten times banished,   2072
So Suffolke had thy heauenly company: 2076
Why onely Suffolke mourne I not for thee?   2100
To France sweet Suffolke: Let me heare from thee: 2122
Enter Lieutenant, Suffolke, and others.   2169
Suf. Stay Whitmore, for thy Prisoner is a Prince, | The Duke of
Suffolke, William de la Pole.   2213
Whit. The Duke of Suffolke, muffled vp in ragges?   2215
*Lieu. Water: W. Come Suffolke, I must waft thee | to thy death.   2283
Pompey the Great, and Suffolke dyes by Pyrats. | Exit Water with
Suffolke.   2306
Qu. Ah were the Duke of Suffolke now aliue,   2577
Qu. My hope is gone, now Suffolke is deceast.   2593
SUFFOLKE = 1*1
SUFFOLKES = 7*1
Yorke. For Suffolkes Duke, may he be suffocate,   131
Winke at the Duke of Suffolkes insolence?   1036
How often haue I tempted Suffolkes tongue   1814
Mischance vnto my State by Suffolkes meanes.   1998
Omitting Suffolkes exile, my soules Treasure?   2099
Suf. Suffolkes Imperiall tongue is sterne and rough: 2289
*Enter the King with a Supplication, and the Queene with Suf-|folkes   2530
King. How now Madam? | Still lamenting and mourning for Suffolkes
death?   2554
SUFFOLKS = 1
And Suffolks cloudie Brow his stormie hate;   1455
SUGRED = 1
Hide not thy poyson with such sugred words,   1745
SUITE = 2
With humble suite: no, rather let my head   2292
But. I haue a suite vnto your Lordship.   2637
SUITES = 1
Begin your Suites anew, and sue to him. | Teare the Supplication.   424
SULLEN = 1
Why are thine eyes fixt to the sullen earth,   278
SUM = 1
Spirit. Ad sum. | Witch. Asmath, by the eternall God,   648
SUMME = 1
Be counter-poys'd with such a pettie summe.   2191

SUMMER = 1
    And after Summer, euermore succeedes   1172
SUMMERS = 2
    In Winters cold, and Summers parching heate,   88
    Like to the Summers Corne by Tempest lodged: 1880
SUMMES = 2
    Large summes of Gold, and Dowries with their wiues,   136
    Leuie great summes of Money through the Realme,   1355
SUMMON = *1
    *Her. I summon your Grace to his Maiesties Parliament,   1247
SUMPTUOUS = 1*1
    *Som. Thy sumptuous Buildings, and thy Wiues Attyre   520
    Is my Apparrell sumptuous to behold?   2733
SUNDER = 1
    Euen as a splitted Barke, so sunder we: 2129
SUNNE = 3
    Or count them happy, that enioyes the Sunne?   1215
    And these dread curses like the Sunne 'gainst glasse,   2045
    Aduance our halfe-fac'd Sunne, striuing to shine;   2266
SUNNES = 2
    Queene. Free Lords: | Cold Snow melts with the Sunnes hot Beames: 1524
    Like to the glorious Sunnes transparant Beames,   1659
SUP = 2
    For you shall sup with Iesu Christ to night.   3214
    Ric. If not in heauen, you'l surely sup in hell. Exeunt   3217
SUPPE = 1
    To suppe with me to morrow Night. Away. | Exeunt.   713
SUPPER = 1
    Our simple Supper ended, giue me leaue,   961
SUPPLANT = 1
    Which feare, if better Reasons can supplant,   1331
SUPPLICATION = 2*1
    Begin your Suites anew, and sue to him. | Teare the Supplication.   424
    *Enter the King with a Supplication, and the Queene with Suf-|folkes   2530
    *Buc. What answer makes your Grace to the Rebells | Supplication?   2539
SUPPLICATIONS = 1*1
    deliuer our Supplications in the Quill.   388
    *Queene. To my Lord Protector? Are your Supplica-|tions   399
SUPPOSED = *1
    *Cade. Wee Iohn Cade, so tearm'd of our supposed Fa-|ther.   2352
SUPPRESSE = 1
    In what we can, to bridle and suppresse   208
SURE = 5*2
    *Peter. Here a comes me thinkes, and the Queene with | him: Ile be the
    first sure.   392
    *Whose Beame stands sure, whose rightful cause preuailes. | Flourish.
    Exeunt.   957
    Hang ouer thee, as sure it shortly will.   1226
    Card. Sirs, take away the Duke, and guard him sure.   1488
    *Queene. So the poore Chicken should be sure of death.   1553
    For sure, my thoughts doe hourely prophecie,   1997
    The king hath sent him sure: I must dissemble.   3005
SURELY = 3
    Is he a Lambe? his Skinne is surely lent him,   1371
    War. As surely as my soule intends to liue   1857
    Ric. If not in heauen, you'l surely sup in hell. Exeunt   3217

SURETY = 2
Shall be the Surety for their Traitor Father.   3111
That for my Surety will refuse the Boyes.   3116
SURFETS = 1
As one that surfets, thinking on a want: 2063
SURFETTING = 1
Till *Henrie* surfetting in ioyes of loue,   263
SURGE = *1
*Ah thou Say, thou Surge, nay thou Buckram Lord, now   2659
SURLY = 1
Vnder the surly *Glosters* Gouernance?   433
SURMIZD = 1
'Tis but surmiz'd, whiles thou art standing by,   2062
SURPRISD = *1
Kin. Why Buckingham, is the Traitor *Cade* surpris'd?   2858
SURPRIZD = 1
Hath slaine their Gouernors, surpriz'd our Forts,   2257
SURPRIZE = *1
*I see them lay their heades together to surprize   2835
SURUEY = 1
And to suruey his dead and earthy Image: 1850
SURUEYOR = 1
To make the Fox surueyor of the Fold?   1555
SUSPECT = 5
If they were knowne, as the suspect is great,   526
For thousands more, that yet suspect no perill,   1452
If my suspect be false, forgiue me God,   1841
Queen. Than you belike suspect these Noblemen,   1890
But will suspect, 'twas he that made the slaughter?   1894
SUSPENCE = 1
That you will cleare your selfe from all suspence,   1440
SUSPITION = 2
Because in *Yorke* this breedes suspition;   603
Pray God he may acquit him of suspition.   1719
SUSPITIOUS = 1
Euen so suspitious is this Tragedie.   1898
SWAIN = *1
Whit. Speak Captaine, shall I stab the forlorn Swain.   2233
SWAINE = 1
Obscure and lowsie Swaine, King *Henries* blood.   2218
SWALLOW = *1
*thee eate Iron like an Ostridge, and swallow my Sword   2933
SWALLOWING = 1
For swallowing the Treasure of the Realme.   2242
SWEARE = 6
Sweare like a Ruffian, and demeane himselfe   196
As if she had suborned some to sweare   1480
And therefore by his Maiestie I sweare,   1999
But when I sweare, it is irreuocable: 2008
Ioyne with the Traitor, and they ioyntly sweare   2589
Sal. It is great sinne, to sweare vnto a sinne: 3182
SWEEPE = *2
*Thy lips that kist the Queene, shall sweepe the ground: 2243
*that must sweepe the Court cleane of such filth as thou   2665
SWEEPES = *1
*She sweepes it through the Court with troups of Ladies,   463

SWEET = 8*3
 With whose sweet smell the Ayre shall be perfum'd,   267
 *_Hum_. O _Nell_, sweet _Nell_, if thou dost loue thy Lord,   290
 With sweet rehearsall of my mornings dreame?   297
 King. Sweet Aunt be quiet, 'twas against her will.   535
 *_Warw_. Sweet _Yorke_ begin: and if thy clayme be good,   966
 Sweet _Nell_, ill can thy Noble Minde abrooke   1181
 No more, good _Yorke_; sweet _Somerset_ be still.   1607
 *_Q_. Enough sweet Suffolke, thou torment'st thy selfe,   2044
 To France sweet Suffolke: Let me heare from thee: 2122
 A Romane Sworder, and Bandetto slaue | Murder'd sweet _Tully_. _Brutus_
 Bastard hand   2303
 Sweet is the Country, because full of Riches,   2696
SWEETE = 2
 But list to me my _Humfrey_, my sweete Duke: 309
 And then it liu'd in sweete Elizium.   2116
SWEETEST = 1
 Their sweetest shade, a groue of Cypresse Trees: 2038
SWORD = 17*8
 And girt thee with the Sword. Cosin of Yorke,   70
 My sword should shed hot blood, mine eyes no teares.   125
 Against this prowd Protector with my Sword.   756
 Come with thy two-hand Sword.   768
 And that my Sword be stayn'd   1031
 And put the Englishmen vnto the Sword.   1587
 But here's a vengefull Sword, rusted with ease,   1902
 But with our sword we wip'd away the blot.   2209
 Broke be my sword, my Armes torne and defac'd,   2211
 *_Beuis_. Come and get thee a sword, though made of a   2320
 Cade. I feare neither sword, nor fire.   2377
 *_Wea_. He neede not feare the sword, for his Coate is of | proofe. 2378
 *London, where we will haue the Maiors sword born be-|fore vs.   2524
 Should perish by the Sword. And I my selfe,   2543
 *my sword therefore broke through London gates, that   2799
 *me. My sword make way for me, for heere is no staying: 2836
 *sword, and yet am ready to famish. These fiue daies haue   2907
 *thee eate Iron like an Ostridge, and swallow my Sword   2933
 Let this my sword report what speech forbeares.   2958
 Sword, I will hallow thee for this thy deede,   2972
 And as I thrust thy body in with my sword,   2983
 Except a Sword or Scepter ballance it.   3000
 Yorke. So let it helpe me now against thy sword,   3245
 Sword, hold thy temper; Heart, be wrathfull still: 3293
 *_Sal_. Now by my Sword, well hast thou fought to day: 3337
SWORDER = 1
 A Romane Sworder, and Bandetto slaue | Murder'd sweet _Tully_. _Brutus_
 Bastard hand   2303
SWORDS = 2
 Whose dreadfull swords were neuer drawne in vaine,   2260
 They'l pawne their swords of my infranchisement.   3108
SWORNE = 3*1
 *_Suf_. A dreadfull Oath, sworne with a solemn tongue: 1862
 King. Lord _Say_, _Iacke Cade_ hath sworne to haue thy | head.   2551
 Against thy Oath, and true Allegeance sworne,   3012
 King. Hast thou not sworne Allegeance vnto me? | _Sal_. I haue.   3179
SWOUNDS _see_ sounds

SYLLA = 1
And like ambitious Sylla ouer-gorg'd,   2252
SYMON = 1
Who said; *Symon*, come; come offer at my Shrine,   825
SYMPATHY *see* simpathy
T = 1
She vaunted 'mongst her Minions t'other day,   470
TAILE = 1
Hath clapt his taile, betweene his legges and cride,   3153
TAINCTURE = 1
Queene. Gloster, see here the Taincture of thy Nest,   940
TAKE = 29*7
And therefore I will take the *Neuils* parts,   252
Here *Hume*, take this reward, make merry man   360
Hume, if you take not heed, you shall goe neere   378
*Take this fellow in, and send for his Master with a Purse-|uant   419
Strangers in Court, doe take her for the Queene: 465
Spirit. By Water shall he dye, and take his end.   660
Stafford take her to thee.   682
By Water shall he dye, and take his end.   694
Glost. Follow the Knaue, and take this Drab away.   907
*take all the Money that I haue. O Lord blesse me, I pray   1137
*take my death, I neuer meant him any ill, nor the King,   1150
Yorke. Take away his Weapon: Fellow thanke God,   1158
King. Goe, take hence that Traytor from our sight,   1162
Seru. So please your Grace, wee'le take her from the | Sherife.   1191
My *Nell*, I take my leaue: and Master Sherife,   1251
To take her with him to the Ile of Man.   1255
Stanley, I prethee goe, and take me hence,   1271
Take heed, my Lord, the welfare of vs all,   1374
Card. Sirs, take away the Duke, and guard him sure.   1488
Ere you can take due Orders for a Priest: 1576
* *Yorke*. What, worse then naught? nay, then a shame | take all.   1610
Then, Noble *Yorke*, take thou this Taske in hand.   1623
Whiles I take order for mine owne affaires.   1625
I take it kindly: yet be well assur'd,   1652
King. Lords take your places: and I pray you all   1713
And let thy *Suffolke* take his heauie leaue.   2020
Embrace, and kisse, and take ten thousand leaues,   2069
Suf. I go. | *Qu*. And take my heart with thee.   2125
Lieu. Be not so rash, take ransome, let him liue.   2197
As would (but that they dare not) take our parts.   2507
Buc. Then linger not my Lord, away, take horse.   2591
a pole, or no: Take him away, and behead him.   2729
*his Tongue, he speakes not a Gods name. Goe, take   2741
*When shall we go to Cheapside, and take vp commodi-|ties vpon our
billes?   2759
*take your houses ouer your heads, rauish your   2805
Clif. Take heede least by your heate you burne your | selues: 3159
TAKEN *see also* tane = 1*1
*you, for I thinke I haue taken my last Draught in this   1134
Say he be taken, rackt, and tortured;   1682
TAKES = 1
And as the Butcher takes away the Calfe,   1511
TALE = 1
I thinke I should haue told your Graces Tale.   1338

TALKE = 4*1
I come to talke of Common-wealth Affayres.	549
His Highnesse pleasure is to talke with him.	802
Lord *Suffolke*, you and I must talke of that euent.	1631
Lieu. Hale him away, and let him talke no more:	2299
*that thou hast men about thee, that vsually talke of a	2672

TALKES = 1
Sometime he talkes, as if Duke *Humfries* Ghost	2090

TALKING = 1
Glost. Talking of Hawking; nothing else, my Lord.	773

TALLONS = 1
Is *Beauford* tearm'd a Kyte? where are his Tallons?	1900

TALLY = *1
*Score and the Tally, thou hast caused printing to be vs'd,	2669

TANE = 1
If you be tane, we then should see the bottome	3305

TANGLE = 1
And flye thou how thou canst, they'le tangle thee.	1231

TANNER = 1
Hol. I see them, I see them: There's *Bests* Sonne, the | Tanner of	
Wingham.	2340

TANTAENE = 1
Tantaene animis Coelestibus irae, Church-men so hot?	742

TAPER = 1
Enter the Duchesse in a white Sheet, and a Taper	1188

TARRAS = 1
Sound Trumpets. Enter King, Queene, and | *Somerset on the Tarras.*	2848

TASKE = 2
I haue perform'd my Taske, and was espous'd,	16
Then, Noble *Yorke*, take thou this Taske in hand.	1623

TASTE = 1
Gall, worse then Gall, the daintiest that they taste:	2037

TAUGHT = *1
Bro. Iacke Cade, the D.(uke) of York hath taught you this.	2474

TAXE = 1
Because I would not taxe the needie Commons,	1416

TE *l.*645 = 1

TEACH = 1
Elianor. Ah *Gloster*, teach me to forget my selfe:	1203

TEARE = 2
Begin your Suites anew, and sue to him. | *Teare the Supplication.*	424
They will by violence teare him from your Pallace,	1958

TEARES = 13
My sword should shed hot blood, mine eyes no teares.	125
Mine eyes are full of teares, my heart of griefe.	1071
To see my teares, and heare my deepe-fet groanes.	1209
Glost. Witnesse my teares, I cannot stay to speake. | *Exit Gloster.*	1265
For I should melt at an Offendors teares,	1426
With sad vnhelpefull teares, and with dimn'd eyes;	1519
Might liquid teares, or heart-offending groanes,	1760
With teares as salt as Sea, through thy vnkindnesse.	1796
Vpon his face an Ocean of salt teares,	1845
That I may dew it with my mournfull teares:	2055
And with the Southerne clouds, contend in teares?	2101
Prayres and Teares haue mou'd me, Gifts could neuer.	2702
No more will I their Babes, Teares Virginall,	3274

TEARE-STAYND = 1
My teare-stayn'd eyes, to see her Miseries.   1187
TEARMD = 1*1
Is *Beauford* tearm'd a Kyte? where are his Tallons?   1900
Cade. Wee *Iohn Cade*, so tearm'd of our supposed Fa-|ther.   2352
TEARMES = 2
The Duke of Somerset, whom he tearmes a Traitor.   2883
I am so angry at these abiect tearmes.   3017
TEDIOUS = 2
I would remoue these tedious stumbling blockes,   339
Weaues tedious Snares to trap mine Enemies.   1646
TEETH = 2
Deliuer'd strongly through my fixed teeth,   2028
Vnlesse his teeth be pull'd out.   2650
TEIPSUM = *1
Card. Medice teipsum, Protector see to't well, protect | your selfe.   777
TELAMONIUS = 1
And now like *Aiax Telamonius*,   3018
TELL = 15*8
Eli. What dream'd my Lord, tell me, and Ile requite it   296
I tell thee *Poole*, when in the Citie *Tours*   436
Yorke. Ile tell thee, *Suffolke*, why I am vnmeet.   560
King. What mean'st thou, *Suffolke*? tell me, what are | these?   576
Hume. Come my Masters, the Duchesse I tell you ex-|pects
performance of your promises.   620
Well, to the rest: | Tell me what fate awaits the Duke of Suffolke?   692
Suffolke. Come to the King, and tell him what Mi-|racle.   788
King. Good-fellow, tell vs here the circumstance,   803
Queene. Tell me, good-fellow,   819
Glost. Tell me Sirrha, what's my Name? | *Simpc*. Alas Master, I know
not.   862
To tell my loue vnto his dumbe deafe trunke,   1846
King. Goe *Salisbury*, and tell them all from me,   1993
And I am sent to tell his Maiestie,   2094
Qu. Go tell this heauy Message to the King. *Exit*   2096
Beuis. I tell thee, *Iacke Cade* the Cloathier, meanes to   2323
*tell the King from me, that for his Fathers sake *Hen-|ry*   2476
*it vp. Fellow-Kings, I tell you, that that Lord *Say* hath   2484
Say. Tell me: wherein haue I offended most?   2730
as heart can wish, or tongue can tell. | *Dicke*. My Lord,   2757
Tell him, Ile send Duke *Edmund* to the Tower,   2892
Cade. Iden farewell, and be proud of thy victory: Tell   2977
Tell me my Friend, art thou the man that slew him?   3065
Yo.Clif. Foule stygmaticke that's more then thou | canst tell.   3215
TELLING = 1
With *Elianor*, for telling but her dreame?   326
TELLS = 1
My Conscience tells me you are innocent.   1441
TEMPER = 2
And temper Clay with blood of Englishmen.   1616
Sword, hold thy temper; Heart, be wrathfull still: 3293
TEMPEST = 5
And this fell Tempest shall not cease to rage,   1657
When from thy Shore, the Tempest beate vs backe,   1802
Like to the Summers Corne by Tempest lodged: 1880
Like to a Ship, that hauing scap'd a Tempest,   2886
To keepe thee from the Tempest of the field.   3197

TEMPTED = 1
How often haue I tempted Suffolkes tongue   1814
TEN = 7*4
  I could set my ten Commandements in your face.   534
  And ten to one, old *Ioane* had not gone out.   720
  Shall blowe ten thousand Soules to Heauen, or Hell: 1656
  Quitting thee thereby of ten thousand shames,   1923
  Embrace, and kisse, and take ten thousand ieaues,   2069
  Suf. Thus is poore Suffolke ten times banished,   2072
  *shall haue ten hoopes, and I wil make it Fellony to drink   2385
  Cade. Well, hee shall be beheaded for it ten times: 2658
  Better ten thousand base-borne *Cades* miscarry,   2824
  *O I am slaine, Famine and no other hath slaine me, let ten   2965
  *ten meales I haue lost, and I'de defie them all. Wither   2967
TEND = 2
  While they do tend the profit of the Land.   212
  And three-fold Vengeance tend vpon your steps.   2018
TENDER = 3
  The ruthlesse Flint doth cut my tender feet,   1210
  I tender so the safetie of my Liege.   1579
  I thanke them for their tender louing care;   1994
TENDER-FEELING = 1
  To treade them with her tender-feeling feet.   1180
TENNE = 2*1
  Peter. By these tenne bones, my Lords, hee did speake   587
  Sirs, what's a Clock? | *Seru.* Tenne, my Lord.   1175
  Glost. Tenne is the houre that was appointed me,   1177
TENT = 1
  We twaine will go into his Highnesse Tent.   3047
TERMD = 1
  Is term'd the ciuel'st place of all this Isle: 2695
TERME = 1
  I'th parts of France, till terme of eighteene Moneths   72
TERMES = 4
  With ruder termes, such as my wit affoords,   37
  I would inuent as bitter searching termes,   2026
  King. In any case, be not to rough in termes,   2898
  But thou wilt braue me with these sawcie termes?   2940
TERRA = 1
  Dic. What say you of Kent. | *Say.* Nothing but this: 'Tis *bona terra,*
  mala gens.   2688
TERRIBLE = 1
  Where death's approach is seene so terrible.   2140
TERRIBLY = 1
  terribly: then the Spirit | riseth.   646
TERRITORIES = 2
  Som. That all your Interest in those Territories,   1380
  Or banished faire Englands Territories,   1957
TERRORS = 1
  All the foule terrors in darke seated hell -- -   2043
TESTIFIE = *1
  *the brickes are aliue at this day to testifie it: therefore | deny it not.   2469
TH *see also* by'th, i'th, o'th, to'th = 2*1
  Th'vnciuill Kernes of Ireland are in Armes,   1615
  Resigne to death, it is not worth th'enioying: 1640
  K. See Buckingham, Somerset comes with th'Queene,   3078

THAMES = 1
kill and knocke downe, throw them into Thames: 2776
THAN *see also* then = 2
His eye-balles further out, than when he liued, 1873
Queen. Than you belike suspect these Noblemen, 1890
THANKE = 8*6
Queene. We thanke you all. *Florish* 45
We thanke you all for this great fauour done, 76
Som. I humbly thanke your Royall Maiestie. 608
Simpc. Yes Master, cleare as day, I thanke God and | Saint *Albones.* 848
Yorke. We thanke you Lords: 1029
Peter. I thanke you all: drinke, and pray for me, I pray 1133
Yorke. Take away his Weapon: Fellow thanke God, 1158
King. I thanke thee *Nell,* these wordes content mee | much. 1720
I thanke them for their tender louing care; 1994
All. God saue your Maiesty. | *Cade.* I thanke you good people. There
shall bee no 2389
Clearke. Sir I thanke God, I haue bin so well brought | vp, that I can
write my name. 2422
Souldiers, I thanke you all: disperse your selues: 3037
Yor. I thanke thee *Clifford*: Say, what newes with thee? 3122
By 'th'Masse so did we all. I thanke you *Richard.* 3338
THANKES = 3
Be full expyr'd. Thankes Vncle Winchester, 73
To entertaine my vowes of thankes and praise. 2866
And so with thankes, and pardon to you all, 2872
THANKFULNESSE = 1
Lend me a heart repleate with thankfulnesse: 27
THAT *l.*20 21 22 23 26 32 *52 *56 61 *63 116 120 123 128 132 138 140
147 148 *221 245 279 292 307 *312 355 *411 *415 416 422 450 458 462
476 498 554 559 568 579 580 582 *627 640 651 *653 657 678 689 730
733 739 *757 792 793 804 838 *840 880 881 *896 951 1025 1031 1040
1041 *1045 1097 *1116 *1137 1162 1177 1184 1208 1214 1215 1227 1228
1229 1259 1274 1279 1306 1311 1315 1320 1361 1373 1375 1380 1392
*1393 1403 1407 1412 1423 *1424 1425 1429 1431 1440 1452 1457 1458
1473 1493 1506 1508 1532 1537 1540 1544 1545 1547 1559 1566 1567
1571 1586 *1591 1593 1594 *1612 1626 1629 1631 1639 1668 1678 1685
1687 1694 1718 1742 1789 1793 1795 1821 1825 1828 1832 1836 *1838
1839 1854 1858 1860 1868 1876 1894 1903 1904 1906 1921 1924 1927
1928 1939 1967 1968 1972 1974 1977 1989 2010 2037 2049 2055 2059
2061 2063 2081 2086 2088 2095 2124 2128 2152 2156 2173 2182 2204
*2243 2244 2272 2278 2301 2318 *2375 *2392 *2395 *2396 *2397 2423
2449 2455 2472 *2476 *2483 *2484 *2486 *2490 2497 2498 2501 2502
2507 *2528 *2533 2538 2550 2556 2603 2617 2621 *2638 *2640 *2654
*2664 *2665 *2672 *2679 2681 2687 2715 *2719 2734 *2756 2782 2786
2793 *2799 2812 2818 *2838 2843 2850 2886 *2906 *2909 2927 *2941
2947 *2960 *2968 *2971 2976 *2979 2982 2997 3025 3030 3050 3055
3064 3065 3069 3074 3091 3094 3110 3116 3132 3142 3174 3190 3200
3206 3210 3242 3244 3259 3260 3276 3312 3322 3340 3342 = 232*54
THATS = 6*3
For that's the Golden marke I seeke to hit: 255
Suff. Thy Wife too? that's some Wrong indeede. 404
Glost. Why that's well said: What Colour is my | Gowne of? 853
And that's not suddenly to be perform'd, 1033
Elianor. That's bad enough, for I am but reproach: 1276
Suff. Why that's well said. Goe, get you to my House, 1699
Cade. By her he had two children at one birth. | *Bro.* That's false. 2459

THATS *cont.*
Iden. Alexander Iden, that's my name,   3068
Yo.Clif. Foule stygmaticke that's more then thou | canst tell.   3215
THE *see also* t', th' = 798*146
THEE *l.*69 70 206 344 436 439 524 527 537 560 561 617 682 804 816 826
  936 1021 1069 *1129 *1135 *1151 1198 1199 1226 1228 1231 1240 1244
  1267 1395 1492 1506 *1612 *1720 1793 1842 1921 1923 1926 1930 1934
  1935 2013 2054 *2060 2061 2064 2066 2071 2073 2100 *2103 2105 2112
  2113 2117 2118 2122 2124 2126 *2136 2141 2181 2205 2223 2227 2246
  2254 2255 2261 2271 2282 *2283 2285 *2286 *2320 *2323 *2414 *2434
  *2515 *2517 *2528 2559 2579 *2663 *2672 2782 2786 2882 2890 2893
  *2933 2936 *2941 *2942 2972 2973 2982 2985 2996 3006 3050 3073 3088
  3101 *3104 *3122 3125 *3195 3197 3201 3207 3220 3225 *3234 3238
  3248 *3250 3285 = 95*28
THEEFE = 2
  Or foule felonious Theefe, that fleec'd poore passengers,   1429
  And like a Theefe to come to rob my grounds: 2938
THEIR *l.*136 167 189 233 234 340 *635 639 670 *671 727 939 955 1042
  1198 1199 1237 1408 1427 1447 1449 1451 1453 1676 1747 1789 1798
  1828 1830 1944 1985 1994 2036 2038 2039 2040 2041 2174 2175 2179
  2180 2257 2348 2393 2499 2500 2545 2573 2582 2587 *2683 *2685 *2756
  *2835 2860 2863 3108 3111 3114 3115 3120 3134 3142 3148 3212 3256
  3274 3317 = 63*6
THEIRS = 1
  Theirs for the earths encrease, mine for my sorrowes.   2102
THEM *see also* 'em *l.*63 124 126 203 232 238 379 400 426 485 551 *588
  604 *615 680 705 846 876 909 1038 1111 1180 1215 1237 1326 1430 1477
  1510 1634 1651 1789 1790 1812 1965 1993 1994 1995 *2023 2024 2036
  2047 2148 2309 *2340 2349 *2392 2462 2495 2497 2544 2549 2571 2576
  2603 2607 2629 2636 *2675 *2677 *2678 2700 2715 *2744 2765 2766
  2772 2776 2780 2785 *2804 2822 *2833 *2834 *2835 2845 *2967 2997
  3043 3149 3317 3345 3349 3350 = 71*16
THEN *see also* than *l.*2 26 172 183 194 217 260 266 315 *387 457 459 464
  472 494 512 646 664 698 730 745 *856 870 886 914 968 1017 1023 1082
  1113 *1145 1277 1280 1317 *1368 1394 1420 1483 1502 1533 1544 *1554
  1601 1605 1609 *1610 1623 *1643 1645 1686 1715 1773 1779 1788 1799
  1835 *1938 2037 2070 2116 2118 2146 2276 2293 2296 2298 2322 2339
  *2345 *2382 2409 *2486 *2490 *2509 2544 2591 2598 2621 2629 2634
  *2642 2649 *2683 *2723 *2742 2825 2851 2865 2936 3020 3036 *3053
  3083 *3137 3199 3215 *3236 3286 3305 = 79*21
THENCE = 2
  From thence, vnto the place of Execution: 1059
  'Tis not the Land I care for, wer't thou thence,   2074
THERE *l.*124 154 280 343 417 *673 710 870 1099 1250 1275 1586 1590
  1597 1602 1608 1634 1870 1971 2077 2313 *2369 *2383 *2390 2401 2624
  *2753 2987 3289 3332 = 25*5
THEREBY = 2*1
  Heaping confusion on their owne heads thereby.   939
  Quitting thee thereby of ten thousand shames,   1923
  Cade And good reason: for thereby is England main'd   2482
THEREFORE = 21*6
  And therefore I will take the *Neuils* parts,   252
  *of this; therefore I beseech your Maiestie, doe not cast   598
  Bulling. Master *Hume,* we are therefore prouided: will   622
  Queene. I, good my Lord: for purposely therefore   1108
  *nor the Queene: and therefore *Peter* haue at thee with a | downe-right
  blow.   1151

THEREFORE *cont.*

And therefore doe they cry, though you forbid,	1976
And therefore by his Maiestie I sweare,	1999
Therefore bring forth the Souldiers of our prize,	2177
1.*Gent.* Ile giue it sir, and therefore spare my life.	2192
And therefore to reuenge it, shalt thou dye,	2195
Therefore, when Merchant-like I sell reuenge,	2210
And therefore shall it charme thy riotous tongue.	2232
Therefore come you with vs, and let him go.	*Exit Lieutenant, and the*	
rest.	2310
men, and therefore should we be Magistrates.	2337
Cade. Therefore am I of an honorable house.	2368
If you go forward: therefore yeeld, or dye.	2447
But. Nay, 'tis too true, therefore he shall be King.	2467
*the brickes are aliue at this day to testifie it: therefore | deny it not.	2469
All. I marry will we: therefore get ye gone.	2473
*more then that, he can speake French, and therefore hee is | a Traitor.	2486
All. No, no, and therefore wee'l haue his head.	2493
Thinke therefore on reuenge, and cease to weepe.	2535
Therefore away with vs to Killingworth.	2580
And therefore in this Citty will I stay,	2583
And therefore am I bold and resolute. *Exeunt.*	2597
And therefore yet relent, and saue my life.	2750
*my sword therefore broke through London gates, that	2799

THEREOF = 1

Euen to affright thee with the view thereof.	3207

THERES = 3*3

There's reason he should be displeas'd at it:	162
There's two of you, the Deuill make a third,	2017
Beuis. Thou hast hit it: for there's no better signe of a | braue minde,	
then a hard hand.	2338
Hol. I see them, I see them: There's *Bests* Sonne, the | Tanner of	
Wingham.	2340
Cade. I, there's the question; But I say, 'tis true:	2461
Dicke. My Lord, there's an Army gathered together | in Smithfield.	2627

THERFORE = *1

*owne Slaughter-house: Therfore thus will I reward thee,	2517

THESE *l.*102 121 127 189 339 359 375 456 458 461 507 577 580 583 *587
604 *671 676 700 704 718 753 955 1035 1238 1245 1329 1358 *1433 1442
1508 *1720 1848 1882 1890 2019 2045 2059 2097 2196 2216 2273 2291
2293 2308 2321 2448 2578 *2663 *2718 2735 2770 *2801 2891 *2907
*2908 2922 2940 *2943 3010 3017 *3053 3094 3143 *3147 3287
3355 = 56*12

THEY = 58*12

THEYL = 2

They'l pawne their swords of my infranchisement.	3108
See where they come, Ile warrant they'l make it good.	3118

THEYLE = 2

And flye thou how thou canst, they'le tangle thee.	1231
Suffer them now, and they'le o're-grow the Garden,	1326

THIGHES = 1

And fought so long, till that his thighes with Darts	1668

THINE = 16*4

'Tis thine they giue away, and not their owne.	233
Why are thine eyes fixt to the sullen earth,	278
to his Lordship? Let me see them: what is thine?	400
Suff. Resigne it then, and leaue thine insolence.	512

THINE *cont.*

Elianor. Not halfe so bad as thine to Englands King,	677
Card. Thy Heauen is on Earth, thine Eyes & Thoughts	736
Glost. Why *Suffolke,* England knowes thine insolence.	750
In thine owne person answere thy abuse.	760
Let me see thine Eyes; winck now, now open them,	846
Glost. What's thine owne Name? | *Simpc. Saunder Simpcoxe,* and if it please you, Master.	868
Ah *Humfrey,* this dishonor in thine age,	1072
And banne thine Enemies, both mine and thine.	1201
Qu. Runne, goe, helpe, helpe: Oh *Henry* ope thine eyes.	1733
Looke not vpon me, for thine eyes are wounding;	1751
Hast thou not spirit to curse thine enemy?	2022
*thou behaued'st thy selfe, as if thou hadst beene in thine	2516
Yorke. Vpon thine Honor is he Prisoner?	3034
That Head of thine doth not become a Crowne:	3091
And shame thine honourable Age with blood?	3170

THING = 6*2

Suff. How now fellow: would'st any thing with me?	396
Suff. Now Sirs, haue you dispatcht this thing?	1697
That euer did containe a thing of worth,	2128
But. The first thing we do, let's kill all the Lawyers.	2394
*thing, that of the skin of an innocent Lambe should	2396
*'tis the Bees waxe: for I did but seale once to a thing, and	2399
You shall haue pay, and euery thing you wish.	3039
Lands, Goods, Horse, Armor, any thing I haue	3044

THINGS = 6*3

Wee'le see these things effected to the full.	359
Haue you not Beadles in your Towne, | And Things call'd Whippes?	883
King. A Gods Name see the Lysts and all things fit,	1110
For things are often spoke, and seldome meant,	1570
Haue you layd faire the Bed? Is all things well,	1702
King. O thou that iudgest all things, stay my thoghts:	1838
*Small things make base men proud. This Villaine heere,	2274
Cade. And hence-forward all things shall be in Com-|mon. *Enter a Messenger.*	2651
As all things shall redound vnto your good.	2901

THINK = *1

*a mans stomacke this hot weather: and I think this word	2914

THINKE = 18*3

But as I thinke, it was by'th Cardinall,	301
Elianor. It is enough, Ile thinke vpon the Questions:	357
Beldam I thinke we watcht you at an ynch.	672
Glost. I my Lord Cardinall, how thinke you by that?	733
Suff. And yet I thinke, Iet did he neuer see.	858
And would ye not thinke it, Cunning to be great,	879
This Newes I thinke hath turn'd your Weapons edge;	932
*you, for I thinke I haue taken my last Draught in this	1134
But soft, I thinke she comes, and Ile prepare	1186
For whilest I thinke I am thy married Wife,	1204
To thinke vpon my Pompe, shall be my Hell.	1217
I thinke I should haue told your Graces Tale.	1338
What are they that thinke it?	1407
Say as you thinke, and speake it from your Soules:	1549
And thinke it but a minute spent in sport.	2053
That thou might'st thinke vpon these by the Seale,	2059
Lieu. What thinke you much to pay 2000. Crownes,	2187

THINKE *cont.*
Hol. The Nobilitie thinke scorne to goe in Leather | Aprons. 2331
Thinke therefore on reuenge, and cease to weepe. 2535
Cade more, I thinke he hath a very faire warning. 2626
But thou mistakes me much to thinke I do, 3127
THINKES = 6*1
Me thinkes the Realmes of England, France, & Ireland, 244
Peter. Here a comes me thinkes, and the Queene with | him: Ile be the
first sure. 392
Me thinkes I should not thus be led along, 1206
That for the beautie thinkes it excellent. 1532
And not a thought, but thinkes on Dignitie. 1644
And thinkes he, that the chirping of a Wren, 1742
Me thinkes alreadie in this ciuill broyle, 2821
THINKING = 1
As one that surfets, thinking on a want: 2063
THINKS = *2
Yorke. Lord *Buckingham*, me thinks you watcht her well: 685
But. But me thinks he should stand in feare of fire, be-|ing 2380
THINKST = 1
Lord Card'nall, if thou think'st on heauens blisse, 2161
THIRD = 5
Yorke. Then thus: | *Edward* the third, my Lords, had seuen Sonnes: 968
The second, *William* of Hatfield; and the third, 971
Yorke. The third Sonne, Duke of Clarence, 994
The fourth Sonne, *Yorke* claymes it from the third: 1019
There's two of you, the Deuill make a third, 2017
THIRDS = 2
Who after *Edward* the third's death, raign'd as King, 979
Who was to *Edmond Langley*, | *Edward* the thirds fift Sonnes Sonne; 1008
THIRSTING = 1
The Rascall people, thirsting after prey, 2588
THIRTIETH = 1
England, ere the thirtieth of May next ensuing. 55
THIS *l.*26 28 76 105 106 *111 112 132 134 170 177 294 295 *298 305 306
337 *353 360 361 *387 *394 *419 428 429 430 431 479 483 501 504 538
578 591 *598 600 601 603 607 634 674 679 691 703 756 762 775 781 783
785 791 799 808 821 *850 *859 861 880 *891 905 907 922 930 932 952
954 962 1000 1017 1024 1047 1072 1099 *1101 1104 1109 1114 *1134
*1153 *1160 1165 1202 1205 1213 1240 1248 1250 1270 1286 1336 *1368
1388 1397 1448 1535 1545 1592 1605 1623 1657 1660 1666 1677 1680
1697 1700 1770 1782 1785 1787 1810 *1852 1861 1898 1929 1933 1943
2001 2056 2058 2096 2097 2123 2130 2131 2154 2156 2157 2180 2181
2182 2205 2228 2231 2241 *2274 2301 *2395 2444 *2456 *2469 *2471
*2474 *2490 *2522 2536 2547 2583 2615 2689 2695 2711
2736 2764 2778 2821 *2833 2867 2869 *2912 *2914 2923 2953 2958
*2969 2972 2974 2998 3025 3027 3046 3126 3176 3189 3204 3235 3271
3309 3325 3343 = 154*30
THITHER = 4
Thither goes these Newes, | As fast as Horse can carry them: 704
Yorke. That *Somerset* be sent as Regent thither: 1593
And thither I will send you *Mathew Goffe.* 2610
And *Somerset* we will commit thee thither, 2893
THOGHT = *2
*Faster the(n) Spring-time showres, comes thoght on thoght, 1643
THOGHTS = *1
King. O thou that iudgest all things, stay my thoghts: 1838

THOMAS = 1*1
*Peter. Against my Master *Thomas Horner*, for saying,   410
The sixt, was *Thomas* of Woodstock, Duke of Gloster;   975
THORNES = 1
To mowe downe Thornes that would annoy our Foot,   1361
THOROUGH = 1
The false reuolting Normans thorough thee,   2255
THOROWLY = 2
To looke into this Businesse thorowly,   954
Yor. Nay we shall heate you thorowly anon.   3158
THOSE *l.*127 1341 1380 1473 1684 2190 2498 2603 2715 3115 = 10
THOU *see also* y *l.*28 185 205 261 280 *290 317 319 321 *334 346 349
   *413 437 513 *518 *576 650 651 652 *653 758 761 762 786 805 *810 812
   820 830 832 835 *840 847 *850 *856 872 873 905 941 1069 1077 1082
   *1136 *1145 1161 1185 1196 1205 1214 1224 1231 1232 1234 1267 1273
   1281 *1393 1394 1396 1510 1599 1608 1623 1639 1723 1748 1774 1776
   1795 1819 1821 *1838 1905 1919 1927 1928 1932 1933 1935 2005 2006
   2009 2022 *2044 2059 2062 2074 2077 2079 2080 2081 *2103 2104 2114
   2123 *2136 2138 2153 2161 2182 2195 2199 2201 2217 2221 2224 2229
   2235 2237 2244 2247 2251 *2286 *2338 *2419 *2420 2431 2453 *2516
   *2518 2521 2557 *2561 *2638 *2659 *2660 *2661 *2665 *2666 *2669
   *2670 *2672 *2674 *2677 *2678 *2679 2680 *2682 *2683 *2713 2725
   2784 *2931 2934 2935 2940 *2943 2950 2951 2954 *2960 *2962 2963
   2975 *2981 3006 3008 3011 *3053 *3062 3065 3067 3074 3086 3088 3099
   3127 3140 3149 3163 3164 3169 3171 3172 3179 *3181 *3193 3199 3215
   3220 *3236 3239 3240 3242 3255 3267 3283 3289 *3337 = 148*55
THOUGH = 10*2
What though the common people fauour him,   165
Som. Cosin of Buckingham, though *Humfries* pride   179
Though in this place most Master weare no Breeches,   538
With ignominious words, though Clarkely coucht?   1479
Though *Suffolke* dare him twentie thousand times.   1911
Vnworthy though thou art, Ile cope with thee,   1935
And he but naked, though lockt vp in Steele,   1940
And therefore doe they cry, though you forbid,   1976
Though standing naked on a Mountaine top,   2051
Queen. Away: Though parting be a fretfull corosiue,   2120
Beuis. Come and get thee a sword, though made of a   2320
And *Henry* though he be infortunate,   2870
THOUGHT = 10*5
And may that thought, when I imagine ill   292
Hum. Me thought this staffe mine Office-badge in | Court   298
Me thought I sate in Seate of Maiesty,   310
Aboue the reach or compasse of thy thought?   320
I thought King *Henry* had resembled thee,   439
*nor thought any such matter: God is my witnesse, I am   585
Card. I thought as much, hee would be aboue the | Clouds.   731
Which he had thought to haue murther'd wrongfully.   1166
Yorke. 'Tis thought, my Lord, | That you tooke Bribes of France,   1402
Glost. Is it but thought so?   1406
And not a thought, but thinkes on Dignitie.   1644
As being thought to contradict your liking,   1964
And thought thee happy when I shooke my head.   2223
Cade. I haue thought vpon it, it shall bee so. Away,   2646
*I thought ye would neuer haue giuen out these Armes til   2801
THOUGHTS = 8*2
If Simpathy of Loue vnite our thoughts.   30

THOUGHTS *cont.*
Banish the Canker of ambitious thoughts:	291
And beares his thoughts aboue his Faulcons Pitch.	728
Card. Thy Heauen is on Earth, thine Eyes & Thoughts	736
Yorke. Now *Yorke,* or neuer, steele thy fearfull thoughts,	1637
My thoughts, that labour to perswade my soule,	1839
For sure, my thoughts doe hourely prophecie,	1997
This breast from harbouring foule deceitfull thoughts.	2736
More like a King, more Kingly in my thoughts.	3021
Then Yorke vnloose thy long imprisoned thoughts,	3083

THOUSAND *see also* 1000., 2000. = 10*4
Shall blowe ten thousand Soules to Heauen, or Hell:	1656
With twenty thousand kisses, and to draine	1844
Though *Suffolke* dare him twentie thousand times.	1911
Quitting thee thereby of ten thousand shames,	1923
*Through whom a thousand sighes are breath'd for thee.	2060
Embrace, and kisse, and take ten thousand leaues,	2069
Ile giue a thousand pound to looke vpon him.	2147
Ma. A thousand Crownes, or else lay down your head	2185
Better ten thousand base-borne *Cades* miscarry,	2824
Shall haue a thousand Crownes for his reward. | *Exeunt some of them.*	2844
*if I might haue a Lease of my life for a thousand yeares, I	2910
*thousand diuelles come against me, and giue me but the	2966
We giue thee for reward a thousand Markes,	3073
Qu. For thousand Yorkes he shall not hide his head,	3080

THOUSANDS = 1
For thousands more, that yet suspect no perill,	1452

THREATENS = 1
Being Captaine of a Pinnace, threatens more	2275

THREATEST = 1
Iniurious Duke, that threatest where's no cause.	678

THRED = 1
Hol. And Smith the Weauer. | *Beu.* Argo, their thred of life is spun.	2347

THRED-BARE = *1
Hol. So he had need, for 'tis thred-bare. Well, I say,	2326

THREE *see also* 3. = 13*1
Enter three or foure Petitioners, the Armorers | Man being one.	384
And you three shall be strangled on the Gallowes.	1061
Shall, after three dayes open Penance done,	1064
Yorke. And I: and now we three haue spoke it,	1582
Enter two or three running ouer the Stage, from the | Murther of Duke Humfrey.	1690
But three dayes longer, on the paine of death.	2002
If after three dayes space thou here bee'st found,	2009
Once by the King, and three times thrice by thee.	2073
But. No question of that: for I haue seene him whipt | three Market dayes together.	2375
*halfe peny Loaues sold for a peny: the three hoop'd pot,	2384
Enter Lord Scales vpon the Tower walking. Then enters | two or three Citizens below.	2598
Rich. My Noble Father: | Three times to day I holpe him to his horse,	3328
Three times bestrid him: Thrice I led him off,	3330
And it hath pleas'd him that three times to day	3340

THREE-FOLD = 1
And three-fold Vengeance tend vpon your steps.	2018

THREW = 1
And threw it towards thy Land: The Sea receiu'd it,	1808

THRICE = 4
Queene. Thrice Noble *Suffolke*, 'tis resolutely spoke.	1568
Thrice is he arm'd, that hath his Quarrell iust;	1939
Once by the King, and three times thrice by thee.	2073
Three times bestrid him: Thrice I led him off,	3330

THRICE-FAMED = 1
Vpon the life of this thrice-famed Duke.	1861

THRIFTY = 1
For they are thrifty honest men, and such	2506

THRIUE = 2*1
Say that he thriue, as 'tis great like he will,	1685
But. If we meane to thriue, and do good, breake open	2526
As I intend Clifford to thriue to day,	3237

THROATE = 1
Beuis. Then is sin strucke downe like an Oxe, and ini-|quities throate cut like a Calfe.	2345

THROATS = 1
Cut both the Villaines throats, for dy you shall:	2189

THROBBING = 1
Heere may his head lye on my throbbing brest:	2537

THRONE = 2
May honorable Peace attend thy Throne.	1093
King. Was euer King that ioy'd an earthly Throne,	2850

THROUGH = 9*4
*She sweepes it through the Court with troups of Ladies,	463
Glost. Let the(m) be whipt through euery Market Towne,	909
When thou didst ride in triumph through the streets.	1185
Leuie great summes of Money through the Realme,	1355
With teares as salt as Sea, through thy vnkindnesse.	1796
Deliuer'd strongly through my fixed teeth,	2028
*Through whom a thousand sighes are breath'd for thee.	2060
And I proclaim'd a Coward through the world.	2212
Will we ride through the streets, & at euery Corner	2771
*my sword therefore broke through London gates, that	2799
Will he conduct you through the heart of France,	2813
*in despight of the diuels and hell, haue through the verie	2837
(As well we may, if not through your neglect)	3307

THROUGHOUT = 1
Staf. Herald away, and throughout euery Towne,	2496

THROW = 4
And nodde their heads, and throw their eyes on thee.	1198
Stanley. Madame, your Penance done, | Throw off this Sheet,	1285
kill and knocke downe, throw them into Thames:	2776
Throw in the frozen bosomes of our part,	3257

THROWES = *1
Glost. Ah, thus King *Henry* throwes away his Crutch,	1489

THRUST = 3*1
And now the House of Yorke thrust from the Crowne,	2262
Iohn. Masse 'twill be sore Law then, for he was thrust	2642
And as I thrust thy body in with my sword,	2983
So wish I, I might thrust thy soule to hell.	2984

THUMPE = 1*2
Salisb. Peter? what more? | *Peter.* Thumpe.	1143
Salisb. Thumpe? Then see thou thumpe thy Master | well.	1145

THUNDER = 2
False Fiend auoide. | *Thunder and Lightning. Exit Spirit.*	667
Suf. O that I were a God, to shoot forth Thunder	2272

THUNDERS = 1
Bullingbrooke or Southwell reades, Coniuro | te, &c. *It Thunders and Lightens*   644
THUS = 17*7
Well, so it stands: and thus I feare at last,   380
As thus to name the seuerall Colours we doe weare.   874
Yorke. Then thus: | *Edward* the third, my Lords, had seuen Sonnes: 968
Thus got the House of *Lancaster* the Crowne.   988
*Suff. Thus droupes this loftie Pyne, & hangs his sprayes,   1101
Thus *Elianors* Pride dyes in her youngest dayes.   1102
*Glost. Thus sometimes hath the brightest day a Cloud: 1171
Me thinkes I should not thus be led along,   1206
Thus are my Blossomes blasted in the Bud,   1386
Be thus vpbrayded, chid, and rated at,   1475
*Glost. Ah, thus King *Henry* throwes away his Crutch,   1489
Thus is the Shepheard beaten from thy side,   1491
Queene. Why do you rate my Lord of Suffolke thus?   1756
Makes them thus forward in his Banishment.   1965
Oh go not yet. Euen thus, two Friends condemn'd,   2068
Suf. Thus is poore Suffolke ten times banished,   2072
*owne Slaughter-house: Therfore thus will I reward thee,   2517
That thus you do exclaime you'l go with him.   2812
And humbly thus with halters on their neckes,   2863
*King. Thus stands my state, 'twixt Cade and Yorke | distrest,   2884
* Yor. From Ireland thus comes York to claim his right,   2992
That thus he marcheth with thee arme in arme?   3050
* Yor. Thus Warre hath giuen thee peace, for y art still,   3250
And in thy Reuerence, and thy Chaire-dayes, thus   3270
THY *l.*149 150 199 202 204 279 282 283 284 *290 320 322 361 *404 499
501 517 519 *520 522 525 527 583 591 *736 737 751 760 768 940 941
*966 967 1022 1073 1077 1082 1089 1090 1093 1131 1141 *1145 1159
1167 1181 1182 1183 1184 1200 1204 1230 1232 1233 1241 1243 1244
1283 1491 1494 1503 1506 1507 1509 1603 1608 *1637 1745 1746 1749
1753 1774 1777 1778 1779 1796 1799 1800 1801 1802 1805 1808 1809
1815 1917 1925 1926 1927 1928 1930 1932 2011 2020 *2044 2047 2054
2058 2076 2080 2106 2107 2111 2113 2115 *2134 2141 2162 2183 *2202
2206 2213 2221 2228 2231 2232 2235 2237 2241 *2243 2253 2279 2280
2284 *2335 *2414 *2419 *2420 2452 2453 *2516 2551 *2671 *2682 2865
*2943 2949 2950 2952 2953 2956 *2962 2972 2974 2976 *2977 2983 2984
2986 2987 2989 *3007 3012 3014 3030 3031 3032 3067 3083 3084 3092
3100 3114 3124 3125 3139 3140 *3147 3157 *3161 3162 3163 3164 3165
3173 3200 3201 *3208 3241 *3243 3245 3251 3268 3270 3293 = 167*29
THYSELFE *see* selfe
TICKLE = 1
Paris is lost, the state of *Normandie* | Stands on a tickle point, now they
. are gone: 227
TICKLED = 1
Shee's tickled now, her Fume needs no spurres,   543
TIDINGS *see also* tydings = 1
King. What Tidings with our Cousin *Buckingham*?   917
TIL = *1
*I thought ye would neuer haue giuen out these Armes til   2801
TILL = 20*2
I'th parts of France, till terme of eighteene Moneths   72
Still reuelling like Lords till all be gone,   236
Then Yorke be still a-while, till time do serue: 260
Till *Henrie* surfetting in ioyes of loue,   263

TILL *cont.*

Till *Suffolke* gaue two Dukedomes for his Daughter.	473
Till we haue brought Duke *Humphrey* in disgrace.	482
Till France be wonne into the Dolphins hands:	565
Till Paris was besieg'd, famisht, and lost.	567
Answere that I shall aske: for till thou speake,	651
*Sirrha Beadle, whippe him till he leape ouer that same | Stoole.	896
Till they come to Barwick, from whence they came. | *Exit.*	910
Till *Henry Bullingbrooke*, Duke of Lancaster,	980
Who kept him in Captiuitie, till he dyed. | But, to the rest.	1003
Till *Lionels* Issue fayles, his should not reigne.	1020
But I am not your King, till I be Crown'd,	1030
Till they haue snar'd the Shepheard of the Flock,	1039
Nor stirre at nothing, till the Axe of Death	1225
By staying there so long, till all were lost.	1602
And fought so long, till that his thighes with Darts	1668
With the rude multitude, till I returne.	1837
*shall be dragg'd at my horse heeles, till I do come to	2523
Till *Henry* be more weake, and I more strong.	3023

TILT = 1

Thou ran'st a-tilt in honor of my Loue,	437

TILT-YARD = 1

His Studie is his Tilt-yard, and his Loues	445

TIME = 14*6

Then *Yorke* be still a-while, till time do serue:	260
Next time Ile keepe my dreames vnto my selfe, | And not be check'd.	327
Duch. Against her will, good King? looke to't in time,	536
Last time I danc't attendance on his will,	566
The time of Night when Troy was set on fire,	637
The time when Screech-owles cry, and Bandogs howle,	638
That time best fits the worke we haue in hand.	640
And many time and oft my selfe haue heard a Voyce, | To call him so.	828
We know the time since he was milde and affable,	1303
When euery one will giue the time of day,	1308
*Which time will bring to light in smooth Duke *Humfrey.*	1359
To keepe, vntill your further time of Tryall.	1438
*Faster the(n) Spring-time showres, comes thoght on thoght,	1643
Ouer whom (in time to come) I hope to raigne:	2450
*the fift, (in whose time, boyes went to Span-counter	2477
*Sallet was borne to do me good: for many a time but for	2915
*and many a time when I haue beene dry, & brauely mar-|ching,	2917
War. Of one or both of vs the time is come.	3233
That Winter Lyon, who in rage forgets | Aged contusions, and all brush of Time:	3322
'Tis not enough our foes are this time fled,	3343

TIMELESSE = 1

As guilty of Duke *Humfries* timelesse death.	1891

TIMELY-PARTED = 1

Oft haue I seene a timely-parted Ghost,	1865

TIMES = 11*2

Bullin. Patience, good Lady, Wizards know their times:	635
Being call'd a hundred times, and oftner,	823
And had I twentie times so many foes,	1236
And each of them had twentie times their power,	1237
Though *Suffolke* dare him twentie thousand times.	1911
Your louing Vnckle, twentie times his worth,	1980
Loather a hundred times to part then dye;	2070

TIMES *cont.*
Suf. Thus is poore Suffolke ten times banished,   2072
Once by the King, and three times thrice by thee.   2073
Cade. Well, hee shall be beheaded for it ten times: 2658
Rich. My Noble Father: | Three times to day I holpe him to his horse,   3328
Three times bestrid him: Thrice I led him off,   3330
And it hath pleas'd him that three times to day   3340
TIMOR = 1
Suf. Pine *gelidus timor occupat artus,* it is thee I feare.   2285
TINKERS = 1
Sent from a sort of Tinkers to the King.   1990
TIS *l.*113 147 148 155 233 *331 729 933 1041 1296 1324 1325 1402 *1424
1439 1539 1547 *1554 1565 1568 1594 1647 1685 1704 1711 1832 1888
1889 1984 2062 2074 *2326 *2399 2461 2467 2503 2643 2689 2788 *3219
*3236 3244 3272 3343 = 37*7
TITLE = 7
Deliuer vp my Title in the Queene   19
Your Graces Title shall be multiplied.   348
Am I a Queene in Title and in Stile,   434
In crauing your opinion of my Title,   963
Or sell my Title for a glorious Graue.   1389
Vnder the Title of *Iohn Mortimer.*   1665
The Title of this most renowned Duke,   3176
TO *see also* too = 490*91, 2*2
Elianor. Art thou gone to? all comfort goe with thee,   1267
Dicke. And worke in their shirt to, as my selfe for ex-|ample, that am
a butcher.   2685
King. In any case, be not to rough in termes,   2898
*broach'd, and beard thee to. Looke on mee well, I haue   2942
TOASTED = 1
Smith. Nay *Iohn,* it wil be stinking Law, for his breath | stinkes with
eating toasted cheese.   2644
TODAY *see* day
TOGETHER = 7*2
Ioyne we together for the publike good,   207
And hauing both together heau'd it vp,   286
Wee'l both together lift our heads to heauen,   287
Then Father *Salisbury,* kneele we together,   1023
I, all of you haue lay'd your heads together,   1465
But. No question of that: for I haue seene him whipt | three Market
dayes together.   2375
Dicke. My Lord, there's an Army gathered together | in Smithfield.   2627
*I see them lay their heades together to surprize   2835
Knit earth and heauen together.   3264
TOLD = 4
Glost. Hadst thou been his Mother, thou could'st haue | better told.   810
Warw. Father, the Duke hath told the truth;   987
I thinke I should haue told your Graces Tale.   1338
And told me that by Water I should dye: 2204
TOM = *1
*and *Will,* thou shalt haue my Hammer: and here *Tom,*   1136
TOMBE = 2
Is all thy comfort shut in Glosters Tombe?   1778
And hang thee o're my Tombe, when I am dead.   2973
TOMORROW *see* morrow
TONGUE = 12*4
So Yorke must sit, and fret, and bite his tongue,   242

TONGUE *cont.*

* *Yorke.* Dispatch, this Knaues tongue begins to double.	1153
Sharpe *Buckingham* vnburthens with his tongue,	1456
But that my heart accordeth with my tongue,	1571
So shall my name with Slanders tongue be wounded,	1768
How often haue I tempted Suffolkes tongue	1814
* *Suf.* A dreadfull Oath, sworne with a solemn tongue:	1862
Were there a Serpent seene, with forked Tongue,	1971
My tongue should stumble in mine earnest words,	2031
And therefore shall it charme thy riotous tongue.	2232
Suf. Suffolkes Imperiall tongue is sterne and rough:	2289
*with the tongue of an enemy, be a good Councellour, or | no?	2491
This Tongue hath parlied vnto Forraigne Kings | For your behoofe.	2711
*his Tongue, he speakes not a Gods name. Goe, take	2741
as heart can wish, or tongue can tell. | *Dicke.* My Lord,	2757
And let thy tongue be equall with thy heart.	3084

TONIGHT *see* night

TOO *see also* to = 13*5

Early and late, debating too and fro	98
Car. My Lord of Gloster, now ye grow too hot,	144
What, is't too short? Ile lengthen it with mine,	285
* *Suff.* Thy Wife too? that's some Wrong indeede.	404
Wife. Too true, and bought his climbing very deare.	839
Now thou do'st Penance too. Looke how they gaze,	1196
The Duke is vertuous, milde, and too well giuen,	1366
* *Suff.* Nay *Gloster,* know that thou art come too soone,	1393
Too full of foolish pittie: and *Glosters* shew	1527
Be poysonous too, and kill thy forlorne Queene.	1777
King. That he is dead good Warwick, 'tis too true,	1832
But. Nay, 'tis too true, therefore he shall be King.	2467
* *Cade.* He lyes, for I inuented it my selfe. Go too Sir-|rah,	2475
*enemies: go too then, I ask but this: Can he that speaks	2490
And if you can, burne downe the Tower too.	2631
Alas, he hath no home, no place to flye too:	2815
* *Cade.* Was euer Feather so lightly blowne too & fro,	2832
Buc. That is too much presumption on thy part:	3030

TOOKE = 7*1

* 1 . *Pet.* I pray my Lord pardon me, I tooke ye for my | Lord Protector.	397
Yorke. 'Tis thought, my Lord, | That you tooke Bribes of France,	1402
I tooke a costly Iewell from my necke,	1806
With that dread King that tooke our state vpon him,	1858
Thy Mother tooke into her blamefull Bed	1917
For sodainly a greeuous sicknesse tooke him,	2087
Cade. O monstrous. | *Wea.* We tooke him setting of boyes Copies.	2405
Tooke oddes to combate a poore famisht man.	2948

TOP = 3*1

From top of Honor, to Disgraces feete?	323
Though standing naked on a Mountaine top,	2051
* *But.* They vse to writ it on the top of Letters: 'Twill | go hard with	
you.	2417
As on a Mountaine top, the Cedar shewes,	3205

TORMENTST = *1

* *Q.* Enough sweet Suffolke, thou torment'st thy selfe,	2044

TORNE = 2

France should haue torne and rent my very hart,	133
Broke be my sword, my Armes torne and defac'd,	2211

TORTURD = 1
Murther indeede, that bloodie sinne, I tortur'd | Aboue the Felon, or
what Trespas else.   1431
TORTURE = 4
You goe about to torture me in vaine.   893
And torture him with grieuous lingring death.   1959
From thee to dye, were torture more then death: 2118
Oh torture me no more, I will confesse.   2145
TORTURED = 1
Say he be taken, rackt, and tortured;   1682
TORTURES = 1
Strange Tortures for Offendors, neuer heard of,   1422
TOSSE = 1
On which Ile tosse the Fleure-de-Luce of France.   3002
TOT = *2
*Duch. Against her will, good King? looke to't in time,   536
*Card. Medice teipsum, Protector see to't well, protect | your selfe.   777
TOTH = 1
Others to'th Innes of Court, downe with them all.   2636
TOUCH = 3
Ready to sterue, and dare not touch his owne.   241
Their touch affrights me as a Serpents sting.   1747
Their softest Touch, as smart as Lyzards stings: 2040
TOUCHING = *1
*an honest man: and touching the Duke of Yorke, I will   1149
TOURES = 1
So in the Famous Ancient City, Toures,   12
TOURS = 1
I tell thee Poole, when in the Citie Tours   436
TOWARD = 2
To morrow toward London, back againe,   953
But. They are all in order, and march toward vs.   2508
TOWARDS = 5
The King is now in progresse towards Saint Albones,   702
And bid them blow towards Englands blessed shore,   1790
And threw it towards thy Land: The Sea receiu'd it,   1808
That slyly glyded towards your Maiestie,   1972
*Cade. Feare not that I warrant thee. Come, let's march | towards
London. Exeunt.   2528
TOWER = 6*1
Enter Lord Scales vpon the Tower walking. Then enters | two or three
Citizens below.   2598
*The L.(ord) Maior craues ayd of your Honor from the Tower   2604
The Rebels haue assay'd to win the Tower.   2608
And if you can, burne downe the Tower too.   2631
Tell him, Ile send Duke Edmund to the Tower,   2892
The Duke of Somerset is in the Tower.   3033
Clif. He is a Traitor, let him to the Tower,   3131
TOWNE = 3
Haue you not Beadles in your Towne, | And Things call'd Whippes?   883
Glost. Let the(m) be whipt through euery Market Towne,   909
Staf. Herald away, and throughout euery Towne,   2496
TOWNES = 4*1
Queene. Thy sale of Offices and Townes in France,   525
You made in a day, my Lord, whole Townes to flye.   915
By meanes whereof, the Townes each day reuolted.   1357
*which sold the Townes in France. He that made vs pay   2654

TOWNES *cont.*
Of some more Townes in France. Soldiers,   2768
TOWNESHIP = 1
*2. *Pet.* Alas Sir, I am but a poore Petitioner of our | whole Towneship.   408
TOWNES-MEN = 1
Card. Here comes the Townes-men, on Procession,   797
TOWRE = 1
My Lord Protectors Hawkes doe towre so well,   726
TOYLE = 1
And did my brother *Bedford* toyle his wits,   90
TRAGEDIE = 2
Will not conclude their plotted Tragedie.   1453
Euen so suspitious is this Tragedie.   1898
TRAGICKE = 1
That dragge the Tragicke melancholy night: 2173
TRAITEROUSLY = 2*1
Harmelesse *Richard* was murthered traiterously.   986
That good Duke *Humfrey* Traiterously is murdred   1825
*art: Thou hast most traiterously corrupted the youth of   2666
TRAITOR = 12*2
**All.* He hath confest: away with him: he's a Villaine | and a Traitor.   2424
*more then that, he can speake French, and therefore hee is | a Traitor.   2486
Ioyne with the Traitor, and they ioyntly sweare   2589
**Kin.* Why Buckingham, is the Traitor *Cade* surpris'd?   2858
The Duke of Somerset, whom he tearmes a Traitor.   2883
**Iden.* Is't *Cade* that I haue slain, that monstrous traitor?   2971
Yor. To heaue the Traitor Somerset from hence,   3054
Which dar'st not, no nor canst not rule a Traitor.   3090
Som. O monstrous Traitor! I arrest thee Yorke   3101
Obey audacious Traitor, kneele for Grace.   3103
Shall be the Surety for their Traitor Father.   3111
Clif. He is a Traitor, let him to the Tower,   3131
I am thy King, and thou a false-heart Traitor: 3140
Qu. A subtle Traitor needs no Sophister.   3191
TRAITORS = 4
Proclaime them Traitors that are vp with *Cade,*   2497
King. Lord *Say,* the Traitors hateth thee,   2579
Loe, I present your Grace a Traitors head,   3060
Clif. Why what a brood of Traitors haue we heere?   3138
TRANSPARANT = 1
Like to the glorious Sunnes transparant Beames,   1659
TRANSPORTING = 1
For Costs and Charges in transporting her: 141
TRAP = 1
Weaues tedious Snares to trap mine Enemies.   1646
TRASH = *1
* *Yorke.* Lay hands vpon these Traytors, and their trash: 671
TRAUELL = *1
* *Weauer.* But now of late, not able to trauell with her   2366
TRAYNE = 1
The very trayne of her worst wearing Gowne,   471
TRAYTOR = 4
Did neuer Traytor in the Land commit.   569
Yorke. Doth any one accuse *Yorke* for a Traytor?   575
King. Goe, take hence that Traytor from our sight,   1162
Say, who's a Traytor? *Gloster* he is none. *Exit.*   1523

TRAYTORS = 2*1
Ile haue thy Head for this thy Traytors speech: 591
*Yorke. Lay hands vpon these Traytors, and their trash: 671
From Treasons secret Knife, and Traytors Rage,   1474
TRAYTROUS = 1
Suff. The trayt'rous *Warwick*, with the men of Bury,   1950
TREACHERY = 1
And wilt thou still be hammering Treachery,   321
TREAD = 1
And tread it vnder foot with all contempt,   3209
TREADE = 2
To treade them with her tender-feeling feet.   1180
And bid me be aduised how I treade.   1212
TREASON = 9*1
Suff. Because here is a man accused of Treason,   573
That doth accuse his Master of High Treason;   579
*Armorer. Hold *Peter*, hold, I confesse, I confesse Trea-|son.   1156
And in his simple shew he harbours Treason.   1348
From meaning Treason to our Royall Person,   1364
I doe arrest thee of High Treason here.   1395
As I am cleare from Treason to my Soueraigne.   1400
And now henceforward it shall be Treason for any,   2620
Of Capitall Treason 'gainst the King and Crowne: 3102
But that 'tis shewne ignobly, and in Treason.   3244
TREASONS = 2*1
Nor store of Treasons, to augment my guilt: 1469
From Treasons secret Knife, and Traytors Rage,   1474
*base and ignominious treasons, makes me betake mee to | my heeles.
Exit   2840
TREASURE = 3*1
Beat on a Crowne, the Treasure of thy Heart,   737
Omitting Suffolkes exile, my soules Treasure?   2099
*Ca. If thou beest death, Ile giue thee Englands Treasure,   2136
For swallowing the Treasure of the Realme.   2242
TREASURIE = 2
Haue cost a masse of publique Treasurie.   521
King. The Treasurie of euerlasting Ioy.   735
TREE = 4
Suff. How cam'st thou so? | Simpc. A fall off of a Tree.   832
Wife. A Plum-tree, Master.   834
Glost. What, and would'st climbe a Tree?   837
Was graft with Crab-tree slippe, whose Fruit thou art,   1919
TREES = 1
Their sweetest shade, a groue of Cypresse Trees: 2038
TREMBLE = 2
Buck. Such as my heart doth tremble to vnfold: 918
But great men tremble when the Lyon rores,   1313
TREMBLEST = 2
Whose name and power thou tremblest at,   650
How now? why look'st thou pale? why tremblest thou?   1723
TREMBLING = 1
And shakes his head, and trembling stands aloofe,   .   239
TRENCHER = 1
Fed from my Trencher, kneel'd downe at the boord,   2225
TRESPAS = 1
Murther indeede, that bloodie sinne, I tortur'd | Aboue the Felon, or
what Trespas else.   1431

305

TRIALL = 1
Beau. Bring me vnto my Triall when you will. 2142
TRIBUTE = *1
*his shoulders, vnlesse he pay me tribute: there shall not 2753
TRIE = 2
Card. My Lord of Yorke, trie what your fortune is: 1614
And trie your hap against the Irishmen? 1619
TRINKETS = 1
Wee'le see your Trinkets here all forth-comming. | All away. *Exit.* 683
TRIPLE = 1
And set the Triple Crowne vpon his Head; 449
TRIUIALL = 1
And yet we haue but triuiall argument, 1543
TRIUMPH = 2
When thou didst ride in triumph through the streets. 1185
Which I will beare in triumph to the King, 2988
TROUBLE = 4
But 'tis my presence that doth trouble ye, 148
And neuer mount to trouble you againe. 477
That henceforth he shall trouble vs no more: 1629
That liuing wrought me such exceeding trouble. 3064
TROUBLED = 2
But I am troubled heere with them my selfe, 2607
My minde was troubled with deepe Melancholly. 3026
TROUBLES = 1
Troubles the siluer Spring, where England drinkes: 2240
TROUBLOUS = 1
My troublous dreames this night, doth make me sad. 295
TROUPE = 1
Oppose himselfe against a Troupe of Kernes, 1667
TROUPS = *1
*She sweepes it through the Court with troups of Ladies, 463
TROWEST = 1
Trowest thou, that ere Ile looke vpon the World, 1214
TROY = 2
The time of Night when Troy was set on fire, 637
His Fathers Acts, commenc'd in burning Troy. 1818
TRUE = 15*3
To conquer France, his true inheritance? 89
Buck. True Madame, none at all: what call you this? 679
Glost. True Vnckle, are ye aduis'd? 769
And I will helpe thee. | *Wife.* Most true, forsooth: 826
Wife. Too true, and bought his climbing very deare. 839
Suff. True: made the Lame to leape and flye away. 913
So long as I am loyall, true, and crimelesse. 1239
**Suff.* Madame 'tis true: and wer't not madnesse then, 1554
Then from true euidence, of good esteeme, 1715
King. That he is dead good Warwick, 'tis too true, 1832
True Nobility, is exempt from feare: 2297
**Hol.* True: and yet it is said, Labour in thy Vocati-|on: 2335
Cade. I, there's the question; But I say, 'tis true: 2461
But. Nay, 'tis too true, therefore he shall be King. 2467
Against thy Oath, and true Allegeance sworne, 3012
And neuer liue but true vnto his Liege. 3076
**Old Clif.* The first I warrant thee, if dreames proue true 3195
As I in iustice, and true right expresse it. 3246

TRUER = 1
Glost. Farre truer spoke then meant: I lose indeede,   1483
TRULY = 1*1
Suff. Ile see it truly done, my Lord of Yorke. *Exeunt.*   1635
He that is truly dedicate to Warre,   3259
TRUMPET = 2
Now when the angrie Trumpet sounds alarum,   3221
Now let the generall Trumpet blow his blast,   3265
TRUMPETS = 6
Flourish of Trumpets: Then Hoboyes.   2
Sound Trumpets. Enter the King and State, | with Guard, to banish the
Duchesse.   1051
Sound Trumpets, Alarum to the Combattants.   1154
Sound Trumpets. Enter the King, the Queene, | Cardinall, Suffolke,
Somerset, with | Attendants.   1706
Sound Trumpets. Enter King, Queene, and | Somerset on the Tarras.   2848
Sound Drumme and Trumpets, and to London all,   3354
TRUNCHEON = 1
Thy legge a sticke compared with this Truncheon,   2953
TRUNKE = 2
To tell my loue vnto his dumbe deafe trunke,   1846
Leauing thy trunke for Crowes to feed vpon. *Exit.*   2989
TRUST = 2*1
King. Farewell my Lord, trust not the Kentish Rebels   2594
Buc. Trust no body for feare you betraid.   2595
Say. The trust I haue, is in mine innocence,   2596
TRUTH = 5
Warw. Father, the Duke hath told the truth;   987
The truth and innocence of this poore fellow,   1165
Glost. I say no more then truth, so helpe me God.   1420
The Map of Honor, Truth, and Loyaltie: 1504
Cade. And to speake truth, thou deseru'st no lesse.   2521
TRY = 1
Say, we intend to try his Grace to day,   1710
TRYALL = 2
Be brought against me at my Tryall day.   1414
To keepe, vntill your further time of Tryall.   1438
TRYDE = 1
Left I the Court, to see this Quarrell try'de.   1109
TUGGD = 1
And tugg'd for Life, and was by strength subdude.   1877
TULLY = 1
A Romane Sworder, and Bandetto slaue | Murder'd sweet *Tully. Brutus*
Bastard hand   2303
TUMBLE = 1
To tumble downe thy husband, and thy selfe,   322
TUMULTUOUS = 1
Why what tumultuous clamor haue we here?   1949
TUNE = 1
Whose dismall tune bereft my Vitall powres: 1741
TURMOYLED = *1
Iden. Lord, who would liue turmoyled in the Court,   2921
TURND = 3
This Newes I thinke hath turn'd your Weapons edge;   932
thou mayst be turn'd to Hobnailes. | *Heere they Fight.*   2963
My heart is turn'd to stone: and while 'tis mine,   3272

TURNE = 3*2
What, Dost thou turne away, and hide thy face?	1774
Or turne our Sterne vpon a dreadfull Rocke:	1791
So should'st thou eyther turne my flying soule,	2114
*dresse the Common-wealth and turne it, and set a new | nap vpon it.	2324
*that euer I heard. Steele, if thou turne the edge, or	2960

TURNES = 1
| And turnes the force of them vpon thy selfe. | 2047 |

TUT = 2*1
Eli. Tut, this was nothing but an argument,	306
Buck. Tut, these are petty faults to faults vnknowne,	1358
*Cade. Tut, when struck'st thou one blow in the field?	2713

TWAINE = 2
| Was broke in twaine: by whom, I haue forgot, | 300 |
| We twaine will go into his Highnesse Tent. | 3047 |

TWAS = 4
King. Sweet Aunt be quiet, 'twas against her will.	535
'Twas men I lackt, and you will giue them me;	1651
But will suspect, 'twas he that made the slaughter?	1894
Now by my hand (Lords) 'twas a glorious day.	3351

TWELUE = *1
| *Seuen Earles, twelue Barons, & twenty reuerend Bishops | 15 |

TWENTIE = 4
And had I twentie times so many foes,	1236
And each of them had twentie times their power,	1237
Though *Suffolke* dare him twentie thousand times.	1911
Your louing Vnckle, twentie times his worth,	1980

TWENTY = 1*2
*Seuen Earles, twelue Barons, & twenty reuerend Bishops	15
With twenty thousand kisses, and to draine	1844
*one and twenty Fifteenes, and one shilling to the pound, | the last Subsidie.	2655

TWERE = 1
| *Buc.* So please it you my Lord, 'twere not amisse | 3070 |

TWICE = 1
| And twice by aukward winde from Englands banke | 1783 |

TWIGS = 1
| Like Lime-twigs set to catch my winged soule: | 2150 |

TWILL = 1*2
'Twill make them coole in zeale vnto your Grace.	1477
*But. They vse to writ it on the top of Letters: 'Twill | go hard with you.	2417
*Iohn. Masse 'twill be sore Law then, for he was thrust	2642

TWIT = 1
| *Suff.* Hath he not twit our Soueraigne Lady here | 1478 |

TWIXT = 1*1
| His fortunes I will weepe, and 'twixt each groane, | 1522 |
| **King.* Thus stands my state, 'twixt Cade and Yorke \| distrest, | 2884 |

TWO *see also* 2. = 11*2
*To change two Dukedomes for a Dukes faire daughter.	231
Till *Suffolke* gaue two Dukedomes for his Daughter.	473
Enter the Witch, the two Priests, and Bullingbrooke.	619
Enter the Maior of Saint Albones, and his Brethren, | bearing the man betweene two in a Chayre.	795
That beares so shrewd a mayme: two Pulls at once;	1097
Enter two or three running ouer the Stage, from the | Murther of Duke Humfrey.	1690

TWO *cont.*

There's two of you, the Deuill make a third,	2017
Oh go not yet. Euen thus, two Friends condemn'd,	2068
Lath, they haue bene vp these two dayes.	2321
Cade. By her he had two children at one birth. | *Bro.* That's false.	2459

Enter Lord Scales vpon the Tower walking. Then enters \| *two or three Citizens below.* 2598

*and strike off his head, and bring them both vppon two | poles hither.	2744
Call hither to the stake my two braue Beares,	3141

TWO-HAND = 1

Come with thy two-hand Sword.	768

TYDINGS = 1

Buc. Health and glad tydings to your Maiesty.	2857

TYRANNIE = 3

That England was defam'd by Tyrannie.	1423
And proue the Period of their Tyrannie,	1449
Vpon thy eye-balls, murderous Tyrannie	1749

TYRANNY = 1

And lofty proud incroaching tyranny,	2264

TYRANT = 1

And Beautie, that the Tyrant oft reclaimes,	3276

VAINE = 4

You goe about to torture me in vaine.	893
But all in vaine are these meane Obsequies, | *Bed put forth.*	1848
Against the senselesse windes shall grin in vaine,	2245
Whose dreadfull swords were neuer drawne in vaine,	2260

VALE = 1

King. Great is his comfort in this Earthly Vale,	799

VALIANT = 4

But wherefore weepes *Warwicke*, my valiant sonne?	122
Cade. Valiant I am.	2372
Weauer. A must needs, for beggery is valiant.	2373
The People Liberall, Valiant, Actiue, Wealthy,	2697

VALOUR = 3*1

His valour, coine, and people in the warres?	86
Cade. By my Valour: the most compleate Champi-|on	2959
am vanquished by Famine, not by Valour. *Dyes.*	2980
The name of Valour. O let the vile world end,	3262

VANQUISH = 1

Should make a start ore-seas, and vanquish you?	2820

VANQUISHED = 2

The fearfull French, whom you late vanquished	2819
am vanquished by Famine, not by Valour. *Dyes.*	2980

VANQUISHT = 2

Sorrow and griefe haue vanquisht all my powers;	935
And vanquisht as I am, I yeeld to thee, | Or to the meanest Groome.	936

VANTAGES = 1

To match with her that brings no vantages.	138

VASSALL = 1

By such a lowly Vassall as thy selfe.	2279

VAULTING = 1

The pretty vaulting Sea refus'd to drowne me,	1794

VAUNTED = 1

She vaunted 'mongst her Minions t'other day,	470

VAUNTS = 1

And such high vaunts of his Nobilitie,	1344

VAUX = 1*1
  Enter Vaux.   2082
  *Queene. Whether goes *Vaux* so fast? What newes I | prethee?   2083
VAUX = 1
VENGEANCE = 2
  And three-fold Vengeance tend vpon your steps.   2018
  Hot Coales of Vengeance. Let no Souldier flye.   3258
VENGEFULL = 1
  But here's a vengefull Sword, rusted with ease,   1902
VENTURE = 1
  *Glost. 'Masse, thou lou'dst Plummes well, that would'st | venture so.   840
VENTUROUS = 1
  I will reward you for this venturous deed: 1700
VERBE = *1
  *Nowne and a Verbe, and such abhominable wordes, as   2673
VERGE = 1
  Wee will make fast within a hallow'd Verge.   642
VERIE = *1
  *in despight of the diuels and hell, haue through the verie   2837
VERTUE = 2*1
  Noble shee is: but if shee haue forgot | Honor and Vertue, and conuers't
  with such,   946
  Vertue is choakt with foule Ambition,   1443
  *Beuis. O miserable Age: Vertue is not regarded in | Handy-crafts men.   2329
VERTUOUS = 4
  Against my King and Nephew, vertuous *Henry,*   293
  That vertuous Prince, the good Duke *Humfrey:*   1040
  The Duke is vertuous, milde, and too well giuen,   1366
  And let my Soueraigne, vertuous *Henry,*   3040
VERY = 6
  France should haue torne and rent my very hart,   133
  The very trayne of her worst wearing Gowne,   471
  Yet by your leaue, the Winde was very high,   719
  Wife. Too true, and bought his climbing very deare.   839
  Cade more, I thinke he hath a very faire warning.   2626
  That with the very shaking of their Chaines,   3142
VEX = 1
  Queene. Not all these Lords do vex me halfe so much,   461
VICTORIE = 1
  God on our side, doubt not of Victorie.   2829
VICTORIOUS = 2
  Braue *Yorke, Salisbury,* and victorious *Warwicke,*   93
  Yo.Clif. And so to Armes victorious Father,   3211
VICTORY = *2
  *This Monument of the victory will I beare, and the bo-|dies   2522
  *Cade. Iden farewell, and be proud of thy victory: Tell   2977
VIEW = 5*1
  My earnest-gaping-sight of thy Lands view,   1805
  And euen with this, I lost faire Englands view,   1810
  Enter his Chamber, view his breathlesse Corpes,   1834
  *Warw. Come hither gracious Soueraigne, view this | body.   1852
  Oh let me view his Visage being dead,   3063
  Euen to affright thee with the view thereof.   3207
VIGILANCE = 1
  Shall *Henries* Conquest, *Bedfords* vigilance,   103
VILDE = 1
  Great men oft dye by vilde Bezonions.   2302

VILE = 1
The name of Valour. O let the vile world end,   3262
VILLAINE = 5*4
falsely accus'd by the Villaine.   586
Yorke. Base Dunghill Villaine, and Mechanicall,   590
Queene. It made me laugh, to see the Villaine runne.   906
*Small things make base men proud. This Villaine heere,   2274
Cade. Here's a Villaine.   2407
All. He hath confest: away with him: he's a Villaine | and a Traitor.   2424
Cade. Stand villaine, stand, or Ile fell thee downe: he   2434
Staff. Villaine, thy Father was a Playsterer,   2452
*Villaine, thou wilt betray me, and get a 1000. Crownes   2931
VILLAINES = 3
away an honest man for a Villaines accusation.   599
Cut both the Villaines throats, for dy you shall: 2189
Qu. Ah barbarous villaines: Hath this louely face,   2547
VILLANIES = 1
And giuen me notice of their Villanies.   1676
VILLIAGO = 1
Crying *Villiago* vnto all they meete.   2823
VINCERE = 1
Why this is iust, *Aio Aeacida Romanos vincere posso.*   691
VIOLENCE = 1
They will by violence teare him from your Pallace,   1958
VIOLENT = 4
But him out-liue, and dye a violent death.   658
But him out-liue, and dye a violent death.   690
Some violent hands were laid on *Humfries* life: 1840
I do beleeue that violent hands were laid   1860
VIRGINALL = 1
No more will I their Babes, Teares Virginall,   3274
VIRGINS = 1
To force a spotlesse Virgins Chastitie,   3186
VIRTUE *see* vertue
VIRTUOUS *see* vertuous
VISAGE = 1
Oh let me view his Visage being dead,   3063
VITALL = 1
Whose dismall tune bereft my Vitall powres: 1741
VNASSAILD = 1
It greeues my soule to leaue thee vnassail'd. *Exit War.*   3238
VNBLOUDIED = 1
Although the Kyte soare with vnbloudied Beake?   1897
VNBOWED = 1
And passeth by with stiffe vnbowed Knee,   1310
VNBURTHENS = 1
Sharpe *Buckingham* vnburthens with his tongue,   1456
VNCIUILL = 1
Th'vnciuill Kernes of Ireland are in Armes,   1615
VNCKLE = 12*1
King. Vnckle of Winchester, I pray read on.   62
Or hath mine Vnckle *Beauford,* and my selfe,   95
Glo. I Vnckle, we will keepe it, if we can: 114
King. Vnckle, what shall we say to this in law?   600
Good Vnckle hide such mallice: 743
Glost. Faith holy Vnckle, would't were come to that.   757
Glost. True Vnckle, are ye aduis'd?   769

VNCKLE *cont.*

King. Why how now, Vnckle *Gloster?*	772
Ah Vnckle *Humfrey,* in thy face I see	1503
King. Goe call our Vnckle to our presence straight:	1709
Proceed no straiter 'gainst our Vnckle *Gloster,*	1714
Where is our Vnckle? what's the matter, *Suffolke?*	1724
Your louing Vnckle, twentie times his worth,	1980

VNCLE = 1

Be full expyr'd. Thankes Vncle Winchester,	73

VNCONQUERED = *1

*dwell in this house, because the vnconquered soule of | *Cade* is fled.	2969

VNCOUERD = 1

Then stand vncouer'd to the Vulgar Groome.	2296

VNCURABLE = 1

Before the Wound doe grow vncurable;	1589

VNCUREABLE = 1

But flye you must: Vncureable discomfite	3314

VNDER = 8*2

A Spirit rais'd from depth of vnder ground,	354
Vnder the Wings of our Protectors Grace,	423
Vnder the surly *Glosters* Gouernance?	433
Vnder the Countenance and Confederacie	920
Raysing vp wicked Spirits from vnder ground,	926
Vnder the Title of *Iohn Mortimer.*	1665
Vnder the which is writ, *Inuitis nubibus.*	2267
*was he borne, vnder a hedge: for his Father had neuer a | house but	
the Cage.	2370
*well for his life. Away with him, he ha's a Familiar vn-|der	2740
And tread it vnder foot with all contempt,	3209

VNDERGROUND *see* vnder

VNDERNEATH = 1

For vnderneath an Ale-house paltry signe,	3290

VNDERSTAND = 1

As more at large your Grace shall vnderstand.	929

VNDERSTOOD = 1

These Oracles are hardly attain'd, | And hardly vnderstood.	700

VNDERTAKE = 1

And will they vndertake to do me good?	352

VNDER-MINE = 1

Haue hyred me to vnder-mine the Duchesse,	374

VNDISCOUERD = 1

And vndiscouer'd, come to me againe,	1675

VNDOE = 1*1

Doe, or vndoe, as if our selfe were here.	1496
*should vndoe a man. Some say the Bee stings, but I say,	2398

VNDOING = 1

Defacing Monuments of Conquer'd France, | Vndoing all as all had	
neuer bin.	109

VNFEELING = 1

And with my fingers feele his hand, vnfeeling:	1847

VNFOLD = 2

Buck. Such as my heart doth tremble to vnfold:	918
When he to madding *Dido* would vnfold	1817

VNFORTUNATE *see* infortunate

VNGENTLE = 1

King. Vngentle Queene, to call him gentle *Suffolke.*	2004

VNGRACIOUS = 1
  And there cut off thy most vngracious head,   2987
VNHALLOWED = 1
  Let neuer Day nor Night vnhallowed passe,   817
VNHAPPIE = 1
  This get I by his death: Aye me vnhappie,   1770
VNHELPEFULL = 1
  With sad vnhelpefull teares, and with dimn'd eyes;   1519
VNITE = 1
  If Simpathy of Loue vnite our thoughts.   30
VNKINDE = 2
  Nor set no footing on this vnkinde Shore.   1787
  Assure your selues will neuer be vnkinde: 2871
VNKINDNESSE = 1
  With teares as salt as Sea, through thy vnkindnesse.   1796
VNKLE = 1
  King. Vnkle, how now? | *Glo.* Pardon me gracious Lord,   58
VNKNOWNE = 1
  Buck. Tut, these are petty faults to faults vnknowne,   1358
VNLESSE = 6*2
  Vnlesse thou wert more loyall then thou art: 1394
  Vnlesse it were a bloody Murtherer,   1428
  Vnlesse Lord *Suffolke* straight be done to death,   1956
  *mine Honour: vnlesse I finde him guilty he shall not die.   2413
  Vnlesse his teeth be pull'd out.   2650
  Vnlesse you be possest with diuellish spirits,   2709
  *his shoulders, vnlesse he pay me tribute: there shall not 2753
  Vnlesse by robbing of your Friends, and vs.   2817
VNLIKE = 2
  Vnlike the Ruler of a Common-weale.   197
  How prowd, how peremptorie, and vnlike himselfe.   1302
VNLOAD = 1
  To you Duke *Humfrey* must vnload his greefe: 83
VNLOOSE = 1
  Then Yorke vnloose thy long imprisoned thoughts,   3083
VNMEET = 2
  That *Yorke* is most vnmeet of any man.   559
  Yorke. Ile tell thee, *Suffolke*, why I am vnmeet.   560
VNNEATH = 1
  Vnneath may shee endure the Flintie Streets,   1179
VNPOLISHT = 1
  Suff. 'Tis like the Commons, rude vnpolisht Hindes,   1984
VNREUENGD = 1
  She shall not strike Dame *Elianor* vnreueng'd. | *Exit Elianor.* 539
VNSOUNDED = 1
  Vnsounded yet, and full of deepe deceit.   1351
VNSPOTTED = 1
  A Heart vnspotted, is not easily daunted.   1398
VNTAINTED = *1
  King. What stronger Brest-plate then a heart vntainted? 1938
VNTAUGHT = 1
  Vs'd to command, vntaught to pleade for fauour.   2290
VNTILL = 9
  Vntill thy head be circled with the same.   283
  But feare not thou, vntill thy foot be snar'd,   1232
  To keepe, vntill your further time of Tryall.   1438
  Vntill the Golden Circuit on my Head,   1658

VNTILL *cont.*
Vntill they heare the order of his death.	1831
Vntill the Queene his Mistris bury it. *Exit Walter.*	2314
Vntill a power be rais'd to put them downe.	2576
Deferre the spoile of the Citie vntill night:	2769
Vntill his Army be dismist from him.	2894

VNTO = 47*3
*espouse the Lady Margaret, daughter vnto Reignier King of	53
Vnto the poore King *Reignier,* whose large style	118
Nay more, an enemy vnto you all,	156
And looke vnto the maine.	218
Warwicke. Vnto the maine?	219
Vnto the Princes heart of *Calidon*:	247
Aniou and *Maine* both giuen vnto the French?	248
As to vouchsafe one glance vnto the ground.	289
Next time Ile keepe my dreames vnto my selfe, | And not be check'd.	327
You do prepare to ride vnto S.(aint) *Albons,*	332
Was rightfull Heire vnto the English Crowne,	581
As I haue read, layd clayme vnto the Crowne,	1001
Yorke. His eldest Sister, *Anne,* | My Mother, being Heire vnto the Crowne,	1005
Who marryed *Phillip,* sole Daughter | Vnto *Lionel,* Duke of Clarence.	1013
From thence, vnto the place of Execution:	1059
The reuerent care I beare vnto my Lord,	1328
Som. All health vnto my gracious Soueraigne.	1377
Glost. All happinesse vnto my Lord the King:	1391
But mightier Crimes are lay'd vnto your charge,	1434
'Twill make them coole in zeale vnto your Grace.	1477
And put the Englishmen vnto the Sword.	1587
Droue backe againe vnto my Natiue Clime.	1784
But left that hatefull office vnto thee.	1793
To tell my loue vnto his dumbe deafe trunke,	1846
Mischance vnto my State by *Suffolkes* meanes.	1998
Thou wilt but adde encrease vnto my Wrath.	2006
Vaux. To signifie vnto his Maiesty,	2085
Beau. Bring me vnto my Triall when you will.	2142
That layes strong siege vnto this wretches soule,	2156
Vnto the daughter of a worthlesse King,	2249
His body will I beare vnto the King:	2316
For I am rightfull heyre vnto the Crowne.	2451
But. I haue a suite vnto your Lordship.	2637
*Normandie vnto Mounsieur *Basimecu,* the Dolphine of	2662
*France? Be it knowne vnto thee by these presence, euen	2663
This Tongue hath parlied vnto Forraigne Kings | For your behoofe.	2711
Vnto the Commons, whom thou hast misled,	2784
Crying *Villiago* vnto all they meete.	2823
Then you should stoope vnto a Frenchmans mercy.	2825
And he that brings his head vnto the King,	2843
To reconcile you all vnto the King. *Exeunt omnes.*	2847
Or vnto death, to do my Countrey good.	2897
As all things shall redound vnto your good.	2901
Vnto a dunghill, which shall be thy graue,	2986
The King hath yeelded vnto thy demand:	3032
Yorke doth present himselfe vnto your Highnesse.	3052
And neuer liue but true vnto his Liege.	3076
That bowes vnto the graue with mickle age.	3174
King. Hast thou not sworne Allegeance vnto me? | *Sal.* I haue.	3179

VNTO *cont.*
   Sal. It is great sinne, to sweare vnto a sinne: 3182
VNTUTURD = 1
   Some sterne vntutur'd Churle; and Noble Stock   1918
VNWORTHIE = 1
   Whose farre-vnworthie Deputie I am,   2000
VNWORTHY = 3
   Som. If *Somerset* be vnworthy of the Place,   495
   Vnworthy though thou art, Ile cope with thee,   1935
   That were vnworthy to behold the same.   2550
VOCATION = *1
   Hol. True: and yet it is said, Labour in thy Vocati-|on: 2335
VOICE = 1
   Lords, with one cheerefull voice, Welcome my Loue.   43
VOID = 1
   Which makes me hope you are not void of pitty.   2698
VOUCHSAFE = 1
   As to vouchsafe one glance vnto the ground.   289
VOW = 2*1
   *him for his fault the other day, he did vow vpon his   596
   What instance giues Lord Warwicke for his vow.   1863
   Who can be bound by any solemne Vow   3184
VOWED = 1*1
   So mightie are his vowed Enemies.   1521
   War. But both of you were vowed D.(uke) Humfries foes,   1886
VOWES = 2*1
   *Vowes Reformation. There shall be in England, seuen   2383
   And vowes to Crowne himselfe in Westminster.   2567
   To entertaine my vowes of thankes and praise.   2866
VOYCE = 2
   Clapping their hands, and crying with loud voyce,   167
   And many time and oft my selfe haue heard a Voyce, | To call him so.   828
VOYDING = 1
   How in our voyding Lobby hast thou stood,   2229
VP = 40*4
   Deliuer vp my Title in the Queene   19
   Deliuer'd vp againe with peacefull words? | *Mort Dieu.*   129
   And hauing both together heau'd it vp,   286
   Seale vp your Lips, and giue no words but Mum,   365
   And Spirits walke, and Ghosts breake vp their Graues;   639
   Away with them, let them be clapt vp close,   680
   Glost. Make vp no factious numbers for the matter,   759
   Had not your man put vp the Fowle so suddenly, | We had had more
   sport.   766
   Raysing vp wicked Spirits from vnder ground,   926
   Ere thou goe, giue vp thy Staffe,   1077
   Giue vp your Staffe, Sir, and the King his Realme.   1086
   And in thy Closet pent vp, rue my shame,   1200
   Mayl'd vp in shame, with Papers on my back,   1207
   And with your best endeuour haue stirr'd vp   1463
   And as the Damme runnes lowing vp and downe,   1515
   To signifie, that Rebels there are vp,   1586
   I will stirre vp in England some black Storme,   1655
   Som. Rere vp his Body, wring him by the Nose.   1732
   That want their Leader, scatter vp and downe,   1828
   And he but naked, though lockt vp in Steele,   1940
   And cry out for thee to close vp mine eyes: 2112

VP *cont.*

 Hold vp thy hand, make signall of thy hope.   2162
 Close vp his eyes, and draw the Curtaine close,   2166
 Whit. The Duke of Suffolke, muffled vp in ragges?   2215
 Now will I dam vp this thy yawning mouth,   2241
 As hating thee, and rising vp in armes.   2261
 The Commons heere in Kent are vp in armes,   2268
 Lath, they haue bene vp these two dayes.   2321
 *it was neuer merrie world in England, since Gentlemen | came vp.   2327
 Clearke. Sir I thanke God, I haue bin so well brought | vp, that I can
 write my name.   2422
 Rise vp Sir *Iohn Mortimer.* Now haue at him.   2439
 *it vp. Fellow-Kings, I tell you, that that Lord *Say* hath   2484
 Proclaime them Traitors that are vp with *Cade,*   2497
 Be hang'd vp for example at their doores: 2500
 *What canst thou answer to my Maiesty, for giuing vp of   2661
 Are my Chests fill'd vp with extorted Gold?   2732
 *When shall we go to Cheapside, and take vp commodi-|ties vpon our
 billes?   2759
 Least they consult about the giuing vp   2767
 Cade. Vp Fish-streete, downe Saint Magnes corner,   2775
 Fling vp his cap, and say, God saue his Maiesty.   2791
 Oh I could hew vp Rockes, and fight with Flint,   3016
 King. *Iden,* kneele downe, rise vp a Knight: 3072
 Heere is hand to hold a Scepter vp,   3097
 Then any thou canst coniure vp to day: 3199
VPBRAYDED = 1
 Be thus vpbrayded, chid, and rated at,   1475
VPON = 42*6
 And humbly now vpon my bended knee,   17
 Nor weare the Diadem vpon his head,   258
 And smooth my way vpon their headlesse neckes.   340
 Elianor. It is enough, Ile thinke vpon the Questions: 357
 And set the Triple Crowne vpon his Head;   449
 Buck. Thy Crueltie in execution | Vpon Offendors, hath exceeded Law,   522
 *him for his fault the other day, he did vow vpon his   596
 *O Lord haue mercy vpon me, I shall neuer be able to | fight a blow: O
 Lord my heart.   612
 Safer shall he be vpon the sandie Plaines,   663
 Yorke. Lay hands vpon these Traytors, and their trash: 671
 A pretty Plot, well chosen to build vpon.   686
 Safer shall he be vpon the sandie Plaines,   697
 Armorer. Masters, I am come hither as it were vpon   1147
 Trowest thou, that ere Ile looke vpon the World,   1214
 To thinke vpon my Pompe, shall be my Hell.   1217
 No, it will hang vpon my richest Robes,   1289
 Immediately he was vpon his Knee,   1305
 Vpon my Life began her diuellish practises: 1340
 The enuious Load that lyes vpon his heart: 1457
 I know, no paine they can inflict vpon him,   1683
 Vpon thy eye-balls, murderous Tyrannie   1749
 Looke not vpon me, for thine eyes are wounding;   1751
 Was I for this nye wrack'd vpon the Sea,   1782
 Or turne our Sterne vpon a dreadfull Rocke: 1791
 I stood vpon the Hatches in the storme: 1803
 And comment then vpon his sodaine death.   1835
 Vpon his face an Ocean of salt teares,   1845

VPON   *cont.*

With that dread King that tooke our state vpon him,	1858
Vpon the life of this thrice-famed Duke.	1861
Set all vpon me, mightie Soueraigne.	1951
And three-fold Vengeance tend vpon your steps.	2018
Suf. A plague vpon them: wherefore should I cursse | them?	2023
And turnes the force of them vpon thy selfe.	2047
That thou might'st thinke vpon these by the Seale,	2059
Ile giue a thousand pound to looke vpon him.	2147
Looke with a gentle eye vpon this Wretch,	2154
Vpon these paltry, seruile, abiect Drudges:	2273
And sooner dance vpon a bloody pole,	2295
*dresse the Common-wealth and turne it, and set a new | nap vpon it.	2324
Enter Lord Scales vpon the Tower walking. Then enters | two or three	
Citizens below.	2598
And heere sitting vpon London Stone,	2616
Cade. I haue thought vpon it, it shall bee so. Away,	2646
*When shall we go to Cheapside, and take vp commodi-|ties vpon our	
billes?	2759
Leauing thy trunke for Crowes to feed vpon. *Exit.*	2989
Yorke. Vpon thine Honor is he Prisoner?	3034
Buck. Vpon mine Honor he is Prisoner.	3035
And that Ile write vpon thy Burgonet,	3200
So beare I thee vpon my manly shoulders:	3285

VPPON = *2

*and strike off his head, and bring them both vppon two | poles hither.	2744
*make shift for one, and so Gods Cursse light vppon you | all.	2807

VPREARD = 1

His hayre vprear'd, his nostrils stretcht with strugling:	1875

VPRIGHT = 1*1

Him capre vpright, like a wilde Morisco,	1671
*Combe downe his haire; looke, looke, it stands vpright,	2149

VS   *see also* let's *l.**68 78 180 181 190 *334 *628 *631 681 803 952 1055
1164 1167 1228 1297 1311 1360 1374 1486 1536 1629 1802 1859 2167
2256 2310 *2355 2508 2526 2580 *2592 *2654 *2727 2770 2794 2817
*3049 3074 3123 3233 3302 3348 3355 = 35*9

VSD = 4*1

There to be vs'd according to your State.	1275
And shall I then be vs'd reproachfully?	1277
According to that State you shall be vs'd.	1279
Vs'd to command, vntaught to pleade for fauour.	2290
*Score and the Tally, thou hast caused printing to be vs'd,	2669

VSE = 3*2

You vse her well: the World may laugh againe,	1260
Or any Groat I hoorded to my vse,	1413
But. They vse to writ it on the top of Letters: 'Twill | go hard with	
you.	2417
Cade. Let me alone: Dost thou vse to write thy name?	2419
Is his to vse, so Somerset may die.	3045

VSUALLY = *1

*that thou hast men about thee, that vsually talke of a	2672

VSURPE = 1

Nor shall proud Lancaster vsurpe my right,	256

VSURPER = 3

said, That he was, and that the King was an Vsurper.	416
And that your Maiestie was an Vsurper.	582
And calles your Grace Vsurper, openly,	2566

VTTERLY = 1
  Is vtterly bereft you: all is lost.   1381
VULGAR = 1
  Then stand vncouer'd to the Vulgar Groome.   2296
W = *1
  *Lieu. Water: W. Come Suffolke, I must waft thee | to thy death.   2283
WAFT = 1*1
  I charge thee waft me safely crosse the Channell.   2282
  *Lieu. Water: W. Come Suffolke, I must waft thee | to thy death.   2283
WAITED = 1
  How often hast thou waited at my cup,   2224
WAKE = 1
  Watch thou, and wake when others be asleepe,   261
WAKING = 3
  By day, by night; waking, and in my dreames,   33
  Sleeping, or Waking, 'tis no matter how,   1565
  Suff. Thou shalt be waking, while I shed thy blood,   1932
WAKT = 1
  It were but necessarie you were wak't: 1973
WAL = 1*1
WALES = 1
  The first, *Edward* the Black-Prince, Prince of Wales;   970
WALKE = 2
  And Spirits walke, and Ghosts breake vp their Graues;   639
  In this close Walke, to satisfie my selfe,   962
WALKES = 1
  And may enioy such quiet walkes as these?   2922
WALKING = 2
  With walking once about the Quadrangle,   548
  Enter Lord Scales vpon the Tower walking. Then enters | two or three
  Citizens below.   2598
WALL = *1
  *could stay no longer. Wherefore on a Bricke wall haue   2911
WALLES = 1
  Climbing my walles inspight of me the Owner,   2939
WALTER see also Wal., Water = 5
  The other *Walter Whitmore* is thy share.   2183
  Whit. And so am I: my name is *Walter Whitmore.*   2200
  Whit. Gualtier or *Walter,* which it is I care not,   2207
  Manet the first Gent. Enter Walter with the body.   2312
  Vntill the Queene his Mistris bury it. *Exit Walter.*   2314
WAND = 1
  And on the peeces of the broken Wand   302
WANDERING = 1
  Rul'd like a wandering Plannet ouer me,   2548
WANT = 5*2
  And choake the Herbes for want of Husbandry.   1327
  I shall not want false Witnesse, to condemne me,   1468
  But yet we want a Colour for his death: 1538
  That want their Leader, scatter vp and downe,   1828
  As one that surfets, thinking on a want: 2063
  *no want of resolution in mee, but onely my Followers   2839
  Clif. Nor should thy prowesse want praise & esteeme,   3243
WANTST = 1
  Why art thou old, and want'st experience?   3171
WAR = 1
  It greeues my soule to leaue thee vnassail'd. *Exit War.*   3238

WAR = 12*5
WARD = 1
I know ere they will haue me go to Ward,   3107
WARLIKE = 1
That dims the Honor of this Warlike Isle: 132
WARME = 1
I feare me, you but warme the starued Snake,   1649
WARNING = 3
What boaded this? but well fore-warning winde   1785
Cade more, I thinke he hath a very faire warning.   2626
I seeke not to waxe great by others warning,   2925
WARRANT = 1*2
Cade. Feare not that I warrant thee. Come, let's march | towards
London. *Exeunt.*   2528
See where they come, Ile warrant they'l make it good.   3118
Old Clif. The first I warrant thee, if dreames proue true   3195
WARRE = 5*1
Your Deeds of Warre, and all our Counsell dye?   104
Rather then bloody Warre shall cut them short,   2544
Wilt thou go digge a graue to finde out Warre,   3169
Yor. Thus Warre hath giuen thee peace, for y art still,   3250
Where it should guard. O Warre, thou sonne of hell,   3255
He that is truly dedicate to Warre,   3259
WARRES = 1
His valour, coine, and people in the warres?   86
WARW = 9*6
WARWICK = 6*4
Salisbury and *Warwick* are no simple Peeres.   460
Inuite my Lords of Salisbury and Warwick   712
·   *Enter Yorke, Salisbury, and Warwick.*   959
Yorke. Now my good Lords of Salisbury & Warwick,   960
Warw. My heart assures me, that the Earle of Warwick   1045
Richard shall liue to make the Earle of Warwick   1048
King. That he is dead good Warwick, 'tis too true,   1832
Warw. What dares not *Warwick*, if false *Suffolke* dare | him?   1907
Suff. The trayt'rous *Warwick*, with the men of Bury,   1950
Yor. Hold Warwick: seek thee out some other chace   3234
WARWICKE see also War., Warw. = 25*6
*Enter King, Duke Humfrey, Salisbury, Warwicke, and Beau-|ford on
the one side.*   3
Gloster, Yorke, Buckingham, Somerset, | Salisburie, and Warwicke.   74
Braue *Yorke, Salisbury,* and victorious *Warwicke,*   93
But wherefore weepes *Warwicke,* my valiant sonne?   122
Warwicke my sonne, the comfort of my age,   198
War. So God helpe Warwicke, as he loues the Land,   213
*That *Maine,* which by maine force Warwicke did winne,   221
Exit Warwicke, and Salisbury. Manet Yorke.   225
Yorke, Salisbury, Warwicke, | *and the Duchesse.*   489
Card. Ambitious *Warwicke,* let thy betters speake.   499
Buck. All in this presence are thy betters, *Warwicke.*   501
Warw. Warwicke may liue to be the best of all.   502
Suff. Peace head-strong *Warwicke.*   570
Yorke, Buckingham, Salisbury, and Warwicke, | *to the Parliament.*   1293
Noyse within. Enter Warwicke, and many | *Commons.*   1822
What instance giues Lord Warwicke for his vow.   1863
Suf. Why Warwicke, who should do the D.(uke) to death?   1883
Enter Suffolke and Warwicke, with their | *Weapons drawne.*   1944

319

WARWICKE cont.

Come *Warwicke*, come good *Warwicke*, goe with mee,	2012
*Enter the King, Salisbury, and Warwicke, to the	Cardinal in bed.*	2132
The Princely Warwicke, and the *Neuils* all,	2259
Bid Salsbury and Warwicke come to me.	3144
*Enter the Earles of Warwicke, and	Salisbury.*	3145
If you oppose your selues to match Lord Warwicke.	3155
* King. Why Warwicke, hath thy knee forgot to bow?	3161
Enter Warwicke.	3218
* War. Clifford of Cumberland, 'tis Warwicke calles:	3219
Warwicke is hoarse with calling thee to armes.	3225
*Alarum. Retreat. Enter Yorke, Richard, Warwicke,	and Soldiers, with Drum & Colours.*	3319
What sayes Lord Warwicke, shall we after them?	3349

WARWICKE = 1
WARWICKSHIRE = 1

Say, if thou dar'st, prowd Lord of Warwickshire,	1905

WAS *see also* 'twas = 68*11
WASH = 1

To wash away my wofull Monuments.	2057

WASHES = 1

furr'd Packe, she washes buckes here at home.	2367

WAST *l.*1928 3267 = 2, 1

Duch. Was't I? yea, I it was, prowd French-woman:	532

WATCH = 4

Yet let vs watch the haughtie Cardinall,	181
Watch thou, and wake when others be asleepe,	261
To watch the comming of my punisht Duchesse:	1178
To sit and watch me as *Ascanius* did,	1816

WATCHING = *1

* Say. These cheekes are pale for watching for your good	2718

WATCHT = 2*1

Beldam I thinke we watcht you at an ynch.	672
* Yorke. Lord *Buckingham*, me thinks you watcht her well:	685
So helpe me God, as I haue watcht the Night,	1410

WATER = 5*1

Spirit. By Water shall he dye, and take his end.	660
By Water shall he dye, and take his end.	694
Smooth runnes the Water, where the Brooke is deepe,	1347
And told me that by Water I should dye:	2204
* Lieu. Water: W. Come Suffolke, I must waft thee	to thy death.	2283
Pompey the Great, and *Suffolke* dyes by Pyrats.	*Exit Water with Suffolke.*	2306

WAXE = 1*1

* 'tis the Bees waxe: for I did but seale once to a thing, and	2399
I seeke not to waxe great by others warning,	2925

WAXEN = 1

What? Art thou like the Adder waxen deafe?	1776

WAY = 8*2

And smooth my way vpon their headlesse neckes.	340
* will come this way by and by, and then wee may	387
and the good Wine in thy Masters way.	1159
Goe, leade the way, I long to see my Prison. *Exeunt.*	1291
Looking the way her harmelesse young one went,	1516
This way fall I to death.	2130
Qu. This way for me. *Exeunt*	2131
* me. My sword make way for me, for heere is no staying:	2836

WAY *cont.*
Is straight way calme, and boorded with a Pyrate. 2887
To giue the enemy way, and to secure vs 3302
WAYLE = 1
And can doe naught but wayle her Darlings losse; 1517
WAYTED = 1
And duly wayted for my comming forth? 2230
WE = 84*12
WEA = 1*3
WEAKE = 1
Till *Henry* be more weake, and I more strong. 3023
WEALE = 3
Vnlike the Ruler of a Common-weale. 197
That smooth'st it so with King and Common-weale. 739
How I haue lou'd my King, and Common-weale: 943
WEALTH = 5*1
The Common-wealth hath dayly run to wrack, 514
I come to talke of Common-wealth Affayres. 549
Hauing neyther Subiect, Wealth, nor Diadem: 2250
*dresse the Common-wealth and turne it, and set a new | nap vpon it. 2324
Haue I affected wealth, or honor? Speake. 2731
Or gather wealth I care not with what enuy: 2926
WEALTHY = 2
And all the wealthy Kingdomes of the West, 161
The People Liberall, Valiant, Actiue, Wealthy, 2697
WEAPON = 2
Yorke. Take away his Weapon: Fellow thanke God, 1158
Shake he his weapon at vs, and passe by. 2794
WEAPONS = 6*1
His Weapons, holy Sawes of sacred Writ, 444
This Newes I thinke hath turn'd your Weapons edge; 932
You put sharpe Weapons in a mad-mans hands. 1653
Enter Suffolke and Warwicke, with their | Weapons drawne. 1944
Your wrathfull Weapons drawne, 1947
Mark'd for the Gallowes: Lay your Weapons downe, 2443
Rich. And if words will not, then our Weapons shal. 3137
WEARE = 6*2
Nor weare the Diadem vpon his head, 258
Though in this place most Master weare no Breeches, 538
As thus to name the seuerall Colours we doe weare. 874
Suff. I weare no Knife, to slaughter sleeping men, 1901
Cade. Marry, thou ought'st not to let thy horse weare 2682
*proudest Peere in the Realme, shall not weare a head on 2752
But thou shalt weare it as a Heralds coate, 2975
This day Ile weare aloft my Burgonet, 3204
WEARING = 1
The very trayne of her worst wearing Gowne, 471
WEATHER = 1*1
*a mans stomacke this hot weather: and I think this word 2914
But I must make faire weather yet a while, 3022
WEAUER see also Wea. = 1*1
Hol. And Smith the Weauer. | *Beu.* Argo, their thred of life is spun. 2347
*Drumme. Enter Cade, Dicke Butcher, Smith the Weauer, | and a
Sawyer, with infinite numbers.* 2350
WEAUER = 1*2
WEAUES = 1
Weaues tedious Snares to trap mine Enemies. 1646

WEDDED = 1
And wedded be thou to the Hagges of hell,   2247
WEE *l.*387 *588 *627 641 642 *1991 *2352 = 2*5
WEED = 1
So one by one wee'le weed them all at last,   485
WEEDS = 1
Now 'tis the Spring, and Weeds are shallow-rooted,   1325
WEEL = 7*2
Wee'l quickly hoyse Duke *Humfrey* from his seat.   176
Wee'l both together lift our heads to heauen,   287
Butcher. And furthermore, wee'l haue the Lord *Sayes*   2480
All. No, no, and therefore wee'l haue his head.   2493
All. Wee'l follow *Cade*,   2809
Wee'l follow *Cade*.   2810
Wee'l follow the King, and Clifford.   2831
Follow me souldiers, wee'l deuise a meane,   2846
Clif. Are these thy Beares? Wee'l bate thy Bears to death,   3147
WEELE = 4*2
Wee'le see these things effected to the full.   359
*presently: wee'le heare more of your matter before | the King. *Exit*.   420
So one by one wee'le weed them all at last,   485
Somerset, wee'le see thee sent away. | *Flourish. Exeunt*.   617
Wee'le see your Trinkets here all forth-comming. | *All away. Exit*.   683
Seru. So please your Grace, wee'le take her from the | Sherife.   1191
WEENING = 2
Whose ouer-weening Arme I haue pluckt back,   1459
Rich. Oft haue I seene a hot ore-weening Curre,   3150
WEEPE = 3
His fortunes I will weepe, and 'twixt each groane,   1522
Thinke therefore on reuenge, and cease to weepe.   2535
But who can cease to weepe, and looke on this.   2536
WEEPES = 3
But wherefore weepes *Warwicke*, my valiant sonne?   122
Weepes ouer them, and wrings his haplesse hands,   238
For *Henry* weepes, that thou dost liue so long.   1821
WEEPING = 2
Makes me from Wondring, fall to Weeping ioyes,   41
I would be blinde with weeping, sicke with grones,   1762
WEIGHTIE = 2
With thy Confederates in this weightie cause. | *Exit Elianor*.   361
What counsaile giue you in this weightie cause?   1592
WEIGHTY = 1
Car. This weighty businesse will not brooke delay,   177
WEL = 1
Buc. Yorke, if thou meanest wel, I greet thee well.   3006
WELCOME = 3*3
King. Suffolke arise. Welcome Queene *Margaret*,   24
Lords, with one cheerefull voice, Welcome my Loue.   43
Elianor. Well said my Masters, and welcome all: To   633
Elianor. Welcome is Banishment, welcome were my | Death.   1067
King. Welcome Lord *Somerset*: What Newes from | France?   1378
WELFARE = 1
Take heed, my Lord, the welfare of vs all,   1374
WELL = 40*15
King. They please vs well. Lord Marques kneel down,   68
The Peeres agreed, and *Henry* was well pleas'd,   230
Well, so it stands: and thus I feare at last,   380

WELL *cont.*

Elianor. Well said my Masters, and welcome all: To	633
See you well guerdon'd for these good deserts.	676
*Yorke. Lord *Buckingham*, me thinks you watcht her well:	685
A pretty Plot, well chosen to build vpon.	686
Well, to the rest: | Tell me what fate awaits the Duke of Suffolke?	692
My Lord Protectors Hawkes doe towre so well,	726
Suff. No mallice Sir, no more then well becomes	745
*Card. Medice teipsum, Protector see to't well, protect | your selfe.	777
*Glost. 'Masse, thou lou'dst Plummes well, that would'st | venture so.	840
In my opinion, yet thou seest not well.	847
*Glost. Why that's well said: What Colour is my | Gowne of?	853
Thou might'st as well haue knowne all our Names,	873
*Glost. Well Sir, we must haue you finde your Legges.	895
King. Well, for this Night we will repose vs here:	952
**in a Cup of Sack; and feare not Neighbor, you shall doe | well enough.	1121
* Salisb. Thumpe? Then see thou thumpe thy Master | well.	1145
This is close dealing. Well, I will be there.	1250
You vse her well: the World may laugh againe,	1260
Suff. Well hath your Highnesse seene into this Duke:	1336
The Duke is vertuous, milde, and too well giuen,	1366
Glost. Well *Suffolke*, thou shalt not see me blush,	1396
Card. It serues you well, my Lord, to say so much.	1419
*Glost. Why 'tis well known, that whiles I was Protector,	1424
The ancient Prouerbe will be well effected,	1470
And well such losers may haue leaue to speake.	1485
Say you consent, and censure well the deed,	1577
Well Nobles, well: 'tis politikely done,	1647
I take it kindly: yet be well assur'd,	1652
To make Commotion, as full well he can,	1664
*Suff. Why that's well said. Goe, get you to my House,	1699
Haue you layd faire the Bed? Is all things well,	1702
What boaded this? but well fore-warning winde	1785
His well proportion'd Beard, made ruffe and rugged,	1879
And 'tis well seene, he found an enemy.	1889
Well could I curse away a Winters night,	2050
I will repeale thee, or be well assur'd,	2064
*Hol. So he had need, for 'tis thred-bare. Well, I say,	2326
Butch. I knew her well, she was a Midwife.	2362
*Clearke. Sir I thanke God, I haue bin so well brought | vp, that I can write my name.	2422
Bro. Well, seeing gentle words will not preuayle,	2494
*Cade. Well, hee shall be beheaded for it ten times:	2658
**well for his life. Away with him, he ha's a Familiar vn-|der	2740
Let them kisse one another: For they lou'd well	2765
**And shew'd how well you loue your Prince & Countrey:	2868
And sends the poore well pleased from my gate.	2928
**broach'd, and beard thee to. Looke on mee well, I haue	2942
Buc. Yorke, if thou meanest wel, I greet thee well.	3006
Euen of the bonnie beast he loued so well.	3231
(As well we may, if not through your neglect)	3307
* Sal. Now by my Sword, well hast thou fought to day:	3337
Well Lords, we haue not got that which we haue,	3342

WENT = 2*1

Sal. Pride went before, Ambition followes him.	188
Looking the way her harmelesse young one went,	1516
**the fift, (in whose time, boyes went to Span-counter	2477

323

WER *l.**312 = *1
WERE *see also* 'twere *l.*121 124 195 303 338 368 450 526 580 583 *588 734
  *757 *1067 *1147 1241 1341 1427 1428 1493 1496 1533 1540 1550 1569
  1602 1669 1694 1766 1840 1851 1860 1882 *1886 1971 1973 1986 2091
  2106 2117 2118 2254 2260 2272 2550 2577 *2676 2766 3071
  *3196 = 45*7
WERT *l.*205 513 812 941 1082 1394 2074 = 7, 2*1

Wer't not all one, an emptie Eagle were set,	1550
Suff. Madame 'tis true: and wer't not madnesse then,	1554
Wer't not a shame, that whilst you liue at iarre,	2818

WEST = 1

And all the wealthy Kingdomes of the West,	161

WESTMINSTER = 2

In the Cathedrall Church of Westminster,	311
And vowes to Crowne himselfe in Westminster.	2567

WET = 1

Nor let the raine of heauen wet this place,	2056

WHAT *l.*85 91 *111 165 208 232 280 285 *296 305 325 346 349 400 *413
  432 508 529 *576 600 624 *653 *655 659 661 *673 679 688 693 695 721
  722 740 782 785 786 *788 805 808 818 830 837 *850 *853 *856 *900 917
  *938 945 1017 1143 *1263 1297 1300 1318 *1378 1407 1432 *1495 *1497
  1507 1592 *1610 1614 1622 1639 1694 1739 1765 1774 1776 1785 1788
  1851 1863 *1907 *1938 1943 1949 *2083 2097 2106 2119 2139 2184
  *2187 2199 2201 2287 2300 *2414 2455 2472 *2539 *2561 *2574 *2661
  2681 2688 *2716 2778 2787 *2796 2826 2842 2926 2958 *3053 3067
  *3122 3138 3164 3227 3239 *3300 3303 3349 = 87*33
WHATERE *see* ere
WHATS = 8*3

*What's yours? What's heere? Against the Duke of	405
Glost. Tell me Sirrha, what's my Name? | *Simpc.* Alas Master, I know	
not.	862
Glost. What's his Name? | *Simpc.* I know not.	864
Glost. What's thine owne Name? | *Simpc. Saunder Simpcoxe*, and if it	
please you, Master.	868
Sirrha, what's thy Name? | *Peter. Peter* forsooth.	1141
Sirs, what's a Clock? | *Seru.* Tenne, my Lord.	1175
**Qu.* Ah what's more dangerous, then this fond affiance?	1368
For what's more miserable then Discontent?	1502
Where is our Vnckle? what's the matter, *Suffolke?*	1724
And aske him what's the reason of these Armes:	2891

WHATSOERE = 1

Iden. Why rude Companion, whatsoere thou be,	2935

WHEELES = 1

That erst did follow thy prowd Chariot-Wheeles,	1184

WHEN *l.*152 205 251 254 261 292 358 436 *595 637 638 758 782 838 1082
  1092 1185 1211 1308 1312 1313 1323 1349 1512 1802 1804 1817 1873
  2008 2142 2210 2223 2226 *2387 2465 *2509 *2678 *2683 2703 *2713
  *2747 *2759 2766 2780 *2917 2973 3221 = 38*9
WHENCE = 1*1

Till they come to Barwick, from whence they came. | *Exit.*	910
*Sent his poore Queene to France, from whence she came,	984

WHERE *l.**312 313 333 343 664 698 761 812 985 1100 1273 1347 1724
  1900 2052 2077 2079 2111 2140 2143 2146 2240 *2524 3118 3166 3168
  3255 3308 3309 3332 3335 = 30*2, 2*1

That they will guard you, where you will, or no,	1977
Can I make men liue where they will or no?	2144
**Say.* Heare me but speake, and beare mee wher'e you | will:	2692

WHEREAS *see also* where = *1
  *the Realme, in erecting a Grammar Schoole: and where-|as   2667
WHEREFORE = 3*2
  But wherefore weepes *Warwicke*, my valiant sonne?   122
  **Suf*. A plague vpon them: wherefore should I cursse | them?   2023
  But wherefore greeue I at an houres poore losse,   2098
  *could stay no longer. Wherefore on a Bricke wall haue   2911
  Or wherefore doest abuse it, if thou hast it?   3172
WHEREIN = 3
  Who can accuse me? wherein am I guiltie?   1401
  *Alarums to the fight, wherein both the Staffords are slaine. | Enter Cade
  and the rest.*   2511
  Say. Tell me: wherein haue I offended most?   2730
WHEREOF = 3
  By meanes whereof, the Townes each day reuolted.   1357
  By meanes whereof, his Highnesse hath lost France.   1405
  Whereof you cannot easily purge your selfe.   1435
WHERES = 4*1
  Iniurious Duke, that threatest where's no cause.   678
  **Qu*. Are you the Butcher, *Suffolk*? where's your Knife?   1899
  Mich. Where's our Generall?   2430
  Cade. Where's Dicke, the Butcher of Ashford? | *But*. Heere sir.   2513
  But where's the body that I should imbrace?   2538
WHERESOERE = 1
  For wheresoere thou art in this worlds Globe,   2123
WHEREWITH = 1
  Knowledge the Wing wherewith we flye to heauen.   2708
WHERE-ERE *see* wher'e
WHET = 1
  And whet not on these furious Peeres,   753
WHETHER *see also* where = 1*1
  Warw. Whether your Grace be worthy, yea or no,   497
  **Queene*. Whether goes *Vaux* so fast? What newes I | prethee?   2083
WHICH *l.**221 224 279 491 964 *989 1166 1331 *1359 1567 1678 1687
  1870 2190 2207 2267 *2336 2498 *2654 2698 *2913 2986 2988 3002 3090
  3303 3342 = 21*6
WHILE = 11*3
  While these do labour for their owne preferment,   189
  While they do tend the profit of the Land.   212
  While as the silly Owner of the goods   237
  While all is shar'd, and all is borne away,   240
  While his owne Lands are bargain'd for, and sold: 243
  Then Yorke be still a-while, till time do serue: 260
  While Gloster beares this base and humble minde.   337
  **Hume*, that you be by her aloft, while wee be busie be-|low;   627
  Suff. Thou shalt be waking, while I shed thy blood,   1932
  *picke a Sallet another while, which is not amisse to coole   2913
  **Iden*. Nay, it shall nere be said, while England stands,   2946
  But I must make faire weather yet a while,   3022
  That I haue giuen no answer all this while: 3025
  My heart is turn'd to stone: and while 'tis mine,   3272
WHILES = 3*1
  **Glost*. Why 'tis well known, that whiles I was Protector,   1424
  Whiles I take order for mine owne affaires.   1625
  Whiles I in Ireland nourish a mightie Band,   1654
  'Tis but surmiz'd, whiles thou art standing by,   2062

WHILEST = 2
    For whilest I thinke I am thy married Wife,   1204
    As he stood by, whilest I, his forlorne Duchesse,   1221
WHILST = 3
    For whilst our Pinnace Anchors in the Downes,   2178
    And yeeld to mercy, whil'st 'tis offered you,   2788
    Wer't not a shame, that whilst you liue at iarre,   2818
WHIPPE = *1
    *Sirrha Beadle, whippe him till he leape ouer that same | Stoole.   896
WHIPPES = 2
    Haue you not Beadles in your Towne, | And Things call'd Whippes?   883
    Enter a Beadle with Whippes.   894
WHIPPING = *1
    *Now Sirrha, if you meane to saue your selfe from Whip-|ping,   890
WHIPT = 1*1
    Glost. Let the(m) be whipt through euery Market Towne,   909
    * *But.* No question of that: for I haue seene him whipt | three Market
    dayes together.   2375
WHISPERS = 1
    And whispers to his pillow, as to him,   2092
WHIT = 3*1
WHITE = 2
    Then will I raise aloft the Milke-white-Rose,   266
    Enter the Duchesse in a white Sheet, and a Taper   1188
WHITE-HEART = *1
    *you should leaue me at the White-heart in Southwarke.   2800
WHITHER *see also* whether = 1
    I care not whither, for I begge no fauor;   1272
WHITM = 1
WHITMORE see also Whit., Whitm. = 3
    The other *Walter Whitmore* is thy share.   2183
    Whit. And so am I: my name is *Walter Whitmore.*   2200
    Suf. Stay *Whitmore*, for thy Prisoner is a Prince, | The Duke of
    Suffolke, *William de la Pole.*   2213
WHO *l.*417 513 747 825 979 997 1003 1008 1012 1013 1373 1401 1492
    1556 1583 1650 1829 1868 *1883 *1892 1895 2174 2246 2536 *2727 2790
    2792 *2921 2996 3056 3152 3184 3321 3322 = 30*4
WHOLE = 5
    That Suffolke should demand a whole Fifteenth,   140
    2. Pet. Alas Sir, I am but a poore Petitioner of our | whole Towneship.   408
    You made in a day, my Lord, whole Townes to flye.   915
    Mens flesh preseru'd so whole, doe seldome winne.   1604
    in the mouth with a Speare, and 'tis not whole yet.   2643
WHOM *l.*300 641 925 972 1070 *2060 2450 2734 2784 2819 2883 3004
    3061 3100 3256 = 14*1
WHOS = 2*1
    Who's within there, hoe?   710
    Say, who's a Traytor? *Gloster* he is none. *Exit.*   1523
    *I was neuer mine owne man since. How now? Who's | there?   2400
WHOSE = 20*4
    Vnto the poore King *Reignier*, whose large style   118
    Whose Church-like humors fits not for a Crowne.   259
    With whose sweet smell the Ayre shall be perfum'd,   267
    Whose bookish Rule, hath pull'd faire England downe. | *Exit Yorke.*   271
    Whose name and power thou tremblest at,   650
    *Whose Beame stands sure, whose rightful cause preuailes. | *Flourish.*
    Exeunt.   957

WHOSE *cont.*

From whose Line I clayme the Crowne,	995
Death, at whose Name I oft haue beene afear'd,	1269
Whose ouer-weening Arme I haue pluckt back,	1459
Whose floud begins to flowe within mine eyes;	1500
Whose dismall tune bereft my Vitall powres:	1741
Was graft with Crab-tree slippe, whose Fruit thou art,	1919
Whose Conscience with Iniustice is corrupted.	1941
With whose inuenomed and fatall sting,	1979
Whose farre-vnworthie Deputie I am,	2000
Suf. Thy name affrights me, in whose sound is death:	2202
Lieu. Poole, Sir *Poole*? Lord, | I kennell, puddle, sinke, whose filth and dirt	2238
Whose dreadfull swords were neuer drawne in vaine,	2260
Burnes with reuenging fire, whose hopefull colours	2265
Lieu. And as for these whose ransome we haue set,	2308
*the fift, (in whose time, boyes went to Span-counter	2477
As for words, whose greatnesse answer's words,	2957
Whose Smile and Frowne, like to *Achilles* Speare	3095

WHY *l.*172 *274 276 278 504 560 *571 691 748 *750 772 *853 *856 1083 *1095 1241 1274 *1424 1621 1686 *1699 1723 1756 1779 *1883 1946 1949 2100 2201 *2561 2725 *2858 2935 2936 3011 3027 3086 3138 *3161 3171 3240 = 30*12

WICKED = 2*1

Raysing vp wicked Spirits from vnder ground,	926
King. O God, what mischiefes work the wicked ones?	938
By wicked meanes to frame our Soueraignes fall.	1346

WIDDOW = 1

To wring the Widdow from her custom'd right,	3188

WIFE = 12*3

Enter Duke Humfrey and his wife Elianor.	273
And the Protectors wife belou'd of him?	318
and Lands, and Wife and all, from me.	403
Suff. Thy Wife too? that's some Wrong indeede.	404
As that prowd Dame, the Lord Protectors Wife:	462
More like an Empresse, then Duke *Humphreyes* Wife:	464
Suff. What Woman is this? | *Wife.* His Wife, and't like your Worship.	808
Simpc. Alas, good Master, my Wife desired some	842
Of Lady *Elianor*, the Protectors Wife,	921
And for my Wife, I know not how it stands,	944
King. Stand forth Dame *Elianor Cobham*, | *Glosters* Wife:	1053
For whilest I thinke I am thy married Wife,	1204
Sometime Ile say, I am Duke *Humfreyes* Wife,	1218
Cade. My wife descended of the *Lacies*.	2363
King. Come wife, let's in, and learne to gouern better,	2902

WIFE = 7

WIL *l.*2385 *2644 *2719 = *3

WILDE = 2

Him capre vpright, like a wilde Morisco,	1671
As wilde *Medea* yong *Absirtis* did.	3281

WILDERNESSE = 1

A Wildernesse is populous enough,	2075

WILL *see also* hee'l, hee'le, Ile, shee'le, they'l, they'le, 'twill, wee'l, wee'le, you'l *l.*113 114 149 153 171 177 185 224 251 252 266 341 352 381 382 383 *387 452 476 484 496 505 511 541 563 *622 642 675 826 898 933 952 1073 1078 *1149 1226 1245 1250 *1288 1289 1298 1308 1316 1324 1332 *1359 1388 1440 1453 1470 *1497 1522 1541 1574 1605 1617

WILL *cont.*
1620 1626 1628 1650 1651 1655 1684 1685 1700 1894 1934 1958 1977
*1991 2048 2064 2142 2144 2145 2193 2241 2287 2316 2317 2318 2388
*2391 *2438 *2471 2473 2494 2504 *2517 *2522 *2524 2545 2583 *2592
2610 *2671 2693 *2728 2771 2782 2786 2787 2790 *2797 *2806 2813
2871 2893 2900 2972 2985 2988 3047 3074 3107 3116 3133 3135 3136
*3137 3154 3274 3278 3280 3282 3316 = 108*19, 5*3

King. Sweet Aunt be quiet, 'twas against her will.	535
Duch. Against her will, good King? looke to't in time,	536
Last time I danc't attendance on his will,	566
*and *Will,* thou shalt haue my Hammer: and here *Tom,*	1136
King. Cold Newes, Lord *Somerset:* but Gods will be | done.	1382
And so should these, if I might haue my will.	2196
Peace with his soule, heauen if it be thy will.	3251
So was his Will, in his old feeble body,	3334

WILLIAM = 4*2

Charles, and William de la Pole Marquesse of Suffolke, Am-|bassador	51
And *William de la Pole* first Duke of Suffolke.	304
The second, *William* of Hatfield; and the third,	971
William of Windsor was the seuenth, and last.	976
Salisb. But *William* of Hatfield dyed without an | Heire.	992
Suf. Stay *Whitmore,* for thy Prisoner is a Prince, | The Duke of Suffolke, *William de la Pole.*	2213

WILLING = 1

Ile send them all as willing as I liue:	3043

WILLINGLY = 4

Armorer. And I accept the Combat willingly.	609
As willingly doe I the same resigne,	1088
And euen as willingly at thy feete I leaue it,	1090
Somerset. My Lord, | Ile yeelde my selfe to prison willingly,	2895

WILLINGNESSE = 1

I would expend it with all willingnesse.	1450

WILT *l.*321 *334 *653 2006 2138 2199 *2931 2940 3164 3169 = 7*3

WIN = 3

Aniou and *Maine?* My selfe did win them both:	126
Which I will win from France, or else be slaine.	224
The Rebels haue assay'd to win the Tower.	2608

WIN = *1

WINCHESTER see also Win. = 3

King. Vnckle of Winchester, I pray read on.	62
Be full expyr'd. Thankes Vncle Winchester,	73
Hum. My Lord of Winchester I know your minde.	146

WINCK = 1

Let me see thine Eyes; winck now, now open them,	846

WIND = 1

If Wind and Fuell be brought, to feed it with:	1606

WINDE = 3

Yet by your leaue, the Winde was very high,	719
And twice by aukward winde from Englands banke	1783
What boaded this? but well fore-warning winde	1785

WINDES = 2

King. The Windes grow high,	779
Against the senselesse windes shall grin in vaine,	2245

WINDSOR = 1

William of Windsor was the seuenth, and last.	976

WINE = 2

and the good Wine in thy Masters way.	1159

WINE *cont.*
 The pissing Conduit run nothing but Clarret Wine 2618
WING = 1
 Knowledge the Wing wherewith we flye to heauen. 2708
WINGED = 1
 Like Lime-twigs set to catch my winged soule: 2150
WINGHAM = 1
 Hol. I see them, I see them: There's *Bests* Sonne, the | Tanner of
 Wingham. 2340
WINGS = 3
 Vnder the Wings of our Protectors Grace, 423
 Haue all lym'd Bushes to betray thy Wings, 1230
 Who with their drowsie, slow, and flagging wings 2174
WINKE = 1
 Winke at the Duke of Suffolkes insolence, 1036
WINNE = 1*1
 *That *Maine*, which by maine force Warwicke did winne, 221
 Mens flesh preseru'd so whole, doe seldome winne. 1604
WINNERS = 1
 Beshrew the winners, for they play'd me false, 1484
WINTER = 2
 Barren Winter, with his wrathfull nipping Cold; 1173
 That Winter Lyon, who in rage forgets | Aged contusions, and all brush
 of Time: 3322
WINTERS = 2
 In Winters cold, and Summers parching heate, 88
 Well could I curse away a Winters night, 2050
WIPD = 1
 But with our sword we wip'd away the blot. 2209
WIPED = 1
 Ne're shall this blood be wiped from thy point, 2974
WIPT = 1
 Why yet thy scandall were not wipt away, 1241
WISDOMES = *1
 King. My Lords, what to your wisdomes seemeth best, 1495
WISE = 2*1
 Bewitch your hearts, be wise and circumspect. 164
 Beleeue me Lords, were none more wise then I, 1533
 But. If this Fellow be wise, hee'l neuer call yee *Iacke* 2625
WISEDOME = 1
 Now is it manhood, wisedome, and defence, 3301
WISEDOMES = 1
 Her words yclad with wisedomes Maiesty, 40
WISH = 4
 as heart can wish, or tongue can tell. | *Dicke.* My Lord, 2757
 As I do long and wish to be a Subiect. 2855
 So wish I, I might thrust thy soule to hell. 2984
 You shall haue pay, and euery thing you wish. 3039
WISHD = 2
 Because I wish'd this Worlds eternitie. 1270
 And so I wish'd thy body might my Heart: 1809
WISHED = 1
 For loosing ken of *Albions* wished Coast. 1813
WISHEST = *1
 Somerset. And in the number, thee, that wishest | shame. 1612
WIT = 2
 With ruder termes, such as my wit affoords, 37

WIT *cont.*
And yet herein I iudge mine owne Wit good;   1534
WITCH = 4
With *Margerie Iordane* the cunning Witch,   350
Dame *Elianor* giues Gold, to bring the Witch: 367
Enter the Witch, the two Priests, and Bullingbrooke.   619
The Witch in Smithfield shall be burnt to ashes,   1060
WITCH = 1
WITCHES = 1
Dealing with Witches and with Coniurers,   924
WITCHT = 1
Am I not witcht like her? Or thou not false like him?   1819
WITH = 220*39
WITHER = *1
*ten meales I haue lost, and I'de defie them all. Wither   2967
WITHIN = 6*4
Wee will make fast within a hallow'd Verge.   642
Who's within there, hoe?   710
Within this halfe houre hath receiu'd his sight,   791
Whose floud begins to flowe within mine eyes;   1500
* *Yorke.* My Lord of Suffolke, within foureteene dayes   1632
Noyse within. Enter Warwicke, and many | *Commons.*   1822
A noyse within. | *Queene.* What noyse is this?   1942
* *Commons within.* An answer from the King, my Lord | of Salisbury.   1982
* *Within.* An answer from the King, or wee will all | breake in.   1991
*art thou within point-blanke of our Iurisdiction Regall.   2660
WITHOUT = 3*3
* *Englands owne proper Cost and Charges, without hauing any* | *Dowry.*   66
Would make thee quickly hop without thy Head. | *Exit Humfrey.*   527
Without Discharge, Money, or Furniture,   564
* *Salisb.* But *William* of Hatfield dyed without an | Heire.   992
*for a stray, for entering his Fee-simple without leaue. A   2930
Should raise so great a power without his leaue?   3013
WITHSTAND = 1
Killing all those that withstand them: 2603
WITHSTANDING = 1
Yet not withstanding such a strait Edict,   1970
WITH-HELD = 1
Run backe and bite, because he was with-held,   3151
WITNESSE = 5*3
Warw. That can I witnesse, and a fouler fact   568
*nor thought any such matter: God is my witnesse, I am   585
*knees he would be euen with me: I haue good witnesse   597
For he hath witnesse of his seruants malice: 606
Glost. Witnesse my teares, I cannot stay to speake. | *Exit Gloster.*   1265
I shall not want false Witnesse, to condemne me,   1468
Witnesse the fortune he hath had in France.   1595
*middest of you, and heauens and honor be witnesse, that   2838
WITS = 1
And did my brother *Bedford* toyle his wits,   90
WITTED = 1
Suff. Blunt-witted Lord, ignoble in demeanor,   1915
WIUES = 2*3
Large summes of Gold, and Dowries with their wiues,   136
* *Som.* Thy sumptuous Buildings, and thy Wiues Attyre   520
May euen in their Wiues and Childrens sight,   2499
*And we charge and command, that their wiues be as free   2756

WIUES *cont.*
    *Wiues and Daughters before your faces. For me, I will   2806
WIZARD = 1
    Hath made the Wizard famous in his death: 3292
WIZARDS = *1
    **Bullin.* Patience, good Lady, Wizards know their times: 635
WOE = 2
    King. Ah woe is me for Gloster, wretched man.   1772
    Queen. Be woe for me, more wretched then he is.   1773
WOES = 1
    Nothing so heauy as these woes of mine.   3287
WOFULL = 1
    To wash away my wofull Monuments.   2057
WOFULST = 1
    Suf. A Iewell lockt into the wofulst Caske,   2127
WOLDST *l.**3104 = *1
WOLUES = 3
    For hee's enclin'd as is the rauenous Wolues.   1372
    And Wolues are gnarling, who shall gnaw thee first.   1492
    And now loud houling Wolues arouse the Iades   2172
WOMAN = 5*2
    Art thou not second Woman in the Realme?   317
    And being a woman, I will not be slacke   341
    Duch. Was't I? yea, I it was, prowd French-woman: 532
    **Bulling.* I haue heard her reported to be a Woman of   625
    Suff. What Woman is this? | *Wife.* His Wife, and't like your Worship.   808
    * *Queen.* Fye Coward woman, and soft harted wretch,   2021
    Was by a begger-woman stolne away,   2463
WOMANS = 1
    If it be fond, call it a Womans feare: 1330
WOMENS = 1
    To giue his Censure: These are no Womens matters.   507
WONDER = 2
    Was made a wonder, and a pointing stock | To euery idle Rascall
    follower.   1222
    These few dayes wonder will be quickly worne.   1245
WONDRING = 1
    Makes me from Wondring, fall to Weeping ioyes,   41
WONNE = 7
    Hath wonne the greatest fauour of the Commons,   200
    Till France be wonne into the Dolphins hands: 565
    By flatterie hath he wonne the Commons hearts: 1322
    But all the Honor *Salisbury* hath wonne,   1988
    For they haue wonne the Bridge,   2602
    Is not it selfe, nor haue we wonne one foot, | If Salsbury be lost.   3326
    Saint Albons battell wonne by famous Yorke,   3352
WONT = 1
    'Tis not his wont to be the hindmost man,   1296
WOODS = *1
    *I hid me in these Woods, and durst not peepe out, for all   2908
WOODSTOCK = 1
    The sixt, was *Thomas* of Woodstock, Duke of Gloster;   975
WORD = 7*1
    Say but the word, and I will be his Priest.   1574
    The Duke was dumbe, and could not speake a word. | *King sounds.*   1728
    For euery word you speake in his behalfe,   1913
    Dread Lord, the Commons send you word by me,   1955

WORD   *cont.*
Had I but sayd, I would haue kept my Word;   2007
Cade. Bee it a Lordshippe, thou shalt haue it for that | word.   2638
*a mans stomacke this hot weather: and I think this word   2914
in: and now the word Sallet must serue me to feed on.   2919
WORDES = *3
King. I thanke thee *Nell,* these wordes content mee | much.   1720
Staf. And will you credit this base Drudges Wordes,   2471
*Nowne and a Verbe, and such abhominable wordes, as   2673
WORDS = 20*3
Her words yclad with wisedomes Maiesty,   40
Deliuer'd vp againe with peacefull words? | *Mort Dieu.*   129
Looke to it Lords, let not his smoothing words   163
Seale vp your Lips, and giue no words but Mum,   365
His words were these: That *Richard,* Duke of Yorke,   580
King. Say man, were these thy words?   583
*words: my accuser is my Prentice, and when I did cor-|rect   595
Or else conclude my words effectuall.   1335
And lowly words were Ransome for their fault: 1427
With ignominious words, though Clarkely couch?   1479
Hide not thy poyson with such sugred words,   1745
My tongue should stumble in mine earnest words,   2031
Lieu. First let my words stab him, as he hath me.   2234
Suf. Base slaue, thy words are blunt, and so art thou.   2235
Thy words moue Rage, and not remorse in me: 2280
Bro. Well, seeing gentle words will not preuayle,   2494
O let me liue. | *Cade.* I feele remorse in my selfe with his words: but   2737
As for words, whose greatnesse answer's words,   2957
I cannot giue due action to my words,   2999
His sonnes (he sayes) shall giue their words for him.   3134
Yor. Will you not Sonnes? | *Edw.* I Noble Father, if our words will
serue.   3135
Rich. And if words will not, then our Weapons shal.   3137
WORK = *1
King. O God, what mischiefes work the wicked ones?   938
WORKE = 3*2
In England worke your Graces full content.   453
*Earth; *Iohn Southwell* reade you, and let vs to our worke.   631
That time best fits the worke we haue in hand.   640
To dreame on euill, or to worke my downefall.   1367
Dicke. And worke in their shirt to, as my selfe for ex-|ample, that am
a butcher.   2685
WORKEMEN = 1
Beuis. Nay more, the Kings Councell are no good | Workemen.   2333
WORKES = 1
To see how God in all his Creatures workes,   723
WORLD = 15*3
A world of earthly blessings to my soule,   29
As frowning at the Fauours of the world?   277
Inchac'd with all the Honors of the world?   281
Be my last breathing in this mortall world.   294
*World. Here *Robin,* and if I dye, I giue thee my Aporne;   1135
Trowest thou, that ere Ile looke vpon the World,   1214
You vse her well: the World may laugh againe,   1260
This *Gloster* should be quickly rid the World,   1535
Sits in grim Maiestie, to fright the World.   1750
What know I how the world may deeme of me?   1765

WORLD *cont.*

The World shall not be Ransome for thy Life.	2011
For where thou art, there is the World it selfe,	2077
With euery seuerall pleasure in the World:	2078
Aye me! What is this World? What newes are these?	2097
And I proclaim'd a Coward through the world.	2212
*it was neuer merrie world in England, since Gentlemen | came vp.	2327
*the World to be Cowards: For I that neuer feared any,	2979
The name of Valour. O let the vile world end,	3262

WORLDLY = 2

Hast thou not worldly pleasure at command,	319
For with his soule fled all my worldly solace:	1855

WORLDS = 2

Because I wish'd this Worlds eternitie.	1270
For wheresoere thou art in this worlds Globe,	2123

WORME = 1

The mortall Worme might make the sleepe eternall.	1975

WORNE = 1

These few dayes wonder will be quickly worne.	1245

WORSE = 4*1

Yorke. I neuer saw a fellow worse bestead,	1112
Glost. Entreat her not the worse, in that I pray	1259
Might happily haue prou'd farre worse then his.	1609
Yorke. What, worse then naught? nay, then a shame | take all.	1610
Gall, worse then Gall, the daintiest that they taste:	2037

WORSHIP = 3

Suff. What Woman is this? | *Wife.* His Wife, and't like your Worship.	808
Erect his Statue, and worship it,	1780
Brothers, and worship me their Lord.	2393

WORST = 1

The very trayne of her worst wearing Gowne,	471

WORTH = 5

Was better worth then all my Fathers Lands,	472
Resigne to death, it is not worth th'enioying:	1640
Your louing Vnckle, twentie times his worth,	1980
That euer did containe a thing of worth,	2128
Contenteth me, and worth a Monarchy.	2924

WORTHIE = 1

Card. That he should dye, is worthie pollicie,	1537

WORTHLESSE = 1

Vnto the daughter of a worthlesse King,	2249

WORTHY = 4*1

Warw. Whether your Grace be worthy, yea or no,	497
Is worthy prayse: but shall I speake my conscience,	1362
More then mistrust, that shewes him worthy death.	1544
Suff. Here is my Hand, the deed is worthy doing. | *Queene.* And so say I.	1580
*that cause they haue beene most worthy to liue. Thou	2679

WORTHYER = 1

Dispute not that, *Yorke* is the worthyer.	498

WOULD *see also* I'de *l.*134 222 339 447 448 527 *597 *731 879 1075 1091 1349 1361 1416 1450 1545 *1575 1598 1600 1762 1792 1798 1817 1843 1888 1925 2007 2025 2026 2035 2052 2507 2578 2700 2749 *2801 *2921 2996 3313 = 35*5

WOULDST *l.*396 837 *840 1240 1795 2557 = 5*1

WOULDT = *1

Glost. Faith holy Vnckle, would't were come to that.	757

WOUND = 2
Before the Wound doe grow vncurable;   1589
It is applyed to a deathfull wound.   2121
WOUNDED = 2
So shall my name with Slanders tongue be wounded,   1768
And sent the ragged Souldiers wounded home.   2258
WOUNDING = 1
Looke not vpon me, for thine eyes are wounding;   1751
WOUNDS = 2
And are the Citties that I got with wounds,   128
Feare frames disorder, and disorder wounds   3254
WRACK = 1
The Common-wealth hath dayly run to wrack,   514
WRACKD = 1
Was I for this nye wrack'd vpon the Sea,   1782
WRACKE = 1
Humes Knauerie will be the Duchesse Wracke,   381
WRATH = 3
Thou wilt but adde encrease vnto my Wrath.   2006
Clif. Hence heape of wrath, foule indigested lumpe,   3156
Shall to my flaming wrath, be Oyle and Flax: 3277
WRATHFULL = 5
Barren Winter, with his wrathfull nipping Cold;   1173
To free vs from his Fathers wrathfull curse,   1859
Your wrathfull Weapons drawne,   1947
Bro. But angry, wrathfull, and inclin'd to blood,   2446
Sword, hold thy temper; Heart, be wrathfull still: 3293
WREN = 1
And thinkes he, that the chirping of a Wren,   1742
WREST = 1
Buck. Hee'le wrest the sence, and hold vs here all day.   1486
WRESTED = 1
That Doyt that ere I wrested from the King,   1412
WRETCH = 3*1
And binds the Wretch, and beats it when it strayes,   1512
Queen. Fye Coward woman, and soft harted wretch,   2021
Looke with a gentle eye vpon this Wretch,   2154
Die damned Wretch, the curse of her that bare thee: 2982
WRETCHED = 3
King. Ah woe is me for Gloster, wretched man.   1772
Queen. Be woe for me, more wretched then he is.   1773
For yet may England curse my wretched raigne. | *Flourish. Exeunt.* 2903
WRETCHES = 1
That layes strong siege vnto this wretches soule,   2156
WRING = 2
Som. Rere vp his Body, wring him by the Nose.   1732
To wring the Widdow from her custom'd right,   3188
WRINGS = 1
Weepes ouer them, and wrings his haplesse hands,   238
WRIT = 5*1
His Weapons, holy Sawes of sacred Writ,   444
Now pray my Lord, let's see the Deuils Writ.   687
This hand of mine hath writ in thy behalfe,   2231
Vnder the which is writ, *Inuitis nubibus.*   2267
But. They vse to writ it on the top of Letters: 'Twill | go hard with
you.   2417
Kent, in the Commentaries *Caesar* writ,   2694

WRITE = 3*3
2.*Gent.* And so will I, and write home for it straight.   2193
Weauer. The Clearke of Chartam: hee can write and | reade, and cast
accompt.   2403
But. Nay, he can make Obligations, and write Court | hand.   2410
Cade. Let me alone: Dost thou vse to write thy name?   2419
Clearke. Sir I thanke God, I haue bin so well brought | vp, that I can
write my name.   2422
And that Ile write vpon thy Burgonet,   3200
WRITS = 1
Let vs pursue him ere the Writs go forth.   3348
WRONG = 3*1
Suff. Thy Wife too? that's some Wrong indeede.   404
Thou neuer didst them wrong, nor no man wrong: 1510
And haue no other reason for this wrong,   3189
WRONGD = 2
I will subscribe, and say I wrong'd the Duke.   1332
If euer Lady wrong'd her Lord so much,   1916
WRONGFULLY = 1
Which he had thought to haue murther'd wrongfully.   1166
WRONGST = *1
Id. How much thou wrong'st me, heauen be my iudge;   2981
WROUGHT = 1
That liuing wrought me such exceeding trouble.   3064
Y = *1
Yor. Thus Warre hath giuen thee peace, for y art still,   3250
YARD = 1
His Studie is his Tilt-yard, and his Loues   445
YAWNING = 1
Now will I dam vp this thy yawning mouth,   2241
YCLAD = 1
Her words yclad with wisedomes Maiesty,   40
YE *l.*144 148 *397 529 769 879 1298 2287 2300 2473 *2723 2734 *2751
2787 *2796 *2797 *2801 = 13*6
YEA = 3
Warw. Whether your Grace be worthy, yea or no,   497
Duch. Was't I? yea, I it was, prowd French-woman: 532
Yea Man and Birds are fayne of climbing high.   724
YEARE = 1
This first yeare of our raigne.   2619
YEARES = *1
*if I might haue a Lease of my life for a thousand yeares, I   2910
YEE *l.*2625 = *1
YEELD = 5*1
And force perforce Ile make him yeeld the Crowne,   270
Let *Yorke* be Regent, I will yeeld to him.   496
And vanquisht as I am, I yeeld to thee, | Or to the meanest Groome.   936
If you go forward: therefore yeeld, or dye.   2447
And yeeld to mercy, whil'st 'tis offered you,   2788
Clif. He is fled my Lord, and all his powers do yeeld,   2862
YEELDE = 1
Somerset. My Lord, | Ile yeelde my selfe to prison willingly,   2895
YEELDED = 2
Before I would haue yeelded to this League.   134
The King hath yeelded vnto thy demand: 3032
YEERES = 2
I saw not better sport these seuen yeeres day: 718

YEERES *cont.*
  Queene. I see no reason, why a King of yeeres   1083
YES = 2*1
  Eli. Yes my good Lord, Ile follow presently.   335
  **Simpc.* Yes Master, cleare as day, I thanke God and | Saint *Albones.* 848
  Maior. Yes, my Lord, if it please your Grace.   885
YET = 39*3
  Yet let vs watch the haughtie Cardinall,   181
  Elia. What saist thou man? Hast thou as yet confer'd   349
  Yet haue I Gold flyes from another Coast: 369
  Yet I doe finde it so: for to be plaine,   372
  Yet am I *Suffolke* and the Cardinalls Broker.   377
  Yet must we ioyne with him and with the Lords,   481
  Spirit. The Duke yet liues, that *Henry* shall depose: 657
  The Duke yet liues, that Henry *shall depose*:   689
  Yet by your leaue, the Winde was very high,   719
  Glost. A subtill Knaue, but yet it shall not serue: 845
  In my opinion, yet thou seest not well.   847
  Suff. And yet I thinke, Iet did he neuer see.   858
  Your Lady is forth-comming, yet at London.   931
  It fayles not yet, but flourishes in thee,   1021
  Yet so he rul'd, and such a Prince he was,   1220
  Why yet thy scandall were not wipt away,   1241
  Yet by reputing of his high discent,   1342
  Vnsounded yet, and full of deepe deceit.   1351
  For thousands more, that yet suspect no perill,   1452
  And yet, good *Humfrey,* is the houre to come,   1505
  And yet herein I iudge mine owne Wit good;   1534
  But yet we want a Colour for his death: 1538
  And yet we haue but triuiall argument,   1543
  I take it kindly: yet be well assur'd,   1652
  Yet doe not goe away: come Basiliske,   1752
  Yet he most Christian-like laments his death: 1758
  Yet Aeolus would not be a murtherer,   1792
  Yet not withstanding such a strait Edict,   1970
  Yet did I purpose as they doe entreat: 1996
  Oh go not yet. Euen thus, two Friends condemn'd, 2068
  Yet now farewell, and farewell Life with thee.   2071
  Yet let not this make thee be bloody-minded,   2205
  Neuer yet did base dishonour blurre our name,   2208
  If he reuenge it not, yet will his Friends,   2317
  **Hol.* True: and yet it is said, Labour in thy Vocati-|on: 2335
  in the mouth with a Speare, and 'tis not whole yet. 2643
  Yet to recouer them would loose my life: 2700
  And therefore yet relent, and saue my life.   2750
  For yet may England curse my wretched raigne. | *Flourish. Exeunt.* 2903
  *sword, and yet am ready to famish. These fiue daies haue 2907
  *eate no meate these fiue dayes, yet come thou and thy 2943
  But I must make faire weather yet a while,   3022
YFAITH = *1
  **Armorer.* Let it come yfaith, and Ile pledge you all, | and a figge for
  Peter.   1127
YIELD *see* yeeld
YIELDED *see* yeelded
YNCH = 1
  Beldam I thinke we watcht you at an ynch.   672

YOAKE = 1
Ah *Humfrey*, can I beare this shamefull yoake?   1213
YOCLIF = 2
YONG = 2
Enter yong Clifford.   3252
As wilde *Medea* yong *Absirtis* did.   3281
YOR = 8*5
YORK = *3
   Buck. Your Grace shal giue me leaue, my Lord of York,   707
   Bro. Iacke Cade, the D.(uke) of York hath taught you this.   2474
   Yor. From Ireland thus comes York to claim his right,   2992
YORK = *1
YORKE see also Yor., York. = 63*9
The Queene, Suffolke, Yorke, Somerset, and Buckingham, | on the other.   5
And girt thee with the Sword. Cosin of Yorke,   70
Gloster, Yorke, Buckingham, Somerset, | Salisburie, and Warwicke.   74
Braue *Yorke, Salisbury*, and victorious *Warwicke*,   93
And Brother Yorke, thy Acts in Ireland,   202
Yor. And so sayes Yorke, | For he hath greatest cause.   215
Exit Warwicke, and Salisbury. Manet Yorke.   225
So Yorke must sit, and fret, and bite his tongue,   242
A day will come, when Yorke shall claime his owne,   251
Then Yorke be still a-while, till time do serue: 260
And in my Standard beare the Armes of Yorke,   268
Whose bookish Rule, hath pull'd faire England downe. | *Exit Yorke.*   271
*That the Duke of Yorke was rightfull Heire to the | Crowne.   411
* *Queene.* What say'st thou? Did the Duke of Yorke   413
And grumbling *Yorke*: and not the least of these,   456
As for the Duke of Yorke, this late Complaint   483
Yorke, Salisbury, Warwicke, | and the Duchesse.   489
Or *Somerset*, or *Yorke*, all's one to me.   492
Yorke. If *Yorke* haue ill demean'd himselfe in France,   493
Let *Yorke* be Regent, I will yeeld to him.   496
Dispute not that, *Yorke* is the worthyer.   498
I say, my Soueraigne, *Yorke* is meetest man   555
That *Yorke* is most vnmeet of any man.   559
Pray God the Duke of Yorke excuse himselfe.   574
Yorke. Doth any one accuse *Yorke* for a Traytor?   575
His words were these: That *Richard*, Duke of Yorke,   580
Because in *Yorke* this breedes suspition;   603
Enter the Duke of Yorke and the Duke of Buckingham | with their Guard,
and breake in.   669
Enter Yorke, Salisbury, and Warwick.   959
* *Warw.* Sweet *Yorke* begin: and if thy clayme be good,   966
The fift, was *Edmond Langley*, Duke of Yorke;   974
The fourth Sonne, *Yorke* claymes it from the third: 1019
Shall finde their deaths, if *Yorke* can prophecie.   1042
Shall one day make the Duke of Yorke a King.   1046
*an honest man: and touching the Duke of Yorke, I will   1149
And *Yorke*, and impious *Beauford*, that false Priest,   1229
Yorke, Buckingham, Salisbury, and Warwicke, | to the Parliament.   1293
My Lord of Suffolke, Buckingham, and Yorke, | Reproue my
allegation, if you can,   1333
And dogged *Yorke*, that reaches at the Moone,   1458
Suff. Ah *Yorke*, no man aliue, so faine as I.   1546
Yorke. 'Tis *Yorke* that hath more reason for his death.   1547
Som. If *Yorke*, with all his farre-fet pollicie,   1596

337

YORKE cont.

No more, good *Yorke*; sweet *Somerset* be still.	1607
Thy fortune, *Yorke*, hadst thou beene Regent there,	1608
Card. My Lord of Yorke, trie what your fortune is:	1614
Then, Noble *Yorke*, take thou this Taske in hand.	1623
Suff. A charge, Lord *Yorke*, that I will see perform'd.	1626
Suff. Ile see it truly done, my Lord of Yorke. *Exeunt.*	1635
Manet Yorke.	1636
Yorke. Now *Yorke*, or neuer, steele thy fearfull thoughts,	1637
How they affect the House and Clayme of *Yorke.*	1681
And now the House of Yorke thrust from the Crowne,	2262
The Duke of Yorke is newly come from Ireland,	2877
King. Thus stands my state, 'twixt Cade and Yorke | distrest,	2884
And now is Yorke in Armes, to second him.	2889
Enter Yorke, and his Army of Irish, with | Drum and Colours.	2990
Buc. Yorke, if thou meanest wel, I greet thee well.	3006
Buc. Yorke, I commend this kinde submission,	3046
King. Buckingham, doth Yorke intend no harme to vs	3049
Yorke doth present himselfe vnto your Highnesse.	3052
Then Yorke vnloose thy long imprisoned thoughts,	3083
Som. O monstrous Traitor! I arrest thee Yorke	3101
To say, if that the Bastard boyes of Yorke	3110
The sonnes of Yorke, thy betters in their birth,	3114
Clif. This is my King Yorke, I do not mistake,	3126
Enter Yorke.	3226
War. Then nobly Yorke, 'tis for a Crown thou fightst:	3236
Clif. What seest thou in me Yorke?	3239
It shall be stony. Yorke, not our old men spares:	3273
Meet I an infant of the house of Yorke,	3279
Alarum. Retreat. Enter Yorke, Richard, Warwicke, | and Soldiers, with Drum & Colours.	3319
Saint Albons battell wonne by famous Yorke,	3352

YORKE = 35*9

YORKES = 2

*them to me in the Garret one Night, as wee were scow-|ring my Lord of Yorkes Armor.	588
Qu. For thousand Yorkes he shall not hide his head,	3080

YOU = 156*39

YOUL = 2*1

That thus you do exclaime you'l go with him.	2812
Ric. If not in heauen, you'l surely sup in hell. *Exeunt*	3217
Qu. What are you made of? You'l nor fight nor fly:	3300

YOUNG = 1

Looking the way her harmelesse young one went,	1516

YOUNGER = 1

Succeed before the younger, I am King.	1016

YOUNGEST = 1

Thus *Elianors* Pride dyes in her youngest dayes.	1102

YOUR *1.*8 10 11 20 46 71 84 92 104 106 107 108 146 164 168 345 348 *353 356 365 *399 *401 *420 424 452 453 486 497 508 533 534 550 556 578 582 *584 592 *598 608 622 683 *707 709 719 721 725 734 741 749 766 775 778 780 798 806 809 *813 883 885 *890 *895 899 923 928 929 931 932 933 963 1030 *1043 1055 1063 1065 1074 1086 1103 1107 1126 *1140 *1191 *1193 *1247 *1253 *1257 1275 1285 1319 1320 1321 1336 1338 1380 1421 1434 1435 1438 1440 1446 1463 1465 1466 1473 1477 1487 *1495 *1497 1549 1614 1619 1650 1713 *1899 1914 1947 *1953 1958 1961 1964 1966 1967 1968 1969 1972 1980 2018 *2185 *2382 2389

YOUR *cont.*
   2443 2444 2503 *2539 2553 2566 2581 2590 *2604 2611 2637 2641 2703
   2712 *2718 *2747 2748 2749 2789 *2798 *2802 *2804 *2805 *2806 2817
   2827 2857 2864 2867 *2868 2871 2873 2876 2901 3037 3052 3060 3066
   3155 3159 3307 3316 = 143*36
YOURS = *2
   *What's yours? What's heere? Against the Duke of   405
   **Mate.* And so much shall you giue, or off goes yours.   2186
YOURSELFE *see* selfe
YOURSELUES *see* selues
YOUTH = 4*1
   What? did my brother *Henry* spend his youth,   85
   Simpc. But that in all my life, when I was a youth.   838
   *art: Thou hast most traiterously corrupted the youth of   2666
   To loose thy youth in peace, and to atcheeue | The Siluer Liuery of
   aduised Age,   3268
   And like a Gallant, in the brow of youth,   3324
ZEALE = 1
   'Twill make them coole in zeale vnto your Grace.   1477
  &*l.*15 *31 244 *264 *312 344 *673 *736 *960 *1101 *2364 *2468 *2485
   *2515 *2723 2771 *2832 *2868 *2917 *3243 3320 = 4*17
&C *l.*645 = 1
1 = 4
1CIT = 1
1GENT = 3*1
1NEIGHBOR = *1
1PET = *3
1PRENT = *1
1000 = *1
   *Villaine, thou wilt betray me, and get a 1000. Crownes   2931
2 = 1
2GENT = 1
2NEIGHBOR = *1
2PET = *3
2PRENT = 1
2000 = *1
   Lieu. What thinke you much to pay 2000. Crownes,   2187
3NEIGHBOR = *1